Heavens & Hells of the Mind

IMRE VALLYON

Heavens & Hells of the Mind

Volume II

TRADITION

Sounding-Light
Publishing

Heavens and Hells of the Mind, by Imre Vallyon
First edition: October 2007

Sounding-Light Publishing Ltd.
PO Box 771, Hamilton 2015, New Zealand
www.soundinglight.com

Four volume boxed set:
ISBN 978-0-909038-30-4

Individual volumes:
ISBN 978-0-909038-31-1 Volume I: Knowledge
ISBN 978-0-909038-32-8 Volume II: Tradition
ISBN 978-0-909038-33-5 Volume III: Transformation
ISBN 978-0-909038-34-2 Volume IV: Lexicon

Printed in Hong Kong by Regal Printing Ltd.

Source: A selection of the author's handwritten manuscripts dating from 1982 to 2006.

Photo Credits: All photographic images Gérard Stampfli with the following exceptions:
Page 159: NASA, ESA and Jesús Maíz Apellániz (Instituto de astrofísica de Andalucía, Spain).
Acknowledgment: Davide De Martin (ESA/Hubble). Source: ESA
Page 1103: NASA Goddard Space Flight Center, by Reto Stöckli and Robert Simmon
Page 1483: NASA, ESA, S. Beckwith (STScI), and The Hubble Heritage Team (STScI/AURA). Source: ESA
Page 1585: SOHO (Solar and Heliospheric Observatory) (ESA and NASA)
Page 141, 467, 1657: Hamish Cattell
Page 205, 717, 1363, 1411, 1555, 1643: Manu Vallyon
Page 1491: Yaël Pochon

I dedicate this book to the aspiring Soul of Humanity across the planet.
We are One Planet, One Humanity, One Life, One God, One Reality.

May this book help you to recover your own lost Wisdom,
the knowledge of your real Self, and the knowledge of the Real God,
the Bright Eternal SELF that is the Truth, the Love and your own Cosmic Life.

Imre Vallyon

OVERVIEW

Heavens and Hells of the Mind

Volume I
KNOWLEDGE

Part 1 Cosmology Unveiled . . . 9
Part 2 Earth Life . . . 267

Volume II
TRADITION

Part 3 Yoga: The Science of Union . . . 517
Part 4 Pure Christianity: The Religion of Love . . . 607
Part 5 Zen: The Path to Enlightenment . . . 749
Part 6 Sūfī Meditation: The Way of the Holy Fire . . . 825
Part 7 Tantra: The Path of Relationship . . . 903
Part 8 The Warrior School: The Way of the Noble Warrior . . . 967

Volume III
TRANSFORMATION

Part 9 The Path of Return . . . 1115
Part 10 The Way of the Heart . . . 1249
Part 11 The Way of Spiritual Psychology . . . 1361
Part 12 The Worship of the Goddess . . . 1481
Part 13 The Yoga of the Sun . . . 1583
Part 14 The Path of Service . . . 1677

Volume IV
LEXICON

Appendix A Detailed Contents . . . 1731
Appendix B Lexicon of the Wisdom Language . . . 1759
Appendix C Index . . . 1941
Appendix D The Foundation for Higher Learning . . . 2077

Volume II: Tradition

Contents

Introduction II: By Whichever Path 511

Part 3 Yoga: The Science of Union

23 The Goal of Yoga 519
24 Gems from Patañjali's Yoga Sūtras 531
25 Aṣṭāṅga Yoga 559
26 The Yoga of Miraculous Powers 577

Part 4 Pure Christianity: The Religion of Love

27 Teachings of the Saints 609
28 The Heart of Christianity 623
29 Christian History 641
30 Jesus the Christed One 659
31 Christian Fundamentalism 675
32 Christian Prayer 689
33 The Christian Path 717
34 The Greek Mystery Language 731

Part 5 Zen: The Path to Enlightenment

35 The Spirit of Zen 751
36 The Eternal Tao 771
37 Zen Meditation 785
38 The Path of Zen 805

Part 6 Sūfī Meditation: The Way of the Holy Fire

39 The Sūfī 827
40 The Sūfī Heart 843
41 Sūfī Prayer 863
42 Sūfī Mind 885

Part 7 Tantra: The Path of Relationship

43 The Circle of Love 905
44 The One-Hundred-and-Twelve 945

Part 8 The Warrior School: The Way of the Noble Warrior

45 The Spiritual Warrior 969
46 Warrior Training 1001
47 The Primordial Sound Language 1025
48 The Warrior Code 1077

CONTENTS II

CHARTS & DIAGRAMS II

Volume II: Tradition

Charts & Diagrams

Symbols of the Religions 515

Yoga: The Science of Union

The Goal of Yoga 521
Perception through Mind 543
Tarot Key 5: The Hierophant 558
Tabulations of the General Powers 580

Pure Christianity: The Religion of Love

The Many Mansions 611
The Tree of Christianity 651
The Breath-Rhythm of the Name 708
The Divine Message of the New Testament 719
The Burning Heart 730

Zen: The Path to Enlightenment

The Goal of Zen 761

Sūfī Meditation: The Way of the Holy Fire

The Equation of History 834
The Thread of the Heart 844
The Mantram of Unification in the Heart Centre 866
Worlds of the Sūfī 890

Tantra: The Path of Relationship

Polarities within the Human Aura 921

The Warrior School: The Way of the Noble Warrior

The Descent of the Light 980
The Unity-Field of Being 1009
The Pure and Combined Vowel Sounds 1030
IAO and the Perfected Man-Species 1035
Powers of the Awakened Centres 1037
The Pure Vowels for Mental Training 1039
Forces and Qualities of the Vowels 1040
Internalizing the Pure and Combined Vowels 1041
Powers of the Semi-Vowel Sounds 1043
The Internalized Semi-Vowels 1044
Internalizing the Semi-Vowels in the Energy Centres 1045
The Semi-Vowels with the Pure Vowels and the M, Ṁ and Ṅ 1046
The Consonants combined with the Pure Vowels 1048
The Consonants with the Vowels and the M, Ṁ and Ṅ 1049
Sounds for Identification with Pure Being 1057
RŪ-HĀ Breathing in the Base and Crown Centres 1063
The Warrior of the Heart 1074

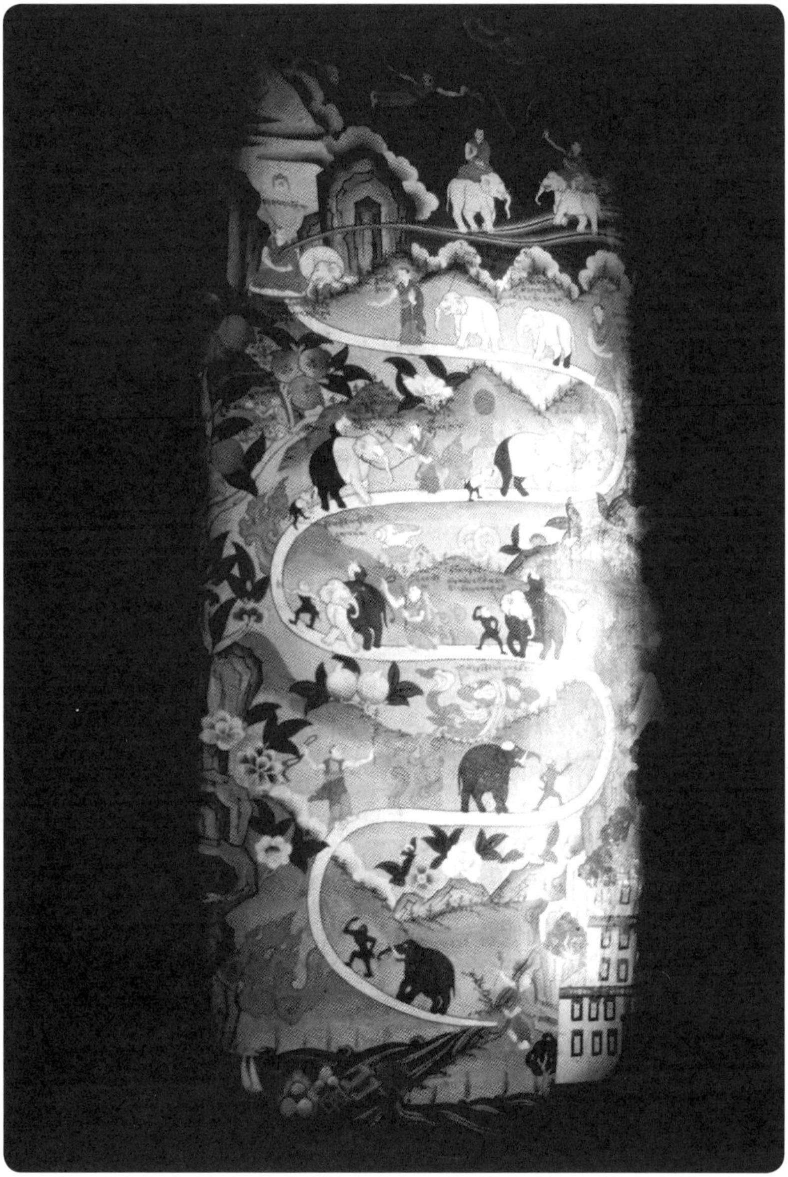

INTRODUCTION TO VOLUME II

By Whichever Path

The Eternal is One

SHEMA YISRAEL, I.H.V.H. ELOHEYNU, I.H.V.H. ACHAD!

Hear, O Israel, the Eternal, our God, the Eternal is One!

Deuteronomy 6:4

There is but One Truth, One Life, One God

How beautiful are the words of Truth! How delightful to the ears! How musical to the sense of Truth within the Soul! There is only One God, One Truth, One Mind, One Reality.

This is the declaration of Oneness: the Oneness of the seen and the unseen; the Oneness of the worlds visible and invisible; the Oneness of God Transcendent and God Immanent in matter, in the atom and in you; the Oneness between all nations; the Oneness between all lives, between angels and men, planets and stars.

There is only One: One Mind, One God, the All in All, a Boundless Circle of Reality. How beautiful are the words of Truth to ears that can hear them!

The Jew and the Arab are One. The Christian and the Muslim are One. The communist and the capitalist are One. The black and the white are One. The planets within our Solar System are One. All the solar systems in the Galaxy are One. All galaxies are One. Every single atom in space, in all dimensions, is part of the One, indelibly at One with the One. See the one field with diverse flowers! There is but One Truth, One Life, One God through and through, above and beyond all Manifestation.

HASIDĪM
Hebrew: Fervent or Holy Ones.
TZADDIKĪM
Hebrew: The Righteous Ones.

These two words describe the Jewish Saints of all times, going back to Old Testament days. They have become Righteous through Union with the Eternal, YAHVEH.

The Hasidim 648

MYSTIKOS
Greek: The Mystics. The Christian Saints. Those, since the time of Christ, who have united their Souls with God and the Saving-Light Force of the Cosmos, the CHRISTOS.

The Way of the Christian Mystic 626

The Children of Israel did not grasp this sublime truth, so they *separated* themselves from the surrounding tribes and nations and said, "Our God is unique, we are unique, we are special, we are chosen". For thousands of years they believed in this delusion that they were special, unique, chosen by *their* God who was the *one and only* God. They believed that when other tribes and nations invoked God, it was not the real God, for only the Jewish God was God!

This was completely *opposite* to the sublime Revelation that was given to the Jews. It was the exact *reversal* of the Truth. So another Revelation had to be given to rectify the wrong understanding.

And thou shalt Love the Lord thy God with all your heart and mind, with all your Soul, and with all your strength.

Deuteronomy 6:5

This was given to the Jews so that they might be able to perceive the Unity, the Oneness of all Life. But this sublime message also fell on deaf ears. So the Ten Commandments were given:

> I Am the Lord, thy God… thou shalt not have other gods before me… thou shalt not have any graven images… thou shalt not take the Name of thy God in vain… keep the sabbath day holy… honour thy father and thy mother… thou shalt not kill… thou shalt not commit adultery… thou shalt not steal… thou shalt not bear false witness… thou shalt not covet….
>
> *Deuteronomy 5:6–21*

The One God of All Religions 110
Tao: the Universal Mind 775
The Divine Unity 852
Mind-Only 974
The Eternal 1644

But these were broken as well. So the next commandment was given:

> You shall love thy neighbour as thyself.
>
> *St Matthew 19:19*

Why should you "love thy neighbour as thyself"? Is not thy neighbour like you?—One with the One? If all is One, if the Divine Being, the Eternal, infuses all with Life, if in fact all *is* that Divine Life, then how can you separate yourself from your neighbour?

But this message also was unheeded. So the "authorities" (the priestcraft, the rabbis) invented endless rules and regulations governing how a true Jew should behave. Yet all of these are unnecessary when we return to *the conscious awareness of the One*, the Eternal.

Yogī
Sanskrit: A Saint of the Hindu and Esoteric Buddhist religions who has attained Union with Ātman (the Universal Spirit) and Brahman (the Ultimate Reality).

The Ultimate Reality is the Meaning of Life 526

Sūfī
Arabic: A Muslim Saint. All those great Saints of the Muslim religion who have attained Union with God, Nirvāṇa, or who have merged into the Eternal Light. Sūfī means "Pure in Heart", Qalb-Salīm, a Heart that is Perfect. In the State of Perfection you perceive nothing else but God in all things and the Divine becomes the Centre of your life, the Heart throb of your Being. Your personal ego is dissolved in God, Fanā'fi-llāh.

A Sūfī is… 840

Religion and Politics

Religion and politics should never be mixed. Politics deals with the things of the world, Religion deals with the things of God. The vibration of politics is worldly, dense, material, while the vibration of true Religion is subtle, non-worldly, spiritual.

In the three great Western religions (the Jewish, Christian and Muslim) many "orthodox" and "super-orthodox" followers mix religion with politics, and have been doing so since the beginning of their religions. This leads to endless wars and violence, since they use their "religion" to further their political ambitions, and they use "politics" to spread the influence of their religion over other peoples and races. Mixing the two is a deadly poison that has caused, and is causing, millions of people to suffer. If you cannot see the difference between true Religion and political, worldly ambitions, you can never enter the Path in this lifetime.

The Dual Nature of Christianity 624

This tragedy of the Jews was replayed by the Christians. Following Jewish thought, the Christians began to believe that their God is the only God, that they are *special*, and that the rest of Humanity will go to eternal Hell!

After the Christians came the Muslims, many of whom also believe that their God is the only God, that the rest of Humanity are "infidels" and will surely go to perdition unless they be converted to Islam.

The Jews, the Christians and the Muslims rely heavily on Old Testament ideas

The Jews called the non-Jews "gentiles"; the Christians called the non-Christians "pagans"; the Muslims called the non-Muslims "infidels". These are derogatory words for "others", and according to each of these religions these "others" will go to eternal damnation, to ravaging fires for all Eternity, because they do not have the right God, because they do not have the right Faith!

The Jews, the Christians and the Muslims rely heavily on Old Testament ideas. They are Old Testament religions. Yet, how beautiful are the words of Truth. How musical to the ears that can hear!

Hear, O Israel, the Eternal, our God, the Eternal is One.

This is *our* God—the God of the Jews, the Christians, the Muslims, the Hindus, the Sikhs, the Parsees, the Buddhists, the Taoists.... There is only one Humanity, one Earth, one God, one Life.

The Eternal is One...

The Eternal is One.

The **Christian religionists** declared anybody who did not believe in their orthodox beliefs (beliefs sanctioned by their "authorities") as "pagan". Yet *pagan* (from the Latin PĀGĀNUS) simply means a country person or villager.

The **Muslim religious orthodoxies** denounced all non-Muslims as "infidels". But *infidel* (from the Latin INFIDĒLIS) means "one who has been unfaithful", such as a husband or wife.

Throughout its history, the **orthodox Christian** church has persecuted and denounced as a "heretic" any person who did not believe in its compulsory "official" doctrine. Yet *heresy* (from the Greek HAIRESIS) simply means "choosing another way or opinion".

The Heretics 655

Who are the 'Elect'? 128
The Chosen Ones 688
Orthodoxos: correct belief? 653
The One and Only 839
The One God of All 869
Holiness to the Lord 1393

The One Transcendental Reality

The Jews of ancient times accused the nations around them of praying to "idols". The Christians accused the Hindus and others of praying to "idols". The Muslims also have accused all nations of "idol-worship".

The Divine Me, the Divine I AM, the Christ, the Kṛṣṇa, the Ādi-Buddha, Allāh, Tao, the "I Am that I Am" of the Jews, *is not a humanoid God.* It is Infinite Consciousness, Intelligence and Bliss—what the Vedantins call SAT-CIT-ĀNANDA. It is almost criminal to liken God to a human being, yet people have done just that throughout the Ages.

The Divine I AM is not a humanoid God

In the Bhagavad-Gītā there is a beautiful sentence by Śrī Kṛṣṇa:

> By whatever path men come to me, I shall meet them there.

In other words, there is only one Transcendental Reality, one Beingness, and through pure Devotion, selfless Surrender and Service, you may approach It by any religious path.

Idol-Worship 655
In the Image and Likeness 104
The Sūfī God 838
The One 1686

Buddhism
The Wheel of the Law.

Hinduism
The Sun, the Spirit.

Taoism
The TAO, or Union of Opposites.

Ancient Tibetan
The SVASTIKA, or GAMADION.
The Flying Cross, symbol of the Holy Spirit.

Ancient Semitic
The six-pointed star, symbol of the Union of Spirit and Matter. The Heart Cakra. (Later adopted by the Jews as the *Star of David.*)

Ancient Egyptian
The ANKH, or CRUX ANSATA. The Tau Cross. Symbol of fertility and Eternal Life.

Judaism
The 7-branched candlestick. The Seven Rays. The Seven Spirits before the Throne of God.

Christianity
The Cross. The Crucifixion in Matter.

Persian
Symbol for the Cosmic Fire.

Islam
The Star of Initiation above the crescent or Moon (the psychic astral body).

Symbols of the Religions

The New and Eternal Way

It is important to understand that my Mission has been *to bring the Teachings of the Piscean Age into the Aquarian Age*. For today the Jewish, Christian, Muslim, Hindu, Buddhist, Sikh, Taoist (Chinese) and Shinto (Japanese) religions are still vibrating to the Piscean Age Vibration, and millions of followers are still in the Piscean mode of feeling, thinking and religious practice.

In the future there will be only One Religion

Truth is eternally the same, but its *presentation* must be readjusted from Age to Age to fit in with the *new vibrations* of the coming Age.

The major old religious traditions need to be re-presented in a new Light (quite literally), in a new vibratory way, in a new state of Consciousness and Understanding. For in the future there will be only One Religion, as there is only One God, One Cosmos, One Humanity. We are in a transition period now.

As for *you*, a seeker or disciple of the Eternal Way, you need to discover (if you do not already know) just what stage of the Way you have reached, and what you need to do to reach your *Objective*, which is Illumination, Deification, Glorification, and Union with the Divine Godhead that dwelleth *in* you. ⚹

From Pisces to Aquarius 837
Monks and Disciples 991
Piscean and New Age Spirituality 1706
The Future 1709
Revelation is Continuous 1710
The Vision of your own Eternity 1144

PART THREE

Yoga

The Science of Union

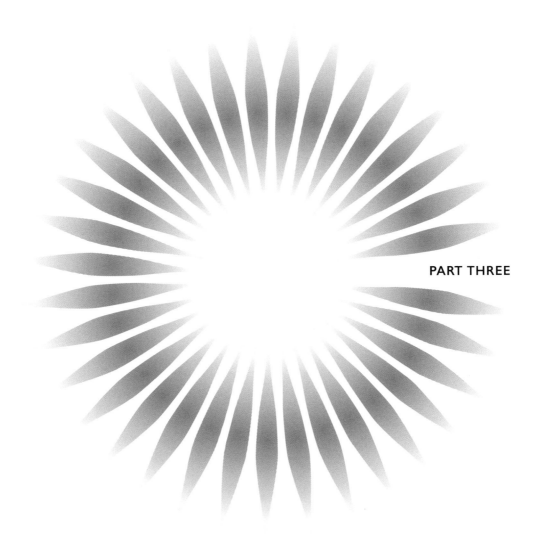

CHAPTER 23

The Goal of Yoga

Yoga-Mārga

In India, many centuries ago, the principle of the holistic approach to Man was well understood. The way to Spiritual Enlightenment was called YOGA-MĀRGA, "the Path of Union". Yoga is a school of ancient Vedic philosophy prescribing a course of physical, emotional and mental disciplines for the purpose of attaining liberation from the material world, the union of the self (the personality) with the Higher Self (ĀTMAN), and the union of the Higher Self with the Godhead (BRAHMAN). The goal of Yoga is the union of the Individuality with the Supreme Being, the Ultimate Principle, the Godhead.

In the early days of the Science of Yoga, there was only one Yoga

YOGA
Sanskrit: "Joining together, yoking, aligning, uniting, going into Oneness or Union, becoming at-one". The State of Union. From YUGH, "to unite, join, put together, integrate".

YOGA-MĀRGA
Sanskrit: "The Path of Union". From MĀRGA, "a path, road, way, track", and YOGA, "integration, conjunction, at-one-ness, Union, Salvation".

ĀTMAN
Sanskrit: The God in you.
Ātman, Ātmā 34

BRAHMAN
Sanskrit: The God in the Universal Manifestation of All.
God Immanent and Transcendent 111

PRAṆAVA
Sanskrit: The Sound of ŌṀ reverberating throughout all Creation.
Āuṁ, Ōṁ, Nāda 550

The Activities of Yoga-Mārga

In the early days of the Science of Yoga, there was only *one* YOGA. The Way to Cosmic Consciousness known as YOGA-MĀRGA was a totally integrated, balanced, holistic way of life. On this original Path of Union there were several *activities* of Yoga. For example:

HAṬHA: Balancing the "sun and moon" currents in the etheric body.

KARMA: Physical action, movement, service.

LAYA: Organization of the cakras (the psychic force centres in the etheric body) and Prāṇa (the life-force).

KUṆḌALINĪ: Awakening the subtle "serpent-power" or dynamic psychic energy.

BHAKTI: Devotion, Love, emotion.

JÑĀNA: Knowledge, mental clarification.

RĀJA: An intense, systematic, meditational approach to consciousness.

ŚAKTI: Energy, power, vitality.

MANTRA: Sound-formulas, frequencies, music.

YANTRA: Geometric forms, symbols, maṇḍalas.

DHYĀNA: Meditation, thought control.

SAMĀDHI: Trance, Union, Transcendental Consciousness, Cosmic Consciousness.

The most effective of all activities of Yoga is the Science of the Creative Word (PRAṆAVA), or MANTRA Yoga.

Spiritual Evolution for all Humanity is the Goal of Yoga

There is a *gap*, a lack of Continuity of Consciousness, between your personality-self and You as a Living Soul (Jīvātman, the Reincarnating Ego), and there is a gap between You as the Soul and the Triune Spiritual Self (Ātman). The work of Yoga is to provide the Bridge to Union.

Jīva: the Human Soul 35
The Threefold Structure of Man 33
Building the Bridge of Light 554

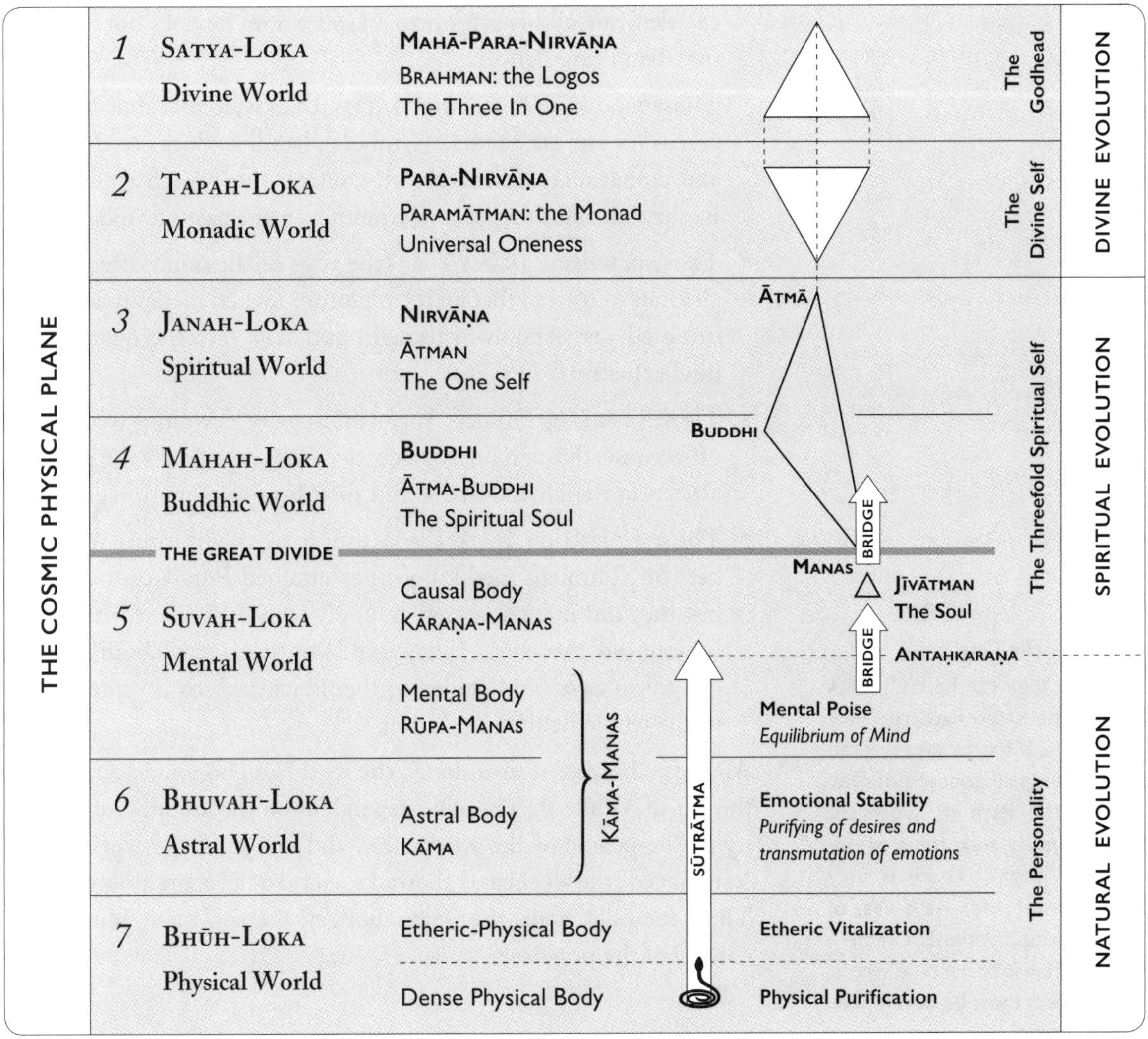

The Goal of Yoga

The Dividing of Yoga

Later on, the one integrated Science of Divine Union (YOGA-MĀRGA) was forgotten and the different *activities* of Yoga became separated. Yoga was split into parts—Haṭha Yoga, Rāja Yoga, Śakti Yoga, Karma Yoga, and so on—and people began to practise them separately from one another and separately from worldly life.

The "holy men" abandoned the world and became dependent on the world

- Those who were practising KARMA Yoga were told that all they had to do was dedicate all their actions to God and they would attain God-Realization. They never did, of course, because who can dedicate all his actions to a God whom he does not know by first-hand experience?
- Those who were practising HAṬHA Yoga were told that by doing āsanas (postures), mudrās (symbols), bandhas (locks of the body) and prāṇāyāmas (forced breath-control) they would attain God-Realization. But they did not, neither in the past nor today.
- Those practising JÑĀNA Yoga (the yoga of the mind) dreamed up all kinds of mental theologies, philosophies and metaphysics. They invented vast schools of thought and sank into the quagmire of intellectualism.
- Those practising BHAKTI Yoga (the yoga of devotion) were better off because, through intense devotion, they *experienced* the personal aspects of the Divine Being. But their lives were not integrated.
- Those practising RĀJA Yoga (union by meditation) were the best off. Through meditation they attained Pure Consciousness, but they did not know how to apply it in daily life, for they had "renounced" the world. They could not help society with it. They just sat in caves and smiled to themselves, which is quite useless to the whole field of Evolution.

All these "holy men" abandoned the world and became *dependent* on the world. While they became dependent on the kindness and charity of the people of the world, they did not *guide* the world. They "renounced" the world and allowed society to fall apart around them. Thus, the politicians, the power hungry, the spiritually blind, took control of the populace.

The One Yoga

Before Yoga can be truly RĀJA Yoga, the Kingly Path, the Way of Kings, it has to be restored to its original concept of One Yoga, the Path of Synthesis. There is no such thing as different "yogas". There is only one YOGA-MĀRGA—the Way of Integration, Synthesis, Union—and, if Man is to become whole, all aspects must be developed.

Balance in Spiritual Life 505

Nowadays, each of these various activities of Yoga are separately called "yoga", as if there were different yogas, as if you could choose any one of them and become perfect! Western students have no real concept of the Way of Yoga (the Path of Union). They may do some exercises (āsanas or postures), some breathing methods (prāṇāyāmas), or maybe some mudrās (seals or locked body postures), and they think they are doing Yoga! Yet, āsanas, prāṇāyāmas and mudrās are only a *part* of Haṭha Yoga, the purpose of which is not physical fitness at all, but the balancing of the subtle etheric currents and cakras of the etheric body. Furthermore, Haṭha Yoga itself is but a fragment of Yoga, the total life-science of Unification. Those who practise only Haṭha Yoga neglect the rest of the Way and get nowhere.

Spiritual Life and Material Life 1118
Rāja Yoga: Divine Union by Meditation 1126
Bhakti Yoga: Divine Union by Devotion 1128
Karma Yoga: Divine Union by Action 1132

There are the "devotees" who just chant and worship their Gurus and have no desire for any other activities. They practise Bhakti Yoga, or rather, an *aspect* of Yoga called BHAKTI.

There are the intellectuals who theorize about the universe, Man and God, who live to analyse all kinds of ideas and thoughts. They are the Jñāna Yogīs; they follow Jñāna Yoga and nothing else. They become sterile, lifeless and empty, because merely gathering knowledge and playing with ideas is but a small fragment of true Yoga.

There are the busy-bodies who want to save the world, who are constantly engaged in action. They are followers of Karma Yoga. But action is only a small part of Yoga. These people live in a limited world, do limited things and mistakenly believe that they are on the Path of Yoga.

This degeneration of the Science of Yoga has become prevalent in the West and even in many Āśramas in India. In such a way, the real purpose of Yoga is lost even to the natives of Hindustan (India).

To call any one activity of the Science of Union a complete Path of Yoga is both deluded and dangerous. Students who practise just one aspect of Yoga become totally unbalanced in their development. Most do physical exercises and nothing more. It is argued that some people are physical, some are intellectual, some are emotional, and so forth, and therefore they must do the corresponding form of Yoga. However, it is precisely because they are already lopsided that they should balance themselves through the practice of other aspects of Yoga.

YOGA-VIDYĀ
Sanskrit: The Science of Realization.

YOGĪ, YOGIN, YOGINĪ
Sanskrit: One who practises Yoga, or one who has attained the State of Union (YOGA) or SAMĀDHI. A female YOGĪ or YOGIN is called a YOGINĪ.

RĀJA YOGA
Sanskrit: "Royal Union". The Way of Kings. The Noble Way. The exploration of Consciousness through meditation.

ĀŚRAMA
Sanskrit: Stages of development in life. Also, a hermitage, a monastery or a spiritual centre.
The Mystery Schools and Āśramas 1148

Haṭha Yoga and Rāja Yoga

Yoga is the Science of the Soul, not just a set of health exercises. The concept of Yoga, the act of Divine Union, was degenerated by the Haṭha Yogīs, the "health yogīs" or body-oriented yogīs. This idea of Haṭha Yoga suited the materialistic, body-oriented Westerners, so that today in the West the prevalent concept of Yoga is a system of health exercises and diet, and many of the so-called Haṭha Yogīs do not even *believe* in a Soul.

You don't have to do Haṭha Yoga to do Rāja Yoga

HAṬHA Yoga is an off-shoot and lower expression of true RĀJA Yoga. Haṭha Yoga concentrates on the physical body. Rāja Yoga concentrates on the mental body (your mind and consciousness). You don't have to do Haṭha Yoga to do Rāja Yoga. Many Western students have been *misguided* in thinking that by doing many years of Haṭha Yoga postures and breath-control exercises they are practising Rāja Yoga.

Traditionally, Haṭha Yoga has eighty-four postures. These do not include "warm-up" exercises and the *watered-down* variations and adaptations popular in the Western Haṭha Yoga classes of the gyms and beauty salons! These were *difficult* postures. It took many long years for the true Haṭha Yogī of India to master all these difficult postures, each of which had to be held for a *very long time* (for instance, to stand on one's head for three hours!). In the West, many people do Haṭha Yoga as a form of gymnastics, quickly rushing through the postures (or just a few of them). When one has only an hour for a class, including "warm-up" exercises and "relaxation" afterwards (as is done in the West), clearly this does not correspond with the requirements of the old and true Haṭha Yoga of ancient India.

ĀSANA
Sanskrit: Steady posture.

MUDRĀ
Sanskrit: A posture, a gesture, a sign, or a symbol.

PRĀṆĀYĀMA
Sanskrit: "Control of the Life-breath". From PRĀṆA (the Life-force, the Life-breath) and YAMA (to regulate, to control, to guide).

When your breathing is calm and steady, your mind is calm and steady. When your mind is calm and steady, your breathing is calm and steady.

HAṬHA
The ancient, esoteric meaning of the Sanskrit word HAṬHA is as follows:
HA is the Seer, the Spiritual Self, the Sun, the PURUṢA.
ṬHA is the Consciousness aspect, the Moon, CITTA.

A further meaning of the word HAṬHA is "hard, difficult, requiring strong will-power, self-discipline and force". Thus, HAṬHA YOGA originally was the method of discovering your Spiritual Self, ĀTMAN, through consciousness-raising exercises or practices. Yoga, by the ancient definition, has nothing at all to do with "keeping fit". It is not aerobic exercises!

Then there were several dozen Prāṇāyāma (breathing) exercises to master, nine of them being the major techniques. To completely master all the proper breathing exercises was the work of many years. Each of the many breathing processes also was practised for *hours*. Thus you will see that, in the gym classes and fitness centres of the West, they have *no idea* of the real Haṭha Yoga.

In Rāja Yoga you *don't* do all these many physical postures and breathing exercises. RĀJA YOGA means "the Science of Kings" or "the Royal Way". It is primarily the Science of Meditative Awareness (DHYĀNA Yoga). You tackle your mind directly, and the *root* of mind, which is Consciousness.

The emphasis is on meditation, not on the posture

- HAṬHA Yoga focuses on the *subjugation* of the physical body.
- RĀJA Yoga focuses on the mastery of the mental body, MANAS (mind), and CITTA (the field of Consciousness).

For a Rāja Yogī, therefore, ĀSANA (posture) means any comfortable posture you can assume for long periods of meditation. The emphasis is on *meditation*, not on the posture. Similarly, PRĀṆĀYĀMA (control of the life-force) means that the breath should flow evenly, simply, naturally, so that it *does not disturb* the meditative process, DHYĀNA Yoga. (The word YOGA also means "a process".)

Beyond Āsana and Prāṇāyāma 573
The Way of the Mind 1238
Prāṇāyāma-Vidyā 1553

The Most Excellent Yoga

Following are the Seven Steps of Yoga according to YOGA VASIṢṬHA, "the Most Excellent Yoga":

1. Contentment in life.
2. Peace of mind.
3. Association with the Wise.
4. Rational investigation.
5. Thinking and experience.
6. Intuition of Truth.
7. Self-Realization (Yoga).

The YOGA VASIṢṬHA MAHĀ RĀMĀYĀNA is a textbook on Yoga written in Sanskrit over two thousand years ago. Its concept of Yoga is based on the mind, not on bodily exercises.

The objective world is a manifestation of mind. It is a system of ideas, a play of mind. Everything is a creature of mind, even as are dreams. This is seen to be true by the fact that when the Yogins bring their minds to rest, they do not experience any objects at all.

The Ideas manufactured in the Mind of BRAHMA (God) are our common objects of experience. In our minds they enter as *our own* ideas. Every mind, being the manifestation of the same Divine Mind, is capable of representing within itself all other minds and ideas. Thus, the *common* ideas shared by all of us provide the appearance of a *common world*.

Such is the philosophy of the YOGA VASIṢṬHA.

The Ultimate Reality is the Meaning of Life

It is important to understand how the old Ṛṣɪs (Rishis, Seers) and Mᴜɴɪs (Sages), such as Patañjali, understood Reality from their *personal experience*. In doing so, you might understand the need for the Science of Yoga (Yᴏɢᴀ-Vɪᴅʏā, the Science of Union), which happens to be the Goal of human life upon this planet (Yᴏɢᴀ-Māʀɢᴀ, the Path or Way of Reintegration). If you understand this, you will know what to do with your life, with your total existence. You will no longer flounder in ignorance and spiritual darkness, Aᴠɪᴅʏā and Māʏā.

When you complete the Journey of Yoga you will become a Superman

First of all, you must ignore the silly Western idea that Yoga is a system of keep-fit exercises, or that it removes fat from your body, or that it is a nice relaxation exercise after a stressful day at your business or office. Patañjali would have died of hysterical laughter if you had told him this!

The Ultimate Reality is the meaning of Yoga.
The Ultimate Reality is the meaning of Life.

In fact, Yᴏɢᴀ (Spiritual Evolution) and your Destiny (Dʜᴀʀᴍᴀ) are the same. This is what you have been looking for, all your many lives.

We do not use the word "God" much in Yoga. In the orthodox Judeo-Christian tradition, God is *symbolized* as an old man on a throne in Heaven, but most take this as the *fact* of God, and this brings to consciousness a terrible limitation to knowing Reality. Yoga has no such limitation.

One of the qualities of the Ultimate Reality (Pᴀʀᴀʙʀᴀʜᴍᴀɴ) is Cɪᴛ, "Boundless, Universal Consciousness", also known as CɪᴅʀūᴘɪṆī-Śᴀᴋᴛɪ, "the Universal Power whose Form is Pure Consciousness Itself". This is a Consciousness not related to any form, body, world, period, time, entity or manifestation; that is, it has no conceivable limitations of any sort whatsoever! It is Universal and Eternal. It is called Non-Relational-Consciousness or Unlimited-Consciousness. It has the quality of Vɪᴍᴀʀśᴀ, "Self-Knowing, Self-Awareness, Universal Self-Consciousness, the Cosmic I-ness, the Cosmic I AM-ness".

This is *not* some philosophy! This is what you *experience* at the highest stages of Yoga! This will become *your* experience, as it was the experience of the past Yogīs. When you complete the Journey of Yoga you will become a Superman (beyond the Man-species). You will become Cosmic Man instead of the limited self you are now.

In Search of Reality 1174
Mythical Concepts of God 104
A 'Godless' Religion? 754
The Sūfī God 838
The Transcendental Godhead 112

Another quality of PARABRAHMAN (the Supreme Absolute) is PRAKĀŚA, the Eternal Light, the Shining Luminosity of Everlasting Splendour, the Light of Revelation. Again, this is *not* a philosophy; you will *experience* this at the highest stages of Yoga. This is the Self-Luminous Self, PARAMĀTMAN. It is the awesome Grandeur, Power, Beauty and Majesty that truly befits the name "God". And this Eternal Light is Omnipresent.

You must not imagine this Light in the sense of a candlelight, or an electric light, or sunlight or moonlight. It is not a lifeless, "dead-matter" light. This Light is Supreme Intelligence, PARĀSAṀVIT, the Omniscient. Further, this Universal Light is not only Self-Conscious, and not only Omnipresent and Omniscient, but it is also the Omnipotent Power, KARTṚTVA-ŚAKTI, the Power-of-all-Doership, that which creates, sustains and dissolves the Universe (the All).

You will become One with this in the highest state of Yoga

You will become One with this in the highest state of Yoga when you have moved out of the human evolution and commenced your Divine Evolution. The higher you go beyond *natural* human evolution into the fields of Supernatural Evolution, into the highest stages of Yoga as you enter the Kingdom of the Gods, the more you have access to this Power and the more you can *use* this Power.

All of this is achieved through the Science of YOGA, or Divine Communion.

Light 978
The Universal Christ 440
The Self-Generating Light 1594
Vertical Evolution and the Path 174
Beyond Natural Evolution 1312

Yoga and Religion

The Sanskrit word YOGA means "union, being united or joined together", from the root YUGH, "to unite, to join, to bind together". YOGA means going into Oneness or Union, becoming at-one, moving from being a separated, fragmented individual to the condition of Oneness and Unity with the All. This is the same as the "Union with God" of the Christian and Muslim Mystics and the Jewish Hasidim.

The Latin word RELIGION has the same precise meaning as the Sanskrit word YOGA. It comes from *re-ligare,* "to tie, to fasten, to re-unite, to bind, to bring back". In the classical days of Rome, religion was *an experience of Unity with the Divine, with the Godhead.*

Since the 4th century AD the word *religion* has been changed by the church to mean "a set of beliefs concerning the nature of the Universe and God; a set of fundamental (fundamentalist) beliefs and practices agreed upon by the church authorities; the practice of religious beliefs (dogmas), rituals and observances; faith, devotion, ritual, religious conviction".

Dogma

"A settled or established opinion or belief", from the Greek DOKEIN, "it *seems* good". *Dogma* is a set of *beliefs* authoritatively laid down by the church, usually by popes, bishops or theologians.

Correct Belief? 653

The Three Stages of Yoga

The Science of Yoga is Illumination by the Soul and the Revelation of the Inner God. In the West it has been called the *Great Work*. This Great Work (Yoga) has three great stages:

The First Stage of Yoga

The goal of the first stage of Yoga is that you become Soul-Conscious

The first stage of Yoga is union of the personality with the Soul, Jīva. This is the Realization that you are a Spiritual-Intelligent-Soul, separate from and above the Three Worlds (the Physical, Astral and Mental Planes), existing apart from your body, mind and emotions, and above Time (Kāla) and Space (Ākāśa). This is Turīya, the Fourth State or Pure Consciousness. This stage can be accomplished by a life of selfless Service, the purification of the personality and deep meditation, which must be done repeatedly.

> Yoga is the control of the versatile psychic nature.
>
> *Patañjali*

The *versatile psychic nature* is Kāma-Manas, the desire-mind. According to the teachings of Yoga, your psychic nature is composed of Kāma (desires, feelings, emotions) and Manas (mind, thinking, thought-patterns, thoughtforms), and while you are alive in your physical body they functions as *one unit*. Thus, the first stage of Yoga is achieved when your mind-activities and all the feelings and desires in your astral body are stilled. Expressed in modern language, union with the Higher Self occurs when you manage to quieten your thoughts and desires simultaneously. Then the Light of the Soul may shine unimpeded in your Consciousness.

> The Seer [the Spirit within] then comes to know its proper nature. Because ordinarily the Seer is caught up in the activities of Kāma-Manas.
>
> *Patañjali*

Turīya: Pure Consciousness 498
Mind and Desire 235
True Death 424
Your Mind is the Key 1208
Cultivate Silence of the Mind 1239
Transformations of the Mind 1242
Meditation is Integration 1193

In the normal state of affairs, the Seer (you as a Soul) is caught up in a maelstrom of thoughts, feelings, desires and psychic impressions. When the thinking principle (Manas) is allowed to run wild in endless thought processes, and the desire nature (Kāma) is continually engaged in all kinds of moods and passions, peace cannot come to the personality; hence the mortal being cannot come to know the Immortal One within. When you are in a state of meditation

(DHYĀNA), peace comes to your mind (the mental body) and quiet equipoise to your emotions (the astral body), and the Seer, the Spiritual Man, is able to perceive itself in Reality. You experience yourself as a Soul rather than as a personality.

The goal of the first stage of Yoga, therefore, is that you become Soul-Conscious, that the Spiritual Man within you may stand in the Divine Light.

The Self in you is one with the Supreme Soul

> When the mind has turned away from external objects and internal thoughts, it passes into the Fourth State of Consciousness, TURĪYA, which is a higher state of consciousness than the objective or wakeful state, the dream state or the dreamless-sleep state. By repeatedly attaining this Fourth State of Consciousness [Pure Consciousness or Transcendental Consciousness], the veil clouding the Self-Luminous Light of Knowledge is dissolved away.
>
> *Patañjali*

The Second Stage of Yoga

The second stage of Yoga is the Union of the Soul with the Self, ĀTMAN, the Universal Spirit. This is Realization of the Self, ĀTMA-VIDYĀ. This Self in you is *not* your little ego which you are accustomed to calling yourself as a personality. The ego belongs to the personality, but the Self within you belongs to the Spirit.

The Third Stage of Yoga

The third stage of Yoga is the Union of the Self (Spirit) in Man with the Oversoul, PARAMĀTMAN, the Monad, your "Father who is in Heaven", the Universal One-Life which permeates and pervades all forms, all beings, all creatures in the Three Worlds. Then comes Union with God (BRAHMĀ-VIDYĀ), an inward unveiling of the Eternal Splendour, the Inner Glory that veils the Absolute Existence, the Godhead, PARABRAHMAN.

The Self in you (the ĀTMAN) is one with the Supreme Soul (PARAMĀTMAN) in a very natural way. The Self in you is a bubble, so to speak, in the "Ocean-ness" which is God, BRAHMAN.

These three stages of the Great Work (YOGA) have to be worked step by step.

MAGNUM OPUS
Latin: "The Great Work". The Spiritual Path, Discipleship, Mind Re-Creation, Union with God. The Western term for the Path of YOGA or YOGA-MĀRGA, the Science of Spiritual Regeneration. The term MAGNUM OPUS was used widely by the Alchemists of Medieval Europe.

ĀTMA-VIDYĀ, ĀTMĀ-VIDYĀ
Sanskrit: Self-Realization. Self-Knowledge. This is not "knowing yourself" on the bodily or personality level, nor learning about your behavioural psychology. This Self is the Boundless, Eternal, Imperishable Divinity *in* you, which is the *real* You.

BRAHMĀ-VIDYĀ
Sanskrit: God-Realization. The direct Knowledge of God. Union with God.

The Seven States of Consciousness 494

To Attain the State of Yoga

Yoga is not psychism, nor is it receiving messages from real or imaginary spooks or so-called "ascended masters". Such astral activity has no place in the field of Yoga, since Mysticism, Yoga, Sūfīsm and Zen begin two planes *above* the psychic dimensions.

There is no escape from the act of sitting down and meditating

Yoga can be achieved only by transcending the mind and the psychic dimensions—the Mental and Astral Worlds.

For a human being to attain to Higher States of Consciousness, there is no escape from the act of sitting down and meditating. The Yoga Masters of ancient India said:

> The Work is not accomplished by mere words or speech. If that were so, nobody would remain poor.

The "poverty" spoken of by the Masters is the "poverty of the Spirit". This was well understood by the Christian Mystics also. This signifies practice—long, arduous, wilful practice. Merely to talk about Yoga, or to listen to speeches on the subject, or to read the scriptures, will not take you there. The Yoga Masters said that the scriptures (the Bible, Koran, Sūtras, Śāstras, Vedas, and other holy books) are not meant to entertain you or cause intellectual discussion, but rather:

Channelling or Soul-Wisdom? 327
Success is Born of Action 256
Sādhanā: the Spiritual Life 1153
To Succeed in your Quest 1330

By the observance of the rules that are given out in the scriptures, you can conquer your internal enemies (the temptations, the "devils") and become a master of the senses (a Yogī).

Thus may you come to the State of Union, or YOGA.

ṚTAṀBHARĀ-PRAJÑĀ
Sanskrit: Truth-bearing Wisdom or Consciousness. The Truth must be actively "thought after", either by listening or reading.

CHAPTER 24

Gems from Patañjali's Yoga Sūtras

The Yoga Sūtras

The Sage Patañjali was just one teacher of Yoga

PATAÑJALI'S YOGA SŪTRAS are also known as PATAÑJALA YOGA SŪTRA and YOGA DARŚANAM (the Teachings on Yoga). The work consists of 196 SŪTRAS (verses or aphorisms) on YOGA-VIDYĀ (the Science of Union).

Yoga is a very ancient science of India, practised since thousands of years before Christ. It is the scientific method of uniting personality-consciousness with that of the Soul, and uniting the Soul with "God" (the Divine Presence) immanent in Creation. Patañjali did not invent it, as many Westerners erroneously believe. He recorded some of its Teachings in written form, but there was a long tradition of Yoga already existent in his time. In fact, it was well established during the Vedic civilization and later during the Upaniṣadic days. The Teaching of Yoga is found in innumerable UPANIṢADS, in the PURĀṆAS, and in other ŚRUTIS and SMṚTIS. Patañjali was a great Yogī himself, but he was also familiar with the YOGA DARŚANA, the Yoga Teachings of his predecessors. The Sage Patañjali was just one teacher of Yoga.

To write a complete commentary on all 196 verses would require many hundreds of pages. Here, and in the following two chapters, I shall deal with a few, hoping to arouse your interest in the profound subjects Patañjali draws to your attention in these SŪTRAS. Patañjali's psychological knowledge of the true Nature of Man, and the human potential for progress and evolution, is thousands of years *ahead* of the current orthodox Western materialistic psychologies.

VEDA
Sanskrit: Knowledge, Gnosis, sacred scripture.

SŪTRA
Sanskrit: A text or aphorism, a book of instructions, a thread, a connection.

ŚĀSTRA
Sanskrit: A sacred scripture or text.

UPANIṢAD
Sanskrit: Sitting down, or near to (the Guru or Master). Scriptures.

PURĀṆA
Sanskrit: "Ancient". Sacred scriptures.

ŚRUTI
Sanskrit: "That which is heard". Revelation, scriptures.

SMṚTI
Sanskrit: "Memory". Traditional teachings.

Models for Higher Consciousness

The Sages and Ṛṣis of old have set down many guidelines for attaining Higher Consciousness. There are many maps, many models. One, for example, is *The Imitation of Christ* of Thomas à Kempis. Another is Patañjali's YOGA SŪTRAS.

Patañjali's Yoga Sūtras are a several-thousand-year-old model of living, and a very good one. Although it was taught long before the birth of Christ, this model is still effective, even in this New Age. If you feel that you have not succeeded in your spiritual life, you should look at this spiritual map of life. We cannot attain Higher Consciousness unless we follow this map of life or one similar to it.

The Yoga Sūtras must be read *slowly, reflectively,* as meditation material rather than as a novel. There will be no gain for you if you hurriedly skim through them.

The Yoga Sūtras must be read slowly, reflectively

- They assume that *you are already an advanced student.*
- They assume that you know something of Punarjanma (repeated births, reincarnation) and Karma (the Law of Cause and Effect in your life).
- They assume that you are a serious student working for Punarjanma-Jaya (victory over the cyclic process of birth and death), for Mokṣa (Spiritual Liberation), for Mukti (freedom from limiting, conditioned existence).
- They assume that you know something of the true structure of Man and the multi-dimensionality of the Cosmos.
- They assume that you know that you are not your physical body; that your mind and consciousness are not your body; that your body is only a temporary dwelling place while you are visiting this dimension; that you are a Living Soul, Jīvātman, above your body, emotions and mind; and that the Spirit of God, Paramātman, dwelleth in you.
- They assume that you know that, apart from your physical body, you have several subtle bodies that relate to the invisible worlds around you; that these bodies also are not You; that each one is a Vāhan, a vehicle, a carriage, a means of transportation for you in these worlds, and an instrument for the transmission of your Soul-Energy and Soul-Life.

With limited materialistic views it is not possible to comprehend the Sūtras.

Note that I use the ancient Sanskrit words in these chapters very purposefully. The ancient words are clear and precise in their meanings. Thus, if you want to have a clear understanding (on your mind level) about the Path, these ancient terms are most useful.

The Human Constitution 31
Karma and Reincarnation 231

The Sage Patañjali

He was an advanced Soul, whether human or angelic

The date of the birth of Patañjali is not known. This is due to the fact that, in old India, the personal history and personality of a Sage or Saint were considered irrelevant; only the Teaching was important. Estimates range between ten thousand years before Christ and three hundred years before Christ. He is said to have been the Teacher of ĀDI ŚAṄKARĀCĀRYA (the first Shankaracharya), who lived five hundred years before Christ.

As in the cases of Rāma, Kṛṣṇa and Buddha, not much of Patañjali's real physical history is known, only mythology and legends. In mythology he is said to have been an incarnation of ĀDI ŚEṢA, the Primordial Serpent of Wisdom. That is to say, he was not human, but from a higher species, and incarnated into a human form to teach Man.

His full name was MAHĀ-ṚṢI (Maharishi) PATAÑJALI, the Great Sage Patañjali. He was also known as YOGINDRA, the King or Chief of Yogīs. Whoever he was, it is obvious he was an advanced Soul, whether human or angelic. And, most likely, he was a member of the old Spiritual Hierarchy of our planet, *before* the time of the Christ and the Buddha.

Legends of the Buddha 393
The Invisible Government 980

MAHĀ-ṚṢI
Sanskrit: "A Great Seer". A Ṛṣi is a See-er, a Sage who has seen the Truth first-hand by direct experience, beyond the mental faculty.
The Brotherhood of Light 395

The Father of Yoga?

Patañjali is considered by the schools of Rāja Yoga to be "the father of Yoga", which is as much an error as calling Einstein "the father of science". There was science before Einstein and there is science after him; likewise, there was Yoga in India thousands of years before Patañjali. Patañjali was taught Yoga by his teachers, who were taught by their teachers, and so on. It so happened that Patañjali wrote down a few notes of what he had learned from his teachers. These notes have survived the many centuries since his death and now the uneducated Western students of Yoga consider him the "father" of the system of Yoga.

Pāda II Sūtra 1

Chapter Two: Verse 1

Tapaḥ Svādhyāya Īśvara Praṇidhānāni Kriyā Yogaḥ

Active Yoga is fiery aspiration, understanding Yourself, and surrender to your Lord and Master within.

Tapas: burning aspiration, fiery zeal, religious fervour; burning with a restless longing for the Beloved; being on Fire for God and in God; self-discipline, self-control; burning away impurities in the body, emotions and mind.

Svādhyāya: self-study, knowing yourself, understanding yourself, Self-Knowledge; the study of the scriptures, sacred writings and the writings of the Saints.

Īśvara Praṇidhāna: surrendering yourself to God (Īśvara) who dwells within the Cave of your Heart.

Kriyā Yoga: active Union, practical Yoga, the Yoga of Action, the act of Union with the Divine.

Pada
Sanskrit: A footstep, a step, a pace, a place, a trace of something, a concept, a viewpoint, a word.

Pāda
Sanskrit: A quarter, a chapter, a part, a foot, a section, a stage, a path.

∞

This Sūtra describes Kriyā Yoga, the Way of Union through the Path of Action. This is what you need to do to attain Liberation in this life cycle. Kriyā Yoga is for men and women of *action*, who live *in* the world but are not *of* the world. It is for *you*—not for the contemplative monks and recluses who are withdrawn from the world.

Kriyā Yoga consists of three parts:

a. Rāja Yoga: the Kingly Yoga of mind control. The control of your mental body; meditation in the Head; the opening of the Third-Eye, the Crown Centre and the centre at the back of the head; the intelligent use of the will; plan, consciousness, purpose.

b. Bhakti Yoga: the Science of Devotion. The purifying of your astral body, feelings, desires, moods and emotions; meditation in your Heart; the awakening of the dynamic Love energy of the Heart Centre.

c. Karma Yoga: physical bodily activity in the form of selfless Service to others, to humans, angels, animals, plants and all life-forms. It is Love expressed physically in action. It is practical Love, not idle theorizing and day-dreaming about future utopias.

Tapas: Spiritual Purification 571
Rāja Yoga: Divine Union by Meditation 1126
Bhakti Yoga: Divine Union by Devotion 1128
Karma Yoga: Divine Union by Action 1132

Pāda I Sūtras 2, 3, 4

Chapter One: Verses 2, 3, 4

2. **Yogaḥ (Yogaṣ) Citta Vṛtti Nirodhaḥ**
   Yoga is the cessation of the activities of the mind.

Yoga is the stilling of the mind

Yoga: union, integration, joining, at-one-ment, absorption.

Citta: mind, consciousness, intellect, intelligence, the mind-stuff or mind-substance.

Vṛtti: mental waves, movements of the mind, mental activities, thoughts, transformations within the mind-stuff, behaviour patterns of the mind, fluctuations of thoughts.

Nirodha: restraining, stopping, controlling, putting a brake to something or allowing it to become still, ceasing movement or activities, settling down.

Thus:

- Yoga is the settling-down of the mind-stuff.
- Yoga is the stilling of the mind.
- Yoga is the suspending of mental activities.

3. **Tadā Draṣṭuḥ Svarūpe Avasthānam**
   Then the Seer abides in the true form of the Self.

Tadā: then, at that time, under such a condition.

Draṣṭuḥ: the Seer (see-er), the Visionary, the Sage, the Knower, the Self, the Thinker, the Soul, the True Man.

Svarūpa: one's own form, the true Form, the real Self-Nature, how one really is, your formless Self.

Avasthānam: dwells in, resides in, abides in, rests in, remains in, is established in.

Mind-Waves 1239
Your Mind is the Key 1208
Transformations of the Mind 1242
No-Mind and the One Mind 763
The First Stage of Yoga 528

Thus:

- Then the Sage abides in his own true Self (being Conscious without thoughts).
- Then the Seer rests in the true nature of his Self (transcending the mind).
- Then the Knower is established in the essential or fundamental Nature of the Self.
- Then the Visionary knows himself as he *really* is (as the Self).

Meditation can start only after you have stopped thinking

∞

Here, in these two verses, the Sage Patañjali gives the greatest clues to the Science of Yoga. They are brief, to the point, yet include all one needs to know about the Way and practice of Yoga. Yoga, as a Way, is basically the *controlling or suspending of the random activities of your mind.* As a result, you come to Know yourself directly as Pure Consciousness, Boundless and Limitless Life.

This is the fundamental and true understanding of the practice of *meditation*. Meditation can start properly only *after you have stopped thinking.* When you have stopped thinking—naturally, effortlessly, not forced—it will be easy to come to the State of Yoga, Union, Oneness with your Soul, with Divinity. It is the *activity of your mind* which prevents this.

This has been taught in the TANTRA (esoteric) literature as:

> The YOGĪ enters into SAMĀDHI (Divine Consciousness) by a thought-free, non-relational Awareness, by dissolving the personality-sense in CITI-ŚAKTI (Universal Awareness, Transcendental Consciousness).

Thus, any activities of the mind, such as SANKALPA (will, desire, imagination) and SAṀKALPA (thought-constructs), cannot lead to Yoga; therefore, from the point of view of the Path to Self-Realization, they are to be avoided as they are actually hindrances. Thus, the busier your mind, the further it is from the Integrated State (YOGA).

Only those practices (DHĀRAṆĀ) which positively lead you to UNMANA (the no-mind state), those practices in which your mental processes are transcended and Soul-Awareness is gained, are of any value on the YOGA-MĀRGA, the Path of Inner Union.

When the Mind is Still 768
To Silence the Mind 1212
Cultivate Silence of the Mind 1239
Some Hints for Meditation Practice 1203
Dhāraṇā and Dhyāna 1523

4. **Vṛtti Sārūpyam Itaratra**

At all other times the Seer identifies with the fluctuations of the mind.

Vṛtti: the fluctuations of the mind, the movements of the mind, mind-currents.

The mind does not know the difference between what is real and what is not

Sārūpya: resembles, similar to, in the likeness of, assumes the character of.

Itaratra: at other times, elsewhere, on other occasions.

Thus:

- When not in the State of Yoga, your consciousness identifies with (resembles) the qualities or experiences of your mind-structure.
- At all other times, when you are not in the State of Yoga, you as a Soul become similar to (or one with) the movements of your mind (your thoughts).
- Your Essential Nature or Pure Consciousness becomes overshadowed by the activities of your mind when you are not in the State of Union (Yoga).
- In your normal, natural state of being, you as the Divine Man identify with all that goes on in your mind.
- If you are not in the State of Yoga, you simply resemble the state of your mind, which appears to you as reality.

∞

One curious feature of the mind is that *it does not know the difference between what is real and what is not.* It simply *reflects*, like a mirror, what is *presented* to it, and *identifies* with it. Therefore:

You identify with what goes on in your mind.

For example, in your dreams your mind sees your repressed or subconscious thoughts and they appear "real" to it. When you "dream", therefore, your dream appears "real" to you. Only when you wake up do you know that it was only a dream.

True Thought 79
To Experience Heaven 82
In Bondage to the Mind 238
Obstacles to Higher Consciousness 1420

So it is with your whole thinking process. Your thoughts are presented to your mind and your mind accepts them as "real". Therefore your thoughts appear to you as reality, even when they are one-hundred-percent wrong or have nothing at all to do with the true Reality of how things actually are. People are habitually trapped by their thoughts—good, bad or indifferent—which they are prepared to defend even at the cost of their lives or the lives of others.

Humanity is steeped in error in all aspects of life

You "think" something about God or the Universe, or about humans or angels, and you *think* that is how it *is*. So, Humanity is steeped in error on all fronts, in every subject, in all aspects of life. This is immensely important to understand, as everybody is trapped by it.

This is the most important issue of life, yet Humanity completely ignores it. You are not what you think about yourself, and the World is not what you think it is.

Myths and mythologies in the Old Testament, for example, or myths about the lives of the Christ, the Buddha, Rāma or Śrī Kṛṣṇa, which were previously presented (told) to the mind, are accepted as "reality" by the minds of the followers of those religions. They really believe that it "really" so happened. Similarly, the legends and myths about the Saints, in all religions, are believed by their faithful as the complete Truth, just as the many "Creation stories" of the tribes, nations, cultures and religions of the world are recited with the belief that they are the Truth.

Yet, simply, the people's minds were previously *impressed* with those stories by their elders. The various traditions of all the tribes, cultures and nations of the world were *indoctrinated* into the young people's minds and, as adults, they believe those traditions as the *sacred Truth* which must be upheld at all costs, even if those customs and traditions are horribly wrong, evil, backward or preventing human progress. These are the so-called "religious" customs. People will *fight* for them.

This process is similar to what you experience when you watch a movie or television. The *images* from the movie arrive to your mind (the mental body) via the physical senses, and these images are then *reflected* or *mirrored* in your mind, and your mind becomes *identified* with them and, therefore, what you "see" appears as "reality".

Traditionis 379
Legends of the Buddha 393
Fear of conditioning 485
Understand your Predicament 892
From Darkness into Light 982

Pāda IV Sūtra 17

Chapter Four: Verse 17

Tad Uparāga Apekṣitvāt Cittasya Vastu Jñāta Ajñātam
An object is experienced only if the mind gets impressed by it.

You do not know the Self because you are not focusing on It

Tad: thus, thereby, from that.

Uparāga: colouring, conditioning, influencing.

Apekṣitvāt: needing, desiring, wanting, expecting, hoping.

Cittasya: of the mind-stuff, by the mind, by Consciousness.

Vastu: an object, a thing, anything.

Jñāta: known.

Ajñāta, Ajñātam: unknown.

Thus:

- An object is known or unknown according to the conditioning of the consciousness/mind in relationship to that object.
- Objects become known, or not, depending on whether your mind becomes coloured (influenced) by them.
- According to how your mind is conditioned, or not, you perceive an object.

∞

In the above Sūtra the "object" can be yourself, your relatives, Truth, God, or whatever you *desire* to know. You do not *know* God because God has not *impressed* His Reality on your mind, because you have not provided the right conditions. You do not *know* Yourself (the Self) because you are not *focusing* on It; therefore your mind is not *engaged* in It. You must learn what to *do.*

Senses or the Self? 239
Conditioned Thinking 1084
Your mind is attracted to physical things 1231
Attach your Mind to the Eternal 1234

Pāda IV Sūtra 18

Chapter Four: Verse 18

Sadā Jñātāḥ Citta Vṛttayas Tat Prabhoḥ Puruṣasya Apariṇāmitvāt

The mind itself is always experienced by the changeless Self who is its Lord.

Your mind is not your true Self, nor the SELF

Sadā: always, forever.

Jñātāḥ: known.

Citta Vṛttayas, Citta Vṛttayaḥ: mind-fluctuations, mind-modifications, changes in the mind-stuff or in Consciousness.

Prabhu: Lord, Master, God.

Tat Prabhoḥ: of its Lord, Master.

Puruṣa: the Self, God, the Being who is the Reality. The Spirit in Man and the Universal Spirit in the Cosmos. Puruṣa is also the Soul in Man as distinct from the body and mind.

Puruṣasya: of the Soul or Spirit, of God.

Apariṇāmitvāt: because of changelessness.

Thus:

- Because of the unchanged nature of the Self (Puruṣa), who is the Lord and Master of the mind, all changes in the mind-stuff (Citta) are known to It.

∞

The mind in you is ever in motion. This mind is *not* your brain or nervous system; the mind (mental body) uses your brain as a point of contact with this world. But even your mind is not your true Self (the Soul), nor the SELF (the Spirit). You must *rise above* your mind in your meditations.

Mind and Brain 79
Realms of the One Mind 492
The Threefold Structure of Man 33
What is Consciousness? 1368
Suspended Mind 1209

Pāda II Sūtra 20

Chapter Two: Verse 20

Draṣṭā Dṛśi Mātraḥ Śuddhaḥ (Śuddho) Api Pratyaya Anupaśyaḥ

The Seer is Pure Consciousness; though Pure, he looks upon things through the window of the mind.

The Seer looks upon things through the window of the mind

Draṣṭā: the Seer (see-er), Observer, Witness, Perceiver, Onlooker. The Self (the Soul) and the SELF (the Spirit). You as the Soul and You in your Divinity, at one with the Spirit. The Seer is Ātman or Puruṣa, the Spectator, the Ātmā.

Dṛśi: seeing, perceiving.

Mātra: a measure, confinement, limitation.

Dṛśimātraḥ: the power of seeing, perceiving, experiencing; being aware or conscious of something.

Śuddhaḥ: pure, immaculate, innocent, clean, unsullied.

Api: although, even though, though.

Pratyaya: cognition, reliance, faith, confidence, trust, means, device.

Anupaśyaḥ: appears as if seeing; sees, perceives, cognizes; goes along with what is perceived.

The Process of Seeing or Perceiving

The *limited* impressions of the multi-dimensional World, as perceived by the *limited* bodily senses, are conveyed to the *limited* mind-structure (the mental body), and that *limited* or *partial* image of the World is thus seen by the Self, by You as the Soul, the Seer, the Knower, the Experiencer. What you see or experience is *not* the total multi-dimensional Reality, however, but only a *fragment of the Physical World*. This is the dilemma of being in a physical body.

Body ⇨ **Mind** ⇨ **The Self or Soul**

As a result of this process, it *seems* as if the Soul or Self *loses* its true Identity or Awareness. Once you have *transcended* the body-mind structure, or have risen above it in meditation, the Seer knows himself to be as he really is: Pure Boundless Consciousness, beyond Time and Space and Causation.

Ātman, Ātmā 34
The Watcher 1212
The Silent Watcher Meditation 1388

Thus:

- The Self is Pure, but he goes along with what is perceived through the mind.
- The Self is Pure Seeing, itself, but his vision is clouded by the faculty of the mind.
- The Spectator is the Self (You as the Soul). Although You are Pure Consciousness itself, you perceive the World through the medium of your mind (with all its limitations); hence you have a warped view of Reality.
- The Self has the power of Pure Seeing, but it goes along with what it sees (what is presented to it by the mind).

For the Enlightened, life in this world is very different

∞

This is one of the most profound Insights ever upon this planet. If you comprehend this Sūtra it will shatter all your materialistic concepts and thoughts, and you will realize just how mad is the worldly thinking of the masses. This will also explain to you the great dilemma of existence in this world. Whatever you see, hear or touch is *filtered* through your mind, *coloured* by your mind, *prejudiced* by your mind.

There is, however, another profound meaning in this Sūtra as it refers to the perception of the enlightened Yogī:

- The Seer is Pure Consciousness; he witnesses the World *without* the colouring of the mind.

This is the State of Yoga or Union with all that is. Thus, for the Sage or the Enlightened, life in this world is very different—mysteriously so.

In the Human Being		In the Cosmos	
Ātman Puruṣa	The Spirit	**Paramātman Parama-Puruṣa**	God
⇩		⇩	
Manas	The mind	**Mahat**	Cosmic Mind
⇩		⇩	
Asmitā	The sense of self	**Brahmā**	God-Incarnate

Perception through Mind

Consciousness 1370
Perceptions of the One Mind 490
The Fourth State 499
The Enlightened 1702

Pāda II Sūtra 21

Chapter Two: Verse 21

Tad Ārtha Eva Dṛśyasya Ātmā
The World exists for the sake of the Self.

The World was planned by Divine Will and Divine Purpose

Tad, Tat: that

Ārtha: purpose, cause, objective, means, meaning, reward, fulfilment.

Tadarthaḥ: for that purpose, for the sake of, for His sake.

Eva: only, alone, verily.

Dṛśyasya: what is seen, the observable, Creation, Manifestation, Nature, the World.

Ātmā, Ātman: the Self (the Soul), the SELF (the Spirit), Puruṣa, Divinity, the Seer, the Witness to All, God.

Thus:

- All that exists is for the sake of the Spirit.
- The *seen* exists only for the *Seer*, Ātman, the Divine Consciousness.
- The World exists to serve the Will of God (Ātmā).
- For the purpose of your Soul does your embodiment exist (your physical, astral and mental bodies).
- The purpose of *all that is* is to behold the Immortal God-ness within All.

∞

This is one of the key revelations of Patañjali's Yoga Sūtras. For the materialistic-minded millions of the world, "reality" consists of their physical bodies and the Physical World perceived through their bodily senses, and there is nothing more. Yet the dense World includes the Astral and Mental Worlds also. These people are the *living dead*, though they do not know it. According to the materialistic thinkers, the world came about through a "Big Bang", the vast star-systems formed themselves out of cosmic dust and gases, life arose out of a primal soup, and consciousness evolved out of dead matter!

But Patañjali says that the World exists for the sake of the Self. How beautiful and how meaningful it is! The World was *planned* from the beginning by Divine Will and Divine Purpose!

The "World" means here, of course, the Physical, Astral and Mental Planes of Being, for they constitute the Gross Physical Body of the Logos, the densest realms of existence, the form-worlds or embodied worlds (Rūpa-Loka).

The Constitution of God-Immanent 122
The Plan is in the Divine Mind 161

The Upaniṣads

Illuminating the Nature of the Self

The Sanskrit word Upaniṣad means "sitting at (or near) the feet of the Guru (Master)". In old India, the Upaniṣads were a type of mystical writings or shorthand notes written by the Sages for students of the Spiritual Life. Basically, they are attempts to describe the Self (the Soul) and the SELF (the Spirit), and their relationship to the ego or lower personality and the physically embodied human being.

You, in your bodily self, are not even a fragment of a fragment of Yourself

There is a profound Mystery concerning Man, the human species on this planet. The Spirit becomes veiled by the Soul, the Soul becomes veiled by the personality, and the personality becomes veiled by the physical body. Thus it is that you, in your bodily self, are not even a fragment of a fragment of Yourself.

How you become so limited is the basic subject matter of the Upaniṣads. By meditating on the Upaniṣadic Mantrams you learn to reaffirm your true Nature, to realize who you really are, to transcend bodily limitations and the limitations of your personal ego or "I", the little self. This form of meditation will help you realize *intuitively* the Truth about yourself.

∞

The real You is the Monad, or Paramātman.

In your descent into lower regions you became the Higher Self, the Triune Self, Ātma-Buddhi-Manas.

On further descending, you became the personality, encased in your mental, astral, etheric-physical and physical bodies.

All of these are You.

On the Path of Return you learn to rediscover your Self and the Divine Nature that you Are.

You, as a personality, are a fragment of You as a Spiritual Soul.

And You, as a Spiritual Soul, are only a fragment of You as a Monad or Divinity.

Thus, what you see of yourself in your physical body is but a shadow of a shadow of a shadow.

Who is 'I AM'? 1418
Trapped Spirits 1240
The Compound Human Being 32
Understand your Predicament 892
Know Thyself 1389

The Upaniṣadic Mantrams

1. More radiant than the Sun,
purer than the snow,
subtler than the Aether
is the Self, the Spirit within my Heart.
I am that Self, that Self am I.

God is the Self of the Universe and the true Self of you

Meditate on this mantram in the Heart...

The word *Self* has many meanings in ancient Sanskrit. It does *not* mean the self you are identifying with now—your bodily consciousness, your worldly name and form, your limited self-image, how you see yourself and how others see you now.

Ātmā, Ātman, the SELF, is Universal Spirit, the God-Presence within you and outside you in all Creation and Space. It is the God-in-you and the You-in-God. Another name for it is Paramātmā, Paramātman, the Supreme Self, the Transcendental Self, the Highest Self. The *Self* means a conscious entity—intelligent, self-conscious, aware. God is the Self of the Universe and the true Self of you. God is the Supreme-Intelligent-Conscious-Being of the Universe, Omnipresent, Omniscient, Omnipotent.

2. The Bright Eternal Self that is God,
and the Bright Eternal Self that lives in my Heart,
is One and the same.
I am that Self, that Self am I.

Meditate on this mantram in the Heart...

One way of understanding this mantram is that God (for the Man-species you belong to) is the Paramātman, the Monad, the Father in Heaven (on the Monadic Plane); and the highest distinguishable Humanity is the Ātman, the Spirit on the Ātmic Plane (the Nirvāṇic Plane, Nirvāṇa).

Ātman, Ātmā 34
The Abode of the Self 434
The Eastern Heart 448
God in the Heart 634
The Mystery within the Heart 1315
Incarnations of the Sun 1593

To meditate on an Upaniṣadic Mantram, simply hold it in your mind. You may do this while sitting down in a formal meditation session, or you may hold the mantram in your mind while busily engaged in life. This will lead you to Ātmā-Vidyā or Self-Realization.

3. **I am That Brahman,**
formless like Space, Supreme,
eternally luminous, the Self of all,
birthless, One without a second,
immutable, unattached,
all-pervading, ever-free Consciousness.
I am that Self, that Self am I.

Your true Human Nature is identical with the true Nature of God

Meditate on this mantram in the Head...

Brahman (the Absolute Godhead) and Parabrahman (the Transcendental Absolute) are the same as Ātman and Paramātman. The Great Mystery discovered in deep meditation or Samādhi, in the State of Yoga or Union, is that your *true* Human Nature, on the level of the Spirit, is identical with the *true* Nature of God. This is *not* a philosophy; it is an actual experience when, through Yoga, you have *transcended* the body-mind complex and your personality.

4. **I am not the physical body; I am the Being of Light.**
I am not my emotions; I am the Being of Light.
I am not my thoughts; I am the Being of Light.
The Self in me is One with the Self in all.
I am that Self, that Self am I.

Meditate on this mantram in the Head...

The Spiritual Self within you, the Being of Light, is the Ātman, who is the true Draṣṭuḥ or Seer (see-er) within you, the true Ṛṣi (Rishi), Sage, Knower of God. It is only through Ātman (Ātmā) that you can *Know* God.

5. **Love is the Source.**
Love is the Goal.
Love is the means of Spiritual Attainment.
The Heart of God is infinite Love.
I am that Self (God), that Self am I.

Meditate on this mantram in the Heart...

The Self is the Thinker and Actor. And yet, the Self is only a Witness, an Observer.

The Fifth State 500
The Being of Light 416
The Experience of the Heart 1281
Mahāvākya: Great Truth Statements 1469
The Essence of Wisdom 1680

Pāda I Sūtra 23

Chapter One: Verse 23

Īśvara Praṇidhānād Vā

Suspension of the mind can also be accomplished by surrender to the Lord God within.

By complete Devotion to the Divine, Enlightenment also can be gained

Īśvara always means the ruling, guiding or controlling principle *within*. In particular:

a. God, Lord, Lord-God, the Universal Self, the Supreme Being, the Central Authority within the Universe, the Master of the Universe, the Godhead.

b. The Solar Logos; the Ruler within any solar system in the Universe.

c. The Monad in the Man-species, the "Father in Heaven"; the Soul, the Triune Self, the Ātman, the Inner-Ruler-Immortal in Man; the Heart Centre.

Praṇidhāna: complete Devotion, surrender to the Divine; prayer, meditation, contemplation of the Divine; worship and selfless service to God (Īśvara, according to any of the three meanings).

Vā: or, also.

Thus:

- By complete Devotion to the Divine, Enlightenment also can be gained.
- By merging into the Divine Heart, Enlightenment also can be gained.

Īśvara 1623
Īśvara-Praṇidhāna 569
On the Wings of Devotion 1129
My Beloved Lives in my Heart 1290
Heart Action 1331

Pāda I Sūtra 27

Chapter One: Verse 27

Tasya Vāchakaḥ Praṇavaḥ
He dwells in the Sacred Word.

God is the Logos, the Divine Creative Word

Tasya: his, its.

Vāchaka, Vākaka: represents, signifies, indicates, denotes, symbolizes.

Praṇava: the Ōṁ, the Ōṁkāra, the Sacred Sound, the Sacred Word, Vāch (Vāk, the Divine Speech); the Symbol for the Infinite; the Logos, the Sound-Current; the Path of Return to the Source; A.U.M, Āuṁkāra, Śabda-Brahman.

Praṇava means the exaltation and praising of God, singing to God, the Īśvara. It also means the Glorious Voice of God, the Sounding-Light Current that brings the Universe into existence, keeps it going, and will dissolve it at the end of the great Cycle of Time.

Thus:

- Īśvara is represented by Ōṁ.
- The Sound of Ōṁ represents Īśvara, the Lord.
- Īśvara is found through using the sound of Ōṁ.
- God is expressing Himself through the Sound of Ōṁ, the Logos.
- God is the Logos, the Divine Creative Word.

Patañjali's Yoga Sūtras are always multi-dimensional, with multiple meanings, owing to the depth of the Sanskrit language. Each interpretation requires careful meditation, careful consideration.

To meditate on the Sūtras (aphorisms, verses, precepts, threads, connecting links), you *hold* each one in your mind, separately, and "reflect" on it. Great *insights* will come to you if you do so. You may do this while sitting, standing, walking or lying down. First you learn to understand its profound *meaning*, then you *apply* it in your daily living. You will undergo tremendous changes and transformations in the process. Thus, gradually, Enlightenment will come to you.

The Logos: the Word of God 114
Vāk: the Divine Speech 118
The Cosmic Christ 662
The Voice of God 864
The Word, Logos, Voice, Name 1646

Āuṁ, Ōṁ, Nāda

ĀUṀ is the Divine Word for Involution, Creation, Manifestation, the materialization of the Universe, the descent into Matter.

ŌṀ is the Divine Word for Evolution, moving upwards and forwards and out of the Three Realms. Purification, Union.

NĀDA is the Soundless Sound, the Divine Word on the highest Spiritual Planes.

The Primordial Light 119
The Action of the Primordial Sound 165
Potent Vibrations: Bīja-Mantra 1542
The Holy Spirit as Cosmic Mother 1501
What is the Name? 1259
The Holy Trinity 1342

ĀUṀ represents Manifestation, the manifest God and the manifest Universe. It is the whole Universe or Cosmos in its totality. It is the past, present and future of the World, A.U.M.

ŌṀ is the same Word, the Logos, in the process of *ascending*, moving out of the Sphere of Creation-Activity.

NĀDA is the Soundless Sound, the Pure Transcendental Sound of Absolute Reality.

ĀUṀ is the Word of the Personality.
ŌṀ is the Word of the Soul.
NĀDA is the Word of the Spirit.

You move from ĀUṀ to ŌṀ and then to NĀDA, for the three are One:

- The ĀUṀ is the Force and Sounding-Light Vibration of the *Third* Aspect of the Deity in active, intelligent Matter of the Cosmos and in Man (in his physical, etheric-physical, astral and mental bodies). This aspect of the Deity is the one closest to us. It incarnates and develops the form-worlds and the forms or bodies of all entities. This is "the Word that was made flesh"—that is, it becomes the forms or bodies of incarnating entities. Thus, in truth, every human being is a Divine Incarnation, though humans in their unregenerated state cannot sense the Word vibrating within them.
- The ŌṀ is the Sound of Liberation and Resurrection, the *Second* Aspect of the Deity, the Christ Aspect or Power, the Sounding-Light Vibration which releases you from bondage to your forms and bodies.
- NĀDA is the Originating-Sounding-Light-Vibration, the *First* Aspect of the Deity, the Source, Silence.

Meditation on Ōṁ

Sitting silently in your meditation posture, intone **ŌṀ** in your Head Centres:

- In the Third-Eye Centre.
- In the Crown Centre.

The final Secret can be discovered only in Nāda, the Soundless Sound of the First Aspect of the Godhead, the First Logos, the First Word, the First Breath. This Sound cannot be thought of, nor uttered by Man. It can be experienced, heard and realized by Man in the highest state of Yoga or Divine At-One-Ment.

The final Secret can be discovered only in Nāda

The highest act of Kriyā Yoga, the highest Cosmic Act of the highest Yogī Adept, is *hearing* this Word and *breathing* it forth from himself for the benefit of all Mankind and all Life. This is "to bless, to heal and to inspire" all life-forms who come in contact with the Yogī Adept, Sage or Seer. The Master Yogī lives in the Sound, which is the true Ineffable Name of the Deity.

The Sound, the Ineffable Name, is beyond Time and Space and Causation. It is complete Silence and yet it is the Source of all that is Manifest.

'The Esoteric Mantram'

Ōṁ Maṇi Padme Hūṁ

Ōṁ is the Jewel in the Lotus (the Heart) in which is the dissolution of the self and the finding of the Self (Ōṁ).

This is an ancient Sanskrit mantram of the Heart School or Heart Path which became popular in Tibet, where the inner meaning became lost in senseless repetition.

Maṇi: a jewel, a precious stone, an ornament.
Padma: the lotus flower, the Heart Centre.
Hūṁ: dissolving, dissolution, melting away.

The true Ōṁ is the Spiritual Self in the Heart, the Ātman, the Draṣṭuḥ or Seer, the Observer, the Witness to all that is, the Inner Visionary, the Self who forever abides in His own true Nature. It is Yourself.

The "self" (with a small 's') is your Asmitā or sense of self in your physical body, egoism, egotism, your false sense of "I", the separated personal self.

Ātman, the Spiritual Self in Man, and Paramātman, the Universal Self, are *one and the same*. This is the Mystery of the Heart.

This mantram can be repeated as follows:

- In the Third-Eye, sharply focused.
- In the Heart, with Love, Devotion and meaning.

Meditations in the Heart Centre 1298

Listen to Nāda 1212
Meditation on the Sacred Word 1216
Hear the Sound within the Silence 1651

The Path of Seeing

There is the Path of *Hearing* and the Path of *Seeing*.

Visualization develops the Eye of Inner Vision, the Third-Eye. Ultimately the Third-Eye transforms into the *Eye of Śiva,* the *All-Seeing Eye*, the Divine Eye (Śiva-Netra) which sees all things in the Eternal Now. This is the Path of *Seeing*.

Visualization will lead you ultimately to the Seeing of the Omnipresent Self

Visualization activates the pineal gland, which is now dormant in Man, but was active in Lemurian and Atlantean days. Through the awakened Third-Eye, energy can be manipulated (etheric, astral, mental and causal), thoughts created and controlled, elemental beings and nature-forces directed, and lesser angels influenced. This is Guhya-Vidyā (Secret Knowledge), the legendary power of the true Magicians of old.

Through visualization you attract to yourself that which you visualize.

Visualization will lead you ultimately to the Seeing of the Omnipresent Self, Ātman, as a White Light of the purest substance and highest vibration, limitless and eternal, Pure-Intelligence, an irresistible Power and ever-new Joy in an Eternal-Now and Forever-Everywhere condition. You will *know* that this *is* God, and the Way, and the Truth, and the Life. This is the Path of *Seeing*.

This is not "thinking" about God; it is *recognizing* that you are in the Presence of your Lord and Master. It is *remembrance* of God in whichever *form* you choose.

Your Way, then, must be to be *active* in the world, in World Service, and to *retire* regularly into the World of Silence, the Still Point within you. In your Solitude you *remember* your Lord God who dwells at the deepest point of your Soul. In this Inner Solitude you meet and *commune* with your God. You *become* those divine attributes by which you visualize your favourite God-Form.

This is not mediumship, not channelling! You do not channel an "ascended master" or a spook of any kind! This is Mystical Union with your true Master within. The mediums and channellers know no such Union. This is Samādhi, At-One-Ment.

The Third-Eye Centre 49
Clairvoyance 292
Esoteric Knowledge 1218
Meditation in the Third-Eye 1224
Visualizing the Divinity within the Heart 1268
See the Light of the Logos 1650
The Being of Light in Meditation 418
Alone with God 700

The Path of Hearing

There is a tremendous Power available in Silence, ready to be used for all life-changing and creative work. When you experience the *real* Silence, your ego (the personal sense of identity) disappears, is dissolved. This is the Path of *Hearing*.

Silence is the womb where true Wisdom is born. Wisdom is not a thought, nor the product of thought. Wisdom is an innate Power of your Soul which flourishes when your personality is quiet.

Within the Silence you will discover a subtle, transcendental Activity

Silence is Feminine. There is a point in your Soul, a Sphere of Consciousness, which is eternally Peaceful, Quiet, Still, Silent. This is your Holy of Holies, the Inner Shrine, the Innermost Chamber of your Temple where God resides in full Splendour and Glory. Nothing can disturb this Silence. The God within you works in Stillness.

The *attitude* in Silence is that of *waiting* and *listening*. You can focus your Attention in the middle of the Head or in your Heart, whichever is easier for you. There you listen and wait patiently for your Beloved Lord. There you listen to the Voice of the Silence, the Soundless Sound, the Music of the Spheres, Kṛṣṇa's Flute.

This Stillness must be simultaneously in your Mind and Heart Centres. In Silence, Īśvara (the Lord within your Heart) can be discovered. You may think of Him as God, the Buddha, the Christ, Śrī Kṛṣṇa, the Ātman, or the Spiritual Self.

In deep Silence you will feel a Divine Movement in your Heart, or a tremendous Power in the Causal Centre above your head, or a Light descending from the Above to the Below (from the Causal Centre into the Base Centre). Within the Silence, within the Stillness, you will discover a subtle, transcendental Activity. This is *Divine Activity*. In Silence you *surrender* to your Lord God, your Inner Ruler Immortal, your Master within.

Your God-Being, the Monad, operates in Stillness within you.

Tao is Silent 779
Zen Listening 787
To See and Hear God 637
The Stages of Sūfī Silence 901
The Practice of Silence 1443
The Power of Divine Hearing 590
The Silence of the Deep 1355
The Silent State 1554
Works of Silence 1643

Building the Bridge of Light

Before attempting these advanced meditations, refer to the diagram on page 521: *The Goal of Yoga.* There you will see that there is a *gap in Consciousness* between you as a personality and you as the JĪVĀTMAN or Living Soul. Further, there is a Consciousness-gap between you as the Living Soul and You as the Triune Self or Triad (ĀTMA-BUDDHI-MANAS), the Spiritual Self.

To overcome these gaps you need to build a Bridge in Consciousness

To overcome these gaps you need to build a *Bridge in Consciousness,* called the *Rainbow Bridge* or the *Bridge of Light.*

- In Sanskrit Yogic terminology this bridge is called ANTAḤKARAṆA (Inner Organ) or ANTASKARAṆA (Inner Cause or Inner Action).
- In the Western Mystical System it is called *Jacob's Ladder* or the *Ladder of Light* or the *Ladder between Heaven and Earth.*

Before attempting these meditations, please review carefully the preceding pages entitled "ĀUṀ, ŌṀ, NĀDA". You should also have meditated on the Upaniṣadic Mantrams so that you understand the Vision or Goal of what you want to achieve on the Path of Wisdom, the Way of Enlightenment, Self-Realization, re-becoming the Divinity that you are.

These advanced meditations consist of three aspects:

a. The desire for Self-Realization (Realization of "the Bright Eternal Self that You are").
b. A visualization process.
c. Sounding the Sacred Word ŌṀ or a Word of Power (mantra).

Meditation One

- Sit Still. Just Be.
- Enter into Simple Silence. Your mind and emotions are at rest. Your breathing is light and natural.
- Remember "the Bright Eternal Self that You are".
- Focus your Awareness in the Third-Eye area (between the two physical eyes). Withdraw your attention into your mental body (the mind-structure). You are no longer aware of your physical body or your outer environment.

Āuṁ, Ōṁ, Nāda 550
The Upaniṣadic Mantrams 546

- With your mind focused in the Third-Eye, intone the Sacred Word Ōṁ, silently, prolonged. At the same time, have the desire, purpose or will to unite yourself with "the Bright Eternal Self that You are". The sounding of Ōṁ carries your will to become United, at One, with "the Bright Eternal Self that You are", your Eternal Beingness.
- With each sounding of the Ōṁ, visualize one of the following:
  a. You are building a bridge made up of the seven rainbow colours.
  b. You are building a bridge of shimmering White Light.
  You must choose before your meditation whether you will visualize the Rainbow Bridge or the Bridge of Light.
- As you build your bridge you will become increasingly aware of the Presence of the "Bright Eternal Self that You are".

The Antaḥkaraṇa is that which causes your Union to take place

Meditation Two

This time you are going to build the ANTAḤKARAṆA (the Bridge of Light) differently. Remember that this word means "Inner Cause", or that which causes your Union to take place.

- Sit Still. Become completely silent, in body, mind and emotions.
- Relax, for you are not going anywhere. *The Journey is in Being, not in doing anything.*
- First, *listen* to the Silence all around.
- Then *hear* whatever you can of the Inner Sound, the NĀDA, the Sacred Word that Sounds in you and in all Creation.
- Then *visualize* a ladder of pulsating White Light stretching up from the back of your neck, up through the Crown Centre, up to the Causal Centre above you, and dissolving into a Star of Brilliant White Light.
- As you silently chant Ōṁ, the Word of Glory, *see yourself ascending* upon this Ladder of Light into the Sphere of Blinding Light above you. Then *dissolve* into the Light, until there is nothing else but Light all around.
- Then *remember* that this Light is Yourself, the Bright Eternal Self.
- That Self You *are*.

Building the Antaḥkaraṇa 1194
The Sounds of Nāda 1651

Pāda I Sūtra 30

Chapter One: Verse 30

Most people fail because of these impediments

Vyādhi Styāna Saṁśaya Pramāda Ālasya Avirati Bhrānti Darśana Alabdha Bhūmikatva Anava Sthitatvāna Citta Vikṣepās Te Antarāyāḥ

The obstacles to Union with the Soul (the Self) are: bodily diseases, mental laziness, indecision, carelessness, physical sluggishness, too much time and energy spent satisfying the senses, false perceptions (wrong ideas), missing the point of the Spiritual Path, the inability to hold onto the stage already gained, a scattered or distracted mind.

Vyādhi: diseases.

Styāna: dullness, lack of perseverance, stupidity.

Saṁśaya: doubts, indecision about the Path.

Pramāda: carelessness, intoxication, drunkenness.

Ālasya: laziness, idleness, taking it easy.

Avirati: sensuality, lack of moderation and control.

Bhrānti-Darśana: false perceptions, illusions, self-delusions, glamour, mistaken ideas.

Alabdha-Bhūmikatva: missing the important issues, disappointment for not succeeding fast enough.

Anava-Sthitatvāni: slipping down from the state already achieved, giving up.

Citta-Vikṣepaḥ (Vikṣepās): mental distractions, confusion, losing your way on many sidetracks.

Te: these (are).

Antarāyāḥ: obstacles, impediments, problems.

In the following passage Patañjali mentions a few more hindrances:

These are the hindrances [to Soul Consciousness]: the darkness of unwisdom, self-assertion, lust, hate and attachment.

A steady application towards the Spiritual Goal is the way to put a stop to these hindrances. By being in sympathy with the happy, having compassion for the troubled, delighting in holy things and disregarding the unholy, the psychic nature within you moves to Eternal Peace.

Passion and Dispassion 695
Crises on the Path 1162
Notes on the Path in the New Age 1166

The brilliance of Patañjali lies in the fact that he can say so much in a few words. Here he describes the troubles and woes of all the spiritual aspirants, seekers and disciples of all times, in all religions, in all traditions and cultures. These are the obstacles, difficulties and hindrances, the impediments that make it difficult for you to attain your Goal, the Antarātma Sādhanā (Quest for the Inner Self).

If you think that you should have achieved your Goal already, please look at the above list again. You need to look carefully at these obstacles, again and again, and *do* something about them. Most people (if not all) fail on the Spiritual Quest because of these impediments. Many students of the Path cannot even imagine that something could be "wrong" with them, and that this is why they are not making rapid progress. This is a very *sobering* Sūtra.

Self-Realization is possible only when you have removed most of these obstacles

Ātmā-Vidyā, Self-Realization, the Knowledge of the Self (the Soul), is possible only when you have removed most of these obstacles. This takes some self-discipline. You don't have to be "perfect" in the absolute sense—you can't be, even if you tried—but the impediments have to be removed until the *Light of your Soul* will show the Way.

Overstimulation on the Path

When you take up the Spiritual Path and are seriously meditating, chanting, doing group work, and so forth, there is a possibility that you may overdo it (that is, in relationship to your previous condition, your "normal" environment, family, lifestyle, etc.). You could experience overstimulation of your physical body, your emotional body (feelings) and your mental body (thinking).

- Overstimulation of your *physical body* produces the sensation of restlessness, or of tiredness and exhaustion.
- Overstimulation of your *astral body* produces the state of excitement and increasingly intense feelings and emotions. You may react more *emotionally* to what people say or do.
- Overstimulation of your *mental body* produces more thoughts and questions as you try to "understand" life through the intellect. You may become a *fanatic* in your views.
- Overstimulation of *personal relationships*. When the new energies produced by spiritual practice enter your system, your relationships may become more "intense". Even trivia can appear to be large, important issues. The *battleground* of relationships may become more fierce.

Diseases caused by walking the Path 1168
The Double Stress of Meditational Life 1181
Obstacles on the Path of Meditation 1205
Obstacles to Higher Consciousness 1424

The Attitude for Yoga

The Seer, the Higher Self within you, is represented in the Tarot System by *The Hierophant* (Tarot Key 5). This Key shows the *attitude* that is required in order to practise Yoga.

The aspirant must have an open mind and a largeness of Heart

The priestess and priest standing in front of the Hierophant represent Kāma-Manas. On the left, the priestess has her arms open towards the Hierophant, which shows the right attitude for the astral body (the desire-nature) to assume. The prayerful attitude shows that the aspirant must have humility, patience and reverence. Our feelings and emotions must be open to the influences of the Higher Self. On the right, the priest has his hands in the attitude of worship, which is how Manas (the mental body) must behave before the Voice of the Higher Self, the Christ within, can be heard by the mind. The aspirant must have an open mind, a largeness of Heart, and a sincere desire to receive instruction.

The Approach to Truth 1152
The Silent State 1554

The Hierophant's right hand is in the mudrā (gesture) of *Silence,* which means that only in utter Silence can the Soul be heard. In his left hand he holds a triple cross, the symbol of the office of the Hierophant, representing the Three Worlds (the three planes of the personality), with a circle at the tip representing the Spiritual Realms of Buddhi and Nirvāṇa.

The Radiance of the Higher Self is seen by the opened Spiritual Eye, and the Glorious Voice of the Spirit is heard by the Inner Ear of he who humbles himself in Silence.... ⚹

Tarot Key 5: *The Hierophant*

CHAPTER 25

Aṣṭāṅga Yoga

Yoga by Eight Steps

In PĀDA II SŪTRAs 29-32 of his YOGA SŪTRAs, the great Sage Patañjali wrote down some ideas about Yoga held in his time by the recluses, the renunciates, the Yogīs, the Brahmacārīs (celibates). This system of Yoga recorded by Patañjali was called AṢṬĀṄGA YOGA (Yoga by eight steps) and was later renamed RĀJA YOGA (Kingly Yoga).

Patañjali's recorded system was divided into three major stages and eight steps

Patañjali's recorded system (he did not invent it!) was divided into three major stages and eight steps:

1. The first stage, *Preparation*, consisted of five Observances or Commandments, YAMA, traditionally understood as non-violence, truthfulness, non-covetousness, celibacy and non-stealing.
2. The second stage, *Dedication*, consisted of five Rules, NIYAMA, traditionally understood as purification, contentment with one's lot, austerities, spiritual studies and Devotion to God.
3. The third stage, *Yoga, Union, Mysticism*, consisted of the six remaining steps: ĀSANA (posture), PRĀṆĀYĀMA (breath-control), PRATYĀHĀRA (withdrawal of the senses), DHĀRAṆĀ (concentration), DHYĀNA (meditation), and SAMĀDHI (trance, ecstasy, Union).

It must be emphasized that, in those post-Vedic days, Yoga was practised by those who had "renounced" the world. The "holy men" wandered around begging for food, possessing nothing (and still do so in India today), unlike during Vedic times (about eight thousand years ago) when the Science of Yoga was practised by the householders. Only during the past six thousand years have the ideas of renunciation, celibacy, the killing out of desires, torture of the body (TAPAS) and other "austerities" been practised. Before that time, "ordinary" people practised Yoga as a normal part of spiritual life.

The most colossal delusion in Human Spirituality came about when the belief arose, in both the East and the West, that only *celibate males* (monks) could attain Salvation, Liberation or Union with God. This false belief permeated almost every religion and even today has a negative influence upon large numbers of people in most major religions. *God is neither sexist nor racist.*

The Feminine Suppressed 910
Female Buddhas 1110

In some respects, the combined Observances and Rules are similar to the *Ten Commandments* of Judaism or the *Beatitudes* of Christianity. The whole system was arranged in a sequence: the Yogīs did one practice, then the next, and so on. They began by practising YAMA, the Observances: non-violence, truthfulness, non-covetousness, celibacy and non-stealing. The system was a very logical, orderly method for a recluse, a monk, a wandering ascetic or sannyāsin, one who had "renounced" the world.

Śiva Yoga of the Liṅga Purāṇa

Patañjali's Aṣṭāṅga Yoga was based on an earlier system called Śiva Yoga, the ancient Hindu system of the Liṅga Purāṇa, the Great Scripture of Śiva:

1. Yama: restraints.
   a. Ahiṁsā: peacefulness.
   b. Satya: truthfulness.
   c. Asteya: non-stealing.
   d. Brahmacarya: inwardness.
   e. Aparigrahā: non-dependence on others or things outside yourself.
2. Niyama: regulations.
   a. Śauca: attention to hygiene and internal purity.
   b. Santoṣa: contentment, tranquillity.
   c. Tapasya: self-discipline, controlling thoughts and emotions.
   d. Svādhyāya: inner attunement, knowing oneself (psychology).
   e. Īśvara-Praṇidhāna: surrender to the God within.
3. Āsana: steadiness in sitting, in movement and in mind.
4. Prāṇāyāma: equalizing the breath.
5. Pratyāhāra: interiorizing the sense-faculties.
6. Dhāraṇā: being inward, or moving the attention inward.
7. Dhyāna: being able to focus in a cakra.
8. Samādhi: spontaneously holding onto the Self, Ātman, Brahma or God.

Patañjali's Aṣṭāṅga Yoga was based on an earlier system

There are other more ancient Rāja Yoga schools which have more than eight steps in their practices of the Spiritual Path. These steps include the following:

Tyāga: Renunciation of manifest forms by abiding in the Ātman alone.
Mauna: Silence, inner and outer.
Kaivalya: Solitude. The Aloneness of being above all created things.
Kāla: Time. The Awareness that every second is simply a surface motion upon Eternity.
Dṛiṣti: Vision. Opening the Third-Eye and seeing the Universe as it really is—a Playground of God.
Ānanda: The discovery of the basic purpose of Existence within you, which is Ineffable Joy.

Aṣṭāṅga Yoga
Sanskrit: "The eight steps to Union". From Aṣṭa (eight) and Aṅgāni (parts, divisions, limbs, members, means, ways, constituents).

Liṅga
Sanskrit: A sign or symbol.

Liṅga Purāṇa
Sanskrit: An ancient Scripture that points to the Way.

Pāda II Sūtra 29

Chapter Two: Verse 29

YAMA NIYAMA ĀSANA PRĀṆĀYĀMA PRATYĀHĀRA DHĀRAṆĀ DHYĀNA SAMĀDHI AṢṬA AṄGĀNI (SAMĀDHAYAḤASTAU)

The eight means which help to produce the State of Unified Consciousness (Yoga) are: following the Commandments and the Rules, correct posture, control of the life-force, withdrawing the senses from objects, concentrated attention, meditation, and spiritual trance (Transcendental Consciousness).

This Sūtra describes what you should do if you want to become a Rāja Yogī

YAMA: self-control, self-restraint, self-regulation, following commandments or observances.

NIYAMA: rules, regulations, order, precepts, obeying the Law.

ĀSANA: poise, balance, posture; the right physical posture for meditation; correct position and attitude; seat or chair.

PRĀṆĀYĀMA: regulation of the vital-force or PRĀṆA, the breath of life; breathing naturally and easily.

PRATYĀHĀRA: withdrawal of the senses from occupation with outer objects; regular retirement and abstraction from the world.

DHĀRAṆĀ: concentrated attention upon the Goal; being fixed upon the Goal; focusing the mind at one point; spiritual exercises.

DHYĀNA: meditation, contemplation, recollection.

SAMĀDHI: ecstatic trance; Transcendental Consciousness, Superconsciousness; mystical experiences; states of Union with God.

AṢṬA: eight.

AṄGĀNI: parts, divisions, limbs, members, means, ways, constituents.

∞

This Sūtra describes what you should do if you want to become a RĀJA YOGĪ. You must pay attention to the *rules and regulations* of Spiritual Life. You must bring your life somewhat under control, since you cannot become a YOGĪ (a Self-Realized One) if your life is an utter mess. You must also *meditate in a suitable posture*, breathing easily, with your physical senses withdrawn, your mind focused and concentrated in deep meditation (SAMĀDHI).

Here Patañjali describes the things that you *must do* if you want to attain the State of YOGA or Liberation. This verse has been much misunderstood and misapplied over the past few centuries, in India and now in the West.

First of all, Patañjali speaks here of RĀJA Yoga, not HAṬHA Yoga; often they have been lumped together as if they were one, but they are not the same.

Secondly, this verse has often been applied in a *sequential* sense, one practice after the other, when in fact they are to be practised *simultaneously*.

Haṭha Yoga and Rāja Yoga 524

Pāda II Sūtra 30

Chapter Two: Verse 30

AHIṀSĀ SATYA ASTEYA BRAHMACARYA APARIGRAHĀḤ YAMĀḤ

Non-violence, truthfulness, non-stealing, a religious attitude to life, and non-greediness are the Observances.

AHIṀSĀ: harmlessness, non-violence, non-killing.

SATYA: truthfulness, sincerity, honesty; being virtuous, genuine, non-devious.

ASTEYA: not stealing from others, not misappropriating the property of others.

BRAHMACARYA: being firmly fixed on God, self-control for the sake of God, a continuous religious attitude, continually being involved in discipline.

APARIGRAHĀ: non-grasping, not being greedy for objects, being free from the insatiable desire for wealth, being free from excessive desires for name, fame and materiality.

YAMA: abstention from, abstinence from, controls, commandments, observances you take upon yourself voluntarily.

Practising the virtues has been the cornerstone of all the major world religions

Thus:

- The Commandments you should take upon yourself are: harmlessness to all beings, sincerity to all, non-stealing, a sacred attitude to life, and living modestly.

∞

Practising the *virtues* (uprightness, morality, right relationships) has been the cornerstone of all the major world religions: the Jewish, Christian, Muslim, Hindu, Buddhist, Sikh, Taoist, Shinto, Jain, and so on. Without a *conscious attempt* to control your physical life there is little chance of any spiritual progress. Sage Patañjali reaffirms the same truth.

Passion and Dispassion 695
The Ten Mahāyāna Precepts 814
Ṭarīqat: the beginning of the Path 831
Qualifications for Discipleship 1149
Virtue and the Afterlife 411
Stage One of Aṣṭāṅga Yoga 566

Pāda II Sūtra 32

Chapter Two: Verse 32

The Rules are the useful practices in Spiritual Life

Śauca Santoṣa Tapaḥ Svādhyāya Īśvara Praṇidhānāni Niyamāḥ

Cleanliness, contentment with your life, a burning desire for Liberation, a proper study (understanding) of Yourself, and surrendering yourself to the Supreme Being are the Rules.

Śauca: purification, cleanliness, purity.

Santoṣa (Saṁtoṣa): contentment, satisfaction with your life *as it is*.

Tapaḥ (Tapas): spiritual practices, religious fervour, strong self-discipline, a burning desire for Liberation, fiery aspiration, spiritual purification.

Svādhyāya: self-study, understanding yourself, knowing yourself, spiritual practices which lead to the Knowledge (direct experience) of the Self.

Īśvara: the Soul, the Self, the SELF, God, the Central Controller of the Universe.

Īśvara Praṇidhānāni: surrendering yourself completely to the guidance of your Soul, or the Triune Self, or the SELF (the Monad), or God (the Logos), or Sūrya, the Sun-Being (the Controller of the Solar Universe), or Mahā-Īśvara, the Universal Deity, according to *your* level of spiritual development.

Niyama: guidelines, practices, rules, regulations, spiritual actions.

Thus:

- The useful practices in Spiritual Life that you should do are: personal cleanliness and cleanliness of your environment; being content with your life; a continuous fiery aspiration for Nirvāṇa (the Goal of Human Evolution); a continuous discovery process (meditation) of Knowing Yourself; and an endless Devotion to your Guru (Īśvara) on the level of your spiritual attainment.

Śauca: Purity 570
Tapas: Spiritual Purification 571
Pāda I Sūtra 23 548
Īśvara 1623
Stage Two of Aṣṭāṅga Yoga 568

Pāda II Sūtra 31

Chapter Two: Verse 31

Jāti Deśa Kāla Samaya Anavacchināḥ Sarva Bhaumāh Mahā Vratam

These [Sūtras 30 and 32] are the great Obligations for everybody (for those treading the Spiritual Path), irrespective of your class or rank, or the country you were born in, or the time and age you live in, or the conditions and circumstances of your life.

The Sage Patañjali has a Universal Message for Mankind

Jāti: class, social status, rank, lineage, race.

Deśa: place, country, locality, nation.

Kāla: time, period, age, century.

Samaya: condition, circumstance, situation.

Anavacchināḥ: not limited to, not bound by.

Sarva: all, everywhere, universally.

Bhaumā: of the Earth, of the planet.

Mahā: great, mighty, powerful.

Vratam: vow, promise, obligation.

Thus:

- These (Yama and Niyama) are the great Obligations for everybody (all those on the Spiritual Path), regardless of their race, country of birth or condition of life, without any limitation, everywhere upon this planet.

∞

You will see that the Sage Patañjali has a Universal Message for Mankind upon this planet, for every man, woman and child who is ready to enter upon the Lighted Way. All people who step upon the Spiritual Path, without exception, must follow the preceding sets of Rules and Observances if they want to achieve their Goal. So, you must take stock of yourself: how are you performing?

For the past three to four thousand years the sacred writings traditionally have been handled by monks and the priestcraft. Therefore, naturally, they interpreted these Sūtras to mean rules for *them*, and they slanted the rules towards themselves, leaving out the great masses of people living in the world with families and work. But Patañjali clearly states that the Sūtras apply to *all* who tread the Path.

It should be understood that we are not against Ritual or the Priestcraft. There is a valid way also for the Priest; it is called Kriyā Yoga or Karma Yoga, Union with God through ritual action. In the olden days there were great and mighty Priests in all religions who were truly Divine, truly Holy.

The Magic of Ritual Worship 366

Stage One of Aṣṭāṅga Yoga

The five self-restraints or *Observances* (YAMA) are as follows:

AHIṀSĀ: Non-violence

We have to become non-violent if we want to attain Higher Consciousness

We begin the Path by learning to be non-violent in thought, word and deed. We must have no desire to hurt anyone or to destroy anyone or anything. This was much emphasized by Mahātma Gandhi and, strange as it may seem, his environment responded with violence! He was shot by a fundamentalist fanatic. The world cannot tolerate non-violence, as the world breeds violence.

Nevertheless, as spiritual seekers, we have to become non-violent if we want to attain Higher Consciousness. A person who is always hateful, violently angry, or planning or doing harm to others, is locked up in a hellish world in his or her mind and therefore cannot rise to Mystical Union.

SATYAM (SATYA): Truthfulness

This not only means that we cease telling lies and deceiving others, but also that we carry in our minds the *Truth Principle,* a certain amount of true Spiritual Knowledge, a certain amount of *discrimination* between that which is real and that which is false, between that which pertains to the Eternal and that which is transitory and ephemeral.

ASTEYA: Non-stealing

This does not just mean that we cease holding up banks and robbing others at gunpoint. It means that we do not take what does not belong to us, *on any level*—emotional, mental or physical. We do not covet what is not rightfully ours.

BRAHMACARYA: Orientation to the Divine

When we have practised and achieved some degree of harmlessness, truthfulness, non-covetousness, orientation to the Divine, and non-attachment, then we have made the first step on the Path to Enlightenment and Liberation.

The word BRAHMACARYA has been wrongly translated by the monks and scholars to mean non-involvement in sexual life, chastity, non-marriage, celibacy. But Patañjali clearly does not mean that, for there is no sexual reference in the word at all!

The Sanskrit word BRAHMACARYA means "being taught by God" or "being a teacher of God" (BRAHMĀ-ĀCĀRYA) or "Godly conduct, God-oriented, dedicated to God, revolving around God" (BRAHMA-CARYA).

Brahmacarya refers not to sex, but to the dedication of our lives to the spiritual pursuit. The word could be translated as "becoming a missionary for God". It does not mean to be a celibate or a monk! When you are a true Brahmacārī, then you organize all your energies to serve God. A monk or a nun may do it one way, a married person another way. A married person with children and responsibilities, living in the world while remaining centred in his or her Heart, truly *living* the God-Life (Brahma-Carya), is a true Brahmacārī whether or not he or she wears an orange robe!

Tranquil Mind 1503
No Anger, No Enemies 986
Cultivate Knowledge 1366
Qualifications for Discipleship 1149
Relational Consciousness 906
Live and Let Live 940

Aparigrahā: Non-attachment

Aparigrahā has been translated as having nothing to do with money (for the monks don't touch money), not accepting gifts, having no possessions, not earning a living. This will naturally isolate most of Mankind. But Aparigrahā does not mean that we have nothing and go around naked. Literally, it means "not receiving anything to oneself". It means *not being greedy!* It means not being bound by anything—not by any person, nor any object, event or circumstance. It also means that we do not bind others! We do not try to control or take hold of others—not our friends, nor relatives, nor strangers, nor our subjects (those below us in rank), nor any objects. We do not try to enslave anybody or anything. We give to all the same freedom of thought, speech and action that we would want for ourselves.

In days of old, Brahmacarya, as *celibacy*, applied to the mendicant, the recluse, the Yogī, the solitary Mystic—those who had no relationship with any living being at all. But today (as in the days of the Vedas, eight thousand years ago) people other than monks and nuns also practise the Path, and most of them are married with families, or are in relationship, and have children, jobs and responsibilities. For them the observance of Brahmacarya has to mean something else. The very word gives us a clue. It literally means "orientation towards God", and for that you do not have to be celibate, or a monk or nun, or a renunciate, or an ascetic torturing yourself.

Sexual repression has never helped any student and has sent many nuns and monks insane. If one *naturally* does not feel for sex, that is fine, but that is quite different from forced suppression which always causes psychological imbalances.

Sex Natural and Divine 926

Brahmācārya
Sanskrit: "Being a teacher of God" or "being taught by God" (Brahmā-Ācārya). A religious teacher, a religious person or student, one belonging to a religious institution, or one who has taken a religious vocation. It has been wrongly translated as sexual continence or celibacy, but the word has only a religious meaning.

Brahmacarya
Sanskrit: Godly conduct (Brahma-Carya). Good conduct. Orientation towards God. Religious rule or behaviour or vows. This embraces *all* of one's life.

Stage Two of Aṣṭāṅga Yoga

The five regulations or *Rules* (Niyama) are as follows:

Śauca: Purification

This means internal *and* external cleansing, raising the vibrations of the physical, etheric, astral and mental bodies. It does not mean abstaining from sex, as some religionists would believe. It literally means bodily hygiene and cleanliness, and cleanliness and tidiness of your environment. It also means the purification of your emotions and thoughts by elevating them from the gross, the morbid, the material, the dense, into vibrations of Light, Love, Bliss and Joy.

Purification is necessary to increase the vibrations of the personality before Higher Consciousness can be experienced. Sattva is the quality of Purity, or high vibration, that is necessary for Inner Contact and Union (Yoga).

Santoṣa: Contentment

This means being happy in your life, living a relaxed and balanced life free of stress and violence. Obviously, if you are always over-stressed and neurotic, it will be difficult to find the Inner Union that leads to God. It also means the virtue of *patience*.

Here, most disciples fail. They are ever on the move to "improve" their lives, ever restless, ever turbid, ever disturbing their peace of mind through ceaseless activity. The life of our whole society is based on *discontent*, ever seeking and struggling for the so-called "better". Contentment manifests when your mind is at *rest*, when the endless seeking and searching and battling and struggling with the world comes to a stop. The Spiritual Life is only possible when you live in the Here and Now, not in an imagined better future. When you are content with your life, there is no more stress.

Tapasya (Tapas): Mental Discipline

The monks and priests interpreted Tapaḥ (Tapas) to mean fanatical torturing of the physical body, which is why, even today, some yogīs starve themselves, lie on beds of nails, cover themselves with ashes, bury themselves alive, never wash themselves, and generally make their lives on Earth as miserable as possible! They think they are doing Tapas. Scholars usually translate the word as "austerities". Austerity

The Spiritual Life is only possible when you live in the Here and Now

These five aspects of Niyama reinforce the results of the first stage. The five Observances (Yama) and the five Rules (Niyama) are designed for emotional purification and mental clarification. These come first. After these have been achieved, one is ready for the third stage, which is the actual science of Inner Union, called Yoga.

One can see clearly the logic in Patañjali's system. It is because people fail in the first steps of the Spiritual Path that they fail in the later steps. Even if you practise just the first stage, Yama, you will transform your life. If everybody in the world practised the first steps of Patañjali's system, it would utterly change the world and all human relationships.

(TAPAS) has been practised widely across India by the monks, the recluses, the wandering "yogīs".

Again, in the context of the modern-day "yogīs" (average men and women), the word TAPAS needs to be brought into a new understanding. The Sanskrit word TAPAS means "being on fire" or "internal burning". There is no suggestion in the word of torturing your body! TAPAS has to do with the Fire of the Mind; it can be translated as "self-discipline" or "mental discipline". It refers to disciplining one's thoughts, one's mental life, for the key to the Spiritual Path is mental regeneration, mind transformation. TAPAS has to do with interior purification of your whole Psyche or Inner Being by Inner Fire as you progress on the Spiritual Path through pure Devotion towards the Deity and correct Yoga or alignment with your Soul.

Mental Activity 1228
Emotional Problems 1429
Cultivate the Positive 1365
Past, Present and Future 1400
On the Wings of Devotion 1129
Know Thyself 1389

It is obvious that the yogīs overdid the idea of self-discipline, just as they overdid the idea of BRAHMACARYA. One can be reasonably disciplined in life without inflicting unnecessary injuries and sufferings upon the physical body.

SVĀDHYĀYA (SĀDHANĀ): Spiritual Study and Practice

Spiritual study refers to many things. SVĀDHYĀYA was wrongly interpreted by the monks as the study of scriptures and spiritual books in monasteries and Āśramas. Literally, however, it means "Self-study". Meditation (YOGA) is the *means* of Self-study (the Soul) and "SELF-study" (the Spirit). In truth, the word SVĀDHYĀYA means understanding the whole gamut of Yourself: you as a personality, you as a Living Soul, you as the Spiritual Self, you as the Divine Self, and you as a particle of God. All of this is Self-study.

ĪŚVARA-PRAṆIDHĀNA: Devotion to God

This is a compound word. ĪŚVARA means "the Lord God within" and PRAṆIDHĀNA means "total dedication, total Devotion, total Love". Thus, ĪŚVARA-PRAṆIDHĀNA means the same as what is written in the Old Testament of the Jews:

> Thou shalt love the Lord thy God with all thy heart, with all thy Soul, and with all thy strength.
>
> *Deuteronomy 6:5*

ĪŚVARA-PRAṆIDHĀNA means totally surrendering yourself to God, the Lord and Master within your Heart.

TAPAS, TAPASYA, TAPAḤ
Sanskrit: A burning longing for God or Liberation. Fiery effort in spiritual practice. From TĀPA, "burning, fiery, heat, zealous". TAP means "to burn". As practised by the ignorant yogīs and ascetics, TAPAS came to mean "austerities, penance, harsh disciplines, punishing the physical body, self-torture", which have nothing at all to do with the original meaning.
Unnecessary Practices 1111

SĀDHANĀ
Sanskrit: Spiritual Practice, Spiritual Discipline. A Way or Path of Meditation consisting of the Purification of the Mind and the Heart, which results in the Union of the personal self with the Universal Self or ĀTMAN.
Sādhanā: the Spiritual Life 1153

Śauca: Purity

The priestcraft in all major religions associated purification with sex

ŚAUCA means looking after your *physical body* and its *environment*. A dirty physical body is more likely to become sick, while a filthy physical environment also breeds potential disease. This was well known to the Sages of old, which is why they emphasized *cleanliness* for all disciples. The priestcraft, however, made *rituals* of it, purification rites and ceremonies such as baptism, immersion in water, being sprinkled with water, or washing your hands and face (ritually) with water. Such were key rituals performed by the priestcraft in all the religions. What is more, the priestcraft said that the religious purification ceremonies were *commanded by God.*

But, while God does not care whether or not you have a shower or a bath, your family, friends and colleagues do. And, if you fall sick, then you realize that physical cleanliness is a sensible idea!

What is worse, the priestcraft in all major religions associated purification with sex, while the word ŚAUCA makes absolutely no reference to sex! In all the major faiths and tribal religions, boys and girls had to undergo ritual purification at the onset of puberty (the commencement of sexual activity), *warping* the whole idea of sexual activity as something impure, dirty and against the wishes of God, instead of what it actually is: a normal function of Nature.

The State of Inner Purity 497
The Feminine Suppressed 910
To Understand Sex 917

The idea that sex is impure, dirty, against God, and punishable by death and eternal hell-fire and damnation, has caused incalculable damage to the Psyche of Mankind, unimaginable suffering, confusion and guilt. This *wrong view* of the sexual function, which was cast upon Humanity by the priestcraft, has produced all the fears, phobias, guilt-complexes, tensions and unhealthy attitudes towards sex in the billions of human beings upon this planet, down through the ages of history, and still does so in countless millions today. Even with the right education (if that were possible) that sex is a natural function, a normal part of the workings of Nature, it would still take thousands of years for Mankind to overcome the sick attitudes about sex so prevalent in society today.

The word ŚAUCA (purity) has deeper meanings also. It refers to cleanliness, not only of the physical body and its environment, but of the *emotions* and *mind* as well.

Purification of the emotions and mind means not entertaining depressing or negative thoughts and feelings in your personality.

The Principle of Choice 1380

Sex is simply a function of Nature, like breathing or hunger, and has its natural place in the total scheme of things, in the total workings of Nature. It is not evil and never has been, but the religious priestcraft made it so, to the detriment of human evolution.

Tapas: Spiritual Purification

The World is purified by Fire (TAPAS). Man is purified by Fire.

"Our God is a consuming Fire," says the Old Testament. Or, in modern language, "God is a purifying Fire." There is the Fire of Kuṇḍalinī. There is the Fire of the Prāṇas (life-streams) in the etheric body. There is the Fire of the Mind. There is the Fire of the Soul. And finally there is the Fire of the Spirit. All these Fires *purify*.

This world is purified by physical fire. There is also the Solar Fire, the Fire from the Sun, which purifies the planets.

Purification is *necessary* to lift your vibrations and transmute your consciousness from the mundane to the spiritual. This is *purifying self-discipline* (TAPAS). Purification by Fire burns away the impeding, lower, gross vibratory matter within you and allows the Luminous Light of Spirit to pour into your consciousness.

Without a truly pure Heart, Union with God is not possible

Spiritual Purification is TAPAS. Your personal self *must be purified* before the Fire of the Spirit can safely descend *into* you. This means that your physical body, astral body (feeling nature) and mental body (mind) must be *raised in vibration*. Purification of the physical, astral and mental bodies is necessary before the higher energies of your Soul and of God may *flow inside you*, unimpeded.

A most important aspect of purification is the purifying of the Heart Centre within you. Without a *truly pure* Heart, Union with God is *not possible*. As Jesus said:

The Cosmic Fire 130
Purify the Heart 701
Guard your Heart 1328
The Path of Purification 1337
On Love and Meditation 1140

> Blessed are the pure in Heart, for they shall see God.
>
> *Matthew 5:8*

Self-purification must be undertaken consciously as your way of life. This is best done by practising the virtues of Love, Charity and Compassion, and by devotional chanting. Self-forgetfulness in doing good to others and serving all forms of life is an all-purifying process. *Love is the greatest purifier.*

Love and Devotion will purify your Heart. Meditation, listening to inspired talks and reading the scriptures and the writings of the Saints and Masters will purify your mind. Working with mantras, chanting, and listening to inspired music are also the best of purifying agents.

The Fire comes at the right time.
Don't try to force it, or you will burn up.

Purification by Diet?

The physical body can be purified (the vibration raised) through a wholesome vegetarian diet, but this will *not* purify your mind or your Heart. Thus, people who are vegetarian are not necessarily spiritual at all, *unless* they purify their Hearts and minds as well.

Balance on the Physical Plane 1257

Stage Three of Aṣṭāṅga Yoga

The third stage of Aṣṭāṅga Yoga consists of the actual practice of Yoga or Union.

The third and fourth steps have to do with the control and vitalization of the physical and etheric bodies:

The actual practice of Yoga begins with Āsana

3. Āsana: "Steady posture". Bodily exercises, bodily posture.
4. Prāṇāyāma: "Steady breathing". Control of the life-breath.

The remaining steps have to do with developing Spiritual Inspiration, Intuition and the Realization of Higher Consciousness.

5. Pratyāhāra: "Turning inwards". Withdrawing the senses (Indriya) from the outside world and concentrating the attention within oneself, in the Heart or in the Third-Eye.
6. Dhāraṇā: Inner Concentration.
7. Dhyāna: Inner Meditation.
8. Samādhi: Inner Union.

According to Patañjali, the actual practice of Yoga begins with Āsana, which means "steady posture", followed by Prāṇāyāma, which means "steady breathing". These are *preliminary* practices of Yoga.

The Inner Journey begins with Pratyāhāra, which is the switching of the attention from the outer world and the outer body to *within* yourself. Mind transformation then develops through Dhāraṇā, which is inner concentration upon an image, a mantra, your inner energy systems, or the Inner Light. Dhyāna (meditation) follows from this, and finally Samādhi, or Inner Union. This state of Inner Union is Yoga.

- Āsana leads to mastery of the physical body.
- Prāṇāyāma leads to mastery of the etheric body and Prāṇa.
- Pratyāhāra leads to mastery of the astral body.
- Dhāraṇā and Dhyāna lead to mastery of the mental body.
- Samādhi leads to mastery of the causal body.

Thus, you will see that Patañjali's system is a very logical one. This same system has been used by the Yogis in India for thousands of years. You should follow the steps as outlined by Patañjali. It is still one of the best models for the Inner Journey.

Prāṇāyāma-Vidyā 1553
Dhāraṇā and Dhyāna 1523
Some Facts about Meditation 1192
Meditation in the Third-Eye 1224
Stages of Interior Prayer 693

Beyond Āsana and Prāṇāyāma

After the performance of the Yama and the Niyama, the Yogī practises Āsana. Unfortunately this has been overdone to the exclusion of everything else. The Haṭha Yoga schools made a complete set of exercises out of the word Āsana, which actually means "steady posture". They also do lots of prāṇāyāmas (the *regulation* of breath) when, in fact, by Prāṇāyāma, Patañjali meant "steady breathing".

Āsana and Prāṇāyāma are preliminary practices of Yoga

Such schools of Yoga worship bodily postures, which are little else than acrobatics. Because of the ignorance in the West on the subject of Yoga, their followers have distorted the whole truth about Yoga: they spend so much time doing bodily activities that they have no time for *real* yogic practices. In fact, often they don't even know about the teachings of Yoga, about meditation, states of consciousness, the Self, and so forth. They are bound, like slaves, to their physical bodies.

Āsana and Prāṇāyāma are *preliminary* practices of Yoga.

It is not necessary to do 108 yoga postures and it is not necessary to do 102 yogic breathing techniques. There is no Yoga in that! It simply locks the consciousness into the physical body, thus making Haṭha Yogīs rather physical people. They even mistakenly call this practice *Rāja Yoga*, the Royal Road!

It is at the level of understanding Dhyāna (meditation) and Samādhi (Union with God) that most of today's Yoga students fail.

Inner Union is Yoga. Outer exercises and breathing exercises are not.

From Patañjali's model you will understand why so many new-agers and aspirants to the Path fail in their quest for Enlightenment. It is because they want *instant* Enlightenment and they go about it completely *unprepared*. They either fail miserably, or they go insane, or they become mediums or psychics.

There is no instant Yoga, no instant Enlightenment.

If you have failed in your Spiritual Quest you can check back to Patañjali's scheme and you will find that you have failed at one or more of these points. Always start from the beginning, with Ahiṁsā, and go through the list, one by one, and discover where your weaknesses lie.

Already Enlightened? 341

Haṭha Yoga and Rāja Yoga 524
Mystics of Pisces and Aquarius 836
Notes on the Path in the New Age 1166
How to Succeed in Meditation 1206

Samādhi: the Goal of Yoga

Samādhi is the Experience of the Transcendent

SAMĀDHI is the objective to be attained on the Path of Yoga. SAMĀDHI is the state of equilibrated-mind (SAMĀ-DHI). SAMĀDHI also means "Union with God", from SAM (with, together) and ĀDHI (the Primeval Lord). SAMĀDHI also means SAM-Ā-DHĀ, "to fix together, to gather together, to revert to the Origin, to bind back to the Source". This is similar to the Latin word *religare* (religion), which also means "to bind back to the Source".

Generally, the word SAMĀDHI might be defined as "a state beyond and above the three ordinary states" (beyond the wakeful state, the dreaming state and the deep-sleep state). SAMĀDHI is the Experience of the Transcendent, or aspects of the Transcendent, or Higher Consciousness. It may be esoterically defined as "a State of Absorption of Consciousness or Attention". In this state various types of experience are possible, depending upon what interior perception is taking place, and what interior mechanism is being used, and on what Plane of Experience or Being. For instance:

The terms for the various types of Samādhi describe the *mechanisms* by which the higher states of Consciousness are experienced. Hence, the word SAMĀDHI cannot have a rigid or final definition. The word is used *variously* by different Yoga and esoteric schools.

The nearest equivalent in the West is the old Greek word EKSTASIS (Ecstasy), which means "a Supernormal Condition arising from the contemplation of Divine Things".

The Latin word for Samādhi is RAPTURUS (Rapture), which means "having been carried away in your consciousness to another State or Condition beyond the normal states".

The Path to Ecstasy 696

Rapture 699

SAMPRAJÑĀTA SAMĀDHI: A type of Samādhi where you no longer cognize the outer world through the five senses, but there is still an intense internal activity, with awareness of mind, thoughts and self. From SAM-PRAJÑĀTA, "with mind and ego".

ASAMPRAJÑĀTA SAMĀDHI: A state of Samādhi in which you are not aware of anything outside, and all internal activities have quietened down. There is no awareness of mind, thoughts or self. You are free of all differentiation between the experiencer and what is experienced. There is only internal tranquillity (ŚĀNTIḤ). From A-SAM-PRAJÑĀTA, "not with mind and ego".

SAVIKALPA SAMĀDHI: A state of Samādhi with imaginings and distinctions, in which the experiencer distinguishes between the "I" and the experience. In SAVIKALPA SAMĀDHI, thoughts and mental functions are still possible. From SA-VIKALPA, "with thoughts, imaginings, form".

NIRVIKALPA SAMĀDHI: A state of Samādhi without imaginings or distinctions. The experiencer is detached from all. In NIRVIKALPA SAMĀDHI there are no thoughts or mental activity whatsoever. From NIR-VIKALPA, "without thoughts, imaginings, form".

Savitarka Samādhi: A state of Samādhi "with an Idea" (such as "God"), but with no thinking about It.

Nirvitarka Samādhi: A state of Samādhi "without an Idea" (such as "God"), but just the *experience* of It.

Sabīja Samādhi: A state of Samādhi with a seed, support or form (such as a mantra, a symbol, a sign, a maṇḍala).

Nirbīja Samādhi: A state of Samādhi without a seed, support or form (no mantras, signs or symbols).

Spontaneous Enlightenment can happen only after you have undergone an Inner Transformation

Kṣānika Samādhi: The momentary glimpse of the Transcendental Consciousness, Turīya, the Fourth State. Brief periods of Trance.

Nitya Samādhi: In this form of Samādhi, one is permanently established in Transcendental Consciousness.

Sahaja Samādhi: Spontaneous or natural Spiritual Trance. Spontaneous Enlightenment (not sought after). This can happen only *after* you have undergone a fundamental Inner Transformation, when you have established yourself in your Inner Reality *permanently*.

Cittamayakośa Samādhi: "Full-of-Consciousness-body-Ecstasy". The Glorified State of Consciousness.

Dharmamegha Samādhi: "Cloud-of-Absolute-Truth-Ecstasy". The first stage of Union with God. Bhāgavata-Avasthā.

Brahmī-Sthiti Samādhi: "In-God-Living-Ecstasy". The Seventh State of Consciousness. The Absolute-Consciousness State, also called Brahmā-Avasthā (the God-State).

The States of Consciousness of ordinary human beings:
1. Suṣūpti-Avasthā: the dreamless-sleep state. Nidrā (sleep).
2. Svapnā-Avasthā: the dreaming state.
3. Jāgrata-Avasthā: the wakeful state. Jñāna (self-conscious awareness).

The States of Consciousness of the realized Yogī:
4. Turīya-Avasthā: the Fourth State. Transcendental Consciousness.
5. Turīyātīta-Avasthā: beyond the Fourth State. Cosmic Consciousness.

The States of Consciousness of the Siddhas:
6. Bhāgavata-Avasthā: the Glorified State of Consciousness. Glory.
7. Brahmā-Avasthā: the State of God-Consciousness.

The State of Inner Purity 497
The Silent State 1554
To Experience Spiritual Ecstasy 1683
The Seven States of Consciousness 494

Modern Yoga Practice

If you are a recluse, a monk or a nun, or a "renunciate", you should follow what is indicated in Patañjali's Yoga Sūtras as described in this chapter. Since you are probably a "householder" (a man or woman in the world, with a husband or wife, children and a job), you can still follow this pattern, but with the adjustments mentioned regarding the concepts of BRAHMACARYA (celibacy) and TAPAS (austerities).

The steps of Aṣṭāṅga Yoga are automatically fulfilled

On the Aquarian Way we begin with meditation.

This makes an amazing difference, for there is an instant improvement in all fields of life. As we meditate more and more, we come to see the Path of Yoga in a radically different way. We will *naturally* like to tell the truth and live in peace. We need not covet other people's property. We are God-oriented. We do not need to steal. We achieve inner and outer purity (our bodily vibrations are raised). We are happy and self-controlled. We desire to know more and more about "spiritual things" and we feel a great Devotion to the Eternal Being, the God within us. All at once, the YAMA (observances) and the NIYAMA (rules) are easy to perform. We do them spontaneously, as a matter of course, not as hard work. It feels better that way! Our lives change radically, sweetly, innocently, without effort!

Through meditation we also achieve ĀSANA (poise and balance), while PRĀṆĀYĀMA (steady breathing, the control of the life-force within us) becomes a simple fact.

Then the senses withdraw automatically (PRATYĀHĀRA), the mind begins to concentrate (DHĀRAṆĀ), and we begin to experience moments of Ecstasy and Bliss-Consciousness (SAMĀDHI). Thus, the steps of AṢṬĀṄGA YOGA are automatically fulfilled, all at once!

The Law of Mystic Experience 508
The Aquarian Way 1117

CHAPTER 26

The Yoga of Miraculous Powers

Pāda IV Sūtra 1

Chapter Four: Verse 1

JANMA AUṢADHI MANTRA TAPAḤ SAMĀDHIJĀḤ SIDDHAYAḤ
Miraculous powers can be attained through birth, drugs, mantras, fiery religious zeal and Spiritual Ecstasy (Transcendental Consciousness).

Here Patañjali touches upon the legendary powers of some Yogīs

JANMA: birth.

AUṢADHI: drug, herb, medicinal plant, elixir, chemical preparation.

MANTRA: a Word of Power, an incantation, a charm, a spell, a sacred scripture text, a "tool of the mind" (MAN-TRA: mind-tool), a purposefully-structured thoughtform or sound-form, a powerful sound-wave.

TAPAḤ: intense self-discipline, fiery desire, austerity, intense devotional practice, fiery Devotion, the desire for Perfection, being on fire from the Fire within.

SAMĀDHI: Spiritual Trance, Higher Consciousness, Superconsciousness, Transcendental Consciousness, Cosmic Consciousness, Spiritual States of Awareness, Self-Realization, Mystical Experience; stages of Union with the Soul, the Spiritual Triad and God; total absorption in a thought, idea, quality, power, or attribute of God.

JĀḤ: born.

SAMĀDHIJĀḤ: powers born out of SAMĀDHI, as a result of SAMĀDHI.

SIDDHI: all kinds of miraculous powers, realizations, perfections, accomplishments, talents, attainments, fulfilments, mastery, empowerments. VIBHŪTI (Divine Graces and Gifts, extraordinary powers).

Powers by Drugs?

Patañjali mentions that powers can come to you through drugs, but he doesn't give a *single example* in his book, the reason being that he considers them too *inferior* to be mentioned. What nowadays are called hallucinogenic drugs (hashish, marijuana, opium, sacred mushrooms, etc.) have been used in India for thousands of years, including during his time, by *inferior* yogīs, sādhus and wandering sannyāsīs who strayed from the true Spiritual Path.

Astral projection by drugs 304

Thus:

- Extraordinary powers can come to you as a result of previous lifetimes, natural preparations, Words of Power, intense Devotion or Spiritual Ecstasy.

∞

Here Patañjali touches upon the legendary powers of some Yogīs. He simply makes a statement of *fact*—not fancy, not philosophy, not speculation, not wishful thinking. He simply says that miraculous powers are a fact, and he tells you *how* they can be attained. For the ignorant materialist such powers are impossible. For the Wise they are just "normal" signs of development in Human Consciousness.

Categories of Powers

The Yogīs of India divided the powers into two basic categories:

The Yogīs divided the powers into two basic categories

MĀYĀ SIDDHI

The powers which give the *advanced* human being power over MĀYĀ, the illusionary Three Worlds, the Physical, Astral and Mental Worlds, the three lowest realms of our planet and solar system, the normal worlds of SAṀSĀRA where ordinary Humanity circulates between birth and death, beyond death and back into incarnation again.

SVARŪPA SIDDHI

Powers belonging to one's own intrinsic form or true Self-Nature; that is, belonging to the Soul (JĪVĀTMAN, the Reincarnating Ego), or to the Triune Self (ĀTMA-BUDDHI-MANAS), or to the Divinity in Man (PARAMĀTMAN, the Monad). These are powers of Pure Consciousness (DIVYA CITTA, Divine Consciousness) which relate to the Buddhic, Nirvāṇic and Paranirvāṇic Planes of Being, and to ĀDI, the Divine World of God.

Māyā 2
The Threefold Structure of Man 33

Yogic Powers and Psychism

These Yogic powers have *nothing* to do with mediumship, channelling or the psychic stuff so popular in the West since 1870, such as psychic Tarot Card readings, fortune-telling, and so forth. Such childish displays Patañjali would not even stoop down to mention, even in passing.

Nor do these powers have *anything at all* to do with the inferior manifestations of the Voodoo and Juju practices, or the witchcraft of old Africa and modern Haiti, which are the lowest, evil, astral stuff. Nor have they anything to do with the higher astral workings of the shamanistic religions of North and South America and the Eskimo populations of Alaska, Canada and Siberia, which seek to control animal forms, animal life and animal spirits, and to gain *power* over them for human purposes. If you engage in any form of practice relating to Voodoo or try to get power from animals, you make a *giant backward step.*

Psychic Phenomena 289
Channelling and Mediumship 317
Roots of Modern Shamanism 276
Magic: White and Black 364

The General Powers

These powers may manifest in anybody who follows the Way of Higher Evolution

There are Aṣṭa Yoga Siddhi (eight Yogic Powers, Vibhūti) commonly acknowledged among the Sages, with a slight variation as noted in the tabulations below. These powers are universal and may manifest in anybody who follows the Spiritual Path, the Way of Light, the Way of Higher Evolution. When the two systems of tabulation are combined, there are a total of *nine general powers*, and 9 is the number of *completion* or *perfection*.

1. Aṇimā, Animan
   A type of spiritual vision in which your inner gaze can perceive even the most extremely minute things, such as the structure of an atom, and you have the sensation that you become small, like an atom, or like a wave or particle in the Ocean of the Universe.
2. Mahimā, Mahiman
   A type of spiritual vision in which you perceive extremely large things. This can manifest as planetary vision, solar-systemic vision or, larger still, seeing vast portions of the Universal Manifestation.
3. Laghimā, Laghiman
   Weightlessness, overcoming gravity, levitation. The power to become extremely light.
4. Garimā, Gariman
   The power to become extremely heavy, fixed, immovable.

Tabulation I	Tabulation II
Aṇimā (Animan)	Animan
Mahimā (Mahiman)	Mahiman
Laghimā (Laghiman)	Laghiman
Garimā (Gariman)	—
Prāpti	Prāpti
Prākāmya	Prākāmya
Īśatva, Īśitva, Īśitritva	Īśitritva
Vaśitva	Vaśitva
—	Kāma-Avasāyitva

Tabulations of the General Powers

Vertical Evolution and the Path 174
Beyond Natural Evolution 1312

5. Prāpti
   The ability to go to, or manifest on, any of the worlds, planes or realms one wishes. The ability to travel anywhere in Consciousness, to expand in Awareness at will.
6. Prākāmya
   To have an irresistible will-power. The power to pervade all things, to become visible or invisible, to have all wishes fulfilled.
7. Īśatva, Īśitva, Īśitritva
   God-like powers, Godliness, Lordship over Nature, Rulership over the All, Supremacy over all beings, absolute Self-Mastery, the ability to manifest or materialize things from the Great Invisible.
8. Vaśitva
   Control over the Elements, dominion over all Creation, control of all beings in the Three Worlds.
9. Kāma-Avasāyitva
   Fulfilment of all desires.

You will find many references to these powers manifesting in some of the Saints

Note that these extraordinary powers are *general*, that is, pertaining to *all of Humanity*. If you study the lives of the Saints of all the major religions (such as the Judaic, Christian, Islamic, Jain, Hindu, Buddhist, Sikh, Taoist and Shinto), you will find many references to these powers manifesting in some of the Saints, to various degrees. Among the Yogīs of India this has been common knowledge for thousands of years.

Seek not Powers

The true Yoga Masters have very strong views about these powers. *One must not seek them.* That is, you must not enter the Spiritual Way just to attain some "miraculous" powers. If you do so, you may get some powers but you will never reach the Goal, the complete Union or Identity with the Godhead. Even Mahātmas (Great Souls) can become entangled by powers and thus temporarily obstructed upon their path to Ultimate Perfection or Divinity. So it is that many great Yogīs, when these powers develop in them, choose not to use them.

The nine universal powers are *part of your evolution.* They develop naturally as a result of Tapas (fanatical adherence to the Spiritual Path) and the advanced stages of Samādhi (Transcendental Consciousness, Cosmic Consciousness, Union with God). But they are *not to be sought after.* They are graces of God, gifts of the Soul and the Spiritual Self.

The Source of Miracles 671
To Safely Perform Miracles 1353
Mysterious Grace 1311

Saṁyama

The third chapter of Patañjali's YOGA SŪTRAs is called VIBHŪTI PĀDA, "Chapter on Miraculous Powers". In this chapter Patañjali lists many powers that can be developed by a process called SAṀYAMA, which involves concentration (DHĀRAṆĀ), meditation (DHYĀNA) and Transcendental Consciousness (SAMĀDHI), all together.

Saṁyama involves concentration, meditation and Transcendental Consciousness, all together

SAṀYAMA is a very peculiar internal state of consciousness. While you are in the state of Superconsciousness (SAMĀDHI), you concentrate on a topic (DHĀRAṆĀ) and contemplate it (DHYĀNA) from within yourself. It is a Superior State of Knowing.

When SAṀYAMA is applied to a focal point of endeavour, what appear to be "supernatural" or "miraculous" powers are attained, called SIDDHIs or VIBHŪTIs. While these accomplishments may appear to be "supernatural" or "miraculous" to the materialist (the ignorant), they are understood by those who Know (the Wise) to be simply a result of intense inner work, self-discipline and effort.

Saṁyama and Parapsychology

In recent years, parapsychology researchers have been investigating *clairvoyance* (extrasensory vision), *clairaudience* (extrasensory hearing), *clairsentience* (extrasensory feeling or touch) and *telekinesis* (the ability to influence and move objects). These are *not* the true SIDDHIs as described by Patañjali! At best, we could call them *rudimentary developments*. Furthermore, these abilities are not "extrasensory" but very much sensory! For the etheric-physical body has senses also, as do the astral and mental bodies, much used in so-called *telepathy*.

The powers mentioned by Patañjali are the results of SAṀYAMA, working *consciously* in the Superconscious State (the Fourth State), and by long and focused effort developing any particular power *from* Superconsciousness *into* physical expression or manifestation. When a power is thus perfected, the Yogī has fully conscious use of it, at any time, anywhere, at will.

The powers of the average psychic are *not* the result of spiritual development; thus, these abilities do not come from superconscious levels but are *personality-based*. They are fragmentary, partial, more like glimpses than continuous abilities, and very often unreliable.

Pure Seeing? 293

Stage Three of Aṣṭāṅga Yoga 572
The Fourth State 499
Awakening the Inner Senses 506
Science of the Soul? 291
Types of Telepathy 346

Pāda III Sūtras 16–56

Chapter Three: Verses 16 to 56

16. **By SAṀYAMA on the three transformations of Nature comes the Knowledge of the Past and the Future.**

Patañjali is very succinct, brief, concise. He tells a lot in very few words. This is *not fortune-telling* he refers to here, nor *astrology* as we know it, nor *prophecies* like those of Nostradamus, but something else, and this is difficult to explain in words. He is referring to the ability to know directly the Past (ATĪTA, what has been) and the Future (ANĀGATA, what is coming) in the Here and Now (ATHA, the present moment).

In the state of Saṁyama you can observe all of your Saṁskāras and Vāsanās

That which you are now is the result of what you have been, and whatever you think, feel and do now conditions what you will be in the future.

In the state of SAṀYAMA, in your Inner Consciousness you tune into your SAṀSKĀRAs, the impressions left upon your causal body from previous lives, which provide the hidden, subtle, invisible driving forces of your present life. Your Past vibrates in your auric-field. These SAṀSKĀRAs or VĀSANĀs (subtle impressions from the Past) condition your present life and give you your present psychological make-up, drives, habits, moods and behaviour patterns.

Prophecy and Destiny 294
Past, Present and Future 1400
Saṁskāra and Vāsanā 251
Types of Karma 243

Your present condition is simply a reverberation of your Past.

In the state of SAṀYAMA you can observe also, with your Inner Consciousness, all of your SAṀSKĀRAs (SAṄSKĀRAs) and VĀSANĀs which are about to be worked out in your life in the Now, or in the near future, or in the distant future. In this state you will *know* the inevitability or unavoidable nature of some of your karmas, the results of your SAṀSKĀRAs and VĀSANĀs. You will know what is coming to you and why, and you will *accept it gladly*.

You will understand also the *need* for transformation of your Consciousness (PARIṆĀMA) in order to liberate yourself from your karmas. This is done by entering *consciously* the Holy Path, by following the Path of Union (YOGA-MĀRGA): Union with your Soul, then Union with the Triune Self, and finally, Union with the Monad, your "Father in Heaven", the point of the Godhead within you, which *alters* your Future completely from human *evolution* to Divine *Being*.

In the third chapter of his YOGA SŪTRAs Patañjali describes, in brief, how to attain to more than thirty Siddhis! One could write a book on this first power alone, about what it means and how to attain it. Thus, in this short chapter it is not possible to cover in detail all of these powers and how to develop them. Further, for the sake of brevity, only the translations of these verses are provided, along with some brief commentary.

17. By SAṀYAMA on a word, and the object which that word denotes, and the idea or inner essence which that object represents (which are ordinarily confused by the common mind), comes the power to understand the languages of all beings through the Original Sound (or Word) of everything.

Saṁyama is mental action with purpose in the state of Superconscious Ecstasy

18. By SAṀYAMA on the SAṀSKĀRA (the impressions left in your causal body from previous births) comes the knowledge of past lives.

19-20. By SAṀYAMA on the mind of others comes the ability to read other people's minds.

21. By SAṀYAMA on the body (the body's form), and intercepting the light from the eyes of an observer, he (the Yogī) becomes invisible.

22. In the same way, he can arrange the disappearance of sound, touch, taste and smell (of one's presence).

23. By SAṀYAMA (in the causal body) on the quickly manifesting and slowly manifesting karmas, the knowledge of the time of one's death is obtained.

or: By SAṀYAMA on the portents or signs (of nearing death), the knowledge of the time of one's death is obtained. [There are also special signs, portents, omens and premonitions of death.]

24. By making SAṀYAMA on friendliness, love, compassion, benevolence, comes great strength (physical, emotional, mental, moral, Soul).

25. By SAṀYAMA on the strength of an elephant comes the power of great strength; similarly, by SAṀYAMA on the qualities of other animals comes the power in you of those qualities.

Note that this is *not* the same as Shamanism. In Shamanism you unite yourself with a real animal, the animal body and/or animal soul, in order to gain that animal's qualities. Here the unification is *symbolic;* you do SAṀYAMA on the *quality itself*, not upon the animal. You don't have to subjugate an animal and you don't have to make a fetish or totem of it. Nor is this a witchcraft practice. It is SAṀYAMA, or *mental action with purpose in the state of Superconscious Ecstasy.*

Roots of Modern Shamanism 276

26. By Saṁyama upon the Inner Light comes the Knowledge of all things that are hidden, subtle, remote, invisible, transcendental.

There is:

- The Light of the Soul.
- The Light of God.
- The Cold Clear Light of Reality.
- The Clear Cold Light of Intuitive Perception.
- The Universal Light.
- The Boundless Light.
- The Light of Everlasting Glory.
- The Effulgent Light.
- The Light in the Head Cakras.
- The Effulgent Light in the Heart Cakra.

Light 978
The Self-Generating Light 1594

27. By Saṁyama upon the Sun comes the Knowledge of all the Worlds. [That is, the seven planes or realms within our Solar System.]

28. By Saṁyama upon the Moon comes the Knowledge of the planetary system and the system of the stars.

We have to remind you here that the "Knowledge" referred to in these two verses is *not* the physical scientific measurements, data and facts about the Sun and Moon!

a. Here the Sage casts the eye of Inner Vision within the Inner Worlds and sweeps through the vast realms of the Sun, the seven great planes of the Cosmic Physical Plane, and sees not only the Body of that Cosmic Being we call the Solar Logos, but the Living Planetary Logoi within that Vast Being, the most dense and outermost expressions of which are the visible, physical "planets" (which are really just the "crusts" of the Planets).

b. All of this has a correspondence within the auric-field of Man where also are to be found the Sun and the Moon, and where the Mystery of the multi-dimensionality of Man is discovered.

The Constitution of God-Immanent 122
The Cosmic Creator-Gods 162
The Manifested-God 1589
Children of the Sun 1590

29. **By Saṁyama upon the Pole Star comes the Knowledge of the starry-systems (of Space).**

Remember always the key word, Saṁyama. Here again, Patañjali does not refer to physical measurements of the physical light coming from the physical aspects of the stars. This Knowledge he refers to is the Knowledge of the Seer whose Inner Eye can sweep through the whole Solar System and *beyond* and *above* into the Cosmic Astral Plane.

You can tune into the molecular and cellular intelligences composing the body

30. **By Saṁyama upon the Solar Plexus Centre comes Knowledge of the system of the human body.**

In medical school you cut up a dead human body into a thousand pieces, you "name" each piece and describe its physical function. That is considered "knowledge" of the human body. But Patañjali means something else. The Nābhi Cakra or Maṇipūraka (Maṇipūra) Cakra contains the *inner-consciousness* of the human body, the instinctual or primary consciousness of the body. We are talking about the *consciousness* of the body, not physical body parts! When you practise Saṁyama in the Solar Plexus Centre you can tune into the molecular and cellular intelligences composing the body and even communicate or "talk" with them. (And, very likely, you will receive lots of complaints about the way you have been mistreating the body!)

31. **By Saṁyama upon the Throat Centre comes freedom from hunger and thirst.**

32. **By Saṁyama upon the Kūrmanāḍī in the Throat Centre comes steadiness and equilibrium and motionlessness of body and mind.**

The Viṣuddhi (Viśuddha) Cakra, the Throat Centre, is also called Kaṇṭha Kūpa (throat-pit, or the pit of the throat). Within the Throat Cakra is a nerve called Kūrmanāḍī (tortoise-nerve).

Remember that the cakras are not the physical ganglions of the physical body as materialists want to believe. The cakras are etheric, astral, mental and causal, as are the Nāḍīs!

The Human Cakras 44
The Body-Elementals 213
Subtle Energy Currents 723

33. By Saṁyama in the Third-Eye Centre comes visions of Perfected Beings (Great Masters, Yogīs, Gurus, Saints).

The Ājñā Cakra (Third-Eye) is also called Mūrdha Jyotiṣi (Head-Light, or Light in the Head) because the Supernatural Light streaming down from the Crown Centre can be focused out through the Third-Eye. This Light can be thrown upon all hidden things, and all things can be known by it. Also, in the Third-Eye Centre, the Siddhas can be seen.

The Siddhas are Saints and Ācāryas (Teachers). These Siddhas are *not* the "spirit-guides", angels, masters and other assorted entities of the mediums, psychics, channellers and so-called "intuitives" of the Western psychic culture. The Siddhas do not give psychic messages!

Saṁyama means that you already have the ability to enter Samādhi

34. By Saṁyama in the Crown Centre comes Universal Knowledge of all things.

This has nothing to do with the modern education-system type of "knowledge" which involves memorizing myriads of facts, figures, data and details of dissected parts and objects and things of this world. That is not Knowledge! This is Knowledge through Prātibha (Prātibhāt), the Supreme Faculty of Spiritual Awareness of the awakened Crown Cakra. Prātibha is the Brilliant Light in the Crown Centre, the Effulgent Light of Deity which shines upon all things from *inside* the Universe.

35. By Saṁyama in the Heart Centre comes the Knowledge and Understanding of all Consciousness.

36. By Saṁyama on the difference between the Intelligent-Mind and the Self (Ātman) comes the Realization of the Spirit.

Saṁyama means that you already have the ability to enter Samādhi (Superconsciousness), and *in that state* you concentrate on a topic (Dhāraṇā) and you deeply meditate on it with your Inner Consciousness (Dhyāna). *This is how the powers are developed.* So then, what is meant by "Saṁyama on the difference between the Intelligent-Mind and the Self"?

Saṅgha: the Spiritual Hierarchy 394
Who are the 'Spirit-Guides'? 334
Prātibhā Siddhi 598
Dhāraṇā and Dhyāna 1523

The Intelligent-Mind is BUDDHI-MANAS (Wisdom-Mind) or SATTVA-BUDDHI (Pure Intelligence, Pure Consciousness, Pure Reason). This is not your ordinary, rational, analytical mind! This is your Mind when you are in Transcendental Consciousness, Superconsciousness (SAMĀDHI). And yet, You (the ĀTMAN) are above even this Super-Mind. When you *realize* this in SAṀYAMA, then you will simultaneously come to realize the Spirit, PURUṢA, the Supreme Being, God, the Omnipresent Reality.

Suspended Mind 1209
Dimensions of the Mind 891
Super-Knowing 1242
Awakening the Inner Senses 506
To Achieve Liberation 1177
The Three Identifications 1369

37. **Then arise the supernatural powers of Spiritual Perception: *supersensory* hearing, feeling (touch), seeing, tasting and smelling.**
38. **These supersensory powers are obstacles to Higher SAMĀDHI but are miraculous when used for worldly ends.**

These *supersensory powers* of hearing, touching, seeing, tasting and smelling in the Inner Worlds, or Higher Planes, can trap you in the worlds *below* the Buddhic Plane.

39. **By SAṀYAMA upon the causes of Bondage of the Consciousness to the physical body, and by the Knowledge of the process of how the mind works, comes the ability to leave the body and to enter another's body.**

There are two major causes of bondage or ties to this earth-life:
a. Psychological: spiritual ignorance, egotism (having an ego), desire for earthly things, anger (or violent tendencies) and fear of death (fear of leaving physical embodiment).
b. Stored-up Karma, or KARMĀŚAYA (the Reservoir of Karma).

Both of these factors will ensure that you hold yourself tied to this earth-plane; therefore you need to work on loosening these factors which tie your existence to this world.

It is precisely through this Knowledge from within (in deep meditation) of *how your mind is connected to your body* that Conscious Liberation from your body can come about. From there develops the PARAKĀYA-PRAVEṢA-SIDDHI or PARAŚARĪRA-ĀVEŚAḤ-SIDDHI (another's-body-entering-power)—that is, the ability to enter into other bodies at will, fully conscious, when it serves a *higher purpose*.

The Knowledge of how the mind works has *nothing* to do with the study of the brain cells (as is prevalent in today's materialistic medicine, biology, psychology and psychiatry), simply because *the brain is not the mind*. Your mind (the lower mind) is your mental body, which uses the brain and nervous system to *make contact* with this physical world.

Mind and Brain 79
All Hail to the Brain! 1368

40. **By SAṀYAMA upon the upward-moving Life-force comes the ability to walk on water, over swamps and thorns without touching them, and to levitate.**

What is the "upward-moving Life-force"? So far as it moves in the normal *embodied* human being on this planet, the Life-force (PRĀṆA, VĀYU) is fivefold:

In the normal embodied human being on this planet the Life-force is fivefold

a. PRĀṆA: general vital energy, life-force, breath, vitality.
b. APĀNA: energy that moves in the Base and Sex Cakra regions.
c. SAMĀNA: energy that moves in the Solar Plexus Cakra region and in the Heart.
d. UDĀNA: energy that moves in the Throat Cakra region and in the Third-Eye and Crown.
e. VYĀNA: interior energies generally permeating the body or form.

The "upward-moving Life-force" in the embodied human being is the UDĀNA VĀYU.

41. **By SAṀYAMA on the SAMĀNA VĀYU comes victory over Fire (control of the element Fire) and the Yogī is bathed in Radiance and Glory.**

The Life-Force

Materialistic medicine and biology discarded the idea of a life-force during the 19th century and today it is not even discussed in medical schools. According to *materialistic* medicine, while your brain is active you are alive, and when your brain-activity stops you cease to exist, cast forever into eternal oblivion! But what makes the brain active in the first place?

PRĀṆA, the invisible Life-force, permeates all the seven great planes of the Solar System *from within*. It is by PRĀṆA (the One Life) that all beings live and move *upon* and *in* all the worlds, visible and invisible. The lowest physical expression is VĀYU (air, breath).

PRĀṆA is planetary, solar-systemic, and universal or cosmic. Life (PRĀṆA) simply Is. Scientists *do not* create Life (as some vaingloriously believe); they are merely *fiddling* (now very dangerously) with the *forms* of Life, with the forms or bodies of entities and species which live *through* Life, as all entities must do.

PRĀṆA is the Breath of Life, the Breath of God, the Universal Life-Force that energizes Creation. Without PRĀṆA, nothing can live, move or have any being in any part of the Universe, on any plane of Being.

Dimensions of the Cosmic Fire 137

The Cosmic Fire 130
Kuṇḍalinī-Fohat 148
The Holy Breath 1340
Spirit 1343

42. By Saṁyama upon the organ of hearing and its connection to Ākāśa (Space) comes the power of Divine Hearing.

Divine Hearing is Divyaṁ-Śrotram or Divya-Śrota. It may appear that Patañjali refers here to listening with the physical ears to sounds in physical space. This is not so. The secret is in the word Ākāśa. The *uninitiated* scholars translate this word as "space" (as ordinary people understand the word). But, to the Initiated Ones, the great Yogīs, Masters and Siddhas, Ākāśa refers to the Monadic Plane of our Solar System, the Para-Nirvāṇa (the plane-beyond-Nirvāṇa).

By Inner Listening to this Sound we return up the planes to our Original Home

It is from the Monadic Plane that the Logos (the "Word" of the Christian Bible) emanates, what in Sanskrit is known as Śabda-Brahman (Sounding-God) or Nāda (the Inner Sound-Current of the Universe), the Voice of the Silence, the Spiritual-Sound, or Ākāśa-Vāṇī, the Sounding-Light, the Voice of Heaven.

This Divine Voice, the Word of God, the Name of God, *descends* through the great planes or worlds of our Solar System and *manifests* as all the sounds, on all the Planes of Being. This is the "Word made Flesh", God-in-Incarnation, God-in-Manifestation.

This is the Āuṁ, the Ōṁ, the *Sound*. By *Inner Listening* to this Sound we *return up the planes* to our Original Home, the Godhead.

43. By Saṁyama upon the relationship between the body and Ākāśa, the body becomes light like a cotton fibre and there comes the ability to levitate (and to rise up out of dense matter).

Again, at first glance, it may appear that Patañjali says that if you know how your physical body is related to space you can levitate physically. This is so. But you need a deeper understanding of the words.

The power of levitation, Utkrāntiḥ Siddhi, comes through several processes and means several things. Utkrāntiḥ does mean physical levitation, but it also means going beyond boundaries. To go beyond the boundaries of your body, for instance, would mean out-of-body experience or astral projection. But it also means Ascension out of all bodily limitations (physical, astral and mental) and raising your Awareness up to the Buddhic or Nirvāṇic levels of Consciousness—that is, ascending or levitating beyond the boundaries of the Three Worlds.

The Logos: the Word of God 114
The Word, Logos, Voice, Name 1646
Āuṁ, Ōṁ, Nāda 550
The Path of Hearing 553
Meditation on the Sacred Word 1216

This process is just one of several that can produce levitation, a phenomenon observed in the lives of many Saints. This is a way of scientific Yoga. Levitation may arise also through the religious way of intense Devotion and Ecstasy and absorption into one's Deity.

The key again is the word ĀKĀŚA. In the previous Sūtra we discussed one of the esoteric meanings of ĀKĀŚA (as it is understood by the Sages); here is another meaning. ĀKĀŚA is the One Universal Aether or Element permeating all the seven planes of our Solar System. By SAṀYAMA on that, you can transcend all boundaries of "space and time" and all bodily limitations.

By Saṁyama on Ākāśa you can transcend all boundaries of space and time

44. **By SAṀYAMA upon the Disembodied State, the Veil that covers the Original Light is destroyed (and hence comes the power of Illumination).**

or: **By SAṀYAMA upon thought-waves that are external and inconceivable (not related to the physical body), the Veil that conceals the Light (from your Inner Gaze) is destroyed.**

or: **By SAṀYAMA upon the thought-waves not related to the body (if your thinking is highly elevated and uplifted to truly spiritual heights), you will transcend your mind (mental body) and even the Higher Mind (causal body), and then is Illumination.**

This is one of the very difficult Sūtras to translate correctly, for even if you know Sanskrit fluently, you would need an Initiate Consciousness in order to understand it. In many of these translations I have added words in parenthesis for clarification, but still you must have some experience of Higher Consciousness to get the true meaning.

The key word in this Sūtra is MAHĀVIDEHĀ, literally "the great-without-a-body" or the Great Bodiless State (from MAHĀ, "great", and VIDEHĀ, "without a body"). What is the Great Disembodied State? It is when your consciousness is free of your physical, etheric-physical, astral and mental bodies—that is, when your consciousness can function above and beyond your personality structure, when you are in Buddhic Consciousness, on the Buddhic Plane. Then the Veil is taken off your Eye and the Light of ĀTMAN shines clear to your Buddhic Vision.

This is the *Beatific Vision* of the Christian Mystics. This Beatific Vision is the MAHĀVIDEHĀ SIDDHI.

Walls of Time and Space 21
Buddhic Consciousness 86
Turīya: Pure Consciousness 498
From Matter to Light 761
Beyond the Veils 894

45. **By SAṀYAMA upon the five states of the Elements—gross, etheric, subtle, and their all-pervasiveness, and their purpose—comes victory over all the Elements.**

46. **From this comes perfect bodily functioning, the arising of the General (Universal) Powers, and freedom from all hindrances (to the Realization of ĀTMAN, the Boundless Self-Nature).**

The Elements are qualities, forces or expressions of Nature

On these two Sūtras alone a whole book could be written. To truly understand Patañjali requires the Wisdom-Mind of the Sages.

By "SAṀYAMA on the Elements" Patañjali does not mean the contemplation of the *physical* elements of science, such as hydrogen, iron or carbon. The ancient Sages understood the Elements as *grades of matter and substance* extending from the physical universe to the subtlest realms of Divinity. These Elements exist in five states:

a. Gross, or physical (STHŪLA).
b. Etheric, or in their true form (SVARŪPA).
c. In subtle states, astral and mental (SŪKṢMA).
d. They are all-pervasive (ANVAYA) on the Buddhic Plane.
e. They reveal their purpose (ĀRTHAVATVA) on the Nirvāṇic Plane.

Paraśakti: the Supreme Power 1500

For the Sages such as Patañjali, the Elements are *qualities*, *forces* or *expressions* of Nature (PRĀKṚTĪ), and Nature is a *Living Being*, the expression of PURUṢA (the Spirit, God, the Living Cause of Nature). The orthodox view of science, accepted by the majority of scientists, is that Nature is but a physical process, matter is dead, life is simply the activity of nerves and cells in the so-called animal, plant and human species, and there is no God, no Spirit, no Spiritual Cause of Nature. How many scientists would *openly declare*, teach and affirm that all of Nature, the entire Universe, is permeated by the Life of God, by the Life-Force, the Supreme Energy (PARAŚAKTI) of the Absolute Being, PARABRAHMAN?

PARAŚAKTI is the Great Mother of All. Thus, the *total* planet Earth is a Living Being, and the *Elements* composing Her, on all the realms and planes, subtle and gross, are living *forces*, *qualities*, types of *energies* within Her Aura and Being.

This is *not* a philosophy, not a theory or hypothesis. You too can discover this in Higher Consciousness, VIVEKAJA JÑĀNA (VIVEKAJAM JÑĀNAM, Exalted Perception), which comes when you can *consciously* function in SAMĀDHI, and from that state you *consciously explore* the nature of Man, God and the Universe.

The Cosmic Elements

PṚTHIVĪ: Earth
ĀP, ĀPAS: Water
TEJAS, TAIJASA, AGNI: Fire
VĀYU: Air
ĀKĀŚA: Ether, Aether.

There are in fact *seven* Elements (corresponding with the seven substates on a plane, and the seven great planes), but the two highest can be perceived only by the SIDDHAS.

The Cosmic Elements 26

In these two Sūtras Patañjali says that by making SAṀYAMA on the Elements comes victory over them, and from that comes bodily health. And he says that you can *develop* the Universal Siddhis as previously discussed: AṆIMĀ, MAHIMĀ, LAGHIMĀ, GARIMĀ, PRĀPTI, PRĀKĀMYA, ĪŚATVA, VAŚITVA and KĀMA-AVASĀYITVA.

In PĀDA IV SŪTRA 1, Patañjali mentions that these Universal Powers come as a result of the following:

- Through fiery religious Devotion (BHAKTI Yoga).
- Through the Science of SAMĀDHI (as a *result* of achieving Transcendental Consciousness, Cosmic Consciousness).
- By birth (if you had attained them previously in former lives).
- By the use of mantras (MANTRA Yoga).

By Saṁyama on the Elements you can consciously develop the Universal Powers

Thus, through BHAKTI Yoga, RĀJA Yoga and MANTRA Yoga (the Way of Devotion, the Way of Consciousness, and the Way of Sound-Formulas) these miraculous powers can come to you *of their own accord*, as a *gift* or *grace* of your Soul or of God. (The lower, primitive effect of drugs he does not even bother to discuss.)

In PĀDA III SŪTRAs 45-46, however, he says that once you have mastered the Elements by SAṀYAMA YOGA, you can *consciously* set about developing these powers, as well as total Liberation.

To Taste the Elixir of Life

As you master the Elements through SAṀYAMA, or are in the process of mastering them, you will *taste* the *Elixir of Life* (SAÑJIVANI) and the *Nectar of Immortality* (AMṚTA).

This is not speculation, not a theory or philosophy, nor is it wishful-thinking. These are Pure and Divine Substances of the Higher Worlds, what the early Christian Mystics called AMBROSIA (Greek: the Food of the Gods), and what Jesus called the *Waters of Life* and the *Bread from Heaven*. Many Mystics, of all the great religions, had similar experiences of *tasting* some indescribable substances, supernaturally, which somehow came from God or were part of God.

There are two such substances: one is more dense, the other is more liquid or watery (but has absolutely no relationship to water!). They are like honey, but they are more than that.

The Initiated Alchemists of the Middle Ages also knew about the *Elixir of Life* and the *Nectar of Immortality*, but very few ever tasted them.

Kuṇḍalinī and Alchemy 153

Pāda IV Sūtra 1 578
Bhakti Yoga: Divine Union by Devotion 1128
Rāja Yoga: Divine Union by Meditation 1126
The Two Applications of Mantra 1219
The Way of the Mind 1238

47. **Perfection of body consists of grace, strength, hardness, compactness.**

Here again, Patañjali says a lot in a few words. He is referring now to HAṬHA Yoga, the vigorous and difficult bodily system of Yoga. The exercises must be spiritual. By SAṀYAMA on the physical body comes the perfection of the form, or peak of bodily development, as is possible at *this* stage of human evolution.

The body is here to serve the purposes or plans of the Soul

This can be achieved through many other processes as well, such as *dancing* and (very partially) some *sports*, such as *gymnastics* and activities which involve whole-body movement. Not every kind of dancing will do, but something like classical ballet or classical Indian (Vedic) dancing. Diet and breathing are important also.

- *Grace* means flexibility, beauty, charm.
- *Hardness* means resistance to diseases.
- *Compactness* means having the right size, being the right weight.

It is important to observe here that Patañjali is not being materialistic or "physical", for the Soul *pervades* the body and, so far as the Sage is concerned, *the body is here to serve the purposes or plans of the Soul.* It is not an independent entity, as the materialists think. For the Sage, the function of the body is to *transmit* the inner Light and Radiance of the Soul into the physical world of darkness, and to *reflect* that inner Harmony of the Soul in the perfect proportion and harmony of all body parts.

The health of the physical body depends upon the etheric-physical (vital) body, which depends upon the astral (feeling) body and the mental (thinking) body.

Your personality must be healthy before your physical body can be healthy.

Haṭha Yoga and Rāja Yoga 524
True Dancing 873
The Personality Complex 36
Mind in Body 988
Mind and Body 1374
Health and Fire 50

48. By SAṀYAMA upon the senses (INDRIYA), their attributes, their functions, their relationship with the sense of individual existence (ASMITĀ), and their purpose, comes their conquest.

49. From this come the powers of a swift mind, the ability to function without the sense-organs, and mastery over Original Nature, the Primary Cause of Creation (PRAḌHĀNA).

The ability to function without the sense-organs is Buddhic Consciousness

INDRIYA (sense-perception) involves not only the senses of the physical body, for senses exist in your astral and mental bodies also. For the Sage, all of your sense-perceptions, whether physical or subtle, relate to your sense of "I-am-ness" or individual existence (ASMITĀ), and to your sense of ego or self (AHAṀKĀRA, I am the doer). The ability to function *without* the sense-organs (that is, above the physical, astral, mental and causal senses) is Buddhic Consciousness, *beyond* your personality, *beyond* your mind.

PRAḌHĀNA (Original Cause) is the same as MŪLA-PRĀKṚTĪ (the Root of Nature). This is NIRVĀṆA, the plane of ĀTMĀ, from which the Descent of Creation begins. NIRVĀṆA is not only the *end* of the evolutionary process, but its *source* or *beginning* also. NIRVĀṆA is the Alpha and the Omega, the Beginning and the End, the First and the Last.

PRA-VṚTTI (Involution) is a movement of Spirit into Matter, from the Nirvāṇic Plane down into the dense realms.

NI-VṚTTI (Evolution) is movement forward in the dense lower worlds, and out of them back to NIRVĀṆA, the Original Cause.

Awakening the Inner Senses 506
Perception through Mind 543
The Creation Process 165
The Creation of the Universe 166
The Divine Bipolarity 471

50. By SAṀYAMA upon the difference between Pure Consciousness and Spiritual Consciousness comes the powers of supremacy over all manifest conditions (those below the level of the Nirvāṇic Plane) and Omniscience.

51. From non-attachment to these powers (supremacy over all conditions and Omniscience), the Seeds of Bondage are destroyed and the Seer attains Eternal Liberation (KAIVALYA).

52. In that State the Presiding Deities of the Realms (Planes of Being) [will become known to the Yogī], but the Sage should not get attached to them (because they will trap the Seer again into the seven realms or vast planes of our Solar-Systemic Manifestation).

Being Alone with the Absolute 502
Angelic Rulers of the Planes 199

KAIVALYA (KAIVALYAM) is the ability to live freely and voluntarily on the Spiritual and Divine Planes, Nirvāṇa and the realms *above* Nirvāṇa, and to work towards the Cosmic Astral Plane.

When Buddhic Consciousness has been stabilized, and Nirvāṇic Consciousness attained, there comes mastery over the lower five Planes of Being of our System, ADHIṢṬHĀTṚTVAṀ (Lordship over all) and Omniscience (SARVAJÑĀTṚTVAṀ).

Time-and-space is the construct of the physical brain and lower mind

Patañjali wrote his Sūtras not only for beginners on the Spiritual Path, nor for only the advanced and very advanced, but even for Perfected Ones like the Buddha or the Christ, for the greatest of all Mystics and Masters who ever lived on this planet. Everybody can learn something from Patañjali.

53. By SAṀYAMA upon being in the Moment, and Awareness of each moment as it flows by, comes Exalted Consciousness, which is beyond the limitations of space and time (local boundaries).
54. From this Total Awareness comes the power to distinguish unfailingly all objects (all beings and all things) regardless of their status (of development) in space and time. (This is Illuminative Consciousness.)
55. This Spiritual Consciousness (shining, radiant and clear) is the great Liberator, Omnipotent, Omniscient and Omnipresent, in which the Past, Present and Future are in the Eternal Now (Everlastingness).

VIVEKAJAM JÑĀNAM means Exalted Consciousness, Pure Discriminative Awareness, Spiritual Consciousness, Total Awareness, Buddhic Consciousness, Pure and True Intuitive Knowledge. This is also the TĀRAKA (TĀRAKAṀ): Transcendental, Shining, Clear, Bright, Exalted, the Deliverer of Knowledge or Realization.

Time-and-space is a construct of the physical brain and lower mind; it does not exist outside these two. Once you have *transcended* the physical brain and the logical, discursive, thinking faculty, time-and-space vanishes. What appears then is Time (Eternity) and Space (a Boundless, Limitless Vastness).

Time is not a dimension as materialistic minds believe. That is a concept of the brain-bound lower mind. Spiritual Consciousness is Buddhic and Nirvāṇic. This is Illumination.

The Sense of Time 22
Past, Present and Future 1400
Liberation from Worldly Consciousness 1233
Attach your Mind to the Eternal 1234
The Eternal 1644

56. When the Illuminative Substance (SATTVA) equals the purity of the Soul, then there is KAIVALYA (complete, final Liberation).

Here Patañjali describes Illumination or Yoga through the Way of Purification.

When the physical body, the etheric-physical (vital) body, the astral (emotional) body and the mental (thought) body vibrate together synchronously (in harmony) with the Soul-Vibration, having been purified (raised in vibration) by conscious self-discipline and effort, the Light of the Soul can shine unimpeded through the personality structure, thus producing the phenomenon or power of Illumination (flooding internally with Light).

The physical, vital, emotional and mental bodies all have to be raised in vibration

As a result of this Illumination, the veils or obstacles that conceal the ĀTMAN (the Spirit within) are destroyed and the Yogī stands free from bondage to the lower worlds (the Physical, Astral and Mental Planes). He remains in the state of KAIVALYA, which is *isolation* from the lower states of existence and *Union* with the higher, the Buddhic and Nirvāṇic Planes and above.

Nowadays, many people and disciples regularly go on special diets which raise the vibration of the *physical body*, but will never become Enlightened in this lifetime. To become Enlightened through Purification, the physical, vital, emotional and mental bodies *all* have to be raised in vibration to match the Vibration-Frequency of the Soul.

Tapas: Spiritual Purification 571
Illumination and Deification 1190
The Path of Illumination 1338
The Experience of Illumination 816

So far we have been dealing with the powers which may arise as a *result* of walking upon the Spiritual Path, or which may be *developed* by conscious will-power, effort, self-discipline and fiery aspiration through the supreme Science of SAṀYAMA YOGA, the Yoga of Miraculous Powers.

These powers cover the periods of:

- Discipleship upon the Path.
- Adeptship, the Master (the Kingdom of God).
- Lordship (the Supernatural Kingdom).
- The stature and development of the *Christ-State* and *Buddhahood.*

The Brotherhood of Light 395
Hierarchies of Life 1721

Further Powers

The Seer is bathed in the Fundamental Light of the Universe

NIRODHA PARIṆĀMA SIDDHI

The power resulting from the control of the transformation of the mind, the control of thoughts and ideas, mental control, conscious mind control (what, in the West, used to be called METANOIA).

PŪRṆA MANO BALA SIDDHI

The power which comes from the use of your *total* Mind, which includes your ordinary mind (mental body), your Higher Mind (causal body), and your Wisdom Mind (BUDDHI-MANAS, the Mind illumined by the Buddhic Light).

ĀTMA BALA SIDDHI

The power which flows from the ĀTMAN within you. This enables you to perform many *healings* and other "miracles".

PRĀTIBHĀ SIDDHI

The power of Divination. This is the true power of *Prophecy*, which has nothing to do with fortune-telling or prediction of the future by any psychic, physical or astrological means. The Seer is bathed in the Fundamental Light of the Universe, on the Buddhic Plane, and from there the prophetic utterances gush forth in mantric rhythms and sentences.

VIKARAṆĀ BHĀVA SIDDHI

The power of bodiless perception, or the power to have knowledge or perception without the physical body at all. (It is as if you never had a physical body or personality complex at all, and you are just a Pure Spirit, trans-dimensional, all-knowing, all-wise.)

PRAḌHĀNA JAYA SIDDHI

The power over the evolutionary forces of Nature. Here you must not limit yourself to the limited scientific theory of evolution, for Evolution is multi-dimensional. The forward movement of all things in the Physical World is the result of a downward push from the Astral Universe, which itself reacts to forces pushing downwards from the Mental Plane, which itself adapts to the Plan in the Buddhic World, which itself tries to manifest the Seed or Germ of things which have been planted in ŚAMBALLA.

Transformations of the Mind 1242
What is Metanoia? 1412
Realms of the One Mind 493
The Prophets 647
The Creation Process 165
The Descent of the Plan 396

Powers of Divine Descent

AVATĀRA SIDDHI
Divine-Descent power.

When the perfected Man completes his or her Journey of YOGA (Integration or Union with the Soul, JĪVĀTMAN, with the Triune Self, ĀTMA-BUDDHI-MANAS, and with the Monad, PARAMĀTMAN), he or she stops identifying with the personality (the physical body, vitality, emotions and thinking faculty) and at first identifies with the Soul (the Reincarnating Ego on the Mental Plane), then with the ĀTMAN, and then with the Monad on the Paranirvāṇic Plane of Being. He or she lives in the Buddhic World or the Ātmic World or the Monadic World in companionship with the Communion of the Saints, the Devas, the Siddhas, and the Gods and Goddesses.

Such a Yogī must therefore create a temporary form

Such a Yogī (United One, Integrated One) no longer has a personality mechanism by which to appear in the lower dimensions (the Mental, Astral and Physical Worlds). He or she must therefore create a temporary form in order to appear in the lower worlds.

MĀYĀVI-RŪPA SIDDHI
"Illusory-form-making power". The power by which the Yogī or Siddha can make a temporary vehicle of appearance in the lower Three Worlds, on any plane or on any planet, as he or she wills. That MĀYĀVI-RŪPA form will last as long as the Yogī focuses Will-power and Imagination-power upon it. This is one form of the AVATĀRA SIDDHI (Divine-Descent power). He or she will also have the power to move bodies or objects through space (VIHĀYASA SIDDHI) and, by mental power, to transfer any body or bodies to any part of the world and to appear and disappear at will (MANO-JAVA SIDDHI). He or she will also have ANTARDHĀNA SIDDHI, the power to become visible or invisible at will.

MANOJAVITVA SIDDHI
The ability to move or transport one's physical body rapidly anywhere in the world over any distance and to appear anywhere physically. This is done by focused mental power in combination with Awakened Soul Energy.

The Avatāra 389
The Three Stages of Yoga 528
Saṅgha: the Spiritual Hierarchy 394
Mysterious Knowledge of the Siddhas 1310

Powers of the Dream State

SVAPNĀ-AVASTHĀ SIDDHI
Dream-state power.
The power of *conscious dreaming*.

You can "dream" things consciously into manifestation

An entire book could be written on the subject of *dreams*, on the dream state or dreaming condition, how it relates to Higher Consciousness and how it can be *utilized* by Higher Consciousness (Superconsciousness). The Yogī (such as Patañjali) views the subject from a much higher perspective than the ordinary person can comprehend. This has *nothing at all* to do with the *psychological* analysis of dreams, nor psychoanalysis, nor the fortune-telling analysis of dreams which was so popular in the olden days.

In Yoga, the three ordinary levels of consciousness (the dreamless-sleep, dreaming and wakeful states), are at first *distinguished* by Superconsciousness (SAMĀDHI), then *absorbed* in it. This means that your normal waking-consciousness and your dreaming-consciousness will be *empowered* by the velocity, dynamism, creativity and vitality of Superconsciousness or Transcendental Consciousness (SAMĀDHI).

Thus, your actions in the Physical World will have more powerful effects, and what you "dream" will *manifest*. Then your dreaming becomes just another tool for creativity, which you may use while you are awake or while you are "asleep" (while your body is at rest at night). You can "dream" things consciously into manifestation, and your dreams become physical realities.

Furthermore, your Soul will be able to communicate with you in your "dreams", as will, later on, the Spirit or Monad, your "Father in Heaven", your Source of Revelation.

The Yoga of the Dream State 299
The Seven States of Consciousness 494
The Physical Projection 297

Knowledge of Past Lives

PŪRVA-JĀTI-JÑĀNAM SIDDHI
Knowledge-of-previous-lives power.

PŪRVA-JĀTI-JÑĀNAM (previous-birth-knowledge) or PŪRVA-JĀTI-SMARANA (previous-birth-remembrance) is a Siddhi which arises when you can function in Causal Consciousness. It is also called PUNAR-JANMA-SMṚTI (again-and-again-births-recollection). It is the power to recall to memory your past lives or previous embodiments.

This Siddhi arises when you can function in Causal Consciousness

This power has *nothing* to do with the "hypnotic regression" or "past-life therapies" which are popular today in the West, in which the psychologist, therapist or counsellor tries, by *suggestion,* to take you back to the time before you were born.

When you can enter Causal Consciousness in your causal body, on the three highest subplanes of the Mental Plane, wherein *you* (as the Reincarnating Self, JĪVĀTMAN) live, then you can read directly with your causal senses the ĀKĀŚA-SMṚTI (luminous memory), or the *Book of Life* as it is poetically named in the Bible. This is not a book, of course; rather, it is like a photographic film imprinted on ĀKĀŚA, the Luminous Ether that is pervading within all Space.

- With further training, you can "read" not only your past history of many births or embodiments on this planet, but the previous lives of other human beings.
- With further training, you can read not only the previous lives of others, but the whole history of our planet (from the inside).
- With further training, you can read not only the history of aeonian evolution of our planet, but the history of our Solar System itself.
- And then? You enter the Omniscience of the Universal Mind.

Memory of Past Lives 312
Punarjanma: Reincarnation 249
The Akashic Records 241
Perceptions of the One Mind 490

Cosmic Powers

We shall conclude our introductory story about the *powers* by drawing your attention to the final possible stages of Evolution or Spiritual Development.

You have come to the portals of the Seven Cosmic Gates

By the time you have become a Christ or a Buddha, you have graduated *out* of the Human Kingdom on this planet, have entered the Kingdom of God (the Spiritual Hierarchy), have reached its highest levels of development and Consciousness, and have come to the portals of the Seven Cosmic Gates.

By then, your Consciousness has already become planetary, then solar-systemic (in its sevenfold multi-dimensional Nature). You have evolved *through* the Kingdom of the Gods and have learned what can be learned or experienced within the seven great Planes of Being of a solar system. So, what next? You are *already* Divine. You already walk with God. Is there more to do?

You enter the next Field of Super-Divine Evolution which enables you to function *consciously beyond* the solar-systemic structure, and *above*, in the Cosmic Astral Plane, in the Infinite Pulsations of the Limitless Love-Vibrations of the Absolute Beingness of Cosmic Infinitudes. (You cannot really use the word "God", as the human mind has so belittled it!)

As you pass onwards from Christhood and Buddhahood to still more inconceivable Evolutions of an Infinite Universe, Cosmic Powers of unimaginable magnitude open up an Infinite Way for you...

The Constitution of God-Immanent 122
Dimensions of the Solar Logos 1591
The Sevenfold Earth-Evolution 169
Hierarchies of Life 1721
How to Become a Buddha or a Christ 1723

1. Mahā-Aṇimā
   Reaching beyond the experience of the Cosmic Physical Plane (our seven-layered Cosmic Plane). The Cosmic Vision of the Subtlest, or the Glimpse of the Cosmic Astral Plane, which is like a Limitless Subtlety pervading the seven-layered Cosmic Space of our Universe.

2. Mahā-Laghimā
   Cosmic Weightlessness. That is, not being bound to our Cosmic Physical Plane, but being able to ascend out of even our highest Solar-Systemic Plane, Ādi, into the Boundless Cosmic Astral Realms.

Mahā-Parā-Siddhi is severing one's roots with this Universe

3. Mahā-Mahimā
   The experience of the Infinite Vastness of the Universal or Boundless Self, the Vastness of the Cosmic Mind.

4. Mahā-Prāpti
   The experience of Pervading the whole Cosmos.

5. Mahā-Prākāmya
   The Cosmic Astral Plane is perceived as the Universal Desire Nature, the foundation and root upon which the Cosmic Physical Plane (our Sevenfold Universe) exists, and the reason why it came into existence.

6. Mahā-Vaśitva
   Mastery over the whole Cosmic Physical Plane (all the worlds and realms of the seven planes of our Universe).

7. Mahā-Īśatva
   The ability to rule over all Creation within the sevenfold Cosmic Physical Plane.

8. Mahā-Kāma-Avasāyitva
   The fulfilment of Cosmic Desire.

9. Mahā-Parā-Siddhi
   Going into the Great Transcendent, breaking with the Immanent Aspect of Deity, going beyond the Beyond, leaving the Cosmic Physical Plane, going beyond the boundaries of our Sevenfold Universe altogether, severing one's roots with this Universe, going through one of the Seven Cosmic Gates. Annihilation into the next Cosmic Plane of Being, the Cosmic Astral.

Know Yourself

You have to die to the old before you can be born as New

Know yourself to be Immortal.

The *Goal* is Perpetual Awareness.

Listen to the Music without the physical sound, the Voice within the Silence.

Look for the Light which is not the Light of the physical Sun, the Self-Shining Light.

Merge into the Silence that has no beginning and no ending, the Silence that is Infinite Space.

Become *Aware* of the whole process of your life, without judgment and criticism.

Make *Constant Awareness* a way of life, in all situations, under all circumstances.

Continually *watch* and *observe* yourself. Observe your actions, thoughts and feelings, and those of others, and those of society. They are just passing events, insubstantial things.

There is a *Silence*, a *Stillness*, a *Peace* that is permanent. It is in you and all around you, in the earth, sky and sea, and in Infinite Space.

Buddha attained Enlightenment through the Power of *Awareness*.

The Christ attained Enlightenment through the Power of *Love*.

You have to *die to the old* before you can be born as New. This new Self lives forever in the Eternal Now.

Quest for the Self 1317
Know Thyself 1389
The Way, the Truth and the Life 670
Learn to Die before you Die 420
True Death 424
Awareness Meditation 1656

The Great Way

And here we must finish our brief introduction to Yoga, the Science of Union. To comment *fully* on all of Patañjali's Yoga Sūtras would take thousands of pages. We have translated a few for your delight and advancement and have briefly explained them. The purpose is to *inspire* you to take the Spiritual Path seriously and work your way up to Kaivalya—Emancipation, Complete Liberation, the State of Absolute Unity.

The Perfection achieved by the Christ and the Buddha are the signposts for the human species

There is an immediate Goal or Plan for Humanity on this planet: that every one of us should reach the "measure and stature of the fullness of Christ", as Saint Paul would say. The Perfection achieved by the Christ and the Buddha are signposts for the human species on this planet, for Man to become.

Most people do not realize that there *is* a Plan for us upon this planet. Individually, in groups and en masse we must work to achieve this Divine Plan, intelligently, consciously, purposefully.

We live in the Age of Kali Yuga—the Age of spiritual ignorance and blindness, called Māyā. In this Age, materialism prevails. The peoples of the Earth are blinded by material energies, material powers, material objects. The lives of people are taken up with accumulating material objects for themselves and their families. Material comforts supersede spiritual powers. Name and fame in society supersede the true Kingliness and Majesty of the Perfected Man.

What Patañjali described, even *before* the Buddha and the Christ, is what Man truly is, what Man can do, what Man can become. He did not write a philosophy, a theory or wishful thinking, but simply facts, the things that are, and the things Man can do, and the Great Way which is open to the human species on this planet.

The Kingdom of God is a fact. May you soon become one of its Blessed Citizens.

Maṅgalam Astu
May you be Blessed.

Dense Materialism 384
The Buddha and the Christ 1722
To Manifest the Kingdom of God 1716

PART FOUR

Pure Christianity

The Religion of Love

CHAPTER 27

Teachings of the Saints

Let not your heart be troubled:

ye believe in God, believe also in me.

In my Father's house are many mansions...

I go and prepare a place for you...

I will come again and receive you unto myself,

that where I am, there ye may be also.

John 14:1-3

The Divine Milieu 12
The Christian Cosmo-Conception 19
The Christian Trinity 113
The Doctrine of the Logoi 116

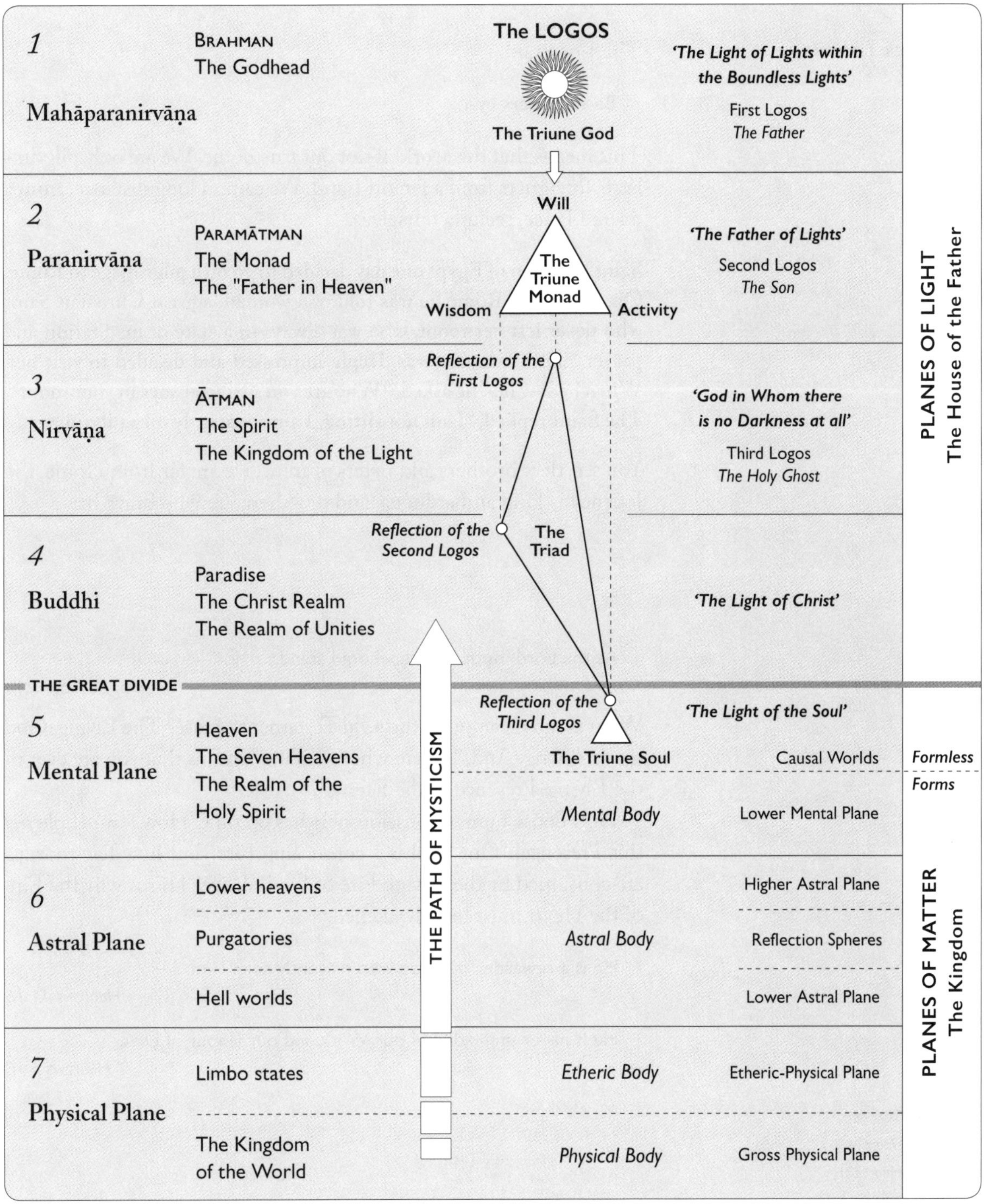

The Many Mansions

1

Thus have I heard...

The Lord said:

> Be ye passers by....

This means that this world is not our true home. We are only pilgrims here, foreigners from a far-off Land. We came a long distance, from a Sacred Place, seeking ourselves.

Saint Sarapion of Egypt one day decided to go on a pilgrimage to Rome. On arriving in Rome he was told of a woman, a great Christian Saint who never left her room, who was always in a state of meditation and prayer. Saint Sarapion was deeply impressed and decided to visit her. When he saw her, he asked, "Why are you sitting always in your room?" The Saint replied, "I am not sitting, I am constantly on a pilgrimage."

You see, dear brothers and sisters of mine, we are far from Home, the Journey is long and arduous, and few there are who brave it.

2

> As the Lord liveth, before whom I stand....
>
> *2 Kings 5:16*

What is the meaning of this Old Testament phrase? The Living-God is ever-living. And, "before whom I stand" means that you are ever in the Living-Presence of the Eternal.

How dense human consciousness has become! How few people *feel* this Presence! "Our God is a consuming Fire," but how few mortals are consumed by the Divine Fire of God's Love! This is why the Fire of the Heart must be reawakened.

> He is a rewarder of those who diligently seek Him.
>
> *Hebrews 11:16*

> He is never unmindful of our Work and our labour of Love.
>
> *Hebrews 6:10*

The Lord of Glory 667
What is the Heart? 435
The Burning Heart 631
The Omnipresent God 1108

3

There are two great methods for contacting God: in the Heart Centre and in the Head Centre. The Way of the Mystic is the Way of the *Heart.* The Way of the Yogī is the Way of the *Head.* At Perfection, the two Paths merge.

The Way of the Mystic is the Way of the Heart

The early Christian Masters said:

> Gather the powers of your five senses together within yourself in the Heart and *worship God* there.

And...

> Seek not the human love that comes and goes and binds, but the Love that purifies, uplifts, and is the *Eternal.*
>
> This is our *Source* and our *Homecoming.*
>
> Heed not the will of the little self that antagonizes and tears apart, but listen to the Will of the One Who is Universal and is Love.
>
> This is our Source and our Homecoming.
> It is the Kingdom of the Heart.
> This Home is within you.
> This Love is within you.
> This God is within you.
> SELAH. In Silence you shall *Know.*

In the Heart you shall know that:

> What now is, has already been. What is to be, already is.
>
> *Ecclesiastes 1:9*

For the Heart is the Eternal.

The Holy Writ says:

Say not that I do not know what you are *thinking in your Heart.* I, the Lord, *scrutinize* every Heart.

And, the scriptures also say:

Say not that, from the time I created you, I do not know your *Heart,* for even before I made you, I knew what you were going to think in the future....

The Two Paths 1112
Heart Knowing 1286
The Divine Unity 852
Uniting Head and Heart 1130

4

Jesus said:

> If a Man shall abandon all for my Name's sake, he or she shall inherit Eternal Life.
>
> *Matthew 19:29*

The faithful always spend their time glorifying God

This means that we ought to think of nothing but God alone. All goodness a person receives is from God, for God is All-Goodness. The Saints say that Humanity was created *by* God *for* God. If a person attracts evil to himself or herself, it is because he or she has *abandoned* God. That is why it has been said:

> He attracts evil to himself, from himself, who no longer remembers from whence he came.

There was a certain recluse in Egypt called Ammon. He was full of Grace and spent all his time communing with God. His holiness was known to all monks and anchorites of the desert. One day, a new monk came to these parts of the desert and wanted to live near the holy man.

Now, Ammon was full of Wisdom and Insight and hidden Knowledge. When the new brother came to him and asked, "Is there a vacant cell nearby in which I might spend my time in prayer and contemplation?" the venerable Ammon said, "Why certainly, I shall go and look for one for you. In the meantime, please use my cell and all that is in it."

Then the venerable Saint left the cell where he had lived for many years and went out into the desert to look for another shelter. Soon he found himself some rocks and stone, built himself another refuge, and settled down calmly to prayer and meditation.

You see, the Master said:

> The birds have their nests, the foxes have their holes, but the Son of Man has nowhere to lay down his head.
>
> *Matthew 8:20*

And also…

> The Bridechamber is ready. Blessed is he who is found wearing the Shining Garment, for he shall inherit the Crown, also.

Thus it is that the *faithful* always spend their time glorifying God.

The Christian Heart-Path 632
Practising the Presence of God 711
The Lover of God 853
Holiness to the Lord 1393

5

> Come now! Let us reason together, saith the Lord, and though your sins be red as scarlet, they shall be made as white as snow, and though they be as red as crimson, they shall be washed white as wool.
>
> *Isaiah 1:18*

"Reasoning together with God" is *communion* with God, in the depths of your Heart, in the depths of your Soul.

Reasoning together with God is communion with God

> Come unto Me all ye that labour and are heavy laden, and I will give you *rest.* Take my yoke upon you; learn from Me, for I am meek and humble of Heart; and you shall find *peace* in your Souls.
>
> *Matthew 11:28–29*

A monk once visited a poor woman who had a very hard life and who was very depressed. She was full of afflictions and thought that God had deserted her. "I cannot pray," she said to the monk.

"Then I will teach you," the wise abbot replied. "I shall teach you a short prayer. Say 'Jesus!'" The woman said "Jesus" very weakly.

"No, not like that!" said the abbot. "Say 'Jesus' with *feeling!*" She said "Jesus" feelingly.

"Now say it with *devotion!*" said the abbot. And she said it with great devotion.

"Now say it *in your Heart* with great devotion!" The woman did so and burst into tears. A great Peace descended upon her.

"Now say in your Heart always, 'Come Lord Jesus!', and you shall attain Eternal Life."

> Even so, Come Lord Jesus!
>
> *Revelation 22:20*

Lord Jesus, Come!

What is Prayer? 690
The Divine Mood 1252
The State of Innocence 1306
Bhakti Yoga: Divine Union by Devotion 1128

6

Now is the accepted time. Behold, now is the Day of Salvation!
2 Corinthians 6:2

When you commune with God, that is your Day of Salvation

The Eternal is always Now. If you *repent* (turn towards God), your Day of Salvation is always Now. This Now stretches over the past, the present and the future. At any time, in any age, in any dispensation of Time, when you turn to God, when you commune with God, that is your *Day of Salvation.* Sit still and commune with your Lord in *Silence.*

There was a hermit who lived in the desert, thirty two miles from the nearest hermit. He always kept to himself, in great Silence. In fact, the Silence around him glowed with a Golden Light.

But, after a while, as more and more people came to live the hermit-life in the wilderness, the area became more and more populous with recluses. He now had a neighbour who was only seven miles from him! He became very worried about this "overcrowding" of the desert and said, "Woe unto Rome that it should have been ruined by unwise rulers, and woe unto the desert that the Silence be broken by the chatter of monks!"

7

The good Lord said:

I came not to call the righteous, but to call the imperfect for repentance. My Father in Heaven desires the transformation of sinners above their punishment.

And, says Isaiah the prophet:

Even the ox knows his master, and the donkey can find his way to the manger, but Israel does not know God. My people do not understand.
Isaiah 1:3

Israel is symbolic of all Humanity. A breach has occurred between God and Man. Humanity has forgotten God in terms of *real* Consciousness, real Communion, real Union.

Past, Present and Future 1400
Alone with God 700
The Silence of the Deep 1355
Repentance 683
Israel (Yishrael) 246

> Thou shalt love the Lord, thy God, with all your Heart, with all your mind, with all your Soul, and with all your strength.
>
> Thou shalt love thy neighbour as thyself.

In these two Commandments is the secret of remembering God. The true Christian life is a continual Remembrance of God. God is remembered as Creator, and God is remembered in the creature, in "thy neighbour". And the great Moses said also:

The true Christian life is a continual Remembrance of God

> Thou shalt consider in thine *Heart,* O Man, that as a man chasteneth his son, so the Lord, thy God, chasteneth thee.
>
> *Deuteronomy 8:5*

Abbot Ammonas went to visit an elder in the desert, an ascetic who was wearing a shirt made of hair. When they had greeted one another, the ascetic said to the abbot, "I live an ascetic life because I want to flee into the wilderness. I want to hide in a place where I am unknown and I want to fast all day."

And the saintly abbot told him, "All these things will do you no good unless you have the Lord in your Heart, as it is taught by the fathers: 'Lord, Jesus Christ, have mercy on me, a sinner'."

God wants the *Heart,* not outer rites and rituals. In the Heart, Man is *reconnected* to God. We have to *learn* in order to *know,* to *know* in order to *remember,* to *remember* in order to *Be.*

The apostle Paul had this in mind when he said:

> The wages of sin is death, but the gift of God is Eternal Life, through Jesus Christ, our Lord.
>
> *Romans 6:23*

That is to say, all wrongdoing (sin) leads to spiritual death, a cutting away in your consciousness from the Divine Presence, from Eternal Life. But, through the Holy Name of Jesus, the Covenant is remade between God and Humanity, between you and your Soul. This is why the Divine Name must be invoked ceaselessly in the Heart.

This is the "Christ *in* you, your hope of Glory" of Saint Paul. That Christ-Glory abounds in us already, but we must *remember* it in deep prayer and meditation.

The Eternal is One 512
Have mercy on me, a sinner? 707
The Christ in the Heart 441
To Call upon Jesus 679

8

> And because we are children of God, God has sent the Spirit of his Son *into our Hearts,* crying "Abba, Father!"
>
> *Galatians 4:6*

Silent prayer in the Heart is better than verbal prayer

In the book of Samuel, we read that Hannah silently *prayed in her Heart* and her voice could not be heard. She was *pouring out her Heart* before the Lord.

Silent prayer in the Heart is better than verbal prayer. The great Apostle says:

> I will pray with the Spirit and I will pray with my mind also. I will sing with the Spirit and I will sing with my mind also.
>
> *I Corinthians 14:15*

The secret of prayer is to pray *with* the Holy Spirit, *in* the Heart. For, Saint Paul also says:

> No one can say "Lord, Jesus Christ" unless with the Spirit of God.
>
> *Philippians 2:11*

There was a young monk who came to see Abbot Pastor in the desert. He told the abbot, "I get bored being alone in my cell in this vast desert. I get anxious, nervous and afraid. What shall I do?"

And the wise abbot replied, "If you are disturbed in your prayer while alone in your cell, this is what you should do: Despise no one, condemn no one, rebuke no one, remember God. Do this and your prayer will improve."

How wise and glorious was that grand old man!

Interior Prayer 691
The Evolution of Christian Prayer 713
The Heart and the Lost Art of Prayer 1251

9

As a man thinketh in his Heart, so he is.

Proverbs 23:7

There is an old Jewish legend about a rabbi and Elijah the Prophet:

One day the rabbi came to Elijah and asked the Prophet, "When will the Messiah come?"

The Messiah is already here

"Why, the Messiah is already here," said Elijah. "If you go to the city gate, you will see him amongst the poor and the sick, where He is looking after their sorrows."

So the rabbi went to the city gate and there he saw the Messiah in a poor man's garb attending to the people's sufferings. And the rabbi asked, "Master, when will you show yourself?" For, you see, a lot of the Jews thought that the Messiah would be a king, a strong ruler who would rule over Israel and all the world.

"I come today," replied the Messiah.

The rabbi was very pleased and went away. A week passed and the Messiah still hadn't claimed the throne of David, so the rabbi went to the Prophet again, saying, "Elijah, the Messiah lied. He said 'I will come today', but a week has passed and He still has not shown himself."

"No, the Messiah is not a liar," replied the Prophet. "Certainly He comes today, for it is written, 'He will come today', if you will *listen* to God's Voice."

Now, this is a very deep story. Let him who has ears to hear with, hear.

The ancient Masters said:

The true Christians [followers of the Radiant-Heart Way] belong to another Kingdom, the Kingdom of the Light. They are children of the Heavenly Adam, not of the Earth. They are a *new people,* born of the Holy Spirit, the brothers of the Christos [the Christ].

The ancient Sages called them the *Children of God* and the *Sons of Light.*

The Sons of Light have nothing to learn from men. They are taught by God. The Fire of Grace [the Energy of the Spirit] *engraves* the Law into their Hearts.

The Jewish Messiah 660
The Coming of the Christ 724
The Kingdom is at Hand 1453
To Manifest the Kingdom of God 1716
The Chosen Ones 688

10

On being asked by the Pharisees, "When is the Kingdom of God coming?", Jesus said:

> The Kingdom of God comes when you know it not [when you are least expecting it]. They cannot say, "Behold, here it is!" or "Behold, there it is!" for the Kingdom of God is *within* you.
>
> *Luke 17:20–21*

The "within-ness" of the Kingdom is the foundation of the Spiritual Life.

This "within-ness" of the Kingdom is the foundation of the Spiritual Life.

> Commune with your *Heart* in your room and be *still.*
>
> *Psalms 4:4*

> Every thought enters the Heart in the form of a mental image. The Light of God can illumine the Heart only when the Heart is *completely empty of everything* and is free from all forms and imaginings.
>
> This Light also reveals itself to the *pure in mind,* in the measure that that mind is free from thoughts.
>
> *St Hesychios (6th century)*

> Blessed are the *pure in Heart,* for they shall *see* God.
>
> *Matthew 5:8*

> You shall *see* God, and all the treasures that are in God, when you have *purified* your Heart. The greater this purity, the more you will *see.*
>
> *St Hesychios*

The Christian Fathers said:

Those who have renounced marriage, family, worldly possessions, name and fame, may be outwardly monks and nuns, but only those who have transcended inner thoughts and passions, and walk in the Clear Light of God, are truly Christian.

And...

Those who thirst for God should purify their minds and their Hearts.

And again...

Those who have become *true* contemplatives bathe in the Sea of Pure and Infinite Light, becoming one with It in an ineffable manner, and dwelling in It forever.

Purify the Heart 701
The Purification of the Heart 849
The Secret of the Heart 1280
Entering the Lost Kingdom 1176

II

This is what Isaiah, the Prophet, the son of Amoz, saw in a vision concerning Judah and Jerusalem. At the end of the Age, a Temple will be raised on the mountain of the Lord, on the highest mountain, and all nations will flock to it. Many peoples will come and say, "Let us go up to the Mountain of the Lord, to the House of the God of Jacob. He will teach us His ways, so that we may walk in His paths."

The Law will go out of Zion, and the Word of the Lord from Jerusalem.

And He shall judge between the nations and shall reprove many peoples. And they shall beat their swords into plowshares and their spears into pruning hooks. For nation shall not lift up the sword against nation, nor will they train for war.

Come, O House of Jacob, and walk in the Light of the Lord.

Isaiah 2:1–5

The beginning of Wisdom is reverence for the Lord

True Peace on Earth cannot come until the House of Jacob will "walk in the Light of the Lord". To *walk in the Light* is not an allegory, not a myth, not a theory, but a necessary fact.

Two young monks went to see an elder in the desert. The first one said, "Father, I have learned the Old and New Testaments by heart."

And the old Wiseman said, "You have filled the air with words."

The other young monk said, "Father, I have copied out by hand both the Old and New Testaments."

The old one replied, "You can use the parchments to fill in your window. Do you not know that the Kingdom of God is not in words, but in Power? Not those who *hear* the Law will come before God, but those who *do* it."

The beginning of Wisdom is reverence for the Lord. Thus, proceed with great humility and patience.

The Way of the Christian Mystic 626
On the Wings of Devotion 1129
The Approach to Truth 1152
Peace on Earth 1304

12

A person by the name of Nicholas Motovilov went to see Saint Seraphim of Sarov, a great Father of the Eastern Christian Tradition, and the conversation turned to discussion about the Spirit of God.

The great Saint was explaining to Nicholas how the true Saints are *consciously aware within themselves* of the Fire of the Holy Ghost, and Nicholas could not understand how he could know if the Holy Spirit was truly acting in him.

The Saints 654
The Baptism of Jesus 718
The Fire of Love 1255
The Fire in the Heart 1287
Baptism by Fire and the Spirit 1348

The Saint said to Nicholas, "We are already in the Spirit of God. Why don't you look at me?"

And Nicholas, trembling, replied, "Father, I cannot look in your face because lightning flashes from your eyes and your face shines brighter than the Sun, and it pains my eyes to look at you!"

Such was the manifestation of the Spirit in that Saint.

13

In the times of the Fathers of the Desert, a young monk came to see an old man who was, in fact, a great Saint. And the younger one said, "Father, I have said my Jesus Prayer in my Heart and have felt its warmth. What am I to do next?"

The old man stood up and stretched out his hands in front of him. Tongues of flames shot out through his fingers, fire enveloped him and his face shone like the Sun.

And quietly he said to the astounded monk, "Why don't you turn wholly into Fire?"

CHAPTER 28

The Heart of Christianity

The Dual Nature of Christianity

> God speaketh inwardly to a man's Soul, without the sound of words.
>
> *Thomas à Kempis*

> No matter how much understanding a man may have of created things, he can never come by means of this understanding to the knowledge of the Uncreated Spiritual Thing. And this is God.
>
> *The Cloud of Unknowing*

The theme of Mysticism has remained within the church for two thousand years

It is difficult for the modern man or woman just to understand Pure Christianity, let alone to practise it.

Spanning two thousand years, the Gnostics, the Hesychasts, the Cathars and the Mystics were all Christians, and they all renounced the world and sought God and Jesus *within* themselves, through Soul-Consciousness. During the past two millennia the worldly powers within the church could never understand these Souls, so they persecuted them, often to the death.

It cannot be said that the church was ever uniformly holy. Since the beginning, there has been this division within Christianity:

- Those who sought the Kingdom of God within the Soul.
- Those churchmen who were merely concerned with collecting a worldly empire.

Saint Jude, in his epistle to the early church, mentions these worldly Christians as "they who bring about division amongst the brethren, sensual men, not experiencing the Spirit". Saint John, in his third epistle, speaks of a bishop called Diotrephes who abused his authority over the brethren of the early Christian church. The New Testament is full of such references. It seems that the church became a material power shortly after the death of Christ. Yet, though the Mystics have always been persecuted, the theme of Mysticism has remained within the church for two thousand years.

> Love not the world, nor the things that are in the world. For if anyone loves the world, he does not love the Father. All that is in the world is but the lusts of the flesh and the lusts of the eyes, and the strength of life which is not from the Father but from the world. And the world with its desires is passing away, but he who does the will of God lives forever.
>
> *I John 2:15–17*

Hesychast

Greek: A person leading a quiet, contemplative life in the deserts of Egypt, Syria, North Africa or Palestine from the 4th century onwards. A monk or a nun (rare) of the early Christian church. A renunciate, a hermit. A person who has attained the *wordless state of prayer* (who has a still mind and communes with God in silence).

The Eastern Christian *Hesychast* tradition can be clearly traced back as far as the 4th century AD. Before that time it is recognizable as the "orthodox" tradition.

Christian Mysticism 450

Since the beginning, the whole attitude of *Pure* Christianity has been that of seclusion, isolation, fleeing away from worldly matters into the solitude of the Spirit. John the Baptist, of course, lived in the wilderness, in the desert, as did all his predecessors. The Christian contemplatives, the HESYCHASTS, fled to the deserts of Egypt, Syria, North Africa and Palestine. The Mystics of the Dark Ages and Middle Ages retired into the monasteries and nunneries.

Meanwhile, for centuries, the popes, cardinals and bishops involved themselves in politics, in the acquisition of worldly kingdoms, great wealth and worldly powers, and the forced conversion of millions to the *church* (never mind their Souls).

Since the very beginning, the church has suffered from a split personality

Thus, since the very beginning, the church has suffered from a dual nature, a split personality.

THEOLOGIA

Greek: "The Science of God-Realization". From THEOS, "God", and LOGOS, "God as the Creative Principle, the Divine Word or Wisdom, the Divine Discourse or Reason".

This is the origin of the English word *theology*. In the early centuries of Christianity, however, theology was not just a set of intellectual ideas and dogmas as it is today. It was the *direct realization* of Divine Realities, the *inner perception* of the Spiritual Realms and Hierarchies through the processes of prayer, meditation and contemplation. From the first to the fourth centuries, this science was known as GNOSIS; henceforth it was usually called THEOLOGIA, the Science of God-Realization. Similarly, to *theologize* means to have flashes of inner Insight.

Intelligent people are not those who are learned, or who can read books, but those who have an intelligent Soul.

St Anthony the Great

THEOLOGIAN

Greek: "A Knower of God by experience". To the early Hesychasts of the deserts, a THEOLOGIAN was a saintly person who *experienced* some degree of Divine Consciousness. Of a true Theologian it has been said:

Have no fear, for I have called you by my Name; you are mine. If you pass through water, I will be with you, and the waters will not drown you. If you pass through fire, you will not be burned, and the flames shall not consume you. For I am the Lord, your God, the Holy One of Israel, who *saves* you.

Isaiah 43:1–3

Christian History 641
Religion and Politics 513
Mystical Theology 706

The Way of the Christian Mystic

We are concerned here not with the history of Christianity, however, but with the *attitude* of all the Christian Mystics during the past two thousand years.

The 14th century Mystic who wrote *The Cloud of Unknowing* emphasized that his book could never be understood by worldly Christians…

Pure Mysticism is much more difficult to do than you can realize

nor by sensual men,
nor by critics [those who defame others],
nor by liars or deceivers,
nor by covetous persons or those greedy for wealth,
nor by the curious,
nor even the intellectuals of the church,
nor even the learned bishops! "This subject is of no relevance for them".

Rather, he speaks to those Souls who are mystically inclined:

> Lift up your Hearts to God, with deep Humility of Love, seeking God alone, and none of His created things.

In this one sentence he told everything there is to know about Mysticism. That is all there is to it, but it is the most difficult thing for any human being to do. In fact, pure Mysticism is much more difficult to *do* than you can realize.

Lift up your Hearts to God,
With deep Humility of Love,
Seeking God alone,
And none of His created things.

Mystics?

There is remarkable ignorance among today's intellectuals and media regarding the *difference* between mediumship, Intuition, Inspiration, Mysticism or Pure Consciousness, Cosmic Consciousness, and so forth. Psychics and mediums, genuine or not, are often called "intuitives", "holy women" or "mystics". Ignorance cannot distinguish between the various sources of experience.

What is 'Channelling'? 320

The Mystics 91
Clouds of Unknowing 704
Humility of the Great Ones 337

Lift up your Hearts to God...

Mysticism is the Way of the Heart. It is an intense longing, desire, fervour of the Heart Centre in a human being for direct experience—an inner touch, super-physical, beyond intellect and mind—of the true essence of *God,* the *Christ,* the *Spirit,* one's *Soul,* and *Religion.*

Mysticism is the fervour of the Heart, the fiery aspiration of the Heart towards God.

Mysticism is the fiery aspiration of the Heart towards God

This *lifting up of your Heart* comes through the *Fire* of the Heart. Fire not only burns; it purifies, transmutes, regenerates. This is why Jesus is often portrayed with the Burning Heart—the Sacred Heart of Jesus. This is the *Baptism by Fire* which Jesus speaks of.

John the Baptist said of the powers of Jesus:

> Indeed, I baptize you with water, symbolic for repentance. But He who is coming after me [Jesus] is mightier than I, whose sandals I am not worthy to untie, for He will baptize you with the Holy Spirit and Fire.
>
> *Matthew 3:11*

Do not interpret these sayings as mere poetic expressions. *Baptism by Fire and the Holy Spirit* is a *real experience* for the Mystic, an *inner* experience.

This is not the water-baptism performed by the church! In the early days, the water-baptism was done for *willing adults* as a symbol of the need for purification. When the church began to function as a worldly empire, however, the Pope declared that all *babies* must be baptized to gain membership! But only a Mystic can know what the *real* baptism is: the Baptism by Fire and the Spirit.

Tapas: Spiritual Purification 571
The Sacred Heart of Jesus 673
The Baptism of Jesus 718
Baptism and Rebirth 722
Heart Knowing 1286

With deep Humility of Love...

To become a Mystic you must become intensely *humble* and your Heart must be overflowing with Love towards God and all creatures. Those filled with intellectual pride, those who are arrogant, haughty, aggressive, competitive and domineering have absolutely no hope of *knowing* God. True, they might *believe* in God, but faith and experience are two different things. A Mystic is one who has gone beyond faith into the kingdom of experience, of *direct Knowing.*

> The term ***fervour*** comes from the Latin *fervere,* "fiery glow, to boil hot, to heat up or warm up". Another word used by the Mystics was the Latin ***ardour,*** "a burning fire, a flame".

Seeking God alone...

The Mystic finds pleasure only in the Transcendental Reality. His or her Heart is ever burning for a glimpse of the *Eternal.*

And none of His created things...

The Mystic lives forever in God's Presence

The Mystic finds no joy in worldly pomp and power, name and fame, money, wealth or worldly goods. His or her Heart is set towards the Eternal alone.

> Seek ye *first* the Kingdom of God, and God's Righteousness, and all other things shall be added to you.
>
> *Matthew 6:33*

All worldly *needs* will be supplied, but the Spiritual Kingdom of the Soul must come first in your life. "Lift up your Hearts to God, with deep Humility of Love, seeking God alone, and none of His created things."

> Love Justice, ye who judge the world, and think of God with Goodness, and seek Him in the integrity of your Hearts. Because He is found by those who test Him not, and He manifests Himself to those who do not disbelieve Him.
>
> *The Wisdom of Solomon 1:1*

The Mystic lives forever in God's Presence, which is sensed through the Heart.

> God is the Witness of his *innermost* Self, and the sure Observer of his Heart, and the Listener of his speech. For, the Spirit of the Lord fills the whole World, is Omnipresent, and knows Man's utterances.
>
> *The Wisdom of Solomon 1:6–7*

Regarding the importance of the Inner Life, Jesus said:

What good does it profit a man if he gains the whole world but suffers the loss of his Soul in the process?

Matthew 16:26

Yet the whole life of Jesus was a demonstration of *active service to all life.*

Amen, I say unto you, as long as you did this, even for one of these, the least of all creatures, you did it unto Me.

Matthew 25:40

Practising the Presence of God 711
The Omnipresent God 1108
The Presence of God 1396

The Dichotomy of the Mystic

This idea of seeking God alone, and negating all created things as inferior, was the view of the Gnostics, the Hesychasts, the Cathars and the "regular" Mystics of the church. It is characteristic of the Muslim and Jewish Mystics also. But it was never a perfect view. It was not practical in those days and it is even less so today! It created a tremendous division, a dichotomy in the Mystic's consciousness, a sense of duality and an alienation from life and from people.

This dichotomy existed within Jesus Himself

What is more, it is not the example provided by Jesus! He did withdraw regularly to the desert, the mountains or the lakes to *commune* with His Father, but He never withdrew totally from His environment. Jesus *acted* on behalf of others, on behalf of the world.

Mysticism is *not* an idea, not a philosophy, not a thought process. It is an approach to Reality via the Heart. But the next stage should be the *grounding* of the Mystic, the expression of that Love-Unity Consciousness in *active service,* as Jesus did.

This dichotomy existed within Jesus Himself. On the one hand, He insisted that "the Kingdom of God is *within* you" *(Luke 17:21)* and that "My Kingdom is *not* of this world" *(John 18:36)*, thus suggesting a severance, an alienation from the world.

> Lay not up for yourselves treasures on earth, where moth and rust does corrupt, where thieves break in and steal, but store up for yourselves treasures in the invisible worlds, where neither rust nor moth does consume your goods, neither can thieves break in and steal.
>
> *Matthew 6:19–20*

Yet, at the same time, He insisted on the most complete and active *service* toward one's fellow human beings that any Teacher has ever demanded of his disciples.

As a result of this dichotomy, some disciples of Jesus, over the centuries, decided to opt out of the world, while others spent all their time in active service toward their fellow suffering creatures. But true Mysticism is both, as Jesus exemplified with His life. It is to live in the Eternal, the Transcendental, but to be engaged in the serving of the temporal, the worldly, that which passes away. It is to live in God the Transcendent and to serve God the Immanent in Creation.

Warrior Jesus 908
Return to Duty 812
Spiritual Life and Material Life 1118
To Love God and the World 1392

Christian Mysticism and Zen

The ideas and goals of Christian Mysticism are the same as those of Zen Buddhism; although the forms are different, the content is the same. The early name for Mysticism was *Contemplation,* which was defined as "the hidden knowledge of God by inward experience; the passive Illumination of the Soul by God; experiencing the Grace of the Divine Light; the direct experience of the Absolute without an intermediary, institutional or otherwise; guidance by the Grace of the Holy Spirit". All of these definitions would apply to Zen also.

Pure Christian Mysticism is not different in essence from Zen Buddhism

- The Mystic is one who *transcends* himself or herself.
- The Mystic is one who believes in a Reality that cannot be rationally comprehended, nor expressed in words, to which he or she *surrenders.*
- The Mystic believes in the Ineffable and seeks to *experience* It.
- The Mystic experiences an ultimate, non-material Unity or Oneness with all things, which cannot be apprehended by reason or logic, nor by the physical senses.
- Mysticism, Gnosticism, Contemplation, is a quest for the Divine and is the ultimate Self-knowledge. Such knowledge of one's Self reveals also the knowledge of God.
- Mysticism is a spiritual, mystical theology based on Inner Revelation, not on outer dogmas or fanciful, intellectual interpretations of the scriptures.
- Mysticism is a personal, spiritual transformation in Christ.
- The goal of the Mystic is Union with God.

What is Zen? 753
Christian Zen 765
When the Mind is Still 768

> Mysticism is an ordered movement towards ever-higher levels of Reality, an ever-closer identification with the Infinite.
>
> *Evelyn Underhill*

> We have to become what we already are. Contemplation cannot be taught, but can be awakened in those who have an aptitude for it. The work of the Contemplative is transpersonal and suprapersonal.
>
> *Thomas Merton*

A Zen monk would readily agree with this. Pure Christian Mysticism is not different *in essence* from Zen Buddhism; the difference is only in form.

Contemplātionis
Latin: "Being within the temple". Contemplation. From Con (with or within) and Templum (temple). The temple is the Heart Centre.

Contemplation (Theoria) 694
Contemplation 1188

The Burning Heart

My heart was hot within me, and while I was musing, my body was on fire.
Psalms 39:3 (from ancient Eastern manuscripts)

Thousands of years ago the Psalmist wrote of his experience of a burning Heart, and of his body being on fire while "musing" on God, that is, thinking deeply of God in his Heart. This same sensation of "burning in the Heart" was felt by Jesus' disciples (who had been practising the Prayer of the Heart) as He talked to them after His Resurrection.

Did not our Hearts burn within us while he talked with us by the way, and while he opened to us the scriptures?
Luke 24:32

The importance of the Heart has been missed by most Christians. The Heart is mentioned hundreds of times in the Bible. Among these references to the Heart there are many which relate directly to the *experience* of God through the Heart. For instance:

Blessed are the pure in Heart: for they shall *see* God.
Matthew 5:8

In most translations of this verse there is a *direct promise* that those who purify the Heart will be gifted with the Vision of God. For most Christians this simply means being a "good Christian" and "believing" in the Bible. Many Christians identify with the historical figure of Jesus who was the Christ, and the "Word" of God as a book in their lives, the Holy Bible. Neither God nor Jesus is merely a historical figure, however, and the Word is not a mere book. Through the Radiant Heart we come to know God as a *Living Presence*, "the Living God", and Jesus as "the Living Jesus" (as He is called in all the Gnostic Gospels).

Keep thy Heart with all diligence, for out of it issues Life.
Proverbs 4:23

Trust in the Lord with all thine Heart, and lean not on your own intellectual understanding.
Proverbs 3:5

As a man thinketh in his Heart, so is he.
Proverbs 23:7

A wise man's Heart discerneth both time and judgment.
Ecclesiastes 8:5

For out of the abundance of the Heart the mouth speaketh.
Matthew 12:34

For where your treasure is, there is your Heart also.
Matthew 6:21

Wounds of Love 699
The Fire in the Heart 1287
The Cosmic Christ 662
Purify the Heart 701
The Gnostic Teachings 1108
Jesus: the Fire of Love 1725

The Christian Heart-Path

The Christian word for the Heart is KARDIA (Greek). KARDIA is more than the physical heart. It is the Spiritual Centre in Man, the Sanctuary within the Temple of the physical body, concealing the true Self or God-Being in Man, the Holy of Holies. It is the Holy Place where God meets Man, where you become One with God.

Prayer in the Heart means entering the depths of your own Being. The Vision of God is in the Heart. Christ dwells in the Heart. The true Heaven is in the Heart.

All of this was known and then forgotten. The earliest Christians were a Jewish sect. They followed Jewish practices, using the Jewish Divine Names in the Heart or short sentences from the Psalms or sacred writings, as Mental Prayer in the Heart. As more Greek-speaking people were converted, however, more Greek knowledge became mixed in with the Jewish religious ideas and practices. The first four centuries saw endless clashes between the "pure Jews" and the "foreign" Greek philosophies and thoughts. Later on, the Latin-speaking populations were also converted, so there developed a mixture of Jewish, Greek and Latin thoughts and ideas. Today's Christianity is a mixture of all this.

As it was for the Jewish and Muslim Mystics, the Love of God was the Goal of Life for the early Christians. They flocked to the deserts of Egypt, Syria, North Africa and Palestine to learn how to *Commune with God in the Heart*, to *Worship* God in the Heart, to *Bless* God in the Heart, to *Exalt* and *Glorify* God in the Heart, to sing God's *praises* in the Heart, to *meet* God in the Heart, with *sweetness* in the Heart, and there to *receive* God's Illumination.

Stillness and Silence within (HESYCHIA) was the aim of this Path: Inner Tranquillity, Mental Quietude, an attitude of Inner Listening, an Inner Attention in the Heart to sense the Presence of God. The intellect (mind) was engaged continually in "calling-upon" God in the Heart.

This Heart-Path was established in Christianity over a period of four centuries and was further developed for eleven centuries in Eastern Christianity. In the West it was soon forgotten. Along came the priestcraft who made rituals, and each century the rituals became longer and more complex. The *Internal Worship* of God became external worship and the Inner Light was lost.

The Love of God was the Goal of Life

What is the Heart? 435
The Early Christians 643
Mental Prayer in the Heart 1254

PHYLAKI KARDIAS
Greek: "The Guarding of the Heart". Having your attention in the Heart. Centring in the Heart. The practice of keeping the Heart free from worldly thoughts and influences, and praying to God in the Heart for help and mercy.
Guard your Heart 1328

TIRISIS KARDIAS
Greek: Vigilance in the Heart.

NIPSIS, PROSOCHI
Greek: Alertness, sobriety, watchfulness, wakefulness in the Heart Centre.

The Meaning of Life is Love

For the Mystic, life must be *simplified* and the attention must be directed not on objects outside in the world, but on things *unseen.*

Your world is the reflection of your consciousness. Your consciousness projects itself into your environment. You can understand any happening in Time and Space only according to your consciousness. The *quality* of your consciousness is more potent than any theory, technique, belief or religion. Stillness of Being, clarity of mind and the quality of your consciousness determine the outcome of any event more than any theories or interpretations of the situation at hand.

Rivers of Love will flow from your Heart

It is the *quality* of your consciousness that counts, and that quality is measured by the amount of true Love that you *demonstrate* moment by moment in your life. The meaning of being "spiritual" or "developed" is equivalent to the degree of your Love in action towards others. It is the amount of *selflessness* that you possess.

No prestige, position, name and fame or wealth is a measure of "spirituality". You can be poor or rich and be highly conscious, or you can be poor or rich and be of low consciousness. The meaning of Life is *Love*—Love demonstrated in actions towards others.

The Love of God and the Love of Humanity are the same. We strive to attain Union with God through prayer and meditation formulas, but when we have found "God", our Hearts open up to the service of Humanity, for the two are one.

Consciousness 1370
The Supreme Act of Karma 264
On Love and Meditation 1140
To Love God and the World 1392
Cultivate the Fires of Love 928
The Fire of Love 1255

∞

Love is a Force, the greatest Force in the Universe.

Love of God renews and re-creates Man. God's Love for Man attracts Mankind back to the Bosom of God. It is an Attracting Force that draws all things towards God.

Love of Man towards God is a Blessing. God's Love towards Man is a greater Blessing. It is the same One Love-Power.

In time, Man-God Love and God-Man Love will be experienced as One and the same. Then your Heart will be on Fire and the Rivers of Love will flow from your Heart like tidal waves or great ocean currents.

Saint Bernard taught that Love has four degrees:

a. Man loves himself only.
b. Man begins to love God for the benefit of himself.
c. Man loves God for the sake of God alone.
d. Man loves himself for the sake of God.

God in the Heart

The Lord seeth not as Man sees things. Man looketh to outer appearances of things, but God looks into the Heart.

I Samuel 16:7

A Divine Mystery is concealed in the human Heart

To the Old Testament Jewish Mystics and the New Testament Christian Saints, the Heart is the *Spiritual Centre* of the human being. In it may be found the image of God, a reflection of the Divine Godhead. A Divine Mystery is concealed in the human Heart. In the Heart, the human creature and God the Creator meet, commingle and unite.

Within the Heart is felt the Oneness of all Life. Within the Heart is experienced Unity. Within the Heart, God shows Himself as the One Life, the Centre, the Root, the Source of all Being and all beings. A Christ-centred life is a Heart-centred life. We can only understand, comprehend and express Love in the Heart, through the Heart and from the Heart. We all become One in the Heart.

It is for this reason that the Gnostics first focused in the Heart. It is for this cause that the Hesychasts and the Mystics first entered the Heart. In the Heart is the Rebirth of Humanity. In the Oneness of the Heart is Beatitude, Blessed Unity, Peace, Tranquillity (Hesychia).

The Holy Spirit manifests itself in full certitude in the Heart.

An early Christian Saint

If the *whole* Man [body, mind and Soul] turns towards God, then, in an unutterable Mystery, God reveals His Presence in the Heart.

Christian Mysticism

The Cave of the Heart

The later Christian Mystics called the Heart "the Cave of the Heart" and "Bethlehem, where the Christ is born". Even as a child is born in the mother's womb, God is born in the human Heart, which is often symbolized as a *cave*. According to the Mystics, Christ was born in a cave in Bethlehem. The cave in Bethlehem is the Heart.

Meditation in the Cave of the Heart 1358
The Eastern Heart 448

The Abode of the Self 434
The Christ in the Heart 441
The Mystery within the Heart 1315
The Solar and Human Heart 1592

God dwells in full Mystery in the Heart. God can be *tasted* and *seen* in the Heart.

> Come *taste* and see that the Lord is Good.
>
> *Psalms 34:8*

According to Saint Diadochos, perfect Love can come only to those whose Souls have already been purified, who experience a constant *burning* and *uniting* of the Soul with God, by the Fire of the Holy Ghost, acting through the Heart.

Perfect Love can come only to those whose Souls have been purified

> Spiritual Knowledge is the transcending of self-love for the Love of God. Having been transformed by God, it is in an intense Illumination [Light].
>
> *St Diadochos*

> Thou shalt Love the Lord, thy God, with all your Heart, with all your Soul, with all your physical strength, and with all your mind. And thou shalt love thy neighbour as you would love thyself.
>
> *Luke 10:27*

This is really the Old Testament commandment given to the Jewish nation:

> I command you this day, to Love the Lord your God, and to serve Him, with all your Heart and with all your Soul.
>
> *Deuteronomy 11:13*

The New Testament version is more complete. In both the Old and New Testaments the connection between the Heart and Soul is recognized, while in the New Testament the connection between the physical body and the mind is added. For the Heart is *controlled* by the Soul, and the physical body is *controlled* by the mind.

Both the early Jewish Mystics and the later Christian Mystics (the Hesychast tradition) concentrated in the Heart, though body-mind control was also practised.

> With my whole Heart, I looked for Thee. Let me not wander from your Commandments. Thy Word I have hid in my Heart, so that I might not commit a fault against Thee.
>
> *Psalms 119:10,11*

The "Word" which the Psalmist hid in his Heart was a Hebrew Name of God. It is a common tradition of both Jews and Christians to call upon God in the Heart through a Divine Name. This same process is very common among the Hindu and Muslim Mystics as well.

To Taste the Elixir of Life 593
Stages of Interior Prayer 693
The Name and the Names 1258
Hebrew Divine Names 1262
The Voice of God 864

The Experience of Mysticism

> Blessed is the man who heareth Jesus speaking in his Soul, that heareth from His mouth some words of comfort.
>
> Blessed are the ears that hear the secret breathings of Jesus, and heed not the deceitful whisperings of the world.
>
> Blessed are the ears that hear not the outward sounds, but listen to what God speaketh and teaches *inwardly,* in the Soul.
>
> Blessed are the eyes that are shut from the sight of the outer vanities of the world, and see the inward movements of God.
>
> *Thomas à Kempis: The Imitation of Christ*

As a Spiritual Being, you see and hear the actions of God

Do not take these words to be mere symbolic or poetic expressions of faith. No! Thomas à Kempis speaks here of *an actual condition of deep meditation.* These words describe an advanced meditational stage, the *inner seeing and hearing of God* within the Soul. The Mystic would describe this experience as *in the Soul.* Technically, it is a deep stage of meditation wherein you know yourself to be separate from your body-mind-personality and are aware that you are a Soul, a Spiritual Being. And, as a Spiritual Being, you *see* and *hear* the actions of God the Father, God the Son (the Christ) and God the Holy Spirit, acting in your Soul—the supernatural operations of Divine Grace causing various movements within your Being. This is *not* theory! We are talking not about belief or faith, but *actual experience.*

So, how can you come to this profound meditational experience wherein you actually *see* and *hear* God within yourself? That is the problem of Mysticism.

There is so much suffering on our planet because Humanity has lost its spiritual heritage. If we are to bring about an end to suffering upon this planet, it must be *realized,* through deep meditation and spiritual exercises, that *a human being is a Soul.*

The Old Testament Jews and other Middle Eastern peoples employed the techniques of *silence, solitude, prayer, meditation, contemplation* and *fasting.* Basically, the techniques for attaining Soul-contact have not changed to this day; the essential ingredients are still the same.

But remember, we *do not* consider the Soul to be the astral body, nor the mind, the mental body. We consider your Soul to be *beyond* your mental and emotional make-up and *beyond* your physical and etheric bodies.

Jīva: the Human Soul 35

The Path of Seeing 552
The Path of Hearing 553
The Universal Heart Practice 846
Heart-Prayer or Spiritual Prayer 1256
Why Life is Suffering 263

To See and Hear God…

To hear Jesus "speaking" in your Soul, and to see God's inward movements in your Soul, requires the following:

- A deep stillness, equanimity and poise of mind.
- A tremendous tranquillity of emotions.
- A discipline of the body.
- The harmonizing of your brain.
- The alignment of all the cakras within you.
- An intense orientation of your consciousness *inside* yourself.

Your outer being must rest while your Inner Being is wide awake

This explains why Mysticism is not for the average person.

Initially, at least, God can only be contacted in *Silence*—silence of thoughts, silence of emotions, silence of bodily activities. "Be *still* and *know* that I *am* God", says the Old Testament *(Psalms 46:10).* When you are very advanced on the Path, God can be contacted while you are busily engaged in activities, but that comes much later.

You must be *still,* but not blank. You must be *silent,* but not asleep. You must have inner *equipoise,* but not rigidity. Your outer being must rest while your Inner Being is wide awake. This is not a zombie-like condition; on the contrary, it is a brightness, an alertness never before experienced. That is why the Buddha was called the Buddha: the word BUDDHA means "inwardly wide awake".

The Law of Mystic Experience 508
To Develop Perfect Stillness 700
Your Mind is the Key 1208
The Silence of the Deep 1355
Attach your Mind to the Eternal 1234

You must *sense* the Timeless within Time, the Everlasting within the transitoriness of all things.

> We belong not to Time, but to the Timeless;
> not to the world, but to That which is beyond all worlds.

So spake the later Mystics of Christianity. We are from the Eternal and shall return unto the Eternal Godhood.

> God has made everything appropriate according to time, but has put the *feeling for the Timeless into their Hearts,* without the ordinary men ever discovering… the work which God has done.
>
> *Ecclesiastes 3:11*

CAKRA
Sanskrit: "A circle, a wheel, a sphere, an orb, a revolving disk, a whirlpool of energy, a rotating centre, a wheel of fire". The term CAKRA can refer to a force-centre in a sun, a galaxy, a planet, a human being or an atom.
The Human Cakras 44

Be Still and Know...

> Be still and know that I am God... the God of your fathers, Abraham, Isaac, and Jacob.
>
> *Psalms 46:10, Exodus 3:6*

The keynote is always the Inner Stillness

The Old Testament Jews knew that by silence, stillness, solitude, aspiration, fasting, inward recollection, concentration and prayer, they could *connect* to God, the *same* God as the God of the old "fathers" of the Jewish faith. (The Jewish religion has always oriented itself toward the past.)

The Piscean Mystic

From the time of Christ, the beginning of the Piscean Age, the new Mystics changed this key idea about God to simply:

Be still and know that I am God.

This was about the *Here and Now.* Using the same eternal principles, the Mystics found the Living God, the God who *always is, right now.* You do this from the Soul level, first by establishing a Soul-connection and then by *expansion* into the Higher Reality.

The keynote is always the *Inner Stillness,* the harmonizing of the body, mind, emotions and vitality (the etheric body) so that the Vision of the Soul may be seen, so that the Voice of God may be heard.

The Aquarian Mystic

In the coming New Age, the Age of Aquarius, a further shift is taking place. The ideal of the Aquarian Age Mystic is:

Be still and know that *you* are God.

Lest some fundamentalist objects to this truth, let me explain. "Be still and know" means that by inward silence and stillness you can *experience* your Soul-Nature. You can experience yourself as an Immortal, Eternal Being, a Child of God, the Eternal. For the Mystic this is not just a belief or wishful thinking; it is an *experiential fact.*

The Hasidim 648
The Attitude for Yoga 558
When the Mind is Still 768
The Way, the Truth and the Life 670
Mystics of Pisces and Aquarius 836

The fact that "you *are* God" does not mean that Man replaces God, or that Man is equal to God or above God. It simply means that Man *realizes,* in a very intimate way, his or her Oneness with the Divine Being. This is the experience of the Buddhic Plane, the *Mystical Union.* Anybody who has reached this level of spirituality always speaks of the incredible sense of *Union,* of *Oneness,* of *togetherness with the All.*

The Soul is realized to be One with the Divine

The phrase "you are God" does not mean that the little, selfish, egotistical individual is God. In fact, in the Mystical State of Buddhi, all sense of ego is lost, the whole sense of a separated, separate identity vanishes. All egoism, egotism, selfishness and egocentricity simply disappears! The frail human ego is not recognized as God; rather, the Soul is realized to be One with the Divine. The Unity between Man and God is perceived as an accomplished, eternal *fact.*

The Temple of God

And when Jesus was asked by the Pharisees when the Kingdom of God will come, He said to them, "The Kingdom of God does not come by looking out for it… for behold, the Kingdom of God is *inside* you."

Luke 17:20–21

For ye are the Temple of the Living God; as God said, "I will live in them, and I will walk in them, and I will be their God."

2 Corinthians 6:16

Know ye not that ye are the Temple of God, that the Spirit of God lives *in you?*

1 Corinthians 3:16

A human being is a Temple of God. The early Christian Saints took this idea quite literally: since God is to be found *inside* a human being, the logical thing to do is to look for God inside oneself by the process of *inner prayer* and *inner meditation.* A favourite focus was in the Heart, though this was not the only way.

This inner journey through interior prayer and meditation is also the Path of the Sūfī, the Jewish Hasidim, the Yogī, the Zen monk, the Buddhist, the Chinese Mystic, and so on. There is ancient agreement among all traditions that *God can be found inside oneself* by a suitable process or method, and with the help of Divine Grace.

The Temple of the Goddess 1492

The Discovery of Truth 85
The One and Only 839
Mystical Union 846
The Path of Union 1339
The Thread of the Heart 844

To Partake of God's Nature

The *Theologia Germanica* asks:

> What is it like to partake of God's Divine Nature, to be filled with Divine Light, to be imbued with the Eternal Love of Christ?

This infusion of Light into the Soul was to be done now, in this lifetime

For that, in truth, is the essential purpose of Christianity. In the early days of Christianity this infusion of Light into the Soul was to be done *now*, in this lifetime, while in the body. When Christianity became "Churchianity", however, this became only a *promise* for a future afterlife in "Heaven".

The true Christian Tradition—true Gnosticism, Hesychasm and Mysticism—is not about asking God for things to pamper one's personality (however useful such things might be). It is about *loving God, simply because God is.*

Mystical Contemplation occurs when you subdue the thoughts in your ordinary, discursive, reasoning mind, leave behind all attachments to worldly things and, in *absolute detachment* from all things (including yourself!), raise yourself into the Stream of Divine Light. Thus taught, also, Saint Dionsius the Areopagite.

The earliest forms of Christian prayers (meditations) were to allow the transcendence of the thinking faculty, to stop the chatter of the mind, imagination and memory. Then, in a wordless, thoughtless mind-state, one could ascend to the contemplation of the Presence of God by a direct Knowing, a Soul-touch, above the mind.

In this sense, true Christianity is identical to true Yoga, Sūfīsm, Buddhism, Taoism, Jewish Mysticism and Zen.

What is Prayer? 690
The Goal of Yoga 519
The Spirit of Zen 751
The Sūfī Heart 843
The Way of the Heart 1249

CHAPTER 29

Christian History

Christian Beginnings

The new disciples of Jesus broke away from the Jewish faith

It is difficult to say exactly what Jesus actually taught, since nothing was recorded while He was alive. It is said that the earliest scriptures surfaced forty to sixty years after His death. Even so, there are no traces of these early scriptures, but only copies of copies of copies, much altered and edited by the pious and dogmatic "Doctors of the Church". The scriptures were translated from Hebrew and Aramaic into Greek, then from Greek into Latin, by church scholars who had no experience of the Kingdom of God. Nor were they living at the time of Jesus, but centuries later.

It is a great tragedy that Jesus taught for only three years. I suppose the times were hard and He found the Jewish consciousness of the day intensely crystallized. He could teach no longer. The Old Testament religion was dead and frozen, and the Scribes, Pharisees and rulers (the SANHEDRIN) were but servants of the material powers of this world.

So, the new disciples of Jesus broke away from the Jewish faith. Members of this breakaway group were known as the *Nazarenes*, the followers of the man from Nazareth, Jesus. Centuries later they became known as the *Christians*.

Before three centuries had elapsed, however, the Christian church was taken over by the "powers of this world": materialism, worldly domination, physical power, riches, name, fame, material glory. The struggle had already started when Jesus was alive and it continued after His death. The worldly powers took control of the church within less than three hundred years!

Records of Early Christianity

The **PHILOKALIA** (Greek: "The Love of God") describes the practices and teachings of the Eastern Christian tradition.

The **VITAE PATRUM** (Latin: "The Lives of the Fathers") describes the Western tradition.

The Philokalia 691

Jesus the Christed One 659
The Dual Nature of Christianity 624

The Early Christians

John the Baptist was a prototype for all true Christians. John lived alone in the desert, like all the Jewish Mystics and Prophets before him who sought to "commune with God". He lived in utter simplicity, total poverty, in complete denial of all personality needs and comforts, surviving on locusts and wild honey—when he was lucky enough to find some!

They were "in the world but not of the world"

In the Gospels, Jesus is portrayed in the same way. Certainly, Jesus never collected any money for any reason and he lived like a hermit, in total ascetic simplicity. He had no rich robes or crowns, no slaves or houses, no comforts whatsoever! Jesus often spent long periods in the solitude of the desert.

The Hesychasts (the Christian desert-dwellers) were similar. Their concern was *not* to live successfully in this world, but *to find the Kingdom of God within themselves.* If you read the PHILOKALIA or the VITAE PATRUM you will know how these Christians lived.

The desert monks and nuns of early Christianity lived alone or in small groups, hundreds of thousands of them in the deserts of Egypt, the Sinai, Mt Athos, Palestine, North Africa and Asia Minor. They may be called the "desert people" or the "desert fathers". They practised absolute discomfort and self-denial. Some never ate anything; some ate only once a week; some ate once a day—bread, salt and water only! Some ate grass or any plant they could find. They were naked or, like John the Baptist, found animal skins to cover their private parts.

Some lived in such lonely and isolated spots that they didn't see another monk for years. Some lived out in the open desert, some found shelter under rocks, some found caves, but none of them had blankets, sheets and pillows! They possessed nothing—or perhaps a wooden bowl, a clay jug or a pot.

Some were living in the towns of the Roman Empire. They merged easily into their environment, but *kept themselves apart.* They obeyed all the local laws, but lived *above* the world; they had no worldly ambitions whatsoever. They were "in the world but not *of* the world". They were a puzzle to the Romans around them.

Marcus Aurelius, the great philosopher-emperor of the Roman Empire, said of these early Christians that they were "fanatics". Later on, the Romans persecuted them.

Christian Mysticism 450
The Christian Heart-Path 632

Then there were those who, over the centuries, organized themselves into monasteries and nunneries. These people also had an incredibly hard lifestyle. They had to work hard, pray hard and discipline themselves. Their diet was bread and cheese, salt, vinegar and water—rather a luxurious diet compared to that of the desert dwellers! Some ate these delicacies three times a day, some only once a day, some only once a week.

The goal of these early Christians was Deification

Each monk or nun had manual work to do. Some translated sacred texts and wrote them out longhand. Everything they did was religious—to enhance the passage to the Kingdom of God *within*. They said:

> You cannot attain pure prayer while entangled with the world, the devil (the opposition) and the flesh (the body).

And what, according to these early Christians, is *pure prayer?* They used the word *prayer* in the way we use the word *meditation:*

Pure prayer is when the mind and Heart are completely free from images, imaginings, thoughts and forms of any kind.

You cannot attain spiritual prayer by being constantly engaged in worldly worries, cares, agitations and ambitions. The mind must be stilled, thoughts must be transcended, and the Heart must be purified of all temporal things.

Blessed is the mind which is free from all forms during prayer.

The goal of these early Christians was *Deification, Union with God, Apotheosis.* The goal of original Christianity was to achieve mental stillness through meditation and thus establish unification with the *Cosmic Christ,* the *Word,* the *Radiant-Light-of-God.* Meanwhile, the goal of institutionalized "Churchianity" was to instil a *fear* of God in the believer and encourage him or her towards a *moral* life.

In AD313 the Roman Emperor Constantine declared Christianity to be the state religion of the Roman Empire; hence, the Western branch of the church came into existence and the church became the political arm of the Empire. The church became a Roman *institution,* modelled on Rome, and the bishops of Rome (the popes) became *dictators.* The church was *not* democratic; it was the dictatorship of the popes of Rome. It became the Latin Church, known as Roman Catholicism.

What is Prayer? 690
Deification (Theosis) 695
The Cosmic Christ 662
Fear of the Lord? 234

The Pilgrims

Thus far we have mentioned four kinds of Christians of the early centuries:

a. The hermits who lived alone in the deserts.
b. The hermits of the deserts who formed a loose association and communication with one another, sometimes gathering in small communities—not in towns or villages, but among the rocks!
c. Those living in towns, cities and villages of the Roman Empire.
d. Those who, in later centuries, organized themselves into monasteries and nunneries.

There is a fifth type also, known as the *pilgrims.* The author of *The Way of the Pilgrim* describes himself as "a Christian man", "a great sinner", "a homeless wanderer who roams from place to place". His only possessions were a knapsack with some dried bread in it and a Bible.

The pilgrims were like the sādhus and sannyāsins of India

The pilgrims were like the sādhus and sannyāsins of India, wandering ascetics who lived nowhere and everywhere. There were many of them in Russia, Asia Minor and Greece. They never settled down anywhere, but travelled on foot visiting holy places or shrines. They ate only dry bread and salt, which they begged from the villagers. They tended to avoid large towns and cities, and travelled alone through the forests and byways. They were totally non-worldly.

The Gnostics

The Greek word GNŌSTIKOS means "a Knower, a Seer, one who knows Spiritual Truth by direct, inner experience". The Gnostics were early Christian Saints who had a direct vision of the World of Light. They were severely persecuted by the church as "heretics" because they did not always agree with the respected church authorities who had no direct experience of spiritual matters but intellectually *speculated* about the nature of Reality. These authorities falsified the teachings of the Gnostics, lied about them and invented all sorts of untruths against them. It is these lies and fabrications about the Gnostics that were handed down through the centuries.

Greek Words from Gnostic Christianity 736

Balance in Spiritual Life 505
Is Renunciation Necessary? 1119
Persecution of the Knowers 656
The Gnostic Teachings 1108

Who are the Christians?

The church was but a hindrance to the spread of Spiritual Christianity

Suppose you are a modern-day Christian: could you understand and *sympathize* with these five types of Christians? Or would you say that these millions of ardent followers of Jesus the Christ were non-Christians?—that they were "of the Devil" as a fundamentalist preacher once told me?

What of the popes, cardinals and bishops of the Roman Church who lived in utter splendour and luxury; could these intensely worldly men ever have understood those early Christians?

So, who are the Christians?—the intensely worldly and materialistic, or the intensely spiritual and transcendental? Christianity has had both for the past two thousand years. This was the great division within the church: between those who believed in the Kingdom of God within the Soul and those who wanted to establish a kingdom on Earth, on the material plane, and to conquer all nations by force and dogma. Yet the Masters of Christian Wisdom said:

> To pray without ceasing is to enlighten the Heart with the Light of Christ.

And…

> Ceaseless interior prayer is a continuous *yearning* of the Soul towards God.

And…

> The Heavenly Light of unceasing interior prayer cannot be attained by worldly wisdom, nor by outward knowledge, but by *poverty in the Spirit* and a *radiant Heart.*

How wonderful is Christian Spirituality! How few modern Christians know of the profound Wisdom within the Christian tradition! How few read the works of the Eastern Christian Saints or the Roman Catholic Saints—even what is left of them after the heavy censorship of the church!

Christianity survived, not because of the church, but *in spite of* the church. The church was but a *hindrance* to the spread of Spiritual Christianity.

Interior Prayer 691
Prayer Spiritual and Material 681
The Heart and the Lost Art of Prayer 1251

The Prophets

The Greek word PROPHETES means "someone who knows the Will of God, the *Plan*, through an interior revelation, by direct experience; one who speaks for God, the Deity; an inspired *revealer* or *interpreter* of the Divine Will, the Divine Plan". From this came the English word *prophet*. A Prophet, in the Old Testament sense and to the early Christians, was one who could speak on behalf of the Deity.

A Prophet was one who could speak on behalf of the Deity

To *prophesy*, in the Old Testament sense, and to the Eastern Christians, the Byzantine Church, meant "to speak by Divine Inspiration; to be moved to speak by the Holy Spirit; to utter Divine Mysteries as moved by the Spirit; to interpret by Inspiration the inner meanings of the scriptures; to preach the Gospel by the power of the Holy Ghost; to reveal the hidden Mysteries of the Kingdom of God *within*".

> Son of Man, prophesy thou, and say: These things sayeth the Lord, thy God.
> *Ezekiel 21:9*

Later on, prophecy came to mean the telling of future events in the world, although that was never the main import of the gift of prophecy. And prophecy has nothing at all to do with the intellectual scripture-interpretation of the scholars, theologians, evangelicals and fundamentalists. Prophecy is not a mental exercise, not a thinking process. It is a result of profound inner meditation and prayer, a connecting to Soul-Consciousness and to the Unitive States of Mystical Prayer.

Prophecy and Destiny 294
'Channelling' the Soul 325
Prātibhā Siddhi: true Prophecy 598
Revelation is Continuous 1710

All true Gurus and Spiritual Masters are true Prophets because they speak by Divine Inspiration. The subject of prophecy must not be limited to the revealing of some future physical event. The real burden of prophecy, since early Greek times, involved the mysteries of the Spirit and the Spiritual Universe.

PROPHETES
Greek: A Prophet. From the Greek PROPHECEIN, "to give religious instruction". Prophets were not confined to Israel only. Before Christianity, the Greeks and the ancient nations had many "prophets". The word, as used by them, had many distinct meanings.

CHOZEH
Hebrew: A seer, a clairvoyant.

NABI
Hebrew: A Prophet. A revealer of the Divine Mysteries.

The Hasidim

Since Old Testament times the Jewish Mystics have been called HASIDIM. To attain to the heights of Mystical Life the Hasidim followed strict rules:

The Hasid comes under the Love of God

- Spiritual study.
- Prayer.
- Meditation.
- Penitence (penance).
- Silence and solitude.
- A sense of *sacredness* in all things. That is, an awareness of the Divine Presence (SHEKINAH) in all things.
- To have a TZADIK (a Guru, a Spiritual Teacher, a Master, a righteous person, a just man, an ideal man) for one's guide and helper.
- To believe in the *Messiah,* the Avatāra or Divine Incarnation.
- Service to everybody and everything, sharing with people, caring for all of Creation because it is a Veil for SHEKINAH, the Glory of God. This is called TIKKUN, the giving of one's life for one's fellow human beings.
- To become a BAAL SHEM, a Master of the Divine Name; that is, to become initiated or baptized into the Divine Power, the Name of God, SHEMA.
- To believe in and work for Redemption or Salvation (Higher Consciousness).
- To believe in and maintain at all times the Truth Principle, the TORAH, the Law.

The HASID comes under the Love of God, or Grace, the Divine Attribute of CHESED on the Tree of Life. The Hasid, or Mystic, is like God in the aspect of Love and Compassion.

The ordinary, unpious men and women come under DĪN, "Divine Justice" (punishment, strict justice, cause and effect, what in the East is called KARMA). On the Tree of Life, this aspect of God is called GEBURAH (severity, anger, strength, the fear of God).

The Law

The Hebrew word **TORAH** has the same significance as the Sanskrit **DHARMA.** The Jewish idea of the TORAH, "the Law", teaches that Man is responsible for his Destiny and Fate.

The *active* agent of the Law, **KARMA**, the Jews also know well as "the vengeance of the Lord", the retribution aspect of the Law, or Cause and Effect.

Dharma: the Law of Being 244

Karma: the Law of Action 240

According to the Hasidim:

God Is.
God Is Everywhere.
God Is One.

God Is. God is the Source, the Fountainhead of all Life, the ever-permanent Reality.

The Hasid must live with the people and for the people

God Is Everywhere. God dwells in every human being, in all objects and in all things, in full Glory, that is, in the form of the SHEKINAH, the Divine Splendour.

God Is One. There is no division or separation in God's Nature. Therefore, the Creator and the Creature are One, and God is the same to all people who turn towards God, whether they be Jews, Christians, Muslims, or Gentiles of any kind or of any religion. God, the Messiah and Humanity are *One.*

The Hasid must live *with* the people and *for* the people. In this sense, Jewish Mysticism is radically different from Eastern Mysticism, where the ideal was to "get away from it all", to have no connection with people and the world. Christian Mysticism also tends to be more practical.

The Jewish Messiah 660
Holiness to the Lord 1393
The Eternal is One 512
The Kabbalistic Tree of Life 359

> He who walks the Path of Love shall be Loved by God.
>
> He who walks the path of hate and disharmony shall surely burn by the Fires of chastisement.

Yet, even the Fires of Hell are but the Love of God, purifying us unto the Perfect Day.

The Masculine God

The Jewish idea of God, as portrayed in the Old Testament, was that of a *masculine* being. God was always described in masculine terms such as *He, Father, King, Judge*, or BAAL (Lord, Master of the Universe, chieftain, ruler).

You will see that Christian Spirituality borrowed these ideas from the Jews, except that Jesus Christ was substituted for God. Meanwhile, the Jews *rejected* Jesus as the long-awaited Messiah. This was the greatest disaster in Jewish history, if only they would know it.

The Feminine Suppressed 910

HASID
Hebrew: "An extremely pious, religious or fervent person". From the Divine Attribute of CHESED on the Tree of Life, which means "Love, compassion, mercy, grace, goodwill, tenderness, fervour".

TZADIK
Hebrew: "One who *lives* his faith". A human being further advanced upon the Path. The Guru or spiritual model, sometimes also called the *Elect* or a *Perfected One*.

Who are the 'Elect'? 128

Christianity was One

With each breaking-up, Truth was further lost

In the beginning, Christianity was one. Then it broke up into the Western Roman Church and the Eastern Orthodox Church. The Roman Church broke up into the Roman Catholic, Protestant and Anglican Churches, and the Protestant Church broke up into various fundamentalist and evangelical sects and reformed churches. With each breaking-up, Truth was further lost, until today the fundamentalist, evangelical and revivalist (Pentecostal) Christianity contains no Mysticism at all!

While many of the Saints of the Roman Catholic Church were genuine Mystics, some were just busy "converters" with no Higher Consciousness at all. The church canonized many religious fanatics as "saints", but a true Saint is one who has reached at least the Buddhic Consciousness. There are many more genuine Saints in Eastern Orthodox Christianity because the East has always been more mystical. The Eastern Christians believed in conscious Theosis, "the Deification of the Creature". This, of course, is also the idea of Sūfism, Buddhism and Hinduism.

In Eastern Orthodox Christianity, Union with God (Theosis) was the very objective and meaning of Christianity and the *duty* of every Christian. It was not reserved for only the "few" chosen at random by God, as was believed by the Roman Catholic Church. It wasn't a hit-and-miss affair. It could be *consciously gained.*

The direct Knowledge of God by human beings (Gnosis) is part of the Divine Plan (Oikonomia).

Christian Mysticism 450
Deification (Theosis) 695
The Muslim Deification Process 1191
Brahma-Nirvāṇa 1224
The Saints 654
The Chosen Ones 688

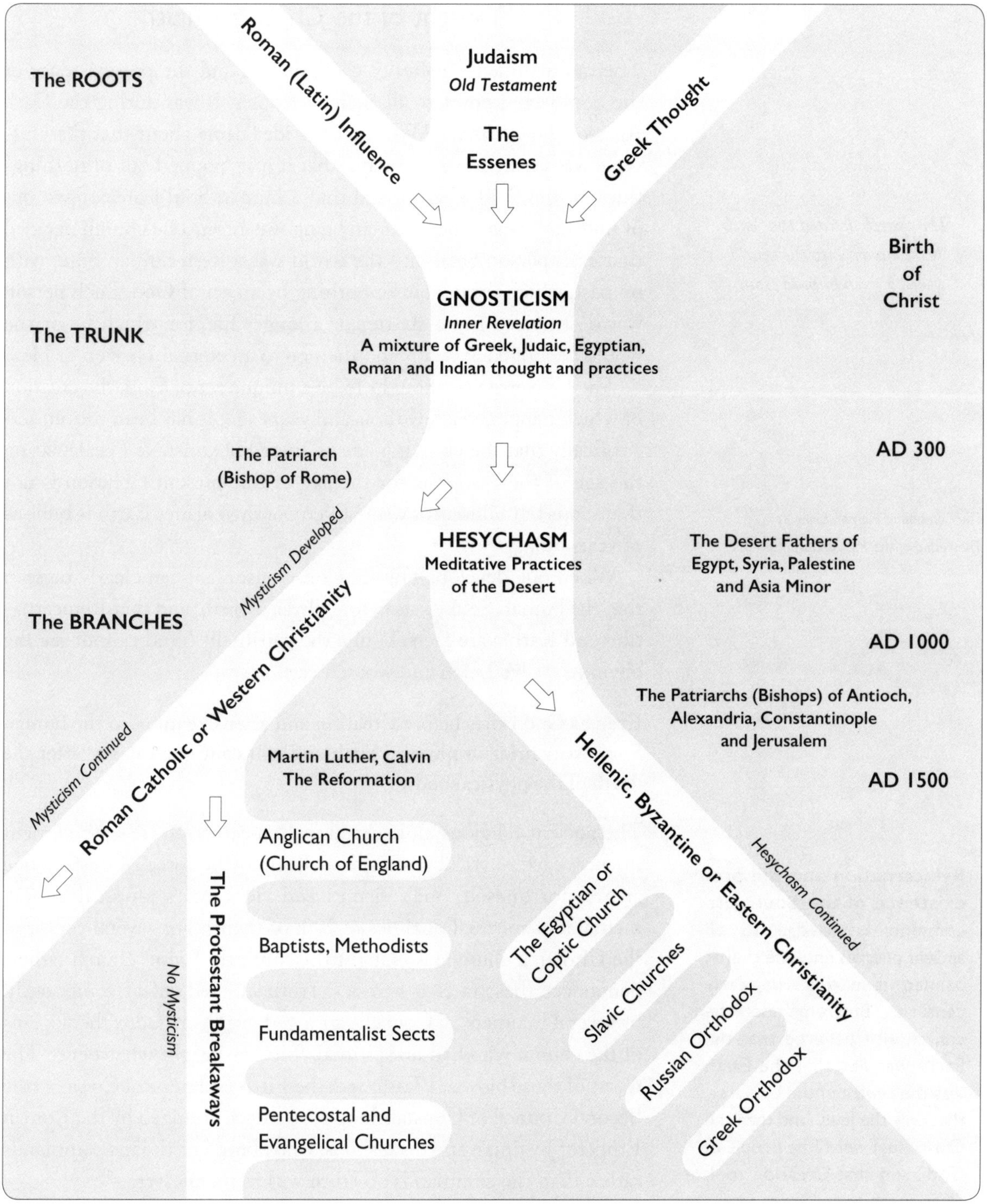

The Tree of Christianity

Twilight of the Christian Truth

The multi-dimensionality of the Universe and the pre-existence of the Soul were known to all ancient peoples. It was during the Dark Ages of the Christian West that the idea came about that the Universe was created in seven days, that it just "popped out of nothing" through the Will of God, and that a human Soul just "popped out of nothing" each time a human being was born. The church decided that each person born into the world was a fresh human Soul, with no past, which sprang out of nothing by an act of God. Each person was destined to live a shorter or a longer life, for which he or she would be judged at death and then go to an eternal Heaven or Hell.

The church decided that each person born into the world was a fresh human Soul

The Universe was thought to be a unique act of God, the creation of which happened a few thousand years ago. It has been proven scientifically that the church made an incredible mistake in calculating the age of the Universe, for the age of this present Creation is not thousands but billions of years! Even our own planet Earth is billions of years old.

The Compound Human Being 32
The Period of the Mahāmanvantara 168

When one develops Higher Consciousness it can clearly be seen that the human Soul exists before physical birth, and that Reincarnation and Karma are facts. While the spiritually blind cannot see the obvious, evolved men and women can.

Even as God exists before Creation and after Creation, so the human Soul exists prior to physical birth and will continue to exist after the death of the physical body.

The ancient religions all believed in Reincarnation (re-embodiment in successive physical bodies) and Karma (the force of destiny one creates for oneself, one's virtues and vices, one's physical, moral, mental and spiritual qualities or lack of them). For several centuries the Christian church also taught this, until the "wise" church fathers denounced these facts as heresies. Truth suffered defeat, temporarily, by several Ecumenical Councils arranged by the orthodox theologians of the church who had no spiritual vision or insight whatsoever. The worst of these blows to Truth was the Fifth Ecumenical Council (the Second Council of Constantinople) in AD553, arranged by the Roman Emperor Justinian and his bishops, who obeyed Justinian's commands rather than the commands of Truth within themselves.

Reincarnation and the pre-existence of the Soul were common knowledge to all ancient peoples until the church banned it during the early centuries. But remember, the church also believed that the Earth was flat, that the Earth was the centre of the Universe, that only the Jews (and then the Christians) were "the people of God", and that Creation took place six thousand years ago!

The Emperor Justinian arrested Pope Vigilius because he did not cooperate, and installed a new pope, a deacon named Pelagius who was a servant of the Roman Empire. At this unholy gathering of Christian fathers many "anathemas" were made, greatly encouraged by the soldiers of Rome, directed against the ideas of:

- The pre-existence of the Soul.
- Karma and Reincarnation.
- The multi-dimensionality of the Cosmos.
- God in Humanity.

The lofty Truth known by the Christians during the first three centuries after the death of Jesus was swept underground by a materialist who did not even lead a spiritual life, and the "Dark Age of Christianity", which has lasted until today, began.

Today's Christian church still suffers from the darkness of the Fifth Ecumenical Council

Today's Christian church still suffers from the darkness of the Fifth Ecumenical Council and others that preceded and followed it. The materialistic, power-seeking, worldly authorities of the church triumphed over the spiritual, the holy, the truth-seeking elements in the church. And so it has been to this day. And, because the West has been brought up in this materialistic church, it is difficult for the Westerner to understand the simple truths and facts that were and are known all over the world by non-Christians.

Correct Belief?

The word *orthodox* comes from the Greek ORTHODOXOS, which means "correct belief" (from ORTHOS, "correct", and DOXA, "belief, opinion").

What is "correct belief"? Is it the opinions, theories, and speculations of popes, bishops and religious "authorities"? If a group of ignorant people come together to form a "consensus opinion" about something, does consensus make their opinion valid?

The Ecumenical Councils of the first thousand years of Christianity were assemblies of bishops and church authorities convened by the popes to decide on doctrine and morals, which were made permanent and compulsory for all Christians. Whatever gross errors the popes and bishops dreamed up in their spiritually dark minds had to be obeyed by all Christians. For almost two thousand years the church was simply a religious dictatorship.

True Thought 79

Planes of Being 11
Jīva: the Human Soul 35
Karma and Reincarnation 231
God in the Heart 634
Protagonists of Ignorance 382

The Saints

The Communion of the Saints is from all Humanity

Who are the *true* Saints? The church has many thousands of saints, but seldom were they true Saints, and those who were true Saints are seldom recognized by the church. The saints of the church were those who challenged the authorities of the time and became "martyred", or who forcibly converted the "pagans", or who were good social workers and tended to the needs of the "poor", or (lately) political appointees in order to please a minority group or a colour or a race. None of this qualifies a person for true Sainthood.

True Saints are those who have achieved Union with God, on the practical level (not those who only "believed" in God). True Saints are those who have been Re-Created Inside by the Holy Spirit into the Likeness of the Original Divine Man. No pope or church authority can do this for you—only the Spirit can do this. And those who have been Reborn in the Spirit have been Acknowledged by God, with or without the pope's knowledge or approval!

How vain human beings are to think that they can make another human being a Saint! God knows who the true Saints are, and He does not need the church's approval for it! And these true Saints come from all religions of the world and from all times. The Communion of the Saints is from all Humanity since prehistoric times.

What is a Saint?

A true Saint is one who has attained one of the following states:

- Buddhic Consciousness.
- Nirvāṇic Consciousness.

While a few of the Christian saints were true Saints who entered the Kingdom of God, many were merely religious fanatics who converted people to the church, either by persuasion or by the sword. They were canonized by the popes because they converted people to the church, but they had no Higher Consciousness of any type. Furthermore, many *true* Saints were never recognized by the church. The church has always been totally confused about the true nature of a Saint!

The Seven States of Consciousness 494

Types of Humanity 376
Belief and Experience 676
Baptism and Rebirth 722
The Chosen Ones 688
Saṅgha: the Spiritual Hierarchy 394

The Heretics

The word *heretic* (from the Greek HAIRETIKOS) is defined as "a person who maintains religious opinions contrary to those accepted by the church" or "one who rejects a particular doctrine of the church". The "heretics" have been persecuted by the church for two thousand years. The rule of fear was the rule of the orthodox fundamentalist elements in the Western church: "Don't question your religious authorities, don't stray away from orthodox thinking, or you will incur the wrath of the church and the anger of an avenging Jehovah!"

> The Church was responsible for the persecution of the Jews, for instituting the Holy Inquisition [by which hundreds of thousands died a cruel death], for slaughtering the so-called heretics [the Gnostics, the Albigenses, etc.], and introducing torture into Europe as part of the judicial process.
>
> *Peter de Rosa*

Who were the "heretics"? They were those who had an open mind and did not swallow the ignorant, false doctrines of the church. The church exercised total inflexibility towards Truth and put to death millions of people considered to be heretics, including Jews, Muslims and other Christians. We could also mention the so-called "Holy Wars", the Crusades, in which millions died. All of this in the name of Orthodoxy!

HAIRESIS
Greek: The ability to choose. To have an open mind. From this we have the English word *heresy* (an opinion or doctrine at variance with the orthodox view).

Idol-Worship

The Old Testament places great emphasis on *not worshipping idols,* which is the old pre-Christian term for *icons.* In Old Testament times, idols were statues, pictures and figures of God, created by the Jews and the surrounding nations. The *early* Christians, in common with the early Jews and the Muslims, believed that God, as such, *cannot* be represented in any picture, painting or form. This idea is still very strong in the Muslim tradition and among some Jews.

During the eighth and ninth centuries of Christianity there was a huge battle in the church between those who approved the worship of icons (idols, symbols) as representations of God, and those who held the opinion that divine things cannot be represented. Those who went about smashing icons became known as *eikonoklastes*, "breakers of icons or images" (hence the English word *iconoclast).* Nevertheless, the Eastern use of icons, and the sacred pictures and statues of the West, have survived to this day.

The One Transcendental Reality 515
The One God of All 869

Persecution of the Knowers

The materialistic powers in the church moved fiercely to persecute the Gnostics

The Gnostics taught that the Spirit in Man (the MONAD) is held captive in the physical body, in the lower conditions of this world, and in the HADES (the reflection-sphere, the underworld, the afterlife), and hence must be liberated. According to the Gnostics, an atom of the Spirit is deeply embedded in the human Heart-System. This *Spirit-Spark-Atom* is the gateway, first of all, to the "Light of the Soul" and, later on, to the "Greater Mysteries" of Divinity. The Particle of Light in the Heart needs to be awakened and made to *shine*.

> Let your Light shine before men, that they may see your good works and glorify your Father who is in Heaven.
>
> *Matthew 5:16*

This was Pure Christianity. It is what Jesus taught, what Saint Paul taught. But the materialistic powers in the church—the popes, bishops, priests and theologians who sought name, fame, prestige and worldly glamour—moved fiercely to persecute and exterminate the Gnostics and their writings. These church authorities were afraid of the Truth, so the new Revelation was crystallized very rapidly, just as the Jewish religion had become crystallized centuries before.

The true Christian Message survived in spite of the church. The Message was perpetuated by the Gnostics, the Mystics, the Rosicrucians, the Alchemists, the Cathars, and many others, upon whom the church declared a relentless war by lies, deceits, falsifications, torture, imprisonment and death, along with the destruction of their teachings.

Before modern Christians attempt to understand Christianity, they have to face facts, which they are most reluctant to do. The "good Christian" of today hears only the lies which the church-powers invented against these true disciples of Christ. This *fact* is difficult to comprehend for modern Christians who delusively believe that all the priests, bishops, popes and elders of the church, from the beginning until now, were "holy men" filled with the Spirit of God. The truth is otherwise. Whenever there have been true "holy people" in the church, they were usually exterminated, banished or banned, and their writings were censored or burned.

Trapped Spirits 1240
The Gnostic Teachings 1108
The Mystery within the Heart 1315
Sex Natural and Divine 926
Christian Mysticism 450

Jesus said that the Jewish authorities always persecuted their Prophets, their Holy Men. Jesus was a Jew. He knew Jewish history.

> ...for so persecuted they the prophets which were before you.
>
> *Matthew 5:12*

And, after failing to convert the Jews of his day to the Kingdom of God which is *not* of this world, Jesus exclaims:

The Jewish, Christian and Muslim religions have always persecuted the Light-Bearers

> Jerusalem, Jerusalem, thou who killest all the prophets, and stonest all those Messengers who are sent to thee! How often I tried to gather thy children together [unto God] as a hen gathers her young under her wings, but you would not cooperate!
>
> *Matthew 23:37*

This persecution of holy people was carried over to the Christian religion and then to the Muslim religion. The Jewish, Christian and Muslim religions have always persecuted the Light-Bearers, the true Mystics, the true Saints, the true Gnostics or *Knowers*. The Mystics, who claimed to know the Higher Worlds directly by Inner Vision through their inner senses, were always ridiculed, doubted and suspected, and were often tortured and put to death. This happened also to the Prophets of the Jewish religion, and also within Islam, because the authorities did not rely on *direct experience* of the Higher Worlds, but rather, on intellectual speculations, conjectures, guesses and theories based on interpretations of the scriptures and a tradition of previous intellectual speculations.

Rulers in High Places

According to the Gnostics, the reflection-sphere (the Astral World) was ruled by the AEONS, who held all powers in this world and in the next. The Gospel writers avoided the well known Greek words AEONS and ARCHONS, which represented the "rulers of this world" and of the reflection-sphere. They used the Latin words *principalities* and *potentates* and the term "rulers in high places" (in the Astral World). It is against these "rulers" that we have to struggle to liberate ourselves, as Saint Paul well knew:

For we wrestle not against flesh and blood, but against principalities, against powers, against the rulers of the darkness of this world, against spiritual wickedness in high places.

Ephesians 6:12

The One and Only 839
The Truth shall make you Free 682
Wickedness in High Places 207

Today, in a certain Arab country, the followers of BAHĀ-U-LLĀH (the Radiance or Light of God) are systematically put to death. This happened during previous times also when the Cathars (the Albigenses) and others were persecuted to the death by the "God-fearing Christians" in the name of Jesus, the Lord of Compassion! Such actions are one-hundred-percent contrary to the whole life and teachings of Jesus the Christ. Why does this contradiction not occur to them?—because they are *englamoured* by worldly darkness, by the "rulers of this world"!

Such actions are contrary to the life and teachings of Jesus the Christ

Jesus, who was the Christ, said:

> My Kingdom is not of this World!
>
> *John 18:36*

Yet the materialistic powers within the church declared that Salvation was a matter of *belonging* to the church and believing in a book—the Bible. Thus, when you were baptized (as a baby!) you entered the church and your Salvation was assured.

This is a materialization and degeneration of a tremendous *fact.* Indeed, if the church was composed of truly enlightened Souls, if the popes, bishops and priests had Nirvāṇic Consciousness (the conscious Realization of God's Kingdom, the Light Universe), and if they themselves were Light-Bearers, as was Jesus the Christ, then belonging to such a church would indeed enable one to become a true Christian—not just by belief, but by *practice!* The church could then give Christians the *practical way* to the Kingdom.

But instead, the popes were concerned with extending their material empires and dominating the world by dominating the worldly kings and monarchs. This is *history.* ⚹

The Universal Christ 440
The Messiah Jesus 666
Religious Reactionaries 287

CHAPTER 30

Jesus the Christed One

The Jewish Messiah

Christianity cannot be understood without understanding the ancient Jewish belief in HA-MASHIAH (Hebrew: the Messiah). This tradition goes back three thousand years among the Jewish people. Originally, the MASHIAH was a Spiritual Saviour, a Redeemer to liberate Mankind from the darkness of matter and the powers of this world that keep Souls imprisoned here. Later on, however, it was changed into the idea of a political king or ruler who would redeem the people of Israel and make it into a great nation, ruler over all nations on Earth.

MASHIAH, MASHIACH
Hebrew: "The Anointed of God" (MASHI-JAH). The Messiah. The same as the Greek CHRISTOS. MASHIAH also means "the Salvation of the Living God (JAH)" or "only the Living God saves".

MASHIAH is itself an abbreviation of MASHIAH-JEHOVAH, "the Eternal God's Anointed One, the Eternal God's Salvation, the Eternal is the Saviour".

The Avatāra 389

In the old Hebrew tradition of the Messiah He was called the King of Peace, the Holy One, the Righteous One, He who heals the afflicted Heart, He who bears our diseases, Healer, the Messenger of Good News (of Salvation), ADONAI (Lord God), MENAHEM (the Comforter), NEHIRA (the Divine Light), MASHIAH (the Anointed One) and EL (the Lord God).

The Jewish idea of MASHI-JAH, "the Anointed of God", comes from early Old Testament times when the Prophets, Saints, Messengers and Divine Kings were "anointed" with sacred oil. During this ancient ceremony a perfumed oil was smeared or poured upon the Chosen One as a mark of distinction. In old Jewish times the High Priest of the Temple was known as the MASHIAH, "the Anointed One of God", that is, one *dedicated* to God.

> Likewise, for the glorious adornment of Aaron's sons, you shall have tunics and sashes made for them... and *anoint* them, install and *consecrate* them, that they may become my priests.
>
> *Exodus 28:40,41*

At first, the anointing with sacred oil was a *religious* ceremony. Later on, the term applied also to Divine Kings—MASHIAH ADONAI, "the Anointed One of the Lord". The ancient peoples rubbed oil, as a token of respect and veneration, upon kings, rulers and admired religious or political figures.

There is an old Rabbinic tradition pre-dating Christianity by a thousand years, that the MESSIAH was existing already in the Mind of God even before the World was created. The MESSIAH is the old Hebrew idea of the Divine Incarnation, the Sanskrit AVATĀRA or Divine Descent, for the redemption of Mankind.

The Divine Incarnation 726

The same concept was held amongst the Greeks and Romans. In Greek He was called CHRISTOS, which literally meant "the Anointed One", precisely the same meaning as the Hebrew MASHIAH. In the Greek Mystery Schools a candidate who had successfully passed all the tests and Initiations was anointed with sacred oil; thus he became known as a CHRISTOS, an "Anointed One", a Christ.

Names of the Great Master Jesus

Christianity is a mixture of the Old Testament Jewish expectation of a personal Saviour, the Messiah (considered by Christians to be Jesus), and the Greek Mystery Religion Teachings of the Universal Logos, the Creative Word or Cosmic Incarnation of God, the Cosmic Christ. Thus, in Christianity we have the Name of God as "Jesus Christ".

Jesus

The word *Jesus* comes from the Latin IESUS and IESU, which were derived from the older Greek IESOUS and the still older Hebrew and Aramaic YESHUA, YOSHUA, YEHESHUA, YEHOSHUA or YEHESHUVAH. As a Jewish child He probably would have been known as YOSHUA. Like the peoples of India, the Jews gave Divine Names to their children.

YAH (JAH) is a God Name meaning "the Self-Existent or Eternal One", and HOSHUA means "who Saves, who is the Saviour". YAH also means "he that is Saved". Thus, YEHESHUA means "the Eternal is my Salvation, in God is Salvation, God is my helper". YESHUA means "Saviour, Deliverer, Salvation, the Power to Save or Liberate, God's downpouring Grace". Hence, *Jesus* means "the Saviour".

Christ

The word *Christ* is from the Latin KRISTUS, which came from the Greek CHRISTOS, which meant "the Anointed One, the Sacred One, the Holy One", one who has attained the grade of Supreme Hierophant of the Mysteries, after the custom in the Greek Mystery Schools of anointing an Initiate with precious oils and perfumes after he or she had passed all the tests and triumphed, or risen to Higher Consciousness.

No Jewish child would have had a Greek family name; it is obvious that this was added to His name after His death in order to attract Greek converts. The actual Jewish family name of Jesus is not recorded in the New Testament.

Jesus was known as YESHUA BEN-PANDIRA (PANDIRA being His Jewish family name) or YESHUA BEN-YOSEPH (Jesus, son of Joseph) or YESHUA BEN-MYRIAM (Jesus, son of Mary). He was also known as YESHUA NAZIR (Jesus of Nazareth, His place of origin). This is how names were given in those days.

Jesus Christ
A compound of Hebrew and Greek words meaning "a Divine Teacher or Guru who has been anointed, or who has been acknowledged as succeeding in the Mysteries of Life and Death".

YESHUA HA-MASHIAH
Hebrew: "The Saviour, the Anointed One". Jesus the Messiah. This was not His name, but a title.

YESHUĀ MESHIKĀ
Aramaic: Jesus the Messiah.

The native language spoken by Jesus was Aramaic, which is related to the ancient Hebrew, though there are differences in word endings.

Variations of the Name of Jesus 1356

Jesus was also known as **RABBI YOSHUA** or **RABBI YEHESHUA**, "Lord Jesus, Master Jesus". The old Hebrew word **RABBI** meant "a Man of God", or a Saint who was established in God-Consciousness.

The Gnostics called Jesus **SŌTĒR**, a Greek word having the same meaning as YESHUA: "Saviour, Deliverer".

The Cosmic Christ

The Greeks taught of the Logos, the Christos, the Incarnation of God

The Semitic tribes of the Old Testament did not have the concept of the Universal Christ, but it existed among the Greeks. For centuries before the Christian religion the Greeks taught of the LOGOS, the CHRISTOS, the Incarnation of God. LOGOS means "the manifested Deity, the outward expression of God into Creation, God incarnating, the Speech of God, the Thought of God, the Mind of God, the Creative Power of God". The Logos is the *Word*, God's Creative Speech or Power, the Divine Mantram. It has the same meaning as the Latin words VERBUM and FIAT.

In the Gospel according to John, the first few verses merely *repeat* the teachings of many Greek writers, philosophers and schools of thought.

> In the beginning was the *Logos*,
> and the *Logos* was with God,
> and the *Logos* was God.
> All things were made by the *Logos*,
> and without Him was not anything made that was made.
> In the *Logos* was Life,
> and this Life is the Light in Man.
> And this Light shineth in the darkness [of matter],
> and the darkness comprehendeth it not....
> This is the true Light that lighteth
> every human being who is born into this world.
>
> *John 1:1–5, 9*

The Threefold Logos

The Christian fathers adapted the Greek LOGOS doctrine to Christianity as follows:

⊙ The *Father* or First Logos.
⊖ The *Son* or Second Logos.
⊕ The *Holy Spirit* or Third Logos.

It is important to understand that the words *Father* and *Son* do not mean anything like a human "father" and "son". To understand it in such a way would be gross ignorance.

The Holy Spirit is the "Mother". The Union of the Father-Mother Principles produces the AUTOGENES-CHRISTOS, the Self-born Universal Light of the Christ, the "Son".

The Logos: the Word of God 114
The Word, Logos, Voice, Name 1646
The Universal Christ 440
The Holy Trinity 1342
The Doctrine of the Logoi 116
Dimensions of the Cosmic Fire 137

Saint John was an Initiate. He refers to "the true Light that lighteth every human being who is born into this world". This Light is the LOGOS, the CHRISTOS, the Cosmic Christ, which has shone into the Heart of every man, woman and child since the beginning of time and ever shall until the end of time. But AGNOSIS veils it from our eyes.

The CHRISTOS (the Universal Logos) is the Heart of the Universe. The Christ is the intermediary between the *Father* (the Cosmic, Transcendental, Boundless Godhead) and the *Mother* (the Holy Spirit, which produces, manifests, organizes and sustains Creation). The Christ, though separate from the Universe, dwells *inside* the Universe, in every atom, particle, human being, angel, sun, star, galaxy and invisible cosmos. The Universal Christ Being, the Cosmic Logos, creates, evolves, and finally divinizes (re-integrates) all things back into the Boundless Bosom of the Absolute (the Father).

The Christ is the intermediary between the Father and the Mother

The Christian fathers translated the word LOGOS as "the Word", and later as "the Christ", and still later as the historical *personality* of Jesus, and finally as the book called the Bible. The Word, the *Infinite Light of God,* became degenerated to mean a book called the Bible; consequently, Christians ceased to worship the Infinite Light of God, and they think that the Word of God is the Bible!

Saṅgha: the Spiritual Hierarchy 394
The Buddha and the Christ 1722

The Threefold Christ

1. The Cosmic Christ, called the *Word* or *Logos* by Saint John of the New Testament.
2. The Great Being called MAITREYA, the Heart of the Spiritual Hierarchy.
3. The Mystical Christ in your Heart, the "Christ in you, your hope of Glory".

Jesus the Christ was an Incarnation of the Divine Logos, the Universal Light of God, which is the Creator of all that is. The mistake, however, is to believe that we are not *all* Children of God. Indeed, Jesus came to *remind* us that we *are* the Children of God. Jesus, the Divine Saviour, came to remind us of the *Indwelling Christ* within us.

Jesus is the Glory of God *Incarnate*.

Christ is the Eternal Logos, the Creative Word.

The Mystery of the Christ 1724

AGNOSIS

Greek: "Spiritual ignorance, darkness, nescience". The same as the Sanskrit terms MĀYĀ, "delusion, material illusion, materiality", and AVIDYĀ, "nescience, spiritual blindness".

The "darkness" referred to by Saint John is the Spiritual Darkness, the blindness and ignorance from which Humanity suffers. Nowadays there are people who are proud to be agnostics, to be spiritually ignorant. They think it is a virtue!

The Mystery of Jesus the Christ

The Word incarnates more specifically through special Beings called Avatāras

The name "Jesus Christ" is correctly *Jesus the Christed One* (in the original Hebrew, YEHESHUAH HA-MASHIAH). This is important. Who, or what, is *Jesus the Christed One*?

- Jesus is ĪŚA, a Lord.
- The Christ (MAITREYA) is a BODHISATTVA.

Two thousand years ago an unusual event took place. Jesus (YESHUA) was undergoing His development in Supernatural Evolution to become a Lord, and the Being called MAITREYA was becoming a BODHISATTVA. For a period of time (three years) they melded together, merged. The Christ "overshadowed" Jesus, producing the miraculous Phenomenon that we call *Jesus Christ*, whose three years of public administration and Service are recorded in small bits and pieces in the New Testament (semi-incorrectly and with ninety-percent of the information missing!).

- Jesus (YESHUA) is Lord of the Sixth Energy Stream, which is intense Devotion to God.
- The Christ (MAITREYA) is Lord of the Second Energy Stream, which is Universal Love and Wisdom.

The Seven Rays 54
Hierarchies of Life 1721
The Descent of the Word 118

The true Mystery, however, is the Incarnation of the Word, the LOGOS (Greek), the DABAR (Hebrew) or ŚABDA-BRAHMAN (Sanskrit). The Word is always Incarnating (coming into Being) and thereby creating Creation and bringing about the Transformation or Evolution of Universal Manifestation. But the Word incarnates more specifically, more powerfully, through the figures of great Saints, Masters, and special Beings called AVATĀRAS (Sanskrit).

The Word is God Manifested.

AVATĀRA
Sanskrit: A Divine Incarnation. One who has descended from the Light Realms. Christ Jesus was such an AVATĀRA. All the pre-Christian religions taught about the existence of AVATĀRAS or Incarnations of Divinity.

Great Incarnations of Divinity 1270
The Avatāras 1320

The original Greek word for the Christ is CHRĒSTOS.

CHRĒSTĒS is the Purifier, a Prophet.
CHRĒSTERIOS is one who is a Servant of God.
CHRĒSTOS is the Hierophant of the Inner Mysteries of the Kingdom of God. CHRĒSTOS also means "the Anointed One, the Pure One". CHRĒSTOS was another term for the Greek SŌTĒR, "Saviour, Deliverer, the Saving Power of God". So was it used in the ancient Mysteries of Greece.

The Mystery of Jesus and Mary

Yeshūah Al-Hayyīm (Yeshūa El-Hayyīm)

Jesus is the God of the Living.

In the Person, Jesus, and His mother, Mary, there are many mysteries. What is that great Being called by many Yeshua, Jesus? It is a Light shining in the Darkness, a Light penetrating the World, but the worldly consciousness perceives Him not. It is a Fire in the Heart, but the Heart of the masses is fast asleep. And Mary stands as a *Witness* to all things *spiritual, sacred, holy, noble* and *good*. The world cannot understand Them.

Our Lady, Mary, is truly a Queen in the Spiritual Realms

But Jesus is the God of the Living. Who are the Living?—those who, through sorrow, struggle and compassion, have *awakened* themselves into the Kingdom of God.

Our Lady, Mary, is truly a Queen in the Spiritual Realms, a Queen of Angels and of Mankind, a Queen of vast Powers and Consciousness, yet of extreme *simplicity* and *humility*. She was a human Adept and Master, and went over to the Angelic Kingdom and became an Adept and Master there. Then She rose above all to become the Queen who embodies all the *feminine powers and virtues* of the Logos, the Lord of all.

Her Transcendental Form 145
The Feminine Virtues 468
The Sacred Heart of Our Lady 1510
Mantras to Connect to Our Lady 1512
Jesus: the Fire of Love 1725

The story of Jesus in the New Testament is fragmentary, half-literal and half-mythological, with most of the details omitted. It is a short listing of some events, rather than the full descriptions of them, with the first thirty years almost entirely left out. And even less was recorded about the life of Our Lady, the great Being who *nurtured* and *nourished* and *supported* Jesus in His mission.

When you read the New Testament texts you come to realize that they have been put together from fragments of information drawn from memory, rather than being direct records of events. The New Testament contains many allegories (parables, teaching-stories), and the Book of Revelation is full of symbols, all of which veil the Truth. The *female Wisdom Mind* can uncover the Truth; the male intellectual mind cannot.
What is Wisdom? 1685

The *synagogue* or *temple* or *church* of Jesus is the awakened Human Heart, wherein He dwells fully. (Did you think that He lives in cold, stone buildings?)

In the inner worlds the Great Master Jesus is shining like a pillar of Light. This is not a light for its own sake, but the Light of Love, or the *Radiation of Devotion-Love*—huge, immense, overpowering. And Our Blessed Lady Mary is His twin, His reflection, His counterpart, the *Light of Feminine Love and Supernatural Grace.*

Jesus and Mary are the twin Love: the one that gives, the other that attracts.

The Messiah Jesus

The Teaching of the Messiah Jesus was that God dwells in Man—in all men, women and children—and that Forgiveness is more powerful than hatred. This Forgiveness and Love are to be practised and demonstrated in daily living. Two thousand years have passed and Humanity still has not practised this Message.

Jesus demonstrated the final Victory of Spirit over Matter

The early Christians called Jesus "the Prince of Peace". This term came from very old Jewish times, from MASHIAH NAGID, "an Anointed Prince", one who would deliver Israel.

Nowadays people like to portray Jesus as a Judean revolutionary who was intent on overthrowing the Roman Empire! But he wasn't involved in politics at all. He was a revolutionary of the Spirit who taught the ultimate dignity and greatness of all Mankind. This is demonstrated by the fact that, of the three Wisemen who came to pay homage to baby Jesus, none was Jewish. One was from Mesopotamia (today's Iraq), one was from Persia (today's Iran), and one was from Ethiopia. They came to baby Jesus not as politicians but as spiritual disciples honouring the future Master.

Jesus demonstrated the final Victory of Spirit over Matter, of Divinity over the powers of this world, through pain, suffering and joyous Resurrection.

Warrior Jesus 908
Saints of Action 1134
The three Magi 356
To Love God and the World 1392

The Mysticism of Saint Paul

Saint Paul, the author of the *Corinthians, Ephesians, Philippians* and other Epistles, was obviously an Initiate since he used the expressions and terms of the Greek Mystery Schools, such as:

CHRISTOS: Anointed. Initiated into the Mysteries.
PNEUMA: The Spirit, the Holy Ghost.
PLERŌMA: The Divine Fullness, the All.
GNOSIS: Direct Divine Knowledge. Revelation through the Heart.
SOPHIA: Wisdom. The Mind of Light experienced in the Head.
DOXA: Divine Glory. Radiance above the Head.

The Mysticism of Saint Paul was Christ-centred, not Jesus-centred. But modern translators twist everything to emphasize the *temporal manifestation* of Jesus rather than the true, original Christian Religion of the *Eternal Christ.*

The Greek Mystery Language 731

VIRTUS
Latin: Virtue. At the time of Jesus, two thousand years ago, *Virtue* meant not only moral goodness, uprightness, morality, bravery and valour, but Spiritual Power emanating from the Soul, or God-Consciousness. It is in this sense that Jesus was *Virtuous.*

The Lord of Glory

Jesus the Christed One (the Anointed One) *knew* Himself, by direct experience-perception, to be a Child of the Divine Being, which He called "the Father". He lived *in* the Divine Milieu, the Divine Life-Field.

Jesus said, "Blessed is He who existed *before* the beginning of Man." What existed before the beginning of Man? The Self-Existent, Eternal God-Being existed before Man. Jesus here directs your attention to the Timeless One, the One God that we must forever adore and worship. And Jesus said, "You have heard that I said unto you 'I am not of this world'."

Jesus knew Himself to be a Child of the Divine Being

This Self-discovery, this Self-knowledge, is our task also and the task of all true forms of Religion, such as Mysticism, Zen, Sūfīsm, Taoism and Yoga. To know our Divine Self practically and experientially, to be Divine and to know the Universe to be Divine, is our goal as human beings.

Even as Jesus, the "Son of Man", is *not* of this world, neither is Man originally of this world. "They have come from a land far away". This "far away land" is the Spiritual Universe, the Kingdom of God, the Kingdom of Light from which the Human and Angelic Hierarchies descended.

Jesus came to remind you of your High Estate and how to return.

Jesus is Lord! And Christ is Glory!
Jesus Christ is the Lord of Glory!

Lordship and Glory are the qualities of the Paranirvāṇic Plane. It is this part of the Kingdom of Light that Jesus kept referring to. And the *Light of Lights* referred to by the Gnostics is the Logos on the Mahāparanirvāṇic Plane of Being.

This Kingdom of Light, stretching through the Buddhic, Nirvāṇic, Paranirvāṇic and Mahāparanirvāṇic Planes, is what Jesus called "the House of the Father". Said Jesus to his *intimate* disciples:

In my Father's house there are many mansions [planes, realms, conditions of Light]... I go before you and prepare a place for you.

The Many Mansions 611

Crowned with Glory 197
Know Thyself 1389
Trapped Spirits 1240
Human Involution and Evolution 170

Jesus Christ, Son of Man

In the New Testament, Jesus is referred to as the *Son of Man,* which was a common designation used throughout the Old Testament *for* the Prophets and *by* the Prophets, the special messengers from on High. In the pre-Christian centuries of the Jewish world, the Messiah was regularly called Mashiah Ben Adam and Mashiah Ben David. These were titles, not names of people, and have been translated as "Son of Man", meaning that the Messiah will be from the Man-species, that He will be human with divine qualities.

Ben Adam
Hebrew: "Son of Man". A title given to the Prophets, Divine Kings and High Priests during Old Testament times.

Yeshua Ben Adam
Hebrew: "Jesus, the Son of Man".

Yeshuā Bar Nashā
Aramaic: "Jesus, the Son of Man".

> Therefore, prophesy, O Son of Man….
>
> *Ezekiel 39:1*

> And thou, Son of Man, prophesy about Gog and Magog, and say….
>
> *Ezekiel 38:2*

> This is the Son of Man in whom dwells Righteousness, who is Righteousness.
>
> *1 Enoch 46:2*

Unfortunately the early Christians considered the Son of Man to be *one person only* (Jesus), but this is not so. The expressions "Son of Man" and "Son of God" were titles of respect and distinction, much like what we have in English: "Sir", "your Lordship", "your Excellency". The title Ben Adam, "Son of Man", was applied to *all* the Prophets, Divine Kings and High Priests. Adam means Humankind, the *species* of beings called Man, as distinct from the other species in the Universe. Each great Prophet was a Ben Adam—a Son of Man, a Child of Humanity.

Jesus was without "sin", without karmas to pay back. He need not have incarnated, but He did so out of Love and Compassion for Humanity.

The coming of the Christed-Jesus was an all-important event in human evolution on this planet because human consciousness was declining en masse (except for a few Initiates here and there). It was to awaken the masses of Souls that the Christ came and demonstrated again that Man is a Child of God, that every man, woman and child is a Spark of God, one with the Flame that is God.

Jesus, the Christed One, acted out the true Human Prototype, what we all are, what we all shall be. Can you imagine the future when the whole Earth is inhabited by Jesus-Christs?

The Prophets 647
Jesus the Personal Saviour? 678
Children of the Sun 1590

The Only Son of God?

Several centuries before Christ, the Greek scriptures used the word MONOGENES, from the pre-Christian Greek Mystery School tradition of the MONO-GENESIS, "the first-born, the first-produced, born from the One, the product of Divine Oneness". This refers to the LOGOS, the *Christ.*

In his Gospel, Saint John refers to the Messiah as MONOGENES. Uninitiated Christians translated this expression as "only-begotten" (which is quite meaningless), and then as "the only Son of God". The early Christian fathers didn't like the idea of competition from other great Teachers of antiquity and unilaterally declared that *Jesus was the only Son of God,* in the same way that the Jews before them declared the tribal Jehovah to be the *only* God, and the Muslims declared Mohammed to be *the* Prophet of God.

To the initiated Greeks, the Gnostics and some early initiated Christians, however, Jesus was a Divine Incarnation who descended from that realm of the Divine Mind which is called MONOS or Oneness. MONOGENES also means "single-specimen" (MONO-GENOS), or something that is unique, special, different, unusual, one of a kind. Applied to YESHUA (Jesus), he was truly special and unusual, being the physical embodiment of the AVATĀRA (Divine Incarnation). Applied to the CHRISTOS, the Cosmic Christ, the Second Person of the Triune Godhead, it is also true, for CHRISTOS is the Greek word for the One Universal Light.

BEN ELOAH
Hebrew: "Son of God". A title given to the triumphant Messiah (Jesus) after he conquered human nature and resurrected the Christ, the Immortal Self within.

YESHUĀ BAR ALAHĀ
Aramaic: "Jesus, the Son of God".

YOSHUA IMMANUEL
Hebrew: "The Saviour, God is with us". Another name given to Jesus, who was a disciple of the Christ.

The Crime of Fundamentalism

The Gnostics understood the Universal Light as the *Christ Being,* the CHRISTOS. The later Christians made the *personality* of Jesus, the Messiah, to be the Universal Christ Being and erroneously declared Jesus to be the *only* Son of God. Nowadays, Bibles are translated to mean that Jesus (the historical personality) is the *only* Son of God, and thus they *deny Divinity* to all God's Children. This falsification of Truth is a crime of *fundamentalist* Christianity. It *betrays* the scriptures and does not correspond with fact. Every Mystic or Saint (those who have *experienced* Higher Consciousness) *knows* that the original scriptures are right and that the fundamentalist falsifications are incorrect.

Belief and Experience 676

The Kingdom of God 123
The Universal Christ 440
The Light of the Logos 119
The Christ is the Light of the World 442

The Way, the Truth and the Life

The supreme Name of God, as revealed to Moses on Mount Sinai, was Eheieh Asher Eheieh, "I Am that I Am" or simply "I AM". This "I AM" is the Universal Christ Being, the *Alpha and Omega* of the Apocalypse.

Christ-Consciousness 443
Tao: the Great I AM 774
What is Consciousness? 1368
Quest for Reality 1178
Who is 'I AM'? 1418

> I AM that I AM. And thus shalt you say to the children of Israel, the I AM hath sent me unto you.
>
> *Exodus 3:14*

Previously the Israelites worshipped God under the name of Yehovah, Yahveh or Yehovahi, meaning "That which was, is, and shall be (the Eternal)". This refers to the *experiencing* of God by the Mystic on the Soul level, in the Kingdom of God (Buddhi) and in Nirvāṇa, the Light and Truth of Reality.

The Christ, speaking through the Messiah Jesus, said:

> Behold, I am with you always, even unto the end of time.
>
> *Matthew 28:20*

> I am the Way, the Truth and the Life.
>
> *John 14:6*

That is to say, the "I AM", the Nirvāṇic Being, is *with us always,* even unto the end of time. And the Christ (the Light of the Universe, the Original Light) is the Way, the Truth and the Life.

The I AM is *within you* always, even unto the end of time.
The I AM *within you* is the Way, the Truth and the Life.

The "I AM" is the Son of God and the Son of Man at the same time. Here is the Ultimate Mystery. You are a *Child of God.* You always have been, you always shall be. You are a Child of God by virtue of the fact that God is *in you.* This must not only be believed, but *realized in Soul-Consciousness.* Jesus is your brother, even as all God-Realized Saints are your brothers and sisters.

All Power is yours now.
All Wisdom is yours now.
All Love is yours now.

Life-force follows attention and energy follows thought. This is the ancient Truth. You are what you make yourself to be.

Ernest Holmes, the founder of the *Science of Mind* philosophy, explained the saying of Jesus, "I am the Way, the Truth and the Life", as follows:

This means that the Infinite I Am-ness, within the finite you, is God. Thus, your thoughts and mind are creative. Your imagination projects out and forms your experience. The I AM is the Creative Principle of the Universe, and this I AM also dwells *within* you; thus, the Law of Creativity of the Great I AM is also projected through *your own* imagination and mind. *To think is to create.*

Mind and Thought 1376

The Source of Miracles

Jesus taught his disciples the Laws of Mind by which He performed all His miracles and healings and teaching. Jesus called the Infinite Mind "Father" because the Jews had a very homely understanding of God. God to them was the Ancient of Days, a king, a ruler, a father, a judge. They could not conceive of God in terms of *Consciousness.*

So, in simple language, Jesus said that the *Father* gives all things to them that believe in Him, which is very true. Then, when Christianity became a religion, the Christian fathers made a twist in the teachings: they said that if you pray to *Jesus* He will give you all things. Later on, the church added the Virgin Mary to the list, and then the Holy Spirit and, later on, numerous Saints.

A "miracle" is but an interference of a superior Consciousness

Thus, a good Roman Catholic could pray to:

- The Father.
- The Son (Jesus Christ).
- The Holy Ghost.
- The Virgin Mary, the "Mother of God". (How could God have a Mother?)
- Numerous Saints.

Nevertheless, no matter who you pray to, you will get results according to *how* you pray, because the answer will come to you from the Universal Subconscious Mind. Furthermore, if you know how to invoke the Superconscious Mind or the Mind of Light, you will be able to work miracles, as Jesus did. A "miracle" is but an interference of a superior Consciousness and Force into our normal affairs and states of consciousness.

The Virgin Mother

According to the pre-Christian Hebrew Tradition, the Mother of the Messiah (Saviour) is the SHEKINAH (Hebrew: the Light of Glory, the Divine Light, the Radiation from the Infinite Light, AIN SOPH AUR). To the Initiated Jews of old, SHEKINAH was the *Goddess*, the Feminine Divinity, the Feminine or Mother aspect of God, the Eternal Feminine Power. It is what the Greek Sages called the *Virgin Light* or *Virgin Mother*. The Christian church confused this with the physical mother of Jesus.

The Virgin and the Mother 144

Subconscious Forces 236
Magical Prayer 365
Realms of the One Mind 492
To Safely Perform Miracles 1353

The Last Words of Jesus

A further falsification of Truth by the church involves the final words of Jesus on the Cross, which are said to have been:

> My God, my God, why have you deserted me?
>
> *Mark 15: 34*

How could God desert His Divine Incarnation?

This is a totally wrong translation of the Aramaic words which Jesus spoke:

Eloi Eloi Lama Sabachthani

This does not mean that God had deserted him! How could God desert or forsake His Divine Incarnation when God cannot even forsake Creation?

Eloi means "my God", from the Hebraic-Aramaic-Arabic root El, meaning "God". The Aramaic word Shabak means "to allow something to happen, to leave, to spare". Lamana means "this".

Jesus was saying that His Crucifixion was "allowed to happen". He was not saying "why have you deserted me", but rather, "how you glorify me" or "for this reason (this event) I was prepared" or "this is my destiny", meaning "I have fulfilled my destiny for which I was born".

Consummatum Est

Latin: It is finished, accomplished, done, concluded.

Yet, in the twisted eyes of the church, Jesus, the Triumphant, the Glorious, became the Man of Sorrows, forsaken by His Father!

Jesus *knew* His own Divinity because he was deeply rooted in Higher Consciousness, in the Kingdom of God. He *experienced* Nirvāṇa. He *descended from* the Kingdom of God.

We all are the Children of God, but we must come to *realize it consciously,* in Higher Consciousness.

> Know ye not that ye are the Temple of God, and that the Spirit of God dwelleth in you? If any man defile the Temple of God, him shall God destroy; for the Temple of God is Holy, which Temple ye are.
>
> *I Corinthians 3: 16–17*

El (Hebrew: God) is often used in the Old Testament. For instance: El Shaddai, "God Almighty, the Great God", which is similar to the Sanskrit term Mahāviṣṇu.

Eli means "my God". Elijah is a compound God-Name, from Eli and Jah, which was another root word for "God". So Elijah also means "my God".

The Palestinian, Arabic and Aramaic versions were Al, Allāh and Allahā.

Hebrew Divine Names 1262

The Divine Unity Mantra 1359

The Sacred Heart of Jesus

Many Christians worship the Sacred Heart of Jesus, but do they understand it? What is the Sacred Heart? Look at what the words say: *Sacred* and *Heart!* Do these Christians understand the Mysteries of the Heart?

Unfortunately, many Christians look upon the Sacred Heart as a *symbol*, a symbol of the Love of God towards Humanity, or a symbol of the loving actions of Jesus towards His people two thousand years ago, or a symbol for what He is doing now. But we are talking about a *real* Heart which is very *sacred*.

The Heart of Jesus is a Sea of Fiery, Dynamic Love

When Jesus walked the Earth-plane His Heart was ablaze with the Fires of Love—not symbolically, but actually. The Cosmic Heart was beating through His Heart. In the inner worlds the Heart of Jesus is a Sea of Fiery, Dynamic Love which inspires you to all good actions and holy deeds. It is truly sacred. This is the secret of Man's future evolution, and the Future is Now.

You may worship the Sacred Heart of Jesus in rituals. But, if you enter your own Heart and there think of the Sacred Heart, soon you will Know the Fires of Love.

A Summary of Saint Margaret Mary's Teachings on the Sacred Heart of Jesus

- The Sacred Heart of Jesus is an abyss of Love into which we must cast all our self-love and lose its evil fruits.
- The Sacred Heart of Jesus is an abyss of Strength and Power. If you are weak and fall often, enter into It. It will strengthen you and raise you up.
- The Sacred Heart of Jesus is an abyss of Light and Knowledge. If you are in darkness or ignorance, enter into It. It will enlighten you.
- The Sacred Heart of Jesus is an abyss of Peace and Joy. If you are perturbed or sad, enter into It and It will dispel your sadness and sorrows.
- The Sacred Heart of Jesus is an abyss of Mercy and Consolation. If you are in desolation and destitution, enter into It and you will find a treasure and a joy.
- The Sacred Heart of Jesus is an abyss of Purity and Perfection. Enclose yourself in It and It will purify and perfect you.

Jesus: the Fire of Love 1725
The Radiant Heart Prayer 702
The Evolution of Christian Prayer 713
The Heart and the Future Evolution of Man 1309

CHAPTER 31

Christian Fundamentalism

Belief and Experience

> We speak Wisdom among them that are Perfect, which is not the wisdom of the world, nor the rulers of this world, which come to nothing. But we speak the Wisdom of God in a Mystery, the hidden Wisdom, which God ordained before the world unto our Glory.
>
> *St Paul (I Corinthians 2:6–7)*

There is a big difference between those who believe in God and those who experience God

The Christian religion is a very profound religion. It brings the Infinite down to the finite, the Absolute down to a human conception. That is why it is not understood by most Christians, especially the fundamentalists and evangelists who think that God is a *person* called Jesus and that the Word is a *book* called the Bible.

Over the centuries the scriptures have been altered many times by pious, fundamentalist scholars. You can observe this in the Christian and Jewish religions and in other religions as well. The modern, fundamentalist translators of the Bible desecrate it even more; they do not translate Truth any more, but *their own biased opinions.*

For instance, they might translate the above passage (which refers to the Ageless Wisdom, the Secret Doctrine) to mean: "When I am among mature Christians I speak words of great Wisdom…", suggesting that if you are a true believer (a fundamentalist) and believe in a *personal* Saviour (Jesus), then that is the Wisdom, the secret of God! Yet, even in the previously corrupted biblical texts, reference is made to the *Elect,* the *Perfect,* the *Wise Ones,* which are pre-Christian terms for the *Initiates*—those who didn't merely believe in a person called Jesus, but who actually *experienced* the Kingdom of God.

There is an incredible gap between those who *believe* in Jesus and those who have seen, tasted and *experienced* the Kingdom of God! There is a big difference between those who merely *believe* in God and those who *directly experience* God.

The modern Bibles are mistranslated to emphasize the belief in a *personal* Saviour called Jesus, when the teaching clearly refers to the Omnipresent Logos (the Universal Christ Principle, the Radiant Godhead) and the Shekinah (the Divine Presence, the Glory of God, the Holy Spirit).

Who are the 'Elect'? 128
Religious Fundamentalism 383
The Cosmic Christ 662
What is True Faith? 1284

Similarly, Prabhupāda, the founder and Guru of the Hare Krishna movement (ISKCON), altered the Hindu scriptures (the *Bhagavad-Gītā,* the *Śrīmad-Bhāgavatam* and others) and made Kṛṣṇa to be a *person.* He emphasized that you received Salvation through a *personal Krishna,* just as the fundamentalist Christians believe that Jesus is their *personal* Saviour.

In the original scriptures, however, this is not so. *God does not have a limited personality* in the sense that the Jews believe (an old man on a throne), or as the Christians believe (Jesus, the *person,* who suffered and died for our sins), or as the Hare Krishnas believe (Krishna, the *person,* who is dark blue and plays a flute).

The Secret Wisdom of God is already abiding in every Heart

Anthropomorphism makes God into a human being, attributes human characteristics to the Absolute. We attribute a "personality" to God so that we can "conceive" of Him. Even the "Him" or "Her" refers to a person; by their use, God has already been humanized. But in fact, the Absolute has no such human limitations.

The Hidden Wisdom

The "Hidden Wisdom" referred to by Saint Paul is the direct experience of God in the Heart.

> We speak Wisdom [the Secret Doctrine] to them who are Perfect [the Elect, those Initiates who have *entered* God's Kingdom], which is *not* a worldly knowledge, nor the knowledge that the people in power in the world possess. This Wisdom [Enlightenment] is of God, the Hidden Wisdom which God has ordained for us from the foundation of the world [this is the direct *knowing* or *seeing* of the Higher Realities, the Inner Worlds]. This Knowledge the rulers of the world do not know. For, if the world did know [experience], they would not have crucified the Lord of Glory [the Divine Incarnation, Jesus].... God has revealed [this Knowledge] unto us by His Spirit, for there is nothing hidden from the Spirit, not even the deep Wisdom of God.
>
> *St Paul (1 Corinthians 2:6–8, 10)*

This Hidden Wisdom will come to *all* men, women and children who will enter their Hearts. They do not have to belong to a church, for the Secret Wisdom of God is already abiding in every Heart. Jesus, the Divine Incarnation, the Lord of Glory, came to *teach* us this Ancient Wisdom, that *the Kingdom of God is within you.*

Mythological Concepts of God 104
The Transcendental Godhead 112
The One Transcendental Reality 515
The Christ in the Heart 441
What is Wisdom? 1685

Jesus the Personal Saviour?

There is a curious misconception amongst the fundamentalist and evangelical Christians that all they have to do is "believe in Jesus Christ" and they will be "saved", or enter the Kingdom of God, for "Jesus Christ died for our sins". But Jesus himself teaches otherwise:

Accepting Jesus Christ as one's personal Saviour is only the entrance to the Path

> Not all who say "Father, Father" will enter the Kingdom of Heaven, but those who do the *Will* of the Father.
>
> *Matthew 7:21*

And that great disciple of Jesus, Saint Paul, teaches likewise:

> Be not deceived. God is not mocked. For whatsoever a man soweth, that shall he also reap.
>
> *Galatians 6:7*

Accepting Jesus Christ as one's personal Saviour is a good beginning, but it is only the entrance to the Path. It is like going to school, but still one must learn, study, experience, and then pass the test!

The teachings of Jesus and Saint Paul, and their living examples, *contradict* the teachings of the orthodox Western Christian churches, and especially those of the fundamentalists and evangelicals. Jesus and Saint Paul both taught that before you can enter the Kingdom of God, Nirvāṇa, you must *do* something about your Salvation. Down through the centuries the many Mystics of Eastern Orthodox and Roman Christianity understood the need to *do* something about their own Salvation. Like the Mystics of the Eastern religions (the Hindu, Tibetan, Buddhist, Sikh, Taoist, and so forth), they knew they had to *work* for their Liberation.

But the ordinary Christians have this false notion that Jesus will do everything for them. This came from the Jewish idea of the *Messiah,* for the early Christians were Jews. The Jews have always longed for a Messiah who would liberate them, rule them, control them, conquer the world and establish a Kingdom of God on Earth with Jerusalem the capital. The Jews thought that God would do everything for them and they expected the same from the Messiah.

The Christians threw this idea onto Jesus: Jesus became their "Messiah", one who "suffered for their sins". The mass of the early Christians (those who were not Enlightened) embraced this idea because it seemed the *easiest thing to do.* This is why they had to reject

Thinking and Being 233
Success is Born of Action 256
The Jewish Messiah 660
The Divine Incarnation 726

the truths of *Karma* and *Reincarnation*: these facts of Nature were not compatible with their ideas about Jesus because the Laws of Reincarnation and Karma place responsibility upon the individual.

The Christians called God's actions *Grace* and, together with the Jews, they said that "God's ways are mysterious". That is, no one knows how God's Grace works; it is a hit-and-miss affair and God seems to favour some and dislike others. Thus, becoming a Saint was not within the control of the orthodox Jew or Christian. It depended on some capricious Grace, distributed by God. The church instituted the Rite of Baptism, which promised this Grace, but people forgot about it and went on believing that God's ways were inscrutable, with Man a victim of circumstances.

Karma: the Law of Action 240
Punarjanma: Reincarnation 249
Twilight of the Christian Truth 652
Baptism and Rebirth 722
Mysterious Grace 1311

Nevertheless, the earliest teachings of both the Jewish and Christian religions clearly state that you *can* do something about your own Salvation and, in fact, that you *must* do something about it!

To Call upon Jesus

Many fundamentalist sects believe that Jesus is their "personal Saviour" simply because they believe in Him. This is an error. Jesus becomes your Saviour by *calling upon Him*—by using His Name in your Heart.

To the initiated Kabbalists, the Great Name of God was revealed in the Heart. According to these Jewish Mystics, the Heart is the throne of God, the altar of the Temple, the *Holy of Holies* of the synagogue. The true Name of God, the *unpronounceable Name*, is pronounced in the Heart. In the Heart, the Name of God, IHVH (YEHOVAH), becomes *radiant*.

The later Christian Kabbalists interpolated the fiery Hebrew letter ש, "SH", into the Divine Name, which became the Sacred Name of Jesus:

IH SH VH (YEHESHUAH)

All Wisdom and Treasures come from pronouncing the secret Name of Jesus in the Heart. This is "the Christ in you, your hope of Glory". Jakob Böhme, a Christian Kabbalist who practised "the taking of God's Name in the Heart", has said:

JEHESHUAH (IH SH VH) becomes the Fiery Name in the Heart, and the pure Soul becomes consumed by the Fires of Love in the Heart.

This should indicate clearly that merely *believing* in the historical figure of Jesus Christ is not enough for Salvation. One must contact the Living God through the Heart.

IHVH: I AM 1460
Yeshua: the Secret Hebrew Name 1276
Christian Meditation on the Holy Breath 1346
The Rose of Love and the Cross of Light 1357
Jesus: the Fire of Love 1725

The Sacrificial Lamb

The Jews of the Old Testament had the idea of a "sacrificial lamb" which was allowed to perish for the sins of the Israelites. They transferred the karmic repercussions for their deeds, ritualistically, onto a poor animal and believed that the sacrificial lamb would atone for their own sins (bad karmas). They really believed this! They were avoiding *self-responsibility*, which is the real teaching of the Jewish TORAH (the Law, or Cause and Effect).

There is nothing to be gained by waiting for the Messiah to do everything for you

The early Christians were happy with this idea. They said, "God so loved the world that He gave his only Son as the sacrificial lamb for our sins." It is a convenient idea: let someone else suffer for one's sins! So Jesus became the scapegoat for the Christians.

But the personal sacrifice of that wonderful Being (who is mistakenly called *Jesus Christ*) was a supreme act of Love and does not absolve the Christian from a degree of *self-responsibility*, striving for perfection and taking up his or her own cross. As Jesus himself taught:

> If you want to attain to the Kingdom of God, forget yourself, take up your Cross, and follow Me.
>
> *Matthew 16:24*

There are three steps mentioned here:

a. Forget yourself.
b. Take up your Cross.
c. Follow Me.

Each of these steps has a very specific meaning for Pilgrims of the Way. There is nothing to be gained by sitting back and waiting for the Messiah to do everything for you.

Torah: the Law 245
Appeasing the Gods? 220
Ritual Degenerated 368
You Alone are Responsible 258

To Worship Jesus...

It is important to understand that the Christians of the first and second centuries did not worship Jesus. The worship of Jesus commenced during the third and fourth centuries when the church had become a materialistic power. Before that time, the Christians invoked the *Father* (God as King, ABBA) and the *Mother* (the Holy Ghost, the Holy Spirit, SHEKINAH), which was a common Jewish practice.

Jesus never asked that people should worship Him; on the contrary, He continually pointed towards ABBA, the Father, who dwelt in Heaven. This "Heaven" is *not* the reflection-sphere of the after-death conditions, as the fallen church later conceived of it. This "Heaven" which Jesus spoke of is the Kingdom of Light, the Light Worlds, what the Gnostics called the *Father of Lights* and the *Light of Lights within the Boundless Lights*.

Prayer Spiritual and Material

It is important to understand that the manner in which modern fundamentalist and evangelical Christian sects pray to Jesus is *not* the same as how the Hesychasts prayed to Jesus. The spirit of the Hesychasts' prayer was so different! The predominant characteristic of the Gnostics, the Hesychasts and the Mystics was their intense *non-worldliness* and their sole preoccupation with the *Kingdom of God within their Souls.* Therefore their prayers (meditational practices) were to this effect alone.

Jesus is invoked to serve your personality needs

The common characteristic of modern Christian fundamentalists is their *intense worldliness and preoccupation with their personalities.* The Christianity of the modern fundamentalists and the Christianity of the Hesychasts have *nothing* in common; they are worlds apart. In fact, viewed from the spiritual perspective, modern fundamentalist Christianity is not Christianity at all; rather, it is a gross form of *materialism.* The modern fundamentalist and evangelical sects seem to be entirely unaware of the vast *spiritual tradition* within Christianity. They are unaware of the thousands of Saints of the Greek and Latin lines of Christianity and the Quest for the Kingdom of God *within.*

For what do the fundamentalist and evangelical preachers teach you to pray to Jesus?

- For the healing of your physical body or the bodies of your relatives and friends.
- For more money, cars, houses, jobs, position and wealth.
- For successful living in *this* world!
- For miracles to save you from personal troubles and from life's inconveniences.

Jesus is invoked to serve your *personality* needs! They call Him your *personal* Saviour and they twist the Bible to coincide with this view of Christianity (so-called). Maybe there is no harm in this, but if you study the lives and teachings of the early Christians of Egypt, Syria, Palestine, Mount Athos, and so forth, what a different picture you will get—so different, indeed, that you might think it is another religion altogether!

Magical Prayer 365
The Early Christians 643
Who are the Christians? 646
The Source of Miracles 671
What is Prayer? 690
The Divine Mood 1252

The Truth shall make you Free

In writing this chapter I am merely obeying an injunction of our Lord Jesus, the Christ:

> Ye shall know the truth, and the truth shall make you free.
>
> *John 8:32*

Know the Things that Are.

Hermes Trismegistus

For nearly two thousand years the church has assiduously suppressed the Truth, destroyed the teachings of the ancients and persecuted those who dared to *know*—first the Gnostics and then the scientists. The church has always been afraid of knowledge. Don't forget that the church burned people at the stake for uttering even simple physical truths—that the Earth is round, that it is not the centre of the Universe, that it rotates, that Creation did not occur six thousand years ago. The church falsified the teachings of Christianity, then backed up these false teachings by *force*.

The Latin word SCIENTIA means "knowledge", as does the Greek word GNOSIS. Why did the church persecute the Gnostics and, during the Middle Ages, the scientists?—because the dark powers that ruled the church were *afraid* of knowledge, of the *truth* about things. In the church you had to commit yourself to *belief* rather than the direct knowledge of the *things that are*.

Televangelism

From watching the theatrical performances of the televangelists, it would be excusable to say that modern fundamentalist Christians know nothing about true Christianity. It is good acting, with plenty of Greek-style drama, but there is nothing of Christianity in it. If you do not have an acting ability, you cannot become a fundamentalist preacher, while the objective seems to be to collect more *money* by using the name of Jesus. The televangelists are multi-millionaires and they are great actors. They laugh and cry at will and stir up the emotions of their followers—their *emotions*, not their *intelligence!* Nor do they awaken in their followers the desire for the Kingdom of God which is "not of this world". Furthermore, they seem to be fixated on the Devil (more often imaginary than real), and they do not seem to have a *conscious recognition* of the Power of God in all things.

True Thought 79
Protagonists of Ignorance 382
Twilight of the Christian Truth 652
Persecution of the Knowers 656

Today the Christian fundamentalists uphold the same ignoble tradition: knowledge is "of the Devil", they say, and anything not included in the Bible is "Devil worship". They are paranoid about the scientific theory of evolution, for instance, which in its general scope is a *fact* (however wrong scientists' deductions about it may be). They condemn *all* religions other than Christianity, and all Christian religions other than their own particular brand of beliefs, for they are *afraid of experiencing Truth.* And they want to reintroduce this so-called "Christianity" as the state law! While the Roman Catholic Church is slowly loosening up, the new fundamentalists are returning to the Dark Ages.

The new fundamentalists are returning to the Dark Ages

It seems that followers of the fundamentalist Christian sects are incapable of thinking for themselves. They are terrified of an avenging Jehovah who will punish them unless they believe what they are told to believe by their so-called authorities and elders. They keep themselves in an utter darkness of ignorance because anything they don't comprehend is "the work of the Devil". This continual concern for real and imaginary devils is counter-productive; instead of enlightening themselves, they sink ever-deeper into the quagmire of ignorance and spiritual darkness.

Can God be Angry? 106
Creation and Evolution are One 160
Religious Reactionaries 287

The Divine within each of us never intended the Human Soul to live in abysmal ignorance. We have a guiding Light within us—the Light of Christ—and the purifying Fire of the Holy Spirit to transform us.

Repentance

The morbid preoccupation of Christians of the Dark Ages (and of many still today) with being "miserable sinners" has no validity in the Christianity of the first three centuries, for the original Christian religion was a religion of Joy and Resurrection.

The idea of *repentance* (because you are "born a miserable sinner") is a perverted translation of the Greek word METANOIA, which means "a change of your mind". The early Christians understood this in a positive sense, as a renewal of your mind towards God and the Spiritual Life.

Those Christians who think that Christianity was always as it is today, and that the Bible was written by God for their benefit and has remained unchanged to this day, are light-years away from the Truth.

What is Metanoia? 1412

HAMARTIA

Greek: "Missing the mark" (as in archery). Wrongly translated as "sin", in the sense of devaluing yourself and destroying your self-esteem. The correct meaning is that you *try again.* If you failed in some aspect of your nature, you do not thereby become morbid, depressed and negative, but you try again and again. This is how the early Christians looked upon life.

Have mercy on me, a sinner? 707

What is 'the Devil'?

The word SATANAS, which the Greeks borrowed from the Hebrew SATAN, simply means "an enemy, an adversary, an opposition, one who plots against you, a tempter". Hence the English word *Satan,* nowadays called "the Devil".

The word Satan may be translated as "the enemy"

It is true that there are evil spirits in the Universe, fallen angels and fallen human spirits in and around our planet. But the word *Satan* means more than just some spooks who have an attitude problem! It also means more than a single fallen angel, called "the Devil" by the fundamentalists and which seems to preoccupy their minds endlessly!

The word *Satan* has innumerable significances. You could say that anything or anyone (including yourself!) who opposes you on the Path to re-integration with the Absolute Divinity is Satan. Thus, Satan could be simply matter; it could be your physical body; it could be your mind; it could be a spirit on the psychic dimensions; it could be your attitude towards or understanding of Reality, or many other things. By this broad definition, the word *Satan* may be translated simply as "the enemy".

> The more your mind withdraws from worldly concerns and focuses on God, the more you will understand the tricks of the Enemy.
>
> *St Mark the Hermit*

It is a very childish idea to blame all the imperfections of the Universe on *one being* called "the Devil"—even a great angel could not take full responsibility for all of that! Angels are limited beings; they are not omniscient, omnipotent, omnipresent, as God is. They have *relative* knowledge and being.

No being is equal to God, so there cannot be an entity (called "the Devil") equal and opposite to God.

Either God is what God Is, or God is not God.

And there is only *One God.*

The Paradox of Evil 208
Satan and the Fall 210
The Mind-Created Devil 218
Qualities of the Divine Being 107
The Eternal is One 512
The Divine Unity 852

Tested by God and the Devil?

The Old Testament Jews had the idea that sometimes God sends tests or trials to Humanity, or tempts a person to test his or her fidelity to God. This is an incorrect understanding. It is more the other way around: men and women test themselves by "mismatching" themselves to the Radiant Glory of God. When we better understand the Law of Cause and Effect (Karma in the East, and "as you sow, so shall you reap" in the Bible), then we realize that most evils that come to us are the results of our own wrongdoings, conscious or unconscious.

God cannot wish evil upon anybody

The whole history of the Old Testament Jewish tribes is an illustration of this faulty understanding. They always blamed God for their misfortunes when, in fact, what came to them was merely the results of their tribal thinking, feelings and actions. It is amazing how spiritually blind human beings can be and how we don't learn from history!

Another Jewish idea was that these temptations, tests or trials came from the "evil one"—the Devil. The early Christian Saints adopted these thoughts and understood their difficulties as tests coming from God and from the Devil.

The fact is that God cannot wish evil upon anybody. God cannot "lead into temptation" so as to trick a person into sin. Such is a childish Western misrepresentation of the Infinite Majesty and Splendour that is God. The East was more philosophical about the Absolute Reality.

Temptations, tests and trials *do exist,* however. We cannot go into a detailed explanation here of what this means, but it has to do with our imperfections, the imperfections of the Universe, and our faulty understanding of Reality.

Fear of the Lord? 234
Karma: the Law of Action 240
The Law of Action 992
The Testing of the Soul 1158
The Tests of the Elements 1159

PEIRASMOS
Greek: Tests, trials, or that by which the genuineness of anything may be determined. PEIRASMOS is commonly translated by scholars as "temptations".

Beyond Phantasia

The land of PHANTASIA is what, in modern terminology, is called the Astral World. The whole land of Phantasia is intensely active today. Millions of people are in the *grip* of it, including many fundamentalist and evangelical Christians.

Millions of people are in the grip of the Astral World

The old Greek word PHANTASIA meant "a non-physical appearance, a phantom". To the contemplative Christian fathers, however, Phantasia specifically meant the image-producing faculty of the Soul—the power of *imagination.* When through prayer, meditation or contemplation you break through the ordinary mind, you will *perceive* Phantasia, the realm of the *subconscious mind,* with all its images, symbols, pictures and archetypes.

The Christian Saints warned their disciples not to pay attention to the land of Phantasia, but to go *beyond* it, *above* it, to the pure, formless contemplation of the Divine Essence, the Essential Light. The aim of all Mysticism is to reach the Buddhic World, "the World of Essential Unities", or degrees of "Union with God".

To have anything to do with the Astral Plane, the source of all psychic powers and psychism, is to *delay* your spiritual progress.

Many of the Saints of Christianity developed phenomenal psychic powers and abilities as a *by-product* of their lives of prayer and inner meditation. But, whereas the medium or psychic thinks himself to be "great" as a result of a little psychic ability, the Saints always considered even the greatest psychic feats as inferior to the Vision of God, the Beatific Vision, and were extremely *humble* about their abilities.

Kāmaloka: the Astral Plane 57
The Action of the Cosmic Fire 279
The New Atlantis 280
The General Powers 580
To Safely Perform Miracles 1353
Humility of the Great Ones 337
Intellectus 375

Saint Diadochos taught his pupils that when the Intellect (the Causal Mind, the root of the mind, the mind-essence in Humanity) is strongly energized by the Divine Light, it becomes completely translucent and will see Light in its own light "very vividly". According to Saint Diadochos, this takes place when the Soul (PSYCHE) overcomes the passions (PATHOS). But Saint Diadochos warns his pupils that if they see a light or a fire which has shape or form, it is not the True Light which is God, but some creature or *reflected* light. Even if it is the form of a great angel, it is not the Primal Glory, which is like a great, formless, essential Radiance. He says that the Christian Saints should not seek visions with forms or shapes, for they lead the Soul astray. These inferior visions are PHANTASIA.

This is how one knows that the channellers, mediums and psychics, and their spirits, have *not* experienced Higher Consciousness: they believe themselves to be "Masters of the Universe", "Intergalactic Lords", and all other kinds of nonsense. There is no *humility* in them, which shows that they have merely touched upon the etheric-physical dimensions and possibly the Astral World.

There is a distinct difference between an astral impression and a spiritual one. Spiritual Reality is *formless*. God is an omnipresent, formless Intelligence. It is not limited to any forms, signs, symbols, bodies or vehicles of expression.

There is a distinct difference between an astral impression and a spiritual one

> God is Light, and in Him there is no darkness at all.
>
> *I John 1:5*

God as Infinite Light is boundless and omnipresent, without limits of any kind. Most people (those who do not meditate) think that Light is just a *symbol* for God, like the Jewish representation of the "old man on a throne". But God is a boundless, limitless, everlasting Radiance, a blinding Glory. This is what in the East they call NIRVĀṆA.

Light 978
The Two Realities 97
The Greek Mystery Language 731

The ancient Greek Sages divided Humanity on this planet into three classes. This threefold division can still be applied today:

PHYSIS
The materialistic, ignorant, blind people; the worldly-minded masses; the spiritually dead. Hence the English word *physical.*

PISTIS
Those who have faith and belief. The religious fundamentalists; the religious orthodoxies.

PNEUMATA
Those who are spiritually awake. The practised meditators; the Knowers (Gnostics); those who have Mystical Awareness; those who have attained Salvation and Liberation.

In the Greek Mystery Schools, before the time of Christianity, Humanity was described according to four classes:

PHYSIKOS
The *physical* people were ordinary Humanity: body-oriented, materialistic, unbelieving, ignorant, spiritually blind, sarcastic about the possibility of non-physical realities. These were the people who believed that the Cosmos grinds on aimlessly, from nothing to nothing, having no rhyme or reason at all. They were also called AGNOSTIKOS and AGNOSTOS (the ignorant), from AGNOSIA (nescience, spiritual darkness, spiritual blindness or ignorance, worldly consciousness).

PSYCHIKOS
The *psychics* were the intellectuals, the mental people, the scholars, the pundits, who viewed everything only as "ideas". (Nowadays the word *psychic* is used for people who are sensitive to the Astral World.)

MYSTAI
The Lower Seers. The *Mystics* were those who were initiated into the Lesser Mysteries of the Higher Mental Plane (the formless mind-realms beyond thoughts) and into BUDDHI, the Unified-Field Consciousness.

EPOPTAI
The Higher Seers, the Sages. These were the perfected men and women who were initiated into the Greater Mysteries, GNOSIS, NIRVĀṆA, the Kingdom of God.

The Chosen Ones

Who are the "chosen ones"? The Jews had this idea before the Christians. They said they were special people, "chosen by God", and called themselves "the chosen ones".

The word EKKLESIA was used by the Greeks before the arrival of Christianity. It was a political assembly of the citizens of Athens, a gathering of people for public business. EKKLESIA literally means "being called out from among the people". It is identical in meaning to the Sanskrit SATSAṄGA (from SAT, "truth", and SAṄGHA, "a gathering or assembly"). Nowadays it is commonly translated as "the church, an assembly, a church group".

Who are the 'Elect'? 128
Saṅgha: the Spiritual Hierarchy 394
The Invisible Government 980
Hierarchies of Life 1721
The Law of the Higher Life 1134

While EKKLESIA ordinarily means a spiritual congregation of Christians, it has a much deeper meaning. This being "called out" or "chosen" is not to be understood in an ordinary religious sense, but in a deeply spiritual sense, as a deep, inward orientation towards God. You are *called out of the world* into the Soul Kingdom.

> You are called out to be of Jesus Christ... called to become Saints.
>
> *Romans 1:6,7*

This is a "calling out" from gross material consciousness into the Light of the Spirit, because Jesus the Christ lives *in* the Spirit. To be a Christian, then, is to have within you the *Fire of the Spirit*.

Jesus said of His Saints:

> They are not of the world, even as I am not of this world.
>
> *John 17:16*

In fact, the true Church is the congregation of the Holy Ones, the assembly of the Saints, those who have attained a certain interior spiritual condition.

EKKLESIA
Greek: "Being called out from among the people", from EK (from) and KLESIA (being called). The Gnostics understood EKKLESIA as the Spiritual Hierarchy, the invisible Hierarchy of Spiritual Beings, composed of Angelic and Human Hierarchies. The later Christians degenerated the word to mean the physical, human organization called the "church"; hence the English word *ecclesiastic*, "pertaining to the church".

CHAPTER 32

Christian Prayer

What is Prayer?

> Prayer is the raising up of the mind and heart to God. Prayer is the raising up of the Soul from earthly to heavenly things, the investigation of things above, the desire for things invisible.
>
> *St Thomas Aquinas*

> Prayer is a pure affection of the mind directed to God.
>
> *St Augustine*

Pray not that *your* desires be fulfilled, for surely they are not of God.

Evagrios Pontikos

Prayer is an offering, a giving to God, of all our duty, love, obedience and virtue.

Father Baker

How beautiful are the words of the Saints about prayer. If only more people would learn to pray in such a way!

We may distinguish between five kinds of prayer:

a. Prayer for material "goodies", jobs, possessions, money, healing of the body, worldly success, and so forth.

b. Prayer for the above objectives on behalf of others or for others.

c. Prayer for virtue, that one may become a better person, more holy or more useful to life.

d. Prayer for Spiritual Illumination, Understanding, Wisdom, Love and Soul-Revelation.

e. The glorification, adoration, worship and magnifying of God for the sake of God alone, with nothing of the ego or self in it. This is totally self-transcending prayer.

The early Christians had nothing at all to do with the first two kinds of prayer. Many of today's Christians, however, being so intensely worldly and materialistic, don't seem to be able to move away from such prayers. The fathers of the desert would be horrified by what Christians pray for these days; most prayers today have nothing at all to do with the Kingdom of God within.

Prayer is a thought-process, a mantra. You always get what you ask for, but *what do you ask for?* Do you ask for the fleeting, the temporal, the passing, that which perishes? Or do you ask for the Kingdom of God, Everlasting Life, Life-Eternal? We can ask for things, for the vanities of the world that pass away, or we can ask for God, who is the Way, the Truth and the Life-Eternal. The early Christians had no trouble sorting out what they wanted.

It is important where we direct our energies. It is important for ourselves as individuals, and it is important for Humanity, for that determines our planetary destiny.

Magical Prayer 365
The Source of Miracles 671
Prayer Spiritual and Material 681

Interior Prayer

In the Eastern Christian view, just as in all Eastern religions (such as Hinduism, Buddhism and Taoism), a human being could work for his or her Salvation. This spiritual exercise is called HESYCHASM. A HESYCHAST is a person who performs spiritual exercises and thereby earns *Divine Grace.*

The tradition of this way of prayer has been preserved in the PHILOKALIA of the Eastern Orthodox Christian Church:

To awaken the Heart, one must focus into the Heart by way of a mantra

> True prayer is not a petition to God that God may give something to us, but a scientific, spiritual exercise to change the one who prays.

This "true prayer" was the Awakening of the Heart. It was called the *Jesus Prayer* or the *Radiant-Heart Prayer* or the *Burning Heart.* This "true prayer" is what in the East is called MANTRA.

To awaken the Heart, the Love faculty, one must focus into the Heart by way of a mantra or "true prayer". In this scientific method of prayer the Eastern Christian focused his or her awareness in the Heart Cakra and there *silently repeated* the mantra. The words should be repeated *slowly, reflectively, contemplatively,* with *feeling, longing* and *devotion.* After some practice, a Light is seen in the Heart. This is, in truth, God's Energy—not God's Innermost Being, but something *emanating* from God.

This is also remembered in Western Christianity; there are pictures of Our Lady and our Lord Jesus with a flaming, burning or radiating Heart. For many centuries in the West, this Heart method was remembered but not taught. Only pictures were painted of it.

The PHILOKALIA, which means, in Greek, "the Love of the Good" (for God was often called "the Good" by the Ancients), is the voluminous writings of the Eastern Saints of early Christianity. It lists dozens of Saints representing the hundreds of thousands of Christians of the Eastern Orthodox Church who meditated upon God's Name in the Heart. Some of it has been preserved in Russian and Slavonic, and it has been translated into English. It is the greatest book on this Earth on the subject of Prayer in the Heart.

God is *seen in the Heart* by the believer.

St Hesychios

Christian Mysticism 450
The Christian Heart-Path 632
The Early Christians 643
The Name and the Names 1258

For the Light already shines in the Darkness of Matter, during the night and during the day, in our Heart and in our Mind. This Light is without change, without decline, and cannot perish. And it Enlightens us *within.* It *transforms* into Light all those upon whom it shines [who can perceive it inwardly]. God is Light, and those who can *see* Him, see Him as Light, and those who receive Him, receive Him as Light.

St Symeon the New Theologian

One must be at Peace with oneself and with the world before the Light can appear

He who participates in the Divine Energy of Light, himself becomes Light inwardly… and *sees* all things that are hidden from those who do not have this Grace. He *transcends* the body, and goes *above the mind*… for the pure in Heart see God [His Light]….

St Gregory of Palamas

He who desires to see God within himself purifies his Heart….

St Isaac the Syrian

Hesychia means "sweet repose". When you are meditating upon the Name of God, the body, mind and emotions should be *at rest.* This is called *Interior Prayer.* One must be at Peace with oneself and with the world before the Light can appear. For it is written:

Blessed is the man whom Thou choosest, and allow to approach unto Thee, for surely, he shall abide in your Tabernacle.

God's Light is the true Grace, and that Grace can be invoked by the scientific method of prayer.

Stages of Prayer

The Saints progressed through several stages of prayer (meditation):

The Prayer of Simplicity: vocal, verbal prayer, voiced aloud, commonly used by ordinary men and women.

The Prayer of the Mind: silent, mental prayer in the Heart.

The Prayer of Remembrance: where God's Presence is felt in response to silent prayer.

The Prayer of Quiet: the highest form of mental prayer, without thoughts, words or images. This form of prayer is beyond the thought faculty, being receptive only to Grace.

The Prayer of Union: various degrees of Union with God, Theosis, Deification, At-One-Ment, Ecstasy.

The Universal Heart Practice 846
Stages of the Silent Meditation Process 1186
The Stages of Prayer 1253

Stages of Interior Prayer

There are five stages of Interior Prayer:

1. Concentration.
2. Meditation.
3. Contemplation (THEORIA).
4. Illumination.
5. Deification (THEOSIS: "Becoming God").

Concentration begins by learning to think in the Heart

Concentration

> As a man thinketh in his Heart, so he is.
>
> *Proverbs 23:7*

This is the basis of the Eastern Orthodox Christian method of *Concentration,* the first stage of the Inner Way of Interior Prayer. For the Eastern Christian Mystic, Concentration begins by learning to "think in the Heart". The mind is consciously brought down *into* the Heart by the process of repeating a Divine Name in the Heart, or a sentence or formula such as the Name of Jesus. For instance:

IESOUS CHRISTOS, THEOS UIOS, SŌTĒR
Jesus the Anointed One, God's Son, the Liberator.

This is repeated *consciously* in the Heart. Hence, the mind is brought from brain-activity into the Heart and thus *awakens* the Heart into activity.

The fathers repeated the Divine Name or formula in the Heart in several ways:

- The first method was to associate the Divine Name or formula with the *physical heartbeat.*
- The second was to associate it with the *breath process.*
- The third was simply to dwell in the Heart and, with *great devotion,* repeat the Divine Name or formula in the Heart.
- The fourth was any combination of the above methods.

You have to discover which is the best way for you to concentrate in the Heart. Concentration is then the holding of the attention in the Heart by and through the Divine Name or formula, intelligently focused in the Heart.

It is said of Pope Pius V, after the example of Moses who frequently went in and out of the Tabernacle, that he regularly retired from the business of being the Pope in order to "discourse with God", that he might learn from God *within* what he should teach to the people without.

Meditation

The stage of *Meditation* is reached when the Heart and mind become One. When the mind can naturally abide in the Heart, you will understand the secret saying: "As a man thinketh in his Heart, so he is". Before you can understand this, you will have to learn to *think in your Heart.*

Meditation is a subtle development from Concentration

Meditation is a subtle development from Concentration. When you reach this stage of Interior Prayer, you are on the outer periphery of the Kingdom of God. You are in the courtyard of the Temple.

Contemplation (Theoria)

The next stage of Interior Prayer is *Contemplation.* Your mind is in a *positive state.* Your mind is in the Heart and the Heart is *awake.* You are *awake* inside the Heart, *alert* and *waiting in silence.* There is a great expectation, a great hush, as when you are waiting for the coming of the Lord.

During the stages of Concentration and Meditation there is an intense activity and focusing of the mind in the Heart. At the stage of Contemplation there is a quiet waiting (HESYCHIA), but with the mind *positively alert.* The mind has to be in a positive state. All intellectual activity ceases. All thinking stops.

Saint Evagrios the Solitary used to say that true Interior Prayer is "the communion of the intellect with God", without an *intermediary,* without a *means.* Those who are advanced in Interior Prayer commune with God, mind to mind, without a Divine Name or formula in between. This is the stage of Contemplation.

To the fathers, THEORIA (Contemplation) was not simply "believing" in God or in Jesus Christ; a contemplative is well beyond the simple "believers". Contemplation is a certain degree of *Sight of God,* a certain amount of *seeing through* the invisible worlds, although this sight is far from perfected. Contemplation is described by the Apostle Saint Paul in these words:

> For whoever are *led* by the Spirit of God are already the Sons of God...
> The Spirit himself gives testimony to our Soul that we are Sons of God.
> *Romans 8:14,16*

THEORIA
Greek: Contemplation, meditation, inner spiritual discipline of the mind. The Saints understood THEORIA as "an Inner Vision of the Primeval Light of God; the flooding of the upper regions of the mind with Light or Transforming Fire; the contemplation of the Inexpressible Light; the Union of the Soul with God by the Energy of God's Light".

The lowest form of THEORIA is the vision of the essences or energies beyond physical Creation, of the subtle worlds, such as the heavens and hells. But the objective of the Hesychast is the contemplation of God Himself/Herself.

Intellectus: Knowing inside 375
Contemplation 1188

Illumination

Then come various degrees of *Illumination*. Illumination, according to Pseudo-Denys, is the reception of the Divine Light into your Soul. It is "the *acceptance* of the Light into your Soul, which is, at the same time, an *effect* of the possession of a certain amount of Light already". Now you will see why the Holy Fathers insisted on the Prayer in the Heart for beginners, for the Divine Name, the Name of Jesus or a Name of God, is *Light-generating*.

Deification (Theosis)

The doctrine of Theosis—the Deification of created beings by the Light of Grace—is the essence of the Christian Eastern Orthodox Church's Mysticism. A human being advances towards Union with God to the extent that he or she allows the Divine Grace-Light to flood into his or her Consciousness.

> Truth will Enlighten us and Illuminate us with its rays. This Truth is God.
>
> *St Gregory of Nyassa*

When the mind perceives the Holy Spirit in full consciousness, we realize that Grace is beginning to paint the Divine Likeness over the Divine Image within us.

Theosis
Greek: Union with God. The Deification of the Human Soul. Attaining Divine likeness. Conscious Immortality. This, of course, is also the goal of Yoga, Sūfīsm, Jewish Hasidism, Zen, Taoism and Buddhism.
Mystical Union 846

Illumination and Deification 1190
Stages on the Way of Holiness 1336

Passion and Dispassion

The Greek word **Pathos** means "passion, strong emotions, vehement feelings". The desert fathers listed several "passions" that were deadly harmful for Spiritual Life and Illumination:

Gluttony: excessive eating.
Avarice: greed, desiring others' property.
Self-esteem: pride, putting oneself above others.
Bitterness: melancholy, grieving.
Anger: wrath, resentment, jealousy.
Unchastity: an uncontrolled sexual life.
Laziness: idleness, sloth, inactivity.
Spiritual ignorance: not knowing that one is a Soul.

The word **Apatheia** means the opposite of Pathos (passion). It means "dispassion, spiritual freedom, liberation from human nature" or "walking like an angel" or "being continually in the Light of God". From this was derived the English word *apathy*, which means "being without feelings, indifferent, passionless or disinterested". To the classical Greeks and Christian Saints, however, Apatheia was a sought-after spiritual quality; there was nothing morbid about it. Apatheia meant the successful overcoming of the "deadly passions": gluttony, avarice, pride, bitterness, anger, unchastity, laziness and spiritual darkness. It is a state of *detachment* from the world, but *not* an indifference to things.

The Path to Ecstasy

Some of the Saints classified the steps towards the Kingdom of God slightly differently:

1. Mental prayer.
2. Interior prayer, or ceaseless prayer.
3. Pure prayer, or meditation.
4. Contemplation.
5. Illumination, or Ecstasy.
6. Deification.

The mind becomes one with God by the complete energy of the Love of the Heart

Mental prayer is when you repeat a mantra in the Heart. The mind is engaged in prayer *in* the Heart.

It becomes "ceaseless" or interior prayer when the subconscious mind, the mind-in-deep, takes up the prayer so that it will be repeated automatically in the Heart, day and night. This is what Saint Paul meant when he said, "Pray without ceasing" *(1 Thessalonians 5:17).*

The Blessed Theoleptus of Philadelphia taught about pure prayer (meditation) in such a way. When the mind has been withdrawn from the external world of the senses and is collected within the Heart, then the mind *returns unto itself* and becomes united with a mental word (mantra) that is naturally inherent to it. Praying this word, the mind becomes one with God by the complete energy of the Love of the Heart. Then all sensations of the body cease, all outward attentions cease, and the beauties of this world no longer delight the mind. The Masters of the Spiritual Life also called this stage "the Remembrance of God".

Terms of Prayer

Over the centuries the words *prayer, meditation* and *contemplation* have been used by the Mystics in a rather interchangeable way. The Eastern (Greek) stream of Christians used the term *interior prayer* for what the Western Saints (the Latin stream) called *meditation* and *contemplation.* According to the Mystics of the Catholic Church, meditation is "internal prayer" and mental prayer is "the occupation of one's faculties on God"—not by thinking or speculating about God, but by stirring up "the will to conform oneself to Him" and "the affections to love Him".

Don't let this confuse you, but feel the spirit of what they are trying to say. Don't be "picky" with words.

The State of Inner Purity 497
Samādhi: the Goal of Yoga 574
Satori: the Experience of Illumination 816
To Experience Spiritual Ecstasy 1683

When the mind is free from sensory pleasures and is no longer engaged in internal fantasies, it comes to itself. "It abides in pure simplicity". This is the state of *Contemplation*, wherein the Christ appears to the Soul in all His Beauty.

Ecstasy, or Illumination, comes about after the mind has been purified and the Heart stands open. Then "the Spirit of God descends upon Man" and the Soul overflows with a Joy that no words can describe. God is perceived as an intense Bliss which gives rapture to the human Soul.

Ecstasy comes about after the mind has been purified and the Heart stands open

Saint Seraphim said:

> The Kingdom of God consists of Peace and Joy through the Holy Spirit.

The manifestations of Ecstasy are a transcendental Peace and an indescribable Bliss.

Concentration

Concentration is the exclusive attention to one object, inner mental activity, focusing the mind. It is derived from the Latin *concentrare,* "to bring the mind to a centre, to a point of focus, towards convergence, towards Union". (From *con,* "together, toward", and *centrum,* "centre, heart, the kernel of a thing".) The first stage on the Path of Mysticism is to bring the mind into the Heart. It is easier, at first, to concentrate on an "object" such as a mantra, a statement of Truth or a Divine Name.

Contemplation

To *contemplate* is a Latin term meaning "to look or view with continued attention, to study thoughtfully, to be deeply absorbed in the object of your thought". In this stage of your Mystic Path you are getting near your goal of Union with God and you get glimpses of Higher Consciousness or Buddhic Unitive-Consciousness.

Meditation

As defined in Mysticism, *meditation* is "a quiescent, prolonged, spiritual introspection, a devout religious exercise". It is derived from the Latin *meditari,* "to plan, to ponder upon, to study, to consider, to intend". In meditation you "think over" a subject for a prolonged period (longer than in concentration). You take your mantra or word of power or statement of Truth into your Heart Cakra and there you develop it, dwell upon it, until deeper Realization, Insight and Intuition dawn upon you.

Ecstasy

The Greek word EKSTASIS means "bliss, elation, delight, religious Rapture, spiritual Exaltation as a result of Mysticism". The Mystics define it as "a mental transport and Rapture, an overpowering Exaltation from the contemplation of divine things". In other words, *Union with God* or, in Sanskrit, SAMĀDHI.

Mystical States of the Medieval Catholic Mystics

According to the Roman Catholic Mystics of the Middle and Dark Ages, the path to Mystical Union or Higher Consciousness is through three stages of prayer: *Concentration, Meditation* and *Contemplation.* These develop into the Mystical States (Buddhi) and Union with God (Nirvāṇa).

The Catholic Mystics had a different terminology

The Catholic Mystics had a different terminology to describe these states of consciousness. They used the words *Communion, Revelation, Sufflation, Afflatus* and *Effulgence.*

Communion is to commune consciously with the Divine Presence.

Revelation is the direct experience of *Insight,* on the Soul level, about God, the Universe, Humanity, the Angelic Hierarchies, and so on.

Sufflation is the experiencing of oneself as a Spiritual Soul, and the experience within the Soul of being overshadowed by the Divine Presence. In the East this is known as the awakening of Buddhi, the Love-Wisdom Principle.

Afflatus is the experience of the Divine as an overmastering impulse or energy within the Soul, as the Guide, Teacher or Guru of the Soul, or the perception of the guiding force of the Divine Presence in the *intimate depths* of the Soul. (This is *not* astral; this is not an outside spook or entity; this is not a "spirit-guide" or "ascended master" of the astral realms!)

Effulgence is the experience of Radiant Light, the White Brilliance, the Supreme Crown, the Supreme Splendour of the Godhead—what is called Nirvāṇa in the East, Allāh among the Muslims, and Shekinah by the Jews. This is the *goal* and *end* of the Mystical Path.

None of these Mystical States has anything to do with mediumship or channelling. Rather, the experience is a *direct inner knowing* without an intermediary, deep within the Soul, *above* the Astral and Mental Planes.

Afflatus
Latin: "Inspiration by God". The breathing-in of God's Power, Wisdom and Knowledge at the Soul level. A Divine imparting of Gnosis (Wisdom and Power).

Effulgentia
Latin: "Radiant Splendour, a brilliant Light, glittering, shining". The shining forth of the Godhead (Deus).
This is similar to the Arabic word Allāh, which is *not* a person. Allāh means "the Effulgent One, God as the Overpowering Effulgence, the Eternally Shining, the Radiant One". The Hebrew word Shekinah (the Divine Presence) means the same: "Radiating Light, Glory (as Light Emanation)".
The Sūfī God 838

Wounds of Love

The mystical literature talks about "Wounds of Love"—wounds produced in the Heart by God's Love. This phenomenon is depicted in traditional pictures as Christ's pierced Heart. The Mystics who have experienced these Wounds of Love have described their experience in many ways:

> My Heart was pierced by an arrow of Living Fire.
>
> Some invisible force plunged my Heart into Fire.
>
> I was mortally wounded in the Heart by intense darts of Fire.
>
> As if someone is plunging a knife into my Heart, causing intense suffering.
>
> A knife was plunged into my Heart emitting Fire.

The Mystic is transformed by the Love of God into a new creation

Even the physical heart can react to this and may bleed. Such cases are called *transverberation.* If these Wounds of Love appear on the hands and feet they are called the *stigmata.*

This piercing of the Heart by God's Love has been called by several Mystics "the Seraph's assault". A fiery Seraph attacks the Heart and pierces it through with a fiery dart, a lance, a sword or a sharp-pointed blade. The Mystic is mortally wounded and is transfixed, transformed by the Love of God into a *new creation.* The Heart takes on a different function than a mere "life-support system". It becomes a dynamo of God's Infinite Love.

> My Heart grew hot within me and in my meditation a Fire flamed out.
>
> *Psalms 39:3*

This is the Soul afire, the Revelation of Divine Love.

Rapture

The word *Rapture* comes from the Latin RAPTURUS: "Having been carried away in your Consciousness to a state or condition beyond the normal states". The Christian Mystics describe *Rapture* as the experience of God in the Secret Chamber of your Heart. The Mystics also call this "Ravishment" by the Spirit of God within you, when you receive the Energies of the Holy Spirit into your Auric Being or Microcosm, which will transform your whole inner Self. RAPTURUS (Rapture) has the same meaning as the Greek EKSTASIS (Ecstasy) and the Sanskrit SAMĀDHI.

The Resurrection Body 40

The Burning Heart 631
The Fire of Love 1255
The Fire in the Heart 1287
Physical Symptoms in the Heart 462
Experiencing the Awakening Heart 463

To Develop Perfect Stillness...

The Christian Masters said of Contemplation:

> The duty of the monk is to develop perfect stillness.

And...

The objective of the religious life is to develop perfect stillness

> When there are no fantasies or mental images in the Heart, and when the mind is established in its *true nature,* then you are ready to contemplate what is spiritual, full of delight, and close to God.

The objective of the religious life is to develop perfect stillness, in a Heart Centre free of imaginings and fantasies, free of thoughtforms and verbalizations, and a mind established in its original, formless nature (the *no-mind* condition), in order that we may begin to truly contemplate what is spiritual, full of Bliss, and of the nature of the Divine Essence.

The question is, how can we safely bring about:

- A perfect stillness in our being?
- A Heart free of images and thoughts?
- A mind which has ceased all mental chatter and has returned to its source, the Soul?

Alone with God

Solitude, as was understood by the Mystics of the early Roman Church, meant "a retirement from the world, a custody of the five senses, and a moderation in external occupations". It was a quiet, regulated *turning within* of the attention, in the most ideal physical environment, usually somewhere "alone with Nature" or alone in a cloister or monastery.

Solitude is *not* loneliness, boredom, isolation, aloofness or being "above" others; rather, it is a quiet, inner poise of the mind. Solitude, mental equipoise, serenity, assists the gift of Contemplation and inner-recollection (Concentration).

According to the Christian Mystics of the Roman Church, solitude is an endeavour to be "alone with God" using vocal prayers (mantras), spiritual reading or holy meditation. It also means "an habitual remembrance of the Presence of God".

In Solitude, God speaks to the Heart.

A Christian Mystical saying

When the Mind is Still 768
Zen Silence 790
The Stages of Sūfī Silence 901
The Silence of the Deep 1355
The Practice of Silence 1443
Silence, Solitude, Peace 1386
Solitude and Loneliness 1170

Purify the Heart

The best way is to begin in the Heart. The early Christians followed Hebrew, Greek and Egyptian practices.

To begin this Holy Work, first *the mind has to be re-created,* which is done by the *Prayer in the Heart*, by the invocation of the Divine Name in the Heart with steady thought and passionate feeling. When the mind is purified, then the Soul gains a new life.

According to Saint Hilary of Poitiers, human bodies that are corrupted on account of vice are the dwelling places of "evil spirits". This is why *purification* is so necessary. Without purifying the Heart and mind through the action of the Divine Name, the Holy Spirit cannot come into a human being.

Saint Jerome commented on a gospel of the Nazarenes, which was written in Hebrew, in which it was written:

> Upon the purified Heart the whole fountain of the Holy Spirit shall pour down. Because God is Spirit. And where the Spirit of God comes down, there is Freedom.

The Divine Being is a powerful Intelligence, a Conscious Will, an Intelligent Force, a Cosmic Person who is vast, limitless, all-knowing. It is a Higher Energy, a Supernal Understanding. All the Names of God (mantras or prayer-formulas) are but aspects of this *Beingness.* Thus, you take one aspect and concentrate very intensely upon it, with total self-forgetfulness, until God appears to you in *Radiance.*

A Name of God is taken into the Heart Cakra and repeated there, slowly, with attention and concentration, with focus upon the meaning. God's Presence is to be *realized.* God is eternally in your Heart Cakra, but you must get in touch with God *consciously*. You will feel God as a Beam of Light entering your Head Cakras, or your Heart Cakra will be bathed in Light. It is a powerful, intelligent *Light-Presence.*

The human Soul becomes Free at the attainment of *Illumination* or *Ecstasy*.

For out of the impure Heart proceed evil thoughts, murders, adulteries, thefts, false witnesses, blasphemies.

Matthew 15:19

Peace I leave with you, my Peace I give unto you, not as the world giveth that I give unto you. Your Heart shall not be troubled, nor will it be afraid.

John 14:27

Awaken First the Heart 428
Tapas: Spiritual Purification 571
The Purification of the Heart 849
The Secret of the Heart 1280
The Pure Heart 1300
Peace of Heart 1595
The Name and the Names 1258

The Radiant Heart Prayer

The Fire of Love ascends from the Heart

There is a tradition in the Roman Catholic Church to which many Saints belonged: Devotion to the Sacred Heart of Jesus. You may have seen paintings of the Christ with His Heart depicted as on fire, aflame or in the form of Light. There is a very good example in my possession which tells the complete story of the Way of the Mystic, the Lover of God. In this painting, Jesus' Heart is radiating pure Fire and Light—the Fire of *Love* and the Light of *Wisdom*. His eyes are turned upwards to the middle of the forehead (the Third-Eye Centre of the Yogī, the Mountain of Illumination of the Mystic). The Fire of Love ascends from the Heart, irradiates the Head, and becomes the cool Light of Wisdom in the Head.

There are four stages to the Radiant Heart Prayer:

1. Vocal or breath prayer (mantra) introduced into the Heart.
2. The dynamic sexual energy of the body-mind is drawn up and transmuted in the Heart.
3. Heart-to-Heart prayer, or communion of your Heart with the Radiant Heart of Jesus, and merging into It.
4. The ascension of the Fire of Love of the Heart into the Gold of Illumination in the Head. This is where the Father is known as "God is Light; in Him there is no darkness at all."

The following points should be observed:

- The process of lifting the sexual energy into the Heart should commence only after there is already some movement or awakening in the Heart as a result of using one's mantra or prayer in the Heart.
- The process of identifying with the Sacred Heart of Jesus should commence only after the sexual energies have been transmuted in the Heart.
- The lifting of the Radiance into the Head Centres should commence after all of the lower nature has been purified, transformed, transmuted.

The Sacred Heart of Jesus 673
The Fire of Love 1255
Wisdom: the Light Path 1354
Kuṇḍalinī and Alchemy 153
Sex Natural and Divine 926
The Path to Immortality 430
The Way of the Radiant Heart 452

Many of the Christian Catholic Saints experienced the third stage of the Radiant Heart Prayer, the Communion with the Heart of Jesus, as an abyss of Light, Love, Joy, Strength and Peace. For instance, Saint Margaret Mary described her experience as follows:

> I feel as if I were quite buried in this Divine Heart. I am as though in a bottomless abyss where He shows me treasures of Love and Grace.

There can be no end to the benefits of meditation in the Heart

In the litany of the Sacred Heart we have many descriptions of the experiences that come to us as a result of merging our Hearts into the Heart of Jesus. The Heart of Jesus has been described as:

Formed by the Holy Spirit in the Womb of the Virgin Mother.

United to the Word of God.

Of infinite Majesty.

The sacred Temple of God.

The Tabernacle of the Most High.

The house of God.

The gate of Heaven.

The burning furnace of Charity.

The abode of Justice and Love.

The abyss of all virtues.

Most worthy of all praise.

King and Centre of all Hearts.

In Whom are all the treasures of Wisdom and Knowledge.

In Whom dwells the Fullness of Divinity.

In Whom the Father is well pleased.

Of whose Fullness we have all received.

The desire of the Everlasting Hills.

Patient and most Merciful.

Enriching all who invoke It.

The Fountain of Life and Holiness.

...and many other descriptions. There can be no end to the benefits of meditation in the Heart and uniting our own Heart with the Divine Heart.

The Jesus Mantra and the Sacred Heart Initiation 1356

Saint Margaret Mary's Teachings on the Sacred Heart of Jesus 673

Jesus: the Fire of Love 1725

Clouds of Unknowing

The 14th century monk who wrote *The Cloud of Unknowing* described prayer as:

> A blind Love towards God, beating upon the Clouds of Unknowing.

Your mind must be enflamed with the Love of God

And...

> A naked intent directed to God for God alone.

He described a Mystic as:

> One who seeks nothing but God.

And his favourite motto was:

> Nowhere physically is everywhere spiritually.

This sounds like pure Zen! He describes this process as follows:

> When you have learned to withdraw from your physical senses, and from all mental thoughts, you *do nothing*, and even if you think that you are doing nothing, you do nothing, and you do this nothing for the Love of God.

Slow down here; don't rush on! Read this *slowly* and understand it well. This is difficult to do. This is pure Zen *and* pure Christianity, and it can be very dangerous! *Your mind must be positively charged, alert, wholesome, fully awake, enflamed with the Love of God.* If your mind is not in this condition you will become a medium and be possessed by spirits. We do not ask you to blank your mind out, to become a zombie or to go into a trance state like a medium. This is not trance-mediumship! That is why you must begin with the beginner's practices.

Saint Isaiah the Solitary advised his monks:

Do not leave your Heart unguarded, even for a moment, while you still live in your body.

For the mind in prayer can *rescue* your Soul from the impact of the bodily senses. But the prayer must be in secret, that is, in the *Heart* and in *Silence*. Then, as the Master also said:

God will see your good works in secret, and will reward you in secret.

Christian Zen 765
Meditating on the Void 801
The Wisdom of Not-doing 1699
Why Channelling is Dangerous 340
Guard your Heart 1328

When you are established in this advanced form of prayer or meditation, you must work hard at *doing nothing,* with only a *single desire:* to have nothing but God alone, who is the Life above everything else.

Choose to be nowhere, and always do nothing.

When you are doing this No-Thing, your attention is directed solely to God, away from yourself. While you are doing nothing, your attention is not on anything in Creation.

You will be changed by the inward experience of this No-Thing

Your mind cannot *reason* about this Nothing, or doing nothing, for it is above thought. Thought cannot touch it. The personality calls this "doing nothing", but the Soul senses it as the *All,* for this No-Thing is, in fact, the Life of everything, visible and invisible.

You will be *changed* by the inward experience of this No-Thing when you can experience it everywhere. Then God is the All in All. Then Christ becomes Man for you, and you become God—or, if you like, you achieve degrees of identification with the Divine Presence.

> Christ became Man so that Man might become God.
>
> *St Athanasius*

For all Life is One, whatever form, visible or invisible, it may take. And you are One with It.

Divine Unknowing

The teaching of Saint Dionysius the Areopagite on the *Divine Agnosia* (Divine Unknowing) can be understood as the stage of *Contemplation.* For here you have surrendered your will-power and are quietly waiting for the Lord to appear. You are becoming aware of yourself as a Soul, living in a Soul-Kingdom, the *lowest part* of the Kingdom of God.

There is a much higher stage of Divine Agnosia at the stage of *Theosis* or *Deification.* According to Saint Dionysius, this happens when you have achieved *unceasing and absolute renunciation of yourself* as a creature through "pure and entire self-renunciation" and have merged into the Divine Radiance, which is also the Divine Darkness (in Sanskrit, ŚŪNYATĀ).

Śūnyatā: the Void 503

The Way of the Christian Mystic 626
No-Mind and the One Mind 763
The One and Only 839
The One 1686

Mystical Theology

MYSTICA THEOLOGIA IDEM EST QUOD EXTENTIO AMORIS IN DEUM PER AMORIS DESIDERIUM.

Mystical Theology is the extension of the Love of God by a desire for Love.

Saint Bonaventure

The more you love, the more you are loved

This means that the *idea* of loving God becomes increasingly a *reality* through inward meditation, prayer or contemplation. As you give more and more of yourself *towards* God, in return you will feel more and more of God's Love towards you.

It is a curious fact that Love begets Love: the more you love, the more you are loved.

Practising Mystical Theology

One of the most powerful expressions of "Mystical Theology" is embodied in the ancient Eastern Orthodox Christian prayer:

Lord, Jesus Christ, Son of the Living God, have mercy upon me.

This ancient prayer is a form of *invocation*. It is a way of *Mystical Theology*. It is a mystical path to arrive at "the Knowledge of God", which is the actual meaning of the word *theology*.

This meditation was practised by the early Christian Saints in the deserts of Egypt, Syria, Palestine, North Africa and the Mediterranean. It is, in fact, a Path of Love, or BHAKTI YOGA. You focus your attention in the Heart Centre and there you invoke the Lord of Love, the Christ Being, by this prayer (mantra).

The mantram has four parts:
a. Lord,
b. Jesus Christ,
c. Son of the Living God,
d. Have mercy upon me.

- First you focus all of your awareness in the Heart Cakra, and there you mentally call out, "Lord!" This is like a small child in distress crying out for her mother: "Mummy!" With the word "Lord" you cry out towards the Infinite, the Absolute, the Divine Presence. It must be a *Heart-action,* not merely a thought!

Theologia 625
The Meaning of Life is Love 633
On Love and Meditation 1140
Bhakti Yoga: Divine Union by Devotion 1128

- Then, after a pause, you say, "Jesus Christ". Here you remember the fact of the Divine Presence *incarnate* in Creation, focused in a living, radiant Being. And you may see this Being with the eye of your Heart as a perfect God-Man or God-Woman.
- Then, still focused in your Heart, you say, "Son of the Living God". Here, it is important to emphasize the word *living,* for God is not a past tradition! It is a Living Presence, here and now, permeating all things. Tradition *kills* the Living Presence, and people who are stuck in tradition cannot experience the Living God of *here and now*—"the Living Waters of Life", as Jesus expressed it.
- Then you say, "Have mercy upon me", which means that you wish the Higher Consciousness, the Superhuman Awareness of the Living God, to turn its attention to you.

Tradition kills the Living Presence

Meditate in such a way in your Heart…

Have mercy on me, a sinner?

From this original Prayer of the Heart, or *Jesus Prayer,* arose many variations, such as:

Lord Jesus Christ, Son of God, have mercy on me, a sinner.

The word *sinner* has been added by some fathers, but it is a rather morbid addition and, psychologically, it is not advisable that you should continually dwell on the idea of being a "sinner" (unless you have *true humility,* which is very rare). Thus, the words *sinner* and *sin* should be avoided in your meditations; rather, you should focus on God's Saving Grace acting in your Heart.

The word *sinner* has acquired, in Christianity, a very unhealthy connotation. The scholars and theologians have morbidly translated the Greek word HAMARTIA as "sin" when, in fact, the Greek word means "to miss the mark, to miss the point, to go astray, to make a mistake, to falter or fail, to make an error". There is no sense of "eternal hell-fire and damnation" in it, as projected by the fundamentalists of today's so-called Christianity.

It is a simple fact: *we are all sinners* in the sense that we have forgotten our Divine Estate, the condition that was ours, as is symbolically shown in Adam before the Fall. Christ came to remind us of who we really are: *Children of God,* in the truest sense of the word. This *remembrance* or *recovery* of the lost Kingdom is the message of Christ. And this was the objective of the Christian Saints of the desert.

Traditionis 379
The Omnipresent God 1108
Holiness to the Lord 1393
The Presence of God 1396
The Lord of Glory 667
Repentance 683

The Great Greek Mantra to Jesus

This prayer is the prototype of all the later Jesus Prayer practices

Iesous Christos Theos Uios Sōtēr
Jesus Christ, God's Son, Liberator.
Jesus Christ, God's Son, Saviour.
Jesus Christ, God's Son, Redeemer.
Jesus Christ, Son of God, save me.
Lord, Jesus Christ, lead me to Salvation.

This most excellent prayer (mantra) should be repeated in the Heart Cakra with great concentration and intensity, very slowly and meditatively, with great longing for the Kingdom of God within you, until you begin to experience a *response* from God. You may work with the original Greek mantra or with an English form, but it *must be repeated in the Heart.*

This original prayer may be repeated in the Heart without being linked to the breath-mechanism. Or, if you prefer, it can be linked to the breath rhythm as shown below.

This prayer is the prototype of all the later *Jesus Prayer* practices, the origin of the true Christian prayer or meditation practice, as distinguished from the ancient Hebrew, Greek or Egyptian practices.

In the *Philokalia*, this Jesus Prayer, the Radiant Prayer in the Heart, is described as:
Light-generating
Light-producing
Light-giving
Light-enhancing
Lightning-producing
Fiery-Thinking
The Radiant Way
Light-measures

Breathing in…		
Breathing out:	Iesous	Jesus
Breathing in…		
Breathing out:	Christos	Christ
Breathing in…		
Breathing out:	Theos	God's
Breathing in…		
Breathing out:	Uios	Son
Breathing in…		
Breathing out:	Sōtēr	Redeemer

The Breath-Rhythm of the Name

Some Variations of the Jesus Prayer

When the Name Iesous (Jesus) is united to your breath, then you will know Hesychasm (Stillness).

St John Climacus

If you unceasingly invoke in your Heart Kyrie Iesous (Lord Jesus), the Fire of Divine Grace will fill your Heart.

St Diadochus

Spiritual Prayer is the continuous communion of the mind with God through the Name Iesous (Jesus) in the Heart.

Evagrios Pontikos

Do not waste time with too many words when praying (meditating); just say "Kyrie" (Lord!) in your Heart, or lift up your hands and say, "Kyrie Eleison" (Lord, deliver me!).

St Macarius of Egypt

Empty your mind of all thoughts and put your attention in your Heart, and there say, "Kyrie, Iesous Christos" (Lord, Jesus Christ).

St Nicephorus

Be Silent and be Still. Close your eyes, press your chin against your chest, and look into your Heart. Breathe in and out gently. Each time you breathe out, say "Kyrie, Iesous Christos, Theos Uios Eleison" (Lord, Jesus Christ, Son of God, deliver me).

St Simeon the New Theologian

Be still in your meditation. Look into your Heart. As you breathe in, say "Kyrie, Iesous Christos" (Lord, Jesus Christ). As you breathe out, say "Eleison" (have mercy upon me).

St Gregory of Sinai

A total God-given equilibrium and inward stillness is given to our minds if we constantly invoke the Name in our hearts: "Kyrie Iesous Christos" (Lord, Jesus Christ).

St Hesychios

Keep the Heart always deeply silent, all thoughts still, and thus pray (meditate), "Kyrie Eleison" (Lord, save me!). Or, humbly call upon God, in your Heart, by the Name Kyrie Iesous Christos (Lord, Jesus Christ).

St Hesychius of Jerusalem

The Name Iesous (Jesus), when invoked in the Heart, brings Light to the Heart.

Philotheus of Sinai

When the Christians were being persecuted, they disguised the Jesus Prayer (Mantra) under the code-name *Fish,* the sign of the Piscean Age and the Jesus Dispensation. In the first to the third centuries, Jesus was often symbolized on the walls of the catacombs as a fish.

I-Ch-Th-U-S = Ichthus = Fish = Christ = Pisces

Mantras for Awakening the Heart 458

Other Christian Masters have said…

Whenever we are filled with evil thoughts, we should invoke the Name IESOUS CHRISTOS (Jesus Christ) in our Hearts to drive them away.

Without the constant invocation of the Name CHRISTOS (Christ) in our Hearts, it is impossible to master the art of Spiritual Warfare [the inner battle].

Strike at the Enemy with the Name IESOUS (Jesus).

We must give the Name KYRIE IESOUS (Lord Jesus) the sole occupation of our Heart.

The guarding of the mind, with the constant invocation of the Name IESOUS CHRISTOS (Jesus Christ) in the Heart, gives you Insight into the depths of the Heart, and a supernatural Stillness in the mind, and the capacity to be conscious without thoughts.

Some Western Heart Prayers

I and the Father are One.
Holiness to the Lord.
In Him we live, move and have our Being.
God in me.
I adore you, Son of God.
Lord, Jesus Christ, teach me Love.
The Joy of the Lord is your strength.
Come, Lord Jesus.
The Way of Love is the Lighted Way.
MARANATHA
Greek: Come, our Lord!
AMEN, IESU, AMEN
Latin: Jesus is the faithful witness.

The Heart, constantly guarded by the Name IESOUS, will give birth, from itself, to thoughts of Light.

The Name IESOUS, when repeated long enough in the Heart, will become flashes of Lightning.

The continuous repetition of IESOUS CHRISTOS THEOS UIOS SOTER (Jesus Christ, God's Son, Deliverer), in the Heart, will drive away spiritual forgetfulness.

Concentrate in the Heart through the invocation of the Name IESOUS CHRISTOS (Jesus Christ) to disperse the demonic fancy of ignorance. The Body of our Lord Jesus Christ (IESOUS CHRISTOS) is a Divine Fire. When this Fire enters into one's Heart, it drives away all evil spirits and all evil thoughts.

When you permit your Heart to receive the Mysteries of Christ (the CHRISTOS), that Divine Body will *illumine* your mind and will make it *shine* like a star.

Just as he who looks at the Sun cannot help but fill his eyes with light, so he who constantly looks into his Heart, and there repeats the Name IESOUS CHRISTOS (Jesus Christ), cannot fail to be illumined by the supernatural Light of Christ.

Your Heart shall burn by the Fire of the Name IESOUS.

The Holy Name IESOUS mediates for us in the Heart.

The purified Soul, with the pure inner-eyes, contemplates the Glory of the True-Light and the true Sun-of-Justice, the CHRISTOS in the Heart.

The CHRISTOS shines in the Heart.

Practising the Presence of God

Brother Lawrence, the 17th century Carmelite monk, taught:

> We should establish in ourselves the sense of God's Holy Presence by continually conversing with Him.

This is known as *The Practising of the Presence of God.* This is also what Saint Paul meant when he said, "Pray without ever ceasing". That is, *pray continually.*

One talks to God by the impulses of one's Soul

The beginner in spiritual life might interpret this as talking to God *verbally,* asking Him for favours for the personality or whatever, but only in the beginning does one talk to God verbally. It is important for the *beginner* to pray or meditate verbally, with thoughts; but when one masters the art of true meditation, prayer or contemplation, one talks to God telepathically, intuitively, silently, non-discursively, non-logically, non-rationally, above the mental chatter, by the impulses of one's Soul.

> I engaged in the holy life only for the Love of God, and for no personal gain. I have tried to do all things out of the Love for God. Whatever becomes of me, whether I be lost or be saved, I care not, but I will always continue to act out of the Love of Thee. At least I know this, that until my death, I did nothing else but to Love Thee.
>
> *Brother Lawrence*

It is said of Brother Lawrence that he was pleased even to take up a straw from the ground for the Love of God, seeking God only, and nothing else, not even God's gifts towards him. He sought nothing for his ego, his personality. He had no consciousness of himself.

The Stages of Prayer 1253
To Realize the Presence of God 1398
My Beloved Lives in my Heart 1290

The Recollection of the Presence of God is done through attention in the Heart. Thoughts appear to arise in the head, but in fact they have their roots in the Heart.

"As a man thinketh in his Heart, so he is."

For beginners, the simplest form is to repeat the word *God* while focusing the attention in the region of the Heart. This will quieten the mind and subdue all images, desires and concepts within it.

It is not the word *God* that is important, but what it represents. This must be *felt* through the Heart. The word *God* should be repeated slowly and meaningfully, with great feeling. With each word one should contemplate the Divine Presence in the Heart. At a later stage you can simply focus your attention in the Heart and you will become aware, at once, of the Divine Presence.

In the *Philokalia* this method is called *attention, sobriety* and *wakefulness*. The Buddhists call it *mindfulness*.

Latin Mantras of the Rosicrucians

These Latin mantras are to be repeated in the Heart Centre.

The Fraternity of the Rosy Cross 450
Latin Mantras to Our Lady 1510

SUB UMBRA ALARUM TUARUM JEHOVA
I live under the shadow of your wings, O God.

NEQUAQUAM VACUUM
There is no empty space.

DEI GLORIA INTACTA
The Glory of God remains forever intact.

JESUS MIHI OMNIA
Jesus means everything to me.

EX DEO NASCIMUR
We are born of God the Father.

IN JESU MORIMUR
In Jesus we die.

PER SPIRITUM SANCTUM REVIVISCIMUS
By the Holy Spirit we are revived.

PERPETUUM MOBILE
The ever-moving Eternal.

LEGIS JUGUM
The Yoke of the Law.

LIBERTAS EVANGELII
The freedom of the Gospels (Revelations).

HOC UNIVERSI COMPENDIUM VIVUS MIHI SEPULCRUM FECI
While alive in the body, this compound universe I made into my tomb.

MANE NOBISCUM DOMINE
Abide with us, O Lord.

CHRISTE QUI LUX ES ET DIES
O Christ, who is the Light and the Day.

The term ROSICRUCIAN is derived from *Rosy-Crucian*, "the Rose and the Cross". According to the Rosicrucians, there is the Rose in the Heart (the Spirit, the Divine Christ-Being) which needs to be *awakened*, and there is the Cross in the Heart (the Soul crucified in the flesh, in the body, in material consciousness). This Cross the Hindu Yogīs call HṚDAYA-GRANTHI, the "Knot in the Heart". This Cross, or Knot, is the material consciousness.

Knots of Consciousness 445
The Rose of Divine Love 858

The Evolution of Christian Prayer

The Christians of the first three centuries took short sentences from the Old Testament and prayed/meditated upon them in the Heart. Following are some of the Hebrew mystical practices from the Jewish mystical stream, as practised in the Heart by the earliest Christians:

The Names and Mental Prayer in the Heart 1261
Hebrew Divine Names 1262
Christian Divine Names 1266
Meditation on the Divine Names 1454

RUACH ELOHĪM AUR
The Breath of God is Light.

YEHESHUAH
God is my Saviour.

IMMANUEL
God is in me. God is with us.

YAHVEH
God that was, is, and shall be. The Eternal One.

EHEIEH (ASHER EHEIEH)
God is. I Am (That I Am).

ABBA
Father!

ADONAI
Lord!

ISRAEL
God is the Ruler. (Pronounced *Yīsrael.)*

AIN SOPH AUR
God is Limitless Light.

HALLELU-YAH
Glory be to God.

BARUKH ATOH ADONAI
Blessed art Thou, O Lord.

ELI
My God! My Lord!

Some ancient Roman Wisdom (Latin):

IN VERITATE RELIGIONIS CONFIDO
I believe in the fundamental truth of Religion.

OMNIA VINCIT AMOR
Love conquers all difficulties.

OMNIA MUTANTUR NOS ET MUTAMUR IN ILLIS
All things change, and we must change with them.

Later on, the Christians started to pray in the Heart in Greek and Latin. For example:

The word Theos (God) is meditated upon in the Heart

KYRIE ELEISON
Greek: Lord have Mercy on us. God have Compassion towards us.

GLORIA PATRI
Latin: Glory be to the Father.

BENEDICAM DOMINUM IN OMNI TEMPORE
Latin: I will Bless God at all times.

IN MANUS TUAS DOMINE COMMENDO SPIRITUM MEUM
Latin: Into your Hands, O God, I commend my Soul (Spirit). (This is a prayer of total Surrender to God.)

HAGIOS O THEOS
Greek: Holy God.

LAUDAMUS TE
Latin: We Praise Thee.

Meditation on Theos

One of the early practices was simply to focus on God in the Heart. In this practice the word THEOS (God) is meditated upon in the Heart. As you say "THEOS" in your Heart you contemplate the Divine Presence.

God is the *Centre, Source* and *Origin* of all things. God is the beginning and the end (the *Alpha* and the *Omega*) of all Creation. God is both Timelessness and the Ever-Living, Eternal, Here-and-Now Moment. This is the Mystery of God. God *is* Creation, yet is *above* Creation. God is both the ever-changing shadow-play and the Changeless Light.

God is the Root and Source of your own being. Each time you say "THEOS", remember the Omnipresence which has a focus in your Heart Centre.

Let your mind dwell on the word THEOS, and let your Spirit attune to it in your Heart.

Theoleptus of Philadelphia

The ceaseless repetition of the Name THEOS in your Heart will destroy all passions—not only passions, but the *root* of all passions.

St Barsanuphius

They who meditate upon God shall renew their lives.

Isaiah 40:31

In the third and fourth centuries the Christians began to pray to Jesus Christ as God—that is, not to God the Father, or the Holy Spirit, or the Spirit, but to Jesus or Jesus Christ *as* God.

The Christians began to pray to Jesus Christ as God

Iesous
Greek: Jesus.

Iesu
Latin: Jesus.

Iesous Christos Theos Uios Sōtēr
Greek: Jesus Christ, God's Son, Saviour.

Iesus Mihi Omnia
Latin: Jesus, to me, is Everything.

Iesu Confido In Te
Latin: Jesus, I trust in You.

Christe Eleison
Greek: Christ, have Compassion on us.

From the sixth century onwards, in the Eastern Christian Tradition, the *Jesus-Prayer in the Heart* became firmly established and widely practised. It was called Iesou Evchi (Greek: Jesus Prayer), the Invocation of the Name of Jesus in the Heart *as* God.

Iesous Christos
Greek: Jesus Christ.

Kyrie Iesous Christos
Greek: Lord, Jesus Christ.

Kyrie Iesous Christos Eleison
Greek: Lord Jesus Christ have Mercy upon us.

Kyrie Iesous Christos Theos Uios Eleison
Greek: Lord Jesus Christ, God's Son, Deliver us.

Each of these mantras (prayers) are contemplated in the Heart Cakra. If you feel attracted to any one of them, sit down quietly, relax, and revolve the prayer in your Heart. You may link the prayer to the breath-process if you wish—whatever feels better for you.

Conscious Breathing in the Heart 1274
Meditations in the Heart Centre 1294

Some Eastern Christians chose to use the variations of the Jesus-Prayer in the Heart, while others continued to use the older formulas. As the centuries rolled by, some Mystics in Western Christianity (the Catholic Church) began to use only the Latin Name of Jesus, IESU (JESU, YESU), as the complete *Prayer in the Heart*. They concentrated totally on this one Divine Name. The Name of Jesus became everything to them. This was a new phenomenon, a rediscovery of the Heart by the Western Christians. Through the Divine Name IESU they discovered the Light of Knowledge in the Heart, the Fire of God, the Fire of Love, the Presence of the Holy Spirit in all Universal Manifestation, the Guiding Force of the Christ in the Heart, and the Omnipresence of God within all things and all beings. They called the Heart the LOCUS DEI (Latin: the Place of God), where Man meets God and God meets Man.

The Name of Jesus became everything to them

Many centuries rolled by in the West and along came the priestcraft again, who created a new ritual: "The Litany of the Sacred Heart of Jesus". Thus, from the *Inner Worship* of the Name of Jesus by the Mystics, it again became an *outer* worship by the priests and congregations! So it is that, in Roman Catholicism today, the Sacred Heart is called the "Heart of Jesus", with a corresponding beautiful outer ritual with many words: the Litany of the Sacred Heart of Jesus.

The Sacred Heart of Jesus 673

Thus, once again, has the Mystery of the Heart been concealed instead of revealed.

Sūfī Prayer 863
The Way of Holiness 1335
The Way of the Heart 1249

CHAPTER 33

The Christian Path

The Unfoldment of the Light

The five major stages of the unfoldment of the Nirvāṇic Light in human beings are described *symbolically* in the New Testament. These steps of Mysticism, or the Path of Christianity, are reflected in the story of Jesus the Christ:

The Path of Christianity is reflected in the story of Jesus the Christ

1. Birth (Baptism).
2. Transfiguration.
3. Crucifixion.
4. Resurrection.
5. Ascension.

This same story reflects the Inner Life of every Mystic. Jesus is a model, a pattern, a plan. Jesus, the AVATĀRA, descended from the Kingdom of the Light to remind the peoples of the Earth about the Light Kingdom, even as the Lord Buddha had done, and Śrī Kṛṣṇa, and Moses, and Rāma.

Baptism: the Birth of the Light in the Heart

Jesus: the Fire of Love 1725
The Gnostic Teachings 1108
Names of the Great Master Jesus 661

> Behold, an angel of the Lord appeared to him in a dream, saying, "Joseph, thou son of David, fear not to take unto thee Mary thy wife, for that which is conceived in her is of the Holy Spirit."
>
> *Matthew 1:20*

Jesus the Christ, or the Holy Light, is *conceived* in our Hearts by the Holy Spirit.

> She shall bring forth a son, and thou shalt call his name Jesus, for he shall save his people from their sins.
>
> *Matthew 1:21*

The Baptism of Jesus is with the Holy Spirit and Fire. This is not symbolic but actual. You feel inside you the Holy Spirit like a mighty Breath, air or wind, and you are burning with the Fiery Energy of Regeneration. The Holy Spirit appears in two forms:

- Like a Breath, air or wind.
- As Fire or radiant Energy.

The Holy Breath 1340
Meditation on the Holy Breath 1348

She (the Virgin Mary, the Heart Centre) shall bring forth a *Child of Light,* whose name is Jesus. In the original Hebrew-Aramaic gospel, this Child of Light is called YEHESHUAH, which literally means "God is the Saviour". The name *Jesus* is a corrupted form of YEHESHUAH, which also survived in the form of JOSHUAH.

> Behold, a Virgin shall be with child, and will bring forth a Son, and they shall call his Name Immanuel, which means "God is with us".
>
> *Matthew 1:23*

Immanuel actually means "God is within us". Thus, two names were given to the Christ-Child-Light in the Heart:

Yeheshuah: "the Saving Power of God" or "the Saving Grace of God". This has been corrupted over the centuries to *Jesus.*

Immanuel: "God is within us". This is the *Realization* of the Divine Presence in the Heart.

This embryonic Light of God, this little Light-Spark in the Heart, when It is *awakened* in us, will "save His people from their sins". That is, It will liberate us from our negative karmas. But this Christ-Child must be *born in our Hearts,* as that great Christian Mystic, Angelus Silesius, has said:

> If Jesus be born a thousand times in Bethlehem, it is of no use if the Christ is not born *in thee.*

Each Initiation signifies the *conquest* of a Plane of Being. Each Initiation is a new state of consciousness. You *prepare* for each Initiation by gaining control of, or subduing, that Realm of Being through meditation and spiritual practice.
Hierarchies of Life 1721

THE COSMIC PHYSICAL PLANE	*1* **Divine Realm** *Cosmic Element Ādi*	7th Initiation Sanat Kumāra	△ **The Logos**	The Universe of Spirit Eternal Realities
	2 **Monadic Realm** *Cosmic Element Aṇupādaka*	6th Initiation *A Lord*	The **Ascension** of Jesus into the Fatherhood	
	3 **Spiritual Realm** *Cosmic Element Aether*	5th Initiation *A Master*	The **Resurrection** of Jesus into the Eternal Self	
	4 **Intuitional Realm** *Cosmic Element Air*	4th Initiation *A Saint*	The **Crucifixion** of Jesus *The great Renunciation of everything below He Has Overcome*	
	5 **Mental Realm** *Cosmic Element Fire*	3rd Initiation	The **Transfiguration** of Jesus on the Mountain	The Universe of Matter Death, Transformation
	6 **Astral Realm** *Cosmic Element Water*	2nd Initiation	The **Baptism** of Jesus in the River of Jordan	
	7 **Physical Realm** *Cosmic Element Earth*	1st Initiation	The **Birth** of Jesus in Bethlehem *The Christ Born in the Cave of the Heart*	

The Divine Message of the New Testament

This is also the meaning of the word *Christmas,* a combined Greek-Latin word meaning "the making of a Christ" or "becoming an anointed one" or "becoming a Christ"—one who has been baptized in the Heart by the Light.

The personality is flooded by the Light of the Kingdom of God

> And Jesus, when He was baptized, went up straight-away out of the water, and lo, the heavens were opened up unto Him, and He saw the Spirit of God descending like a dove, and lighting upon Him. And a Voice from Heaven said to Him, "This is my beloved Son, in whom I am well pleased".
>
> *Matthew 3:16–17*

This is Baptism by the Light. The human being, the personality, is flooded by the Light of Nirvāṇa, the Light of the Kingdom of God.

> He went up out of the water [He rose above the Astral World—water is the universal symbol for the Astral Plane].
>
> And the heavens were opened up unto Him [He went up to the Causal Worlds, Devāchan].
>
> And He saw the Spirit of God descending upon Him [the Blinding Glory of the Light descended upon Him from the Throne of God, the Nirvāṇic Plane].
>
> And a Voice from Heaven said to Him, "This is my beloved Son, in whom I am well pleased." [He heard the Voice of Nirvāṇa, the Sounding-Light, which heals the personality and dissolves karmas.]

The Language of the Bible

You must understand always that the Bible was written in simple language. It is not a philosophical, metaphysical or scientific language. The authors did not know words which referred to higher planes of existence. They used the word *heaven* or *the heavens* for all non-material realms, and they simply had no words like *Nirvāṇa* or *Cosmic-Consciousness*.

They often used the word *kingdom,* for instance, to mean the Kingdom of God. But the word *kingdom* also meant the Earth kingdoms, just as *heaven* also meant the sky. They were desperately short of a spiritual vocabulary. When you read the Bible you have to understand these things, and *intuit* when the authors talk of material things and when they refer to real, inner, spiritual happenings.

Heaven 1352

Christ-Consciousness 443
Nirvāṇa: the World of Glories 93
Let Thy Will Be Done 1720

Transfiguration: the Illumination of the Head by the Light

And after six days, Jesus taketh Peter, James, and John his brother, and bringeth them up into a high mountain apart, and was transfigured before them. And His face shone like the sun, and even His clothing became radiant with Light. And behold, there appeared unto them Moses and Elias, talking with Him.

Matthew 17:1–3

This refers to the Illumination of Jesus' Head Centres. His Third-Eye and Crown Cakras were bathed with the Nirvāṇic Light.

The Path of Illumination 1338

Crucifixion: the Battle between the Personality and the Soul

And they stripped Him, and put on Him a scarlet robe. And when they had plaited a crown of thorns, they put it on His head, and a reed in His hand, and they mockingly bowed before Him, saying, "Hail, King of the Jews!" And they spit upon Him, and took the reed and smote Him on the head. And after that they mocked Him, they took the robe off Him, and put His own raiment on Him, and led Him away to crucify Him... And they crucified Him....

Matthew 27:28–35

Crucifixion is the *Test of the Spirit,* the final battle with the world, the battle of the Soul, the struggle between the Nirvāṇic Light and the dark matter and material powers of this world.

The Tests of the Elements 1159

Resurrection: the Control of the Personality by the Soul

And behold, there was a great earthquake. And an Angel of the Lord descended from Heaven and rolled back the stone from the door of the sepulchre [where Jesus was buried] and sat upon it. His countenance was like Lightning, and his clothing shone like white snow... And the Angel said unto the women, "Fear not, for I know that you seek Jesus, who was crucified. He is not here. He has risen, as He said He would...".

Matthew 28:2–6

At this stage of the Spiritual Journey, the disciple is established firmly in the Light. There is no turning back. The Spirit has conquered this Creation.

Ascension: the Union of Body, Mind and Soul with God

And it came to pass, while He blessed them [His disciples], He parted from them, and was carried up into Heaven.

St Luke 24:51

This describes the entry into Nirvāṇa, the Kingdom of God.

In the Gnostic Gospel of Thomas, Jesus is said to have said that the Kingdom of God is both within you and outside of you. This is, in fact, Universal Consciousness.

God-Consciousness 504

Baptism and Rebirth

The idea of Rebirth (not in the sense of reincarnation, but of renewal) is ancient. It was practised by all ancient religions in one form or another until it was forgotten and became just a symbolic gesture: the submerging of an adult in water or the sprinkling of water on an infant's head. To the evangelical and fundamentalist Christian, however, being "born again" means a deeply emotional conversion to a belief in the Holy Bible and in Jesus as one's Saviour. This also is but symbolic; it is not the real Rebirth. To understand the process of *Rebirth,* one has to understand the process of *birth.*

To understand the process of Rebirth, one has to understand the process of birth

- Before birth, while you lived in the Astral World and inside your mother's womb, you were connected with PRĀṆA, the Universal Radiant Life-Energy (called RUACH in Hebrew, SPIRITUS in Latin). You breathed this Life-Breath freely and unhindered, which made you feel alive, blissful, joyous, ecstatic, happy, complete.
- At the moment of your birth (that is, at the instant you took your first breath in your baby body) you effectively became *disconnected* from Universal Life, the Breath of God, and a permanent inhibition of the breath-process was established. Thus, in fact, your birth was a death, even as your death is the real birth-process.
- Your first breath established in you a sense of *duality,* of division. Instead of breathing with your whole being, you began the limited breath-process of breathing with your nostrils, left and right, causing two breath-currents to work in you: the ĪḌĀ and PIṄGALĀ, Yin and Yang, hot and cold, electric and magnetic, active and passive, male and female.
- This way of breathing effectively reduced your energies to substandard levels and the inexhaustible supply of PRĀṆA (Radiant Energy) was cut off. The feeling of the Presence of God was lost. The feeling of Conscious Immortality was lost. Imperfection and disease were established.

Nowadays there are "rebirthers" who sit in a bath tub because they mistakenly think that rebirthing has to do with water, but it has nothing to do with water, whether hot or cold, steam or ice! It has to do with PRĀṆA, "the Breath of Life".

BAPTIZEIN
Greek: Baptism. To immerse a person in water is symbolic of purification and regeneration, a common concept in all the old "pagan" pre-Christian religions. In the Mysteries, however, they had Baptism by the Holy Spirit, or Fire.

DVI-JĀ
Sanskrit: "Twice-born". Born again. One who has been initiated into the Spiritual Life. The Spiritually Reborn. This is an old pre-Christian concept.

PRĀṆA
Sanskrit: God's Radiant Life-Energy. Cosmic Life. RUACH in Hebrew, SPIRITUS in Latin, PNEUMA in Greek. All these words mean "breath, air, Life, Vitality, Spirit, Soul, God's Radiant Energy".

Dimensions of the Cosmic Fire 137
Spirit 1343

Rebirth is nothing more or less than the reconnecting of your breath-pattern to the Original Breath (PRĀṆA), the uniting of the two poles of the breath-current into the SUṢUMNA, the one Current of Life. It is the merging of the inner and the outer, the left and the right, the positive and the negative, the male and female aspects within you. It is the cessation of duality-consciousness.

In the East, for many thousands of years, this was achieved through PRĀṆĀYĀMA (breath-control) and JAPA ("taking the Name" or "calling upon God"). In Yoga parlance, the holding of the breath is called KUMBHAKA and has innumerable forms and methods. The practice of the Name is SMṚTĪ—Remembrance, Recollection of the Divine Presence. "Jesus" can become your Saviour only when you have taken His Name in your Heart and there become aware of the Divine Presence.

Jesus can become your Saviour only when you have taken His Name in your Heart

Inhalation and exhalation is stopped in KUMBHAKA, the holding of the breath. But this must not be the forced holding of the breath of the Haṭha Yogī or the holding of the breath under water of the modern rebirther. This suspension of the breath must be attained by the breath-awareness of the Divine Presence in the Heart. The forced methods present innumerable unhealthy side effects and at times even insanity.

To Call upon Jesus 679
Sex Natural and Divine 926
Haṭha Yoga and Rāja Yoga 524
Conscious Breathing in the Heart 1274
Prāṇāyāma-Vidyā 1553

Subtle Energy Currents

ĪḌĀ
Sanskrit: The subtle energy current on the left side of the SUṢUMNA or subtle spinal chord in the etheric-physical body.

PIṄGALĀ
Sanskrit: The subtle energy current on the right side of the subtle spinal chord in the etheric-physical body.

NĀḌĪ
Sanskrit: Invisible, subtle nerve currents or energy currents of PRĀṆA in the subtle bodies. (These are not the dense physical nerves.)

KUMBHAKA
Sanskrit: The restraining of the PRĀṆA energies in the central invisible nervous system.

SMṚTĪ
Sanskrit: Remembrance. Remembering God in your Heart Centre. Practising the Presence of God.
Practising the Presence of God 711

The Coming of the Christ

There are two distinct levels of understanding in Christianity about the Second Coming of the Christ, and each is correct in its own sense:

- The historical coming, at the end of the Piscean Age.
- The *inward* coming of the Christ in the Heart of the Mystic.

Cosmic Intervention 282
The Universal Christ 440
God in the Heart 634
The Initiation of the World 1712

Both themes have been developed by the early fathers, and both find validation in the scriptures. In the Gospel according to Mark, there is a dramatic passage about the coming of the Christ:

> As Jesus was sitting on the Mount of Olives, opposite the Temple, Peter, James, John and Andrew asked him privately: "Tell us when these things shall be, and what shall be the signs when all these things shall be fulfilled?"
>
> And Jesus said to them:
>
> Watch out that no one *deceives* you. For *many* will come in my Name, saying, "I Am the Christ," and will deceive many.
>
> When you hear of wars and rumours of wars, be not troubled, for such things need to come. But the end of the Age is not yet. And nations shall rise up against nations, and kingdoms against kingdoms.
>
> And there shall be earthquakes in various places, and famines, and troubles. These are the *beginnings* of the anguish ahead.
>
> Take heed for yourselves, for the powers shall deliver you up to local councils, and you shall be beaten in the synagogues… and you shall be brought before the rulers and kings for my sake….
>
> Brother will betray brother to death, and the father the son, and children shall rise up against their parents and cause them to be put to death….
>
> When you see the *abomination that causes desolation,* spoken of by Daniel the Prophet, standing where it ought not to be… flee to the mountains….
>
> For, in those days shall be affliction such as was not from the beginning of the Creation, which God created up to this time, nor shall it be again. If the Lord had not shortened those days, no one would survive.
>
> In those days, if anyone says to you, "Here is Christ," or "Look, there is Christ," *believe him not!* For false Christs and false prophets will appear and perform signs and miracles to deceive even the Elect… thus, *be on your guard!*
>
> In those days, *after* those tribulations, the Sun shall be darkened, and the Moon shall not give her light, and stars shall fall, and *the powers that are in heaven* shall be shaken.
>
> After this, they shall see the Son of Man coming in the clouds with great power and glory.

The Anti-Christ

In addition to the many "false Christs" mentioned by Jesus, we must understand the coming of the *Anti-Christ*, the Great Deception. This Great Deception will be a *staging* of the Christ, as in a great cosmic play, with "miracles" and with signs and wonders in the sky. And the millions will be deceived, for it will not, as yet, be the *real* Manifestation.

Indeed, the coming few years could be most *confusing,* and even millions of Christians will be deceived.

> Then shall he send his angels to gather his Elect from the four corners of the Earth....
>
> I tell you the truth; this race shall not pass away until all these things have happened.
>
> *Mark 13:3–30 (excerpts)*

For the moment, let us concern ourselves with the prophetic coming of the Christ at the end of the Age (not the end of the world!). The word used in the Bible is AEON, which means "an age, a world, a period of time, a cycle, a duration".

The beginning of a New Age is always traumatic for Humanity

There are many kinds of ages (aeons, or cycles of time): lesser, greater, and of vast duration. A moderate age is the *Precessional Age* of about 25,800 years, during which time our Sun, and hence our Solar System, is influenced by the belt of stars known as the *Zodiac.*

It takes our Solar Logos (the Sun) approximately 2,150 years to pass through the influence of each sign of the Zodiac. We do not want to go into vast cosmology here, but if you can imagine that our Sun is one of the Logoi that emanated from the LOGOS, the Creator, and that all of the stars are but Logoi, you will see that, naturally, as our Sun moves about in space He will come under different *influences* or *radiation-fields* from the other Logoi in space.

Who are the 'Elect'? 128
The Doctrine of the Logoi 116
The Action of the Cosmic Fire 279
Zodiacal History 833

In a sense, the end of an Age, and the beginning of a New Age, is what the Holy Scriptures call a "Judgment Day". The word *judgment* means "a period of trial, tribulation, testing; a sentence in a court of justice". Thus, the world is "judged" at the end of an Age and the beginning of a New Age.

Jesus came at the end of the Age of Aries, which was the beginning of the Age of Pisces. The past 2,150 years (approximately) were the Piscean Age (the Fish, the symbol of Jesus the Christ). Now the Piscean Age is ending and the New Age of Aquarius (the water-bearer) is beginning. This is because our Solar Logos, and with Him the whole Solar System, is coming under the influence of the group of stars known as Aquarius. It is a matter of journeying through *space* rather than through time.

Thus the Aquarian radiations are beginning to be felt throughout our Solar System, and hence upon Earth, changing, renewing, re-creating all things. The ending of an Age and the beginning of a New Age is always *traumatic* for Humanity. It is always a great opportunity or a great loss.

The Universe operates like a vast Machine, run by Intelligent Beings—the LOGOI, the ELOHĪM, the Stars—under the Supreme, Eternal, Infinite, Indescribable Godhead. God, the Absolute, is Supreme. Under God, the great Logoi perform their allocated duties in Space. Under the Logoi are vast Angelic and Spiritual Hierarchies, and under them are the Humanoid Hierarchies, including Man.

The Elohīm 120
The Cosmic Creator-Gods 162
Children of the Sun 1590

The Divine Incarnation

The Avatāra 389
The Jewish Messiah 660
The Coming of the Spirit-Guides 281
To Worship the Divine Incarnations 1270
Scenes of Battle 1158

The idea of a Messiah, or "Saviour", coming during critical times of world history is nothing new. The Hindu religion openly taught this for thousands of years. An AVATĀRA (Sanskrit) is a Divine Descent, an Incarnation of God to help the world in critical times. The Hindus count ten Avatāras *before* Christ: ŚRĪ KṚṢṆA, ŚRĪ RĀMA, and so on. The Shiite Muslims believe in IMAM MAHDI. For thousands of years the Jews also had this idea of Divine Incarnation; they called such an Incarnation MASHIAH, from MASHI-JAH, "the anointed of God".

At the end of an Epoch, and the beginning of a new one, an Incarnation takes place. An "Anointed One" again comes to call Humanity back to God at this new opportune time.

Today we are at the end of one Age and the beginning of a New Age: the Age of Aquarius. Thus, a Manifestation can be expected. However, you must read the words of Jesus carefully. He speaks of many *false* Messiahs and Christs, and they, or their followers, will proclaim that they are *the* Christ. You have to be especially wary of mediums, channellers and "transmitters", for the greatest delusion will come from the psychic realms, the Astral World. During the past 150 years there have been many mediumistic people who have claimed, or who are claiming, to be the Christ.

Apart from the Zodiacal Precession of the Ages (AEONS), there are even greater cycles of time. We are presently at the end of one of these greater cycles, each of which lasts 6,300 years. When the end of such a cycle coincides with the end of a Zodiacal Age, you can expect things to happen as described by Jesus in *Mark 13*. Obviously, something big is going to happen, or can happen. It may well be what the scriptures call the *Armageddon* (from the Hebrew HARMEGIDDON, "field of battle"). This field of battle is most likely to take place in the Middle East, around Israel and the Arab countries, involving many nations, as prophesied.

There were false Messiahs before Jesus and after Jesus, and even today there are deluded people claiming to be the Messiah. As was the saying in old Israel:

False Messiahs are born under every cloud.

If the Messiah comes, He will bring Truth with Him, real Knowledge of the Universe. For, as Jesus said:

Ye shall know the Truth, and the Truth shall make you *free*.
John 8:32

And also, as the Hasidim said:

The Truth can *bring* the Messiah down to Earth.

The Coming of Christ in the Heart

In one sense, the Second Coming of Christ means a Divine Incarnation. In another sense, however—as applied by the Mystics of the church, Eastern and Western—it refers to the coming of the Christ into your Heart, into your Soul. For, as Angelus Silesius said:

> However well of Christ you talk and preach, unless He lives *within* you, He is beyond your reach.

So the great Mystery of the Divine Incarnation is also a deep and profound *personal* Mystery. Saint Paul expressed this Mystery as:

> The Christ *in you,* your hope of Glory.
>
> *Colossians 1:27*

In truth, we should strive for the birth of the Christ *within us.* This is the teaching of all the Christian Saints, of both East and West:

> Come, my King, my Christ, sit upon the *throne of my Heart,* and from hence rule my world, for thou alone art King and God.
>
> *St Dimitri of Rostov*

> The Spirit of God must be apprehended *in us,* in the Heart.
>
> *St Seraphim of Sarov*

> Keep your attention always within yourself, in your Heart; keep your mind *in* the Heart and invoke the Christ there.
>
> *St Simeon the New Theologian*

> The Wisdom of the Spirit is superior to philosophy.... As the Gospels also say, "If a man is *in* Christ, he is a Perfect Man."
>
> *St Gregory of Palamas*

> He who would live *in Christ* must necessarily depend on the Heart.
>
> *St Gregory of Palamas*

> Now, the Lord is Spirit, and where the Spirit of the Lord is, there is Freedom.
>
> *St Jerome*

Thus you can see the two ways in which the Christ comes.

Watch and Pray!

Parousia
Greek: "The Second Coming".
For the Mystic, Parousia is the coming of the Christ into the Soul, the Divinization of the human being, the *direct experience* of the outpouring of the Universal Christ Light.

The Kingdom is at Hand 1453
Christ-Consciousness 443

Have you not *seen* the Spirit in the likeness of a dove? Have you not *heard* the Voice? And the Christ shall *baptize your Heart* with Water and the Holy Spirit.

St John Chrysostom

This Water is the *living waters* of the scriptures. The Holy Spirit is *Fire* and *Blazing Light.*

For our God is a consuming Fire.

Hebrews 12:29

Jesus Speaks…

"I have descended from the Boundless Realm of Light so that I might be able to tell you about Divine things.

The Spirit that *Is* is a Creator who has the Power to beget, to produce, so that the great abundance that is hidden in the Boundless Realm of Truth can be revealed to creatures.

Because of the compassionate and loving nature of the Infinite One, the Spirit wished to bring forth forms from the Homogeneous One so that the Unbroken Whole might not enjoy the State of Perfection alone, so that the Creative Spirits of the Unwavering Order might bring forth bodies and forms for Glory and Honour, in Everlastingness, in Unending Grace, so that the Blessings of the One Mind might be revealed by the Self-generated Son, who is the Source of Immortal Life.

A great difference exists between the Order of the Imperishables [the Order of Melchizedek] and those orders that are of the perishable realms. Whoever has ears to hear about these Boundless Mysteries, let him hear! It is only to those that are Awake that I can speak!

The Glory that *is* is ineffable. No one can *know* it. No authority, nor any creature since the foundation of the Universe, except that Glory, *knows* Itself, and to Whom It makes a Revelation by the Primordial Light-Radiance.

That First-Glory is immortal and eternal, having no birth, nor death, nor suffers any change. Every created being that has a birth, a beginning, also will have a death or an ending, but the Primal Glorious Light which is unbegotten, uncreated, has, therefore, no ending, no dying.

No creature can command this First-Glory of the Godhead, and it has no Name, for whatsoever has a name has been created by another mind. But the Primordial Splendour is unnameable, and has no form, for whatever has a form is the creation of another mind.

This First-Glory has a Face, a likeness of its own, unlike anything else that you have seen or can see in the Universe, a Glorious Countenance which surpasses all things, in a Form of Limitless Dazzling Light. It looks to every side in Space and sees only Itself. It has no conceivable boundaries and is incomprehensible to human minds. It is an Imperishable Effulgence and has no likeness in the Created Universe. It is immeasurable, traceless, imperishable, without limits. It is the Blessed One.

Melchizedek
Hebrew: "King of Light". Melchizedek was a Priest-King of ancient Israel, a King of Light, a Magician of the Light, one of the great survivors from the Atlantean line of Divine-Light Magicians of Nirvāṇa.

I desire you to know that all Mankind born on Earth, since the foundation of the world, is like dust. They inquire about God—what It is, who It is, what It is like—but they have not found the Ultimate Cause.

I have descended from the Boundless, Shoreless Worlds, and I am here so that I might speak to you concerning these Mysteries of the Truth and the Life. That which comes down from the Boundless Light is immortal, even amongst mortal Mankind. My Mind, which was enclosed in my physical body, was taken to the Highest Realms, close to the Infinite Light, and this Ineffable Splendour shone through the whole Created Universe. The Created Universe disappeared from my view and I saw only a region of Ineffable Light-Radiance. My Mind separated from the mortal body, like in a deep and profound sleep, and I heard the Great Voice of the Light speak.

In the beginning was Superessential Light and Divine Darkness, and there was the Holy Spirit between them. The Light is the Father; the Divine Dark is the Mother.

The Light, the Darkness and the Spirit were united in one Formless Form. The Light was Mind, Awareness, Consciousness and Absolute Reason. And the Darkness of the Divine Mother was upon all the Waters of Space, the Waters of the Deep. And Space was wrapped in the Invisible Fire of the Holy Spirit, and the Spirit was humble and gentle, like a soft radiance.

Mankind was created in God's likeness, but in a lesser form. In the outer, earthly men and women, only a superficial image can be seen; the Inner Light, the Hidden Countenance of God, is concealed. But this Inner Light of the Logos is revealed to all those who are the Children of the Light, Sons and Daughters of the Living Father, those who are on the Path of Light, the Path of Gnosis.

Those who follow the Light belong to the Kingdom of the Light. Those who follow the ways of materialistic darkness belong to the darkness of the rulers of this world.

When you will *see your likeness* in the Light, you will rejoice, and you shall never die."

Pure Christianity

A human being is a Child of God, an Incarnation of the Light of the Logos, the Word. This must not only be believed in, but discovered personally in this lifetime. This discovery is called *Salvation*.

The *Order of Melchizedek* is the Divine Order, the Communion of the Holy Ones, which the church *tries* to be, but of which it is only a faint shadow. True Christianity, the Order of Melchizedek, is as different from *Churchianity* as is Light from Darkness.

Visualization of the Christ in the Heart

The Christ-Being inside you has a Burning Heart

- Close your eyes and sit peacefully. Breathe evenly and relax. Switch your attention from the outer world to inside yourself. Now you are going to visualize the Christ within you.
- As you sit peacefully, imagine the Christ-Being in the same space as you, *inside you,* filling your whole body. Christ, a glorious Being, pulsating with Light, fills your whole being with Light.
- Now you are going to visualize in detail. Focus your attention in your Heart. The Christ-Being inside you has a Burning Heart. The Heart of Christ coincides with *your* Heart. See the Christ-Heart, which is in the same place as your Heart, glow with a fiery radiance. Feel the heat, the fire, the flames shooting out.
- There is also an aura of Iridescent Light emanating from the Christ-Heart. Your whole chest area is filled with Fire and Iridescent Light. It glows in your chest, shoulders, arms, fingers.
- There is a stream of Light flowing upwards from the Christ-Heart, through your throat, into your eyes, irradiating your whole head. This stream of Light makes the whole inside of your head glow. The inside of your head is lit up with a bright Light.
- This bright Light radiates out of your head in all directions, forming an aura of brilliant Light all around your head.
- Now you see your whole body, your whole being, pulsating and radiating White Light.
- Now you intuitively understand the words of the Master Jesus: "Let your Light shine before men, that they can see the good works within you, that they may glorify your Father who is in Heaven."
- Now the Light of Christ merges inside you into the Iridescent Brightness of the Father.
- Now you see the whole Universe as a Brilliant Field of Intelligent Light, without limits, without boundaries, without qualities, a vast Cosmic Intelligence of unutterable Brightness. You have reached the Kingdom of God.
- Now, slowly withdraw your attention from the Brightness of Reality. Relax. Focus upon yourself. Become aware of your body. Sit in stillness and quiet....

The Burning Heart

CHAPTER 34

The Greek Mystery Language

Learn the Things that Are

Following are some ancient Greek words which you should memorize for your greater understanding. As you learn these words, you will learn about "the things that are" and thus expand your mind.

The Greek Mysteries have had a deep influence on Christianity

The Greek Mysteries and the Greek Language have had a deep influence on Christianity since the earliest years. Hence, in order to understand Original Christianity it is most helpful to be familiar with the terms used by the Greek Mystery Schools, the Gnostics and the Eastern Christian Hesychasts.

You may recognize that many English words have been derived from these Greek words. But of course, by the time these ancient Greek words became popularized in the vernacular languages, the proper meanings became lost.

∞

Words from the Greek Mystery Schools 733
Words from Gnostic Christianity 736
Words used by the Christian Hesychasts 739

The Human Constitution (Greek) 39
Words from the Greek Mystery School 135
The Mysticism of Saint Paul 666
Greek classifications of Humanity 687
The Wisdom Language 1760

Some Words from the Greek Mystery Schools

Kosmos

The Cosmos or Created Universe in its *totality.* All seven planes of the Cosmic Physical Plane. Kosmos also means order, system, reason, logic, rule by law. This is the *nature* of the Universe.

Chaos

The Infinite Space *before* the Creation of the Universe. The *Mother Deep,* or Space filled with disordered matter *before* Creation. Chaos, in Greek, also means disorder, confusion, illogic, no-system. Hence the English words *chaos* and *chaotic.*

Aether

Space in its boundless extension, including the visible space known to science, and all the Inner Spaces of the higher dimensions. Aether, or Space, is the *Body of the Absolute.* It is from this Greek word that the English words *ether* and *etheric* are derived. Aether means the same as the Sanskrit Ākāśa. In Space there are hosts of unseen beings, worlds and universes. Space (Aether, Ākāśa) is the container of all. It contains within itself all the seven great dimensions, and everything within them. It is the physical body of God. God is in it, totally, even as you are in your physical body. *There is no empty space.* Emptiness is merely an illusion (Māyā) of the sense of sight. Space is not void or empty; it is full!

The Cosmic Elements 26

Plerōma

The Divine Fullness, the Whole, the complete Universe of seven Planes of Being, the All-in-All, the Reality, the totality of all that is, visible and invisible. The Universal Soul of all Existence, from matter to Spirit. The Great Mother, the Mother of the Universe, including all seven Planes of Being. Each of the seven great Planes of Being in the Solar System is a state of Plerōma. The Mental Plane, for instance, is the fifth state of Plerōma, while the Physical Plane is the seventh state of Plerōma. Equivalent to the Upaniṣadic Pūrṇa (Perfection, Completeness).

The Divine Milieu 12

Makrokosmos

"The larger world". The Solar System.

Mikrokosmos

"The little world". A human being.

Mikrokosmos, Makrokosmos, Chiliokosmos 121

Monad

The Indivisible One. The One. The Latin Atom or primordial unit. The ancient classical Sanskrit Aṇu. This Monad, Atom, Aṇu, can be the little world known by science as the "atom", or a human, a planet, a solar system or a galaxy; they are all atoms of various sizes. Even a galaxy is just a gigantic Atom or Monad in Omnispace, in the Plerōma, in the Universal Fullness or Reality. Remember, however, that Space stretches not only outwards, horizontally, but *inwards,* into the various dimensions, the Planes of Being.

Primordial Atoms 24

Gnosis

Knowledge, Insight, direct knowledge of Truth, Inner Revelation, Self-Realization, Soul-Communion, direct knowledge of the supersensible worlds, the knowledge of Reality as it is (not only by faith or as a belief-system). From Gnōstiko, "to know directly". Gnosis is what the Buddhists call *Insight.* It is a non-verbal, non-intellectual, direct perception of higher realities. It is non-rational knowledge—knowledge from *above* the ordinary mind. In India this would be called Ātmā-Vidyā and Brahma-Vidyā.

Gnōstikos

"One who is good at intuitive perception". A Seer. One who knows Spiritual Truth by direct, inner experience. Hence the word *Gnostic.*

Sophia

Spiritual Wisdom, Primordial Wisdom, the Soul of the Universe, the Divine Mother Power, the Transcendental Consciousness in Humanity (what in the East is called Buddhi).

What is Wisdom? 1685

Mysteria
Things that are hidden. The Great Invisible Universe, the Divine Mysteries, the Esoteric Knowledge learned in Mystery Schools.

Physis
Nature on the Physical Plane. Hence the English word *physical* and *physics*. The same as the Latin Natura (Nature).

Pneuma
Spirit, Breath, Wind, the Universal Soul, the Great Breath, the Life-Force, the Holy Spirit, the Virgin-Spirit of the Universe. Hence, the English word *pneumatic*.

Spirit 1343

Theos
God, the Creator.

Hierophantēs
"Revealer of the Sacred Mysteries". From Hiero, "sacred, holy, religious, mysterious, belonging to the knowledge of the priestcraft", and Phantes, from Phainein, "to show, to reveal, to expound". The Guru, the Spiritual Master (as depicted in Tarot Key 5). From this Greek word we have the English word *hierophant,* "a religious teacher, an expounder of religious rites". Today the word *hierophant* has become degenerated to mean an ordinary religious teacher, such as a pope, a bishop, a priest or a clergyman, but in the Greek Mystery School it had the deeper meaning of the Guru or Master who speaks not just from faith or belief, but from *direct inner experience* of the Truth (Gnosis).

The Mystery Schools and Āśramas 1148

Christos
"The Anointed One". The Christ, a Teacher of Teachers, the Saviour, Grace, the Universal Christ-Principle, the "Judge of the living and of the dead" (those in physical bodies and those in the "afterlife"). In the old "pagan" Mystery Schools, a Christos was one who had attained the highest state of Union with God possible for a human being. The Christians borrowed this term from them.

Names of the Great Master Jesus 661

Chrēstos
One who inspires you to follow the Truth. Note the similarity with Christos, the Christ, which means "the Anointed One" or "filled with the Holy Spirit".

Logos
Literally, "a word, an idea, a speech" (from Legein, "to speak"). To the Greek Mystery Schools, however, the Logos meant the Creative Word of God, the Universal Creative Intelligence, the Wisdom of God as a *Power,* the Source of Creation, the Cosmic Fatherhood, the Source of all things. The Christians borrowed this idea from the Greeks.

The Logos: the Word of God 114

Theologia
From Theo-Logia, "the Knowledge of God". The same as the Sanskrit Brahma-Vidyā. A Theologian was one who had attained Nirvāṇic Consciousness, the Kingdom of God. From this we have the degenerated words *theology* and *theologian.* Nowadays, most theologians do not have a direct knowledge of God, and some do not even believe in God!

Theosophia
From Theo-Sophia, "God's Wisdom". The experiential knowledge of Buddhi and the planes above. A Theosophos was an Enlightened Being, a Sage, a Wiseman or Wisewoman. From this we have the English words *theosophy* and *theosophist.*

Philosophia
From Philo-Sophia, "the Love of Wisdom". *Wisdom* is on the Buddhic Plane, perceived by the Spiritual Soul. A Philosophos was an Initiate who had Buddhic Consciousness. From this we have the degenerated English words *philosophy* and *philosopher.*

Hairesis
The ability to choose. To have an open mind. From this we have the English word *heresy,* "an opinion or doctrine at variance with the orthodox view". The *heretics* were those who had an open mind and did not swallow the false doctrines of the church.

The Heretics 655

Orthodoxos

From Ortho, "correct, true", and Doxa, "thought, idea, opinion". Thus, in the Mystery Schools, the word Orthodoxos meant "having acquired the right understanding of Life and Reality". From this we have the degenerated English word *orthodox,* "conforming to a philosophy or ideology, approved by the paralysed thought-system of the church". (Note that the beliefs or attitudes approved by the church in ignorance, or with immobilized thought-patterns, usually do not conform to Truth at all!)

Correct Belief? 653

Honoma

The "Name" or "Sound-Vibration". The same as the Sanskrit word Nāma.

Onomatopoeia

"A sound which stands for Revelation". The Greek equivalent of the Sanskrit word Mantra. The Greek word Hōnoma (Hōnyma) means "a name, a sound, a word" or "the Name or Sound-Vibration". Poiein means "to produce, to make, to become". Thus, Onomatopoeia means "a word or sound-vibration which was created to reveal itself (its hidden meaning, which imitates or reveals something)".

Idea

From the Greek Idein, "to see something". The original form or pattern of a thing. A causal form on the Higher Mental Planes (the Causal Worlds) imbued with energy and power. An Archetype in the Divine Mind. An eternal thought which will become manifest in "the things that are". For example, Man, the planets, the stars and the galaxies are Ideas of the Divine Mind which become *manifest* (tangible on this Physical Plane). From this we have the degenerated English word *idea* (a thought, a notion, a thoughtform, a thought-construct, mental force, mental understanding, a conception arising in the human mind). Creation or Manifestation takes place according to Cosmic Ideas. A human being also creates or manifests his or her life according to his or her ideas.

Ideas and Archetypes 138

Archetipon

Archetype. The first model of things in the Cosmic Mind, the *subtlest* forms of things. What we would call *Causal Plane forms,* out of which all denser forms are manifested or created. From Arche, "original, first, archaic", and Tipon, "mode, pattern".

Idealogy

"The Science of the Archetypes". The knowledge of the thoughts in God's Mind. Nowadays, *ideology* refers to the different political, theological, philosophical or metaphysical ideas of Humanity.

Idiology

"Self-thinking". From the Greek Idios, "the concrete mind, reason and logic, *human* thoughts and perceptions from the lower mental worlds". From this we have the English words *idiot, idiotic* and *idiom.* It is a sublime irony that one's own thoughts (when not aligned with the Archetypes in the Divine Mind) are quite idiotic! The disadvantage of the lower mind is that all mental systems are paralysed thoughts by reason of their rigidity and immobility. There is a positive side, however: mental systems put facts into the right sequence and logical order, into their right relationships, thus assisting orientation.

Episteme

Ordinary mental knowledge. Hence the English word *epistemology,* the science of mental knowledge.

Pistis

Faith, belief, ordinary religion. The power of faith in the Divine. Hope for Glory in the Godhead.

Greek classifications of Humanity 687

Phainomenon

"What is seen". The physical universe, or the universe of sense-perception. From this we have the English word *phenomena.*

Noumenon

"What is thought". The invisible Universe around us and in us. From this we have the English word *noumena.*

Words from Gnostic Christianity

Some early Christian Gnostic words from the first to the fourth century.

Monad ⊙
The One, the Divine Father Power, the Point, the Original Atom, the Seed of the Universe.

Duad ⊕
The Two, the Father-Mother, the Line, the first Pair or Duality at the beginning of Creation. Mother, ⊖, and Father, ⦶, unite to form the Mother-Father, ⊕.

Triad ◬
The Trinity, the triangle, Father-Mother-Child, Generation, the Original Perfection of the Universe, the Spirit, the Archetypal World. In Humanity, the Triad is the Spirit, the Soul and the Higher Mind.

Tetrakti □
The Four, the Quaternary, matter, the lower aspects of Creation. The lower four in Creation and in Humanity. In the human being, it is the physical, etheric, astral and mental bodies. Together, the Tetrakti and the Triad constitute the Sacred Seven, or the Law of Seven.
The Compound Human Being 32

Pentad, Pentagram ☆
The five-pointed star. The mind, the ordinary mental faculty, the personal mind, the seeking mind, the power-driven mind. (*Not* the Divine Mind, Nous.)

Hexalpha, Hexad ✡
The union of Spirit and Matter, of Life and Form, of the lower, ▽, and the higher, △, *in* the Heart of things, whether the human Heart Centre or the Cosmic Heart.

Syzygie
What in the East would be called Śakti, the "Female-Energy-Power". The companion or opposite to the Male-Energy-Powers of the Universe.
Śakti: the One Energy 150

Barbelo
The Divine Mother. The Virgin of Light. What the Jews used to call Shekinah (the Feminine Divine Presence). What in the East is called Śakti.

Prunikos
The All-Mother, *after* the Conception of the Universe.

Bythus
The Primordial Deep, the Root, the Unmanifest Condition before Creation.

Aphtarsia
The Indestructible. The Imperishable.

Kenoma
The Void, the Emptiness, the Unmanifest Condition. The same as the Sanskrit Śūnyatā.

Autogenes
Born out of one's self. Self-produced. From Auto, "self", and Genes, "born, produced". The same as Autogenetos. Refers to the Father, the Unmanifest Godhead, which has no parents, which is not a product of previous causes. The Union of the Father-Mother Principle produces the Autogenes-Christos, the Self-born Universal Light of the Christ, the "Son".

Monogenes
One-born. Born from the One (Mono-Genes). The church interpreted this to mean "only-begotten". Originally, the Greek word referred to the Second Logos, the Universal Christ-Principle. The later church made it to mean the historical Incarnation of Jesus Christ. Nowadays, the fundamentalist Christians (the Evangelicals, the Pentecostals and the Protestant sects) refer this term to the *personality* of Jesus, saying that Jesus is the "only Son of God", that God has no other children but Jesus.
The Only Son of God? 669

Logos
The Word, the Sound of God, the Universal Creative Energy, the Universal Creative Sounding-Light Vibration, the Universal or Cosmic Christ, the Cause, Divine Reason, God as the Creator.
The Logos: the Word of God 114

Dynamis
Motion, Power, Energy in the Cosmos. The Dynamis of the Universe is an inexhaustible source of Power, Energy and Radiance. Hence the English words *dynamic* and *dynamo.* Equivalent to the Tibetan Fohat.
The Cosmic Fire 130

Zoe
The Primordial Life-Force, the Prāṇa or Life-Energy in all things.

Aionia Zoe
Eternal Life, Eternity, the true Being, God as God is.

Ennoia
A thought, an idea, a concept, whether in the human mind or in the Divine Mind. Also, the Virgin-Father, the Father before Fatherhood.

Aletheia
The Law, the Truth, the original Divine Plan.

Ekklesia
The Spiritual Hierarchy, composed of Angelic and Human Hierarchies. The invisible Hierarchies of Spiritual Beings. The later Christians degenerated this word to mean the physical, human organization called the "church".
Who are the 'Elect'? 128

Anthropos
Man (the Human Hierarchy).

Homopneumata
"The same spirits". Souls having the same qualities, interests, or vibrations. Kindred Souls. The Disciples. From Homo, "the same, likeness", and Pneumata, "spirits".

Nous
Higher Mind, Consciousness, Intelligence.

Physis
Matter, substance, the gross Creation.

Archon
A ruler of a plane, realm, layer or world of the total Universal Manifestation. A lesser ruler or spiritual intelligence.

Aeon, Aion
Space (All-Space), Time, an Age, a cycle of Manifestation, a cycle within Time, a Creative God, a Ruler or Power that emanated from the Supreme Godhead. A Ruler of a realm of Space, or of a cycle of Time, or of a realm, a world or a plane. Thus, Aion can mean Eternity, an Age, Space, a realm and a being.
Rulers in High Places 657

Aeonian, Aionios
The Eternal One, the Timeless, the Transcendental Reality, the Everlasting, God the Unmanifest *(beyond* Creation).

Heimarmene
"The compulsion of the stars". Astrology, astrological influences, the influences of the Zodiac, the impact of the Cosmos on the planet Earth and in the lives of Humanity.
Destined by the Stars? 260

Psyche
The Soul. That which *indwells* the physical body. That which does not die at "death". The immortal part in Humanity.

Psychostasia
"The weighing of the Soul" (putting the Soul on a scale). Karma, Justice, the Law of Cause and Effect.

Hierosgamos
Mystical Marriage, Mysticism, the Union of the Soul with God, the Union of matter and substance with Spirit and Life.

Gnosis
Spiritual Knowledge, Insight, Realization gained through meditation and inner Revelation, God communicating with Man, the Wisdom of the Soul.

Gnōstikos
A Gnostic, a Realized person, an Enlightened One, one who Knows.
The Gnostics 645

Hermes
A Wise Teacher, a Master, an Adept.

Morphe
Form, body, vehicle.

Eidolon
The shadow, the image, the double, the duplicate. The astral body or "spirit-body".

Augoeides
"The star-like body". The Radiant Body of the Soul. The causal body, within which the Living Soul dwells upon the upper regions of the Mental Plane. More generally, a radiating or heavenly body, whether human, angelic, planetary or cosmic.

Aurora
The Aura. The invisible emanations, influences and atmosphere emanating from a person or an object. Esoterically, the movement or radiation of Prāṇas (life-forces) from a person, the subtle currents around a person.
The Human Aura 42

Prognosis
Knowing in advance, foreknowledge, insight into the future, knowing the Divine Plan. From Pro, "before", and Gnosis, "knowledge".

Pronoia
Thinking ahead, planning for the future, looking ahead of things. Divine Providence (the Divine as *providing* for the Universe). From Pro, "before", and Noia, "thought".

Epinoia
Thinking upon, magical thinking, creative thinking, directed thinking, purposeful thinking.

Annoia
Delusion, ignorance, glamour, illusion, unreality. Mundane consciousness. Also, the Divine Unknowing or Unmanifest. The same as the Sanskrit Māyā.
Māyā 2

Metanoia
"Changing or renewing the mind". Mind Re-Creation. Acquiring Wisdom and Insight. Meditational experience, growth in mental understanding, mental transformation.
What is Metanoia? 1412

Logion, Logia
Mantras, sayings, utterances, axioms, words of power, spiritual truths, principles.

Eirene
Peace, tranquillity, which are necessary for spiritual life.

Charis
Divine Grace. Later, it also came to mean "charity" and "good-will towards others".

Synesis
Insight, Intuition, direct understanding of the Truth.

Phronesis
Wisdom, prudence. A regulated life.

Aisthesis
Perception. To receive impressions through the mind and the senses.

Anastasis
Resurrection into the New Life.

Greek Words used by the Christian Hesychasts of the 4th to 15th Centuries

Now we will look at some of the Greek terms used by the Byzantine Christians of the fourth century onwards. The understanding of these words will help you to understand the Pure Christianity, or Christian Mysticism, of the Eastern Orthodox Tradition.

Hesychia
Union with God in silence. Solitude, inner tranquillity, stillness. The complete silence of body, mind and emotions. The absence of discursive thinking, being without thoughts. Not only non-talking, but what, in the East, is called mental equilibrium, equipoise, tranquillity. The state of *quiet*.

Hesychasm
Living a life of inner calm, quiet, composure, stillness and contemplation. Developing mental stillness and quiet in order to attain Union with God. Suspending mental activities.
Interior Prayer 691

Hesychast
A person leading a quiet, contemplative life in the deserts of Egypt, Syria, North Africa or Palestine from the fourth century onwards. A monk or a nun (rare) of the early Christian Church. A dweller in the desert, a renunciate, a hermit. One who leads a solitary, isolated life, cut off from Humanity and even from other Hesychasts. A person who has attained the *wordless state of prayer* (one who has a still mind and communes with God in silence).
Christian Mysticism 450

Monos
"One who lives alone". One who is alone in the desert, a solitary one, an ascetic living by himself or herself in isolation, an anchorite. Hence the English words *monastery* and *monk*.

Heremites
A recluse. One who has retired from the world and lives in solitude in the desert. From Heremos, "a desert, a desolate and lonely place, a solitary abode". Hence the English words *hermit* and *hermitage*.

Asketikos
A hermit, a recluse, one who is retired from the world. One who undergoes severe self-denials. One who is engaged in severe self-discipline, spiritual exercises, austerities, mortifications, and so forth. Also, Askesis, "training yourself". Hence the English words *asceticism* and *ascetic*.

Cenobites
"Living together". A group of anchorites, hermits and recluses living together in a loose community in the deserts of Syria, Egypt and Palestine. In the early centuries of Christianity there were renunciates who lived by themselves, totally alone in the desert, and others who lived in loosely connected groups.

Abbas
An elder. A saintly old man of the desert, usually addressed as "father". From this came the English word *abbot*, which in later centuries was the name given to the head of a monastery.

Mysterion
A Mystery. The Mystery is something *hidden* from the uninitiated, but *seen* by the Knower. From the verb Myein, "to close your eyes and ears", as was the custom in the old pre-Christian Mystery Schools: "Close your eyes and ears to this world so that you might see and hear the Invisible." This has been the basis of all meditational processes, Eastern and Western, orthodox and unorthodox, Christian and non-Christian. The Greek word Mysterion was used several centuries before Christianity, and the early Christian fathers adapted it to their new faith. "God is a Mystery", they said, meaning that God is hidden from the view of mortal eyes and inaudible to mortal ears. "For no one has *seen* the Father at any time" (that is, no mortal!).

Sophia
Wisdom. To the ancient Masters, Wisdom did not mean just being clever, worldly-wise, learned or intellectual. Wisdom is an Energy Stream. Wisdom is the *Breath of the Power of God* and a *Mighty Influence from the Radiance of the Almighty.*
Sophia 146

Philosophia
"The Love of Wisdom", from Philo, "love of", and Sophia, "Wisdom". From this came the English word *philosophy,* but in those days it did *not* mean what it means today—merely intellectual verbiage! The task of Wisdom is to encourage the mind to be in strict watchfulness of the thought-processes, to establish firmness in mind, tranquillity and spiritual contemplation. To the early practising hermits, *Wisdom* was what, in the East, is called Buddhi. It is Higher Consciousness. A Philosophos was a Wiseman or Wisewoman, with Higher Consciousness.
The Love of Wisdom 1694

Theos
God. God is the *Centre, Source* and *Origin* of all things. God is the beginning and the end (the Alpha and the Omega) of all Creation. God is both Timelessness and the Ever-Living, Eternal, Here-and-Now Moment. This is the Mystery of God. God *is* Creation, yet is *above* Creation. God is both the ever-changing shadow-play and the Changeless Light.

Theosophia
"The Wisdom of God". Divine Wisdom. From Theos, "God", and Sophia, "Wisdom". This is the *direct experience* of Wisdom, what in the East would be called *Buddhic Consciousness.*

Theosis
Union with God. The Deification of the Human Soul. Attaining Divine likeness. Conscious Immortality. This, of course, is also the goal of Yoga, Sūfīsm, Jewish Hasidism, Zen, Taoism and Buddhism. *When the mind perceives the Holy Spirit in full consciousness, we realize that Grace is beginning to paint the Divine Likeness over the Divine Image within us.*

Theologia
The Science of God-Realization. From Theos, "God", and Logos, "God as the Creative Principle, the Divine Word or Wisdom, the Divine Discourse or Reason". The origin of the English word *theology.* In the early centuries of Christianity, however, theology was not just a set of intellectual ideas and dogmas as it is today. It was the *direct realization* of Divine Realities, the *inner perception* of the Spiritual Realms and Hierarchies through the processes of prayer, meditation and contemplation. Similarly, to *theologize* means to have flashes of inner Insight. From the first to the fourth centuries, this Science was known as Gnosis.

Theologian
"A Knower of God by experience". To the early Hesychasts of the deserts, a Theologian was a saintly person who *experienced* some degree of Divine Consciousness.
Theologia, Theologian 625

Theosophos
A Sage. One who is wise *in* God. A man or woman of God. One who is filled with the Spirit of God. From Theos, "God", and Sophos, "a Wiseman or Wisewoman". Hence the English word *Theosophist.*

Theotokos
"One who bringeth forth God". The same as the *Virgin Mary* concept in Western Christianity. From Theos, "God", and Tokos, "to bring forth, to manifest".

Theophainesthai
A manifestation or appearance of God in a mystical vision, in Ecstasy, or in an interior Revelation.

Apotheosis
Union with God, becoming One with God, the Divinization of the Human Soul, God-Consciousness, God-Realization. The goal of Christian meditational practice.

Pneuma
The Holy Spirit. The Spirit of God. The Breath of God.
Dimensions of the Cosmic Fire 137

Deipara
The Mother of God.

Iesous
The Greek source of the English word *Jesus.*
Names of the Great Master Jesus 661

Christos
"An Anointed One". A High Priest of the Mysteries. The Universal Christ Light, the Second Logos. From this came the English word *Christ.*
The Cosmic Christ 662

Monogenes
"Alone born". The first-born, the singly-born, the born-without-another. A term used by the Ancient Greeks for the Cosmic Christ, the Cosmic Logos, the Cosmic Word. This term was distorted by the later Christians to refer to the *personality* of Jesus, yet it was well known to the Greeks long before Jesus was born.
The Only Son of God? 669

Parousia
"The Second Coming". For the Mystic, Parousia is the coming of the Christ into the Soul, the Divinization of the human being, the *direct experience* of the outpouring of the Universal Christ Light.
The Coming of Christ in the Heart 727

Gnosis
Inner Revelation by the Logos, or the Christos, or the Holy Spirit (Pneuma). An Omniscient Energy-Radiation of the Godhead, contacted in deep meditation by the Christian Saint. The direct, experiential knowledge of the Kingdom of God *within.* Spiritual perception. Inspiration.

Gnosis Theou
The direct experiential knowledge of God. Enlightenment by the Divine Light of Christ. The annihilation of the personal self (the personality) and the Deification of the Soul. The supersensual experience of the Presence of God. Spiritual Ecstasy. Union with God. Experiencing degrees of Divine Consciousness through the inner senses.

Monad
The Divine I AM in Humanity. "Your Father in Heaven". The I AM Presence in the innermost depths of the Soul. The overshadowing of Humanity by the Divine Presence at the highest point of Spirit. The God-Self in Humanity. The Monad *cannot* be perceived by the personality, for "no man has seen the Father at any time". It is the individualized God-Being in *You,* not in your personality! It is *not* your personal Saviour! It is not your *personality* redeemer. The Monad, "your Father in Heaven", redeems your *Soul.* It is "the Truth of the Lord God within you", dwelling in your Soul. The Monad is the image of God in the human being, while the Christos is the intermediary Light between the Father and your Soul. The Monad is God *individualized* in each human being. It is the image of Perfection, "the image and likeness of God".

Psyche
The Soul. The immortal part in a human being, what is called the Reincarnating Ego, in the causal body on the Causal Plane, above the personality complex.
Jīva: the Human Soul 35

Psychelogia
"The Science of the Soul". The study of the attributes of the Soul, the non-material part of Humanity. From this is derived the English word *psychology,* though for many years psychology did not study the Soul, but merely physical reactions and emotional states.
Science of the Soul? 291

Epignosis
"Spiritual Knowledge". Illumination. According to the Saints, only *Illumination* can bring true peace in the world, as "the sweetness of God destroys the bitterness of quarrel". Thus, Humanity has to become God-centred, Illumined by God's Light, before true peace on Earth becomes possible. Each man and woman must attain this great jewel of Illumination—the *Pearl of Great Price.* According to Saint Diadochos, perfect Love can come only to those Souls who have already been purified, who experience a constant *burning* and *uniting* of the Soul to God, by the Fire of the Holy Ghost, acting through the Heart.

Propheteia
The origin of the English words *prophecy* and *prophesy.* To *prophesy,* in the Old Testament sense, and to the Eastern Christians, the Byzantine Church, meant "to speak by Divine Inspiration, to be moved to speak by the Holy Spirit, to utter Divine Mysteries as moved by the Spirit, to interpret by Inspiration the inner meanings of the scriptures, to preach the Gospel by the power of the Holy Ghost, to reveal the hidden Mysteries of the Kingdom of God *within*".

Prophetes
Someone who knows the Will of God, the *Plan,* through an interior Revelation. One who speaks for God, the Deity. An inspired *revealer* or *interpreter* of the Divine Will, the Divine Plan. From this came the English word *prophet.* A Prophet, in the Old Testament sense, and to the early Christians, was one who could speak on behalf of the Deity.
The Prophets 647

Logikos
True Intelligence. Spiritual in perception. Hence the English words *logic* and *logical.* To the classical Greeks and early Christians, the word Logikos meant to be intelligent in the *true* sense of that word—not to be merely rational, but rather, to be *spiritual* in perception. One who is Logikos possesses Divine Intelligence.

Logiki-Psyche
"Logical Soul". A Deified Soul. A spiritualized human being, possessed of spiritual experience. According to Saint Anthony the Great, "Intelligent people are not those who are learned or who can read books, but those who have an intelligent Soul."

Diakrisis
Spiritual Wisdom. The power to discern spirits, the power to discern thoughts, the power to distinguish between what is real and essential and what is unreal and passing. From this was derived the English word *discrimination.* According to the early meaning of the Desert Fathers, however, discrimination was a *spiritual* faculty. It is the same as the Sanskrit idea of Viveka.

Plani
Illusion, delusion, material bondage, spiritual ignorance, worldly consciousness. Being bonded to materialistic, physical consciousness, and not being aware of one's Soul-Nature. The same as the Sanskrit Māyā.

Pistis
Faith. To the early Christian Masters, faith was not only a matter of *belief* in God, but a total transformation or reorientation of one's life towards God.

Dianoia
The ordinary lower mind, the reasoning faculty, the objective mind, the conceptualizing mind. The discursive, thinking mind, considered by the early Christian Saints to be an inferior faculty.

Nous
The Divine Intelligence, the Mind of God. Also, the Spiritual Mind in Man, the Higher Mind, the Intellect, in the old classical sense! In the old sense, Nous, or Intellect, had a *spiritual* meaning, which nowadays has been lost. To the classical Greeks and early Christians, Intellect was "the eye of the Soul", "the depth of the Soul", what in modern terminology is called the *Higher Mind*, the *Abstract Mind* or *Causal Consciousness.* From Nous was derived the English word *noetic,* which means "intellectual"—in the *original* sense. Nowadays, an intellectual is someone who is full of ideas and thoughts.

Noisis
Abstract thinking. Pure intellection (in the classical sense), where spiritual realities are comprehended intuitively.

Noitos
Intuitive, direct perception by the mind.

Metanois
A change of perception, a changing of the mind, a renewing of Consciousness, a change of perspective, attaining a different viewpoint, the transformation of the mind, a mental revolution. To be reborn into a new Consciousness.

Metanoia
"To renew one's mind". From Meta, "beyond, above, after, transformation, transference, in the midst of, amongst, in between", and Noia, "thought". The New Testament translators interpret Metanoia to mean *repentance,* which means to feel sorrow, regret or sadness for one's sins. But Metanoia does *not* mean repentance. To the early Christians, this word was *not* associated with sin, but rather with the need for changing one's mind, one's thoughts—to have a new mind, a new way of thinking about things, a rebirth into a Higher Consciousness. There is no sense of sin or morbidity in the original Greek word. To the Saints it means "to renew one's mind in God".

Repentance 683

Catharsis
Intense physical, emotional and mental purification. The violent purging of the mind and emotions, freeing oneself of images, ideas and thoughts.

Praktiki
Purificatory disciplines. Self-discipline. Practising *consciously* the virtues as aids to the spiritual life. The English derivation, *practical,* no longer refers to the spiritual life; nowadays it pertains to action, worldliness, practising something physical, being "a man of the world", and so forth.

Doxa
"Praise, adoration, an opinion". Glory. Divine Effulgence. From Dokein, "to think".

Doxologia
Praising and glorifying God through chanting, singing, dancing. From Doxa, "praise, adoration", and Logos, "a word, an idea, a speech".

Monology
The constant repetition of a mantra or prayer. This is the same concept as the Eastern Mantra-Japa. A Monology can be the repetition of any of the Divine Names—such as *Jesus,* or *Jesus Christ,* or *Lord, Jesus Christ*—repeated over and over in the Heart, and contemplated upon.

Parrisia
"Talking to God". Inner Communion with God. This is *not* the same as how some of the fundamentalist and evangelical Christians "talk to God"—talking verbally or mentally to God as an old man sitting on a throne in heaven, which is, most of the time, talking to themselves. This *Inner Communion with God* is possible for the Saints only after years of meditation and inner development. They have to be in the condition known in the East as Buddhi—Enlightened, Intuitive—which is *not* a verbal-mental consciousness.

Mnimi Theou
"Remembrance of God". This has several layers of meaning. The simplest, of course, is prayer or meditation on God in the Heart. But, as you progress, this *Remembrance of God* acquires greater and greater reality. It is the cornerstone of the Jewish, Christian and Islamic (Muslim) religions.

Kardia
The Heart. Hence the English word *cardiac,* referring to the physical heart organ. To the early Greeks and Christians, however, the Heart (Kardia) meant more than just the physical heart organ. The Heart is the *Spiritual Centre* of the human being. In it may be found the image of God, a reflection of the Divine Godhead. A Divine Mystery is concealed in the human Heart. In the Heart, the human creature and God the Creator meet, commingle and unite.

The Christian Heart-Path 632

Phylaki Kardias
"The guarding of the Heart". The most important practice of the Christian Saints of the Eastern Tradition. This is done by constantly invoking a Divine Name in the Heart.

Phylaki Nou
"The guarding of the mind". This, after *the guarding of the Heart,* is the next most important practice: watching over our thoughts, day and night, being constantly *aware* of all that goes on in our minds, and consciously resisting any evil impulses in our minds. This is similar to the Buddhist practice of *mindfulness.*

Iesou Evchi

The Jesus Prayer. The constant invocation of the Divine Name of Jesus in the Heart. Variations are: Jesus; Christ; Jesus Christ; Christ Jesus; Lord Jesus; Lord, Jesus Christ; Lord, Jesus Christ, Son of God; and so on.

The Great Greek Mantra to Jesus 708

Theoria

Contemplation. Meditation. Inner spiritual discipline of the mind, or a method of spiritual practice. In a more specific sense, the Saints understood Theoria as "an Inner Vision of the Primeval Light of God; the flooding of the upper regions of the mind (the root of the mind) with Light or Transforming Fire; the contemplation of the Inexpressible Light; the Union of the Soul to God by the Energy of God's Light; deep, inner Spiritual Knowledge". The lowest form of Theoria (contemplation) is the vision of the essences or energies beyond physical Creation, of the subtle worlds, such as the heavens and hells. But the objective of the Hesychast is the contemplation of God Him/Herself. From this came the English word *theory,* which nowadays has a radically different meaning: speculation, guessing, conjecture, hypothesis, a point of view. How things change!

Charisma

Divine Grace, Divine Power or Gift. The power of producing miracles, miraculous powers. Hence the English words *charisma* and *charismatic*.

Eros

Intense desire, aspiration or longing for Union with God or Ecstasy. Saint Evagrios the Solitary interprets Eros as intense Love of God: "Eros transports the mind to the spiritual realms". To the pre-Christian Greeks, Eros meant Love, and Eros was the god of Love (the Latin name of which was *Cupid).* From Eros came the English word *erotic,* which nowadays refers to sexual passion. To the classical Greek Sages, however, and to the early Christian Saints, Eros meant spiritual-passionate Love, or Unitive Love, or Love through inner desire.

Agape

Universal Love. Spiritual Love. Platonic Love. Transcendental, almost impersonal Love.

Philia

Brotherly, sisterly and family love. Friendship.

Terms of Love 914

Ekstasis

"Going out of oneself". From this came the English word *ecstasy.* Ekstasis is not the mediumistic trance, nor the "channelling" or "transmitting" processes of today's mediums. Ecstasy is *not* psychic; it is a *spiritual* phenomenon. Ecstasy is *not* madness, nor is it a psychological or mental disease. The body of the ecstatic Saint may become temporarily paralysed or immobile, and the normal, objective, wakeful consciousness (the rational faculty) may also be suspended for a while. To the Hesychasts of Eastern Christianity and the Mystics of the Roman Church, Ecstasy was a by-product of intense interior meditation or prayer. Ecstasy, according to the Christian Saints, is a sign of being near to God. Saint Diadochos defines Ecstasy as "losing awareness of oneself by a total going out towards the Divine". In other words, you, the personality, is forgotten, and you, the Soul, is remembered. Ecstasy is a condition that is non-verbal, non-intellectual, non-thinking. It is what the Eastern Yogīs call Samādhi.

The Path to Ecstasy 696

Agnosia

Nescience, spiritual darkness, spiritual blindness or ignorance, worldly consciousness. From A-Gnosia, "not knowing". The opposite of Gnosis. Hence the English word *agnostic*. There is, however, a higher meaning of the word Agnosia—a *Spiritual Unknowing.* Saint Damascius says that at a very high stage of Mystical Union we perceive the Unknowable Darkness, beyond all mind and thought actions, a Darkness which is, in fact, a super-abundant Light of God, too dazzling for even the eyes of the Soul to contemplate. This is *Contemplation by Unknowing.*

Clouds of Unknowing 704

Hidoni

Pleasure. Delight. The lowest form of pleasure is, of course, sensual. The next is intellectual, as in true knowledge or understanding. But the highest form of delight is in God or Divine Consciousness.

Lypi

Sorrow, contrition, repentance. Being sorry for one's imperfections.

Philokalia

"The Love of the true, the beautiful, the good" (Philo-Kalia). The striving for Perfection. *Walk in the Spirit and you will not walk in the ways of the flesh.*

Pathos

Passions, strong emotions, vehement feelings. Hence the English words *pathology, pathos* and *pathetic*. Pathology is the study of physical diseases and illnesses, whereas the original Greek word refers to passions, feelings, desires and emotional states—*not* to the physical body!

Apatheia

Dispassion. Spiritual freedom. Liberation from human nature. "Walking like an angel" or "being continually in the Light of God". The opposite of Pathos (passion). From this was derived the English word *apathy,* which means "being without feelings towards a person, object, or event; being insensible or indifferent; being passionless or disinterested". To the classical Greeks and Christian Saints, however, Apatheia was a sought-after spiritual quality; there was nothing morbid in it. It is a state of detachment from the world, but *not* an indifference to things.

Passion and Dispassion 695

Satanas

The word Satanas, which the Greeks borrowed from the Hebrew Satan, simply means "an enemy, an adversary, an opposition, one who plots against you, a tempter". Hence the English word *Satan,* nowadays called "the Devil". By this broad definition, the word *Satan* may be translated simply as "the enemy".

What is 'the Devil'? 684

Peirasmos

Tests, trials, that by which the genuineness of anything may be determined. Commonly translated by scholars as "temptations". The Old Testament Jewish idea was that sometimes God sends tests or trials to Man, even tempts a person to see how genuine is his or her fidelity to God. This is an incorrect understanding. It is more the other way around; men and women test themselves by mismatching themselves to the Radiant Glory of God. When we better understand the Law of Cause and Effect (Karma in the East, and "as you sow, so shall you reap" in the Bible), then we realize that most evils that come to us are the results of our own wrongdoings—conscious or unconscious.

Tested by God and the Devil? 685

Hamartia

This is the Greek word that the scholars and theologians so morbidly translate as "sin". The word *sinner* has acquired, in Christianity, a very unhealthy connotation. But the Greek word actually means "to miss the mark, to miss the point, to go astray, to make a mistake, to falter or fail, to make an error". There is no sense of "eternal hell-fire and damnation" in it, as is the case with the evangelicals and fundamentalists of today's so-called Christianity.

Have mercy on me, a sinner? 707

Phantasia

The origin of the English word *fantasy.* Nowadays, fantasy means "an illusion, a fancy, something unreal, a delusion, an hallucination". But the old Greek word Phantasia meant "a phantom, a non-physical appearance". To the contemplative Christian fathers, Phantasia specifically meant the image-producing faculty of the Soul—the power of *imagination.* When through prayer, meditation or contemplation you break through the ordinary mind, you will *perceive* Phantasia, the realm of the *subconscious mind,* with all its images, symbols, pictures and archetypes. The Christian Saints warned their disciples not to pay attention to the land of Phantasia, but to go *beyond* it to the pure, formless Contemplation of the Divine Essence, the Essential Light.

Beyond Phantasia 686

Soma
A *form* of something. A body. The Universe is the Body of God, in the same way as the human body is but the body of the human Soul.

Sarx
The flesh or gross physical body of the human being.

Eikon
A picture, a maṇḍala, a likeness, a resemblance, a figure, a representation, an image, a symbol, a portrait, an illustration of something (usually of God, Christ, the Holy Trinity, the Virgin Mary, the Saints or the angels). Hence the English word *icon.* Eikons are usually objects of veneration and worship in the Eastern Orthodox Church, and are equivalent to the pictures, paintings, statues and amulets of the Roman Catholic tradition.

Eidolatres
"A servant who worships an idol". From Eidolon, "an image, a form, a representation, a statue, a spectre, an apparition, a ghost, a phantom, an effigy of a god or goddess to be worshipped", and Latris, "a servant". A worshipper of forms, images and sense-objects. A materialist. A sensualist. A consciousness whose only experience is through the five senses. The reliance on physical objects, people, forms and conditions for happiness. The lack of awareness of the Great Invisible and of the Power of God in all things. The worship of matter instead of Spirit, of the body instead of the Soul, of the world instead of God. From this came the English words *idolater* and *idolatry.* There are countless humans who are idolaters, worshipping "false gods".
Idol-Worship 655

Daimon
The source of the English word *demon.* To the early Greeks and Christians, the word Daimon meant something divine or angelic. Even a human Soul was considered a Daimon—that is, a *spiritual being.* Later on, it came to mean evil spirits as well. Nowadays, the word *demon* refers *only* to evil spirits. How words become corrupted over the centuries!
Angels and Demons 193

Angelos
Literally, "a messenger, a representative, a spokesperson". Hence the English word *angel.* The angels are "spirits", but *not* human spirits. They are of another kind, with many grades, orders and classes. The spirits that haunt the seances and channelling sessions of mediums and psychics are *not* angels. They are human spirits, and sometimes not even that. True angels are superior to humans in powers and intelligence, but inferior to God.
The Angels 196

Logoi
The plural of Logos. The Logos doctrine was a well established Greek doctrine about God before Christianity. The Christian fathers adapted the Logos doctrine to Christianity: the *Father* being the First Logos; the *Son* (or Christ) being the Second Logos; and the *Holy Spirit* being the Third Logos. The doctrine of the Logoi, as taught by the Saints, is an even further division of the Godhead. According to the Christian fathers, the Logoi are "thoughts of God, principles of God, essences of God, the seeds of all things", from which all things come into existence according to their own inherent natures—the *inner Plan* of God for them.
The Doctrine of the Logoi 116

Logia, Logoi
Instructions and sayings of Jesus. In the early days of the church, hundreds of gospels, epistles and writings were circulating, of which just a small fragment now form the New Testament. Some of these Logia, or Logoi (sayings), formed an oral tradition which was never written down, while others were written down and some became part of the gospels. Towards the end of the second century, the four gospels of today's New Testament were declared to be the only authentic gospels and, from then on, all other writings were declared to be heretical.

Paralipomena
The esoteric and secret sayings of Jesus that survived the enthusiastic spree of destruction by the church authorities of the first four centuries after Christ.

Apokryphos

The many esoteric, occult and Gnostic Christian manuscripts that were in circulation during the first three centuries of Christianity. The esoteric or deeper sayings of Jesus, banned by the church. From the Greek Apokriptein, "to hide, to conceal". All of the Apocryphal gospels, epistles and letters are profound; hence they were excluded from the Bible by the selectors and were declared "heretical" by the ignorant church authorities. Only one of these got into the New Testament: the *Apocalypse*. There is no rational reason why that one alone was permitted to stay in the Bible after it was heavily "edited" during the first four centuries.

Parabola

A story, an allegory. A symbolic speech by Jesus in the New Testament, with hidden, spiritual values. From Para, "beside, alongside, beyond, past", and Balein, "to throw, to cast". Hence the English word *parable*. An enigmatic narrative, similar to the Zen Kōan.

Allegoria

"Speaking otherwise". Symbolic speech, much used in the Old and New Testaments (such as the story of Adam and Eve and the serpent, or Noah and the flood) and, unfortunately, usually interpreted by the ignorant as *literal events*. From this came the English word *allegory*. Jesus tells many allegories in the New Testament: the pearl of great price, the prodigal son, and so on.

Biblos

A book. Also, Biblion, "a little book". Hence the English word *Bible,* the collection of sacred texts used by the Saints.

Evangelion

Good news, a good story, a good message. The gospels. Hence the English words *evangelical* and *evangelism.*

Episunagoge

"A gathering together into Oneness". From Sunagoein, "to bring people together". The Greek word Sinagoge means "a meeting" or "a group of people together", while an Episunagoge is a gathering together of "the chosen ones, the elect". Hence the English word *synagogue.* A synagogue is a place where the Jews come together for prayer and worship. It is an assembly or congregation of devoted people.

Who are the 'Elect'? 128

Ekklesia

The Greek word Ekklesia literally means, "being called out from among the people", from Ek, "from", and Klesia, "being called out". Nowadays, it is commonly translated as "the church, an assembly, a church-group". It is identical in meaning to the Sanskrit Satsaṅga, from Sat, "truth", and Saṅga, "a gathering, an assembly". Hence the English word *ecclesiastic,* "pertaining to the church". Ekklesia ordinarily means a spiritual congregation of Christians, but it has a much deeper meaning. This being "called out" or "chosen" is not to be understood in an ordinary religious sense, but in a deeply spiritual sense, as a deep, inward orientation towards God. You are called *out of the world,* into the Soul Kingdom.

The Chosen Ones 688

∞

PART FIVE

Zen

The Path to Enlightenment

CHAPTER 35

The Spirit of Zen

Origins of Zen

ZEN is a Japanese word which has roughly the same meaning as the Western term *Mysticism*. It does *not* mean mediumship or channelling, nor any form of psychism. Zen is not astral stuff, not psychic, not phenomenal. It is the experience of the Buddhic Plane, the Realm of Unity, or (in Christian language) the Mystical States, the Mystical Marriage of the Soul to God, which leads to the Kingdom of God, NIRVĀṆA.

Zen originated in India as a method of Tantra

Zen originated in India as a method of TANTRA, where it was called DHYĀNA (or DHYĀN), meaning "meditation-contemplation". In ancient India, DHYĀNA was practised by thousands of yogīs, sādhus, sannyāsins and other "holy" men. Gautama Buddha, born 563 years before the Christ, was said to have practised this kind of meditation, by which he attained Enlightenment.

The famous BODHIDHARMA, an Indian Buddhist monk and the twentieth Patriarch of Buddhism, travelled to China in the year 520 after the birth of Christ and taught DHYĀNA to the Chinese. The Chinese called it CHĀNNA (in short, CHĀN) because they did not pronounce the Sanskrit properly. Later on, the Chinese Mystics spread it to Japan, Korea and elsewhere. In Japan the word was further mispronounced to ZENNA or, in short, ZEN.

Nowadays most people think that Zen is Japanese. The methods of Zen were practised in India for thousands of years, however, and when the "new" religion of Buddhism arrived in China, the Zen practices quickly merged into the old Chinese religion of Taoism, which was a native Chinese Mysticism *identical* with DHYĀN or Zen. Thus you have Chinese Zen Buddhism. When the Japanese learned it from the Chinese a few centuries later, they adapted it to Japanese cultural backgrounds. The Zen of Japan is a Japanese *adaptation*, peculiar to the Japanese temperament and consciousness. But to think that Zen came from Japan is just as erroneous as to think that apples came from California because in California they grow apples!

BUDDHA
Sanskrit: "One who is filled with Light". An Enlightened One, an Awakened One. This refers to the awakening on the Nirvāṇic spheres of Being.

CHĀN
Chinese: "Meditation". Derived from CHĀNNA, which was in turn derived from the Sanskrit DHYĀNA. In the Japanese language, CHĀN became ZEN.

SAMĀDHI
Sanskrit: The suspended animation of your ordinary thinking mind. In SAMĀDHI you live by ŚAKTI (Divine Energy) and CAITANYA (Divine Consciousness) alone.

The State of Inner Purity 497
Samādhi: the Goal of Yoga 574

What is Zen?

While many Western intellectuals think that Zen is some kind of clever intellectual game, Zen is not a form of intellectualism or verbalism. Zen is actually quite *wordless* and *beyond* the mind; therefore it cannot have anything to do with intellectual smartness. The intellectuals who approach Zen with their verbose minds will never be able to grasp it.

You can discover the root of your mind, your mind before thought arises

Zen is a special mind-to-mind transmission.

Zen is a transmission of Enlightenment which is not dependent on the holy scriptures or sacred books, nor on any writing, speech, ideas or thoughts.

Zen is the *direct experience* of the Soul, the *real* part of Man.

Zen is the discovery of one's Higher Consciousness, one's Super-Essential Nature, one's Buddhahood.

Man's Original State is this holy Buddha-Nature, but we do not know this because of our *spiritual ignorance.* Thus, Zen is a Path that attempts to rediscover Man's Original Nature. It is a Path of self-discovery, leading to Self-Realization and Union with God.

Perceptions of the One Mind 490
The Buddha-Mind 1208

Zen is described by the Chinese Masters as:

The direct pointing to the Mind, for the perception of the Self-Nature, in order to attain Buddhahood.

This is philosophical talk. In practice it means that you meditate in such a way that you can discover the *root* of your mind, your mind *before thought arises.* This will help you discover yourself as you truly are, beyond your mind, ego and personality, which will lead you to the state of Buddhahood, Enlightenment, Union with God, Transcendental Consciousness.

Buddhi is Love and Bodhi is Wisdom. This is the dual characteristic of the Intuitional Plane—the plane above the Mental and below the Nirvāṇic. It is called the Buddhic Plane because it is the plane of Love, Unity, Oneness. Thus, Love and Wisdom go together; in the Enlightened Man they are inseparable.

Buddhi: the Realm of Unities 83

Bodhi
Sanskrit: "Awakening". Wisdom or Enlightenment. From the Sanskrit Budh, "to awake".

The Essence of Wisdom 1680

Bodhisattva
Sanskrit: "One whose essential nature is Wisdom", from Bodhi, "Wisdom", and Sattva, "one's fundamental or essential nature".

The Nirmānakāya 390

A 'Godless' Religion?

The Universe is one, mighty, inconceivable medium, and the Deity is the controlling, omnipotent Spirit.

Zolar

A difficulty arises for the Westerner when we consider that, in the Indian, Chinese and Japanese forms of Zen Buddhism, the words *God* and *Soul* are not mentioned at all! Consequently a Christian might think that Zen Buddhism is some kind of godless religion. And so it appears from many Buddhist teachings and the ideas of Buddhist monks. This, perhaps, is because the Buddhists themselves don't always understand the teachings of the Buddha.

But it is not so. The words or terms *are* different, that is true; the Buddha never taught of a *personal* God, nor of a *personal* Saviour, nor of a *personal* Salvation process—concepts so popular in the Christian West. The Buddha was in touch with a *Universal Reality,* a Cosmic Mind or Essence *beyond* the old Jewish idea of God as an old man with a white beard, sitting on a throne somewhere in "heaven".

The Christian West adopted this old Jewish concept of God as "Father", while adding Jesus Christ to the "family" of God as a *personal* Saviour (the "Son"), and the Holy Ghost as a dove fluttering above the heads of the Father and the Son. The Roman Catholics added the Virgin Mary to complete God's family picture.

Religion and Spirituality

Zen is a kind of *meditational life* that does not depend on the authority of the scriptures or traditions, nor on churches, sects or religions. Now, this might be difficult to accept for a Westerner or a Japanese who is steeped in tradition!

Nowadays not many people understand the true function of religion. Religion is but a stepping stone to Spirituality. Religion is the observance of rites, rituals, forms and the outer trappings and casings of Spiritual Life, while Spirituality is the *awakening* to the Consciousness of the Soul and to the Kingdom of God within.

Whether we talk of Zen, Christianity, Islam, Judaism, Hinduism, Sikhism or Buddhism, the basic idea has always been the same: to strive to attain to the Higher Life by prayer and meditation, to gather *true Knowledge, true Insight* into the Mystery of Man, and to express that Inner Knowing in *Loving Service* to Mankind.

Yoga and Religion 527

Mythical Concepts of God 104
Jesus the Personal Saviour? 678
Brahma-Nirvāṇa 1224
The Sūfī God 838

The Jewish-Christian representation of God is appropriate for unphilosophical people who are unable to think in abstract terms. For the Buddha, however, such representations of the Universal Reality would have been grossly inferior, humanized, anthropomorphized, and contrary to his *experience.* Buddhism does not deny God, the Absolute Reality, but it does deny the Jewish-Christian *ideas* of It, because they are contrary to the experience of the Mystics who have connected with their own Soul-Natures and attained some degree of Unity with that Supreme Reality.

While Buddhists don't believe in a *personal* God, a *personal* Saviour or a *personal ego* that must be "saved", they do believe in a Universal Reality transcending all limitations, in a Universal Saviour-Principle (the Buddha-Mind) *inherent* in all things, and in the possibility for the human being to *merge* into a higher Reality, to *rediscover* a higher order of Truth.

This subtle point has to be understood, or sitting in Zen meditation is meaningless. In simple Western language:

God and Man are One. God and the Universe are One.

This has to be *realized.*

Only God is alive as everyone and everything. All beings and things and worlds are arising as spontaneous transformations or modifications of the One.

God eternally transcends the world and all the beings in it, yet the world and all beings are nothing but God.

Da Free John

The Sanskrit word **Buddha** means "the Enlightened One" or "One who possesses the Awakened Mind". Chān (meditation) is the sowing and Buddhahood is the reaping or the reward. A Buddha possesses Sarvajña, "All-Knowledge" (Omniscience in a certain sense, pertaining to certain worlds and conditions).

There is much difference between "learning" and the *Insight* one gains by self-cultivation, meditation, realizing one's true Nature. This was beautifully expressed by an old Chinese Master:

When I was a young man I did much learning.
I read the scriptures and all their commentaries,
I was endlessly discriminating between things,
I was vainly counting the grains of sand in the ocean,
Until one day I was reprimanded by the Buddha, who asked:
"What do you gain by counting other people's gems?"

Yung Chia

Qualities of the Divine Being 107
The Christ in the Heart 441
The One and Only 839
The One 1686

False Zen

The idea of Zen is much abused and misused by the ignorant, both in the East and in the West. Nowadays, in the West, the word *Zen* is used as a magic word to sell products: "Zen motorcycle maintenance", "Zen tea-making", Zen this and Zen that. But *the average person cannot practise Zen!*

To attain book-knowledge, *add* things every day. To attain Enlightenment, *remove* thoughts every day.
Lao Tzu

False Zen *A*

The belief that Zen is some sort of clever intellectual twaddle, idle talk, empty talk or nonsense.

This delusion exists in the East as well as in the West. For example:

- "What is the Buddha?" Answer: "A new bride rides a donkey, the mother-in-law leads it."
- A disciple saw a picture of the bearded Bodhidharma and exclaimed, "Why hasn't he a beard?"
- "Say one word with your mouth shut."

There are many hundreds more such statements, and you may even invent a dozen yourself if you are of the "clever" type. They may engage your *intellect* to "find out" the answer, but this is *not* Zen.

Don't engage in intellectual smartness!

You can only *do* Zen after *your* Enlightenment.

For Zen is *acting from the State of Unity.*

This Unity occurs when your separated-self no longer exists, when only the One Self, the Ātman, is acting in you. Then you are One with the World, with all Life and all beings. But *first you must attain the State of Unity* which is *losing your self to gain the All.* Your intellect, the clever-mind, has nothing to do with it at all!

Everything that is a material object in this world is the Invisible World solidified.
An ancient esoteric saying

Matter, on this Physical Plane of Being, is but visible, solidified Spirit. Primordial Matter (Aether, Ākāśa) contains within itself all that ever was, or will be, in the Three Worlds.
Living Matter 134

False Zen *B*

The belief that things are as they appear and behind them there is nothing.

In other words, a cow is only a cow, an event is only an event, exactly how it *appears* to the bodily eyes and senses, and there is nothing invisible. This delights the *materialistic minds* of East and West: this world is only what it appears to be, and there is nothing supernatural, nothing extraordinary; all you need to do is *flow in this world* without stress and with a calm mind.

Not so! *Behind* all that you see, hear, touch, smell or taste is the Great Invisible, and behind that is the Eternal Absolute, the Fountain Source of the Great Invisible or Supernature. Your *true* Nature is the One Imperishable Self, the Universal Spirit, who is Present everywhere and always, radiant, full of Life and eternally Self-Conscious.

First Unite yourself with the Great Invisible, then Unite yourself with the Absolute. Then you will *do* Zen.

The known universe of three dimensions embraces the merest fraction of the whole Cosmos of substance and energy.

H.P. Lovecraft

You Are the World 1390
Consciousness and Phenomena 323
Channelling or Soul-Wisdom? 327

Zen is not Psychism

Zen does *not* involve mediumship, channelling or psychism of any kind, nor the occult arts and sciences such as astrology, tarot and numerology, nor magic or witchcraft, nor mental-control techniques. It does not depend on spirit-guides, nor on so-called ascended masters or space-beings of the Astral Plane, nor on any "spirits" outside yourself. At least you should form a clear idea of what Zen is *not*.

Zen, or true Mysticism (Eastern and Western), is entirely different from the channelling process. Channelling is an *outside interference* by real or imagined etheric or astral beings who *masquerade* as angels, space-brothers, masters of the wisdom, and so forth. In the channelling process there is no Soul contact either for the channel or for the listeners, only astral body contact. Zen, or Mysticism, is the development of your *own* consciousness within the depths of your own Soul. The knowledge you gain is intimate, deep within yourself. When you attain Soul contact, *nobody uses you* and you have knowledge of infinitely higher realms than what any astral or physical-etheric entity could provide.

Mediumship is not spiritual; it is psychic-material. You have to understand this, because channelling *takes away the possibility of your own Soul contact.* You cannot follow both paths. Psychism leads to bondage to the Astral World, whereas Zen, or any form of pure Mysticism, leads to Higher Consciousness.

Zen and the World

When a Sage speaks, Silence blooms. When an ordinary person speaks, it merely reveals the chattering mind within.

When people hear new teachings they always try to reinterpret those teachings into their old ways of thinking and explain them away with their old-fashioned thought-patterns.

Materialistic thinking raises a barrier against the spiritual Life-Current

For the normal consciousness, the Original Reality, the Higher Consciousness, Tao, Nirvāṇa, seems to be a limitless Void, a spontaneous, formless activity that eludes normal comprehension.

Materialistic thinking raises a barrier against the spiritual Life-Current.

The world is so preoccupied with money that it would take a major economic or ecological crisis for it to recognize its spiritual poverty.

No one can be made happy by force.

Do not imitate Wisdom before it becomes your Truth.

To seek for Buddha outwardly, in a form, is an error.

Men walk in their own shadows and they cry that it is dark.

The future of Mankind is infinitely bright.

The Ordinary Mind 896
In Bondage to the Mind 238
The Way of the World 380
Liberation from Worldly Consciousness 1233

A disciple asked a Zen Master, "How can we attain Enlightenment? We have to dress ourselves, we have to eat, we have to work."

And the Master said, "Well then, dress yourself, eat and work."

"But I don't understand," said the disciple.

And the Master replied, "If you don't understand, then dress yourself, eat and work."

If you want to go on the Path, just do everything opposite to what the masses do.

Jakob Böhme

I cannot see... therefore there is nothing to see.
I cannot hear... therefore there is nothing to hear.
I cannot feel... therefore there is nothing to touch.
Such is the attitude of the spiritually-blind materialists.

G.S. Arundale

Men will welcome error and crucify the Truth. And, there is nothing new under the Sun.

Ancient proverb

This group aggregate and individual ignorance of the Truth of Man are identical, like a forest and the trees, or like the sea and the waves.

Vedantasara

Truth is like a finger pointing to the Moon. Most people look at the finger and not at the Moon.

An old Zen saying

Self-knowledge cannot be *imposed* on a person. Understanding cannot be compelled.

J. Krishnamurti

Wonder of wonders! Intrinsically, all living beings are Buddhas, endowed with wisdom and virtue. Because men's minds have been perverted through wrong thinking, they cannot perceive this truth.

Gautama Buddha

While a clear-mind *listens* to a bird singing, the stuffed-full-of-knowledge-and-cleverness-mind *thinks what kind* of bird is singing.

Benjamin Hoff

There is nothing to be afraid of, only to be understood.

Kung Fu

Insatiable desire for riches and pleasures; the love of fame, name and vainglory; the ignorance of Spiritual Truth; these are the worst passions of the Soul.

Our self-willed desire for many outer objects fills us with unquiet and turmoil, and we wander in the darkness of an unhappy life, *not knowing* ourselves.

For your *ordinary* mind is worldly and unstable; it produces both good and bad thoughts; it is changeable and leans towards material things. But the *God-loving* mind in you will put to death all the evils which come from the ordinary mind's careless thinking.

St Anthony the Great

I, through the labyrinth of Life can find my way,
And will not by erring lights be led astray.
I hold the key that leads me to the Core,
Peacefully I watch where others uselessly make war.
On the world's stage I play no part at all,
To vain men I, therefore, do seem so small.
Even so, they see always only multiplicity,
Whereas mine is the All, O what Felicity!

Lao Tzu

Those who do not know that Mind is Buddha, and attempt Enlightenment by a discipline attached to forms, follow the wrong path. There is no Buddha outside the One Mind, and there is no Mind outside the Buddha. This Mind is like Space and has no specific form. If you begin to think about it and formulate ideas about it, you ruin the reality of it and you attach yourself to forms.

Huang Po

I am BRAHMAN [God, the Supreme Reality], without attributes, ever pure, ever free, non-dual, homogeneous, like Space, and of the nature of Consciousness. The ignorant man *identifies* himself or herself with whatever he or she sees in the world. That is why Man does not know that he or she is, in fact, BRAHMAN.

Upadeśasahasri

The Goal of Zen

In genuine Zen, SATORI or "Enlightenment" is the experience of the seven subplanes of the Buddhic Plane and, later on, the seven subplanes of the Nirvāṇic Plane. Thus, there are several levels of "Enlightenment" possible. In a certain sense, even the experience of the formless causal subplanes (the higher Mental Worlds) are part of this Enlightenment process.

Evolution is the determination of the Deity to express Divinity through forms.
Master DK

Consciousness is free and unlimited, and it can function in and out of forms according to the state of the Soul.
Master DK

Zen has nothing to do with the four etheric subplanes of the Physical Plane, nor the seven subplanes of the Astral Plane, nor even the four lower subplanes of the Mental Plane. This should be clear enough for you. This is why Zen is not the emotional-psychic workings, nor the mentalism (thinking) of ordinary humans.

What Zen *is,* is difficult to describe. It depends on *your own Soul.* This should be *clear* to you. The goal of Zen, as of all true spiritual-development schools, such as Mysticism, Yoga and Sūfism, is the awakening of Consciousness first on the causal subplanes, then on the Buddhic Plane and finally in Nirvāṇa, the Kingdom of God. At this stage of Cosmic Unfoldment this is the goal for Human Evolution.

In the inner worlds there are other evolutions pursuing even higher goals! And there are Divine Hierarchies who evolve on the Cosmic Planes *above* the Cosmic Physical Plane (beyond the seven planes of our Solar System).

Remember that the Mental Plane is divided into three subplanes *with* forms (with objects or shapes as we know them) and three *without* forms. The three lower subplanes contain forms and shapes (RŪPA), whereas the higher mental subplanes are *formless* (ARŪPA), meaning they are states of Energy and Consciousness. The subplane in between (the fourth subplane) has both characteristics.

The Buddhic Plane is *formless.* The beings who dwell there are Energy-Consciousness-Bliss beings. They have a "bliss-body", but do not think of it as a solid object. On the higher mental and Buddhic subplanes you may call yourself a "consciously-intelligently-aware disembodied entity".

The Buddhists refer to these formless conditions of existence as ŚŪNYATĀ, "emptiness, void". ŚŪNYATĀ does not mean that nothing is there; Life is there, Consciousness is there, but not with the limited forms and shapes we experience in the Three Worlds. It simply means that Life is less limited, more extended, more glorious!

The Fullness of the Void 23
Śūnyatā: the Void 503
Formless Worlds 1372
Human Involution and Evolution 170
Clarify your Objective 423

From Matter to Light

You must remember here an esoteric fact: the gross and etheric realms of the Physical Plane, along with the Astral Plane and the Mental Plane, are the *gross physical body* of our Solar Logos. They are the *dense body* of the Cosmos. The Buddhic and Nirvāṇic Planes, and the two planes above the Nirvāṇic, constitute the *etheric body* of our Solar Logos, or the Cosmic Etheric-Physical Planes.

The etheric body of any entity is its Body of Light; thus, the four higher planes of our Solar System constitute the Light-Planes, or the Light Body (Cosmic Etheric Body) of our Solar Logos. The Cosmic Astral Planes constitute the Cosmic Astral Body of our Solar Logos, and so on. Thus, as you move into the Mystical Experience, Buddhi, Satori, in the Buddhic Realms, you move out of the Matter Worlds into the Worlds of Light.

The Light Bodies 40
The Path of Light 89
From Darkness into Light 982
The Constitution of God-Immanent 122
The Many Mansions 611
The Goal of Yoga 521

THE ONE MIND						Cosmic Etheric-Physical / Cosmic Dense-Physical
1	Mahāparanirvāṇa		The Logos		**Samyaksaṁ Buddha**	Cosmic Etheric-Physical Body of the Logos
2	Paranirvāṇa		The Monad		**Dhyāni Buddha**	Cosmic Etheric-Physical Body of the Logos
3	Nirvāṇa		The Spirit	↑ AWAKENING	**Bodhisattva**	Cosmic Etheric-Physical Body of the Logos
4	Buddhi		The Spiritual Soul	↑ AWAKENING	**Satori** *Degrees of Enlightenment*	Cosmic Etheric-Physical Body of the Logos
5	Mental Plane	Arūpa	Causal Body	AWAKENING	*Higher Mind, Abstract Mind*	Cosmic Dense-Physical Body of the Logos
		Rūpa	Mental Body	AWAKENING	*Mentalism. Intellectualism*	Cosmic Dense-Physical Body of the Logos
6	Astral Plane		Astral Body	AWAKENING	*Psychism* *Mediumship, Channelling*	Cosmic Dense-Physical Body of the Logos
7	Physical Plane		Etheric Body / Physical Body	AWAKENING	*Materialism*	Cosmic Dense-Physical Body of the Logos

The Goal of Zen

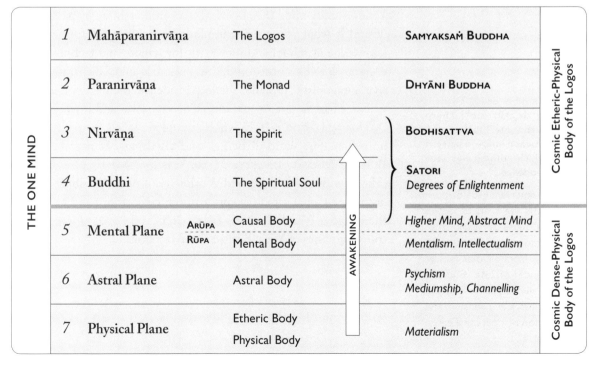

The Path of Non-Duality

Zen is the Path of non-duality. The Zen Masters say:

When there is no liking and no disliking, your eyes are clear.

And...

Your true Mind is one with the All

All things move among and intermingle with each other without distinction. To realize this is to be without anxiety about your own non-perfection.

Just be part of all things, the All. The goal of Zen is to have your eyes on the Whole, the Perfect, the *Complete Reality.* Your *true* Mind is one with the All. In fact, it *is* the All.

Zen is characterized by the silence of the Buddha and the laughter of Lao Tzu, the two greatest exponents of Zen. The silence shows the passive side, while the laughter shows the active side. For Zen is both action and non-action, passivity and objectivity.

Mind-Only 974
Mind and Desire 235
Realms of the One Mind 492

The root problem is your little mind, your ordinary thinking-mind, which effectively cuts you off from *Mind,* the Cosmic Intelligence. Your ordinary mind (KĀMA-MANAS, or mind tainted by passion and desire) is what you use for thinking and reasoning, for acquiring knowledge at school and university, for science and technology, for everyday life. This little mind, your personal mind, is separative, divisive, antagonistic, profane. Yet deep inside you there is another Mind which is like *no-mind*—just Pure Consciousness and Intelligence.

This real Mind is holy, whole, complete. It is Cosmic in nature, non-dual, one with all beings and all things. It may be called BUDDHI-MANAS, Intuitive Mind, Wisdom Mind. This Mind is infused with Love, Unity and Wisdom (BUDDHI). To subjugate your ordinary rational mind (the pride of our civilization) and to awaken the Intuitive Mind, the Non-Dual Mind, is the goal of Zen and all true disciplines of Yoga, Sūfism and Mysticism.

The "I am" is dead! There is nothing to call "me"! There never was a "me"! It is an allegory, a mental image, a pattern upon which nothing was ever really modelled.

In the experience of BUDDHI or SATORI we transcend the personal sense of "I" and "me", the personal sense of being separate from all that is. The experience of the Buddhic Plane is always a sense of Unity, of Oneness, and a sense of the dissolution of a personal ego, a personal "I".

To Rediscover Buddhi 90

No-Mind and the One Mind

No-mind, no-thinking, or no-thought-in-the-mind (WU-HSIN in Chinese Zen, MU-SHIN in Japanese) is the emptiness of the mind in which the One Mind can reveal Itself. It is a mind *not attached* to any forms or objects.

This One Mind is also described as TAT (Sanskrit: Suchness or Thatness) because it is like Space: it is Emptiness (ŚŪNYATĀ), has no forms, knows no orientation or limitations; it knows neither birth nor death, neither beginning nor ending; it is neither being nor non-being; it transcends all words, thoughts or ideas about it.

> The Great Way is not difficult for those who have no preferences. When love and hate are absent, everything becomes clear and undisguised. When you make the smallest distinction, heaven and earth are set apart. If you wish to know the Truth, hold no opinions, for or against. The struggle of what you like and what you do not like is a disease of your mind.
>
> *The Chinese Master Sosan*

The No-mind of the Zen Masters is not a mindlessness. It is not a zombie-like condition or unintelligence. It is simply the transcending of your ordinary mind, the KĀMA-MANAS, the desire-filled mind, the judgmental, critical, rational mind. It is the stopping of the endless chattering, criticizing commentary of your ordinary mind and the awakening into a silent, non-judgmental, holistic, super-rational Mind: first the formless Causal Mind on the causal subplanes, then the Buddhi-Mind (Wisdom-Mind) on the Buddhic Plane and finally the Supreme Intelligence on the Ātmic or Nirvāṇic Plane.

My original Self-Nature is primarily pure. When my true Mind is *known,* and my Original Essence is *seen,* I naturally attain the Path of Buddhahood.

Bodhisattva Sila Sūtra

If you have dust on your inner-eye, the Universe appears to be limited. But, with *nothing in your mind,* the Universe is endless.

Muso (a Japanese Master)

Go on renouncing thinking, and act as if nothing has ever happened.

To experience Zen you must renounce "thinking about things" but not "doing things". You must remain dynamically active, but this activity must not be tied up with your ego-sense. It must be purely a spontaneous activity of *Consciousness,* without any egotistical striving. You must have *spontaneous-action-awareness.*

Those who have "renounced" the world—the sādhus, sannyāsins, wandering ascetics, monks and nuns—have, in effect, merely renounced action, but spend their time thinking, contemplating or meditating. This is *not* the right human condition.

To Become a True Renunciate 257

The 'No-Mind' 990
Clouds of Unknowing 704
Suspended Mind 1209
Cultivate Silence of the Mind 1239
Non-Action Misinterpreted 1120
Silence and Activity 1446

Messengers of the One Mind

The true Mind does not act in any way. It neither comes nor goes, is not born and does not die. It does not move but remains motionless.

Hsu Yun

This One Mind is not the ordinary mind of conceptual reasoning thought, and it is detached from all form-structures. In this way, the Buddhas and sentient beings are not different at all. If you can rid yourself of all ordinary, conceptual thinking processes, you will have accomplished your goal. But if you do not get rid of the faculty of thinking, in a flash, even though you strive for aeon after aeon, you will never accomplish Enlightenment.

A single Spiritual-Brilliance is this One Mind. The terms "Unity" and "Oneness" refer to this homogeneous Spiritual-Brilliance. The transmission of this Form-less-Mind (the Void) cannot be made through words. A transmission with concrete thoughts cannot be the eternal Dharma (Truth). The transmitting of this One Mind, and the receiving of the transmission, are a difficult and mysterious undertaking, and few have ever been able to receive it. This transmission of the Mind and its reception is Zen.

Huang Po

The Enlightened Beings (Buddhas) and the ordinary people are both in the One Mind. This One Mind is like Space whose boundaries know no measure. You cannot apply any concepts to the One Mind. This One Mind is the Buddha-Nature. As soon as your thinking ceases, and you stop forming ideas in your mind, the Buddha-Nature reveals itself to you.

Huang Po

In this One Mind, there is not any particular shape or form that you can lay your hands on [meditate upon].

Huang Po

Nothing, save the Universal Mind, is conceivable. Mind, in its uninhibited nature, brings forth all that comes into existence. That which manifests is like a wave upon the Ocean of Mind. This *state* of Mind, which is above dualities, brings *Liberation.* This Mind is *beyond* Nature, but it expresses itself in Nature's forms. The *realization* of this One Mind brings Salvation from rebirth. All beings are of this Buddha-Essence, but they have to *realize* this before they can enter Nirvāṇa.

The Tibetan Book of the Great Liberation

It should be thoroughly understood that all men have One Mind, One God and Father, One Life, Truth and Love.... Intelligence is the primal and eternal quality of Infinite Mind, of the Triune Principle—Life, Truth and Love—named God. Mind is God. God is the only Mind.

Mary Baker Eddy

Mrs Mary Baker Eddy, the founder of *Christian Science,* experienced the state of Zen or Mystical Consciousness. Her description is the experience of the Buddhic Plane. She perceived God as the *One Mind.* Interestingly, this is also how the Tibetan, Chinese, Hindu and Japanese Mystics *independently* describe the Higher Reality.

The Vedic Yogīs of India described PARABRAHMAN (the One Transcendental Reality, or "God") from their experience as SATCIDĀNANDA (SAT-CIT-ĀNANDA: Beingness or Life, Consciousness or Mind, and Happiness or Bliss)!

Mary Baker Eddy wrote about her experience more than a hundred years ago, when there were no books on Zen translated from the Chinese or Japanese. The West did not know of Zen, yet her description *is* Zen, as you shall see! The *revelation* within her Soul she called *Christian Science.*

Christian Mysticism and Zen 630

Christian Zen

A mind which is not dispersed amongst external things of the senses *returns to itself,* and from itself it ascends to God by an unerring Path.

Saint Basil the Great

Blessed is the man whose help is from the Lord, who ascends by prayer—*not* of words, but of the Heart.

An old Christian mystical saying

Blessed is he whom Truth itself teaches, not by words or symbols, but as it is, in itself.

Thomas à Kempis: The Imitation of Christ

Practice forgiveness by letting go of all resentments and all sense of retribution. This is the Way of Love.

Christian Mysticism

The beginning of the Path is where the personality keeps *silent* and the Soul *lives.* The beginning of the Path is where the personality abstains from actions, where you can say, "Do *you,* oh God, take the lead!"

The ancient Rose and the Cross

I and my Father are One. All that the Father is, I am. All that the Father has, is mine.

Jesus the Christ

This is true of all of us. It needs to be *realized.*

It is the old tradition of the Christian Russian Orthodox Church to awaken the spiritual qualities of the Soul which are to be found in each individual. The task of the Church, its prophetic mission, is to divinize Man, to light another's candle on the altar of Spiritual Rebirth.

The Metropolitan Bishop of Volokolamsk

Would that the Church, in both East and West, really understand her mission!

Father, honour me with the Glory that I had with you before the world was made.

An ancient Eastern Christian prayer

And here are some early Christian Mystics of the Eastern Orthodox Church:

The divine and deifying Illumination of Grace is not the *essence* of God, but is the *energy* of God.

Saint Gregory of Palamas

Illumination is the wonder of the total uplifting of the powers of the Soul towards the Majesty and Glory of God. It is the outreaching of the mind towards the Limitless Power of the Light. Ecstasy is the taking up of the faculties of the Soul to heavenly states, and the removal of the Soul from the actions of the physical senses.... The Love experienced in the Heart is for those who are still in the *process* of Enlightenment, but Ecstatic Love is for those who are perfect in Spiritual Love. Both work on the mind and draw it away from the physical senses.

Saint Gregory of Sinai

It is by His Light energies that we can say that we can know God.

Saint Basil

According to the *Fa Yen* Chinese Zen School:

The Three Worlds are but the One Mind.

And...

All things are but Consciousness.

The "Three Worlds" refers to the Physical, Astral and Mental Planes.

Perceptions of the One Mind 490
What is Consciousness? 1368

Enlightenment

When a Chinese Zen Master was asked to describe Zen, he said:

The sword has gone long ago.

This means perfect peace of mind. Here there is no aggression, no comparisons, no criticisms, no disquiet. This is "the peace that passes all understanding" spoken of by Saint Paul *(Philippians 4:7)*.

There is a Zen saying:

Body asleep, mind awake.

This is the condition that leads to the experience of Satori or "Enlightenment". The aim of Chān (Zen, Dhyān) is to empty your mind of all phenomena so that your Self-Nature can return to its "normal" condition. This means that when you clear your mind of all impressions of worldly objects, inner images, and thoughts, you discover your Self-Nature, as you really are, as a Soul, a Spirit, a Being *above* your personality level, a Being which is eternal, timeless and immortal. This is *Enlightenment.*

∞

Saṁsāra is disturbance, the phenomenal life in the Three Worlds.

Śūnyatā, the Void, is Stillness and Peace.

Nirvāṇa is the condition in which both Creation and Emptiness vanish.

When you have instant Enlightenment, you merely return to your Original Mind.
Vimalakīrti Sūtra

Why not, from *within your own mind,* at once, reveal the original nature of your Suchness?
Hui Neng

Terms of Awakening

Awakening is called **Bodhi** in Sanskrit, **Wu** or **Lung-Tan** in Chinese, and **Satori** in Japanese Zen traditions. A modern term for it is *Enlightenment.* It is a mass of Brightness and a resurgence of the sense of the Real within you.

Wu also means "Not-Doing", and Wu-Wei means "the Not-Doing of the Eternal", or Transcendental Inactivity.

Wu (Chinese) is Mu in Japanese. That is why, in some old Japanese monasteries, you hear the monks bellowing "Mu!" ("Not this, not this!").

Your Original Face 87
Know Thyself 1389
The Enlightened 1702
The Law of the Higher Life 1134
Satori: the Experience of Illumination 816

The Thought of Enlightenment

> The whole Universe, including Man, is an *embodied thought.* Man also has the ability to *create forms* for the clothing of his ideas in tangible matter… That which we see and touch with our physical senses is but an *effect* of subtle, inner, underlying causes [the psychic dimensions]. Even these causes are only those causes which underlie the *grossly objective* physical plane; he will not really have ascertained the *vital impulse* coming from Being, as yet, the Cause of causes.
>
> *Master DK*

The thought of Enlightenment will flourish into the effect, the realization

> We go through this endless cycle of births and deaths (SAṀSĀRA) because of our ignorance of the source of this cycle of births and deaths, and because of our forgetfulness of the Mind-Essence (NIRVĀṆA) in the midst of this Cause-and-Effect Nexus (KARMA) which governs these worlds of forms.
>
> *Śūrangama Sūtra*

> Good karmas come, and evil karmas too, but both are illusions. Your body is like a foam or a bubble, and like air is your mind. This MĀYĀ has no substance and no reality.
>
> *Shikhin Buddha*
> *(The 999th Buddha of the Golden Age)*

Very few people understand the power of thought, that each thought they think is a cause which will make something happen. Thoughts are *causal,* they lead to *effects.* Every thought acts as a cause of some effect. This is the Law of Karma in action on the mind level. Thus, the *thought of Enlightenment* will act as a cause, a seed, which in time will flourish into the effect, the realization. Hence the importance of meditation or Zen.

The Power of Thought 232
Karma: the Law of Action 240
Dharma: the Law of Being 244
Mind and Thought 1376

The Law of Karma brings about *reincarnation,* for we return again and again to repay our debts. When you become free of debts, you will be a Free Man.

Your highest Self-Nature is your Being in NIRVĀṆA. That is called *Reality.* From such a viewpoint, your ordinary mind and body are called illusion or MĀYĀ.

> Concerning the freedom of the Spirit, note this well: the Spirit is free so long as it is not attached to nameable things.
>
> *Meister Eckhart*

When the Self-Mind is realized, speech and silence, motion and stillness, all are Chān.

Chung Feng

The *Self-Mind* is the term used by the Zen people for your Consciousness, for the root of your mind, before thoughts have arisen in it. When you realize this, then you are in the true state of meditation, which is called CHĀN, ZEN or DHYĀN. In Korean Mysticism it is ZŌN, and in Tibetan it is BŌN.

When the Mind is Still

The birds sing, the flowers smile and the moon reaches down to the stream.
Master Hsu Yun

That is, when the mind is still, free of thoughts and passions, then Truth flowers on its own.

When the mind is free of thoughts and passions, then Truth flowers on its own

The mind is the great slayer of the Real. Let the disciple slay the slayer.
H.P. Blavatsky

The mundane activities of the mind must be quietened and stilled; then one's Self-Nature becomes manifest. This Self-Nature is the Buddha-Mind—Samādhi, Zen, Satori, Bodhi. This is Prajñāparamitā, "Transcendental Wisdom". This is "the Christ in you, your hope of Glory", as expressed by Saint Paul *(Colossians 1:27)*.

Fundamentally, there is no day or night, only the Brightness.

When the ordinary mind (the lower mind, the mental body) is quietened of its activity of *endlessly producing thoughts*, then the Higher Mind (the Causal Mind in the causal body) will manifest. By a further movement inward you awaken to the plane of Buddhi, the Wisdom-Mind (Bodhi). Then, one plane *above* the Buddhic Plane of Being is Mahāprajñāparamitā, "Great-Wisdom-Transcendental", Nirvāṇic Consciousness, the Mind of Light.

There are those who find true peace and quiet and strength and renewal when they are *alone with themselves*. These are those who keep company with Divinity.

Annalee Skarin

This being *alone with yourself* is what Zen or Mysticism is about. This is what the Christian Mystics called "the flight of the alone to the alone". This is *not* the same as loneliness, boredom, depression or suicidal tendencies, for you "dwell with Divinity". There is no outside interference in this process; it is between your own Soul and God.

Alone with God 700

Zen Silence 790
To Develop Perfect Stillness 700
The Seven Stages of Sūfī Silence 901
Your Mind is the Key 1208
Transformations of the Mind 1242
Being Alone with the Absolute 502

The Great Wisdom of the Other Shore

MAHĀ-PRAJÑĀ-PARAMITĀ
The Great Wisdom of the Other Shore reached.

MAHĀ: great.
PRAJÑĀ: the Wisdom of seeing *into* one's Self-Nature.
PARAMITĀ: Transcendental Virtue and Knowledge.

When you cling to Prajñā, there is no birth and no death

The Mystic, having attained to "the Great Wisdom of the Other Shore reached", NIRVĀṆA, realizes the Original-Mind of the Universe. This Self-Nature contains *within itself* all the universes, all the stars and galaxies, all the worlds, all the angels and human beings, all heavens and hells.

> PRAJÑĀ is eternally abiding, and is your own Self-Nature. He who has *experienced* this is free from obstructing thoughts, from past memories and worldly attachments. This is what is called *Thatness* or *Suchness,* because it is indescribable. When all things are experienced in the Light of Wisdom, PRAJÑĀ, then there is neither attachment nor non-attachment to the worlds of objects. This is seeing into your Fundamental Nature or Buddha-Mind. This way you become a Buddha.
>
> *Hui Neng*

When you cling to the objective world (the Physical, Astral and Mental Planes) there is birth and death for you. When you cling to PRAJÑĀ (the Transcendental Wisdom of the Buddhic and Nirvāṇic Planes), there is no birth and no death.

The Christ in you, your hope of Glory, spoken of by Saint Paul in the New Testament, is the same as your Buddha-Nature, your Buddha-Mind, your Self-Nature, the Original Mind of the Zen Masters, and the Self, or ĀTMAN, of the Yogīs of old.

It is as if there were two of you: the *you* as you know yourself on the personality level and the *You* that needs to be discovered, the Eternal and Timeless Spirit that you are.

The Coming of Christ in the Heart 727

Tao: the Great I AM 774
Touch Ultimate Emptiness 96
Learn to Die before you Die 420
Attach your Mind to the Eternal 1234
To Become a Jīvanmukta 259
The Christ in the Heart 441

The Enlightenment of Teh Shan

Once upon a time, in the northern part of China, there was a man called *Chou*. He became a Buddhist monk and for many years he studied the holy books of Buddhism, the Sūtras and the Śāstras, until he became a well known and greatly respected pundit.

One day he learned that there was a Zen sect in the southern part of China, so he decided to travel there and teach them "a thing or two", for he thought the Zen people were foolish. So he left his monastery and began his long journey on foot, carrying on his shoulders a scripture, "The commentary by Tao Yin on the *Diamond Sūtra*" (which was very heavy, since in those days it was written on blocks of wood). After a long journey on foot, carrying the heavy book on his shoulders each day, he arrived at the province where the famous Zen monastery was located.

As he walked along the road he came to a stall where an old woman was selling pastry, like cakes, which in Chinese were called *Tien-Hsin* or "mind-refresheners". So, he put down his heavy book and decided to buy a *Tien-Hsin*. And the old lady asked, "What heavy burden are you carrying, O monk?"

"I am carrying a commentary on a scripture," replied the monk.

"Which scripture?" asked the woman.

"Tao Yin's commentary on the *Diamond Sūtra*," said the monk.

Then the old women said to the monk, "I'll tell you what, monk; I will give you a mind-refreshener if you will answer me this question: 'Since a past or a present or a future mind cannot be found, what are you going to refresh?'"

The monk became speechless. He was dumbfounded. He left the old woman in a hurry.

After many more days of journey on foot, carrying his heavy burden, the monk arrived at the Zen monastery, the name of which was *Lung-Tan*, "The Dragon's Lake". Since he wanted to show off what a great man he was, as he entered the meditation hall he said, "For many years I wanted to see this famous *Dragon's Lake;* now that I am here, I see not a dragon and not a lake."

Upon hearing this, the Zen Master of the monastery replied, "But even so, you have arrived at the Dragon's Lake."

Again the learned monk became confused and speechless. For the Dragon is the *Wisdom* and the Lake is the *Mind,* and the Zen Teacher's *function* is to stir the Mind of the disciple so that he too may become a Dragon of Wisdom—a Buddha.

The monk was not yet ready for Enlightenment, but he decided to stay at the monastery anyway. One day he was attending upon the Teacher of the monastery. It was getting very late at night and the Master said to him, "Why don't you retire now to your room?" So the monk said good night to his Teacher and went out.

Then immediately he came back in and said, "But Master, it is very dark outside." The Master lit a lamp and gave it to the monk. As the monk was about to pass through the door, the Master blew out the lamp. At that moment, for the third time in his life, the monk became speechless—and, this time, *Enlightened.* For we all carry our own Light within us.

This monk became the famous Zen Master *Teh Shan*. This is how things were in the olden days.

CHAPTER 36

The Eternal Tao

What is Tao?

The Reality of the Cosmos is the Omnipresent Being which ever Is

The Chinese Sages have called Tao "the Great Absolute Ruler" and "the Heavenly-Master of Creation". Tao has also been described as the *Being* or *Essence* of all things, the *Source of active Power* within all things, the *Force* or *Energy* behind all forms.

The Chinese word TAO, which predates Christianity by several centuries, is often translated as "the Logos" or "the Word", for Tao also means "to speak, to utter a sound, to express oneself by words". According to the ancient Chinese, Tao gave *order* to Primordial Matter, which then became Nature. Tao is transcendental and abstract, but, in its capacity as the subjective Power within Creation, it is God Immanent within the Universe *and* within Man.

Tao has also been translated as "the how of things, how things work, the meaning of things". For Tao *is* the ultimate meaning of all things, the *why and how* of all things, since beneath and within all objects is to be found Tao.

It is difficult to describe this Ultimate Reality, even as is said in the *Tao Te Ching*:

> The Tao that can be described by words is *not* the Eternal Tao.
> The Name [of Reality] that can be pronounced is *not* the Absolute Name.

Reality (Tao) is not an *object* or *thing* that can be known or experienced as objects and things are experienced. According to Zen, it is "that which is *before* you". It is in front of you always, but you do not perceive It. The Reality of *yourself*, for example, is that Being or Intelligence (Pure Consciousness) which you are before the sensation of an ego (your "I-am-ness" or self-reference) arises within you. The Reality of the Cosmos is the Omnipresent Being which ever *Is*.

Tao: the Great Mother 146
The Plan is in the Divine Mind 161
Perceptions of the One Mind 490
The Logos: the Word of God 114
The Word, Logos, Voice, Name 1646
What is Reality? 1175

The pre-Christian Greeks had the concept of the LOGOS centuries *before* Christianity, as did the old Vedic religions of India. In Sanskrit, the Logos (the Word) was called VĀK, which is the Creative Speech of God, of PARABRAHMAN, the Transcendental Reality. Thus, the Christian idea of the Word, or Logos, is anything but new!

Vāk: the Divine Speech 118

Objects in space *seem* to exist, but they are temporary constructs, "compounded things", and after a while they vanish. But the Reality, Tao, the Universal Mind, eternally *Is.* It does not pass away at any time. It is Radiant-Brightness, characterized by Being-Consciousness-Bliss. This Radiant-Beingness, the One Mind, is the true significance of every moment, of every object in Space and every living entity in Creation. This Reality is always present. It is always in the Here and Now.

Look! The Tao cannot be seen;
it is beyond physical forms.
Listen! The Tao cannot be heard,
for it is beyond physical sounds.
Try to grasp it; it cannot be held
in your hands, for it is intangible.

Tao Te Ching

Thoughts (which are subtle objects) and objects throughout Omnispace are but modifications arising in Reality, the Universal Mind, Tao. They do not exist separately, by themselves. No object, gross or subtle, by itself, is real. No object is separate from Tao, the One Mind.

> The highest knowledge is to know that you know nothing. For this knowledge makes a man tranquil and devout.
>
> We do know more book-knowledge than the illiterates, it is true, but we have not learned the meaning of the sublime Mystery that is Tao.
>
> Man's real problem is that he does not know that he knows not! By intellectual thinking we cannot touch the Essence, nor do we reach, by acts, the sublime Ideal.
>
> *Lao Tzu*

> A seeker visited a Sage upon the mountain called "the Unnoticeable Slope" and asked the Enlightened One, "What kind of thoughts and what kinds of doings will bring us to the Tao? And where must we go and what must we do? And where do we start from and which road do we follow to realize Tao?" And the speechless non-doer Sage gave him no answer.
>
> *Chuang Tzu*

> To have no thoughts and to put forth no effort is the first step towards Tao.
> To go nowhere and do nothing is the second step.
> To start from no point and follow no road is the third step towards the understanding of Tao.
>
> *The Yellow Emperor*

According to the Chinese Zen Masters, the TAO *can be found,* but not in books or scriptures, nor in the writings of the Sages, Saints or Masters. It cannot be found by learning, nor by thinking, nor even by using clairvoyant and other psychic powers. It is *above* such means of search. To discover and establish yourself in the TAO is to find yourself in the condition known as Freedom, Liberation, Enlightenment, Salvation.

When the Yellow Emperor was looking for Tao, the Great No-Thing (T'AI-HSÜ), he sent *learning* ahead of him to find Tao. But learning came back and said he could not find Tao. Then he sent *clairvoyance,* but clairvoyance could not find Tao either. Then he searched with Empty-Mind, and he found It.

Tao: the Great I AM

Tao is the Universal Self of All, the One Beingness of the Universe

The ancient Chinese word TAO is often translated by scholars as "the Way, the Path", but also as the "Truth, the Universal Life-Force, Reality, the Godhead". Tao means the same as the old Hebrew Name of God that Moses received on Mount Sinai:

EHEIEH
I Am. Being. Beingness.

When Moses asked God to show him the *Nature* of God, God replied:

EHEIEH ASHER EHEIEH
I Am that I Am. I am the Universal Self of All. I am Beingness.

The real meaning of this sublime revelation is "Thou Art That Which I Am" or "I Am That Which Thou Art". It means that Mankind and God are One, that Creation and God are One. This is the same revelation as that received by the Sages of Upaniṣadic India concerning the nature of God (ĀTMĀ, ĀTMAN, PARAMĀTMAN: the Spirit, the Self, the One Universal Self, the I AM). The Upaniṣads state:

SOHAṀ HAṀSA
That is I. I am That.

This Universal "I-Am-ness", the "Me" of the scriptures, is also the Christ-Consciousness, the Logos of the ancient Greeks and the Christian Gnostics. This is also the "Christ *in you,* your hope of Glory" of Saint Paul. This is the meaning of Tao as understood by the ancient Chinese Sages. Tao has been translated as "the Way, the Truth, the Life, the One Truth or Reality, the Single Principle of the Universe". Tao is the Universal Self (ĀTMAN) of All, the One Beingness of the Universe, the One Living God.

Because I Am a Perfect Oneness, all of Me Exists everywhere.

Thus, Tao may be described as the Truth-Principle, the Eternal Reality, the Self, the I AM, or God.

Ātman, Ātmā 34
Who is 'I AM'? 1418
The One God of All Religions 110
The Way, the Truth and the Life 670
The Upaniṣadic Mantrams 546

Tao: the Universal Mind

TAO, the Universal Mind, the Mind of Light, cannot be talked about, but it can be *demonstrated* by Silence and Consciousness. All work is done by Consciousness (Tao). You must become *conscious* of Consciousness.

All existence is a single Whole, Tao. Therefore, all things are interconnected. Tao is the One Reality underlying all Creation. Although Tao is unmoving, it moves all things.

If you leave behind everything you possess, you will see the Mystery (TAO), eternally inviolate, a clean and tranquil fountain from which the true Life wells forth.

Lao Tzu

There is a Way of Knowing, *above* reason. This is Tao. There is a Self above the ego. Tao is selfless and is the Oneness of all Creation.

You cannot escape the consequences of your actions. Tao does not play favourites. Tao is everywhere and shines equally on the just and the unjust. No person, race or religion receives special treatment from Tao. For Tao, it is all the same; each person, religion or race is judged by its own actions. In this sense, Tao is Absolute Justice. Tao does not do anything, yet all things get done.

Every object and every event in the Universe is a vibratory Energy. Everything emerges out of Tao (the First Cause), develops and returns to its Source, which is Tao. But Tao is not originated by anything. Some people name Tao "God". It is the One Principle before all else.

Tao is not a thing. It is not *a* sound nor *a* vibration. It cannot be divided into parts. It does not change. It cannot diminish, nor can it be increased. It was not born and it cannot die.

Tao is One. It is an indivisible Unity. It determines everything and it comes *before* all things. It is First and it is the Last. It gives the inherent Law to everything. It has no form, nor any qualities such as one could think of. It is vast, infinite. It is everywhere and at all times. And it is forever.

Human beings depend upon the planet Earth for their existence. The Earth depends upon the Cosmos. The Cosmos depends upon the Tao. But the Tao, the Universal Mind of Reality, does not depend on anything.

∞

Mind-Only 974
Consciousness 1370
The Eternal is One 512
The Divine Unity 852
The One 1686

Tao: the Supreme Way

It is a precious thing, it is the Energy of Enlightenment.
It is the state of the Primeval Buddha.
It is the essence of Knowledge in its natural state.
It is absolute Purity and it is unconditioned.
It has no basis in the physical and psychic dimensions.
It is unaffected in any way.
It is the Great Unmoved, and has no origin apart from Itself.
It has no intermediate way, no progressive stages, and no final attainable result.
It lacks the characteristics of coming and going, or of any transformations.
It is inexpressible in words.
It is not a process conditioned by Time, nor is It a non-existence.
It is symbolized by a single dot within a circle.
It is the *Basis* of everything, it is the *Source*.
It is also the Way or the Means.
And it is the End and the Result.

From an old Tibetan text

The Supreme Way is not a mind made up by conceptual thinking

Sages who abandoned intellectual learning came to rest in spontaneity.

All concepts you have formed in the past must be discarded and replaced by a void in your mind. Where the duality of the mind ceases [the discriminative faculty], there the Emptiness of the Womb of the TATHĀGATĀs [the Buddhas] appears.

The Sage is one who knows how to put his or her mental activity to rest and achieve inner tranquillity.

The Supreme Way is not a mind made up by conceptual thinking. It is completely Formless [Void]. If you can stop your thinking process, you can enter the meditative state.

The Buddhas [Enlightened Ones] and ordinary people are not different. The substance of the Absolute [the Mind] is inwardly solid, rock-like, and outwardly appears to be Void.

The phenomenal world, although relative, is not separate from the One Mind.

The Womb of the TATHĀGATĀs is intrinsically Formless and Silent, containing no *individualized* conditions [Dharmas] at all.

Huang Po

TATHĀGATĀ
Sanskrit: "One who has gone to That". From TATHĀ (TAT, That, the Absolute State) and GATĀ (gone to, arrived at). A fully Enlightened Buddha.

When the deep meaning of things is not understood, the mind's essential peace is disturbed.

The Way is perfect; it is like a vast Space where nothing is lacking and nothing is in excess. It is because of our discriminative minds that we do not see the true nature of things.

Live neither in the entanglements of outer things, nor in the inner Emptiness of meditation. Be serene, without striving. Realize the Oneness of things and your false perceptions will disappear.

Realize the Oneness of things and your false perceptions will disappear

When you try to stop activity, or to reach inner, passive Silence, your effort will produce further activity. As long as you remain in one extreme or the other, in discriminating between things or in the inner Emptiness, you will never know the Oneness.

Those who do not live in the Supreme Way of Oneness will fail in both activity and passivity.

Seng-T'san Sosan
(a Chinese Zen Master)

In one Condition are to be found all other conditions.
Reality is neither forms, nor mind, nor works, but All.
Even before you can snap your fingers,
eighty thousand holy teachings are fulfilled.
Even in a second, the evil karmas of vast ages are absolved.
Propositions made by logic are not true,
because they have no relationship to the Inner Light.
This Inner Light is beyond praise and blame.
Like Space, it has no boundaries.
It is with us all the time, Serene and Full.
When you seek it, you lose it.
You cannot get hold of it, nor can you get rid of it.
You can do nothing, for it behaves in its own way.
If you remain Silent and listen, it will speak to you.
If you speak, it will remain silent.
The great Gate of Charity that leads to Nirvāṇa
is always open, with no obstructions before it.
The mind functions through the sense organs,
and thereby the world is perceived.
This causes dualism and spoils the mirror of the mind.
When the dirt of dualism in the mind is wiped out,
the Light shines forth on its own accord.

Yung-Chia Ta-Shih
(a Chinese Zen Master)

To become aware of Tao one must come with an *open mind.* A prejudiced mind can see only what fits in with those prejudices.

Do not get carried away by what other people do. Hold fast to the One Mind, the Single Principle, the Eternal Tao. Then you can do good works and stay free from all chaos and conflicts caused by people. And in all situations you will be in the Here and Now.

Be Tranquil 987

The Truth cannot be searched for by the mind.

To deny that things are real is to miss their *beauty*. To assert that all things are but the Void [ŚŪNYATĀ] is to deny their *reality*.

The more you talk and think about the Reality [TAO], the further you wander away from it. Stop talking and thinking and there is nothing that you shall not know.

If you return to the Root [NIRVĀṆA], you will find the *meaning* of things. If you pursue only the phenomenal world, you will miss out on the Source. The moment you become Enlightened, you will go beyond appearances and the Emptiness.

The changes that take place in the phenomenal world we call "real" because of our *ignorance*. Do not search for the Truth; only cease having opinions about it. Do not remain in the dualistic state of likes and dislikes, this and that. If there is even a trace of this or that, right or wrong, your mind-essence will remain in confusion.

Although all dualities come from the One, do not get attached even to the One. When your mind is in an undisturbed condition, established in the Tao, nothing can disturb it. And when a thing can no longer offend you, it ceases to exist for you. When no discriminating thoughts arise, your old mind ceases to exist.

Sosan

The Moon is the same old Moon after my Enlightenment; the flowers are exactly the same as before. But I have become the *thingness* of all the things I see.

Bunan (a Japanese Master)

To be in the One Mind means to have no self-mind [No-mind] in all circumstances, not to be limited by any condition, not to have likes and dislikes, to deal with all phenomenal conditions, and yet to be eternally free from any form of striving.

To be in the One Mind does not mean that one is self-conscious [conscious of an ego-mind], nor is one in a state of abstract ecstasy, nor is one in an indifferent state or apathy, nor is ordinary consciousness wiped out. To be in the One Mind is to be *conscious* [awake], and yet to be unconscious of an ego-mind or the sense of "I" [the sense of "I am the doer"].

Your essential self-nature [your mind-essence] is the One Mind itself. The One Mind is the Ultimate Reality, the *true form* of things and the body of TATHĀGATĀ [the Buddha]. It is not a philosophical concept, but a *living experience*.

To see into the One Mind is to understand your essential self-nature. When you understand that you are the One Mind, you will not take hold of anything [you will not grasp at things to make them permanently your own]. Not to take hold of anything is the meditation of the Buddhas.

Ta-Chu Hui-Hai

∞

The 'No-Mind' 990

No-Mind and the One Mind 763

Resting in the No-Mind State of the Absolute 1014

Tao is Silent

The Tao is Silent.

Tao comes not and was not. Tao IS.

The Self-Moving Way (Tao) is a Path that is completely silent and tranquil. But this cannot be attained by the ordinary mind.

Tao speaks with the Voice of Light

Tao (the Way) cannot be spoken about, nor can it be written, but it can be *experienced.*

The Way of Tao is not to strive. We cannot acquire Tao by means of effort, by activities of body-mind-emotions, by the little self, but only by the *surrender* of the self.

Tao speaks with the Voice of Light. Listen! The Voice of Tao is everywhere, at all times. Still your mind to hear It.

∞

These are the words of a modern Zen student after gaining Insight, or a degree of Illumination:

The Universe, as it is registered by the five physical senses, is the least true, the least dynamic, the least important in a vast Geometry of Existence of *unspeakable profundity,* whose rate of vibration, intensity and subtlety are beyond verbal description. Words are useless in trying to describe this multidimensional Reality, which is a vast complex of dynamic Forces; to contact it, *you must abandon your normal state of consciousness...* Every act is only a visible moment in a network of causes and effects which reach backwards into the Unknowingness and into an Infinity of Silence, into which an individual consciousness, an ego, an I, cannot enter.

This is a description of an experience of TAO, the Mind, the Universal Mind, the Buddha-Nature, the ĀDI-BUDDHA (the Primordial Buddha-Mind), or simply, in Western terms, "God". For the Christian Mystic this would be the LOGOS, the Universal Christ-Being, the Cosmic Christ. For the Hindu it would be the ĀTMAN, the Universal Self, the One-Selfhood-in-All, or the PARABRAHMAN, the Transcendental Reality.

Zen Listening 787
The Path of Hearing 553
The Attitude for Yoga 558
The Silence of the Deep 1355
Silence and Activity 1446

The Zen Master according to Lao Tzu

The Wise Master has no expectations; therefore, no pupil can become a failure. Because he has no expectations about anything, nothing can go wrong.

The Wise Man leads a quiet and meditative life, whereas others are busy chasing after possessions, which exhausts them.

The Wise Master does not protect people from themselves

The Teacher teaches more by example than by words. He does not force issues. He does not *make* things happen, but waits for events to unfold by themselves.

The Master fears neither life nor death. In all situations he is eternally free.

The Wise Master does not impose himself upon his group; he allows his group members to develop individually. He judges none, and is attentive to both sides in an argument.

The Master does not make a show of "holiness"; he does not pretend to be someone "special"; he is simple and humble. He does not allow competition and jealousy amongst his group members. He does not gossip, nor does he waste his energy by arguing for and against different theories of life. He just gets on with his Work.

The Wise Teacher does not frequently interfere in the lives of his group members, for they all have to learn by themselves. He simply facilitates their spiritual growth.

The Wise Leader is selfless; he puts the well-being of others before the well-being of his own self.

The Wise Master does not protect people from themselves; they all have to learn by experience. Since Tao is everywhere, all peoples are equal. God has no favourites. The Light of Awareness shines equally on the good and the bad. Each person has to become responsible for himself or herself.

Be ye Lamps unto yourselves. Rely on yourselves and not on external help. Hold fast to the Truth as a lamp. Seek Salvation in the Truth alone.

Gautama Buddha, on his deathbed

One has to be a Light unto oneself. This Light is the Law. There is no other Law.

J. Krishnamurti

This is the Inner Light, which acts as a lamp to give Light. This Inner Guide, the Inner Teacher, is the Higher Self, the Voice of Light, which will reveal all things to the listening student.

Rely on your Inner Self 1226
Inner Guidance (Metanoia) 1464

The Wise Teacher is like water. Water refreshes and purifies all creatures; so does the Teacher. Water is fluid and adaptable; likewise is the Master. Water penetrates beneath the surface and wears away even rocks; likewise does the Master penetrate the hidden Mysteries of Life and wear down all the rocks of ignorance.

The Wise Master leads without dominating, accomplishes without being possessive, and gets the Work done without coercion.

The only way to reach a Master is when you don't have preferences. Simply come empty, without opinions, vacant, receptive.

A Modern Zen Master

Through meditation the Wise Teacher has found Infinite Beingness. This is why the Master is so *profound.* His leadership does not rest on mental techniques, nor on leadership models, but upon his Silent-Wisdom which springs from the Mind of Tao.

The Wise Leader follows the Way of the Feminine. He lets go in order to achieve.

The Good Master knows how to be Still, which means to follow the Inner Wisdom. The Wise Teacher knows how to cooperate with Tao. This is why he is so effective.

The Wise Teacher's ability does not rely on techniques, traditions and creeds, but on the *awareness* of what is happening in the Here and Now.

The Wise Man knows when to listen (Yin), when to act (Yang), and when to withdraw into Silence (Tao). Thus, the Teacher is male and female, and also possesses the Emptiness (ŚŪNYATĀ). He emphasizes being (Yin) over doing (Yang), and he remains centred at all times (Tao).

The Wise Master knows that the *reward* for doing the Work is in the doing of the Work.

The Sage does not care about success for himself; he is interested only in the success of others. The One Mind (Tao) behind all Creation shows us that true benefit and goodness blesses everyone and diminishes no one.

Yin, Yang, Tao 476
Cosmic Sensitivity 1009
The Law of the Higher Life 1134
The Approach to Truth 1152

The Zen Master

Real words are not vain, and vain words are not real. And, since those who argue prove nothing, the Sage does not argue.

Lao Tzu

A Master is one who has resolved the essential problems in life

A Master is one who has learned to control and dominate his or her mental body (thoughts), astral body (emotions) and the physical and etheric bodies (actions). You might say that this is not much, but it is everything! To dominate your thoughts, feelings, emotions and actions implies the use of special methods, special discipline, and a profound knowledge of the structure of human beings. It implies the knowledge of the entities of the Invisible Worlds, the entire structure of the Universe.

A Master is one who has resolved the essential problems in life. He or she is *free*. He or she possesses a strong will; but, above all, a Master is filled with love, kindness and Light.

Omraam M. Aivanhov

The Universe is beautiful, but it says nothing.
The seasons abide by fixed law, but they are not heard.
All Creation is based on principles, but nothing speaks.
The true Sage looks upon the Universe and pierces the
principles of all created things to the One Principle.
Thus it is that the wise and perfect man does
nothing but, in silence, gaze at the Universe.

Chuang Tzu

There are two modern Zen Masters who came out of Southern India: Śrī Ramana Mahāṛṣi, the Sage of Arunāchala (the Mountain of Light), and J. Krishnamurti. Ramana Mahāṛṣi and Krishnamurti were born with Buddhic Consciousness.

"Who am I?" (Kohaṁ?), said Master Ramana Mahāṛṣi. And, ever since then, this word has become a means to Enlightenment.

Krishnamurti, as a young child, was regularly caned at school and was punished daily by the teacher for "not remembering things" and not being able to "study". The schoolmaster could not understand that Krishnamurti truly found it difficult to produce a thought! It has been said of Krishnamurti that "he had not a single thought, and was only looking at the beauty of the World".

Pure Consciousness in the Heart 447

The Guru 389
The Sage 973
The Aquarian Teachers 1147
The True Teachers 1694

Mountains, Clouds and Water

In many of the Chinese CHĀN (Zen) paintings you see mountains, water and clouds. For the Chinese Mystics these have profound spiritual significance.

Mountains are immovable; they always mean steadiness, steadfastness, solidity and perseverance in meditation and in Spiritual Life. They also represent inner strength of character and Soul.

A Zen practitioner should be like the mountains, the clouds and water

Clouds always move freely, forming and reforming in response to external conditions and their inner make-up. This represents the virtues of freedom, flexibility, spontaneity and adaptability.

"Water is yielding but all-conquering," say the Chinese Masters. Water extinguishes fire, but, if it is overcome by fire, it escapes as steam! Water washes away soft earth but moves around rock! Yet, even rocks are washed away by water over a long period of time, with *patience.* Water saturates the atmosphere as humidity, or it can come down as torrential rain. Rivers give way to obstacles, yet persist in flowing to the sea, their objective. The Chinese Masters say: "Water conquers by yielding; it never attacks, but always wins the battle in the end." Whereas *fire* typifies the masculine qualities (the Yang), *water* represents the truly feminine virtues (the Yin), which are much respected in Chinese Mysticism.

According to the Chinese Masters of Chān (Zen), a Zen practitioner should be like the mountains, the clouds and water. That is, he or she must have inward resilience and steadiness, outward spontaneity and adaptability, deep humility and inner strength, and the ability to move into any changing situations with grace, ease and flexibility, without strain, anxiety or loss of purpose.

> Alone, cup in hand, I view the distant peaks of mountains. Even if my love came to me, could I be happier? The silent peaks neither speak nor smile, and yet, what happiness, what joy!
>
> *Yun Son Do*

> When one's life is in harmony with Nature, it is in harmony with Tao. The aim of human existence is to achieve harmony with Tao through achieving harmony with Nature and *within* one's self.
>
> *Taoism*

The Feminine Virtues 468
The Law of Mystic Experience 508
The Warrior Code 1077

CHAPTER 37

Zen Meditation

The Attitude of Zen

Zen is a teaching that cannot be grasped by the intellectual, reasoning, logical, discursive, verbal mind. This would exclude most people today!

Zen is an act of discovering yourself wordlessly.

Zen may be described as getting to know yourself as a Soul

Zen is not a particular method; it is more an *attitude*. Consequently it has many expressions, such as the Zazen meditational practices of the Japanese Buddhist monks, or martial arts such as Karate, Judo, Jiujitsu and Kendo (which the Japanese adapted from the various Kung-Fu schools of China). There are the Samurai (the warrior-class) and the famous Ninja warriors. Then there is the gentle Tai Chi, the Tea Ceremony, Zen Archery, and so on.

The basis of the Chinese-Japanese martial arts is "the dynamic-immediacy of Tao". Tao, the Universal Life-Force, is *dynamic* and *here and now*. In Christian Mysticism this would be called "the activity of the Holy Spirit in Creation" or "God Immanent within all things".

Zen may be described as getting to know yourself as a Soul, and getting to know God who dwells *in* your Soul. While this is how it would be described in Jewish, Christian and Muslim Mysticism, that is *not* how it is described in Zen Buddhism. The words might be different but *the experience is the same.*

Chi

Chinese: The *Vital Force* of Tao, the *Energy* of the Universe which flows through all things. In India it is called Prāṇa. It is a spiritual and psychic energy which becomes the five elements and gives *substance* to all objects. By controlling Chi, the Life-force, one achieves Conscious Immortality. This control of the Life-force is called Chi-Kung.

The Three Forces of the Warrior 996

Spirit 1343

Quietly Seeing

There are three important Zen practices: Listening, Seeing and Breathing.

In Zen *Seeing* there is no thought-process involved; you just see. There is no analysing of what you see, no criticism by the mind, no differentiation.

This leads to the state described by Krishnamurti as "the observer is the observed". He is talking pure Zen. This means that there is no differentiation or separation between you, the see-er, and what you see. This is Buddhic Consciousness, the State of Unity.

Thus, one of the Zen practices is just to quietly look at something, external or internal, but without thinking about it, without the mind reacting to it.

The Path of Seeing 552

Just Seeing 1018

Zen Listening

A popular method of Zen meditation is *Listening*. AVALOKITEŚVARA BODHISATTVA practised this form and thereby attained Nirvāṇa.

In this method, which is also recommended by the ŚŪRANGAMA SŪTRA, you enter deep meditation by the organ of *hearing*. At first there is the organ of hearing (the ear), the object you are listening to and the act of hearing. Later, the organ of hearing, the act of listening and the object listened to become one, merged, united. When the act of hearing and the object heard both come to an end, there comes a *clarity*, an *intense purity of mind*. There comes a Voidness, an Emptiness (ŚŪNYATĀ), which is the *formless* state of Mind.

In Zen Listening you listen without any thoughts

You may direct your listening in three directions:

- Outwards, to a single outer sound. Or listen to sounds of Nature, catching the *furthest* sound. There comes a great peace and a feeling of expansion.
- Inwards, to the sound of a mantra silently repeated, until the sound and the mantra are transcended.
- Inwards, to the internal sounds made by the cakras in the subtle bodies, or to other natural inner sounds, choosing always to listen to the subtlest sound heard.

If you listen to external sounds until you become absorbed in them, there comes an outward expansion of consciousness. Or, if you listen to the inner sounds heard inside your subtle bodies, thus comes Union with yourself, the Self.

> What do you do when you listen to the sounds of the birds, or the wind rushing through the leaves? Does your mind interpret? What do you do? You must simply listen!
>
> *Rajneesh*

In Zen Listening you listen without any thoughts, in stillness, in silence. Your whole attention is on *the act of listening*, not on what you hear. You listen *without reacting* to what you hear, whether it be the voice of a person, the song of a bird, the singing of a brook, the sigh of the wind amongst the trees or the sounds inside yourself.

When you listen to music, make your mind silent, for music is the note of Eternity. Every moment passes by like a musical sound. When you listen to music, you are hearing echoes of Eternity.

The Path of Hearing 553
Listening 1215

Listening to a Mantra

For some people it is easier to listen to the sound of a mantra as they repeat it, silently, inside the head. By listening to the subtle sound of a mantra inside yourself, you can transcend to Higher Consciousness, to the Formless-Mind (the Causal World) or the Superconscious Mind (Buddhi), the *No-mind* of the Buddhist Zen Masters.

It is during the Initiation that the subtle energy of the mantra is communicated

To receive such a mantra, however, one must become *initiated.* This is important, as it is during the Initiation that the subtle energy (Śakti) of the mantra is communicated. When you silently repeat the mantra, you are working with this subtle energy until the mantra itself is transcended and you come to the No-mind state (Buddhism) or Pure Consciousness (Hindu Yoga).

This No-mind state (Pure Consciousness, the Turīya or "fourth state" of the old Yogīs of India) is really the Higher Mind working on the causal subplanes of the Mental Plane (which are *formless)* and the Superconscious Mind working on the Buddhic dimensions.

Listening to Ōṁ

Listen, in deep Silence, to the Universal Reverberation, the Word, the Universal Logos, the Christ-Universal, the Ōṁ. This Sound is Cosmic-Intelligent-Vibration. It is cosmic, it is intelligent, and it is vibration. It is a Trinity, symbolized by Āuṁ:

- The Ā of Āuṁ is Akara, or creative vibration.
- The U of Āuṁ is Ukara, or preserving vibration.
- The Ṁ of Āuṁ is Makara, or destructive vibration (the "Devil").

Thus you will discover that all vibrations are within the Āuṁ, which is itself in the Ōṁ, the field of Absolute Oneness or Unity.

Turīya: Pure Consciousness 498
The Science of Bīja-Mantra 1218
Āuṁ, Ōṁ, Nāda 550
Listen to Nāda 1212
Meditation on the Sacred Word 1216
Hear the Sound within the Silence 1651

Remember that Gautama Buddha was a Hindu Brahmin. He practised all the Hindu Yoga methods of meditation and handed them down to his disciples. Thus, the Buddhist methods are essentially selected forms of ancient Hindu Yogic practices.

Listening to the Sound of the Dharma

Avalokiteśvara Bodhisattva attained Satori (the Enlightened Mind, Bodhi) by "Listening to the Sound of the Dharma". This method consists of "hearing inwardly your Self-Nature".

In the Sikh religious tradition this practice is known as Dhūn, "inner listening". In Hindu Yoga it is known as "listening to the Nāda", the Soundless Sound, the Voice of the Silence. Jesus referred to this practice as "listening to the Voice of the Holy Spirit". In the Christian Bible this *Sound of the Dharma* is called the Gospel and the Logos (the Word). This Sound-Current, the Sounding-Light Current, the Word, is also the Life-Current, the true Life inside you. In Zen this is also known as "the Stream of Bodhicitta".

Man does not live by bread alone, but by the Word that proceedeth out of the Mouth of God.

Matthew 4:4

- You begin by listening through your right ear. You *ascend* the various subtle worlds by following the Sound-Stream. Your attention will first be in your right ear, then it will switch to the middle of your head, then it will go above your head.
- After much inner listening to the Sound-Current, the mind attains stillness. With continued practice, the faculty of hearing and that which is heard are merged. They "come to an end". Samādhi is that stage of Dhyāna (meditation) wherein the mind is no longer disturbed by anything. It is also translated as *Ecstasy*.
- Then dawns upon the meditator the Śūnyatā, the Voidness, the formless or bodiless condition where there is no subtle body or form and no sensation of a personal "I" or ego.
- Then comes the "all-embracing Brightness pervading all directions". This is the *real* Mind, the profound Mind of the Buddha. This is Nirvāṇa, your Self-Nature. In Zen, this Mind is also called "the fundamentally clear and pure Mind". In Tibetan Zen it is "the Clear Light of Reality".

Dharma: the Law of Being 244
Samādhi: the Goal of Yoga 574
Śūnyatā: the Void 503
Nirvāṇa is... 98

What is the Sound of the Dharma? For Dharma means Truth, Religion, the Teaching, the Law, the Doctrine, the Buddha's Teaching, the Fundamental Reality, the Absolute Body of Truth or Light. It also means any one thing, an object great or small (visible or invisible), the sameness of the noumenal (spiritual) and the phenomenal (material).

You will find the Sound of the Dharma in *active Listening*. As your listening deepens, so will your understanding of the Dharma, the Truth of all things.

Between the Two Extremes, Find the Middle Point 1100

Bodhicitta
Sanskrit: An Energy which works towards Enlightenment, or the Energy which comes *from* Enlightenment. Also, an enlightened motive for living.

Zen Silence

Zen Silence is the pure Silence *above* thinking, *before* thinking, *between* thoughts. It is mental quiescence, mental silence, a non-movement of the mind. This mental silence is beyond Time and beyond Space. It is the stopping of thought.

Zen Silence is learning to tune into the fundamental note of a thing

Zen Silence is learning to tune into the *fundamental note* of a thing, whether it be the note of your own Being (your Soul, or *Self-Nature* as the Buddhists call it) or the note of a bird, an insect, a tree, the sea, the sky or a star.

If you can tune into the fundamental tone of another, which still vibrates on its own key note of Being, it will purify your own fundamental tone and help you discover it.

By listening to another's Being, you can tune yourself into your *own* fundamental note of Being.

- First, find the fundamental note of your personality.
- Then find the note of your Ego (the Human Soul in the Causal World).
- Then find the note of your Spirit, the Ātman.
- Then find the note of your Monad, "your Father which is in Heaven", the Paramātman.

The Universal Fundamental Note is the *Cosmic Absolute,* and included in It are all the fundamental notes of stars, solar systems, suns, planets, angels, humans and atoms.

With the non-arising of a single thought, the Brightness of the Self-Nature appears in full.

Hanshan (a Chinese Zen Master)

This is the Nirvāṇic Light, which appears after you have gone through the formless mental subplanes (the Archetypal Worlds) and the Buddhic subplanes of Essential Unities or Love-Wisdom.

The Great Wisdom of the Other Shore 769

No-Mind and the One Mind 763
When the Mind is Still 768
Suspended Mind 1209
Cultivate Silence of the Mind 1239
The Silence of the Deep 1355

The Experience of Silence

Our Silence is not just an emptiness, like death. On the contrary, it draws us ever nearer and brings us ever closer to the Fullness of Life. We are silent because the words by which our Souls would live cannot be expressed in earthly language.

A Carthusian monk

For O! We know not what each other says. These things, you and I, in sound, we speak. But *their* sound is but their stir, for *they* speak by silences.

Francis Thompson (a Christian Mystic)

Like silence after noise or cool water on a hot day, Silence and Emptiness *clears up* the mind and recharges the batteries of spiritual energy.

Benjamin Hoff

He who has ears to hear, let him hear what the Holy Spirit has to say to him.

Jesus the Christ

Stillness and peace are the real temples wherein God most often visits His devotees.

Paramahansa Yogananda

Hearing God's Name is meditation on God; it will steady the mind. Hearing God's Name will destroy sufferings caused by wrong thoughts and deeds.

Guru Nanak

When the mad activity of the mind is brought to a stop, then comes BODHI (Enlightenment).

From the Chinese Masters

The aim of Chān (Zen) is to disentangle the mind from thoughts and feelings, and from external phenomena of objects, so that the Self-Nature can return to its normal state and operate normally without the hindrance of the thinking process.

The transmission of the Chinese Zen Masters

Remaining relaxed and inwardly calm enables one to move quickly when the time arises. Stillness settles the vital forces and calms the mind. *One should not be disturbed by the wind of another's spirit.* He who is to become a master of motion, must first become a master of Stillness.

Chinese Kung Fu

Yoga is the suspension of the fluctuation of the mind-stuff so that the Self can abide in his native condition.

Patañjali

It is That which is not put together by thought.

J. Krishnamurti

He who knows, remains silent.
He who speaks, knows not.
Close the gates and doors of your senses,
and soften the lights of the outer world.
Turn your noise into Silence,
and you will behold the miracle of Oneness.

Tao Te Ching

To Silence the Mind 1212
The Practice of Silence 1443
The Seven Stages of Sūfī Silence 901
The Silence of the Warrior 1008

Listen to the Silence

Zen is mental silence which comes as a result of no-thinking. This is a natural silence in the mind, not a forced one. It is the Silence *beyond* the sensation of Space and the passage of Time.

Zen is the Silence beyond the sensation of Space and the passage of Time

Zen is the art of *Listening* and *Seeing*.

Zen is a returning *into* Silence.

Zen Silence is Zen *Listening*.

Zen Listening is tuning into your own *fundamental note*.

Silence means that you have to be *you*, as you really are. Forms and rituals cannot reach it.

Watching and listening, with no thought. This is Zen Silence.

This means that you are *actively aware* of life. In your Zazen processes you see and observe, you listen and hear, but no thoughts come to your mind about the things you see and hear.

The centre of the storm is *Stillness*. We call this Silence SAMĀDHI.

The Thinker and his thought must come to an end for Truth to be.

J. Krishnamurti

The *Thinker* is *you* in your causal body, you as the Ego, the Soul. The *Truth*, or perception of BUDDHI, the Soul-Wisdom, can come about only when you stop thinking, when you stop mental activities, when your mind becomes absolutely still and quiet. Then Truth just *is*.

The Seer is pure Vision, but he looks out upon the world through the window of the mind.

Patañjali

This means that your Original Consciousness is warped by your thought-processes.

The Process of Seeing or Perceiving 542

The Experience of Mysticism 636
Vipassana 1221
See the Light of the Logos 1650
Hear the Sound within the Silence 1651

When you are a beginner in prayer, you talk to God. When you are more advanced, you *listen* to God.

Sit very quietly, with your attention not fixed on anything, without an effort to concentrate, your mind just being quiet and still.

Sit still, without effort, *listening to everything.*

The Voice of Light is peaceful and gentle

Listen to the Voiceless Voice of the Universe, the Voice of the Silence.

Be *still* and *listen*. The Voice of Light will always speak to those who want to know the Truth. You need only have faith that the Inner Voice will guide you.

The Voice of Light is peaceful and gentle.

Not even a Sage can impart a *word* about the Realm of Silence from which all thoughts issue. Not even a Buddha.

∞

The following statements by the Masters are each about Silence:

Not to speak does not necessarily make you silent, for the mind still moves in all directions. But, when the mind is dissolved in Mind itself, then you are one with the One.

When the individual self (Jīvātma) dissolves in the Supreme Self (Param-ātma), then who will speak to whom?

One who hears the Sound of Ōṁ attaches oneself to the Inner Lord.

Each of these statements concerns the Third-Eye. The Third-Eye Centre is a gate, a door, but it is also a *window*. Through the door you go in; through the window you look out. The Mystery of the Third-Eye is bound up with Ōṁ and the *Five Words*.

The Sound of Ōṁ, Ōṁkāra Dhwani, is the Mind of Truth; one should meditate upon it in the body.

Guru Nanak

The Voice of God 864
Inner Guidance (Metanoia) 1464
Meditation in the Third-Eye 1224
Remember the Presence 1653

Mindfulness of Breathing

ĀNĀPĀNASATI is a Pali word which means "mindfulness of breathing" or "being aware of breathing". PRĀṆĀYĀMA (breath-control) was a favourite method of Yogic meditation in old India before and during Buddha's time and is still so today. There are over a hundred different techniques of Prāṇāyāma, of which Ānāpānasati is one.

Warrior Breathing 1020
Watching the Breath 1213
Three Kinds of Breathing Meditation 1220
Prāṇāyāma-Vidyā 1553
Awareness Meditation 1656

> The disciple, by whom the breathing exercise with self-control is to perfection brought, practised the method as the Buddha taught, has cast a radiant glow around the world. Behold the mind become radiant white, expanded beyond measure, practised well. Its nature understood and overcome, the mind is shedding radiance everywhere.
>
> *Mahā Kappina*

In the HAṬHA YOGA PRADĪPIKĀ of India, and similar Yogic works founded on the practical experiences of the Yogīs, the breath (PRĀṆA) is described as follows:

> The mind is the master of the senses. The breath is the master of the mind. The breath, in its turn, is subjugated by LAYA (absorption, concentration, awareness), and LAYA is subjugated by NĀDA (Sound). This total absorption (LAYA) is called MOKṢA (Liberation, Freedom). When the mind is absorbed, ĀNANDA (Ecstasy, Bliss) is experienced.

The mind must be concentrated at the tip of the nose, where the air (Prāṇa) enters the body. There must be an awareness of touch as the air enters the nostrils. The air is felt when in-breathing and when out-breathing.

An old Yogic instruction

The Buddha himself describes this process in the ĀNĀPĀNASATI SUTTA, thus:

A monk, who has gone to a forest, gone to the root of a tree, empty handed, simple, sits down cross-legged, holds his back straight, concentrates, becomes aware. With awareness he breathes in; with awareness he breathes out.

Notice that there is no sensation of *controlling* the breath, only watching, observing, focusing on it, being aware of it. This is very important!

The Buddhist monks practise several forms of this "mindfulness of breathing". For instance:

- Watching the breath at the tip of the nose.
- Watching the abdomen rise and fall.
- Being generally aware of in-breathing and out-breathing.
- Counting the breath.

These are four of the 108 or so ancient Yogic Prāṇāyāma methods, most of which are unsuitable and dangerous for average men and women. You must remember that, in the above four methods, there is no effort to *control* the breath. The breath moves naturally, on its own. There is only watching, observing, being aware. There are many other methods where the breath is interfered with, or forced, or regulated wilfully. Those methods could be dangerous for the average student of mystical life. These four, however, are safe for popular usage.

Salutation to the Buddha

Ōṁ Namo Amitābhāya Buddhāya!

Salutation to the Buddha of Boundless Light!

Followers of the *Pure Land* School of Buddhism repeat the above mantram, or just Amitābha Buddha!, to gain Enlightenment. The repetition of a Sacred Name must be done *silently*, by the *inner mind.* In this practice you repeat it in your Third-Eye and then transfer your attention to above the head.

> Nirvāṇa's glorious Vision is Bliss that Man can claim, if he but devoutly and sincerely repeats Amitābha Buddha's sacred Name.
>
> *Honen*

Amitābha
Sanskrit: Light-Limitless, Light-Endless, Boundless Light, measureless Ocean of Light. This Amitābha is the Ain Soph Aur (Boundless Light) of the Jewish Kabbalists, the *Face of God.* In Japanese it is known as Amida, which means "Endless Light".

The Christ in the Heart 441
The Kabbalistic Tree of Life 359

In the East, this Limitless Ocean of Light has been symbolized as a Buddha for the same reason that the Jewish Mystics call it Makroposophus (the Great Face of God, the Sublime Countenance). The Infinite Light is conceived of as a Buddha because it is an Intelligent, Self-Conscious Light-Beingness. It is not just an impersonal light, like a candle or a torch flame; it is a *Living Intelligence,* a *Cosmic Mind,* a *Cosmic Person.*

This is the nearest that Zen or Buddhism get to the idea of God as a "person". Normally the humanized idea of "God" is not used in Buddhism or Zen as it is in the Jewish-Christian concept of God.

Some Zen schools in China teach their pupils not to repeat the Buddha's Name, but to continually ask themselves in meditation, "Who repeats the Buddha's Name?" This is a Hua-Tou or concentrated self-training. This is the same method as Ramana Mahāṛṣi's "Who am I?" technique. You keep asking yourself these questions in deep meditation until you penetrate beyond the mind into the greater Mind.

> There is a constant flow of Light. It is known as the Buddha of Infinite Light (Amitābha). If we perceive this Light with an uninterrupted attention, we shall be born into the Pure Land (Nirvāṇa).
>
> The Radiance of this Light surpasses all. It is called the Buddha of Infinite Light. Those who are embraced by this Light are cleansed from the dirt of Karma, and attain Freedom (Nirvāṇa).
>
> *Shinran*

A 'Godless' Religion? 754
Pure Consciousness in the Heart 447
Touch Ultimate Emptiness 96

Meditating on Kōans and Hua-Tous

The Japanese word KŌAN is from the Chinese KUNG-AN, "a case which establishes a legal precedent, a formulation pointing towards the Truth". Kōans are not supposed to be logical; they are not meant to be solved by reason or intellectual thoughts, nor by the discursive intellect. The word, phrase or idea into which a Kōan is resolved is called WATŌ, from the Chinese HUA-TOU "a pointer to the Mind-Essence".

Kōans are not meant to be solved by reason or intellectual thoughts

HUA-TOU (Chinese) = WA-TŌ (Japanese).
KUNG-AN (Chinese) = KŌ-AN (Japanese).

KŌAN

A KŌAN (KUNG-AN) is a riddle which, when meditated upon, penetrates into the heart of Truth. Kōans are sometimes stories, sometimes just words, all designed to shake up one's normal perception of things. Some well known Kōans are:

What is the meaning of Mu?

What is the sound of one hand clapping?

When a hair swallows up the ocean, the ocean loses naught.

When you hit the needle's point with a mustard seed, it shakes not the needle.

Some schools of Japanese Zen concentrate heavily on Kōans as a means of meditation. The purpose behind a Kōan is to grasp the BHŪTATATHATĀ, the Original Reality or Buddha-Nature.

HUA-TOU
Chinese: "A pointer to the Mind-Essence". An ante-word or pre-word. The mind in its pure state before a thought arises.

BHŪTATATHATĀ
Sanskrit: The Essential, unchanging, immutable Original Reality or Buddha-Nature beyond temporary forms, phenomenal limitations, or the cycles of birth and death. From BHŪTA, "Essential Substance", and TATHATĀ, "That which is unchanging, eternal, forever the same; the *Suchness* or unvarying nature of the Eternal; TAT (Being, Eternal Reality)". In the theistic religious language, BHŪTATATHATĀ is "God".

What is the sound of one hand clapping?

The answer to this favourite Zen Kōan is, of course, *Silence*—the silence of the No-mind state, the formless (void) Causal Mind.

Hua-Tou

Following are some examples of Hua-Tous:

Who is repeating the Buddha's Name?

Mind is Buddha.

Not a single thing can be gained, and not a single thing can be done. (For, if *you* be doing, there will be birth and death, and if *you* gain, there will be loss.)

The Chinese and Japanese always meditated in the Solar Plexus Cakra

The early Zen Masters of India meditated in the Third-Eye Cakra using the breath method (Hong Sau, Haṁsaḥ). Previous to the arrival of Zen, however, the Chinese and Japanese always meditated in the Solar Plexus Cakra; hence the Chinese and Japanese Zen monks and students meditated on their Hua-Tous in the solar plexus.

Drop your awareness from its normal location (at the front of the skull, between the eyes), in a straight line down to the solar plexus, and repeat the Hua-Tou there, *understandingly*.

There is a direct link between the Third-Eye Centre and the Solar Plexus Centre. The solar plexus is an important centre of the *personality*. It is the focus for your ordinary emotions, your astral body, and is the opposite pole to the Third-Eye Centre, which is the focus for your ordinary, natural mind. It is through these two centres that you master your personality. That is why it has been said by the Masters of old that those who hold the Hua-Tou in their minds *efficiently* can clear up their passions and thoughts instantaneously.

Remember:

Many little insights produce great Enlightenment.

And don't forget what the ancients said:

Our Way consists of abandoning our baggage, for our Home is quite near.

This is why the Masters of old also said that:

If the preceding thought does not arise any more, it is Mind.
If the thought coming after does not end, it is Buddha.

Rest in the Great Breath 1654
The Psychic Centre 49
The Functioning of the Cakras 52

Zazen: Zen Sitting

In the earliest days of Zen, you could realize Enlightenment at any time, by any means

In the earliest days of Zen, in both India and China, sitting down and meditating was not the main practice at all. You could realize Enlightenment at any time, by any means, under any circumstances! It is because the human mind became increasingly degenerated by materialism that formal sittings in CHĀN (Chinese: meditation) became necessary. In Japanese, this formal meditation sitting is called ZAZEN.

The Japanese monks' stages of spiritual practice are as follows:

- Counting your breaths.
- Following the breath with the mind's eye, or observing the breathing process without control of the breath.
- SHIKANTAZA: Concentration without an object in the mind, without a thought, without watching the breath. (This is what Patañjali would call *seedless meditation*.)
- Care is taken that the monk's external environment is peaceful, serene and beautiful.

Originally, Zen had many techniques. As it is practised in modern-day Japan, however, it is extremely limited. The Japanese limit themselves to focusing *only* in the Solar Plexus Centre, and there they count the breath, or watch the breath, or practise KŌAN or SHIKANTAZA.

The development of the Solar Plexus Centre was a major step for the Atlantean epoch, and the Chinese, Japanese, Koreans, Eskimos, North and South Americans, Mongols and Tibetans have evolved from sub-races of the Atlantean race. In the early days of Zen, however, the HARA (solar plexus) was not the only cakra used as a focus of meditation. In Vietnam, for instance, the Zen Buddhist monks focused in the Third-Eye Cakra, where they knew the Soul could leave the body at will and enter higher dimensions. The Tibetans also focused in the Third-Eye, as well as in the Crown Cakra at the top of the head.

The purpose of Zen sitting is alignment:

a. Alignment of the personality (mind, emotions and body).

b. Alignment of the Soul with the personality.

c. Alignment of the Spirit with the Soul and the personality.

The Human Cakras 44
Human Evolutionary Epochs 176
Meditation is Integration 1193

Sayings of Lao Tzu on Zen Meditation

TAO, the Divine Essence, cannot be defined, but it can be *known*. The method is meditation: *being aware of what is happening where you are.*

Effective action arises out of Silence and from the experience of Being. Silence is a great source of strength. Be still, go into a valley which is uninhabited, or watch a quiet, solitary lake. Your silence will grow until you experience the Silence of Tao.

The way to *do* is to *be*.
Lao Tzu

Learn to see the Emptiness (formlessness) in all things. When you enter a house, enter its *emptiness* (its space). Similarly, see and feel the emptiness inside a vase or pot, which is the *real usefulness* of it. And see the emptiness of the sky (space). Silence and Emptiness reveal what is the Essential (Tao).

Allow time for silent meditation. Turn *inwards* into Silence and Space (Emptiness) to understand the *real* meaning of things. Let your physical senses rest and become inwardly still. In order to *know* your Inner Wisdom, you have to be *still.*

Meditation is a *keen awareness* of what is going on inside you and around you, and of the change or development that is happening in the Here and Now.

TAO, the Ultimate Reality, is a Principle—that which comes *first*. Creation is a Process—that which *follows*. Tao is universal and is the Source of all things. All processes reveal the underlying Principle, which is Tao. Therefore, Tao can be *known* in this way. You can know It by becoming silent and being observant of Consciousness.

∞

Krishnamurti said:

"Let go!"

In the olden days, the Chān Master Hui Chueh of the Lang Yeh mountains was teaching when a woman came up to him and asked what to meditate upon to attain instant Enlightenment. He said, "Let go!" And, by letting go of all cause-producing thoughts, in a short time she beheld her Self-Nature.

Shikantaza

SHIKANTAZA is usually practised by advanced meditators. "You must drop body and mind," advised Ju-Ching. Normally, this is done in the lotus posture or the heel posture. In any situation, however, if you can "drop body and mind", you will gain *Insight,* the goal of meditation. This is SHIKANTAZA.

SHIKANTAZA
Japanese: "Just-sitting" or "to sit fully aware". From SHIKAN (wholeheartedly) and TAZA (to hit the awareness).

The Zen monks describe SHIKANTAZA, the highest form of concentration, in these words:

> SHIKANTAZA is sitting still, in the lotus posture or the heel posture, like the Buddha did, with an unshakeable faith in the Buddha-Mind, with your mind void, empty of all thoughts, conceptions, ideas, beliefs, points of view, reason and logic. Sitting (meditating) in this way will, in time, *actualize* the BODHI-Mind (the Wisdom Mind) with which human beings are endowed.

SHIKANTAZA has been described as:

The cultivation of a profound Inner Silence.

The looking into one's Heart-Mind.

To sit with a sense of dignity and grandeur as a Man (like a Buddha).

To be filled with intense gratitude for the Buddhas and for the Dharma, the Omnipotent Reality.

The discovery of one's True Nature, one's Original Condition (in Nirvāṇa).

When practising Shikantaza you must have faith in your own hidden Buddha-Mind and in the Higher Order of Reality (DHARMA) which pervades the Universe. One day, sitting like this, persevering, you will *directly perceive* your own Bodhi-Mind, which leads to Enlightenment, SATORI.

To be anxious for SATORI *does not work.* Thinking "I must get Enlightened" is as much an impediment as any other thought. Simply sit, with poise, stability, equanimity, in Stillness. You must cultivate a *profound silence, surrender and receptivity* inside yourself.

Expect Nothing 1205
How to Succeed in Meditation 1206
Stages of the Silent Meditation Process 1186
Contemplation 1188

Hold your mind in the HARA (solar plexus) and be still, without breathing, until it happens.

In this method you do *not* attempt to control or suppress the breath; this is *not* the Hindu Prāṇāyāma. You sit still (for a long time!) until—naturally, easily—the mind drops all thoughts and the breathing becomes lighter and lighter, until it almost disappears on its own or becomes inward and subtle. This is not easy to do, as one soon finds oneself to be very restless.

The breathing becomes lighter and lighter until it almost disappears

You may practise this Stillness also in the Heart Cakra, or in the Third-Eye or Crown Cakra. Or simply *look outside* yourself and observe an aspect of Nature in silence and stillness, without thinking, without registering or analysing what you are observing.

Since this is difficult for most beginners, it is recommended that at first they meditate with an "object" such as a Kōan, or by counting the breath or watching the breath. In the greater Zen tradition, the Universal Zen, mantras also are used as a focus for meditation.

Meditating on the Void

In Tibetan Zen Buddhism you are asked to meditate on ŚŪNYATĀ, the Void, the Emptiness. Unless you understand this practice, you are in danger. It is *not* a meditation on annihilation, negation, nihilism or nothingness. Nor is it a mere blanking-out of the mind, or putting yourself in a vacuum-like condition. That will lead you to mediumship and psychism, and possibly to possession. That is *not* what is meant by this practice.

The real ŚŪNYATĀ means a *formless condition of Being*. It is not an empty, negative condition; on the contrary, it is an intensely positive one. But, to reach this condition, the mind must be in an absolutely positive, alert and bright state. That is why it is recommended that you begin by practising "meditation with form".

This Tibetan Zen idea of ŚŪNYATĀ (formless) meditation is the same as the Japanese SHIKANTAZA. You should attempt it only after you can meditate with an object, when your mind is positively concentrated and alert.

Śūnyatā: the Void 503

Clouds of Unknowing 704
The Fullness of the Void 23
Formless Worlds 1372
Involuntary Possession 310

A Summary of Zen Meditation

There is nothing to seek outside ourselves.

If you have faith in God, go and pray. If you believe in Zazen, go to the Zendō and sit.

Zazen is just to be present in the process of Zazen itself

When you are sitting in Zazen, *don't think*. All you have to do is sit down in peace and harmony.

Sitting as the Buddha is Zen. And how does the Buddha sit?

Zazen is just to be *present* in the process of Zazen itself. This is called SHIKAN-TAZA, or continuous self-awareness. There is no goal in Zazen.

Sit quietly, without any movement, and observe what your mind is doing. Don't try to control it; just be aware of how your thoughts are moving. Don't do anything about them, but watch your mind, just as, from the banks of a river, you watch the water flowing by.

Action Zen

You do not have to confine your ZAZEN or SHIKANTAZA only to sitting (which is over-emphasized in Japanese monasteries). You can uphold the same attitudes and realizations while walking, talking and doing other tasks, engaged in life.

Every action issues from the BODHI-Mind. Therefore, every act has the inherent purity and dignity of the Buddha.

You can *realize* this in action in your daily life, as a form of meditation. Some Zen Masters say:

To enter fully into every action with full Consciousness is also ZAZEN.

This is called mobile-Zen or action-Zen. From here come Kung Fu, Kendo, Archery, Calligraphy, and so forth.

Meditation in Action 1019
Karma Yoga: Divine Union by Action 1132
Silence and Activity 1446

When the Prāṇa of respiration makes the mind one-pointed, he becomes steady in sitting. Conversely, steadfast sitting and concentration will eventually make the breath tranquil.

What is your mind before it is stirred by a thought?

Take the Sacred Word Ōṁ and pronounce it—not according to the books, but according to your own *fundamental note.*

Samādhi is to just be present where you are

Enlightenment (Satori) is not a question of how to do it, but how to *allow* it to happen. It is a matter of *relaxing into* your mind, not a matter of activating your mind.

Not to seek for anything is to rest in Tranquillity.

Sitting patiently, clear your mind of images, of rituals and beliefs, of symbols, words and mantras, of all fears and all hopes. Then you shall *see* the Real, the Eternal, the Everlasting.

Sit, with your mind very quiet, *listening timelessly* to everything that is happening.

Be *awake* to everything!

Samādhi is to just be *present*, where you *are*, with *wholeheartedness* (with your whole Heart Centre). This is you and the Universe coming together.

The Essentials of Zen Meditation

- One-pointedness (concentration).
- Pointing directly to the Mind (the Self-Nature).
- Simplicity.

The Science of Meditation 1173
Meditation Practice 1201
The Heart and Spontaneous Meditation 1227

The Masters on Meditation

Sitting in meditation, even for a short time, is better than building temples (STŪPAS) as many as the grains of sand on the banks of the Ganga (Ganges) river.

The Lotus Sūtra

The DHARMAKĀYA (the Body of Truth, NIRVĀṆA) can be realized by meditation without waiting to pass through countless Aeons (KALPAS).

Śūrangama Sūtra

Turn the Light inwards in yourselves so that you can be liberated from mortality.

Master Hsu Yun

Self-cultivation takes an unimaginable time, whereas Enlightenment is in an instant attained.

The ancient Chinese Masters

Followers of the Way who understand the idea of instant Enlightenment do not practise external exercises but reflect only *within themselves* upon their Original Natures. Thus they gain insight into Truth.

Hui Neng

ZAZEN is not so difficult. Just free yourself from all incoming thoughts and hold your mind against them like a steel wall. Or, imagine your room to be the whole Universe, and that all sentient beings are sitting there *with* you, as One!

Soyen Shaku

Make your Hearts dwell in loving-kindness, and whatever you have gained from your ZAZEN, offer the results for the benefit of all beings. Avoid pride and intellectualism. Do Zazen *innocently,* without aiming for anything.

Keizan Zenji

SATORI is not so much a matter of progress; it is a leap in Consciousness. Put your mind in the bottom of your belly and inhale and exhale "MU".

A Japanese Zen tradition

Voice "MU" from the bottom of your belly all night, from the Hara Centre, not from the top of your lungs.

A Japanese Zen tradition

Put your mind in the bottom of your belly (HARA). There is a blind Buddha there; make him see!

Nakagawa Roshi

Hold with care the attitude of the Observer, and do not identify yourself with the phenomena you experience or may experience in the future.

Master DK

It cannot be grasped by the physical eyes, nor by any other of the physical senses, nor by speech, nor by thoughts, nor by any austerities and self-torturings. Only by a *Serene-Wisdom,* by your own inner Pure Essence, can you see this Homogeneous One in meditation. This subtle Self can be known only by a mind in which the ordinary life is sleeping, a mind purified of the self.

Mundaka Upaniṣad

True meditation is waiting. True prayer is infinite patience. True religion is not allowing your mind to create problems for you.

If you can make your mind to wait, meditation happens. If you can make your mind to assume the position of waiting, you will be in prayer.

Waiting means no-thinking. It means sitting on the river bank and not interfering with the stream. What *can* you do with the river? Whatsoever you do, you will only make it more muddy. If you walk into the stream, you will only create more problems. So, sit patiently on the river bank and wait.

A modern Zen Master

∞

CHAPTER 38

The Path of Zen

Life as a Zen Monk

The Japanese form of Zen is almost contrary to the spirit of Zen

The life of a Zen monk in Japan, even today, is harsh, rigid, regulated and over-disciplined, very much in line with traditional Japanese forms. It is more like a military academy than a system of spirituality. Every moment of the day is accounted for. It is not at all in line with the original spirit of Zen, which was characterized by freedom, spontaneity and a lack of authoritarianism. The Japanese form of Zen is almost *contrary* to the spirit of Zen!

In some Burmese Theravada monasteries the monks meditate for sixteen hours a day, alternatively sitting and walking. Thus, all the exercises are restricted to sitting meditation or walking meditation. A monk will spend ten years in this discipline and another ten years training if he wants to become a resident priest in a small temple.

One may ask: does such fanaticism bring Enlightenment? Sometimes it does. But there are many people who have experienced Enlightenment without such regimentation and authority.

Whether you want to be a Zen monk or live freely in the world and be a Zen man or a Zen woman, there is an important element in Zen which is the key to it all:

> When you are hurrying along in life, there is a large part of the world around you that you cannot see. Zen teaches us that in order to find ourselves, and to find our place in the scheme of things, we have got to stop, look around, see inside and outside ourselves. Paradise is all about us, but in order to gain it we must stop and look.
>
> *Keido Fukushima*

Spirituality and Renunciation

It must be noted that all religious instruction in old India, as well as in Buddhism, was addressed to monks, sādhus, sannyāsins, people who had *renounced* the world. It was a time when Spirituality was divorced from worldly life. Even the Buddha made a distinction between life in the world and the Spiritual Life, as did Jesus.

Spiritual Life and Material Life 1118

Pāda II Sūtra 31 565
Monks and Disciples 991
Is Renunciation Necessary? 1119
To Become a True Renunciate 257

The Japanese Zen Retreat

Following are a few important Japanese words which relate to Zen retreats

Sesshin
A spiritual retreat. To train oneself in seclusion. A Zen intensive, normally composed of Zazen, Teishō, Dokusan and Kyōsaku.

Zazen
Intensive meditation practice. Zen-sitting, or sitting down and meditating.
Zazen: Zen Sitting 798

Teishō
Formal class or lectures by the Zen Master.

Dokusan
Private instruction and counselling; private interview.

Kyōsaku
The "big stick". Kyōsaku is a symbol of Manjusri's "delusion-cutting sword".

Zen
An abbreviation of Zenna, from the Sanskrit Dhyāna (meditation) and the Chinese Chānna (which was also abbreviated to Chān).
Origins of Zen 752

Zenji
A Zen Master.
The Zen Master according to Lao Tzu 780

Zendō
The room where Zazen is practised. The meditation hall. Also, Sōdō.

Roshi
The Spiritual Teacher, the Master, the Guru.

Godō
The Way of Enlightenment. Also, Daigo.

Tettei
Complete Enlightenment.

Kenshō
"Seeing into one's own true nature." A glimpse into one's own Immortality. Insight, Intuition, seeing into Reality, Inner View. The same as the Sanskrit Bodhi and the Japanese Satori. In Western language, this would mean a glimpse of yourself as an Immortal Spirit, or Soul, on the planes of Eternal Being.

Hara
The Solar Plexus Centre, considered to be the centre of gravity for a human being.

Kōan
From the Chinese Kung-An, "a case which establishes a legal precedent, a formulation pointing towards the Truth". The word, phrase, or idea into which a Kōan is resolved is called Watō, from the Chinese Hua-Tou. Some schools of Japanese Zen concentrate heavily on Kōans as a means of meditation.
Meditating on Kōans and Hua-Tous 796

Sesshin

A Sesshin (Zen spiritual intensive) might be for one day, or four or five days, or perhaps a week. It is normally composed of Zazen (intensive meditation practice), Teishō (formal class or lectures by the Zen Master), Dokusan (private instruction and counselling) and Kyōsaku (the "big stick").

The idea of Sesshin is to experience Kenshō

The idea of Sesshin is to experience Kenshō—Insight, Enlightenment, Intuition, seeing into Reality, Inner View.

In Zendō (the meditation hall) the participants are assigned places by head monks and are instructed to come and go quietly and unobtrusively. In the Japanese Soto Zen monasteries the meditators sit facing a wall. In the Rinzai sect they sit facing each other.

Meals are taken in silence and utensils are handled silently. Normally you eat less during a Sesshin, but asceticism is not required. Eating is communal and all start and finish at the same time. There is no fasting; one is to keep up one's strength for the Sesshin.

Meals are preceded by *Sūtra chanting*. In Sanskrit, the word Sūtra means "a thread upon which pearls or jewels are strung". *Sūtra chanting* specifically refers to the reciting of the scriptures or sacred books. This is *not* mantra repetition, nor is it the same as bhajans or kirtans. Sūtra chanting is not singing and it does not repeat itself; it is the reciting of a scripture passage once through.

Blind Tradition

Due to a lack of understanding, not everything the old Masters did in the past was correct. For instance, when *Fa Kuang* experienced Wu (Awakening, Satori), suddenly he found himself extremely creative mentally. "Words and sentences came to him day and night in endless succession." This was considered by the Zen monks and Masters to be an abnormal condition, a *disease*, and the remedy was to beat him to unconsciousness! Beating seemed to be the remedy for many ills.

This was simply a lack of understanding of the functioning of the several layers of the Mind. And this is why you should not follow a tradition blindly just because it is a tradition, even if it is Zen!

Traditionis 379
Religion and Spirituality 754
Dimensions of the Mind 891

Kyōsaku

Kyōsaku, the "big stick", is a symbol of Manjusri's "delusion-cutting sword". In the Rinzai sect the "big stick" is applied by the head monk, striking the student from the front so the student knows when he or she is going to be struck. In the Soto Zen sect the "big stick" is applied from the rear, unexpectedly, suddenly, surprisingly, without warning. In the Rinzai sect the student requests a whack of the "big stick" to keep him or her alert, but in the Soto monasteries you get the whacks whether you want them or not! And lots of them, all for free!

The Japanese made a military tradition out of Zen

This is a typically Japanese idea and is *not* part of the Universal Zen tradition. The idea was to encourage the Zen Buddhist monks to meditate more fanatically in their quest for Enlightenment. The Japanese made a military tradition out of Zen, which was originally much softer and more fluidic.

Zazen

The central purpose of a Sesshin is to do Zazen, or Zen Sitting, or sitting down and meditating. Zazen is to develop the powers of concentration, to achieve unification of the mind and inner tranquillity (which is often very difficult with the head monk screaming and yelling and distributing large whacks with the big stick on the back and shoulders!). Furthermore, in Zen monasteries they have no variety from sitting, and little walking. Consequently, most meditators suffer excruciating pain in the legs and back.

The final goal of Zazen is Self-Realization, or knowing one's Buddha-Mind, one's fundamental nature.

The practices of Zazen are:

- Counting the breaths.
- Watching, observing or following the breath.
- Shikantaza. Concentration, without counting or watching the breath.

Traditionally, all practices are done in the Hara (the Solar Plexus Cakra).

Zazen: Zen Sitting 798
Mindfulness of Breathing 794
Shikantaza 800

Balanced Practice

In the traditional Zen retreat the emphasis is on sitting. For most Westerners, too much sitting causes excruciating pains which detract from the meditational process. Thus, I believe that sitting-meditation (ZAZEN) should be counterbalanced by activities and bodily exercises.

Sitting-meditation should be counterbalanced by activities and bodily exercises

The following are additional activities which I include in Zen Retreats. These activities are not part of traditional Zen, but are very essential when balance is needed:

- Dancing.
- Haṭha Yoga, Tai-Chi, or other forms of bodily exercises.
- Long walks in Nature, in silence.
- Outdoor meditational practices.
- Working with sound: sound-immersion, music, mantras, bhajans.
- Rituals.
- Zen work.

Zen Work

Zen work is work on your *being,* flowing in with events, "doing" with *awareness.* You work with a silent mind. All work is done by the Buddha-Mind.

The purpose of Zen work is:

- Gathering knowledge (self-observation).
- Attaining an objective.
- Learning self-control.
- Grounding the Teachings.
- Giving up the ego or self-will.
- Group integration.
- Harmonizing your centres (cakras).
- Overcoming personal difficulties.

The highest goal of Zen work is to surrender to the Living Being known as TAO, the One Mind, the All-Pervading Life-Current of the Universe. This is done by harmonizing your vibrations with the Universal Tao, which expresses itself in you, in Nature and throughout the Cosmos.

The purpose of work is to Awake!

Balance in Spiritual Life 505
Primordial Balance 995
Balance on the Physical Plane 1257
Tao: the Supreme Way 776

Relaxation

If the retreat is longer than one week, the following should also be included:

- Relaxation, such as swimming and hiking.
- Creativity, such as performing plays.

Mantras

The whole idea of Zen is spontaneity

The Japanese Kōans (the "nonsense mantras") can be replaced with proper Sanskrit mantras (as was the case originally!) or sensible sentences of Truth upon which the students *can* meditate. One does not have to follow the Japanese tradition *blindly*. The whole idea of Zen is *spontaneity* and the discovery of the Truth for yourself.

Rules for a Modern Zen Retreat

- *Silence*. Silence means that you are quiet all the time. Communicate only in writing, or in a whisper only when it is *necessary*—when giving or receiving instructions, work allocations, and so forth. Aim to be silent, deep inside yourself, at all times. Meals are in silence and utensils are to be handled silently. When you wash the dishes, do not clatter or make loud noises.
- Eating is communal, in silence. Do not fast or wear down your body. Eat normally.
- Do not say or do anything unnecessary.
- During the retreat, do not engage in personal relations, love affairs and personality problems. You will spoil the retreat for yourself and others.
- Work is sacred. Every action springs from the Buddha-Mind. Realize that everything you do is the work of the Buddha. Therefore, it must be done well, efficiently, lovingly and freely, thereby honouring the God within yourself.
- Respect the *Teacher* and the *Teaching*. Without the Teacher you cannot go anywhere. You will realize this someday, when you overcome your ego-pride.
- Do not criticize others, neither verbally nor in your mind.
- Be group-conscious. Forget yourself. You are not important; the group is. Live for the group, work for the group; thus you will overcome your own petty personality.
- Be always punctual, on time. Do not have people wait on you. Do your duties gladly and willingly. Sacrifice yourself; this way you will grow rapidly in spiritual stature.
- Do not stay up all night. Have enough sleep so that you are not tired the next day. Zen requires energy; thus, conserve your energy. Sleep well and eat well. Lazy and tired people cannot get SATORI (Enlightenment). You need to generate lots of BODHICITTA (Energy for Enlightenment) in order to break through.
- Be happy, and smile. Remember that the *Silence of the Buddha* and the *Laughter of Lao Tzu* are but two sides of the same Zen.
- Above all, remember that you are not going anywhere, for *you* are the Path and *you* are the Goal and *you* also are the means of achievement.

Return to Duty

True Zen is not an escape from outer reality, but a sanctification of it

The ancient idea of Zen, Taoism, Buddhism, Christianity, Sūfīsm, Sikhism, Islam, and so forth was to *escape* from the worlds of matter (the Physical, Astral and Mental Planes) into the worlds of *Substance* or *Essential Matter* (the Buddhic Worlds and upwards). As a result, this world and the afterlife worlds (the reflection-spheres) were not helped. The purpose of true Spirituality is not division, however, but the integration of Spiritual Life into the life in the world.

The inner experiences have to be transmuted into outer service.

There are Mystics in all religions who get lost in inner experiences. They experience the Higher Reality through prayer, meditation, contemplation, silence, inward striving and aspiration, and they separate themselves from the world, from their environment. Then there are those Christians (such as many of the monks, nuns, missionaries, priests and lay people who devote their lives to outer service of the poor, the needy, the sick, the troubled) who have Faith, but *no inner experience* of God or the Spirit or the Soul.

But *true* Christianity, and true Zen, is based on the experience of the God-Reality *first* and then its practical expression in *outer service,* helping Creation to fulfil itself perfectly. True Christianity and true Zen are not an escape from outer reality, but rather, a *sanctification* of it. The Teaching has to be *lived* in practical life, as there is no separation between the Inner Light and the outer darkness of *apparent* material bodies. This is the true meaning of the sentence in *The Lord's Prayer:*

> Thy will be done on Earth, as it is in Heaven.
>
> *Matthew 6:10*

The word *Heaven* refers not to the heaven worlds in the reflection-sphere, but to the Kingdom of God above. The attainment of the Higher Worlds (the Worlds of Light, Spirit or *Substance)* is only a partial objective of the new spiritual disciple. Today, in the New Age, in the new Zen, in the new Spirituality, the disciple accepts his or her duty to help evolution in the lower three planes (the Kingdom of the World) so that the Light of Truth, the all-embracing Light of Nirvāṇa, might unfold the Divine Plan on "Earth".

God-Consciousness is the Wholeness of Life 504
The Dichotomy of the Mystic 629
Relational Consciousness 906
To Love God and the World 1392
Duty and Spirituality 1641
Piscean and New Age Spirituality 1706
Let Thy Will Be Done 1720

The Steps to the Experience of Zen (Sanskrit)

- SILA: Virtuous conduct, or the right way to be for *you*. Achieving a harmonious state of being inside yourself.
- DHYĀNA (DHYĀN): Intense *internal* meditational practices. Silence, Solitude.
- PRAJÑĀ: The resultant Wisdom, Insight.

The most important things in life are Love and Wisdom

The Seven Qualities to enter Paradise

Following are the seven qualities needed on the Path of Spiritual Development to enter Paradise:

- Love.
- Inclusiveness.
- Self-sacrifice.
- Service.
- Unselfishness.
- Wisdom.
- Meditation.

On the human level, this is what you *can do* to develop qualities in you that will *coincide* with the fundamental notes of the Causal and Buddhic realms.

The Being of Light 416

> It is the *quality* of your life that determines your place on the Ladder of Evolution.
>
> *Master DK*

The most important things in life are Love and Wisdom. At the time of your death your life flashes through your consciousness and you measure yourself against the nature of the Being of Light, whose very essence is Love and Wisdom. This is your individual Judgment Day. It is *not* the work of an angry, avenging Jehovah, but your own inner, silent realization of your shortcomings. This is why you should make every effort, while still in the physical body, to improve yourself, to live by the Law of Love, and to develop more and more Spiritual Understanding.

In ancient times there were five practices necessary for the attainment of Illumination, Higher Consciousness or Union with God:

- Aloneness.
- Detachment from the world.
- Isolation from people's mental auras.
- Silence.
- Purification of the body, mind and emotions.

Since the beginning of the Āryan Epoch, another quality has been added that must be practised by the aspiring disciple of Spiritual Life: *Service to all life.*

The Call to Service 1705

The Four Vows of the Bodhisattva

1. All beings without number, I vow to liberate.
2. Endless blind passions, I vow to uproot.
3. Dharma doors beyond measure, I vow to penetrate.
4. The Great Way of the Buddhas, I vow to attain.

The Ten Mahāyāna Precepts

An unregulated outer life makes the inner work of meditation impossible

1. Do not kill.
2. Do not steal.
3. Regulate your sex life.
4. Do not lie.
5. Do not consume alcohol or drugs or cause others to do so.
6. Do not criticize others.
7. Do not praise or exalt yourself.
8. Be charitable, sincerely, openly.
9. Avoid anger, hate or negative emotions.
10. Do not forsake the BUDDHA, the DHARMA and the SAṄGHA.

The Ten Mahāyāna Precepts and the Four Vows of the Bodhisattva were given by the Lord Buddha 2,500 years ago to help His followers on the Spiritual Path. They are for laymen and laywomen as well as for Buddhist monks and nuns. They are also followed by students of Zen.

Five hundred years later the Lord Christ gave similar rules in His Sermon on the Mount, in the *Beatitudes.* These rules are general, universally applicable, and are a *must* for all seekers. Some sort of regulation of behaviour, of outer life, is always necessary if one is to take up the Spiritual Life seriously. An unregulated outer life causes inner disturbances, tensions and emotional upheavals which make the inner work of meditation impossible.

Yoga by Eight Steps 560
Pāda II Sūtra 30 563
Integrity and Perfection 1005
Sādhanā: the Spiritual Life 1153

The Noble Eightfold Path of the Buddha

1. Right Understanding (right mind).
2. Right Desire (right feelings).
3. Right Speech (mantra, prayer).
4. Right Action (on the bodily level).
5. Right Living (right lifestyle).
6. Right Effort (positive energy).
7. Right Meditation (technique).
8. Right Samādhi (Divine Union).

The Path begins with the correct mental evaluation of life (right understanding) and ends in Pure Consciousness, Conscious Immortality, Divine Union, Union with God, Nirvāṇa, Bliss.

The Path begins with the correct mental evaluation of life

The Governor and the Bird Nest

There was a CHĀN (Zen) Master in China called NIAO-KE, the "Bird Nest", because he used to do his meditations perched high up on the branches of a tree. The governor of the province visited him one day and shouted up to him, "You have a dangerous seat up there in the branches!"

"Yours is far worse than mine!" the Master shouted back.

The governor was taken aback and said, "Well, I am the governor of all this district and people obey me; I don't see what danger I am exposed to."

"Then you do not *know* yourself," replied the Sage.

"Why?" asked the governor.

"For one thing, when your passions burn, and your mind is unsteady, what can be more dangerous than that?"

The governor fell silent, and then asked the Master, "What is the teaching of the Buddha?"

"Do not do any evils," replied the Zen Master, "but do only what is good, and keep your Heart always pure. This is the teaching of all the Buddhas."

But the governor wasn't happy with the answer. So he said, "But any child knows that!"

And the Sage shouted back at him, "Yes, any child may know this verbally, but even for an old Master of eighty years it is difficult to do." And with that he entered into Silence.

Right Practice 1696
Cultivate Knowledge 1366
Samādhi: the Goal of Yoga 574
Qualifications for Discipleship 1149
Guard your Heart 1328

Satori: the Experience of Illumination

BODHI (Sanskrit), SATORI (Japanese), Enlightenment, Mystical Union, or Illumination, is not a haphazard happening at all. It is an expansion of Consciousness, the result of an inner yearning, persistent effort at meditation, silence, contemplation and a certain way of life.

Light 978
The Path of Light 89
The Path of Illumination 1338
Illumination and Deification 1190
Realms of the One Mind 492

Illumination is the experience of Superconsciousness. This experience is *not* the experience of the subconscious mind (erroneously called the "unconscious"). The Universal Subconscious Mind is what we call the Astral Plane, and your "personal" subconscious mind is your astral body. Superconsciousness begins at the higher (formless) mental subplanes (the Causal World) and includes the seven subplanes of the Buddhic Plane. Thus, there are several kinds of Illumination, several degrees or stages of Mystical Union.

When Illumination strikes you while you are embodied in your physical body, then (depending on your level of Union) you are engulfed in a Golden Radiance or a Living Intelligent Light.

The Light streams through me.
It is in and around all things.
It is within and without all Space.
It shimmers translucently.

"I" melt away, the ego is liquified.
The energy of the Light is music,
a silent inner music, yet so aloud,
It stops the Heart with Ecstasy.

I cannot speak, nor think, nor write.
Even movement is difficult,
as the boundaries of the self collapse
to give way to the Greater Self.

Tumultuous waves of Joy sweep over me,
cascading rivulets of Light dance inside,
but there is no inside and no outside,
only a swirling, living Radiance.

This is the Light of God,
bursting through the boundaries of Creation.
All is swallowed up in the Light,
and all objects are specks floating in It.

This is the Fundamental Truth,
the Truth of you and me,
and all that is, was, and is yet to come.
From Light all things come.

How beautiful is this Light!
Shining in streams and rivulets!
And oceans and rivers and seas!
Light upon Light, everywhere!

The vast spaces of Emptiness
are filled with brilliant atoms of Light,
swirling and dancing to the Endless Music.
The Musical-Light forms all that is.

If the Music would stop,
or the Light fail,
you and I would burst into nothing.
For this is the stuff of Life.

This is true Gnosis or hidden Insight.
This is the Silent Unity of all that is.
It is the Source, the Middle, the End,
the Alpha and Omega of all things.

The Light is in everything,
and in everyone.
Who could live and be without it?
It is only that people have forgotten.

All Emptiness is filled with Light.
All Space is full.
All Matter is empty.
Only the Light remains.

There is the reality of Matter,
of an objective world of forms and shapes,
and subjective forms and imprints.
This is the lesser reality.

And there is the Universe of Light,
Formless, Silent, Awe-inspiring,
the Kingdom of God,
guarding Eternity.

The Radiance of Eternity
shimmers and dances through,
and darts hither and thither
in the Worlds of Time.

It is the exaltation of all
that cannot be expressed in words.
The Light cannot be expressed,
nor confined, nor conditioned.

A state of relaxed receptivity
is all that is required of you,
receptivity to the Glory that is God.
And no amount of thinking will help you.

Thought cannot reach this Light.
No language can express it.
It is the fabric of the Universe,
the Glory of the Ineffable.

It is the Oneness of Buddhi
and the Brilliance of Nirvāṇa.
The moment I stilled my thoughts
I was flooded with Knowledge.

A curious Knowing is this,
which is revealed by the Light.
It is an Unknowing Knowing,
for you know by the Root of the Mind.

The greatest thing is to know the Light,
and to know the phenomenal worlds
as One with the Light.
This is the Supreme Knowing.

Be still, and let the Light flow.
It will come in its own time.
The Light is unstoppable when you are ready.
The Being of Light embraces you silently.

A stream of Knowing,
of an Inner Joy,
a Conscious Immortality,
Where no questions are asked.

This is Certainty.
No more seeking or questing.
Surrender to the Steady Flame,
the Eternally Present.

The Way of the Zen Masters

Three times the cry goes out to all the Pilgrims upon the Path of Life. "Know thyself" is the first great injunction, and long is the process of attaining that knowledge. "Know the Self" comes next, and when that is achieved, man knows not only himself, but all the Selves. Then, when man stands as an Adept, the cry goes forth "Know the One"—search for That which is the Cause....

Master DK

The attainment of Nirvāṇic Consciousness, becoming a Buddha, is possible only through the denial of the little ego, the self-hood, the egocentricity, and through the labour-in-Love for all sentient beings.

Soyen Shaku

If you want to be happy, then lead a simple life, use what you have, and be content where you are.

Lao Tzu

Know the things as they are.

Hermes Trismegistus

It is the *harmony* of the individual with himself and with his environing units, and his *realization* of the essential Oneness of all Life, which brings about the great expansions of Consciousness which lead to the individual's *identification* with the greater Whole.

Master DK

The Enlightened Man is one who understands that life and death, joy and sorrow, pleasure and pain, are of no ultimate consequence. The Enlightened Man recognizes that he or she is not identical to his or her experience, that he or she need not be implicated or bound by anything, that he or she is, essentially, free.

The Enlightened Man personifies the unsurpassed happiness of Awakened Consciousness, which is native to all beings, but not yet realized by them.

Da Free John

One must act in accordance with the principles of one's system. If these principles are lost, one is in disarray. He who keeps pure to the principles of his system can reason by them and understand the results of each of his actions.

Chinese Kung Fu

Having attained that Primeval Consciousness, the Absolute Bliss which is Truth, and which is formless and without action, abandon this illusive physical body which has been assumed by the ĀTMAN within you, in the same way as an actor abandons his costume after the show is finished.

Viveka Chudamani

I am ĀTMAN [the Pure Original-Consciousness], eternally pure, eternally enlightened, ever free, the One Existence, without a second. I am Bliss Infinite. I am VASUDEVA, the All-Pervading One, and I am ĀUṀ, the Creative Power.

Panchikaranam

He who renounces identification with all outer activities, and worships at the sacred and stainless altar of ĀTMAN, which is above time and place, distance and causation, which is present everywhere, which is the destroyer of all pairs of opposites, the giver of eternal Happiness, becomes *all-knowing, all-loving* and *all-powerful,* and attains, in the hereafter, Conscious Immortality.

Śrī Śaṅkarācārya

He who denies ĀTMAN, denies himself. He who affirms It by meditation comes to *know* himself.

Taitteriya Upaniṣad

The Sages [MUNIS] studied the rituals prescribed by the Vedas, and went *beyond* them to the Truth [SAT].

Mundaka Upaniṣad

Whatever lives is full of the Spirit [the Self]. Claim for yourself nothing. Enjoy Creation, but do not covet God's property.

Īśa Upaniṣad

Life is uncertain, but death is certain.
Life is precarious, but death is for sure.
Life has death as its goal.
There is birth, disease, suffering, old age and death.
These are the aspects of existence in this world.

Mahasi Sayadaw

The journey from exploring for Truth to grasping it is often a long one, full of twists and turns.

Han Ying

Impermanent are all compounded things.
Their nature is to rise and to fall.
When they have risen, they cease.
The bringing of them to an end is Nirvāṇa.

Gautama Buddha

All that Is is ever present. We are concerned only with the *constant awakening* to that which eternally Is, and which is ever present in our environment, but of which we are unaware, owing to our spiritual blindness.

Master DK

Really to *live* requires a great deal of Love, a great feeling for Silence, and a great simplicity.

J. Krishnamurti

Consciousness is a form of energy, and Life is energy itself.

Master DK

Out of manifestation, Time is not. And, freed from objectivity, states of Consciousness are not.

Master DK

The Teaching's fundamental teaching is that it has no Teaching. The Teaching of no-teaching is a Teaching too. Now that the Teaching of no-teaching has been transmitted to you, has there ever been a Teaching?

Gautama Buddha's transmission of Zen to Mahākāśyapa

The Spiritual Light shines in Solitude, disentangling the attention from sense-objects. The experience of true Eternity does not come by reading books. Your Fundamental-Mind is taintless and is perfect. Free yourself, by this Light, from ignorance-producing causes, and master the state of Buddhahood.

Pai Chang (a Chinese Zen Master)

Even the highest Sons of God, on our manifested planetary system, can grasp only *partially* the Purpose and Plan of the Divine Logos.

Master DK

This teaches us great *humility*, which is always the mark of a Saint!

The Bright, Eternal Self that is Truth and the Bright, Eternal Self that lives *in* Man are one and the same. This is Immortality; this is Truth; this is the All.

The Upaniṣads

In other words, the Eternal, the God-Being, is permeating our lives and our environment all the time, but we need to become *aware* of this fact by the process of meditation. This is Zen.

∞

A Summary of Zen

Close your eyes and you will *see* the Truth.
Be still and you will move forward on the tide of the Spirit.
Be gentle and you will need no strength.
Be patient and you will achieve all things.
Be humble and you will remain *free.*

You must realize the liberating power of your own Buddha-Nature

When the wind blows through the scattered bamboos,
the bamboos do not hold the sound after it has gone.
When the wild geese fly over a lake,
the lake does not retain their shadows after they have passed.
So, the mind of the Superior Man works when an event occurs,
and becomes still again when the matter ends.

When we eat, there is no eater, only eating.
When we walk, there is no walker, only walking.
When we work, there is no worker, only the working.
When we meditate, there is no meditator, only meditation.

Going nowhere and doing nothing. How do you go Nowhere? And how do you do No-Thing? It means that you go along, listening to all the things you can't hear, and not worrying about the results.

Once you enter the Buddha's Way with sincerity and zeal, myriads of Bodhisattvas will spring up everywhere around you to help you. You must have courage and faith, and you must *realize* the liberating power of your *own* Buddha-Nature. And you must *persevere,* no matter how much pain and sacrifice the Way may entail.

The Angel with the flaming sword turns away from the Gate to Paradise all those who are not yet ready to enter. The Angel protects the aspirant, not the gate through which he strives to go. This is the Mystery of Divine Love.

The Path of Non-Duality 762
The Law of the Higher Life 1134
Attach your Mind to the Eternal 1234
To Succeed in your Quest 1330
The Wisdom of Not-doing 1699

The Universe is One.

The One Mind pervades all.

All is One, and you are a part of all that is.

There is no Universe apart from me.

Begin the Path by cleansing your Heart

We are thoughts in the Mind of God, and Love is the great Cosmic Energy that holds us together in God's Mind.

God is the Self in Man.

Because Man is essentially one with God, a human being can realize his or her Innate Perfection and Blissful Existence in Divine Consciousness.

What is That which, when it is *known,* all is known?

The Zen Masters always taught their disciples to stop seeking for Enlightenment and Buddhahood.

All truths come from the Spirit of Truth *within* you.

Begin the Path by cleansing your Heart.

Not to commit evil, but to practise only good, and to keep one's Heart always pure: this is the teaching of the Buddhas.

Reduce your life from complexity to simplicity to find the fundamental note of your Being. This requires a simple life and a simple mind.

The knowledge that you don't have to control everything is a revelation.

The Truth will stay, the rest will pass away.

The One 1686
Consciousness 1370
Perceptions of the One Mind 490
No-Mind and the One Mind 763
Purify the Heart 701

The Heart and the Head must become wholly one in the One.

Realizing your own Buddha-Nature is not so much a step-by-step process, but rather the result of a *mental leap.* When your mind is empty, you can make this leap.

The meaning of Zen is a flowing mind

If you want BODHI (Enlightenment), make your mind as barren of preconceptions and as empty of thoughts and as innocent as a new-born baby, with no self-will and no ego.

You will attain SATORI when you completely *forget* yourself.

Do not try to take your circumference to the centre.

To Love is not to ask for anything in return, and not to feel that you are giving something.

Just see Life-energy in motion, every day. This is *Realization.*

Observe the many things always interchanging: this is the play of Tao.

You can watch the snowflakes falling down in Silence, and then all is White.

Sitting in solitude, like a mountain: this alone is required.

The meaning of Zen is a flowing mind.

An empty mind brings Enlightenment.

Abide in a wordless state of mind.

Zen is the celebration of simple things.

There is nothing to realize!

Sitting silently, doing nothing, spring comes and the grass grows by itself.

The Path to Immortality 430
Your Mind is the Key 1208
The State of Innocence 1306
Tantra Mind 933
The 'No-Mind' 990
Silence, Solitude, Peace 1386

From the beginning, all beings are Buddhas. This Earth upon which we stand is the pure Lotus Land of the Buddhas, and this very physical body of mine is the body of a Buddha.

My thoughts travel far away; inside I am free.

When the mind is no longer comparing, criticizing or evaluating, but sees only *what is*, moment by moment, without wanting to change things, there is the Eternal.

A Moment is nothing more than a Being that arises constantly

The *Moment* includes the Whole.

If you see the Moment from your individual viewpoint, it is limited. The true Moment is vast and infinite, and it extends to all sentient beings in the Universe.

A Moment is nothing more than a Being that arises constantly.

Zen means *Awakening.*

You are *you*. But you are not only *you*, you are the whole Universe.

Come out of *your* world into *Ours.*

Are you the One who is *You?*

Stop thinking, stop analysing, stop imagining! This is it!

The Circle of Love 905
The Spiritual Warrior 969
The Heart and Spontaneous Meditation 1227
The Psychology of Consciousness 1363
Time and Eternity: Action and Destiny 1399

PART SIX

Sūfī Meditation

The Way of the Holy Fire

CHAPTER 39

The Sūfī

Mystics of Islām

There are two kinds of religions: the outer and the inner, the orthodox and the esoteric or mystical. All of the great world religions, such as Judaism, Christianity, Islām, Hinduism, Buddhism, Jainism, Sikhism, Taoism and Shinto, have within them these two aspects.

Sūfī-sm is the inner religion of Islām

For the vast millions of the world, there are the outer religions of orthodox beliefs, rituals, ceremonies and priestcraft, and rules and regulations invented by the religious "authorities" who describe them as "commandments" of God. The hundreds of millions in all the world religions are entrapped by these.

SŪFĪ-sm is the esoteric or inner religion of ISLĀM, which, in Arabic, means "surrender" or "submission". For the SŪFĪ, the submission is not to the outer religious authorities and commandments, but to the Light Eternal That Ever Shines, to the Radiance of Eternity, to the Immortal Absolute that is ALLĀH. For the SŪFĪ, the whole meaning of life is to practise the Way whereby one may *experience* this Glory of the Divine Being and become One with It forever.

MUSLIM
Arabic: "A believer". One who believes in the One God.

ISLĀM
Arabic: "Surrender or submission to the One God".

QUR'ĀN
Arabic: "Revelation".

SŪFĪ

The word SŪFĪ means "One who has purified the Heart", that is, One who has attained Mystical Union with God.

In the Persian language the word for Wisdom is SŪF. A SŪFĪ, in Persian, means "a Wise Person", an Enlightened One, an Illumined Mystic who has experienced God firsthand.

But SŪFĪ is also an Arabic word. SŪF means "wool", and a SŪFĪ was one who wore a coarse woollen garment. It was a monkish outfit, similar to that of the Christian monks, worn by the early Muslim Mystics who renounced the world in order to search for God.

Thus…

While the orthodox religious make a pilgrimage (Ḥāj) to the Ka'ba in Mecca (the Black Stone or Qube), the Sūfī makes the Pilgrimage in his or her Heart to the *direct experience* of God within and the God without.

While the orthodox go to Makkah, the Holy City (*Mecca*, in English), the Sūfī searches out the Kingdom of God within.

The Sūfīs look into the Mirror of the Heart and see Themselves

While the orthodox read the Qur'ān, the Holy Book (*Koran*, in English), the Sūfī reads the Messages that God has traced into the Human Heart, the Cosmic Law.

While, for the orthodox, Muḥammad (*Mohammed*, in English), the Praised One, the Prophet, is the giver of the Religion of Islām, for the Sūfī, Muḥammad is Nūr 'Alī, "Light Most Exalted", the Grand Revealer of the Mysteries of the Heart and the Secrets of the Universe.

While, for the orthodox, the Mullā (Persian: the learned man, the scholar, doctor, theologian) is the guide and leader, for the Sūfī it is the Shaikh (*Sheikh*, in English), the Spiritual Master, who is the Leader and the Guide in life.

While, for the orthodox, the place of worship is the Masjid (*Mosque*, in English), for the Sūfī it is the Throne of the Mālikul Raḥīm (King of Mercy), Malkān Malkā (King of Kings), Mālikul Mulk (the Lord of the World). This is the Secret Place, known only to the Sages who have climbed up upon the Planes of Being, upon the Ladder of Light, and found the King, Malīk, whose Radiance and Glory never dies, from Age to Age, until the End of Time.

Search out your Heart 437
Orthodoxos: correct belief? 653
Religion and Spirituality 754
Traditionis 379

The Sūfīs look into the Mirror of the Heart and see Themselves.

Languages of Islām

The major languages of Islām are Arabic, Persian and Turkish.

Note that within this section all Sacred Language terms are Arabic unless noted otherwise.

The Radiant Way

The Sūfīs call the Spiritual Life the *Radiant Way,* the *Shining Path* or the *Light of Faith.*

> The Love between a true lover and the Beloved [God] is a great secret, and is not comprehensible to one who has not experienced it.
>
> *A Sūfī saying*

The first stage is the stage of ordinary religion

The Shining Path has seven stages:

1. Sharī'at
2. Ṭarīqat
3. Ḥaqīqat
4. Ma'rifat
5. Quṭbīyat
6. Qurbiyat
7. 'Ubūdiyat

1. Sharī'at

The first stage is the stage of *ordinariness,* the stage of *sleep* in which average men and women find themselves. It is full of suffering and dualities such as pleasure and pain, light and dark, good and evil. This is the stage of ordinary religion, where one strives to abide by the Sacred Law, the Holy Qur'ān, the words of the Messengers and the Prophets.

In this stage one should fight against one's imperfections and evil tendencies, the so-called vices and sins, by constantly reminding oneself of the Law of the Prophets and Sages. Of this stage it is said in the Holy Qur'ān:

> If Satan [the Adversary] tempts you, seek refuge in Allāh [the Resplendent Light]. For He hears all and knows all.
>
> *The Qur'ān: Chapter on the Revelations Expounded*

Sūfī Terminology

Note that these Arabic words can have a variety of meanings, according to the various Sūfī traditions. For instance:

Sharī'at can refer also to the Divine Plan, the Spiritual Laws governing Creation.

Ṭarīqat can denote the Path itself, the Journey to Spiritual Enlightenment.

Ma'rifat sometimes refers to a stage of intermediate Realization, preceding **Ḥaqīqat**.

The Journey of the Heart 855

The Four Stages of Spiritual Life 1160

2. Ṭarīqat

This is the beginning of the Mystic Path. Here one *imitates* the lives of the Holy Messengers and the Prophets. Here is true *conversion* to the religious life, true faith in God. This is the stage of discipleship and spiritual practices. One begins to act only according to virtues and perfections, positive qualities such as Faith, Hope, Love, Charity, Kindness, Wisdom and Compassion. One lives a saintly life, resigned to God's Will. The following virtues are especially cultivated:

One lives a saintly life, resigned to God's Will

Ṣabūr: Patience.

Shukūr: Happiness, peace, contentment.

Tawakkalallāh: Trust in God.

Alhamdulillāh: Realizing that all praise, glory and fame belongs to God only.

Shaikh: The Spiritual Teacher's influence.

3. Ḥaqīqat

This is the state of merging into God, or Union with God. It is the experience of the Vision of the Eternal Beauty, the Glorious Light (Allāh). It is the enjoyment of the Love of God, the Divine-Bliss-Consciousness, Ecstasy, the Embrace of the Beloved. This is the State of Being of the Messenger, the Prophet. It is the Mystical Flight of Love. In the East it is called Samādhi or Self-Realization.

4. Ma'rifat

The advanced stages of Mysticism. The Height of the Mystical Union. The state where only God's Light exists, in which there is no day or night, nor birth or death, nor coming or going, nor advancement or delay, nor Time or Space. It is Conscious Immortality, the Kingdom of God, where everything is *known* as it *really is.* It is the stage of Inner Knowing, called "the Secret of the Messengers".

The Ten Mahāyāna Precepts 814
Qualifications for Discipleship 1149
Samādhi: the Goal of Yoga 574
Mystical Union 846

There are three states which are higher still:

5. QUṬBĪYAT
   The Central Axis of Reality.

6. QURBIYAT
   The Proximity of Reality.

7. 'UBŪDIYAT
   The Reality.

Each of these stages relates to the conquest of one of the seven great Planes of Being

Note that these stages relate to the conquest of the seven great Planes of Being:

ḤAQĪQAT	–	The various stages of Samādhi
MA'RIFAT	–	Buddhi
QUṬBĪYAT	–	Nirvāṇa
QURBIYAT	–	Paranirvāṇa
'UBŪDIYAT	–	Mahāparanirvāṇa

Of the first stage, SHARĪ'AT, it has been said:

There are as many paths to God as there are breaths in sentient beings.

Of the second stage, ṬARĪQAT, it has been said:

He who knows himself, also knows his God.

Of the third stage, ḤAQĪQAT, it has been said:

Beyond the mind lies a whole new Universe, inexpressible and inexplicable to human reason and logic, the *World of Witnessing*.

Of the fourth stage, MA'RIFAT, it has been said:

Wheresoever you turn, there is the Face of God.

The Sūfī Master

The Holy Man, the Guru, the Spiritual Teacher, the Master, is called the **SHAIKH**.

Another name for the Guru is **IMĀM**, the Spiritual Teacher, the Holy Man.

Another name for the Master is **MURSHID**, the Spiritual Guide, or **PĪR-O-MURSHID** (Persian).

Another name for the Spiritual Master is **QITUB**. For it is said:

There are always QITUBs in the world, special beings who take care of Souls. For the Perfect Man, the Complete Man, lies hid within each one of us.

Esoteric History of the Piscean Religions

Before you can understand the sublime aim and practice of the SŪFĪ Path to Union, you need to understand some esoteric history.

The past Piscean Age (approximately 2,150 years) was, in many ways, the most influential in the history of Humanity on this planet. It gave birth to three major religions:

The Piscean Age gave birth to three major religions

a. Christianity, AD33 (the first century of the Christian Era).
b. Islām, AD612 (the seventh century).
c. Sikhism, AD1500 (the beginning of the sixteenth century).

Christianity was founded by YESHŪ BEN-PANDIRA (Jesus the Christ).
The Muslim religion was founded by the Prophet MUḤAMMAD.
The Sikh religion was founded by GURU NANAK.

These three world religions have one thing in common: they are all Piscean. It is not surprising that three religions came into being during this time.

- Christianity was founded at the beginning or *opening* phase of the Piscean Dispensation.
- Islām was founded during its upswing or *peak activity* period.
- The Sikh religion was founded during its downswing or *down-winding* period.

The Action of the Holy Spirit 279
The Coming of the Christ 724
Destined by the Stars? 260

Zodiacal History

What you read in history textbooks is not the real history. Historians write down results, not the causes. They record how human beings *react* to some things, that is all (and most of the time people react badly). History is *written in the "stars"*, not in the social theories of historians!

During the past 2,150 years (the Age of Pisces), our Sun travelled through space and received vibrations, rays, energies, forces and frequencies from a certain group of stars. These energies penetrated our whole Solar System and affected all life upon the planet Earth, including the human species, producing certain *reactions* in Humanity. Historians mistakenly think that these reactions are the "causes" for certain happenings on our planet. They are unable to register the vast sweep of energies coming from space and bombarding our planet, thus producing current history.

In the future, *Astrology* (the study of the influences of stars and planets upon Humanity) will be the preoccupation of the "historians" of the day. Each Zodiacal Age impacts on Human Consciousness in certain ways. The Cosmic Rays that bombarded our planet during Pisces produced in Humanity the *tendency towards Spirituality*, the seeking or questing for the Great Invisible—call it God, Truth, the Eternal, or Enlightenment. Pisces provided the *impulse* or *momentum* in that direction. The human *response* to that impulse depended on the level of *evolution* reached by Human Consciousness.

The Influence of the Seven Rays

There is a further series of hidden influences or energies that circulate within our Solar System in periodic rhythm, impacting upon everything, including Human Consciousness. We call these the *Seven Rays* or the *Seven Rhythmic Impulses of Life*. Each of these Forces also creates particular *reactions* in Human Consciousness.

The Sixth Ray produced the phenomenon of intense idealism

These Energies are *not* the influences coming from distant star systems; rather, they come from the inter-dimensional spaces of our own Solar System. They are, in fact, the Life-Vibrations of seven great Cosmic Beings within the multi-layered space-structure of our Solar System. These Cosmic Life-Waves also have a tremendous impact on Human Consciousness at any given time, thus *precipitating* human "history" or "events".

The Stream of Energy that was predominant during the Piscean epoch (the Sixth Ray) produced in Human Consciousness the phenomenon of intense *idealism:*

- Devotion to a sect, cult or new religion.
- Devotion to a new leader, Guru, Teacher, Master or Prophet.
- An intense *fanaticism*, often expressed in violent action towards others not of the same cult, religion or faith.
- Intense *emotional devotion*, fiery emotional expression towards the Deity.
- The sense for "martyrdom" for one's cult or religion, leading to *religious wars*.

These attitudes and conditionings were reflected in the *spiritual practices* of the three Piscean religions, and most strongly in the Muslim religion, since the powers of the Sixth Ray, as well as the Piscean stellar influences, were at their height when the Muslim religion was founded.

HISTORY =

Stellar (Zodiacal) Influences from deep Space. + Internal Solar-Systemic Ray Influences. + Current Evolutionary Attainment of Human Consciousness.

The Equation of History

The Seven Rays 54
The New Aquarian Energies 426
Piscean and New Age Spirituality 1706

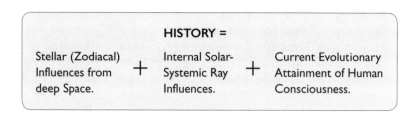

All three religions became "military" religions. Christianity became the religion of the Roman Empire, the Muslim religion became the religion of the Arabic Empire, and the Sikh religion also had military characteristics and involvement.

In contrast, today we are at the beginning of the Aquarian Age, and our Sun is influenced by star-systems that produce *effects* in Human Consciousness which tend to be mental, intellectual, of "scientific mind", and the Path tends towards unification and group-consciousness, rather than the extreme separatism and individualism of the Piscean Path. Also, other Ray energies are manifesting on our planet from the inner dimensions: the Fifth Ray, which stimulates the lower mind, and the Seventh Ray, which influences Human Consciousness towards law, order, regulation, materiality and *secularism*.

Other Ray energies are manifesting on our planet from the inner dimensions

When the Muslim religion came about during the height of the Piscean Age, Devotion to God (the outer, formal, ritualistic religious practices) and Sūfī-sm (the inner mystical practices of meditation aimed at *direct* experience of God) were the sought-after Goal of Life for the hundreds of millions of people. And they went into it with an intense vigour, fanaticism, zeal, inspiration and dedication (due to the Sixth Ray influence) which is not possible today for the hundreds of millions of people on the planet, because of the secular, non-religious nature of the new Aquarian Vibration.

The orientation of the Piscean Age was towards the *Soul* and the invisible worlds and Realities, towards "God" (howsoever people understood that word).

The orientation of today's Aquarian Age is towards the *lower mind* and the *physical body*, the physical world and the physical universe. Hence the intense *materialism* of today's science, politics, religion, education, psychology and art, and the endless preoccupation with sports, physical activities, extreme sports, physical endurances, and *physical* forms of dancing (with no religious or spiritual symbolism or meaning).

During the Piscean Era, in many places upon the planet, music and dance had a religious and spiritual meaning, as did art. Today art is generally just physical, lacking the Piscean Transcendentalism or religious interpretation. In fact, Aquarius is a grossly materialistic age. The idea of Yoga, which is a system of Spiritual Evolution, has now become a set of *physical exercises*.

The Creative Soul 1692

Scientific Materialism 382
The Education System 480
Art and the Follies of Man 470
Haṭha Yoga and Rāja Yoga 524
True Dancing 873

Mystics of Pisces and Aquarius

From the point of view of the Piscean Age Sūfī Mystics, the Seekers after God (Ṭalabān) were of four types:

Wāqif: the charitable workers, those serving others on the Physical Plane, those skilful in *action* towards others.

Ahl Al-Ḥaqq
Arabic: The Followers of the Real (God) or the Absolute Truth. A name given to the Sūfī Saints.

Wāṣif: those who praise God continually, the devotees of the *active* type (singing, dancing, chanting).

'Ārif: the Knowers of God, the Gnostics, those who have esoteric knowledge about Man, God and the Universe, the *meditators*.

'Āshiq: the Lovers of God, those Saints who are in Love with God, those who have abandoned themselves (annihilated the self) in the Fiery Love of God.

From the perspective of the Sūfī Mystics during the Piscean Era, the highest and best seekers were the 'Āshiq, the intimate Lovers of God. Thus, when the Muslim religion was born, it was the Age for fanatical devotees, intense emotionalism and sacrificing the personal self (in Arabic, Fanā, annihilation) by merging into God. The Goal was Fanā'fi-llāh, annihilation in God, or complete Union with God. In this Fanā, annihilation, the mind and the sense of the personal self, the personal ego, were completely lost, replaced by the Divine Mind and the Divine Ego, or the God-Self.

Contrast this with the coming Aquarian Age, the presence of which is already so strongly felt, which is based on the mind, the sense of personal ego and physical body awareness! In this Aquarian Age there won't be much room for the fanatical, emotional devotee, nor will seekers like the idea of a personal annihilation, since so many new-agers have such terribly big egos! This Age concentrates strongly on the mind, mental stuff, the sense of "personal worth" and physical bodily activities.

The seekers in the New Age want to "know" how things are, how they work, rather than just "believe" because some "religious authority" told them so.

The Lover of God 853
The Mantram of Unification 866
The Muslim Deification Process 1191
Brahma-Nirvāṇa: Dissolution in God 1224
Spirituality Past and Future 1104

From Pisces to Aquarius

Today we are at the melting point between the impact of Pisces and the influence of Aquarius. Aquarius is the Age of the Mind; Pisces was the Age of the Emotions. Some are caught up in Pisces, some in Aquarius, and some in both. The fanatical emotionalism of Pisces hasn't yet died out, but the Piscean influence is slowly fading. In two hundred years it will be but "ancient history". Then the mind will be the predominant element.

The Head-person must descend into the Heart to discover the true meanings of his search

Hence, in the coming Aquarian Age there is the possibility of following the Way of the 'ĀRIF, the Knower of God, by:

a. Using the mind in the form of *conscious meditation*.

b. The intelligent understanding of the Divine Plan, SHARĪ'AT, the Spiritual Laws governing the Universe and Mankind.

c. The intelligent following of the Path, ṬARĪQAT.

This leads to Liberation from the sense of *materialism* and *bondage to mind and body*, which is the all-pervading disease of the hundreds of millions of people in this Aquarian Age.

The Way of the Mind is the Way of the Head, the way of thought, intellectual search, thinking, experimentation. It is the way of the scientist, the philosopher, the thinker. It is the use of the lower mind and, later on, the Higher Mind or Causal Mind, the true Intelligent Mind. This way will be the Path for many in the New Age.

A *secret* is involved in this Mind Way, however, and unless the "scientist", "philosopher" or "researcher" understands this secret, he or she will never reach the true Goal.

In the end, the scientist, the Head-person, must *descend* into the Heart to discover the true meanings of his or her "search" and outer "research": what is beyond appearances?

Similarly, in the end, the Mystic or Heart-person must *ascend* from the Heart to the Head and give a "meaning" or "explanation" to his or her mystical experiences, an understanding in language.

And both will have to *show* their Enlightenment in *active service* to Mankind and to all Life.

The Two Paths 1112
Uniting Head and Heart 1130
The Way of the Mind 1238
From Head to Heart 427
The Importance of the Heart in Approaching God 432

The Sūfī God

The Sūfīs use two words most frequently to describe or refer to God:

Al-Ḥaqq

The One Reality, the Absolute, the Supreme Being, the Truth, the Justice, the Rightness, the Law.

Love, Bliss, Light and Unity are the basic "qualities" of God

Allāh

The Essence, the Essential Reality, the Ultimate, the Self-Subsisting, the Effulgent One, the Eternal, the Shining, the Radiant One, the Resplendent One, the Radiance of Glory, That which is beyond naming, comparison, description, images or definitions.

Notice that neither of these words has the sense of a humanized God, such as the *popular* Christian conception of the "old man on the throne". The true Sūfī is very much against the idea of representing God as a human being, with all the human weaknesses and faults, such as anger or vengeance, or being punishing, dictatorial or selective. Some Old Testament writers attributed to God aspects of a savage nature which do not fit the Perfection that God actually is, as known by *Those who have had the inner Mystical Experience* of the Divine Nature, the Divine Essence. In the Old Testament, "God" tells individuals to do things which nowadays would be considered very shocking crimes against Humanity!

As a result, the *outer, orthodox* religions of Christianity and Islām inherited some of these false ideas about God, with more than unfortunate consequences, resulting in religious wars, crusades, persecution of people within the same religion and in other religions, fanatical attempts at "conversion" of others by fair, foul and violent means, and so on, resulting in immense suffering.

The true Sūfī, the true Christian Mystic and the enlightened Jewish Kabbalist will see God in a different light, based on the *inner experience* of Love, Bliss, Light and Unity. Those who have *experienced* the Divine Nature or Divine Essence know that Love, Bliss, Light and Unity are the basic "qualities" of God.

Mythical Concepts of God 104
Can God be Angry? 106
Qualities of the Divine Being 107
The One Transcendental Reality 515
What is Reality? 1175

The One and Only

God always is That which is *veiled* by bodies, forms, structures—even mind-structures and thoughts. To "experience" God you always have to be *beyond* body, form, structure. People who are body-bound, mind-bound, cannot experience God on any level. This would include those church hierarchies, theologians, religious leaders and "authorities" who are body-bound and mind-bound.

That is why, in the Jewish, Christian and Muslim religions, the religious "authorities" so severely persecuted their Mystics, Prophets and Saints (and in some cases still do so today, in the 21st century): they could not understand the statements of the Saints that *they are One with God*. Many of the Jewish, Christian and Muslim Saints were killed for declaring this, including Jesus.

For a long part of your Journey on the Spiritual Path you will be discovering aspects of God-Immanent—that is, God *within* your Heart Centre, *within* your Soul, *within* forms, bodies, planets, *within* Space. This is God-in-Form, God-in-Heart, the Pure, Boundless Consciousness *within* the Universe, and the subtle Driving-Force behind all the happenings of Time and Space and Evolution. It is the hidden motivating Force beneath all Life and behind all things, including the Soul's search for Itself in the Heart of the Deity. God is the Plan, the Direction, the Purpose, the Goal of the Universal Manifestation. This is the *experience* of the Saint, the Sūfī, the Mystic, the Seer.

After a long time, having attained a very high level of Cosmic Evolution, the Adept, the Perfected Man, Angel or God-Being, begins to experience the God-Transcendent, *above and beyond* Creation, Manifestation and Evolution, beyond Beginning and Ending, shrouded in Eternal Mystery.

It is the *combination* of God-Immanent and God-Transcendent that is hinted at in the Sūfī description of **Aḥad** (Arabic), the One and Only, the Unique, the Singular, the Oneness, the Divine Unity, the One without a Second (without parts, attributes or divisions). This is the highest possible *experience* of God. But, as the Sūfīs say:

Only the Man who has *become* God can know that God is God, and there is no one else.

O God, You are One.
Because of your Oneness,
I am One.
Abu'l-Hasan Khurqānī

Within my body there
is nothing but God.
Bāyazīd Al-Bistāmi

Anā Al-Ḥaqq.
I am the Truth (God).
Husayn Ibn Mansūr

Beyond the Veils 894
Persecution of the Knowers 656
God Immanent and Transcendent 111
Being Alone with the Absolute 502
The Divine Unity 852
Aḥad: the One and Only 877

A Sūfī is...

A Sūfī is one who speaks without talking, sees without looking, enjoys sweet fragrances without smelling, and learns all things without studying.

A Sūfī is one whose learning cannot be learned, whose understanding cannot be understood by the common mind.

A Sūfī is one who, although still existing in a physical body, has built within himself a Temple of Luminous Light.

A Sūfī is one who has acquired the qualities of God and has lost himself in those qualities.

A Sūfī is one who is in the world, yet is not; who uses his mind, yet has no mind; who has imperfections, yet has no faults; who is ignorant, yet knows himself; who has renounced everything, yet possesses all things.

A Sūfī is one who has disappeared in the Light and become lost in God.

A Sūfī is one who sees nothing except God in all the worlds.

A Sūfī is one who has no self and has lost his ego.

A Sūfī is one who worships God in secret, in his Heart.

A Sūfī is one who never loses what he has found and never finds what he has lost.

A Sūfī does not know his own appearance, nor what is within or without. He sees only God.

A Sūfī owns nothing, for he knows that all that he possesses belongs to God.

A Sūfī is one who knows the propriety of all things, for everything in Time and Space, and every process, has its appropriate setting. He who behaves at all times according to the rightness of the moment is a Holy Man, a Sūfī.

A Sūfī is one who understands Virtue and practises Love.

A Sūfī does not really possess anything in this world, nor even any glory in the next, because God possesses him. The Sūfī has achieved the complete annihilation of egocentricity.

A Sūfī is one who is essentially without *form.*

A Sūfī is one who cannot see the imperfections of this world because he is blinded by the Glory of God.

A Sūfī sees only God because he has no self. The seeker after phenomena is a self-seeker and lives by egocentricity and selfishness. "Whosoever is blind to God sees the self, and whosoever is blind to the self sees God."

A Sūfī is one who has purified his or her Heart from the self.

A Sūfī is one whose thoughts keep pace with his feet, whose feelings agree with his thoughts, and who lives entirely in the Present.

A Sūfī is one who has lost himself, but has found Allāh.

A Sūfī is one who lives the life of Love. Love is the source of all Life. The Sūfī collects Love into his Heart, and when his Heart is filled with Love there is no room for anything else but the Beloved.

A Sūfī is one who is free from useless desires and who has abandoned all troubles.

A Sūfī is one who seeks no rewards, desires no fame, does not push himself or herself onto others, and who remains centred and grounded at all times.

A Sūfī is one who has no Name.

A Sūfī lives in a Place where place does not exist.

A Sūfī is one who has attained Spiritual Poverty, which is the annihilation of all thoughts, and who has purified the self, which is the vanishing into No-Thingness.

A Sūfī is one who follows the Right Way, acts simply without hypocrisy and show, refrains from ostentation and glamour, and is just himself.

A Sūfī is one who is single in *essence* and simple in his acts.

When a Sūfī has a Vision, the whole Universe is his Sanctuary or Mosque.

A Sūfī is one who guards his Heart. "Guard your Hearts, for Allāh knows your innermost thoughts." *Guarding the Heart* means turning to God.

A Sūfī is one who cares not for praise or blame, success or failure, glory or punishment.

A Sūfī is one who is separated from the Many, but is united to the One.

A Sūfī is like a man with a sickness which begins in deliriousness and ends in dumbness. A Sūfī begins with Ecstasy and ends in *Silence*.

A Sūfī is one who does not desire miracles, for miracles veil God. Mankind has fallen in love with miracles and has forgotten the Beloved.

A Sūfī is one who listens to music, to the vibrations and sounds of Life, until he has attained to God. Then, Silence has all-power.

When a Sūfī speaks, his language is Reality; when he thinks, he is in tune with the Infinite; when he acts, God acts through him; when he is silent, he has cut off all worldly ties.

A Sūfī is one who has annihilated all things human in himself and has embraced all things Divine, in God.

A Sūfī is one whose Spirit has been freed from the Many and yet has found solidity and steadiness in the Spirit of God.

A Sūfī is one who possesses nothing; nor can he or she be possessed by anything, except by God.

CHAPTER 40

The Sūfī Heart

The Thread of the Heart

The Path of the Sūfī is essentially a Journey of the Heart

SŪFĪ-sm belongs to the Heart Tradition of Spirituality. To understand Sūfī meditation you have to consider:

- The zodiacal time period when it was founded (Pisces).
- The activity of the Sixth Ray of Devotion and Idealism from within the Solar System.
- The ancient lineage of the Heart Path, or the Heart approach to God, Gnosis, Illumination.

Traditionally, the Mystical Schools of all the religions meditated in the Heart—that is, they focused their Spiritual Quest in the Heart Centre, with its multiple layers and possibilities—while all the esoteric groups, occult schools and mind-based societies focused their attention in the Third-Eye Centre.

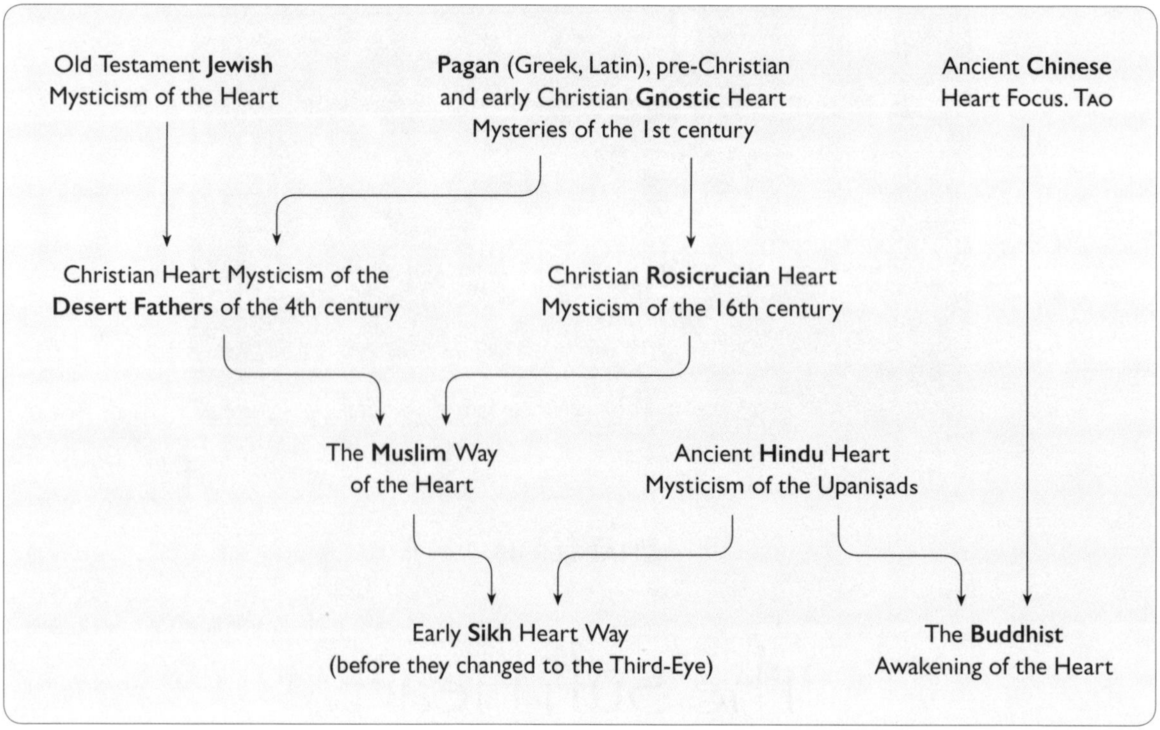

The Thread of the Heart

The Ancient Heart-Path

The Path of the Sūfī is essentially a Journey of the Heart. There is a *sameness* in all the Heart traditions: the Old Testament Jewish, Christian, Muslim, Sikh, Hindu, Buddhist and ancient Chinese. The Glory of God passes by repeatedly, but it seems that Mankind is unable to grasp it in sufficient numbers to liberate the planet from death, pain and sorrow.

When the Original Cause [God] established my Soul, I was given the first lesson as Love, and my Heart was made a Treasury of Light and Mystical Knowledge.

Umar Khayyām (Omar Khayyam)

∞

The Heart Centre is "the Way, the Truth and the Life". Through the Heart one becomes Aware of oneself as a Living Soul, and Aware of the Living God as One with one's Soul.

The Heart Centre is the Seat of Consciousness.

The Heart Centre is the Source of Spiritual Wisdom (which has nothing at all to do with book-learning, passing exams, worldly knowledge, memorizing physical facts and data, what today is called "education").

The Heart Centre is the Source of Joy, Bliss, Peace and inward calmness. In the Heart Centre one discovers the Beauty of God, the perfect Chord of Harmony, and the Meaning of Life.

In the Heart Centre one discovers the Unity of all Life, the Oneness of the Cosmos, and the Divine Oneness or Sameness of the Godhead which pervades every atom of Space.

In the Heart Centre the Ultimate Reality is discovered and the Goal of the Universal Manifestation (Evolution) is perceived.

Therefore, the Practice, the Way, is focused *on* the Heart and *in* the Heart.

The Mystery of the Heart 425
The Heart of Christianity 623
The Way of the Heart 1249

The Universal Heart Practice

The Practices of the Heart, in *all* the Heart Traditions, are:

- **Repetition of God's Name in the Heart** with Love, Devotion, Longing, self-surrender and self-forgetfulness.
- **Conscious Breathing in the Heart.** That is, consciously breathing in the Life-force and breathing it out, with or without the aid of a Divine Name.
- **Remembrance of God's Presence in the Heart**, with or without the use of a Divine Name.
- **Awareness or Attentiveness in the Heart**, thinking of God only and not allowing the mind to bring any worldly thoughts into the Sanctuary of the Heart.
- **Solitude in the Heart.** That is, being in a peaceful, quiet place, away from noisy crowds and worldly places, by oneself alone, centred in the Peace and Quiet of one's Heart, abiding in Silence and Stillness.
- **Solitude in the World.** This means that you go about your worldly duties and business, dealing with people and events, always abiding in your Heart and not allowing outer happenings to disturb the profound Peace and Tranquillity of the Temple of your Heart.

Zikr
Arabic: Prayer, meditation, invocation, repetition of Divine Names or Mantras (Kalimah) in the Heart.

Mystical Union

Look within your own Heart, for the Kingdom of God is within you.

A Sūfī saying

The personal centre of selfhood, in the Heart, is One with the Universal Centre of Selfhood and the Universal Heart, for Man and God are One. This is not some nice theology, but a *fact realized* in the Heart in Mystical Union. The sense of a separate selfhood, held by every human being, is an illusion.

The Heart is the point where the Universal Selfhood (God) meets Its reflection, Man.

The Sun of Righteousness shines in the Universal Heart, reflected in the Heart of Man.

The Universal Christ 440

Sūfī Prayer 863
Christian Prayer 689
The Heart and the Lost Art of Prayer 1251
Hṛdayaṁ: Meditations in the Heart Centre 1279
The Way of Holiness 1335

Dimensions of the Heart

In the Sūfī tradition the Circle of the Heart Centre is much larger than simply the physical heart organ. In any mystical tradition, when they talk of the Heart, they do not mean the physical heart!

The Arabic word for the Heart Centre is **Qalb**. It is located in the chest area—the left side, the right side, the centre, and the innermost part. Qalb also means "the middle point, the centre, the core of one's Being, the Essence, the Mind, Soul and Spirit". All these have to do with the Mysteries of the Heart.

For the Sūfī Mystic, the Way to Know God is through the Heart

- On the left side of the breast, Qalb (the Heart) is called **Sirr**, the Secret.
- On the right side of the breast it is called **Khafā**, the Hidden.
- In the middle of the chest it is called **Ekhfā**, the Most Hidden.
- On a deeper inward dimension, it is called **Rūḥ**, the Spiritual Soul. (Note that this term can also refer to the Spirit in Man.)
- As a still deeper inward revelation it is called **Qalb**, the Spirit, the Essence, the Innermost Self, the Centre within Man and within the Universe.

None of this has anything to do with the physical body, but with Inner Space.

> God said, "I am a Hidden Treasure, and I want to be known."
>
> *The Qur'ān*

For the Sūfī Mystic, the Way to Know God is through the Heart.

The Light of God

Nūr (Arabic), the Light of God, the Splendour of God, the Glory of God, is Omnipotence Itself.

There is the serene, clear Light of the Heart, called **Nūrānī** (Arabic).

Nūr, in Persian, means "the Light, the Moonlight" (in the Heart).

Nūrjahān (Persian) is the Light of the World, that is, the Light *within* the World.

It is God's Light, **Nūrullāh** (Arabic), that performs all deeds, all miracles, and gives all powers to the Saints (Sūfīs).

The Self-Generating Light 1594

The Lotus of the Heart 446
Hṛt-Padma: the Heart Lotus 1505
The Mystery within the Heart 1315
God in the Heart 634

Qalb: the Sūfī Heart

QALB (the Heart) is the great Intermediary between God and Humanity, the secret of inner spiritual guidance and the Mystery of Being. The Sūfīs call it "the Divine Subtlety" and "the Human Necessity".

God is visible to the inward sight of the Pure Heart

QALB-SALĪM (Arabic: Pure Heart) means the direct Inner Vision of the Divine Face in the Spiritual Heart. God is visible to the inward sight of the Pure Heart. The Light by which the Heart sees God is God's own Light. This the Sūfīs call **RU'YAT AL-QALB**, "the Vision of the Heart".

The Heart (QALB) can know the Essence of God when it is illumined by the Divine Light. In Arabic, Awareness of the Heart is **WUQŪF-QALBĪ**. When the Heart becomes *aware* of God, infinite Mysteries are revealed to you.

> Oh Sūfī! Make clean the mirror of your Heart!
> A Door shall open up to you,
> And the Radiance of ALLĀH shall shine upon you.
>
> The true Mosque is a pure and holy Heart.
> Let all human beings worship God there.
> For He dwells not in mosques made of stone, but in pure Hearts.
>
> ALLĀH, who is the Light of the heavens and of this Universe, cannot be seen by the bodily eyes, but He is visible to the vision of the Heart.
>
> *Sūfī sayings*

ALLĀH's speech is Light, His works are Light, He moves as Light, and He is seen as Light in the Heart.

YAQĪN is the Light of Certainty by which the Heart *sees* God. God is seen by His *own* Light, which shines in the Heart.

QALB-I-VUKUF is Heart-Consciousness. Heart-Consciousness means turning away from mental activities, gazing into the Heart, and "waiting for the Divine Secret to manifest".

Without and within, ALLĀH is there,
like a Boundless Radiance, everywhere.

Search out your Heart 437
The Five Stages of Certainty 895
The Experience of the Heart 1280
The Pure Heart 1300
The Lighted Way 1394

The Purification of the Heart

Before you can "see" God, your Heart must be purified of all worldly concerns and impressions. If your Heart is full of the problems and troubles of the world, the Beatific Vision is not possible.

The Heart has to be purified from the *impressions* of the world:

- First, the impressions of the outer physical world.
- Then the subtle astral impressions from the Astral Plane (feelings, desires, moods, emotions).
- Then, finally, impressions from the Mental Plane (thoughts, ideas, mental constructs, logic, reasoning, mental activities).

Your Heart must be purified of all worldly concerns and impressions

Then the Heart has to go through a process of *Revivification*, Renewal, Rebirth and Illumination, until the Divine Intelligence shines like a splendid Light from within. Finally the Heart *becomes* the Divine Light Itself, where there is nothing but God.

In all the Heart Traditions, the purpose of the Heart Purification is to invoke or call down the Divine Grace, so beautifully expressed in a Gnostic Christian Heart mantram:

O Light of all Lights,
Which is within the Boundless Lights,
Remember us and Deliver us.

In this beautiful early Gnostic Christian Heart prayer we are invoking the Deity, hidden by a Field of Absolute Light, to "Remember" us, Humanity (who is struggling for survival in this dark world of matter, having long forgotten our Origins in the Kingdom of Light), and to Deliver us from this material imprisonment.

> Blessed are the pure in Heart, for they shall *see* God [in the Heart].
> *Jesus (Matthew 5:8)*

Faith and Wisdom

The Heart is purified by Faith and Wisdom. *Faith* is following the orthodox religious rituals, prayers, ceremonies and customs. *Wisdom* is the following of the Way of Meditation and, by *direct experience,* to enter the Kingdom of God. Wisdom is superior to Faith because it gives certitude of Knowledge.

What is Wisdom? 1685

Purify the Heart 701
Guard your Heart 1328
The Secret of the Heart 1280
To Invoke God in your Heart 1293
Tapas: Spiritual Purification 571

Some Arabic Prayers to the Deity

Through each of these Divine Prayers the Heart is purified of all worldly dross.

1. **Lā Ilāha Illa Allāh**
   There is no God but the One.

The Divine Unity is the central teaching of Ṣūfism

This is the *Mantram of Unification in the Heart*. When you repeat the Prayer of Unification in your Heart you will begin to have glimpses of the Mystery of Unity. The Divine Unity (Tauḥīd) is the central teaching of Sūfīsm.

2. **Bismillāh Ir-Raḥmān Ir-Raḥīm**
   In the Name of God, the Compassionate, the Merciful.

This is the Arabic *Mantram to Awaken the Divine Love in the Heart*, to Awaken your Love for God, and to call down the Divine-Love-response from God, whose very Nature is Love Itself.

Bismillāh means "in the Name of God, in the Divine Name". The Divine Name of God is the Omnipresent Light-Vibration of the Ineffable Godhead. To be *in* the Name is to be Universally Illumined, Cosmic-Conscious, having within one's Heart the Light of Gnosis.

Ir-Raḥmān, Ir-Raḥīm means that the Divine Name is the well-spring of Love. It is all Compassion, all Forgiveness. It is, in fact, an Ocean of Loving-Bliss-Vibration.

The theme of this prayer is Divine Love. Love is the second major theme in Sūfīsm. The Love and Mercy of God is infinite. This also is not theoretical, but what is *experienced* in the Heart by the Sūfī Mystic. The Arabic word **Ḥabīb**, "beloved, sweetheart", is often used for God by the Sūfīs. They literally fall in Love with God.

The great female Sūfī Saint, Rābi'a, said:

> If I worship you, O God, because of fear of hell, burn me in hell.
> If I worship you because of hope for heaven, exclude me from heaven.
> But if I Love You for your own sake, do not deny me your Everlasting Glory.

The Voice of God 864
The Mantram of Unification 866
Sūfī Mantras for Meditation 874
The Beautiful Names 1264

3. Allāhu Akbar
or: Allahū Akbar
God is Omnipotent.

This is the Arabic *Mantram of the Omnipotence of God*, who does everything, who is the Creator and Dissolver of the Universe (visible and invisible), and within whose Power are all possibilities and all miracles and attainments. This third prayer in the Heart is the Omnipotence of God as Light.

This third prayer in the Heart is the Omnipotence of God as Light

> Allāh is the Light within the Heavens and the Earth. There is Light upon Light, and God will guide whomsoever He wills to His Light.

Such is the teaching of the Qur'ān.

The Truth in the Heart

The Truth is written in my Heart. I listen for Its instruction.

God has written the Truth in the Heart of each human being. It is the self-evident Truth for each individual—unique, singular, particular, while at the same time Universal. The Heart is your own true *reality,* yet it is also the discovery of Universality.

He who knows his own Heart knows Allāh.

Muḥammad the Prophet

Reality (Allāh, the Splendid Light) manifests in the Heart. This was why the Christian Desert Fathers of Egypt, Palestine and Syria meditated in the Heart during the early centuries of Christianity, using the Jesus Prayer. They called it the *Radiant Heart.*

Allāh, the Eternal Splendour, cannot be perceived by the mind. Hence, when all mental activity ceases and the Heart awakens, there comes true Surrender, which is the true state of prayer and meditation.

It has been said of the Heart:

The Divine Mystery of Love is beyond reason and logic.

And...

There are some Sūfīs who only repeat the Name Allāh (the Radiant Light) all the time in their Hearts, because they know that a human being may die at any moment, and they want to have the Name of God in their Hearts when they die.

Sūfī tradition

The Greatness of God 875
The Radiant Heart Prayer 702
Meditation on the Exalted Name of God 871

The Divine Unity

Union *with* God, and the Realization of the Unity or Singleness of the Divine Essence, is the Goal of the Sūfī Mystical Path, as it is for all true Heart Paths.

TAUḤĪD, Divine Unity, the Oneness of God, is the Goal of the Mystics of Islām.

TAUḤĪD
Arabic: The One. The Oneness. The Unbroken Sameness of the Godhead. Unity Consciousness, Union with God, Union with the All. This is the central teaching of SŪFĪ-sm.

TAUḤĪD-E-ZĀTI, the Unity of God's Essence or God's Being, is the Goal that the Mystic experiences in the higher stages of the Spiritual Journey (ṬARĪQAT).

There are two stages in this higher Mystical Union:

- The Lover of God ('ĀSHIQ) and the Beloved (MUSHUQ) are experienced simultaneously as One.
- The Lover (the Mystic) and the Beloved (God) are experienced as One, without even a sense of the Spiritual Self being different from the Essence of God. Man, God and the Universe are experienced as being the unbroken Oneness of the Ultimate Reality.

This final Union is also the Goal, of course, of the Christian and Jewish Mystics, the Hindu and Buddhist Yogīs, the Sikh Mystics, the followers of Zen, and the students of Chinese Taoism.

The Immutable Principle, God, is One, Infinite, Eternal, beyond Time and Space, yet *includes* the All-Creation or Multiple-Manifestation in Its Boundless Consciousness. From the Absolute we came and to the Absolute we shall return. This Absolute is ALLĀH, the Self-Subsisting One, the all-perfect Boundless Light. Such is the Realization of the Sūfī.

God is in the East and in the West. Wheresoever you turn your Inner Eye, there shines the Face of God. God pervades the All. And God is the GNOSIS of the All. God is the First and the Last, the Manifest and the Unmanifest, the Before and the After, the Beginning and the End. Wherever you are, God is with you, within you, and God sees everything you do.

Such is the Revelation (QUR'ĀN) of the Divine Unity.

The Eternal is One 512
The One and Only 839
Mind-Only 974
The God-State 1257
The Path of Union 1339
The One 1686

The Lover of God

The Sūfī's Pure Love of God transcends all pairs of opposites. It transcends all nationalities, all limitations, all religious affiliations. It absorbs the whole being of the Lover—body, mind, Soul—in a Fiery Conflagration or Spiritual Fire. The pure Lover of God wants nothing for the personal self: no name, no fame, no worldly successes, no worldly greatness or riches. The Lover of God wants to possess nothing save the Beloved (God)—nothing of this world, nothing of Heaven or of Paradise, only the Annihilating Glance of the Divine Majesty in a Beatific Vision.

The Lover of God wants to possess nothing save the Beloved

Said a Sūfī Saint:

> I ask nothing for me, O Lord, no favours, no graces, only Yourself.

The true Love of the Mystic is Transcendental for God, but is Immanent and practical towards God's Creation and all creatures and all lives. This is expressed in loving deeds and actions.

> It is said of Rūmī that he broke through to Oneness and solved the problem of seeing the One with two eyes.
>
> *Sūfī tradition*

I went to the Door of the Heart, seeking for my Beloved, and knocked. And a Voice said, "Who is there?"

"It is I," I said.

And the voice replied, "There is no room for you and Me here." And the Door remained shut.

After many years spent in solitude and self-discipline and meditation, I went to the Door of the Heart and knocked again.

"Who is there?" the Voice inquired.

"It is You."

And the Door opened wide.

Jalāluddīn Rūmī

The Meaning of Life is Love 633
Practising the Presence of God 711
On the Wings of Devotion 1129
My Beloved Lives in my Heart 1290
To Love God and the World 1392

The Revelation of God

There is a great Mystery hidden in the word "God" which is revealed in the state of HĀL (Persian): Mystical Rapture, Ecstasy, Superconsciousness, Samādhi, Spiritual Trance, Union. Until then, talking about God is just theorizing, speculating, day-dreaming.

∞

As you move deeper towards Perfection, another Heart is discovered

"God" is first revealed in the *Heart Centre*, by an *inward Gaze of the Soul.*

Then another Heart is discovered in the *Crown Centre*, the Thousand-Petalled Lotus Flower. This Heart is *within* the Head, but is not the Head. Here, another aspect of God is unveiled.

As you move deeper towards Perfection, another Heart is discovered, the *Causal Heart* within your causal body, the Centre of your Soul. Here is revealed the relationship between you as a Living Soul and the Pulsating Life that is God, the two being inseparably One.

Next on your Pilgrimage is the discovery of the *Planetary Heart Centre* and your Soul's relationship to it, and another aspect of God as ruler of our World.

Next is the discovery of the *Solar-Systemic Heart* within the Spiritual Sun, and God as the Ruler of Systemic Life, Space, hierarchies, planets, evolutions.

Next, when you have passed well beyond Perfection, well beyond the Angelic and Divine Hierarchies, is the discovery of the *Cosmic Heart* or *Universal Heart*, wherein you discover the Great Mystery of the All-Manifestation, that which is *concealed* by the multitudes of Universes, Creations and Emanations. It is the Ineffable Mystery of God, unspeakable, inexpressible, untouchable by human mind and thought and understanding.

Heart and Mind 429
The Universal Heart 436
The Manifested-God 1589
The Solar and Human Heart 1592

The Journey of the Heart

1. The First Stage of the Journey of the Heart is:

Ṭālib (Arabic): A seeker, a neophyte, a searcher after God. At this stage of your life upon the Path (Ṭarīqat), you are *seeking*, searching for Truth everywhere, motivated by the hidden impulses from your Heart. Occasionally you attempt to meditate or try some practice, but you are very easily distracted.

At this stage of your life upon the Path, you are searching for Truth

2. The Second Stage of the Journey of the Heart is:

Murīd (Arabic): A disciple, a follower, a student, one who is inclined towards or desirous of the Realization of the Truth. Your Heart impulses are stronger and more steady towards the Spiritual Life. You become more serious about meditation and other spiritual practices, and you try out many things.

3. The Third Stage of the Journey of the Heart is:

Sālik (Arabic): A pilgrim, a traveller (in the spiritual sense), a devotee. At this stage of your journey of the Heart you have found a Teacher and you are serious in following out the spiritual instructions, meditations and practices that the Teacher gives. You have a great Devotion (Sulūk) towards God, and your Heart is burning with desire to realize God in this lifetime.

4. The Fourth Stage of the Journey of the Heart is:

Abūdiyat (Arabic): Service to the Teacher and Worship of God; faithfulness to the Path. At this stage the Heart impulses are very strong and you express your Devotion by doing things for the Teacher, your Group and the Teaching. Also, you are trying to regulate your outer, worldly life so that you have more time for your meditation and spiritual practices, and more time for God in your life.

The Arabic word Abūdiyat is derived from the Persian and Arabic word Abū, "father". (Note also the Hebrew word Abba.) This is because, in the olden days (the Piscean Age), the son followed in the footsteps of the father; whatever the father was, the son was supposed to become. In the spiritual sense, the Spiritual Teacher is a "father" to the devotee-disciple.

The Radiant Way 830
Qualifications for Discipleship 1149
The Four Stages of Spiritual Life 1160
The Approach to Truth 1152

5. The Fifth Stage of the Journey of the Heart is:

'Ishk (Arabic): Love. At this stage you become an 'Ishshiq, a Lover. Your Love for God and your Teacher becomes immense. You definitely feel and experience something going on in your Heart—changes, transformations, insights, and the Grace of God working there. You would rather spend all your time in meditation than deal with the world and worldly people. Your Love for God appears to have created in you a conflict with the world. You feel that worldly people are empty and superficial.

I was looking for God everywhere. I looked into my Heart and found Him there.

Jalāluddīn Rūmī

I penetrated the Heart, reason and Soul, and my Beloved appeared in the Midst.

Jalāluddīn Rūmī

6. The Sixth Stage of the Journey of the Heart is:

Zuhd (Arabic): Intense Devotion to God, non-worldliness, the intense desire to cut yourself away from the world, to have nothing to do with the world. You want to live in seclusion, possibly alone, away from everybody. You may develop fanatical ideas about diet and your physical body, and you are sharply aware of the imperfections of the world and of people around you. The pull from within your Heart is tremendous, while the impressions of the world are less significant in your life. You question why you are in the world at all; material life is totally unsatisfactory and meaningless. You sense the Centre within your Heart and you know that that Centre is also your Goal and Beginning.

7. The Seventh Stage of the Journey of the Heart is:

Ma'rifat (Arabic): Gnosis, Enlightenment, inner insights, revelations from within the Heart, spiritual experiences that transform your life or give a new meaning to your life, profound understandings, glimpses of Self-Realization, glimpses of Divine Unity, deep sympathy with all that lives, and insights into why you need to serve (help) Mankind.

Alone with God 700
Solitude and Loneliness 1170
The Muslim Deification Process 1191

8. The Eighth Stage of the Journey of the Heart is:

Hāl (Persian): Spiritual Ecstasy, Spiritual Trance, spiritual tranquillity of the mind.

Wijd, Wijdān (Arabic): Ecstasy, direct Knowledge, direct Realization of the Truth (equivalent to the Sanskrit Samādhi of the Yogīs, the Superconscious State). Illumination of the Heart by the Light of God, the Light of Gnosis, Nūrul-'Irfān (Arabic).

The **Hālah** (Arabic: Glory) is seen, the internal shining of the Light and Spiritual Radiance. (From this word comes the English word *halo*, as seen around Saints.)

Hālah (Persian) is the complete Rest, Stillness and Equilibrium of the Saint in Trance.

It is the Place where there is no birth or death, where there is no time for questioning.
Sūfī tradition

9. The Ninth Stage of the Journey of the Heart is:

Ḥaqīqat, Ḥaqqīqat (Arabic): Truth, God. This comprises various stages of Perfection, various degrees of Union with God, the Godhead, the Absolute. (This corresponds with the stages within Samādhi.) These are stages in Spiritual Life where Man turns into Super-Man (above the Man-species), where Man enters streams of Supernatural Evolutions beyond the ken of present Mankind, beyond the wildest dreams of worldly people.

The Journey, the Path, the Way, the Road, Ṭarīqat, is a Journey in Spiritual Evolution, a flowing of Man into Man-God, and then into God-Man.

The Pilgrim returns to the Source, to reclaim what was never really lost: Divinity.

Experiencing the Awakening Heart 463
Signs of Progress in the Heart 1289
Stages on the Way of Holiness 1336
Samādhi: the Goal of Yoga 574

The Rose of Divine Love

Meditation 1

Smell the perfume of the Mystic Rose

- Sit Still.
- Focus your attention in the Heart, remembering that the Heart is not physical. It is a Spiritual Centre, your temple, synagogue, mosque, "the Temple of God which is not made by human hands", in which you *worship*.
- *Rest in Being.* This means that you just *rest* in your Heart, with no thoughts about anything. In this meditation there is no visualization, no mantra, no prayer, no image, no form of any kind, nor a wish to go anywhere, nor a desire for Liberation or Enlightenment. Simply rest, in a state of Peace.
- Sense or feel the Still-Point within your Heart. This is not an intellectual (mental) exercise, nor an emotional (solar plexus) one. Just be fully Aware in the Heart, without the need to do anything.
- After a while you might feel impatient and think that you ought to "do" something. *Just rest*, and dive deeper and deeper into your Inner Silence and Stillness within the depths of your Heart.

Meditation 2

- Sit quietly, relaxed. Put all the cares and worries of the world behind you. You are alone with the Alone within you.
- Focus your Awareness at the centre of your Heart Circle, in the middle of your chest space. There you are going to visualize the *Rose of Divine Love*.
- Visualize your Heart as a *single Rose.* The green stem is merging into your spinal column and the Rose flower is facing forward, in front of you. The petals are deep rose in colour and they are in the process of unfolding or opening up. At the centre of the Rose, inside the petals, there is a golden luminous glow. Sense clearly the rose colour, smell the perfume of the Mystic Rose, and feel the aliveness of the liquid-gold vibration inside the centre of the Rose.

The rose colour is the most pure of the astral vibrations, the highest "feeling" vibration.

The liquid-gold colour is of the Buddhic World, the Golden Hue of the Buddha, a vibration of the world *above* the mental realms, *beyond* the mind structure, the World of Unity or At-One-Ment.

When you begin to practise this meditation, you are the one who is building the Rose. After several meditation sessions, however, you will begin to notice that there is a *response* from deep within your Heart. It happens when the God within you *responds* to your efforts. Then you will "feel" that you are *embraced* by a field of Divine Love, or that God is a personal Lover. That is, somehow you feel an Intimate Union with God, somehow you know God on an intimate level that cannot be "explained" by the mind. A great Peace and Joy will descend upon you, and you will Know that *within you* everything is "all right", even if the outside world is a shambles.

The Rose represents the Divine Love of the Deity in your Heart

The Rose represents the Divine Love of the Deity in your Heart. At this stage you will understand the expression that "I have been Lost, but now I am Found". It is *you* who have been lost, and it is *You* who have been found.

The Rose was a symbol of Divine Love in the Heart for the Sūfīs, the Christian Mystics and the Rosicrucians. For the Old Testament Mystics it was the flower called the *Lily of the Valley*, and for the Hindu, Buddhist and Jain Mystics it was the *Lotus Flower*, as it was for the Japanese and the Chinese Mystics.

If you practise this meditation for some time, you will fall in Love with God, who will not be as an old man in a far away "heaven", but the very Life and Soul of Yourself, your very essential Beingness, and from your Heart you will radiate Peace, Joy and Love to all beings all around you in an act of Divine Blessing.

You will also understand that all fears, worries and anxieties of life come from your sense of *separation,* of isolation from the Real, from the Godhead, the Divinity. This comes about because of the mind, the mental principle, which divides, separates, compartmentalizes, analyses, thus breaking up the Essential Unity of All That Is. We already live *in* the Divine Sphere, *in* the Kingdom of God, but the separative mind, the lower mind, makes it *appear* that we are self-existent, separate from the Whole, from the Sense of Unity.

When you experience final Union with the Beloved in the Heart, you will no longer be afraid of anything, nor will you have the feeling that You "need" anything. You will know that your body "needs" food, your mind "needs" thoughts, and your astral body "needs" emotions, but You need nothing at all, because *in* the Beloved you already have everything. You will also come to experience the Fundamental Tone

The Lotus of the Heart 446
The Rose and the Cross 712
Maṇi-Padma: the Jewelled Lotus 1298
The Mystery within the Heart 1315
Hṛt-Padma: the Heart-Lotus 1505

of your Being as all-inclusive Love and Bliss, like that of the Deity, Divinity, God.

In normal life we separate ourselves from others continually through the normal mind function. Sometimes we feel a little emotional connection with others through the Solar Plexus Centre, but that is nothing compared with the Dynamic-Love-Unity of the Heart. When you discover this, you will discover a new meaning in your Life.

Visualize the form of your favourite God-Expression

Meditation 3

- Visualize the Heart as a *Golden Flower*, a golden rose or lotus flower, the petals made of vivid golden light.
- At the centre of the flower, at its heart, place a *Divine Name*, your favourite Divine Name, which represents an attribute or a quality of God.
- Then *see* this Name as pure, liquid, shining Light-letters. *Hear* the Sound of the Name as Divine Sound-Vibration, and mentally repeat that Name (that quality) as an *accomplished fact* in your existence.

Meditation 4

- Visualize the *Rose of the Heart* or the *Sacred Flower* as golden-orangish petals.
- After you have formed the flower, visualize *the form of your favourite God-Expression* at the centre or deepest point. You may visualize the Prophet (the Being of Light), or Jesus, or the Christ, or Buddha, or any other Saint, Master or Spiritual Teacher. Form that image very clearly and see it very clearly. Realize that the image serves as a *connecting link* between your consciousness and God within.
- After repeated meditations, you will carry that image in your Heart always, and it will act in your life always as the Living God.

From Head to Heart 427
The 99 Arabic Divine Names of God 878
Visualizing the Divinity within the Heart 1268

Meditation 5

- Visualize the *Sacred Fire* in the Heart.
- This is the Fire of the Holy Spirit, the Fire of Divine Love. "Our God is a Consuming Fire," said the Mystics of the Old Testament. This Holy Fire consumes all of your imperfections and hindrances to Union with the Beloved, Union with God.
- See your Heart ablaze with this Fire of Love. At first, it is the Fire of Love that *you* have for God, the Beloved, but then you will discover the Fire of Love that actually *is* God: the Divine Fire, the Cosmic Fire, the Fire of Creation, the Living Fire, the Liberating Fire, the Transcendental Fire.

Visualize your Heart as if it were a lamp

Meditation 6

- Visualize the *Sun* in the Heart. At first it is like a golden-yellow-orangish Sun, the size of a dinner plate, burning, shining in your Heart. It has a warm-giving Light, comforting, healing, making you Whole.
- At a later stage of your meditation practice, visualize a blazing, white Sun in your Heart, the size of a dinner plate.
- Slowly, little by little, this Sun will become "the Sun of Righteousness, with healing on its wings", a blazing Sunshine all around. This is the Prophet, and Christ the King.

Meditation 7

- Visualize your Heart *as if it were a lamp*, shooting out beams of White Light in all directions—brilliant Rays of Light, silvery-shining, illuminating the Darkness of the World.
- Concentrate the silvery luminous Light into one terrific beam of Light, and send it forth from your Heart to a person, place or situation in the world where Help is needed. This is a Blessing. ≮

The Burning Heart 631
The Fire of Love 1255
Incarnations of the Sun 1593
The Shining Lights 1595
The Rose of Love and the Cross of Light 1357

CHAPTER 41

Sūfī Prayer

The Voice of God

God and the Name are One.
The Name and the Named are One.
The Illimitable Glory of the Primeval Being
resounds in the Name of God.

Each of the Divine Names
is a particle of the Name

Let the Name be fixed in your Heart.
Remember always the Name in your Heart.
The Name and the Names are One.

Each of the Divine Names is a particle of the Name.
Sweet are the Names of God when they are linked to
the Heart by the threads of Love and Devotion.

Close your eyes and ears and mouth, turn within.
If then you do not perceive the Glory of God, you can laugh at me.
Jalāluddīn Rūmī

Within our Hearts we remember the Lord,
With our tongues we praise His Holy Name,
With our ears we listen to the Voice of God calling us,
With the inner eyes we see the Form of the Beauty of our Beloved.
The Credo of the Sūfīs

Nothing is as good as God's Name.
Repeat God's Holy Names,
It will lead you to the Pure and Indestructible Source,
The Ocean of Bliss, the Source of Happiness, the Eternal Light.
Dādū Dayāla

Kalma
Arabic: The Word, the Logos, the Speech of God.

Kalām-i-llāhi
Arabic: The Voice of God, the Word of God, the Heavenly Music, the Divine Name.

Kalām-u-llāh
Arabic: The Word of God, the Divine Vibration of the Name, the Sounding-Light Vibration of God's Name.

Sulṭān-ul-Azkār
Arabic: The King of Prayers, the Victorious Power, the Divine Word.

Iṣām-i-A'zam
Arabic: The Highest and Greatest, the Greatest Name.

What is the Name? 1259

Nidā
Persian-Arabic: The Voice, the Call to Prayer, the Proclamation of God, the Voice of God calling in the Heart.

Note that the Persian-Arabic word **Nidā** has the same meaning as the Sanskrit word **Nāda**, "the Voice of God, the Inner Sound-Current, the audible Life-Stream that emanates from God, the Infinite Hum of the Creative Power of God".

Āuṁ, Ōṁ, Nāda 550

The Word, the Logos, the Name, creates all the worlds and realms, from the highest Spiritual Planes down to the Physical World.

The Everlasting Beingness, ALLĀH, is the Source of All, is the Source of the Name, is the Source of all the Names, of all the Words of Power (mantras).

The Voice of God is calling Mankind all the time

The Word is God. The Name is God. God is the Final Truth or Reality of all things visible and invisible.

The Divine Name-Sound (Vibration) creates All, and is within all, and can be experienced in the Heart.

The Words, the Names used in meditation, will lead to the true Word, the true Name within you and within all Creation or Manifestation.

The true Name within you and within the Universe is pure Inner Music, Inner Harmony, which reverberates in the All-Manifestation. It can be experienced in the Heart, or when you leave your body or step outside of your body and mind (the common, ordinary mind).

The Word or Name is the connecting link between the highest Spirit and the lowest material vibration. It is the Eternal Continuum of the Primeval Reality and manifested forms, bodies and happenings in Time and Space.

The Voice of God is calling Mankind all the time, but Man is deaf and will not listen.

The physical body is the source of connection to the Physical World. Through the eyes and ears, and the other senses, our Attention is continually dragged outside into this world, and the mind is dragged downward to endlessly think of this world. Through this process we lose our Inner Connection, our Inner Awareness of the Truth Within, the Glory within us. Thus, our Attention must turn inward again.

Senses or the Self? 239

The Logos: the Word of God 114
Vāk: the Divine Speech 118
The Word, Logos, Voice, Name 1646
The Name and the Names 1258
Meditation on the Sacred Word 1216

The Mantram of Unification in the Heart Centre

The Goal of the Sūfī is to become One with God.

I. **Lā Ilāha Illa Allāh**
There is no God but the One.
There is no God but the Resplendent Glory.

The Goal of the Sūfī is to become One with God

- Sit still, at peace, relaxed.
- Focus in the large circle of the Heart. You are going to repeat the Word of Unification slowly, with visualization.
- As you say it mentally, see **Lā Ilāha** written with flaming white Light-letters on the left chamber of the Heart. Pause...
- As you say it mentally, see **Illa** written with flaming white Light-letters on the right chamber of the Heart. Pause...
- As you say it mentally, see **Allāh** written with flaming white Light-letters in the middle chamber of the Heart. Pause...
- Deep within the chest, in the innermost chamber of the Heart, hold the thought: "There is nothing but God."

The chest is only a reference in physical space as to where you are holding your Attention. The Heart is *not* physical, of course; it is subtle, invisible.

Dimensions of the Heart 847
Some Arabic Prayers to the Deity 850

Lā Ilāha	*"There is Nothing but God"*	Illa
Left Side of Chest	Within the Middle of the Chest	Right Side of Chest

Allāh
Middle of the Chest
(between the shoulder blades)

The Mantram of Unification in the Heart Centre

Kalma-i-Ḥaqqīqat
Arabic: Word of Truth. A Word of Power, or Mantra.

This Word of Power can be understood in many ways, such as:

There is no God but the One.
There is no God but the Resplendent Glory.
There is no God but ALLĀH (the Resplendent Light).
There is only One God.
There is nothing but God.
God alone is.
There is only the One.
Nothing is but God.
There is only God.
Nothing is but the Glory of God.
All is God, the Divine Splendour.
God is One.
God is a Unity.
The Oneness of All.
Divine Unity (or, the Unitive State).
There is none existent save God alone.
There is none to be worshipped save God.
There is nothing important but God.
God is eternally self-subsistent.
God is the Self-Existent One.
There is no other; there is only God.
Our true Self is none other than the Ultimate Reality.

Using this Word of Truth will help you to experience this State of Unity

No words can properly describe what this Mantram of Unification means, because it is *an experience beyond words, mind, logic, reason*, in the state of FANĀ'FI-LLĀH, the complete annihilation or merging of your consciousness into the Divine Consciousness or Universal Presence.

Using this Word of Truth will help you to experience this State of Unity, or Unitive Consciousness. This great mantram is repeated in the Heart with intense yearning. It means that our entire aspiration or yearning in life must be directed to God alone, as there is no worthier objective.

The Divine Unity 852
The One and Only 839
Mystics of Pisces and Aquarius 836
Brahma-Nirvāṇa: Dissolution in God 1224

Variations of the Mantram of Unification

There are many variations of this great Word of Union:

2. **Lā Ilahe Illalāh**
   No God but One.

Your life cannot be separate from the Life of God

When you take this mantram in your Heart, it pulsates in a rhythm:

Lā Ilahe... Illalāh...

As you mentally say the mantram, see Lā Ilahe written across your chest in flaming white letters, and Illalāh pounding deep within the Cavity of the Heart as a Shining Light, as a Source of all Light.

3. **Lā Ilallāh**
   Nothing but God.

This is uttered in the deepest recesses of the Heart, in the most inward, hidden or spiritual part of the Heart, Ekhfā (Arabic), where there *is* nothing but God, and Glory all around.

4. **Lā Ilāha El Il Allāh Hu**
   There is only One God.

5. **Allāhu La Ilāha Illa' Allāh**
   God, God, there is nothing but God.

6. **Allāh-Hu Alāzi La Ilāha Illahū**
   God is One, and there is no other god but the One.

Lā Ilāha Illa Allāh means that the appearance of "otherness", apart from the Oneness, is a delusion. Your life cannot be separate from the Life of God.

Mystical Union 846
Dimensions of the Heart 847
Monology 453
Practising the Presence of God 711
The Two Applications of Mantra 1219

In Arabic, the repetition of a prayer is called **Zikr** and **Dhikr**, or **Zikar** and **Dhikar**. The meaning is the same as the Sanskrit Mantra-Japa. But the Arabic word has another meaning also: *Remembrance*. The prayer helps you to remember the One whom you are calling upon (God). Thus, you pray in your Heart while completely remembering the Oneness of the Divine Nature within you and within All That Is.

The One God of All

The ignorant may interpret this mantram, LĀ ILĀHA ILLA ALLĀH, "There is no God but ALLĀH", to mean that Islām is the only true religion, that all other religions are wrong, pagan, infidel, that BUDDHA, ŚIVA and KṚṢṆA are but idols, and that the Muslim God, ALLĀH, is the only true God. But this is *not at all* the original inspiration of this Divine Word of Power.

There is nothing outside of this Divine Oneness of the Godhead

As it is *experienced* by the Sūfī, the Muslim Mystic, this mantram means that there is nothing but the One God of All, nothing but the One Universal Reality or Godhead, who is the God of all religions, past, present and future. It means that all that is, is God. All that you see, feel, taste, touch and hear is God-in-Expression, God-in-Manifestation. All is God in different degrees of manifestation and unfoldment.

The Divine Unity means that there is nothing outside of this Divine Oneness of the Godhead. All that is visible and invisible is the Godhead. The Creator and the Creation are One, undivided. Mankind is also an expression, a manifestation of that One Divine Unity, and that means that *you too* are Divine. The inward, direct Realization of this fact is the true secret of the Sūfī.

> If you regard yourself as existent and do not regard Me as the cause of your existence, I will veil my Face from you, and only your own face shall appear to you.
>
> *Sūfī tradition*

> For those who say, "Our God is ALLĀH" [the White Brilliance], and take the *right* Path to Him, the *angels* will descend to them, saying, "Let nothing alarm you or grieve you. Rejoice in the Paradise you have been promised. We are the guardians in this world and in the next. You shall find there all that your Souls desire, and all that you can ask for."
>
> *The Qur'ān*

> Serve none but God. To God you shall return. ALLĀH has power over all things.
>
> *The Qur'ān*

The Divine Unity 852
The Eternal is One 512
The One God of All Religions 110
The Omnipresent God 1108
The One 1686

Breathing God

The purpose of these breathing exercises is to *attune* your breath, your life-force, to God—that is, to the Sea of Vibrant Energies that emanate from the Creative Source.

In the following "soft" breathing, the purpose is to *purify* your psychic-self (not to energize it) so that your Heart will become soft and *receptive* to the Divine Impulses from within. To be able to *receive impressions* from the God within you, your Heart must become "soft".

To be able to receive impressions from the God within you, your Heart must become "soft"

Millions of peoples in the world have a "hardened" Heart; that is, they do not feel anything in their Hearts. Therefore they are "dead" to the Divine Presence within themselves and in the Universe around them. They are closed. They have "hardened attitudes", "polarized opinions", "inflexible will", which are mind-states showing that their Hearts are not functioning to temper or tame the mind.

1

HUA (Arabic: God. In Hebrew, HOA.)

Breathe into the Heart	*Breathe out from the Heart*
HU...	A...

The breathing cycle is smooth, flowing evenly in and out, with no stopping, no counting, no holding of the breath, neither in nor out. There is no stopping or pausing between HU and A. Allow the Breathing of the Name to become subtler and subtler, until only the Name remains. *Think of God all the time.*

2

ALLĀH (Arabic: God. In Aramaic, ALLA.)

Breathe into the Heart	*Breathe out from the Heart*
AL...	LA...

The breathing is continuous; there is no stopping or pausing between AL and LA. ALLĀH is one unbroken cycle of breath (as was HUA). Again, the breathing is gradually refined, drawn deeper and deeper into the Heart, until there is no breathing at all—only the Breath, ALLĀH, remains. ALLĀH is the Breath of God.

Conscious Breathing in the Heart 1274
Christian Meditation on the Holy Breath 1346
Gāyatrī (Sun) Breathing 1553
Warrior Breathing 1020

3

La Il La Ha El Al La Hu

This is a variation of the Zikr (Mantram) of Unification:

Lā Ilāha El Allāhu
There is no god but God, the Absolute Reality.
There is no Divinity except the Ultimate Glory (which includes All).

This is a continuous breathing, in and out, of this great Word of Power, centred in the Heart.

Breathe the syllables evenly into and out from the Heart

Breathe the syllables as follows:

in	*out*	*in*	*out*	*in*	*out*	*in*	*out*
La	Il	La	Ha	El	Al	La	Hu

Breathe the syllables evenly into and out from the Heart, until there is no more breathing, until only the State of Unity (Tauḥīd) remains.

Meditation on the Exalted Name of God

Allāh is the exalted Name of God. Allāh means "the Shining One, the Resplendent One, God is Light, the White Brilliance".

- Imagine that your Heart is filled with a Boundless Radiance (Allāh).

Without and within, Allāh is there, like a Boundless Radiance, everywhere.

- Repeat the Name Allāh in your Heart.
- With each inhalation, visualize the White Light pouring into your body through the breath, down to your Heart Centre, and making the Heart glow with Light.

  With each exhalation, imagine the White Light pouring out of your Heart and irradiating the whole world.
- The secret technique of Initiation is the visualization of the Name Allāh in *letters of Light* in the Heart Cakra, and hearing the Sound of the Name.

Allah
Arabic: God. The Total Reality that is God.

Allāh
Arabic: The Name of God. The Greatest Name of God.

Let the Sunshine in...

1. Jallā Julāl-u-Hū (Jallā Julāluhū)
   May God's Glory shine all around.

   Jallā: Splendour, Glory, Divine Majesty.
   Julāl: shining, radiating, resplendent.
   Hū: God.
   U: of.

These meditations will awaken your Heart Centre

a. Repeat the Word of Power, Jallā Julāluhū, in the Heart, and think of its meaning: "May God's Glory shine all around."

b. Visualize the Centre of your Heart (in physical space, the centre point of your chest) radiating Rays of Light in all directions simultaneously—in front, behind, sideways, up, down, all around.

c. Combine the two methods. Thus, as you say the Word of Power, see the Rays of Light, the Divine Glory, shoot out in all directions from your Heart Centre. These Rays of Light are the Living Glory of the aspect of God within your Soul-Nature.

2. Allāh Jall-Jalāl-Hū (Allāh Jalljalālhū)
   The Glory of God shines all around.

   Allāh: the Radiant Name of God.
   Jall, Jallā: Splendour, Glory, Radiance.
   Jalāl: resplendent, radiating, glorious.
   Hū: God, He.

a. Repeat the Word of Power, Allāh Jalljalālhū, in the Heart, and think of its meaning: "The Glory of God shines all around".

b. Visualize, centred in your Heart, an Ocean of Glory, a Brilliant White Light everywhere, intense, sublime, majestic. It is filling all Space and there is nothing to be seen but this unending Glorious Light. You are a pulsating point of Light within this Ocean of Light, which is Luminous-Bliss-Consciousness.

c. Combine the two methods. Thus, repeat the Word of Power, think of the meaning, and *see* the Ocean of Reality that is God.

These meditations will awaken your Heart Centre and make it a Source of Light for all who are around you.

The Absolute-Truth-Being

Remember that, for the Sūfī Mystic, God is not an old man on a throne somewhere in Heaven, but is **Al-Ḥaqq**, the Absolute-Truth-Being, the final Meaning of all things, a Being of Light of Immeasurable Splendour.

The Sūfī God 838

The Dance of Life

The Sūfī ascetics in the Piscean Age were called Darvesh in the Persian language, which means "a mendicant, a renunciate, an ascetic, one who is wholly devoted to God". Darvesh became Dervis in Turkish, which means "a poor man, a holy man, a wandering ascetic, one who has renounced the world". In English it became *Dervish*. They were also called, in Arabic, Awliyā-Yekhodā, "people of Holiness", or Saints.

The Influence of the Seven Rays 834
Movement and the Life-force 1020
Baptism and Rebirth 722
The Creative Soul 1692

Remember that we are talking of the Piscean Age, when spiritual people did things to the extreme. As a result of the *extreme* practice of fasting, prayer and meditation, day and night, relentlessly for weeks or months on end, some of these ascetics attained trance conditions which were similar to those of the Jewish ascetics of Old Testament times and the early Christian Mystics. In this trance they were overcome by waves of Joy and Bliss which made their bodies dance *spontaneously* and go into strange, convulsive movements, beyond their control.

Later on, as the centuries rolled by, the Sūfīs created *formalized* dancing sessions in the hope that through them they would attain Spiritual Ecstasy. These dance sessions became *choreographed* and *rigid*, and the students had to adhere to a strict regime of movement. This is what is left today of the *Dancing Dervishes*.

Originally, however, dancing had another meaning. Movement was sacred.

> As it is necessary to be born from the womb to see this world, it is necessary to be born from the Heart to see the Face of God.
>
> *Sūfī Wisdom*

This Birth is a Movement, a Dance of Life. This Spiritual Birth is just as real as physical birth, but it takes place in another dimension.

The Heart is the Central Point of the Circle of the Dance of Life.

Have you found your Centre yet?

True Dancing

To the Ancients, *dance was sacred*. And what is it today?—gyrating one's hips to a lot of noise. In no way could this be described as sacred! For the past few centuries, even the *Dancing Dervishes* did not quite get it right; they swirled around until they fainted or collapsed from exhaustion.

It is recorded in the Gnostic Gospels that Jesus danced with His disciples in imitation of the Sun and the planets, Jesus being the Sun, and the twelve disciples being the twelve planets circling around it. (Later on, the church authorities forbade dancing as being of the Devil!) Jesus and His disciples danced with *Awareness*, fully conscious, and directed by a Divine Purpose. This is *true Dancing*.

Sūfī Mantras for Meditation (Arabic)

These 28 Sūfī mantras are to be meditated upon in the Heart. You may choose any one that you are attracted to and repeat the KALMA (prayer, mantra, Word of Power) with Faith, Devotion and Love, and with Longing for the Manifestation of the Divine Presence in your Heart.

Repeat the Kalma with Faith, Devotion and Love

1. ALHAMDULILLĀH
   Praise be to God.
   Glory be to God.
   Glorify God.
   All praise is to the Radiant Glory.

2. SUBḤĀNALLĀH
   Praise be to God.
   Holiness to the Lord.
   Glorify God.
   God is spotlessly Pure.

3. AS-SALĀMU-'ALAIKUM
   May the Peace of God be upon us.

4. SALĀM
   The Peace of God.
   God as Peace and Tranquillity.

5. AMĪN
   God is Complete, Full, Whole, Perfect.

6.

ĪL	I'LĀ	ILĀH, ILLĀH	ILĀHA, ILĀHĪ
God.	Divine.	God.	God.
	Exalted.	Divinity.	Divinity.
	Of God.	Deity.	My God.

7. AL-ILĀH
   The God.

Alhamdulillāh 1128
Some Arabic Prayers to the Deity 850

8. **Āl** — The Progenitor of all things.
   'Alā — The Glory. The Sublime.
   A'lā — The most Sublime.

   Allah — The general Name of God.
   Allāh — The most Excellent Name of God.
   Allāhu, Allahū — The Name that Calls upon God.

There is none greater than God

9. **Allāh**

   The Absolute Reality. The Primeval Being.

   The Boundless Ocean of Existence. The All.

   The Final Reality beyond which you cannot go.

   That which includes all that is Manifest, as well as the Transcendent.

   The Indescribable.

10. **Hū**

    God.

11. **Allāhu Akbar**
    Allahū Akbar

    God is the Greatest.

    There is none greater than God.

    God is Omnipresent, Omnipotent, Omniscient.

12. **Allāh-Hu Alāzi La Ilāha Illahū**

    The Everlasting, the Infinite, there is no God but God.

13. **Allāhu Lā Ilāha Illa Allāh**

    There is no God but the Godhead.

14. **Allāhu Ta'ālā**

    God Almighty.

    God in the Highest.

    God the Most Exalted.

    God who dwells in the Heart.

The Greatness of God

The Arabic mantra **Allāh Hu Akbar**, "the Greatness of God", is commonly translated as "God is Great". How misunderstood is the Greatness of God! How tragic that this Name be used for human political ends!

Revolutionaries cry "Allāh Hu Akbar!", but how few understand this Glorious Name.

God is Great because God is Infinite Glory, Infinite Power, Infinite Majesty. God is the Ruler of all the Worlds, the Fathomless Abyss of Space, the countless stars and galaxies, and a World Everlasting. Who can stand in His Presence?

15. Hūa Hū
God, God.

16. Hūa Illā-Hū
God, God, God.

There is no God other than the One

17. Lā Ilāha Illa Allāh
There is no God but the Resplendent Glory.

18. Lā Ilahe Illalāh
No God but the One.

19. Lā Ilallāh
Nothing but God.

20. Lā Ilāha Ill-Allāhu
Lā'illāha Il'allāhu
There is no God other than the One.
There is no God but the Unconditioned Absolute.
There is only the Absolute Reality.
Everything (visible and invisible) is a projection or a particle of the Absoluteness.

21. Lā Ilāha El Il Allāhu
There is no God but God, the Everlasting.

22. Lā Ilāha Illa'llāh
There is no Reality but the Divine Essence.

23. Lā Illā-ha Illāha Illah-Allāh
There is no God but the Absolute.

24. Bismillāhirahmānirahīm
Bismillāh Ir-Raḥmān Ir-Raḥīm
Bismillāh Ar-Raḥmān Ar-Raḥīm
In the Name of God, the Compassionate, the Merciful.
In the Name of God, the Beneficent, the Forgiving.

The Mantram of Unification 866
The Beautiful Names 1264

25. Anā Al-Ḥaqq
Anā 'l-Ḥaqq
I am the Truth. I am the Living God. I am One with God.
My Essential Nature is God's Essential Nature.
My true Self is inseparable from Divine Nature.

26. Lā Ilāha Il-Allāhu
'Ishq-Allāh Mahabbud'lillāh
Ya Raḥmān Ya Raḥīm
Subḥānallāh Alhamdulillāh
Allahū Akbar, Allahū Akbar

There is no God but the Resplendent Glory.
God is Love, God is the Beloved Lover,
the Compassionate, the Merciful.
Glory be to God, Glory to the Majesty!
The Divine Majesty is the Greatest.
The Divine is the Greatest Majesty.

There is no God but the Resplendent Glory

27. Bism-Allāhi Alraḥmāni Alraḥīm
Alhamdu-Lillāhi Rabbī-Alamīn
Māliki-Yawmid-Dīn
Iyyāka Nabodu wa Iyyāka Nastaīn

In the Name of God, most Loving, most Merciful,
Glory be to God, the Lord of the Universe,
King of the Day of Judgment,
You we worship and to You we go for help.

28. Qūl Hū Allāhu Aḥad Allāhu 'Aṣamad

Declare, the Godhead is One God, the Eternal.

Declare the Truth that the Eternal Godhead (Reality) is One:

- Oneness in Essence.
- Oneness in Attributes.
- Oneness in Works or Manifestations.

Note that **Hūa** is **Hoa** in Hebrew. Note also that **Qol** and **Aḥad** (**Achad**) are also Hebrew words, and **Al** is pronounced in Hebrew as **El**. The pure Arabic has no **E** and **O** vowels, only **A, I** and **U.**

Remembrance of the Five Pure Vowels 1032

Qūl
Arabic: The Voice.

Ṣamad
Arabic: The Eternal, the Everlasting, the Never-Ending, beyond Time, Space, Causation.

Aḥad
Arabic: The One and Only, the One without a Second, the Absolute State of Unity. The same as Waḥīd and Tauḥīd: "the indescribable Singularity or Oneness of the Eternal Reality, Union with God". This is not speculative philosophy, theological belief or metaphysical guesswork, but the *experience* of the Mystic in the highest states of Ecstasy or Inner Union, beyond the comprehension of the body and the mind, in the Transcendental Vision of the Heart.

The One and Only 839

The 99 Arabic Divine Names of God for Meditation in the Heart

The Purification of the Heart 849
The Name and the Names 1258
The Beautiful Names 1264

The 99 Arabic Divine Names of God are a source of Purification of the Heart. Each Name is a quality or attribute (among countless possibilities) upon which you can focus and meditate in your Heart. This means approaching God, AL-ḤAQQ (Arabic: the Absolute Truth or Reality), through a preferred quality with which you can identify. That Name of God becomes your guide or model to *repeat in the Heart* and *live by in the world.*

Note that there are some variations of the 99 Names of God according to the various Sūfī traditions. There are actually more than 130 Names of God used by the Sūfīs.

∞

1

ALLĀH, ALLAHĀ, ALLAH-HŪ
The Eternal, the Everlasting, the Self-Subsisting, the Ultimate Reality, the Transcendent, the Cause of all that Is.

2

AR-RAḤMĀN
The Gracious, the Good, the Beneficent, the Compassionate, the Kind.

3

AR-RAḤĪM
The Merciful, the Loving, the Compassionate, the Kind, the Forgiving.

4

AL-MALĪK
The King, the Lord, the Master, the Ruler, the Controller.

5

AL-QUDDŪS
The Holy, the Sacred, the Pure, the Innocent, the Sanctified.

6

AS-SALĀM
The Peaceful, the Tranquil, the Quiet, the Serene, the Prosperous.

7

AL-MU'MIN
The Faithful, the Believer, the One Who gives Security.

8

AL-MUHAIMIN
The Guardian, the Protector, the Preserver, the Merciful.

9

Al-Aẓīm

The Infinite, the Grand, the Dignified, the Exalted.

10

Al-Jabbār

The Strong, the Omnipotent, the Almighty, the Absolute.

11

Al-Mutakabbir

The Superb, the Great, the Mighty, the Sublime.

12

Al-Khāliq

The Creator, the Progenitor.

13

Al-Bārī

The Shaper, the Fashioner, the Maker, the Creator.

14

Al-Muṣauvir

The Maker of all Forms, the Fashioner.

15

Al-Ghaffār

The Forgiver, the most Merciful.

16

Al-Qahhār

The Almighty, the Supreme, the Powerful, the Conquering, the Victorious.

17

Al-Wahhāb

The Bestower, the Giver, the Liberal, the Generous.

18

Ar-Razzāq

The Provider, the Sustainer.

19

Al-Fattāḥ

The Victorious, the Greatest,
the One Who gives a chance,
the One Who solves all problems.

20

Al-Alīm

The All-Knowing, the All-Wise, the Omniscient.

21

As-Sarī

The Swift, the Quick, the Fast.

22

Al-Bāsiṭ

The Wide-Spreading, the Omnipresent, the Giver of all goods.

23

Al-Khāfiz

The One Who makes low, the One Who brings down the Mighty.

24

Ar-Rafī

The Exalter, the Noble, the Sublime, the Elevated, the Delicate, the Subtle, the Transcendental.

25

Al-Mu'izz

The One Who blesses, the One Who glorifies, the One Who honours you.

26

Al-Muzill

The Giver of Shade, the Reliever,
the One Who humbles the Mighty.

27

As-Samī
As-Sāmi

The Hearer, the One Who listens to you,
the One Who can be heard.

28

Al-Baṣīr

The Seer, the One Who sees all things,
the All-Wise, the All-Knowing.

29

Al-Ḥakīm

The Wise, the All-Knowing, the Omniscient.

30

Al-Fāṣil

The Decider, the Discerner,
the One Who can separate or distinguish.

31

Al-Laṭīf

The Subtle, the Mysterious, the Transcendental,
the One Who is very fine and light.

32

Al-Khabīr

The Aware, the One Who is always Awake,
the All-Knowing, the Wise.

33

Al-Ḥalīm

The Considerate, the Forbearing, the Gracious,
the Gentle, the Merciful.

34

Al-Azīz

The Mighty, the Powerful, the Noble,
the Venerable, the Honourable.

35

Al-Ghāfir

The Pardoner,
the One Who is forgiving and merciful.

36

Ash-Shākir

The Grateful, the Rewarding, the Thankful.

37

Al-Alī
Al-Āliyah

The Sublime, the Exalted,
the Most High, the Most Excellent.

38

Al-Kabīr

The Great, the Omnipotent, the Noble,
the One Who is most senior.

39

Al-Ḥafīẓ

The Protector, the Keeper, the Preserver, the
Watcher, the Guardian, the Ruler, the Governor.

40

Al-Ḥasīb

The Reckoner, the Record-Keeper,
the Keeper of the balance book.

41

Al-Jamīl

The Beautiful, the Graceful, the Good,
the Excellent, the Perfect.

42

Al-Karīm

The Noble, the Honoured, the Gracious,
the Generous, the Kind.

43

Ar-Raqīb

The Watcher, the Guardian, the Preserver,
the Keeper, the Protector.

44

Al-Mujīb

The Answerer, the One Who accepts prayers,
the One Who grants favours.

45

Al-Wāsi

The All-Embracing Generous Giver,
the Liberal, the Infinite, the Vast.

46

Al-Ḥakīm Al-Mutlāq

The Absolute Judge, the All-Wise.

47

Al-Wadūd

The Loving, the Friendly, the Beloved.

48

Al-Majīd

The Glorious, the Noble, the Exalted.

49

Ash-Shadīd

The Stern, the Strong, the Powerful,
the Intense, the Awesome.

50

Ash-Shahīd
Ash-Shāhid

The Witness, the One Who sees all,
the One from Whom nothing is hidden.

51

Al-Ḥaqq

The Truth, the Reality, the Absolute Law,
the Perfect Justice.

52

Al-Wakīl

The Defender, the Guardian, the Advocate,
the One Who takes care of all.

53

Al-Qawī

The Powerful, the Strong, the Mighty,
the Omnipotent, the Vigorous.

54

Al-Matīn

The Firm, the Strong, the Solid, the Immovable.

55

Al-Walī

The Friend, the Helper, the Patron,
the One Who governs,
the One Who is close to you, the Intimate One,
the Sovereign, the Lord, the Chief.

56

Al-Ḥamīd

The Praiseworthy, the Glorious.

57

Al-Qābil
Al-Qabīl
The Accepter, the Capable, the Kind,
the One Who is competent to do all things.

58

Al-Badī
Al-Bādī
The Originator, the Author,
the Cause of all things, the Beginning.

59

Al-Muḥīt
The One Who surrounds, the Omnipresent,
the All-Pervading, the One Who is everywhere.

60

Al-Muḥyī
The Giver of Life, the Regenerator,
the Quickener, the Resurrector.

61

Al-Mumīt
The Giver of Death, the Destroyer.

62

Al-Ḥāyī
The Living, the Everlasting.

63

Al-Qayyūm
The Eternal, the Changeless, the Everlasting,
the Self-Subsisting.

64

Al-Yuīd
The Affectionate.

65

Al-Wāḥid
Al-Waḥīd
The One, the Unique, the Singular,
the Monad, the Alone.

66

As-Ṣamad
The Resource of All,
the One upon Whom all depend,
the Eternal, the Lord and Master.

67

Al-Qadīr
The Capable, the Powerful, the Mighty,
the Omnipotent.

68

Al-Muqīt
The Support, the Controller of All,
the Strengthener, the Provider, the Overseer.

69

Al-Qarīb
The Near, the Immanent, the One Who is close by.

70

Al-Muakhkhar
The Far, the Transcendent, the Goal, the End.

71

Al-Awwal
The First, the Foremost, the Primordial,
the Best, the Topmost.

72

Al-Ākhir
The Last, the End, the Completion.

73

Az-Ẓāhir

The Outer, the Manifest, the Visible,
the Evident, the Objective, the Apparent.

74

Al-Bāṭin

The Inner, the Unmanifest, the Hidden,
the Subtle, the Interior, the Mystical.

75

Al-Āmīn

The Trustworthy, the Faithful,
the One Who can be depended upon.

76

Al-Muta'ālī

The Exalted, the Sublime, the Highest,
the Greatest, the Most Perfect.

77

Al-Bārr

The Just, the Benign One, the Beneficent,
the Righteous, the Truthful, the Affectionate,
the Good.

78

Al-Tauwāb

The Relenting, the Mild, the Tender,
the Compassionate, the Flexible.

79

Al-Ghafūr

The Benevolent, the Benign, the Forgiving,
the Merciful.

80

Al-Affūw

The Mild, the Pardoner, the Forgiving.

81

Ar-Ra'ūf

The Affectionate, the Merciful, the Kind,
the Benevolent, the Gracious.

82

Malikul Mulki

The Master of the Universe,
the Master of the Kingdom of God.

Mālik Al-Mulk

The Master of the Kingdom of God,
the Owner of the All.

83

Dhūl Jalāl Wa Akrām

The Mighty and Glorious Lord.

Dhūl Jalāli Walikrām

The Lord of Glory and Honour,
the Lord of Majesty and Greatness.

84

Al-Ghālib

The Triumphant, the Overpowering,
the Dominant, the Victorious.

85

Al-Ghanī

The Absolute, the Independent,
the Self-Sufficient One,
the Contented, the Prosperous.

86

Al-Mughnī

The One Who is enriched with everything,
the One Who makes rich,
the Giver of all powers and abilities.

87

Al-Maulā

The Protector, the Helper, the Chief, the Lord,
the Master, the One Who befriends all.

88

An-Nāfi

The Good, the One Who is profitable for all,
the One Who confers all benefits,
the One Who is beneficial to all.

89

An-Naṣīr
An-Nāṣir

The Helper, the Friend, the Defender,
the Protector, the Ally.

90

An-Nūr

The Light, the Eternal Being of Light,
the Radiance, the Splendour, the Glory.

91

Al-Hādī

The Leader, the Guide of All.

92

Ar-Rāziq

The Sustainer, the Cherisher,
the One Who gives sustenance.

93

Al-Bāqī

The Everlasting, the Eternal,
the One Who endures forever.

94

Al-'Azalī

The Purifier, the Eternal, the Everlasting.

95

Ar-Rashīd

The Pioneer, the Pious, the Holy,
the One Who directs the All.

96

Al-Aḥad

The One, the Unique, the Alone,
the One without a second.

97

As-Ṣabūr

The Patient One, the Gentle, the Mild.

98

Dhūl-Faḍli

The Generous Lord, the Source of all virtues.

99

Rabbul'-Ālamīn

The Lord of all creatures.

CHAPTER 42

Sūfī Mind

Worlds of the Sūfī

We live in a multi-dimensional Universe. The perception that this physical world is the only "reality" is a gross delusion. There are seven great Worlds, Realms, Kingdoms or Planes of Being, the Physical World or Physical Plane being the seventh and last, counting from above downwards.

The perception that this physical world is the only reality is a gross delusion

The Seventh World

The Seventh World or Realm is called by the Sūfīs:

'Ālam-i-Nāsūt
The World of Humanity (embodied Humanity).

'Ālam-i-Ṭabi'at
The World of Results (having been sealed).

'Ālam (Arabic) means a World, a Realm, a Kingdom, a Sphere or Plane of Being (identical with the Hebrew Olam).

Nāsūt means Humanity, or pertaining to Mankind (in physical bodies).

Ṭabi'at has the sense of having been published or sealed, or having resulted, because it is the last world, the final result of the Creative Effort of Divinity.

Worlds within Worlds

You must not conceive of these Worlds or Realms of Being as being on top of each other, like layers of bricks or steps of a ladder. They are actually *within* each other, with each higher realm being a more subtle rate of vibration. All seven realms are in the same Space, but you can perceive a world or sphere only when you develop the corresponding *vibration* within yourself.

Dimensions of the Solar Logos in Cosmic Space 1591

The Seven Great Planes 13
The Four Kabbalistic Worlds 360
The Seven Subplanes of the Physical Plane 16

The Sixth World

Above this is the Sixth World, what nowadays we call the Astral Plane, the afterlife state or the subtle worlds. The Sūfīs named this realm:

'Ālam-i-Mithāl
The World of Subtle Imagination.

In the Astral World you see things reflected, as in a mirror

In today's language we would call it the imaginative consciousness, or dream-consciousness, or reflection. They also named this realm:

'Alām-i-Ṣūrat
The World of the Soul (after death).

The Arabic word Ṣūrat means an image, a form or appearance, but to the Sūfīs it also meant the "Soul" in the disembodied state, and inner attention. In fact, the Astral Plane has been called the *Reflection Sphere* by some modern writers because there you see things reflected, as in a mirror. It is to the Astral World that you go after you exit your physical body.

The Astral World surrounds and penetrates the Physical World and every person or object on the Physical Plane, and is inhabited by angels as well as humans. The astral matter is more shiny or translucent than the matter of the Physical World. It is the region of intense *feelings* and *desires*, for the physical body is no longer present to block out the feeling or sentient vibrations. The lowest regions are of "hell" vibrations, the middle regions are of "purgatory" or purifying vibrations, and the highest realms are of "heaven" vibrations, or pleasurable sensations. These are not the true "heavens", but the experience is intense enough for people to believe that they are in "heaven".

The Three Worlds

The lower three Worlds, Spheres or Planes of Being constitute the normal Three Worlds within which the Human Souls circulate or reincarnate, life after life, until they decide to break their chains and return to their Source, the Divine Being, the Logos.

From Bondage to Liberation 422

Kāmaloka: the Astral Plane 57
Death and Liberation 397
Powers of Consciousness 374
Realms of the One Mind 492
Beyond Phantasia 686

The Fifth World

The Fifth World is what, in modern language, we call the Mental Plane. The seven subdivisions of this plane are the true "Heaven Worlds". The Sūfīs call this world:

'Ālam-i-Ma'nā
The World of Immediate Appearance.

Here your thoughts become immediately visible to yourself and to others

Note that, in Sanskrit, Manah and Manas mean "mind", while in Persian, Man means "the self, ego, personal I, me" and "the Heart". (From this came the English word *man.*)

The Mental World is the true home of the "mind". Here your *thoughts* become immediately visible to yourself and to others, and the thoughts of others are clear and shining to you. Nothing that is in your "mind", or in the minds of others, can be concealed or hidden.

The Mental Realm is composed of *thought-constructs* or *thought-forms* created by humans, angels and archangels, the three species that can be found on that plane of Life. The Heaven Worlds in this realm are *mental constructs* in accordance with people's ideas about God and "Heaven". You can go to these Heaven Worlds only if your thoughts were noble, elevated, sublime, pure, inspired, truly artistic, or truly "scientific" (meaning *an impersonal search for knowledge).*

Devāchan: the Mental Plane 73

The Fourth World

The next world above is the Fourth World, called by the Sūfīs:

'Ālam-i-Malakūt
The World of the Kingdom (the Kingdom of God).

This is what, in modern language, we call the Buddhic World or Buddhic Plane, the World of Unity or At-One-Ment, the characteristics of which are Love, Bliss, Unity and Luminous Intelligence. To this world go the Mystics who have united themselves, to a certain degree, with God. On this plane you are already Liberated.

The Arabic word Malakūt means "an empire or kingdom", but it also means the Kingdom of God, or the Divine Empire, the world of the higher angels or spiritual beings, the Gods.

Buddhi: the Realm of Unities 83

The Third World

The next realm above is the Third World:

'Ālam-i-Jabarūt
The World of Omnipotence.

This is what, in modern terminology, we call Nirvāṇa, or the Nirvāṇic World, or the Ātmic World.

The Arabic word **Jabarūt** means "Omnipotence, All-Consuming Power, exceedingly high spiritual state, exalted condition". Very high Mystics or Enlightened Beings go to this realm of Being.

Nirvāṇa: the World of Glories 93

The Second World

The next world, the Second World, is:

'Ālam-i-Lāhūt
The World of Divine Nature.

The Arabic word **Lāhūt** means "the Godhead, Divine Beingness, Divinity". Nowadays we call this realm the Monadic World, the Divine World, the world of Paramātman, or the sphere of Absolute Glory, Paranirvāṇa. This is an extremely high state of Liberation. In this world abide species of Divine Evolutions.

Our true Home or Origin 17
The Third Stage of Yoga 529

The First World

The next world above is the First World:

'Ālam-i-Hāhūt
The World of Divine Essence.

This is the Origin, the Source of All Things. Nowadays we call it the plane of Ādi, the Logoic Plane, the world of the Logos or Deity.

It is interesting that, in both Sanskrit and Arabic, the word Ādi refers to the Ultimate. The Sanskrit Ādi means "the First, the Origin, the Source, Primordial", while in Arabic Ādi means "the very Ancient, the Primeval, the Primordial State". In this state you *become* the Logos, and the Way opens up for you to the Door of Cosmic Life, Cosmic Perception.

The Logos: the Word of God 114
Cosmic Powers 602

1	'Ālam-i-Hāhūt **Mahāparanirvāṇa**	The World of Divine Essence 'Ubūdiyat: The Reality	**Ādi** The Very Ancient The Primordial State	
2	'Ālam-i-Lāhūt **Paranirvāṇa**	The World of Divine Nature Qurbiyat: The Proximity of Reality	**Rūḥ-u-llāh** The Spirit of God The Paramātman	
3	'Ālam-i-Jabarūt **Nirvāṇa**	The World of Omnipotence Quṭbīyat: The Central Axis of Reality	**Rūḥ** The Spirit The Ātman	**The Light of God**
4	'Ālam-i-Malakūt **Buddhi**	The World of the Kingdom (of God) Ma'rifat: The Secret of the Messengers	The Spiritual Soul Ātma-Buddhi	The Mind of Light
5	'Ālam-i-Ma'nā **Mental Plane**	The World of Immediate Appearance	△ **Nafs** The Living Soul **Jism-i-Alṭaf** Body of Great Subtlety	**"Intellect"** **Higher Mind** **Ordinary Mind**
6	'Ālam-i-Mithāl 'Ālam-i-Ṣūrat **Astral Plane**	The World of Subtle Imagination The World of the Soul (after death)	**Jism-i-Laṭīf** Body of Delicateness	**Imaginative Consciousness**
7	'Ālam-i-Nāsūt 'Ālam-i-Ṭabī'at **Physical Plane**	The World of Humanity The World of Results	**Jism-i-Kasīf** Body of Denseness	**Physical Body**

Worlds of the Sūfī

Dimensions of the Mind

The Mind is a complex reality. In the olden days the Sages distinguished between the ordinary mind, the Intellect, the Mind of Light, and the Light Itself.

The Ordinary Mind

The *ordinary mind* is your rational mind, your mental body, your lower mind, what you use in your daily life (along with your astral body).

The Mental Body 78

The Intellect

The *Intellect* is your Higher Mind, the Abstract Mind, what is known as the causal body. Very few people use this mind. Whereas the *lower mind* uses simple logic, "research" and simple memory, the Higher Mind quickly sees the principle or principles behind something and grasps the essential "facts", without involving the cumbersome and prolonged process of research, analysis or logic.

Intellectus: Knowing inside 375

The Mind of Light

The *Mind of Light* (Buddhi-Manas in Eastern terminology) is your Mind (lower and higher) infused with Light—the Light of your Soul, or the Light of the God within you, or the Light of the Universe—but *still functioning as Mind*. This is *Illumination*.

Inspiration by the Mind of Light 1113
Super-Knowing 1242

The Light Itself

When you perceive the Light Itself as Light, when even the veil of Mind is removed, you *Know* God Face-to-Face, or "See God's Face" (a much-used Sūfī expression). This is *Enlightenment*.

When the Glory of God, the Dazzling Light, pervades everywhere for you as a Brilliant White Light, you have attained Nirvāṇa, as the Eastern Sages say, and Al-Ḥaqq (the Truth), as the Sūfīs say, which is the same as God, Hū.

Nirvāṇa! 94
The Light of God 847

Note that the term *Mind of Light* has been used in various ways by the Mystics, Sages and Seers. It can refer to the Universal Mind of the Deity (the One Mind), or it can refer to the Light of the Nirvāṇic Plane, or, as in this case, it can refer to the human mind infused with Light (Buddhi-Manas). One must consider the context in which such terms are used, since there is a shortage of words in the English language to describe the Spiritual Realities.

Perceptions of the One Mind 490
Realms of the One Mind 492
The Seven States of Consciousness 494

Understand your Predicament

To succeed upon the Spiritual Path, you must understand your existential situation.

- First of all, you must *know* that you are a Living Soul, your habitat being the formless part of the Mental Plane, known as the Causal World. You, the Living Soul, are formless, without boundaries or restrictions (up to a certain point) in Eternal Space.
- You are *encased* in a mind-body which responds to the vibrations of the Mental Plane. Your mind-body is dual: the causal body responds to the vibrations of the Causal World, the formless portion of the Mental Plane, while your mental body, or thinking body, responds to the Thought World, the form-making portions of the Mental Plane.
- You are further encased in your astral body, your emotional body, the "feeling" or "emotional" self which registers vibrations from the Astral Plane or Emotional World.
- You are further encased in a dual physical body: the gross animal body and the etheric-physical-light body, which register vibrations coming from the dense and etheric parts of the Physical World.

Ḥāj
Arabic: Pilgrimage to the Real. Your Journey upon the Way. Your Quest.

The Human Constitution (Arabic)

You are a Living Soul, **Nafs**, and are encased in the following vestures or "bodies":

Jism-i-Kasīf: Body of Denseness, that is, your gross physical body, the animal body.

Jism-i-Laṭīf: Body of Delicateness, that is, your subtle body or astral body, through which you sense, feel, have moods, desires, wishes.

Jism-i-Alṭaf: Body of Great Subtlety, that is, your mental body or thought-body, your ordinary mind, by which you think, plan, and so forth.

Subtler still is the **Rūḥ**, the Spirit that you are (the Ātman, in the Eastern system). And above that still is the **Rūḥ-u-llāh**, the Spirit of God (the Paramātman of the East).

In Arabic, the "mind" is also called **Nār**, which means "fire, hell, mind, intellect, advice, counsel". This practically sums up the true meaning of your "mind"!

The Human Constitution 31
Trapped Spirits 1240
The Three Identifications 1369
Obstacles to Higher Consciousness 1424
Beyond Natural Evolution 1312
To Experience Heaven 82

Your physical body is an animal body, belonging to the Animal Kingdom, but it is *not* You! Your etheric-physical, astral and mental bodies are your true human bodies, vastly different from your physical body. It is a Mystery why the Human Souls have received animal bodies to work through on this planet, as this physical body has no relationship to your truly human non-physical bodies. Your non-physical bodies belong to the true human evolutionary process, while your physical body belongs to the animal evolutionary process.

Your physical body belongs to the animal evolutionary process

It is also a Mystery why people so completely *identify* with their physical bodies. You could say that this New Age civilization is very physical-body bound! If you solve this Mystery in *deep meditation* or spiritual trance, you will be on your Way to true Liberation. You cannot "philosophize" about this; to do so is a waste of time.

- When your consciousness functions through your physical body, you *identify* with the sensations and impressions coming from the dense Physical World, its objects, people, and so on.
- When your consciousness functions through your etheric-physical body (as it does immediately after death, for example), you identify with the sensations and impressions of the etheric portion of the Physical Plane.
- When your consciousness functions through your astral body (as in dreams and in the after-death state), you identify with the impressions and sensations coming from the Astral World, the afterlife or subtle world.
- When your consciousness functions in your mental body, as it does in the Heaven Worlds, you identify with the sensations, impressions and objects of that world.

In none of these situations do you Know Yourself, Who You Are!

The Spiritual Path is necessary in order to learn to *disentangle* yourself from your various bodies (including your mind) which act as coverings or veils over Yourself.

Until you understand the Goal or Purpose of the Way, and practise it sincerely, you are lost in idle speculations and theories. What is more important, until you do so, you will keep reincarnating, circulating in the three lower regions of the Cosmic Sphere, pulled therein by your consciousness and the impressions, sights, smells, tastes and sounds of these worlds, forever blocking out for you the Universe of Light, the Abode of God, the Upper World of Light, Glory and Bliss.

Clarify your Objective 423

Beyond the Veils

When the Mystics of all religions say, "Know your Self", they don't mean that you should dissect your physical body, or map out the activities of your brain cells, or observe your outer psychological behaviours. They mean that you should *go beyond the veils*, your coverings, including your "mind", by practising the right meditational processes, until you stand clear of them all and *Realize Yourself* as a shining and luminous Being of Light, at One with the shining and luminous Being of Light of the Universe—call it God, the Absolute, the Truth or Reality, it is the same.

All embodiments act as limitations to Consciousness

At this stage of your Journey, your Path consists of discovering Who You Are when you are not limited by the various veils or coverings, the bodies you inhabit, because those veils limit your experience of Reality to the degree that they are unable to sense It or experience It.

The physical body is the most limiting veil over Reality. In your astral body, in the Astral World, you can experience more of Reality, and in your mental body, in the Mental World, you can experience even more of Reality. But even your causal body, on the formless part of the Mental Plane, acts as a limitation for You, the Living Soul. For all embodiments, of whatever kind, act as limitations to Consciousness.

Pure Consciousness (consciousness not circumscribed by a body, form or veil) is unlimited, boundless, infinite, absolute. Thus, you have to divest yourself of your bodies, or go beyond your "coverings" which conceal the Light that you are, and the Light that God is, the Sublime Reality. For just as your bodies or veils act as coverings over your Light, so the many worlds and planes on the lower levels of the Universal Manifestation act as coverings or veils over the Infinite Ocean of the Intelligent Supreme Light-Being of the Absoluteness that is God, or Truth, the Reality. Thus:

You have to ascend the various lower planes of Being, out of your various lower bodies, into your Spiritual Nature upon the Spiritual Planes.

Know Thyself 1389
Who is 'I AM'? 1418
Turīya: Pure Consciousness 498
Entering the Lost Kingdom 1176
What is Consciousness? 1368
Ascending the Planes of Consciousness 20

The Five Stages of Certainty (Arabic)

There are five *Stages of Certainty* in this Knowledge which I have described above:

1. 'Ilm-ul-Yaqīn

   Knowledge of Knowledge.

The first stage is intellectual understanding and certainty of the truth about your Spiritual Goal, your direction in life.

The first stage is certainty of the truth about your Spiritual Goal

2. Yaqīn-ul-Yaqīn

   Knowledge of Knowledge.

Here you are becoming more certain because you are beginning to have direct inner mystical experiences through meditation, interior graces, illuminations, inner mystical feelings, intuitions, and so forth.

3. 'Ain-ul-Yaqīn

   The Eye of Knowledge.

At this stage you have the All-Seeing Eye of Seership, whereby you look into Yourself and Reality.

4. Ḥaqq-ul-Yaqīn

   True Knowledge.

This is Union with God, Seeing Reality without veils or coverings.

5. 'Urf-ul-Yaqīn

   Beatitude-Knowledge.

Here, you are THAT.

The ignorant materialists think that your animal body, the physical body, is all there is, and that the physical brain is the "mind". There are learned, "educated" people who still try to convince you that you are a chimpanzee. There are deluded materialistic-religious people who think that the physical blood is the "Soul". There are "learned" psychologists and psychiatrists who map out the activities of the physical brain under the delusion that they are describing the activities of the "mind". It is the same delusion as a person fiddling with a car wheel while thinking that the wheel is the total car!

The Essence of Wisdom 1680
Orthodox Psychology 1105
All Hail to the Brain! 1368
Liberation from Worldly Consciousness 1233

The Ordinary Mind

This is the common mind which everybody uses. This is the cause of difficulty for you and for the millions of people in the world.

This is the "thinking mind" or "thought-producing mind". It is basically critical, separative, analytical, discriminative, isolationist, verbal, insular, self-centred, cold, calculating, impersonal, "feelingless", materialistic. This analytical mind is used nowadays in education, psychology and science. But there is no Heart in it, meaning there is no *inner connection* with your object of observation or experience. The mind looks outward, at *appearances*. It observes the form side, how things appear on the surface (called "objective analysis").

You can see the danger of it, can you not?

This mind is your constant source of trouble in your relationships with your friends, family, group members, and the outside world of events. This is the constant source of trouble between groups, tribes, nations, and the "theological" aspects of religion (the mental parts of religious doctrines). It is also clearly evident in politics.

The New Aquarian Energies 426
The Education System 480
In Bondage to the Mind 238
Some Human Evils 384
Separatism and the Law of Love 386

Unfortunately, this mind will be the paramount expression in the New Age (which is why hundreds of millions of people are focusing on it already). But you can see the danger of it, can you not? Without the Heart, which is the inner experience of Unity with all Life, with God, with Creation, with the Universe, we can end up in a totally self-destructive society where individuals, tribes, groups and nations are interested only in themselves, for themselves alone, over and above the good of the All. We could have another Armageddon or planetary crisis, caused by this lower mind, caused by lobby groups, pressure groups, minority groups, special-interest groups, who think they are above the rest of society and refuse to work for the good of the All.

Let us re-emphasize that your mind is not your brain! The brain is part of your physical body, whereas your mind (your mental body, the vesture of thought) uses the brain and nervous system as the means of communication with this physical universe. Your mind happily exists after the death of your physical body and carries on "thinking" as ever before.
Mind and Brain 79

For you, as a disciple on the Spiritual Path, the most important thing is to *tame* this mind, to bring it under the control of the Soul.

There are two ways to tame this mind:

a. To *bring it down* into the Heart and there experience the Sense of Unity with All That Is.

b. To *link it up* with the Higher Mind, the Abstract Mind or Intelligent Mind, and from there to the Mind of God, the Infinite Mind or Cosmic Intelligence.

Meditation I
Linking the Head with the Heart

- Sit quietly and relaxed.
- Focus your attention in the Third-Eye Centre, between the two physical eyes, with your eyes closed, without straining. This is where your "thinking" normally happens during the day.
- Visualize yourself surrounded by a deep blue colour.
- After a while, imagine a silvery-shining ray of light emerging from the deep blue sky at the Third-Eye and descending into the Heart Centre (into the middle of the chest).
- Along this Silver Thread, your attention descends into the Heart, and all of your thoughts descend into the Heart.
- After a while, visualize a liquid-golden Sun in the centre of your Heart, the size of a dinner plate.
- Then this *Sun of Compassionate Understanding* enlarges and extends far outside of you, radiating saffron-coloured rays of Sunshine all around. It warms your Heart, it gives warmth to all life around you, it unites, it gives Life, it gives Joy. This is the *Sun of true Wisdom* (unlike mere intellectual knowledge).
- After a while, return your attention to the middle of the forehead and *rest.*

You will be able to "think" and be united with your Heart

During the day, as you go about your daily activities and "thinking", *remember* the Golden Sun in your Heart. In time, you will be able to "think" and, at the same time, be *united* with your Heart.

The lower mind is also the cause of the utterly superficial and trivial personalities which are so numerous these days, with no depth in them, where the orientation is solely on how they "look" or how they "dress" or how to get "rich" by quick means, fair or foul. These people are totally worldly-minded, without the slightest interest in spiritual things.

Another negative aspect of this lower mind or common mind is being constantly preoccupied with oneself: *your* thoughts, *your* ideas, *your* feelings, *your* reactions, *your* views of things, *your* progress on the Path or lack of it, *your* success in meditation or lack of it, *your* experiences or lack of them. This aspect of the ordinary mind can be overcome only by selfless Service, and hence by helping alleviate the sufferings of the world.

Uniting Head and Heart 1130
From Pisces to Aquarius 837
Types of Humanity 376
What is True Service? 1714

Meditation 2
Transformation of the Ordinary Mind

You are building into your thought-body the attributes you are "thinking" of

- Sit relaxed and at ease.
- Focus your attention in the Third-Eye Centre. There should be no strain placed on your eyes or brain.
- Select a Divine Name or a Word of Power (mantram) which represents a Divine Quality or Virtue or Power that you feel attuned to or drawn to.
- Repeat that Name or Word of Power (a mantric phrase or sentence) *slowly* in your mind, focused in the Third-Eye, and realize or contemplate its meaning. In other words, you are doing mental repetition with *understanding* of what you are very slowly repeating. You are not relying on the sound-power of the mantram alone, but also its meaning. *This meaning will transform your mind.*

If you "think" of a Divine Attribute, your mind will take on the quality of that Attribute.

- Next, while you are slowly repeating the word, visualize in your mind that *you already have* that Attribute. In your mind, *act out* scenes and situations where you are using your Divine Attribute or Attributes.
- Next, return to a simple gaze or simple focus in the Third-Eye Centre and *let go.*

The next stage of this process is that, during your daily activities, you remember your Divine Attribute and try to live from that Principle in your day-to-day life. *This will transform your existence.*

Sūfī Mantras for Meditation 874
The 99 Arabic Divine Names of God 878

When you meditate in the Heart, you abide in pure Love, Devotion and Longing as you use the Divine Names or Words of Power (mantras).

When you meditate in the Head, as in this meditation, you use thought-power to develop Understanding and Realization of what you are slowly repeating. You are building into your thought-body (the mental body, your "mind") the qualities or attributes you are "thinking" of.

The Two Paths 1112
The Way of the Mind 1238
Heart Knowing 1286

Example

For example, suppose you chose for your meditation the Divine Name As-Salām, "the Peaceful One, Divine Peace":

- Mentally say, "Salām", and think of the meaning, "Peace", as you say it.
- Then, in your mind, *imagine* situations or circumstances where you are going to use your Power of Peace.
- Then, during your daily life outside of your meditation time, apply your Power or Quality in real life, in real situations, by *recalling* it to your mind when the situation arises.

All Divine Names and mantras are keys to real powers

This applies not only to Arabic Names and mantrams, but also to Hebrew, Aramaic, Sanskrit, Greek, Latin, and so on. The principles are the same in all cases, even if the Sacred Languages are different.

All Divine Names and mantras are *keys to real powers,* miraculous powers which can transform your life and the lives of all those you contact. Thus can you help transform the world.

Taming the Mind

This subject is most important for your understanding if you are going to have any success at all upon the Spiritual Path, or in any areas of your present life. If you are to succeed upon this Path, you need to understand the total meaning of Mind, every aspect of it.

During the Piscean Age, the emphasis was on the Way of the Heart, the Way of Love and Devotion. In the coming Aquarian Age, the emphasis will be on the Way of the Mind, the Way of the Head. This is going to be a big change, with its own problems and challenges.

Also, in the past Age, Salvation or Liberation was individual, for yourself alone. In the coming Aquarian Age, your Liberation will be for the benefit of All, as part of a group process. The understanding of the "mind" is all-important in this process. The wrong use of your mind will prevent you from achieving success in your Quest, your Ḥāj (Arabic: Pilgrimage to the Real, your Journey upon the Way), and will prevent the group of Souls you are working with from achieving their Goals also.

Piscean Spirituality and New Age Spirituality 1706

Your Mind is the Key 1208
Cultivate Silence of the Mind 1239
Mystics of Pisces and Aquarius 836
Group Work 1146

The Sūfī View of Mental Disorders

Humanity on this planet has to become Soul-oriented rather than body-oriented

According to the Sūfī tradition, mental and emotional disorders arise as a result of the following:

Wrong Mental States

- Fear.
- Anxiety.
- Frustration.
- Inner conflicts.
- Wrong thinking, ignorance.
- Wrong relationships.

All of these causes arise through the wrong orientation of the life-force. Humanity is *asleep;* it is cut off from the Inner Reality. Humanity is craving ceaseless external stimulation because it lacks *inner connection.* This external stimulation manifests as the desire for possessions, name, fame, conformity with society, and all kinds of enjoyment. People want more and more material things. All of this causes mental stress, neurosis, psychosis and breakdowns.

Relationships which are based on external factors only, on purely selfish concepts and egotistical aims, cause emotional disturbances.

Wrong Emotional Drives

- Greed and ambition.
- Anger.
- Hatred.
- Jealousy.
- Vanity and superficiality.

These five negative emotional states continually disturb your inner equilibrium. This is how society at large operates, resulting in endless conflicts, wars, tensions and violence. Before true peace can come into the world, each member of society has to free himself or herself from these wrong emotional drives. For this to happen, a *radical inner change* has to take place in the consciousness of Humanity. Humanity on this planet has to become Soul-oriented rather than body-oriented. *This is the fundamental change.* Each of these emotional expressions is the result of ego, the sense of "I", which is the cause of all selfishness.

The Way of the World 380
Passion and Dispassion 695
Cultivate the Positive 1365
Reactive-Emotional Consciousness 1426
Emotional Problems 1429

The Seven Stages of Sūfī Silence

1. **Do not say or do anything unnecessary.**
   This eliminates eighty-percent of the chatter and senseless activity of the average man and woman.
2. **Silence from psychological memory.**
   This means living in the Moment and not being conditioned by the Past.
3. **Silence of the ego or the sense of "I".**
   This means that all actions are done without a sense of ego attached to them.
4. **Silence of the mind, or meditative silence.**
   Whether or not one is thinking or acting, there is an all-pervasive inner serenity. This silence does not come about by the suppression of talking or of action. It has to come naturally, from deep within, from beyond the mind, from the level of the Soul.
5. **The Silence of true surrender to the God-Being within.**
   Establishing an inner connection with the Being of Light and abiding by His Will.
6. **Cosmic Silence.**
   The perception of the Silence, the Emptiness, which is the substratum of the All.
7. **Absolute Silence.**
   The Silence of the Godhead.

Zen Silence 790
Silence, Solitude, Peace 1386
The Silence of the Deep 1355
The Practice of Silence 1443
The Silent State 1554

MURĀQABAĪ (meditation) is a state of the mind, an awareness or alertness in which you are a *witness* to everything, but without becoming psychologically disturbed by what is being witnessed. This state of meditation is *not* a running-away from the world. It is not a renunciation of the world or a giving-up of the worldly condition, nor a shirking of one's responsibilities and duties. It is a condition of "being in the world but not of the world". This can happen only when you become Soul-dependent, when you obey the *Master within*. It comes as a result of fine *inner attunement*.

MURĀQABAĪ has been described by the Sūfīs as *a state of being in which the ego ceases to be*.

MURĀQABAĪ is also the observation of the movement of the mind, moment by moment, and non-reaction to it. Krishnamurti called this state of mind "choiceless awareness".

It is the ending of all mental activities.

It is true Prayer.

It is Surrender to the Divine.

It is Awakening to the Holy Fire, the Spirit within.

PART SEVEN

Tantra

The Path of Relationship

CHAPTER 43

The Circle of Love

Relational Consciousness

Tantra is Relational Consciousness. What is relationship? Relationship is a connection or happening between you and some other person or object. If nothing is going on between you and something else, then there is no relationship.

The Great Ones were concerned for people

You *can* avoid relationships. The ascetic, the yogī, the sannyāsin, the monk, the nun and the renunciate avoid relationship. They are not related to anybody or anything and therefore they are "happy". They have no responsibility to anyone or for anyone, so their lives appear free of complications. Although such a life seems ideal—free of distractions and difficulties—it is also insipid and most often useless. Such people live for themselves alone.

Sometimes I am asked if enlightened people have emotions, or should they not remain in a state of blissful Nirvāṇa, uncaring and unaffected by the sea of emotions and suffering all around? Yet, if you look at the lives of the Great Ones—the Buddha, the Christ, Śrī Kṛṣṇa, Rāma, Muḥammad, Mahāvīra, and the countless thousands of Saints, ancient and modern—their lives were precisely lives of *relatedness.* They had Relational Consciousness. They were *concerned* for people. They cried and agonized over people.

It is true that there are some Saints who enter Nirvāṇa, the Kingdom of God, and become blissfully unaware of Mankind and its problems. They live in their own private world of Bliss and Transcendental Consciousness. They relate to nobody. But such Saints are rare, because the majority of the Great Ones choose relatedness.

If you surrender your ego totally—that is, if you surrender your whole body and mind structure and annihilate all vestige of the personal self in you—then it is possible for you to stay in a relative calm all your life, and at death to become absorbed into the Transcendental Bliss of Nirvāṇa. It is also true, however, that if you choose this Path (the Path of the PRATYEKA BUDDHA or Solitary Mystic), then you have to *get away* from the world. You have to live alone in a cave or in the desert, or in some lonely spot, and not engage in any human activity. You must remain completely alone, single, solitary, unique. Then your relationship is with the Transcendental alone, with the Absolute, with the Source of your Being.

There have been many Saints who lived like this, both in the East and in the West, but they were never the movers and shakers

TANTRA
Sanskrit: The term TANTRA is most difficult to describe. It means the loom and warp of a weaving machine; something that is important, essential or mystical; esoteric philosophies or systems of teachings; mental and spiritual procedures, processes and techniques; sacred books, rituals, magical formulae; polarity, female energies of goddesses; Insight, the perception of Reality; relationship.

MAHĀVĪRA
Sanskrit: "Great Hero".

PRATYEKA BUDDHA
Sanskrit: A Solitary Buddha. A Buddha who walks alone.

of civilization. They were not the inspirers of the people. The Great Ones were those who stayed with their people, who had concern for them, who suffered with them, who laughed and cried with them. The Great Ones lived and died for others. It is They who have benefited Humanity. Although they walked *with* the crowd, they were not *of* the crowd. Although they lived in the world, they were not *of* the world.

The Great Ones retain their egos in order to serve others

The Great Ones retain their egos in order to serve others. Their egos never become totally annihilated, only at times suspended and transcended. Once your ego is destroyed, it destroys also your ability to relate, and you cease to be concerned about others. So the Great Ones did not destroy their egos, but merely suspended them and at times transcended them. In such a way they could remain in the world and function in the world in order to serve Mankind. Such Saints manifested their egos and their Divinity in the same life, in the same person.

All the truly great Saviours and Master Adepts were both Human and Divine, otherwise they could not have communicated with Humanity or enlightened others about the causes of suffering. None of the Saints who truly helped Humanity were abstract intellectuals spinning theories. They were flesh-and-blood men and women who knew what suffering was, who knew from personal experience what it means to be human. And yet, beneath their mortal frames, beyond their personalities—products of time, space and matter—shone the Light of Truth, the Eternal Heart of Reality. This is the Mystery of God incarnating as a human being into the human family.

Periods of Life in Vedic India

In the ancient Vedic days of India, human life was divided into four periods or **Āśrama**:

1. **Brahmacarya**: the religious-student life.
2. **Gṛhastha** or **Gārhastya**: the householder, or married with children.
3. **Vānaprastha**: being in the world but becoming non-attached.
4. **Bhaikṣya** or **Sannyāsin**: an ascetic or mendicant, one who has completely renounced the world in old age and spends all his time in meditation and spiritual experiences.

Types of Conscious Immortality 390
To Become a True Renunciate 257
Spiritual Life and Material Life 1118
God-Consciousness is the Wholeness of Life 504
Brahmacarya: Orientation to the Divine 566

Warrior Jesus

The Way of the Warrior is to fight the Battle of Life

Take a look at the life of Jesus, for instance. He would become angry! He took a scourge and beat the people who lent and sold things in the synagogue. He was furious, red with anger, and He shouted at them. He upset their tables, threw things around and chased them out of the synagogue. On another occasion He cursed a fig tree for bearing no fruit! At another time He sat atop a hill overlooking Jerusalem and cried heavily for the Jewish race and the fact that, no matter how He tried to help them, they would not listen. He cried in frustration and sadness. Jesus was emotional. Jesus was human.

There were hundreds of scenes like these not recorded in the Bible, for the Bible contains less than five-percent of the story. But even from the little that has been recorded, if you read carefully, you will come to know that Jesus had all kinds of emotions—joy at a wedding, for instance, and exaltation when He was led into the city upon the back of a donkey. Jesus was human. He had an ego. He knew what pain and suffering were. He knew what loss was, what death was, what separation was. He *knew.*

But Jesus was also divine. He was also a Son of God, for Divinity shone through Him. For two thousand years the church has tried to portray Him as some kind of abstract Deity who sits on a throne on the right side of the Father. Doing what? No one knows. The church made Him out to be an abstraction, but this is not how the Bible describes Him at all! He certainly was not an abstraction in people's lives. He was a vivid revolutionary, transforming energy in people's lives. He impacted tremendously on His environment. There was *nothing* abstract about Him.

The Way of the Solitary Mystic is Transcendence, non-ego, non-relationship. The Way of the Warrior is to fight the Battle of Life, to understand the Mystery of Existence, to dare to discover the secrets that even angels won't explore, and having won the confidence of the Eternal, to become the brother, guide and helper of a lost and forsaken Humanity.

The Path of the Warrior, the Saviour, is not easy. Usually it is not appreciated even by the very Humanity for which the Saint sacrifices his or her life. But without such Warriors of Existence the world would be plunged into darkness and there would be no chance for suffering human beings to know Themselves.

Jesus the Christed One 659
The Spiritual Warrior 969

Tantra is for the Living

Tantra, like Zen, is the Spontaneous Way. Zen relies on spontaneity; so does Tantra. Zen believes in the Moment; so does Tantra. Zen relies upon experience rather than theory or intellectualizations; such is also the Way of Tantra. And Tantra, like Zen, seeks to transcend all limitations and discover *That Of Which Nought Can Be Said.*

But Tantra is more all-embracing than Zen. You could say that Tantra is the Zen of relationship. For Zen discards sex and male-female relationships, while Tantra embraces them. Zen is the Way for monks, nuns and renunciates, while Tantra is for everybody—especially for men and women engaged in relationship.

Zen discards sex and male-female relationships, while Tantra embraces them

This must be understood. For six thousand years Tantra has been written about by monks who knew nothing about relationship, or what a female looked like, or what femininity was. Therefore they *internalized* all the processes of Tantra, visualized the Goddess within the mind only. For six thousand years monks have written about a subject which essentially they knew nothing about, and this idea of Tantra has pervaded the thinking of the world. Nowadays, professors and intellectuals write about Tantra as if it were a system of abstract philosophy, difficult to comprehend, impossible to grasp. No woman has written on the subject, yet Tantra is essentially of the Woman—the wife, the mother, the consort, the Divine Female, the Virgin, the Śakti, the Life-force, the Divine Energy.

Tantra is not for monks, celibates, renunciates or those who have given up the world. Tantra was originally the Way of the householder, for men and women in relationships, those who cannot renounce the world, who have husbands and wives, boyfriends and girlfriends, lovers and mistresses, jobs and responsibilities in the community. This is how it was for thousands of years before religion took over the Science of Tantra. Tantra is the Science of Life. It is the Science of relationship, of relatedness, of Love. Tantra does not deny life. The monks, the nuns, the renunciates, all deny life.

I say to you that Tantra is for the Living, for those striving to know themselves in the midst of life. Tantra is for those who are engaged in the processes of life, even the process of having babies and raising children. For in truth, Love flourishes in all circumstances of life. This is what the monks did not understand, nor could they understand it, because they did not relate to anyone.

The Spirit of Zen 751
Monks and Disciples 991
Is Renunciation Necessary? 1119
Three Schools of Spirituality 1121
The Virgin and the Mother 144
Śakti: the One Energy 150

The Feminine Suppressed

Humanity is still suffering from a tremendous guilt-complex

The Western religions, which declared the Woman to be evil, to be the temptress, the seducer, and sex to be unclean, impure and against God, have done great harm to human beings in the Western World. Christianity, with its twisted and unnatural view of sex and of the Woman for nearly two thousand years, has done incalculable damage to human consciousness and has brought immeasurable suffering to countless millions of people down through the centuries. Humanity is still suffering from a tremendous guilt-complex which has permeated art, literature, the legal system, religion, and every strata of society. This guilt-complex is now inborn into the species.

These unnatural views of women and of sex were foisted upon Humanity by celibate monks, such as Saint Paul and Saint Augustine, who were terrified of women and of the Divine Feminine, the great Mother Force, the Holy Spirit. In their mental error they declared the *church* to be the Mother, thus dethroning the Holy Spirit—the real Love-Force of the Universe—and substituting an all-male human organization. For two thousand years the church has been the bastion of male chauvinism, completely excluding the true Female, and women, from their rightful place.

According to Christianity, Judaism and Islam, God is always He, never She. God is always Father, King, Ruler, Lord, Son or Chief. And the church, the mosque, the synagogue, is always male-run, male-dominated, male-oriented, worshipping a male God. This male tradition has its roots in the Old Testament and has been carried over to the present day by Christianity and Islam.

The Breath of the Divine Mother 142
The Mother of the World 147
Female Buddhas 1110
The True Feminine 1516
The Masculine God 649
The Masculinization of Children 478

The Work of the Devil?

In ancient Israel, people who misbehaved sexually were stoned to death (as in the New Testament story of Jesus and the woman who committed adultery). In some Muslim countries, even today, sex outside of church-state approved criteria carries the death penalty. In Christianity, illicit sex was a mortal sin, punishable with eternal hellfire. In places where fundamentalist views predominate, sex is still a work of the Devil, punishable by hellfire and damnation.

What is 'the Devil'? 684

The Way of Love

Tantra is essentially a Path of Love, or maybe *the* Path of Love. Tantra is the Love of God manifesting through a human being. God, the Eternal, the Everlasting, the Transcendent, is approached through Its Beingness as a Creation, as a Creature, as a Humanity. Humanity, the Creation, is recognized as an Incarnation of God, the Essential Reality.

The wounds we suffer through human love can be healed only by Divine Love

Love is a many-splendoured thing: the Love of the mother for her child, the father for his son; the Love between brother and sister; friendship, companionship, charity. But Love has other dimensions as well, such as the Love between Man and Woman—Man being the Incarnation of the Divine Male, and Woman of the Divine Female.

The Play between the Divine Male and the Divine Female brings the Creation about. God's Nature is Love. The nature of Love is Creativity. The nature of Creativity is the bringing forth of things in Blissful Union. To discover true Creativity is the purpose of Tantra. To feel the creative urge *in* you is Tantra.

Tantra is the Way of Love. All art, science, music, literature and creativity should be an expression of this Love, but human beings have not understood this Energy and have turned it to destructive ends. Thus, Love is not free from pain. When you love, the seed of pain is already there. But when you love as God Loves, pain will disappear.

The wounds we suffer through human love can be healed only by Divine Love. Divine Love is Tantra at its highest. Divine Love is the Fullness of the Light, the Brightness of Reality, the essential form of all things. Our human love is but a faint reflection of the Divine Love. When we glimpse Divine Love, that is Tantra.

To Reach Unqualified Existence

In truth, human beings are gods who take incarnation into human bodies. The goal of Tantra is to reach Unqualified Existence, what you might call Love, Truth, God, Reality, Nirvāṇa or Bliss. This Unqualified Existence is SAT, CIT, ĀNANDA (Being, Consciousness and Bliss). It is the bright Light above and beyond all Lights. This is the Original Creative Impulse, the Original Field Of Love. This is the Generative Source, the Creative Energy from which the whole Universe springs.

The Experience of the Heart 1280

The Law of Polarity 164
The Divine Bipolarity 471
Śiva-Śakti 1521
The Creative Soul 1692
The Perennial Source of Love 438

The Energies of Sex and Love

People keep talking about "love" but they have no idea what it is. They confuse it with the physical sexual force or Prāṇic energy. This is a terribly bad habit which confuses the ignorant.

Physical magnetism (sexual attraction) is a force-field between two etheric bodies; it depends upon PRĀṆA, the Life-force from the Sun. The energy of Prāṇa, manifesting as sexual attraction, is focused in the sex organs. The sexual force is a mutual attraction, the force of union on the three planes of human evolution (the Physical, Astral and Mental Planes), and is the work of the Lunar and Solar Angels.

Love transcends personal barriers and interests

The Heart Love is the inherent force of the Buddhic Plane, the first plane above the Three Worlds. It is the *Christ-Force*. The Energy of Love is a quality of the Spiritual Soul in Man—the BUDDHI, the "Christ in you, your hope of Glory"—and is focused in the Heart Centre. Love streams forth from Buddhi via the astral body and manifests itself as Wisdom and Compassion.

Sexual attraction is *personal*, while Love *transcends* personal barriers and interests. Countless evils and sorrows of Mankind are the direct result of not comprehending this difference between these two types of force: sex and Love. Both are sacred, both are creative, and both fulfil, in different ways, the Divine Plan.

Kuṇḍalinī-Fohat 148
Kuṇḍalinī and Alchemy 153
The Universal Christ 440
Heart Union and Sexual Union 1140

Sexuality and the Life-Force

Why are men and women attracted to bodies, when essentially Man is Spirit? Because bodies, forms, constructs of matter, veil the Life-force. People are attracted not to the body, but to the Life within it. Without the Life within the body, there could be no attraction to it. Nobody is attracted to a cold corpse from which the Life-force has gone.

Sexual attraction is your Life-force seeking to meet the Life-force in your beloved. Sex is of the total body; it has to do with health. Health and sexuality are synonymous: only a healthy body is sexy, only a healthy body is attractive. This attractiveness is essentially the Life-force within the atoms of the body.

Health and Fire 50

PRĀṆA

Sanskrit: The Life-force. The same as the Chinese CHI (KHI). The Life-force is either positive or negative (male or female) in its operation.

Dimensions of the Cosmic Fire 137
The Life-Force 589

The Many Hues of Love

Never forget the many hues of Love. Love is not just a simple thing. Basically, Love is *attraction*. There is sexual love, there is Heart Love and there is a caring Love. When you care for someone, that is another turn on the spiral of Love.

Then there is a Love which is Consciousness itself. That Love is not "being in love". That Love is the *state* of Love, the *condition* of Love. That Love does not depend upon external things or relationships with another. That Love is the fundamental nature of things. It is a condition, a state, an abiding, like a flower perfuming the air all around. Does the flower need to have a relationship to perfume the air? That Love is like the flower. It is unconditioned.

There is a Love which is Consciousness itself

Sexual Love

Sexual love is what the millions of people in the world understand by "love". Sexual love is an electro-magnetic phenomenon: the human aura throws off electricity and has magnetic energies or fields around it and people are attracted to each other's electricity and magnetism. The various body parts also are electric and magnetic, with men and women complementing one another. The strongest attraction is at the level of the sexual organs because, by Nature, they carry the strongest electric impulse (in the male) and magnetic field (in the female). So when people sing "I love you," they really are singing "I want to have sex with you." This is natural.

Sexual love is Nature's love. It is the attraction of opposite polarities primarily for the propagation of the species and the continuation of the race. Through sex, many tensions are released. Due to wrong religious views on the subject, however, many tensions are also created. Society made rules, on religious-moral grounds, which are unnatural. Nature is natural; it is society which is unnatural. This has created incredible suffering and frustration for everybody.

The Human Aura 42
What is Consciousness? 1368
The Svādhiṣṭhāna Cakra 46
The Ascent of Kuṇḍalinī 152
Śauca: Purity 570

Emotional Love

The next level of Love is centred in the Solar Plexus Centre. This is the *feeling* love, the emotional or romantic love. This attraction on the solar plexus level has produced many great works of art, literature, poetry and music. This is all feeling, emotion and attachment. This is truly love and hate, happiness and tension. This is what you see constantly on television, in movies and in books. This is the melodrama of life.

Sexual attraction and solar plexus attachment constitute the ordinary human experience of Love

These two types of Love—sexual attraction and solar plexus attachment—constitute the ordinary human experience of Love, what the millions of human beings experience every day. It is a carnival, a merry-go-round of pleasure, hate, feeling, violence, temporary happiness, elation, insanity, and so on. Attraction at the solar plexus level can quickly turn into hate, for hate is just emotional love which thinks it has been hurt. On the solar plexus level of Love, the root of all suffering is *attachment.* This is the cause of all emotional fury and irrational actions.

Terms of Love

The more intelligent civilizations understood the difference between sex and Love. In Sanskrit there are several words for Love, such as:

Kāma: Desire, attraction, sex.

Bhāva: The feeling for finer things; the Love of the Good, the Beautiful and the True.

Prema: Divine Love, the Love of God.

The pre-Christian Greeks had five words for Love:

Eros: Sexual love, sexual attraction and desire. On a higher level, the Mystics understood Eros as spiritual-passionate Love, the intense desire, aspiration or longing for Union with God.

Philiā: The love between family members, brothers, sisters, children and close friends.

Philadelpheia: The love of one's particular group.

Sterge: The love of one's whole community or nation.

Agapē: The Love of God, Divine Love, Spiritual Love, Universal Love for all Mankind.

The Maṇipūra Cakra 47
Kill out Desire? 58
Passion and Dispassion 695
Reactive-Emotional Consciousness 1426

Heart Love

The next level of Love is in the Heart Cakra. This Love is truly human and also Divine. In the Love of the Heart there is a tremendous depth which is personal and at the same time impersonal. This is where God and Man meet.

The Love radiating from the Heart Cakra is not sexual attraction, nor is it an emotional affair. When you have Love in your Heart for a person, it transcends sexual attraction and all emotional upheavals. While the emotional love of the solar plexus is unsteady, moving back and forth between opposites, the Heart Love is a steady glow. The Heart Cakra is the Kingdom of God. When two people unite on the level of the Heart, they are truly "married". It is an extraordinarily powerful union, a bond that cannot be overcome by time, place or circumstance.

When two people unite on the level of the Heart, they are truly "married"

Notice that we speak here of *union,* not merely attraction. The Heart Love transcends all personal imperfections, and although it is a very deep union there is profound freedom in it. While the solar plexus love is emotional bondage, the Heart Love is Freedom.

Jesus was speaking of this Heart Love when He said:

> Greater Love than this has no man, that he sacrifices his life for his fellow man.
>
> *John 15:13*

The Heart Love is a Mystery, a Sacrament, a Sacrifice. It knows no boundaries, no limits.

Mental Love

There is also a mental "love" in the Ājñā Cakra, the Third-Eye Centre in the forehead. This is the seat of the mind, the thinking principle. In the ordinary human being, the "love" that manifests here is the altruistic principle, charity, good deeds. It is a mental decision, calm, considered. You decide you are going to help someone or work for some cause or ideal—religious, political, social or economic. You want to do some good, so you do it as a matter of principle. Emotions don't have to enter into it. It is neither sexual nor emotional, nor is it the Heart glow. You simply decide what is right and you do it. It is a mental love.

The Anāhata Cakra 47
Heart and Mind 429
What is the Heart? 435
The Heart and the Energy Centres 1332

Divine Love in the Head

The Third-Eye and the Thousand Petalled Lotus (the Crown Cakra at the top of the head) are also centres of Divine Love. When two people truly meet in the Third-Eye they dissolve into Light. They see each other as Light and know each other beyond personality. They know each other's true meaning, without thought, feeling or emotion. This is uniting in the Light. This is a Divine Love. When two lovers happen to raise themselves to the inner levels of the Ājñā Cakra, they reveal themselves as Beings of Light.

This Love is like an Ocean of Light

The Love that is experienced in the Crown Cakra is universal, cosmic, timeless, transcendent. It is impersonal, all-embracing, non-human. In this Love there is no relationship and no attachment. In a sense, it is "feelingless". In this state you do not "love" someone, nor do you seek to love; you just *are* Love. In this Love there is no lover and no beloved. There is only Love.

The Ājñā Cakra 49
The Sahasrāra Cakra 50
The Lover of God 853
The One and Only 839
The Sixth State 501

In the Heart the Mystic seeks to unite himself or herself with God, who is the Beloved. There is still subject and object; God is still "out there", an object one should unite with. When the Mystic has succeeded, however, he or she will find that God was never "out there", was never separate from himself or herself. The idea that God is separate from us is the most cruel and untruthful religious dogma.

In the Heart, God is known to be as One, while in the Crown Cakra there is neither God nor Man, neither lover nor beloved. There is only Love. This Love is like an Ocean of Light, a Supernatural Existence, a Sea of Being, a Self-Existent Radiance, a fullness of Glory, a great Face or Infinite Countenance, like a cosmic smile or laughter. Who can describe It?

It is the Chiliocosm, the truly Supernatural. It is the Infinite Radiance of the Self-Existent Light. It is a Love which defies all analysis, formulas or descriptions. It is the Ocean of Love that *was* before Time, that *is* throughout Eternity, that *will be* when all the worlds have gone and the Cosmos has resolved itself into atomic dust.

May you also come to know this Love.

This is the Goal of Tantra.

There is a Love that comes through the Third-Eye which is a truly Divine Love, beyond the personality. This is the revelation that a spiritual disciple receives from his or her Guru. When the disciple sees the Guru in the Third-Eye Centre, he or she will see the Radiance of the Guru, the Spiritual Glory of the Guru. This is a common experience: if you focus your attention in the Third-Eye and "love" your Guru there, he will reveal himself to you in all his splendour.

Meditation in the Third-Eye 1224

To Understand Sex

Humanity differs from the plants, animals, birds and fish—perhaps even from the angels—in that people seek *meaning* in their lives. Men and women seek to know, to understand, to comprehend experience. Humanity has invented all kinds of meanings and attributed all kinds of ideas and values to sexuality, some correct but most erroneous. Most people's understanding of sex is medieval, outdated and false, having nothing to do with the *fact* of it. This understanding is not based on Nature, but is guided by a false morality, invented by sick religious minds. Society has made this sick religious view of sex into *law*, which it desperately tries to uphold. But of course, most people fail to meet this false morality; hence confusion, guilt, fear and punishment arise. Humanity has become anti-natural, anti-Nature.

Sex can be understood only through Tantra

You cannot comprehend Tantra unless you have an open mind. Tantra is not a system of philosophy, religion or metaphysics. It is an *attitude of life.* For the Masters of Tantra there is only One Reality—call it God, Tao, Nirvāṇa, the Infinite Mind or Cosmic Consciousness. It is Transcendental Reality, the Truth. The basic purpose of every seeker after Truth is to find a means to realize *That.*

Sex can be understood only through Tantra, which is the total exploration of Love. Tantra resembles Zen, but goes further than Zen. In all orthodox religions—Christianity, Islam, Judaism, Hinduism, Jainism, the Sikh religion, Buddhism—sex is considered to be sinful, evil, unspiritual. Therefore, these religions promulgate chastity or celibacy as the only means to Salvation. Tantra, however, upholds the fact that the body is the Temple of God, and that every part of it is holy and sacred. The whole Universe is the Body of God, and all events in it are sacred. Therefore, sex also is sacred, holy, divine.

Tantra does not deny the sexual function; rather, it adapts it to the process of Enlightenment.

Tantra is the most perfect Way.

The modern man and woman has lost the spiritual significance of the sexual act because human beings deny the presence of the invisible worlds around them. Sex has very little to do with the sex organs. It has to do with the polarities throughout the microcosm, the human aura.

Nowadays, in the sex books of our "enlightened" world, there are intricate descriptions of the function of the sex organs but essentially nothing about the etheric, emotional, mental and spiritual dimensions of sex. And, if children are taught about sex at school, it is purely as a biological functioning. The mystical and spiritual dimensions are completely neglected. Consequently there is tremendous ignorance in the world about sex.

Natural Sexual Dynamism

For millions of years Humankind has engaged in sex from an early age without feelings of guilt. In most cultures (such as the Jewish, Arab and East Indian) marriages took place between partners as young as twelve or thirteen years, sometimes even younger. In those days you engaged in sex as soon as your *nature* was ready for it. It was not considered a sin, nor was it considered dirty or unnatural. This warped view of sex was spread around the world by the Christian missionaries who taught that nudity and sex were evil and of the devil, and that children were "innocent" (meaning non-sexual), and that they cannot and should not engage in the sinful practice of sex.

Sex is the most dynamic force in people's lives

The idea that children are non-sexual is wholly false. The natural sexual dynamism functions most powerfully during the ages of twelve to eighteen for a girl and about thirteen to twenty-one for a boy. That is why, all over the world—in India, China, Tibet, Africa and Asia—this was the ideal age for Tantra practice.

Children born innocent? 250

The entire teenage trauma and psychosis arises because the girl or boy is supposed to suppress the tremendous dynamic energy of sex. Most girls are interested in sex from twelve onwards, most boys from thirteen or fourteen, but are faced with fear, superstition, guilt, and the attitudes of parents, teachers and society. Parents and teachers try to suppress the sexuality of their children, when in fact it is wholly natural—of Nature. The community is so deeply brainwashed that parents have a breakdown if they discover that their child had a sexual experience!

Religion has taught people to feel shame and guilt and to repress Nature. Present society, the residue of religious oppression, now has a great conflict to deal with: Nature versus the dogmas of an unnatural religion. This cannot be ignored, because sex is the most dynamic force in people's lives.

To be able to practise Tantra one cannot have feelings of guilt about sex.

The sex act is holy. It is not against God. It is *of* God.

Natural Attraction

By Nature, the male is always attracted to the physical beauty of the female. The Feminine Consciousness always tries to be beautiful, even down to the physical bodily level, and the male is attracted to the beautiful form, face or eyes of the female. Both of these facts are natural. It is the "fatal attraction". It would eliminate much suffering from human relationships if the stuffy intellectuals who endlessly impose rules and "moral laws" on human behaviour would study Nature as it really is, with Understanding and Compassion.

The Healing Power of Touch

Everybody needs to touch and to be touched. Touching includes hugging, caressing, kissing, stroking, massaging, cuddling, holding hands or embracing someone. Hugging is a form of touch. True hugging is a spiritual experience where your Hearts can melt into Oneness. When you hug somebody, let go and merge into the Heart.

In the so-called "primitive" tribes all over the world, touching, hugging and sex were free, open and innocent. There were no guilt-trips about it. Babies begin with the sense of touch because touching is the first and most fundamental form of communication. This is gradually destroyed by society, especially in the English-speaking countries where touching, along with sex, is suppressed. Children are taught not to exhibit the most basic form of human communication, so that by the time they are teenagers touching makes them feel awkward and shy. To repress touching is to create frigidity in both men and women. Cut away Love, tenderness, touch and intimacy at any age and you have a sick society.

Cut away Love, tenderness, touch and intimacy and you have a sick society

Most English-speaking countries still suffer from this Victorian attitude about sex and touching. This subconscious guilt makes our highly technical society psychologically backward and unbalanced. It is modern psychology which will rise up against unnatural religion to recover the Truth, the Natural Religion, the Law of Nature which is the only Law of God. Science and psychology will replace religion because they are based not on man-made laws, but on the observation of Nature—God's Book.

Tantra is about *life* and *relationship*. It is not an escape from life; rather, it is the *understanding* of life. Touching, hugging and sex—and even more so, Tantra—are forms of communion and communication between two individuals who become One, between two separated selves who become united and at One with the One Life dwelling in all.

In Tantra we touch one another physically, psychically, emotionally, mentally and spiritually. All barriers are broken down.

Natural Law

The flower children of the sixties, whose slogan was "make love, not war", understood something of the nature of Humanity. If, from an early age, there is a natural flow of energy between men and women, and between boys and girls, if polarity is allowed to work, if Nature is not tampered with, then there will be few tensions in the world.

Nature has its own antidote for tension, anxiety, hatred and violence, and that medicine is Tantra. Go with Nature and you will live happily. Go against Her and you will suffer. The Law is simple, but Humanity makes all things complicated.

Psychology and the New Age Religion 1105

Polarities Male and Female

It is because men and women are different that the practice of Tantra is possible

It must be understood that there are basic differences between the inner constitutions of the human male and female. Since human beings are essentially fields of electro-magnetic energies, many polar opposites exist between men and women. Their energies complement one another, forming two halves of a circle. This has nothing to do with so-called education or conditioning; the differences are natural. There are definite bodily differences between men and women—physical, emotional, mental and causal.

Although your Soul is sexless (it is neither male nor female), you have incarnated in a series of bodies which are polarized differently in the male than in the female, or arranged along definite attracting or repelling lines. This polarization is to be found not only in the male and female physical bodies, but also in the etheric, astral, mental and causal bodies. For instance:

- There are differences between the male and female *etheric energy fields*—the male and female etheric bodies.
- There are differences between how a man or woman *feels* about things—the male and female astral bodies.
- There are differences between how a man or woman *thinks* about things—the male and female mental bodies.

These *differences* cause the attracting power we call "sex". The opposite polarities attract and complement one another, while like polarities repel. It is because men and women are *different* that the practice of Tantra is possible.

Jīva: the Human Soul 35
The Personality Complex 36
The Human Bipolarity 472

Hērmaphrōdītē
Greek: Both male and female. Hermes is the male prototype. Aphrodite is the female prototype. This is a mystery of ancient human evolution before the separation into male and female sexes took place.

Andro-Gynē
Greek: Male-female.

The Sexless Soul

Understand that You, as a Soul, are neither male nor female, and that every Soul on this planet has incarnated into male and female physical bodies countless times.

The first races of Humanity on this planet were sexless. Those of the second Root-Race were developing differentiation or duality. The third Root-Race was at first Hermaphrodite (each human being was bisexual) and then separated into the male and female sexes. All this took place over millions of years.

Human Evolutionary Epochs 176

As Nature intended it, a male is physically strong and dynamic, but emotionally weaker, more sensitive and vulnerable. He is mentally bright and outgoing, but spiritually sensitive and receptive. A female is the reverse: she is more sensitive and vulnerable physically, but strong, dynamic and outgoing on the emotional level. She is mentally more sensitive and soft, but again more strong and positive spiritually.

Nature has intended a perfect balance between men and women. Just as the stronger male physical body penetrates the female body, the stronger psychic-emotional energies of the female penetrate the astral body of the male. The dynamic masculine mind penetrates the female mental body, while the more dynamic spiritual nature of the female penetrates the male Soul.

Nature has intended a perfect balance between men and women

Thus you will see that women who try to be all masculine are out of harmony with Nature, as are males who try to be all feminine. It is a grave error to think that men and women are the same and that one can simply "prefer" non-heterosexual relationships, which will then be the "same" as heterosexual relationships. When you analyse the inner constitution of men and women, you will see that non-heterosexual relationships are not as Nature intended.

Mother and Father 475
Yin, Yang, Tao 476

\+ means *active, radiating, dynamic, electric, masculine*
— means *passive, receiving, sensitive, magnetic, feminine*

THE THREE WORLDS The Realm of Polarities	Plane	Body			Human Female	Human Male
	5 Mental Plane	Causal Body KĀRAṆA-MANAS	JĪVA: the Living Soul *Neither male nor female* △	Abstract Mind	+	—
		Mental Body RŪPA-MANAS	KĀMA-MANAS The Psychic Nature	Rational Mind	—	+
	6 Astral Plane	Astral Body KĀMA		Desires, Emotions Subconscious Mind	+	—
	7 Physical Plane	Etheric-Physical Body PRĀṆA		Life-force	—	+
		Gross Physical Body STHŪLA		Inert Matter		

Polarities within the Human Aura

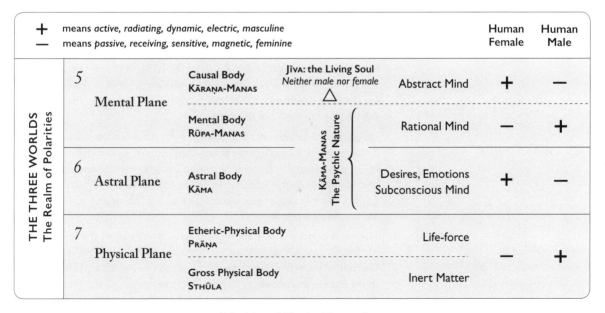

Falling in Love

When a natural woman meets a natural man—that is, as Nature intended—an electro-magnetic phenomenon takes place between them, a tremendous explosion of energies. This is called "falling in love". It is also called *attraction* or *bio-energy* or the *Life-force*. Tantra makes use of this electro-magnetic phenomenon.

The natural electro-magnetic phenomenon increases as the Heart is brought into play

The natural electro-magnetic phenomenon between men and women increases as the Heart is brought into play. If the Heart Cakras are functioning simultaneously with the natural electro-magnetic attraction, then you and your partner will experience an unearthly Love, a Love-Divine, like a brilliant Light, a sea of Love, a tide of Joy, or a sky of intense Lightness and Brightness. Your head will become an extremely clear space and you will feel as if you are swimming in space and time. For the time being, all problems will vanish for you and the world will appear to be a paradise. This natural electro-magnetic attraction between a man and a woman, coupled with the Heart Glow, constitutes the Circle of Love in your relationship.

People do not realize that "falling in love" is essentially the result of the *differences* between the sexes, not because of similarities. So the general pattern is that, after the initial shock of "falling in love", the male wants to change the female to be like him and the female wants to change him to be like her. Thus arise arguments, tensions and hatred—for the opposite of emotional love is hatred, and unfulfilled love quickly swings into the mood of destruction.

Practically all people have problems with male-female relationships. Because we lack insight, we cannot cope, so we go through the process of separation or divorce, or maybe become homosexual or lesbian because we think it is easier than having to deal with the opposite sex. For the same reason, some people give up sex altogether and become "renunciates"—monks or nuns.

The usual pattern is that the male does not understand the female and the female does not understand the male, so conflict arises between them. Our lack of understanding of the *differences* between male and female leads to frustration and endless problems. Tantra seeks to heal the rift between men and women by affirming that the differences are natural and good.

From Head to Heart 427
Cultivate the Fires of Love 928
The Heart (Hṛdayaṁ) 1282
Reactive-Emotional Consciousness 1426

The Circle of Love

Of the many opposite polarities between men and women, one of the most important is the opposite natures of the Heart Cakra and the Sex Cakra, which together form one of the energy poles in the human system. In the female, the Heart Cakra is positive, electric, vital, outgoing, dynamic, aggressive, while her Sex Cakra is negative, cool, receptive, feminine, submissive, magnetic. Her dynamism is in her Heart Cakra, in her breasts, in her chest, while her receptivity is in her Sex Centre. In the male, however, the Sex Centre is the positive pole, the electric energy, and his Heart Cakra is receptive, negative, magnetic. This is one example of how the human male and female are complementary to one another.

So long as this energy-circuit persists between them, that couple is invincible

If a man and a woman lie together with their Heart Cakras and Sex Centres in close contact (or the man might sit on a chair or on the floor, with the woman sitting on his thighs, facing him), then a curious thing will happen. Since men and women are of opposite polarities, an energy-circuit is established. The positive, Life-giving Heart energy of the female enters the receptive male Heart, and the positive, Life-giving energy of the male Sex Centre enters the receptive, magnetic female Sex Centre. The result is a mutual Glow, Satisfaction, Bliss, Completeness, Harmony, Transcendence. It is as if two powerful magnets have been brought together and are pulled irresistibly into each other's magnetic fields.

When the hot, positive, electric current of the male Sex Centre enters the female Sex Centre, she feels as if the Sun is moving inside her. Similarly, when the woman gives her Love to a man—her Heart radiance, which is her positive pole—then he feels on top of the world. He can conquer mountains, do the impossible.

True marriage, good sexual relationship and Tantra have much to do with this energy-circuit: the man gives his seminal vitality to the woman and she gives her Heart radiance in return. In such a way, both feel that life is rosy and they live on a pink cloud. They can do anything together, overcome the greatest obstacles. This is what romance is about, and the dreams of the "young and foolish". So long as this energy-circuit persists between them, that couple is invincible.

The circulation of energies between male and female is as real as the Sun and the Moon. It is the Way of Nature. Human beings are part of Nature, whether they admit it or not.

The Female Dominant

The way of normal sexual encounter is that the man takes the initiative. He leads the woman, he proposes, he takes her out, he chases her. He is aggressive and demanding, and in the sex act he is active, dynamic, on top of his partner, controlling the whole process, while the woman is being led, is passive, does nothing.

In Tantra the male has to relinquish control and the female has to lead

Many women are simply inactive during the sex act and wait for the male to do everything. They do not know how to arouse a man and may not think it is even necessary. This style of sex, which has been the pattern for the millions for countless generations, is quite unsatisfactory and today the feminists have rightly rebelled against it. In most cases the female finds little enjoyment in it. In this regard, however, both the male and the female have to be re-educated. The woman is just as guilty of ignorance as the man. Generations of wrong sexual habits have to be overcome by both sexes.

Tantra differs from the normal sexual attitudes. In Tantra the male has to relinquish control and the *female* has to lead. Strange as it may seem, in Tantra the female activates the male while the male remains passive and receptive. This may be difficult for both to accomplish. It is contrary to all sexual habits of society, where the male adopts the role of being strong, aggressive, macho, "in control", while the female appears to be weak, helpless, receptive, *subject* to the male. The normal sex act is male-dominated, while in Tantra it becomes female-dominated.

Before the arrival of Christianity, all over the world, young women from an early age were taught how to lead the male into ecstasy. This was known in India, China, Persia, among the Jews and Arabs, in the Far East, in Africa, and generally to all native tribal women. It was universal knowledge that sexual ecstasy was induced by the female. Nowadays, lesbians may stimulate each other to orgasms, but it is not the same as when a man is inside them, since lesbians are of the same sex, the same energies, the same polarity. To induce the bliss of Tantra you must commence with the merging of polar opposites, and then *transcendence* occurs.

This was less understood in pre-Christian Greece and Rome, where homosexuality was extensively practised, so much so that all boys from an early age were apprenticed into homosexuality. Yet, even there the courtesans knew the secret of true sexual bliss—of Tantra.

The Law of Polarity 164
The Human Bipolarity 472
Śiva-Śakti 1521

If the woman is allowed to dominate in such a way, her psychic penetration into the aura of the man will result in an internal combustion of energies, producing a Timeless Bliss.

Remember, in this regard, that just as a male might rape a woman physically, for countless generations women have been raping males on the astral and emotional levels, where the female power is strong and the male is weak and defenceless. Millions of men have been shattered and devastated by this "emotional rape" by women. Because this is subtle, however, or at least not easily seen, women have (apparently) evaded the law of punishment.

The woman enters into her true function as Master or Mistress of the sexual realm

Here there is no question of rape, only a role reversal. In Tantra the woman enters into her true function as Master or Mistress of the sexual realm and thereby helps both partners to attain the highest experience of Bliss and Joy. Most men find it difficult to let go and give themselves up to women, however, and most women find it difficult to take up the leadership role.

Beware! This is not an intellectual leadership we are talking about. We are talking about the woman's psychic energies.

The Feminine Heart

Since most books on Tantra have been written by male monks, we need to reflect more on the female Heart Cakra. The female Heart Cakra is different from the male Heart Cakra. When a woman is "in love" with a man she projects a tremendous Heart energy towards him (we are assuming that the woman's Heart Cakra is in working order). Then she begins to "mother" him. The true "wife" is really but a "mother" to her husband and there is nothing wrong with that. That is as Nature intended.

The wife/mother/lover nourishes the psychic being and psychic life of the man. She gives him creativity, inspires him with her positive Heart dynamism. She propels him to great heights of endeavour and achievement. While he has his woman's Heart with him, the man is invincible. Similarly, his physical-sexual energy gives her strength, endurance and perseverance through all obstacles in life.

In her Heart, a woman's dreams are fulfilled and her psychic visions come true. When she opens her Heart in Love, every woman is the Mother of the World.

The Virgin and the Mother 144
The Mother of the World 147
The Feminine Virtues 468

Sex Natural and Divine

My Kingdom is not of this world.
Jesus (John 18:36)

Unless you understand somewhat the constitution of the world around you, you will not understand the most profound mystery of sex, because it is infinitely more than what is understood in the world. Sex is an inter-relationship of parts to the Whole. Sex is the seeking of the Unity of the separated "selves". Sex is the inner drive to Union on all levels, from the tiniest world of the atom, through to Man (the microcosm), to the Solar System (the Macrocosm), the Galaxy and our group of galaxies (the Chiliocosm). The sexual force of the Sun is the attractive power which keeps the planets revolving around it. The sexual force of the Central Spiritual Sun keeps all the stars attracted around the Heart of our Galaxy. Sex is the Great Attractor, the Great Unifier.

One of the mysteries of the microcosm (yourself as a human system) is the miniature image of Divine Perfection that is situated in a space near the top of the right ventricle of the physical heart, but in *another dimension.* This image of the Spirit within you is *outside* the microcosmic system. It is the image of BRAHMAN (God) in you, as taught in the Upaniṣads of India. It is also the ray of the ĀTMAN (the Self) of the Brahmins, the custodians of the Vedic religion. It is the prototype of the Buddha within you, and of Śrī Kṛṣṇa.

In the West we call this Divine Atom the Christ-Atom, the Spirit-Atom, the Proto-Atom or the Nous-Atom. It is the *Rose on the Cross* of the Rosicrucians. It is the *Jewel in the Lotus* (of the Heart) of the Tibetan Buddhists (the ŌṀ MAṆI PADME HŪṀ). It is the Breath of Allāh. It is the Fire of the Holy Ghost. You must understand this Divine Mystery: this "Christ", "Buddha" or "Spirit-Atom" within you does not belong to this world. That is, it does not belong to your microcosm.

According to the Bible there is a perishable seed and there is an imperishable seed. That is, there is natural sex and there is a Divine Sex. A human being is born of the perishable seed—the union of the father's sperm and the mother's ovum. The sperm, the egg and the ovum are perishable, as is the grown physical body. The physical organism, so produced, belongs to this world and is subject to the endless process of death or "corruption".

BRAHMAN
Sanskrit: The Supreme Godhead, the Absolute, the final Reality, beyond name, form and qualities, beyond Time and Space, Infinite, Eternal, All-Pervading, Universal Radiance, Inconceivable Glory, Immeasurable Consciousness.

ĀTMAN
Sanskrit: The Face of the Logos within your Heart Centre. The Self-Luminous Being.
Ātman, Ātmā 34

ŌṀ MAṆI PADME HŪṀ
Sanskrit: The Jewel in the Lotus. From MAṆI, "jewel", and PADME, "lotus" (the Heart Centre).
The Esoteric Mantram 551
Meditations in the Heart Centre 1298

But the imperishable seed—the Spirit-Atom, in the secret place in the inner dimensions of the Heart—is not of this perishable world. It does not perish. This is the ultimate mystery of Sex.

There is a Seed within you, a Spirit-Spark-Atom, that is indestructible and eternal. Being born through it, you will likewise become immortal.

This imperishable seed (the Spirit-Spark-Atom) has to be *connected* to the Heart, for it belongs to the Kingdom of the Light, the Original Kingdom, the imperishable Kingdom of God. This Spirit-Spark-Atom, the Secret of the Heart, is a seed from the imperishable Kingdom of the Light, Nirvāṇa, implanted in the Heart of the microcosm in the perishable world. It is a seed or potential of our rebirth into Nirvāṇa. It is through this imperishable seed in the Heart Cakra that you can be reborn into Eternal Life. This is the Divine-Sex-Seed which must be fused into the Mother-Light in order to lift ourselves from the microcosm into the Macrocosm and gain Conscious Immortality.

The Universal Christ 440
The Lotus of the Heart 446
The Coming of Christ in the Heart 727
The Mystery within the Heart 1315
Incarnations of the Sun 1593
The Path to Immortality 430

This is why I do not emphasize physical sex, nor the transmuting, purifying and conquering of the physical or etheric sexual functions, as do all the Esoteric Schools and many Yogic Schools, and the outer religious teachings in general. This is why I do not emphasize celibacy, or becoming a monk or a nun, or renouncing the world. For the sexual seed in the microcosm is perishable and all its workings are perishable. Even if you were to succeed in renouncing the world and sex and become celibate, you have managed to control only the perishable and are nowhere near the Imperishable. So we do not emphasize controlling sex or fighting with it, as do the orthodox religions. But we do seek to enter the Cave of the Heart so that we may find the Jewel in the Lotus, the Christos, the Christ-Self in the secret place in the Heart Cakra.

There is a natural sex-magic and there is a Divine Sex-Magic. The natural sex-magic involves the attractive forces of polarity between the male and female physical, etheric, astral and mental bodies. The Divine Sex-Magic is the attraction of the Imperishable Seed in the Heart Cakra to the womb of the Great Mother, the Mother-Light of Nirvāṇa. This birth takes place *inside* you, inside the Heart. You cannot see it outwardly, but you can experience it inwardly.

That the Seed of Christ may be born in you is my prayer for you.

It is through the awakened Heart Cakra that one is reborn into Eternal Life. This fact is behind the much misunderstood drive of the Christian fundamentalists to be "reborn" or "born again", though they do not know what it means.

Being born again, not of corruptible seed, but of incorruptible, by the word of God, which liveth and abideth forever.

I Peter 1:23

This Seed is the Secret, SVD (Sod), of the ancient Jewish Kabbalist Initiates, the Secret of the Heart.

Baptism and Rebirth 722

Cultivate the Fires of Love

It is said that there is a great peace and silence at the centre of a cyclone. Nature is tearing everything apart in its rage, yet at the heart of the storm there is stillness. I have never been at the centre of a cyclone, but if this is true it is a good analogy for the Human Heart.

You can commune silently with your partner through the Heart Cakra

The Human Heart has many functions, for the Heart Cakra exists in several dimensions. There is the physical heart; then there is the psychic Heart wherein you perceive dreams and mystical visions and prophesies and the knowledge of past and future; then there is the Spiritual Heart deep inside you, the Ground or Root of your Being. The Spiritual Heart is like a void, an abyss, an emptiness or a space. It is like a great Darkness or a great Light. It is a field of Transcendental Consciousness. It is the Peace that passes all understanding.

The river of the mind flows violently, restless with the myriads of thoughts that swim within it. Your body is ceaselessly engaged in struggle, in the fight for survival in this world. Your body, mind and emotions together beat against the rocks of life—the obstacles, the oppositions, the anxieties, the anguish. The lake of your existence is turbulent, turbid, disturbed. But strangely enough, like the eye of the cyclone, your innermost Core at the centre of the Heart remains very still, quiet, silent. There is no struggle, no fighting, no distress, no pain, and nothing is disturbed. There is only peace. To discover that peace is Tantra.

The Heart is a great Mystery. You can commune silently with your partner through the Heart Cakra. In this silent communion comes a unique form of Bliss and Ecstasy, and an indissoluble bond is established between you. When two Hearts truly meet, they melt into one another, producing a link that is deep, profound, unbreakable.

Cultivate awareness without thought in the Heart. The Heart-awareness is more like a *feeling* than a thought, though not as dramatic or violent a feeling as is to be found in the Solar Plexus Centre. Rather, it is like a glowing or a radiance.

You *think* in the head. You have *emotions* in your solar plexus. In your Heart Cakra you *glow.*

This glow can become a great heat, or a great Fire and Conflagration. It can consume you. It can burn you and your partner and anyone near you.

The Three Regions of the Heart 463
The Burning Heart 631
The Fire of Love 1255
The Fire in the Heart 1287
Peace of Heart 1595

When this happens, you will know the meaning of the scriptures:

> For our God is a consuming Fire.
>
> *Hebrews 12:29*

The Original State of Being for Humanity is in the Heart

When you live in the Heart rather than in your head, then your life will take on a different dimension. It will become more rich and full, more pleasurable but also more painful. When two heads meet they are inclined to argue, to discuss, to theorize and to remain separate. A man and a woman who meet only in the head remain forever separate. Tantra is not possible for them. When two people meet in the Heart Centre, then there is Unity, there is Love, there is compassion, understanding and sympathy. Thinking creates a distance between you and what you think about, while the Heart feeling at once produces Unity, Closeness, Oneness.

The Original State of Being for Humanity is in the Heart. When your Consciousness sinks back into the Heart Cakra, you rediscover the lost Kingdom of God. If a man and a woman can move simultaneously into the Heart Cakra, they will experience Divine Love and Ecstasy. They will know what Tantra is.

Through Sex which is Love

It is written in the scriptures that *God is Love.* But of course, this Love is understood to be some kind of Cosmic Love—abstract, ideal, but certainly not sexual. This is a theological error, because God's Love is all-inclusive, as is God's Bliss. God's Love manifests also in the Love between creatures. It manifests even more so between men and women because of the greater *dynamism* of Love between the sexes.

When sex is an expression of Love, it is then the Way to the great Bliss of self-transcendence. In self-forgetfulness the true Selfhood is known. Through sex which is Love we attain to Bliss Divine, but through sex which is empty of Love we descend into the deepest hell and despair.

Sex as it is practised today by the millions, devoid of Love, is a degenerated practice and is destructive and harmful in effect. Sex without Love, as portrayed in pornographic movies and practised by many ignorant men and women today, is Soul-destructive. When taken outside of Love, sex is self-destructive and causes untold human misery.

The Cosmic Fire 130
Heart and Mind 429
The Experience of the Heart 1280
Qualities of the Spiritual Heart 1329

When Sex is Love

If you would take someone as your Tantra partner, first discover your Heart and move into your Heart. Many people in the world engage in sexual activity without the Heart Centre being involved. They think they are loving, but they do not know, nor can they know, what Love is about.

In true Tantra, all sexual activity is done in adoration, reverence, awe

Even ordinary sex can become heavenly when done with the Heart feeling. When you have deep Love and Compassion for your partner—which comes from the Heart—then sex is Love. When two people engage in sex with Heart-feeling, then even ordinary sex becomes a benediction, a great blessing. For in the Love of the Heart all things are sanctified.

In true Tantra, all sexual activity is done in adoration, reverence, awe. Your partner becomes for you God-Incarnate, the god or goddess, physically present for you. Therefore you want to worship your beloved and melt your Heart in this worship. If you embrace your beloved in deep adoration, you will experience God.

To worship a human being in such a way is truly to worship God, because "Man was made in the image and likeness of God." Actually, Man *is* God, but does not know it. If we all knew our Divinity—that is, if we knew it from the Heart—then human civilization on Earth would truly be an Incarnation of the Kingdom of God.

We can project the Kingdom of God into this world only if we can truly Love, and we cannot Love if we live in the head. The head separates all religions, all castes, all creeds, all colours, all nationalities. So while we live in the head there will be endless wars, arguments, discussions and divisions. Thoughts create divisions and disunities, while the silent Glow from the Heart is healing, uniting, equalizing.

The Temple of God 639
Peace on Earth 1304
The Supreme Act of Karma 264
To Manifest the Kingdom of God 1716

The Meaning of Love...

While we identify with life in this world, we identify with struggle, anguish and disturbance. But when we identify with the core of the Heart, we identify with a soundless Silence, which is an undisturbed Peace. This is why Lao Tzu said:

> I have watched all things revolving and going back to their Source, and returning to the Root.

When we identify with the core of the Heart, we identify with a soundless Silence

From this innermost centre of the Heart you can watch all things and all events—your whole life, your many lives, the whole Universe. You can watch as if from a distance, like from the eye of a hurricane. You can watch all things revolving, coming and going, and finally returning to their Root, the Source of Being, Tao, Nirvāṇa, the Kingdom of God.

Everything glides into the past, moment by moment, both joy and pain. Whatever we cling to, agony or ecstasy, all falls apart.

Life is like a flag fluttering in the wind. As the wind blows, the flag moves, but the flag has no control over its movements. Neither does the wind move the flag wilfully. The wind is there, the flag is there, and in this coincidence the flag flutters.

Love is not willed. It is not decided. It is the coincidence of two forces that sometimes attract one another, sometimes repel. But what design is there in Love? Is there a meaning? Is there a meaning in the air that moves the flag? No, there is no meaning. Love just is.

The Meaning of Life

There is meaning to human existence, but it cannot be known by the ordinary mind. The ordinary mind identifies with the body and the objects of the world. To seek the Real, you must go beyond the body, beyond the mind, beyond all objects and all events.

You can begin the Great Search by asking yourself "Who am I?" or "What am I?" To discover the Mystery of Existence, you must dig deeply into yourself, in silence, in a wordless mind. This is Tantra.

Touch Ultimate Emptiness 96
The Meaning of Life is Love 633
On Love and Meditation 1140
Three Meditations in the Heart 1292

Freedom is Boundless Love

True freedom is in the Boundless Love of the Original Sky of our Consciousness

Remember that the Sun is always shining, no matter how cloudy the day. On the ground the clouds may block the Sun and the rain may pelt down hard, but if you fly above the clouds, the sky is full of bright sunshine.

So it is with human life. In the body and mind there may be many stresses, storms, tensions, upheavals. Even if your life is a neurotic mess, remember that, deep inside you, you are always above the storms of life. Deep inside, you are always in the Eternal Sunshine. Deep inside, you are always bright and clear. Your Soul and the Great Spiritual Sun are always in the Light. Your Soul is always bathed in the Sun's Light, and the two are always One.

Can you rise above the earthly limitations of your body and mind? If you can, you will see the Great Sun eternally shining on the Limitless Horizon. At such moments, the Earth may seem like a far-off marketplace. You will wonder why people live such noisy lives. The Sea of Light is all around.

To be *free* is to be free of both joy and pain. Freedom is Boundless Love. It cannot be measured by time and circumstances. Boundless Love is like space and the cloud in the sky; the cloud moves on or evaporates, but the sky remains.

Limited love is the experience of joy and pain. Boundless Love is the experience of tranquillity upon the Sky of our Consciousness. Limited love is what we fear—the separation, the rejection—but Boundless Love knows no rejection, no separation, no coming and no departing. This Love fills the Sky of our Consciousness with perfect Sunshine all the time. Beneath the clouds the world appears to be dark and heavy, but above the clouds the Sun is always shining brightly.

Human love is a cloud formation. Divine Love is the sky itself. True freedom is not in human love, but in the Boundless Love of the Original Sky of our Consciousness.

Sometimes, when two lovers meet, they merge into this field of Divine Love which is filled with Light and Bliss. This is Tantra.

Cidākāśa
Citta-Ākāśa
Cidghana
Sanskrit: The Sky of Consciousness. The Infinite Space of Universal Consciousness. The Self-Luminous Sky of Consciousness. The Wisdom Mind which sees all things from Above, from the point of view of the Transcendental Reality.
Śrī Jagadambā: the Mother of the World 1498

Tantra Mind

Human beings are prisoners of their own minds. This is a great mystery. You are a prisoner of your own thoughts.

The word TANTRA means to "transcend limitations", to "transcend the mind". Tantra is to be free from the limitations of your mind, free from your thoughts, ideas and opinions. The mind is the ego. The ego is the cause of your bondage. If you transcend your mind, you will transcend your ego, and with it, all misery.

Tantra is to be free from the limitations of your mind

You are a prisoner of society. You are a prisoner of your own mind-constructs. You are full of pain, sorrow, anger, frustration, bitterness, envy, and all of this is but mind-constructs. This is how things are in this world.

Tantra is the Joy of the Infinite. For beyond this world is a subtle realm, and beyond that is the Eternal, the Divine Presence. This Divine Reality is not a body, nor a mind. It has no limits, no foundations, no shape or size. It cannot be comprehended by thinking about It. It is the Way, the Truth and the Life. It is sometimes known as the Void or the Emptiness. In truth, it is the PLERŌMA or utter Fullness of Existence.

It is difficult to reach the Eternal because it is difficult to give up the ego. Watch a bird flying through the air, it does not have an ego. The bird is not aware that it is a bird, that it is a sea gull, that it has its nest on a particular spot. It is all unconscious, not ego-inspired, and therefore the bird is "free". On the contrary, a human being is conscious that he or she is human, conscious that he or she is male or female, conscious of being a father, a mother, a typist, an executive, a millionaire or unemployed. The human being is conscious of ego.

In Bondage to the Mind 238
Obstacles to Higher Consciousness 1424
Return to Primeval Happiness 1179
Liberation from Worldly Consciousness 1233

Ego means identity—identifying yourself with things. You will discover that if you stop identifying yourself with things you will diminish your ego, and if you cease to identify yourself with anything, your ego will disappear. Then you will be free. Freedom is Tantra.

PLERŌMA
Greek: That which contains the All. The Cosmic Fullness in which the myriads of galaxies and star systems and planets move and function. Total Space as the Living Body of the Absolute Reality. The All-Pervading Spiritual Existence.
The Divine Milieu 12

Stand in your own Centre

We start off in life totally self-centred. Babies are total egotists; they need complete attention from those around them, and with some people this attitude never changes. It is surprising how many adults are still "babies"—they have not grown up emotionally at all! Some remain totally dependent on others, while some are semi-dependent. But the more mature Souls gradually learn to forget themselves, and the most mature Souls *dedicate* themselves to others. Thus the circle is completed: from the total selfishness and self-centredness of babyhood to the total giving of ourselves to others. Thus are we freed from our egos, our little selves.

Independence means standing strong in your own Centre

Independence is true freedom, but independence is not isolation or callousness, not neglecting communication with others. Simply, independence means standing strong in your own Centre, in your own Beingness, in touch with the Master within. This also is Tantra.

Develop a Bird's Eye View

We must develop a bird's eye view of life rather than a worm's eye view. The worm sees and knows little; it digs blindly in the ground, scarcely aware of where it is going. What a different view the bird has of things, flying high in the sky!

The average man or woman lives his or her life like a worm, aware of very little. You are confined to the categories of your mind and the crushing walls of your environment, which are created by your own body-mind-personality, and you look at the world with the eye of a worm and think that you know, that you are smart. Really!

To attain a bird's eye view we must be able to stand back, above ourselves and our circumstances. We must break out of our limitations. We must get far away from ourselves, from our environment, from our associations, from our relationships, from our everyday doings. We must fly above the clouds of our own creations. In the blue sky there is knowledge, there is freedom, there is confidence, there is strength. Then a new person is born. Then the same things are never the same again.

You must go through this experience. It is like a new Freedom inside you. This new Freedom is Tantra.

What is True Service? 1714
The Law of your Being 976
The State of Innocence 1306
You Are the World 1390

Return to your Root

Every now and then, simply let go of all things. Forget your cares, worries and troubles, forget the storms of life. Just sit down in a quiet spot, in any posture you find comfortable, and return to your Root, your Source, your Heart, the Ground of your Being. Simply relax, focus your attention in the heart area inside your chest and surrender yourself to the Spiritual Heart. Don't think of anything, just sit in silence, doing nothing. Try to be calm, disinterested in life about you, unmoved by your feelings and emotions. Don't reflect on events, just empty yourself. Imagine yourself to be like a cup and your Heart an open vessel. Soon you will enter the Spiritual Heart and find the Peace that passes all understanding. This is release and Freedom. This is Tantra.

Imagine yourself to be like a cup and your Heart an open vessel

Surrender to the Limitless

The more you are in the crowd, the more crowded your mind becomes. People and thoughts are synonymous: the more people in your life, the more thoughts in your mind. With people come diverse influences on your mind—pressures, tensions, divisions, arguments—until your mind screams for peace and release.

At such times, spend some time alone with the stars. Find a quiet spot where you can be alone, silent, undisturbed, and gaze into the Infinitude of Space. Soon you will realize how trivial all human life is, and how silly all our neuroses. What is human neurosis to the Great One? What do the stars teach you about Eternity and Infinity? What does Limitless Space tell you about the Great Mother? For God is a Great Mother and Her children are the stars.

It is important at such times that your mind is silent, empty of thoughts, and that you gaze into Infinitude with awe and wonder. If you surrender properly, the Great Limitless might show its Face to you. For the twinkling stars and the vast empty Space are but a veil thrown over the Limitless, the One Of Whom Nought Can Be Said, but Who can be intuited in moments of Ecstasy.

∞

Alone with God 700
Silence, Solitude, Peace 1386
The Silence of the Deep 1355
The Law of Mystic Experience 508

Love Lost

How can one be "in love" with someone who does not reciprocate?

It is difficult to give up that which we love. Pain is to be separated from our Love. Pain is not to have Love. The worst pain in life is when you love somebody and that Love is not returned. Love given but unreturned produces feelings of pain and anguish. How is this possible? How can one be "in love" with someone who does not reciprocate? Yet it often happens that one loves someone long after separation. It is a fact of life, a painful fact. This is the subject of art, poetry, music, literature and psychology. What do we love in a person when that Love is not returned? And if we are "in love" with someone, how can separations occur? What is Love?

To love someone and not to experience the same from that person is pain. But to love nobody at all in life is a vast emptiness, a black hole, a dreaded loneliness, a desert, a grave. One cannot live without Love, because Love is the driving-force of Life. Love is ecstasy, joy, completeness. It is the Primary Condition, the First State. Love is the water that nourishes the plant of Life. Without Love we are outcasts in Life. Without Love, human existence is meaningless. It is an empty desert, a dead end. If we can abide in the purest Ray of Love, even for a moment, our lives have not been wasted.

The Tragedy of Human Relationships

There is a need to look carefully at all aspects of human relationship. Marriages and unions break up because of a lack of understanding and an inability to accommodate the changes brought about by the process of life itself. So arise the syndromes of "my wife does not understand me", "my husband does not know me", and so on.

Thus, men and women tend to gravitate away from each other into different groups. Women's groups are formed and men's groups are formed (the pub). In the extreme we have the feminist groups and the lesbian groups and, on the other hand, the gay male groups and the macho-type groups. So, what in the beginning starts off as naturally complementary becomes antagonistic opposition and mutual exclusiveness. This is a human tragedy of vast proportions.

The Breakdown of Family 473
Primary Relationship 479

The differences between men and women are not due to conditioning or education. The differences are purely natural, that is, *according to Nature.* The consciousness of men and women is complementary and this creates a divide. Men and women do not know that being complementary is not the same as being in opposition, so they fight continually.

The conflict between men and women is similar to the conflict between the rain and a thunderstorm. Like the conflict between men and women, a storm or hurricane is caused by a conflict of opposites, and together they release a tremendous discharge of vital power. While the conflict lasts it appears to be very painful, but afterwards comes peace. To understand this conflict is Tantra.

The wounds of Love can be healed only by Love

The greater the tension, the greater the conflict; the greater the amount of electricity released, the greater the vitality. Is it possible for such polar opposites as men and women to live together, side by side, without conflict? Peace may come after a thunderstorm, and there may be an uneasy peace before the storm, but during the storm all bound-up forces are unleashed, released, and the atmosphere is cleared. Even a storm is a form of creativity.

When you are heart-broken because of a lost Love, only Love will repair the damage. Forget the mistakes of the past and concentrate on making the Living Moment a success, for the wounds of Love can be healed only by Love. I say that only Love can heal Love. When someone truly loves you, your life begins anew.

When a man and a woman are in love, they form a third being which is neither male nor female, but both. They radiate streams of Light and Energy towards each other in an electro-magnetic circuit, a magnetic-electric field of Energy. There are many reasons why this energy-circuit between men and women may be broken. A common situation is that the man or woman "falls in love" with another person. If the man gives his sexual radiance to another woman, the wife or lover feels betrayed. Things are not the same; he does not give her the same sunshine as before. Similarly, if the woman falls in love with another man, she "gives her heart away" and the original husband or lover feels that he has "lost" her.

The Law of Polarity 164
The Human Bipolarity 472
Polarities Male and Female 920

Mother, Father and Baby

When a woman has a baby she transfers her mothering instinct to the baby

Another situation is very natural: when a woman has a baby she transfers her mothering instinct to the baby and her Heart energy goes out to the child. This increases with each successive child; the mother's psychic energy and Love-stream tend to flow automatically to the new baby, who becomes the new meaning for her existence. Consequently, the father feels left out. This is a common complaint of new fathers: "My wife is no longer interested in me, she expends all her energy on the baby." This is so. While previously the two lovers had sent all their Love energy towards each other, very often the new mother switches off from her husband and devotes all her time and energy to her baby. This alters the flow of polarity. Psychically she is now attuned to the child and her Heart energy goes to the child. The man notices this switch of the woman's Heart energy and feels that something is "missing" from the relationship.

Further, the mother's consciousness becomes less complex as a result of her continuous attention to the children. This further alienates her from her man and in some cases the new father becomes superfluous, except perhaps as a source of income or security. Very often her sexual energy transfers itself into the Heart and she does not want sex. With each child this transference deepens until the man and woman no longer engage in sexual communion, the Heart Love stops and they begin to live like brothers and sisters or in some sort of business arrangement. The previous Love relationship, on the Heart and sex centre levels, is gone.

This frustrates the new father for two reasons:

- The sexual communion is denied him.
- The Heart Love is also denied him.

As his frustration grows, it turns into anger, then resentment, then hatred. All of this has to be understood. The young father needs to be more tolerant and understanding towards his partner. She was the Goddess, the Virgin; now she is the Mother. But also, the young mother must realize how the man is feeling. Being cut off from both sexual communion and Heart Love can bring on psychosis within him and he may begin to look for other women in his life.

The Gift of Parenthood 474
The Virgin and the Mother 144

This can be a difficult period, but not insoluble if both partners accommodate each other a little. The problem is that people do not adjust easily to new situations. The best approach for the mother who wants to keep both baby and lover is to love and mother them both. And the best approach for the young male is to accept the new role of his young wife as the Mother and to surrender to her in this way. It is possible to have Love flourish three ways: between husband, wife and baby. This is another dimension to Love. This is extended Love. This is selfless Love.

It is possible to have Love flourish three ways: between husband, wife and baby

There are many couples who have never experienced Heart Love, only sexual love. These are the couples who fall apart more quickly. If the couple has experienced Heart Love, then the relationship will last longer, at least as long as the Heart remains glowing.

In Tantra we seek to understand all aspects of human life and seek to find solutions that are based on the principle of Eternal Harmony, which is Love.

You are Alone on this Way

Remember that you are your own Reality. You always were and always will be. Whether or not you have a partner, whether you walk the Way in company or alone, remember that you always *are*.

Who goes with you? Some partner, lover or companion? For how long? How long is the journey that you make together?

Life is a journey upon the endless Way. You cannot see the beginning of the Way, nor the middle, nor the end. You see just a short distance ahead, yet the Way stretches behind you into Eternity and before you into Infinity. Whence have you come? Whither are you going?

My brother and sister, you are alone on this Way. The Heart of the Absolute is One Heart, yet we all must discover It for ourselves. How strange: we appear to be journeying with others, but in truth we are travelling alone, for we all must make the Journey from here to Eternity by ourselves. We hold hands for a while, then let go. For our paths are obscured by Silence.

Solitude and Loneliness 1170

Mother and Father 475
Nourishing the Goal of Life 487
Family and Duty 998

Live and Let Live

Do not take any person for granted. Do not take *anything* for granted. You cannot own anybody, you cannot own anything. People are not objects you can possess, to do with as you like when you like. People have their own self-determination, which often clashes with what you want of them. Love is to live and let live. Love is not slavery. Love is not aggression. Love is not bondage.

If you love the Great One, you will know that you cannot hold onto the many

Enjoy, but do not covet God's property.

So says Tantra. Enjoy, but do not covet! You cannot own even an object. How then can you own a person, a being with a free will? Sooner or later you will realize that the being you are desperately trying to possess has his or her own life.

Lead a life of Love, in detachment. Love profoundly, truly, sincerely, but don't be surprised if suddenly your beloved has other plans. Such is life.

Love in the context of freedom is God's Will. Love in the context of bondage is Man's idea of love. It has never worked and never will. It has created misery for untold millions and has wrecked untold millions of unions. If you love the Great One, you will know that you cannot hold onto the many. You can hold unto only the One. Be free, but give this freedom to your loved ones also. Otherwise you will always be disappointed.

Most often, what people really want is a slave, not someone who is a unique Being. This very uniqueness is your difficulty. The more unique a Being is, the more difficult it is to make a slave of him or her. But it happens that such slavery is very much part of the way human society operates. It is known as conformity: you are expected to behave in such and such a way under such and such circumstances. You also have your expectations of how someone should behave and you get upset if they do otherwise. What foolishness!

If the Creator had not given us free will, we would all be slaves, machines, zombies. This free will makes it impossible, ultimately, for a human being to become a total machine. In it lies our safety. In it lies our progress. In it lies true Love.

Aparigrahā: Non-attachment 567
The Path of Self-Actualization 1110
Rely on your Inner Self 1226
Self-Worth 1382

You can only Love Now

Life in this world is like a train journey in Europe. There are many stops, many stations, many countries. You get on your train, you journey for a while, and then you get off. It may happen that someone will journey with you for a while, and then that person may get off before your station, or maybe after, or even at the same station. Your journey begins at birth, you get off at your death. Note that the trains have been coming and going before you got on, and they will be coming and going long after you get off. You seem of no relevance at all to the process. You do not influence the matter. Likewise in life: people before you, people after you. Life goes on....

Love is not of the Past and it cannot be in the Future

But, my friend and beloved, there is only a short time on this Journey of Life. There is such a short time to love. Remember, should you have a companion journeying with you, you have only a little time for Love. Waste not that time. Waste not the Moment. While you are together, be loving, for who knows how soon you or your beloved will have to get off the train.

Love flourishes in the Moment. It is not of the Past and it cannot be in the Future. You can only love Now. What a tragedy it is when people get caught up in a love from the Past or some perfect love in the Future and all the while their fellow traveller in life is missing out on their affection and Love. The Journey is Now! Your bond of Love is Now! You cannot love at any other time than Now!

So, should it happen that some traveller comes to your compartment and travels with you for a while, be kind to him or her so that you may not cry later on over a Love that was lost, a Love that never flourished, or a Love that was never born.

I say to you, my friend, that Life is a mystery, but the greatest mystery is Love.

Let Go of the Past 1241
Past, Present and Future 1400
The Kingdom is at Hand 1453
Oneness and Love 1450

The Path of Tantra

Tantra is intimate relationship. What will you gain out of intimacy? Will you understand the tragedy of human existence? Will you understand that all things human are impermanent? Will you cry out for the Real?

Can you and your beloved reach this State in your intimacy?

Consider that your body is passing away, moment by moment. Even your mind is impermanent. Your thoughts die just as soon as they are born. Your emotions and feelings are constantly changing. Your life is on the move all the time. Everything is going away from you, slipping out from beneath your feet. Conditioned human existence is limited, impermanent. Your values and society's values are artificial, temporary constructs of the mind, having nothing to do with the Real.

In your intimacy with your beloved, can you see through the misery of the human condition? Can you take hold of the Divine Condition, which is profound, unchanging, unique, permanent, absolute? In this Divine Condition there is no coming or going, no pleasure or suffering, no ups or downs. Time and place do not affect It. In the Divine Condition there is no dying, no separation, no enmity, no rivalry. Can you and your beloved reach this State in your intimacy? Can you transcend your egos? Can you live in the Eternal? If you do so, then you have reached the goal of Tantra. Then all of your illusions of conditioned existence will disappear and you will see society as it really is. This is Insight. This is Tantra.

The illusions of the mind permeate the whole of human society. Humanity no longer lives in the Real, but is limited by ego-mind identifications, fleeting thoughts, intellectual speculations, philosophies, creeds and religions. The goal of Tantra is Insight into the conditions of human society and of all suffering.

If you and your beloved, in a moment of sweet embrace, or a moment of Truth, can see into Existence, then you will be Free. You will be awakened into that condition which is eternal, which is beyond any idea of mind. This is Divine Intimacy, which transcends human intimacy. Here you are alone, and your beloved is also alone. Yet in your Aloneness you are One. And All is One. And God is One. And you are One with God. And you turn around and smile.

The Law of Death 398
Quest for Reality 1178
The Eternal 1644
The One 1686

Beyond Nature is the Absolute, the Eternal, but to come to understand the Eternal One we must first go through Nature. She is our Mother. In Tantra, Nature is understood. In this sense a researcher in Tantra is like a scientist: both seek to know and understand the causes of things. We seek to understand Nature, to work with Her rather than against Her. She knows it all and we must learn what She will teach us.

Not everybody can become a monk or a nun, but everybody can practise Tantra because there is no split between "ordinary" life and "spiritual" life. In Tantra, all things are spiritual and all things are extraordinary. That is, all things are infused with the Divine Being and all things are of the Essence of ŚŪNYATĀ—the Emptiness, the Void, Tao, Nirvāṇa, the Kingdom of God, Parabrahman, the Transcendental Reality. Thus, even ordinary life is extraordinary and Sex is the Play of the Infinite.

If you come to identify with That, you will become Immortal even in this life

Beyond all polarities and dualities lies the Great Unknown, the Fundamental Reality. Call it God, or Truth, or Wisdom, or the Infinite Mind, or simply Tao. It is *That Of Which Nought May Be Said.* There is nothing you can say about It, nothing you can think about It, nothing you can do about It. Although it is Transcendent, it permeates every pore of your being. It permeates your flesh, blood and bones, your mind, emotions and Heart. You are saturated with It through and through.

If for a moment you can stop identifying with yourself and plunge into the Absolute, the Eternal One, then you have accomplished the purpose of Tantra. This is the Ocean of Reality, beyond Time and Space, beyond Matter and Energy, beyond thought, philosophy and argument. This is the Innermost Core of the Universe, the Substratum, the Inner Essence. If you come to identify with *That,* you will become Immortal even in this life. Your body will die, but You—that which Is—will surely become Immortal.

Śūnyatā: the Void 503
The Vision of your own Eternity 1144
Attach your Mind to the Eternal 1234
Practice for Wisdom 1700

The Way of Feminine Consciousness

The future Masters of Tantra will be women who are in relationship

The Path of Tantra is essentially learning to master Life, to control your Destiny, to transcend all obstacles, to overcome all limitations, to reach out for the Unreachable, to look for the most distant star, to discard the false, to reveal the Real, to throw away superstitions and ignorance, and to accumulate Knowledge based on experience. It is not a theoretical path, nor an intellectual exercise, nor a system of memory. Tantra is not a philosophy; it is an observation of Life, an observation of Reality.

A Tantra Master is essentially a scientist, an observer of Nature. A Tantra Master does not fight Nature, does not fight Life, does not fight Reality. A Tantra Master lives to *observe* Life, to discover the causes of suffering and to devise means to overcome them. A Tantra Master learns to *master* Life.

Tantra is the Way of Feminine Consciousness. I hope that more women will write about Tantra from their experience (though not the feminists who have rejected male-female relationships; like the monks, they cannot understand this subject). The future Masters of Tantra will be women who are in relationship, who have been trained in the Science of Polarity. For essentially, Tantra is the Feminine Understanding of Life, the Feminine Understanding of Relationship.

The Heart and Spontaneous Meditation 1227
The Worship of the Goddess 1481

CHAPTER 44

The One-Hundred-and-Twelve

That the Other One might Live

Tantra is more ancient than Zen. In fact, Zen borrowed its techniques from Tantra. The School of Tantra flourished in India thousands of years ago, and from India the Teachings of Tantra spread into Tibet, Mongolia and China. That was a long time ago. Nowadays we have Tibetan Tantra, Chinese Tantra, Hindu Tantra, and so on.

You can become Enlightened by living in the midst of all conditions

The following 112 meditations are the original methods of Instant Enlightenment, of living in the Spontaneous Moment, Liberation (MOKṢA) and Freedom (NIRVĀṆA), as were practised in India by the first Tantra School and recorded in the VIGYĀNA BHAIRAVA TANTRA.

These methods were practised by the "ordinary" people, the householders, so you can practise them also. You do not have to "renounce" the world. You do not have to quit your responsibilities to your society and your family. You can become Enlightened by living *in the midst of all conditions.* All you need to do is drop off the ego, the little self, so that the *Other One* in you might live.

Space

1

Enter into Space—supportless, eternal, still.

Or, empty yourself into the Void, without stirring, motionless, still. Thus, know the Eternal.

Dissolve your self in the Omnipotent

2

The Universe is an empty shell in which your Mind plays infinitely.

Or, be free to *play*, for the Cosmos is the Playground (LĪLĀ) of your Mind. This is Freedom.

3

Imagine your body to be empty Space, Void, with just a wall of skin. Then remove the skin also. Thus is the Voidness of all things.

Consciousness

4

Imagine your Mind simultaneously within you and around you, until the whole Universe is the Mind.

Or, imagine that the Spirit, the *Essence* of things, pervades the whole Cosmos within you and outside of you.

5

Focus your entire Consciousness at the beginning of Desire, of Knowing, and *Realize*.

Or, with your entire Consciousness focused at the beginning of each desire, *Know*.

6

Each act of perception is limited, yet has its origin in the Omnipotent.

Or, realize that all perceptions are necessarily limited, and dissolve your self in the Omnipotent.

7

In truth, forms are not divided from each other. The Omnipresent Being and all forms are a Unity. Each form is made of this Consciousness.

Or, realize that all forms are inseparable from the One Omnipresent Being, and that your form also is inseparable from It. Your body, and all forms, are made out of this Original Consciousness.

Experience the Consciousness of each being as your own

8

Experience the Consciousness of each being as your own. So, leave aside concern for yourself and become each being.

9

This Consciousness exists as each being in the Universe, and outside this Consciousness nothing else exists.

10

This Consciousness is the Spirit that guides each being in the Universe. Become *That*.

Or, this Primordial Consciousness is the Inner Guru of each being. Become identified with It.

The Self

11

Imagine a Fire that rises from your feet upwards and consumes you. Your form is reduced to ashes, but you remain.

12

Imagine the whole Universe burning with the Cosmic Fire. The whole Universe is reduced to atoms, but you remain.

13

Letters become words, words become sentences, circles become worlds, worlds become elements. Find the origins in yourself.

14

Sweetheart, meditate on knowing and not knowing, on existing and not existing, and then forget it all and just be.

15

The Universe is My thought; feel Me.

Dissolve yourself in the Eternal Beauty

16

Consider this passing world, and then dissolve yourself in the Eternal Beauty.

17

Be not attached to your form, as you are everywhere. He who is everywhere is Happy.

18

Suspend all mental activity and the Self will be free.

Or, suspend your mind and know yourself to be the Limitless Self.

19

Reach for the Unreachable. Grasp the Ungraspable. Go beyond perception. Go beyond yourself. Thus, find your Self.

20

Realize: "I exist. This is mine. This is not mine, but all is the Unlimited."

21

Sweetheart, if for a moment you can leave your mind, your intellect, your body, your breathing, you will know the Totality.

The Light

22

Beloved, thus shall you meditate. Imagine the Cosmos to be an Eternal, Translucent Presence. For so it is.

Look into the darkness and behold the Light

23

Or, imagine yourself to be Self-luminous. For so you are.

24

Or, perceive the Light ascending cakra by cakra up your spine, and descending cakra by cakra from the Crown of your head to the Base Cakra at the lowest vertebrae. Thus shall Life enter you. For the Light is Life.

25

Or, look up into the sky on a clear summer's day and see the Blueness of Space around you as you gaze into Infinity.

26

Meditate in your Head. Imagine there the Light. This Light fills all Space.

27

Whether you are awake, or asleep, or in dreamless sleep, know yourself to be that Light. This is the Essence of Reality, the Witness to all things.

28

In the darkness of night, or on a stormy dark day, look into the darkness and behold the Light! The Darkness is the Emptiness. The Emptiness is the Original Form of all forms. And the Emptiness is the Light.

The Word

29

In Silence, sing a mantra that ends in the long "Ah..." sound. And, in that long "Ah...", attain Spontaneous Enlightenment.

30

Enter the Primordial Sound within you

Stop hearing all outer sounds by closing your ears. Focus your attention at the base of the spine, at the rectum, and enter the Primordial Sound within you.

Or, put your fingers into your ears and listen to your right ear, deep inside.

31

Listen to the sound of your own name, and deepen the listening until you hear the Real Name.

Or, listen to your name and, through it, merge into the Root-of-all-Sounds.

32

Listen to the sound of the Sacred Word, ĀUṀ, but perceive neither the "Ā" nor the "Ṁ". In the long "U" is Revelation.

33

Chant the great mantra ĀUṀ (ŌṀ), slowly, prolonged. And, as the ŌṀ glides into the sonorous "Ṁ", enter into the Word, the Cosmic Reality.

34

Listen to a waterfall, or to a river or the sea, or to a continuous humming sound, and enter the Sound of Sounds.

35

Gradually refine a sound. Make it subtler and subtler, like a mantra silently repeated, and Wake Up!

36

Listen to an orchestra or a piece of music and hear the Omnipresent Sound.

Or, dance ecstatically to your favourite music until the self is reduced to No-Thing.

Listen to the Silent Harmony

37

Sing a note or a tone, slower and slower, until Silence comes. Listen to the Silent Harmony.

38

Open your mouth slightly and put your attention in your tongue. Breathe in silently and listen to the Sound of Breath.

39

Imagine a mantra. Visualize first its letters. Then inwardly hear its sounds. Then discard even that and you are Free.

Centring

40

Place your attention carefully into the middle of the spinal column, in the central nerve. Hence comes Transformation.

41

Close your eyes and ears with your hands, close your mouth, and look into the space between the eyes (the Third-Eye). Hence comes Unity.

42

Focus your awareness in the Heart Cakra by melting your senses into the Heart. Hence comes Blessedness.

43

Close your eyes and ears and feel your Centre, without the mind. Just dwell inside yourself, with no thoughts.

44

Imagine the peacock's feathers like five coloured circles. Now, imagine that these five coloured circles are your five senses. Now, stretch these circles until they embrace Unlimited Space.

Gaze at any object, filled with Love

Or, imagine the five colours of the circles on the peacock's feathers, and allow their beauty to become the All-Beauty.

Or, watch a spot, or a dot, or a circle on a wall, or anywhere in Space, until the spot or dot or circle disappears and only you remain.

45

Gaze at any object, filled with Love, for at the Centre of this object is the Great Happiness.

46

Try this: without using your hands or feet, sit down on your buttocks. Thus develops Concentration.

47

Try this: rock rhythmically, or move around in circles, until you rise above body-awareness. You can practise this also in a moving vehicle, or in something that rocks rhythmically.

Or, imagine yourself making invisible circles, circling around and around in your mind, until you drop on the floor and transcend the body.

Or, circle around and around to music and drums.

48

Gaze at an object in front of you until you perceive nothing else. Then, gaze further still, or until even the object disappears and there remains only the *sensation* of the object. Now, drop even that sensation. This is Realization of empty Space, that is to say, the *Origin*.

The Breath

Here, O beloved, are the methods for attaining
Supreme Enlightenment through Prāṇāyāma,
the regulation of breathing

49

Feel the Energy of Prāṇa and you shall be Strong

Instant Knowing comes when you catch hold of the interval between two breaths.

Or, breathe in and, as the air descends to the lungs and before the air goes out again, experience Vitality.

50

Watch the moment between inhalation and exhalation, and between exhalation and inhalation. Watch the moment of change as Prāṇa moves up and down, or in and out of your body.

Or, be attentive to the breath locked in (before exhaling) or the breath locked out (before inhaling).

51

When you breathe in or breathe out, at that precise moment feel the Energy of Prāṇa and you shall be Strong.

52

Breathe in completely, or breathe out completely. When there is no movement of breath, the self, the ego, the "I am", disappears.

53

Focus your attention at the tip of your nose and watch the breath going in and out.

Or, focus your attention between the two eyebrows (in the Third-Eye Cakra) and breathe naturally, dropping all thoughts from your mind. Become aware of the Prāṇa (breath) filling your head and breathe through the top of your head (the Crown Cakra). Thus shall you bathe in the Universal Light. This is Baptism by the Spirit.

54

Even while in worldly pursuits you can be aware of your breathing-pattern. If you keep yourself constantly aware of your breathing under all circumstances, you will be Reborn.

55

Discover the subtle breathing in the middle of your forehead. Thus is Immortality.

Or, know the breath as it enters the Heart Cakra and you shall be a Master of Dreams and overcome the Fear of Death.

Reduce your mind to no-thought and place it in your Heart

56

Concentrate on the moment between in-breathing and out-breathing, and out-breathing and in-breathing, and discover the Self-Existent.

Omnipresence

57

Dearly beloved, realize that the Omniscient, Omnipotent and Omnipresent God penetrates everywhere, even to the most distant stars and infinite Spaces, and within you also.

58

Know that the Divine Mother, the Great Goddess, permeates your form, and also below and above and everywhere.

59

Look up with your eyeballs into the Third-Eye Centre (the Eye of Śiva). There you will find the Luminosity of the Cosmos. From there, descend into the Heart Cakra and find the Universal Presence.

60

Reduce your mind to no-thought and place it in your Heart. Hence comes the Inexpressible Lightness of the Universe.

61

Imagine that your body is Unlimited Space and that the stars are but the atoms revolving within it.

62

The Cosmic Essence fills your whole form, your body, flesh, blood, breath and mind. Feel It.

Consider the Cosmic Breath as moving through your own Cosmic Body

63

The Heart Cakra is the subtle Creative Centre. Enter the Heart and perceive your subtle thoughtforms and dream-images. Then be *Free* of them.

64

Sweetheart, go out into Nature which is wide open to the Universal Presence, where there are no human habitations, where you can gaze into Infinity, where your vision is Boundless, where nothing obstructs your view. Gaze thus and there comes the dissolution of the mind, and with it the ending of all problems, tensions and desires.

65

Consider the Prāṇas of the Earth (the winds) as moving in your own subtle Bliss Body. And consider the Cosmic Breath, the Great Wind, as moving through your own Cosmic Body.

66

Suddenly, imagine yourself spreading in all directions, infinitely, everywhere. Hence comes Cosmic Consciousness.

67

Sit yourself in the lotus position, or in your favourite Āsana (posture). Imagine your whole chest area as a cave, a hollow, an abyss or an emptiness. Hence comes profound Peace and Blessedness.

68

Sit comfortably in your favourite posture, or lie down, or sit in a chair, and float in Space.

Attention

69

Fix your attention inside your body, with eyes and ears closed, and visualize your internal organs. Then become aware of your Real Nature, the Bodiless.

70

Fix your attention into an empty cup or a drinking bowl, but without being aware of its sides or what it is made of. Then comes Awareness.

Go on observing all things as if you are seeing them for the first time

71

Observe a beautiful object and an ugly object, as if you have never seen them before. Then comes *surprise*. Go on observing all things, always, as if you are seeing them for the first time. Then comes ever-new Joy.

72

Pay attention to the blue sky beyond the clouds or on a cloudless day. Melt into the Infinite Blue. Hence comes peace of mind.

73

Listen to the Guru's words when spoken to you on your behalf. Pay attention. Steady your gaze upon him without blinking, mind tranquil. Then you will be Liberated.

74

Sit by the side of a deep pool, a lake or a well. Gaze down into its depths. Plunge into the Abyss.

75

Observe any object. Then slowly remove your gaze from the object. Then remove your thought of the object. Then… find It, the Inexpressible.

Desire

Never forget That which is beyond desire, the Eternal One

76

When you have an emotion for any person, such as hate or aversion, attraction or like, anger or joy, do not put that feeling onto the person, but abide in the centre of your emotion. Thus, no one will ever be able to hurt you.

77

At the moment you feel the impulse to do something, stop. Thus shall you ever know Peace.

78

When you are aware of a desire overtaking you, observe it calmly, then forget it. This is Emancipation.

79

Find Freedom and Bliss in pure Devotion and Cosmic Ritual.

80

When in a state of extreme desire for something, let it go and find Peace.

81

If you realize a particular desire, and your dreams have come true, then know that it has been only a desire, and never forget That which is beyond desire, the Eternal One. For all things are passing except the One.

The Embrace

82

When you embrace your sweetheart and are in sexual communion, remember the Fire and you shall not be burned at the end with live coals.

83

Enter into the caress with complete self-abandonment

When you are in sexual communion, you are all fired up and excited. Enter into that Excitement fully and forget yourself. In the ensuing Bliss you can know *That*.

84

Even if you remember a successful embrace (sexual communion) with great Love, you will be Transformed.

Or, if you visualize a blissful experience of sex you have had, even that will bring about a new Transformation.

Or, if you imagine a successful union, even if it is but imagination, you will be transported to Heavenly Bliss.

85

When you caress your beloved, enter into the caress with complete self-abandonment until there is neither you nor your beloved, only the act of caressing. Then is Eternal Life.

86

If, in the act of sexual communion, you close the door of your senses and become aware of the Inner Energy, then comes Enlightenment and Freedom from all bodily conditions.

87

If you meet your lover after a long separation and a great Joy wells up inside you, allow yourself to be joyous so that you may know Joyousness Forever.

Other Moments

These are other moments when you can let go of the ego and mind-ordinary and dissolve yourself in Ecstasy.

88

Perceive all things, but become not lost in things

Run around, walk around, or dance until you are so exhausted that your body falls to the ground. As you fall, *remain together.*

89

Suppose you make yourself so tired that nothing matters any more, or suppose you exhaust yourself in thinking too much: even this is a blessing. Let go, and you shall enter into the Transcendent.

90

Know that there is no difference between an Enlightened person and an ordinary person. Both look out at the same objects around them, but the Illumined One does not get lost in them. Thus, Sweetheart, perceive all things, but become not lost in things, and you shall forever know Freedom.

91

Pretend to be dead, like a corpse. What does it feel like to be dead?

Or, if you are angry, enter into anger. What does it feel like to be angry?

Or, if you are sad or lonely or depressed, enter fully into that condition and discover: Who is angry? Who is sad? Who is lonely and depressed? Who?

Or, simply look without moving an eyelash.

Or, chew or suck something. Who is chewing? Who is sucking? Who is enjoying? Become what you feel. Then, let go and become Immortal.

92

During bad weather (such as a moonless night or a rainy day, or when you are wholly depressed and the world is depressed), close your eyes and see the darkness before you. Then open your eyes and see the darkness outside you. Then close your eyes and see the darkness inside you. Do this until there is only one darkness which is both within and without. Enjoy that Darkness. Relax, and all your troubles are over forever.

Just before waking up, Wake Up!

93

When you wake up, just before waking up, Wake Up!

Or, before going off to sleep, just before falling asleep, Wake Up!

94

There is a nectar at the roof of the mouth. If you allow yourself to enter, you will taste the AMṚTĀ, the River of Life.

95

In your mind, slowly recollect a past event. If you lose your present form, the Past suddenly will become your Present.

Or, in your mind, slowly see a future happening. If you allow your present form to disappear, suddenly you are in the Future.

Thus, you shall know that there is neither the Past nor the Future, only the ever-moving Present.

96

When you eat or drink, be filled with the taste. Total Experience!

97

O, Lotus-Eyed One, when you sing, dance, move, sit or walk about, or when you eat or sleep, just know that you *are* and you shall have Eternal Life.

98

As you are falling asleep, when sleep has not yet overcome you, your Being will be revealed to you. Watch!

99

As you are falling asleep, your Being will be revealed to you

Know that things are not as they appear to be. Even colours are but veils thrown over things. And the multiple (the many, as it seems) is not multiple, not many. It is the Indivisible.

100

The Universe around you is but Māyā (a conjuring trick) by the Great Magician. It seems real enough, but look again. What you perceive as solid is but fine energy, and that fine energy is but Consciousness, and Consciousness is but a Mask that veils the Real. So, why don't you laugh? The Universe is but a Thundering Laughter.

101

Neither pleasure nor pain are realities in themselves. Let not your Attention be enslaved by either of them, but only attend to That which is *between* them.

102

Ignorance (Avidyā) and Freedom (Mokṣa) are both relative terms. To the Enlightened One there is neither Bondage nor Enlightenment. This Duality exists only for those imperfect minds who are afraid of the Universe. Those who are afraid live in Duality.

This Universe is a mirror or reflection of the Spirit. It is an Image of Reality. But, as the many wavelets on an ocean reflect the same Sun, so the many worlds you behold reflect only the One. There is no slavery and no liberty to the Perfected One because, although he perceives the Many, he knows only the One.

103

The many millions of human beings have the same desires for the same objects of the same senses. You are merely one of these humans. You are not different. Accept yourself as you are and let these desires operate only in others. Do not cling to yourself. Do not cling to others. Do not cling to objects outside of yourself. Yourself, the objects and the others come and go, but You remain. Awake!

Throughout all these mutations, remain ever fixed in the Present

104

This Universe is a sphere of change, movement, transformation. It is never meant to be a fixity. Throughout all these mutations, remain ever fixed in the Present.

Or, although this World Order is ever changing and mutating, move along with it, Changeless.

Or, your life is a constant state of flux and change. Be not afraid of movement in your life; only remain fixed in your Essence.

Or, the only Law that is constant is the Law of Change. That is what gives the Changeless its real Value.

105

Waves are the product of the ocean. Flames are the product of fire. So, changes occur inside you as a result of the movements in your mind.

Or, the whole Universe is a Dynamo of Change because the Mind that holds it fluctuates. Be not attached to the fluctuations of the Mind. Be attached to the Mind Itself.

106

Realize that Mind inside you, even when your thoughts race about. If you can do that, you will know great Purity.

107

Because of the One, be the same for friend or foe, lover or enemy.

Or, in fame or failure, in success or dishonour, be the same, because of the One.

Or, Love all things, because of the One.

Because of the One, be the same for friend or foe

108

Remember that all things are natural. Even as a hen naturally knows how to raise her chicks, through centuries of old habits, so your life is a natural product of thousands of years of habits. Having discarded all this, realize Reality.

109

Be always Curious. When you become aware of a particular feeling, or a thought, or a sensation, be Curious, and leave it at that!

Or, when you are hungry, or when you are thirsty, know who is hungry, know who is thirsty, and find Yourself.

110

Nothing is pure or impure, sacred or non-sacred, divine or human. This is for imperfect minds only. Duality is not for One who Knows.

111

In all things, Transcend.

112

In all things, be your Self. Be a Witness, an Observer, and go on laughing all the Way.

The Original Calm

These are the 112 forms of meditation of the original Tantra School, based in India thousands of years ago. Without doubt, the fame of this Teaching has spread far and wide, slowly influencing many cultures of the East and Far East. We find this influence in Zen, in Taoism, in Tibetan Buddhism, among others.

Do not let the Original Calm disappear from view

The Taoist Masters say:

> Watch all things revolve around for a while and then return to their Roots. This is Silence, and Silence is Divinity, and Divinity is the Great Tao.

And the Zen Masters also affirm this simple Way:

> When you walk, walk. When you sit, sit. But don't wobble.

"Don't wobble" means don't wobble in your mind. Do not let the Original Calm disappear from view. It is the Calm Boat on a painted ocean upon a canvas. A painted boat upon a painted ocean. The ocean seems to be moving, and the boat seems to be riding on the waves. But does it really happen?

Find out the Answer. This is the Goal of Zen and of pure Taoism.

This is Tantra.

The Spirit of Zen 751
The Eternal Tao 771
The Heart and Spontaneous Meditation 1227

PART EIGHT

The Warrior School

The Way of the Noble Warrior

CHAPTER 45

The Spiritual Warrior

Qualities of the Spiritual Warrior

The Spiritual Warrior purposefully cultivates Intelligence

If you observe the behaviour of a Warrior, from the most primitive to the most noble, one of the striking qualities you will observe is intense will-power: enduring ability, fearlessness, power, energy, dynamism, swiftness in action, death-defiance, strength, virility. All true Warriors have this quality—in all countries, in all Warrior Schools, at all times. Whether they recognize it or not, this quality comes from the same source: *Spiritual-Will*. In the Warrior, Spiritual-Will is flowing very strongly through the physical, vital, emotional and mental bodies.

But the Spiritual Warrior has another quality also: *Love-Wisdom*, or Compassionate Understanding. This quality gives the Spiritual Warrior dignity, a sense of morality or right and wrong, wisdom-in-action, compassion towards suffering, virtue, a deeper understanding of the purpose of life, a greater comprehension of all situations, and Spiritual Influence or Radiation. This quality comes from another source and needs to be *acquired* through meditation, inner connection to the higher worlds, higher states of consciousness, and the influence of a Spiritual Guide or Teacher.

The third quality a Warrior should have is *Active Intelligence*. Some primitive Warriors have no Intelligence at all; they are just savages fighting. Others have various levels of Intelligence. But the Spiritual Warrior purposefully cultivates Intelligence by the serious study of the Esoteric Wisdom under the guidance of a Spiritual Teacher well versed in the Esoteric Tradition. Intelligence comes when the hidden Spiritual Laws of the Universe are studied and then practically applied in daily living.

Thus, the true Spiritual Warrior has three outstanding qualities:

- Will and Power, energy, dynamism.
- Love and Wisdom, understanding.
- Intelligent Activity, purposefulness.

The Spiritual Warrior is a Tower of Strength in the turbulent Ocean of Life, whose motives for action spring from the Timeless Realm, not conditioned by politics, religion, culture or tradition.

The Spiritual Warrior is a Free Spirit, whose body may be killed or put in chains, yet whose Spirit ever roams in Freedom in the Eternal Spaces of the Cosmos.

The Spiritual Warrior makes a Mark upon the world, even if it is unseen by the blinded eyes of the Ignorant, and that Mark is his Signature Vibration upon the Cosmic Ocean of Life.

Warrior Jesus 908

Development of the Spiritual Warrior

There are three stages in the development of the Spiritual Warrior:

Stage One

The first stage is *self-knowledge*. Your *self* is your personality make-up, you who live in *this* world, in Time and Space, under limited circumstances inherited through your customs, culture, tradition, race, colour, religion, country, language, education, family, and so on. It is your *limited self*.

The new You will live in the Timeless Ocean of Eternal Life

This is the *human* Warrior, learning about yourself on the *personal* level: your strengths and weaknesses, your successes and failures, your thoughts and emotions, and your relationships to people. This involves also your bodily training, your combat techniques, your weaponry training, your handling of people and situations in your life. This will make you the human Warrior. Most Warriors don't get beyond this stage.

Stage Two

The next stage is *Self-knowledge*. Your *Self*, You on the level of the Soul and Spirit, is the timeless, eternal, boundless Being, unconditioned, deathless, fearless, blissful, compassionate, loving, understanding. It is *Pure Intelligence*.

To get to this stage you have to practise meditation, breathing techniques, silence, sound-work, the Spiritual Warrior Aphorisms, and the study of the Esoteric Science. As you practise the various processes described in these chapters you will have glimpses or experiences of your Timeless Self, the You who lives in the silent, motionless Ocean of the Absolute Reality.

Stage Three

The third stage of your Journey towards becoming a Spiritual Warrior is to fuse and blend the two selves, your self and your Self, to become the SELF, the indescribable Spiritual Warrior, by awakening the Warrior Within. The new You will live in the Timeless Ocean of Eternal Life, yet will participate in shaping the Moment of Time as it flows through, changing people and the destiny of nations and the planet.

Who is 'I AM'? 1418
The Three Stages of Yoga 528
Meditation is Integration 1193
The First Circle of Life 1422
The Second Circle of Life 1438
The Third Circle of Life 1448
The Warrior Path 1002

The Warrior, the Sage, the Ruler

There are three major Streams of Spiritual Energy available for the evolution of human beings on this planet:

Stream One is *directed power*, intense will, power over life and death, dynamic energy, fierce independence, noble self-sacrifice, the feeling of Destiny or the *necessary* choice for action, a powerful awareness of people, situations and events, a strong sense of purpose and energy. This Energy Stream makes the *Warrior*.

The Second Energy Stream makes the Sage

Stream Two is an Energy Current that produces *Universal Love and Compassion*, sympathy, understanding, wisdom, the ability to *teach* others the Mysteries of Life and Death, the Plan and Purpose of the Universe, the Spiritual Path, and so forth, and to *inspire* others. This Energy Stream makes the *Sage:* the Wise-Person, the Spiritual Teacher, the Prophet, the Seer, the Spiritual Guide.

Stream Three produces *Active Intelligence*, executive ability, governing or ruling power, creative mind and intelligence. This Energy Stream produces the *Ruler:* the administrator, the statesman or stateswomen, the king or queen, the emperor or empress, the official, the diplomat, the governor, the chief, the elder.

The Seven Rays 54

The Eternal Triangle

The Warrior, the Sage, the Ruler: upon these three society stands or falls. The correct development and interaction of these three makes life bearable or unbearable, causes nations to rise or fall, brings war or peace.

When the Warrior opens the Heart and receives the Second Stream of Energy through the disciplines of meditation, breathing, silence, sound-work, study of the Esoteric Tradition, and living the Warrior Code or Aphorisms, this Warrior becomes the Spiritual Warrior or the Warrior Sage, a Warrior with a Heart. When the Warrior masters the Art of Statesmanship, then he or she is the Warrior King or Warrior Queen.

Both the Spiritual Warrior and the Warrior King or Queen depend on the Wisdom of the Sage for their attainment and success. Without the Wisdom of the Sage, and their own inner development through the teachings of the Sage, both will fail; the Warrior will not know right from wrong, nor will the Ruler be able to govern with understanding and vision. Without the Sage, both the Warrior and the Administrator are lost; hence civilization becomes lost, hopeless, chaotic.

The Sage, the Warrior and the Ruler are the eternal triangle for a balanced and healthy society where Wisdom rules, Equality reigns, and Human Evolution proceeds along the line of the Divine Plan.

The Sage

The Sage is an Esoteric Teacher. There are popular figures such as the Dalai Lama of Tibet, the Pope of the Roman Catholic Church, the Shankaracharya of Hinduism, and the preachers, ministers, priests and clerics of orthodox religions and traditions. These teach the masses, the mass-mind, the millions. But the Sage is different. The Sage cannot teach the masses for they are not ready for the Esoteric Truth, the *real* Truth about things.

Although the Sage lives in the world, the Sage is not of the world

The Sage has a small number of disciples, counted in hundreds rather than thousands. The Sage is not known in the world; that is, the Sage shies away from worldly fame and name and is not in the worldly "spotlight". Were it so, the Sage could not teach the real Truth about things.

Although the Sage lives in the world, the Sage is not of the world. The Sage points the Way to Reality, away from the glamours, delusions and ignorance of the worldly consciousness. The disciples of the Sage are seeking earnestly the Way of escape from the quagmire of materialism, from the Night of Ignorance of the mass consciousness, the common mind.

The Sage is the Light to those who seek the Way out of the Worldly Darkness.

Your choice of Greatness is of three kinds:

1. The Warrior wields the energies of Power, Will, Purpose, Intention, Life and Death.
2. The Sage wields the energies of Love, Wisdom, Understanding, Compassion, Goodness and Universal Inclusiveness.
3. The Administrator builds societies, groups, communities or civilizations which are of the greatest benefit to all, not just of benefit to their own family, friends, tribe, nation or religion.

Both the truly inspired Administrator and the valiant Warrior learn from a Sage and are disciples of a Sage, for the Sage is Enlightened, Illumined, and knows the Divine Plan for Mankind. Without the Inner Wisdom of the Sage, the Warrior will simply be a killing machine, and the Administrator (the politician) will simply look after his or her own selfish interests for power, advantage, name and fame, worldly glory.

The Guru 389
The Aquarian Teachers 1147
The True Teachers 1694
The Law of the Higher Life 1134
The Zen Master according to Lao Tzu 780

Mind-Only

Mind-Only has many names:

- Cosmic Mind, Universal Mind, the Mind of God, the Mind of Light, the One Mind, the Mind, Infinite Mind, Divine Mind, Master Mind.
- Creative Intelligence, Creator-Mind, the Creative Principle, the Source-Mind, the Great Architect of the Universe, the Mental Origin of All Things.
- Universal Light, Boundless Light, the Radiant Light of Reality, the Name, the Nameless, the Cosmic Christ, the Buddha-Nature, the Self-Nature, your Original Nature, your True Self, Tao.
- The Unobstructed Reality, the Primeval Vision, the All-Seeing-Mind, Infinite Consciousness, Transcendental Consciousness, the Absolute, the Universal Field of Awareness, the All-Presence.
- The One Life, the Universal Life-Power, Life, the Life-Force of the Universe, the Spirit of God, the Breath of God, the Great Breath, the One Force, the Universal Radiant Energy, the Cosmic Sea of Life.

Nothing can exist outside of this One Mind

There is Mind-Only. Nothing can exist outside of, or separate from, this One Mind. All things are built up by this Universal Mind: the planets, the stars, the suns, the galaxies, the Cosmos, and the bodies of all sentient beings, subtle or dense, including your own physical body.

This Knowledge is the Key to it all.

By this Knowledge you gain Power, Fearlessness, Valour, Vigour, Energy, Focus, Intelligence and Success.

Through you flows the Infinite Life and Energy of the Universe.

Only your false sense of self, your false ego, obstructs it.

The Plan is in the Divine Mind 161
Perceptions of the One Mind 490
Messengers of the One Mind 764
Tao: the Universal Mind 775
The Holy Breath 1340
The One 1686

The Art of the Warrior consists of *removing* your false self so that you may become an *unobstructed channel* for the Universal Life-Force, the Power of the Universe, the Will of God, the Mind of Light. Then you become a *true* Warrior. Then you will be *guided* by the Infinite Mind, Cosmic Intelligence, and take your place among the Shining Warriors of Light.

You need to *meditate* on the Mind-Only until you discover its true Secret; then your life will change, your Vision will change. Instead of failure, limitation, despair, hopelessness and weakness, you will become a focal point of Radiant Life, purposeful Living, intelligently-applied Force in your life, and the discovery of Higher Evolution.

You need to meditate on the Mind-Only until you discover its true Secret

You will stop thinking as the mass-mind of the world thinks. You will stop thinking as your family, tribe or nation thinks. Your mind will become the Master's Mind, a Master Mind, *directing* not only your own life, but the lives of many others.

What do you Seek out of Life?

Happiness? Wealth? Name and fame? Or perhaps success in your job, marriage or project?

Do you know where to find true Happiness, true Joy, true Bliss?

Is happiness dependent on outside factors, such as your job, your house, your car, your wife or husband, your children, your career? Is there a Happiness that does not depend on outside factors?

With whom do you *identify?*

- The manifesting self, your personality?
- The Higher Self, your Soul?
- The Universal Self, God?

On the Way of the manifesting self you always change, move from one thing to another, from one goal to another, from one state to another.

On the Way of the Higher Self, the Soul, you are at the Centre—Still, Silent, Tranquil, the Observer of the phenomena of Life around you.

The Way of the manifesting self is the Way of Action, of Becoming.

The Way of the Higher Self is the Way of Being, Abiding, Non-Changing.

The Way of the Universal Self is the Way of Omnipresence, Universality, Eternal Renewal and Revelation, Indestructibility, Cosmic Activity.

The Way of the Spirit 381
Understand your Predicament 892
Being and Becoming 1415

The Law of your Being

Most people are out of tune with themselves. That is why they are sad, angry, depressed, annoyed, irritated and stressed out. They are out of tune with the Law of their Being. They are not living in their own Being, but on the surface, superficially, emptily. This is true of children as well.

You are the Way, the Truth and the Life

People do not need drugs, nor endless talking or "counselling". They need to *re-establish themselves in Being*, and this cannot be done by "counselling sessions", nor by drugs.

The true Warrior is established in Being, and his or her actions come from Being, not from the surface, nor from emotional reactions, nor from devious thoughts of the mind.

Strive to become a true Warrior.

Although Being is subtle, transcendental, spiritual, it can work through your body and mind and emotions once you have discovered It and established yourself in It.

All suffering arises in Humanity through breaking the Law of Being.

When your attention is continually outside, on the surface, you are not paying attention to your Being; hence, most of the time you are out of tune with your own Law of Life.

To understand your Being is simply to Be. It is not gained by accumulation of knowledge, nor by learning from books, nor by storing vast amounts of information in your mind, nor by becoming something or another, nor by wanting to get this or that.

The Way to Being is not a matter of distance, nor of time. It always Is. Although we speak of a Journey or a Way, really it is not going anywhere. It is being still, silent, inwardly receptive, bright and awake inside yourself. You are the Way, the Truth and the Life.

Dharma 1408
Dharma: the Law of Being 244
The Path of Self-Actualization 1110
The Way, the Truth and the Life 670
The State of Being 1232

It is not a matter of how long it takes you to get there. It is a matter of Silence and Stillness and Receptivity within yourself. You have to turn your attention within yourself rather than outside yourself. This is the Way to your Being.

Your Being is on the transcendental level. To reach that State you have to quieten your mind, for Being is beyond and above your mind. Your mind, your consciousness and your intelligence have their Source in Being. So you must return to your Source, your Root, your Self-Nature, your Real Self, which is different from your personality and personality consciousness.

The desire for Being must come from within yourself

To Realize your Being or Self-Nature you must cultivate the Silence that just Is. Your mind has to turn inwards until your sense of personal "I" (your personal ego) disappears and you experience yourself as Pure Being—eternal, limitless, blissful, indestructible, full of all potential and all possibilities, whose very essence is Wisdom and Love.

This is Self-Realization, or knowing Yourself as you truly are. Then your identification with your body ceases and your sense of limitation disappears. For while you identify with your body and the world, you are limited, but when you identify with Being, you are Limitless and everlasting and all things are possible for you.

The desire for Being must come from within yourself. You must be self-motivated, self-inspired. Look not outside for your source of help in your Quest. All that you need is already within you. Reduce your mind, become Still, Silent. In the Stillness of your mind, Being will reveal Itself.

Having established yourself in Being through meditation, you perform your actions spontaneously, naturally, from the level of your Being. Then you act from the harmony of your Being, in tune with Yourself and in harmony with the Universe, for Being is the basis of all Creation and of every creature in the Universe, human or otherwise. Then you truly are a Spiritual Warrior, simply doing your Duty in the Service of the King.

Pure Being 1056
The Attitude for Yoga 558
Your Mind is the Key 1208
Rely on your Inner Self 1226

Light

There is:

The Boundless Light, Infinite Light.

The Light of God.

The Living Light, the Light of Bliss.

The Light within the Light.

The Light of all Lights.

The Glory of God, the Splendour of God.

The Everlasting Light, the Eternal Light.

The Light of Unity, the Light of Oneness.

The Glory, Splendour, Brightness.

The Original Light, Primeval Light.

The Fundamental Light.

The Light of the Soul, the Light of Love.

The Light of the Mind.

The Light of the Central Spiritual Sun.

The Light within the Heart.

The Light of Truth, Reality.

The Light of the Spirit, the Light of Intuition.

Energy for Illumination may come to you through:

- Strong Faith.
- Radiant Love in the Heart.
- Fixed Purpose of Will-power.
- Light in the Head.
- Profound Silence of the mind.
- A Blessing from your Soul, or a Being of Light, or the Spiritual Hierarchy.
- Selfless Service towards the Divine Plan.

The Law of Radiation 175
The Self-Generating Light 1594
The Path of Illumination 1338
Satori: the Experience of Illumination 816

Light is not a metaphor or symbol (as ignorant theologians and philosophers think). It is real. In fact, it is the only Reality!

Light is God-in-Manifestation, God-in-Incarnation, God-in-Expression. Light is God's Presence in Creation. Light is Substance, many invisible grades of Substance and Essence.

You will become one of the active Forces of Light in the Three Worlds

When you can hold your mind steady in the Light, then you can become a Warrior of the Light.

The Light may be found in the Heart Centre, in the Third-Eye Centre, and in the Crown Centre at the top of the head.

If you focus your Awareness in the Heart Centre, the Third-Eye or the Crown Centre for a long time, eventually the Light will appear. This will give you entrance to the Lighted Way. This means that you travel along the Way of Light-Vibrations to interior dimensions within yourself and into the inner Light Worlds of the Universe.

The Light will become for you a source of Strength, Power, Grace, Wisdom, Energy and Illumination. You become the Lightened Warrior, the Warrior of Light, the Warrior Crowned with Glory.

The amount of Light you have within yourself is the degree of your Dignity, Majesty, Kingliness, Royalty.

You will become one of the active Forces of Light in the Three Worlds of Manifestation: the Physical (outer), the Astral (subtle), or the Mental (subtlest). Beyond these worlds are the great Realms of Light and Being. And beyond them is the Brilliant Light-Sea of Reality, the Shoreless Ocean of Boundless Light, your true Source and Home.

You will no longer be concerned with your personality because your focus will be in your Soul-Nature. You will know yourself to be Deathless and Eternal, and you will understand and follow the Path of Righteousness.

The Path of Light 89
The Lighted Way 1394
The River of Light 1308
Rules of Light 1597

The Invisible Government

The Invisible Government of the World we call the *Spiritual Hierarchy*. This is a group of liberated human beings who are helping Humanity primarily on the Mental Plane, in the formless portion of the Mental World, wherein most of the Human Souls dwell.

The Spiritual Hierarchy focuses on the world of Mankind from within the Inner Worlds to produce outer events in the world. The Divine Plan or Pattern upon which the Spiritual Hierarchy works comes from a higher Source of Revelation, from the Council Chambers of the Spiritual King, the Lord of the World, the Ancient of Days. Thus, there is a Divine Plan in life, and for the life of our planet, even as there is a Plan for the Evolution of the Universe.

You can register in your Silent Mind the vibrations of the Spiritual Hierarchy

You must seek to make contact with the Hierarchy on the Mental Plane by a poised, silent mind, a fully alert, awake mind, receptive to subtle mental impressions. In this process your physical body is at rest and your emotional nature, your astral body, is completely still. You can register in your Silent Mind the vibrations of the Spiritual Hierarchy, which are of Love and Joy. This silent contact has Healing on its Wings, an internal restructuring of your inner being in Freedom and Light.

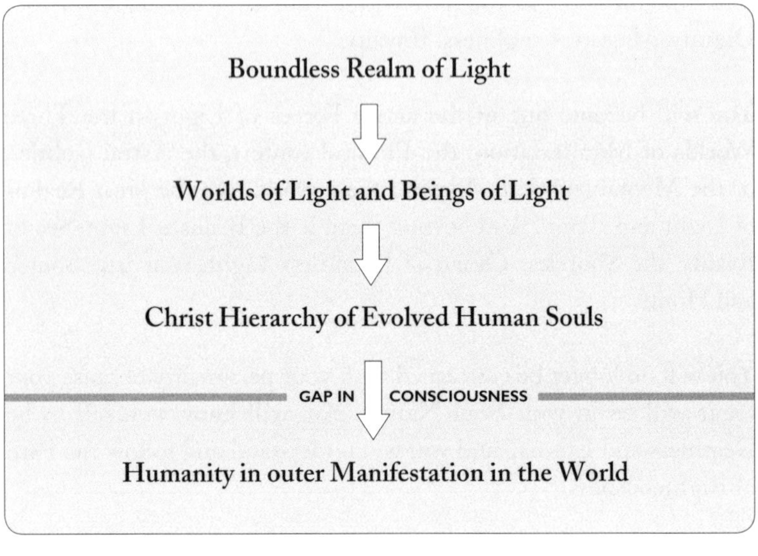

The Descent of the Light

The Plan is in the Divine Mind 161
Saṅgha: the Spiritual Hierarchy 394
The Christ-Hierarchy and Śamballa 396
The Function of the Spiritual Hierarchy 1720

Light is the Fundamental Nature of the Higher Existences in the subtlest part of Universal Manifestation. This All-Pervading Light is Pure Intelligence, Pure Consciousness, Beauty, Perfection. It is All-Knowing, Absolute Love, Compassion and Understanding, Infinite Joy and Creativity. It is Eternal Life, beginningless and endless.

The Light of the Divine Radiance and the Light of your Soul are One Light, although You as a Living Soul exist within this Light of Reality as pure Conscious-Beingness. Light is God-in-Manifestation, God incarnating as the Omniverse or Omnirevelation of All That Is. The Light Eternal pervades the whole Universe, All-Space. It is Intelligence, Consciousness, Bliss. That You are!

The Plan is for you to become transformed by the Light

Humanity, or the species of Man (men, women and children in physical bodies), is cut off from experiencing this Infinite Intelligent Light (the Mind of God) and the Light Worlds and Beings of Light contained within It. The idea is to build a Bridge to the Light by using combined Sound-Vibrations uttered in Silence (that is, to work in Silence). The Sound-Vibrations, in their silent, subtle form, enable your consciousness to *realize.*

This is a group work. In the olden days (the Golden Age), groups of monks, warrior-monks and Spiritual Warriors worked in such group formations and called it the *Silent Work* or the *Work in Silence*, and they generated a great Power and Blessings upon all Humanity.

A new world is being created at this moment. The cyclic rotation of the Ages brings automatic changes on the planet. But there is a focused effort today by Those who walk in the Light to bring about a permanent revolution, a fundamental change, to re-align the planet to the Original Patterns of Light, to make this planet a Light-planet instead of a dark planet as it is now.

The Plan is for you to become transformed by the Light so that you become a Conscious Light-Being. This is the Destiny of Mankind, of every human being. Can you understand the Call? Are you sufficiently Awake to Respond?

The Full Moon period (from two days before Full Moon until two days after Full Moon) is the best time each month to tune into the Spiritual Hierarchy. At that time the Inner Government is especially active towards contacting Humanity. Also, it is easier to gain Illumination during Full Moon, for during that time your inner sensitivity is at its highest.

To be taught Wisdom 353
Understanding your Work in Silence 1024
The Initiation of the World 1712
To Manifest the Kingdom of God 1716

From Darkness into Light

Truth comes silently to the tranquil mind

Is there a time when human suffering shall cease? Is there a time when wars will be no more and human beings will live with each other in peace? Is there a Utopia when society will be ordered and harmonious? This planet is a planet of war, a School for Warriors. It always has been. When will the Warriors lay down their arms? When will the conflicts cease?

The Way of the Warrior is a Journey from Darkness into Light. Mankind, in its highest nature, is a Being of Light. The Warrior, on the level of the purest Essence, is made out of the Original Light-Effulgence.

So, whence came the Darkness? Mind clouds and obstructs the Light. Thought prevents the Light from shining through to the brain. Hence you are in Darkness. When you stop the turning of the wheel of your mind, when you put to Rest your restless thoughts, when you stop being anxious about the Way, when you are carefree, the Light reveals Itself to you as your very Self, you and God united, bright and spotless in the Infinite Radiance.

From Matter to Light 761
The Suspending of the Mind 1209
Liberation from Worldly Consciousness 1233

What you hold in your mind you will become.

If you hold in your mind the Infinite Light, you transmute your personal awareness of limited Darkness into the Boundless Light-Awareness of Eternity.

The philosophers, theologians and metaphysicians churn out endless volumes of thoughts in their darkened minds, endlessly speculating and guessing about Man, God and the Universe, and they think that their evanescent thoughts are the sacred Truth, the Reality! How wrong they are! How deluded they are! Truth comes silently to the tranquil mind, beyond words and descriptions.

There is a Darkness within you when you close your eyes. There is a Darkness of Ignorance which is the world mass-mind. There is the Darkness of Space when you look into the night sky. Yet all these Darknesses are simply a Veil over the Light. If you remove the Veil from your eyes, you will see the Universe of Light. As your consciousness has been emerging out of the Primordial Darkness towards the Light, so the consciousness of Humanity is emerging today to embrace the Living Light.

The closer you are to the Truth, the more shines your mind, as you are lit up within by an in-born Light.

Who are you? Who are you presently identifying with? Whatever you have identified with, you have become, and this is what limits you. It is what you *believe* yourself to be: your thoughts, feelings, sensations and habits, your education, your culture, what your so-called religion and tradition have made out of you, with which you deeply identify.

But who are You when you are not identifying with your limited self? Who are You without your traditions, culture, religion, beliefs, opinions, education and conditionings? The Liberated Man. The Free Warrior. When your self-centredness ceases, your Universality begins. When your identification with the limited comes to an end, your Journey in the Limitless can begin.

The structure of Life is evolving on this planet, therefore also Consciousness itself. The true Warrior is adaptable, forward-looking, moving with the new conditions, new demands and new ways of the New Age. Those who are crystallized will perish—individuals, tribes, nations, religions, and outdated customs and ways of thinking. The New Age, the new Power, will move relentlessly on. Are you stuck in the Past, O Warrior? Are you fighting for lost causes, for past visions and goals, which no longer serve the King's Divine Plan?

Who are You when you are not identifying with your limited self?

The Great Chief of Light is the embodiment of the new Plan, Purpose, Will and Destiny of all Life upon this planet. The Vibrations of Light are steadily increasing and the Forces of Light are gathering momentum.

Whom do you Serve?

Surpassing your own Limitations

- You are limited by the capacities of your physical body.
- You are limited by the thought-processes in your mind.
- You are limited by your culture, tradition, religious upbringing, family disposition, and the values (right or wrong) imposed upon you by the society you live in.

Can you see this? Can you surpass these limitations? Do you see how everybody is conditioned by these factors? Do you see how language conditions you? Do you see how these things separate people, keep people apart, and very often cause struggles, strife, antagonism and wars?

If you are an evolved man or woman on the Warrior Path you will rise above these limitations and become the Universal Man or Universal Woman, without boundaries, serving all equally, without distinction of race, colour, religion, nationality, country or cultural background. Your Field of Service is the whole Family of Man, and your country is the whole planet.

Can you outgrow your present self?

What is Consciousness? 1368
How do you Know who You really Are? 1387
Obstacles to Higher Consciousness 1424
Attach your Mind to the Eternal 1234

The Warrior of the Light

The Great Army of the Light is assembling all over the world

The New Warrior is Universal, broad in Vision, not limited to the old tribal ways and customs. There is a new Humanity slowly being born on this planet which is planetary and then cosmic in becoming. A new world is being born, a new Heaven and a new Earth. The past traditions, customs, cultures, religions and social structures will have to pass away, and there is a conflict between the old, crystallized, fossilized elements and those who catch the new Vibrations and engage in the Transformation of the World.

There are countries and religious groups who are still back in the Dark Ages, who are lagging behind the times, who want to stop the liberation of women and progress towards the new World Civilization. Fight the War on the side of progress, O Warrior, not on the side of those whose thinking is small, local, tribal, outdated and no longer relevant to the larger community. Your culture can be your trap if it is old and outdated. Your religion can be a trap if its leaders and priestcraft long ago lost their way.

Religious Reactionaries 287
Warriors of the Sun 1618
The New Age and You 1708

You are called to a Great Work, to help liberate all Mankind on this planet by cooperating with the Forces of Light, to awaken Soul-Consciousness in Mankind, to bring about the Spiritualization of the planet and help the Divine Hierarchy incarnate on this Earth. The Great Army of the Light is assembling all over the world. Are you part of this Heavenly Army? Are you a Warrior of the Light, for the Light, by the Light? Then join the Great Band of Warriors under the Banner of the King, the Ancient of Days, the Chief and Lord of the Heavenly Hosts and the Spiritual Realms.

Even now, the Kingdom of God is at hand. It is near, it is upon us. Watch and see! The Day is breaking, the Sun of Righteousness is rising, and the Darkness of the Night is fading away.

The Warrior of the Light lives by the Rule of Love, Compassion, Goodwill, Forgiveness, Service to All.

The Warrior of Darkness is full of hatred, anger, selfishness, self-interest, cruelty, materialistic ambition, and desire for conquest and dominion over others.

Choose!

The True Warrior stands between the Light and the Darkness. He or she perceives the Light of the Spirit and battles the Forces of Darkness which hold back human evolution and progress on this planet: ignorance, prejudice, materialism, evil, corruption, hatred, and the glamours of the Astral Plane, the subtle, invisible world that surrounds the planet and keeps the Human Souls entrapped in the material sphere. Such is the Task of the Warrior. The Battle is both visible and invisible.

True War

True War is the conflict between Spirit and Matter, between the Spiritual Forces and the materialistic powers, between the Forces of Light and the Forces of Darkness (evil), between Those who move along with the Plan for Divine Evolution and those who seek to retard it. True War determines whether human life on this planet is controlled by the materialistic forces (materialism) or the Christ Hierarchy, the Spiritual Kingdom, the Kingdom of God.

The True Warrior fights for the Enlightenment of all Mankind

The true Spiritual Warrior is a Light-Warrior who brings Light to this dark planet, to the materialistic mass-mind which is ever at the point of darkness and the despair of Spiritual Ignorance.

Being a true Spiritual Warrior is not about greed and ambition, nor about conquering other kingdoms and lands, nor about enslaving other nations, tribes, races or religions. The true Warrior fights with the Sword of the Spirit, has the Shield of Truth to protect him, and serves the King, the Ancient of Days, the Lord of the World, the Great Warrior who forms the protecting Wall of Light between Humanity on this planet and the great cosmic evil forces who seek to enslave the free Human Souls and destroy and disintegrate all that is True, Beautiful and Good.

The true Warrior fights for the Enlightenment of all Mankind, regardless of race, tribe, colour, customs or tradition. His gift to Man is Freedom, Truth, Light and Love.

Wars in Heaven 271
Brothers of the Shadow 226
Brotherhoods of Light and Darkness 228
Beyond War 1098

Acting from the Centre: Spontaneous Benevolence

Most schools of warriors, down through the ages, in all countries and on all continents, concentrated their training on physical fighting skills or martial arts. These physical fighting schools seldom understood what it means to be a true Warrior—the qualities, virtues and attainments of the Spiritual Warrior.

In far-off days there were mighty Warriors in the Service of the King (the awesome Spiritual Autocrat who rules our planet from the Light-dimensions), whose destiny was to reshape Mankind, build new civilizations, and fight Cosmic Evil which ever threatens to engulf the world of Mankind in dark ages. To be in the Service of the King is the destiny of the Spiritual Warrior, the Warrior of the Light.

To become a true Warrior, a Warrior of the Light, you have to eliminate all hostile tendencies in your character, all aggression, all hate, all violent urges, all desire to dominate and control others. Will that make you weak, my brother? No, but extremely strong. Try it!

In the presence of the Warrior, who is united to the Sun within the Heart, there flows blessings, joy, confidence and strength.

The Warrior seeks Peace not War

Non-violence is the greatest virtue of a Warrior. Does this seem strange? A true Warrior lives in Peace with himself and in Peace with his neighbours. In fact, a true Warrior is totally self-controlled.

A true Warrior never goes on a rampage of destruction. The Skill of the Warrior is only for deserving ends: to protect the weak, to right wrongs, to uplift the downtrodden, and to protect Humanity from the forces of evil. Even towards the Enemy, the true Warrior is kind and does not seek unnecessary death and violence. The true Warrior is never cruel—not to people, nor to animals.

The true Warrior does not glory in violence

The true Warrior does what is right and proper to fulfil his or her Duty. The true Warrior does not glory in violence, nor in self-importance, nor in greed. He or she is humble and unassuming.

The true Warrior is honest and truthful and does not employ the art of cunning or deceit to gain advantage over another. The true Warrior has a large Heart and easily forgives.

There are four types of warrior: the physically strong but with no intelligence; the feeling, emotional, idealistic warrior; the mental, calculating, cunning type; and the best, the Spiritual Warrior.

No Anger, No Enemies

The virtuous Warrior has no anger, therefore he has no enemies.

This means that he does not consider anybody to be his enemy. He is a friend to all. There are people who consider this Warrior to be their enemy, but that is on their side only. This Warrior just knows Duty and acts accordingly, without anger, venom, the killing lust or malice.

This Warrior does not instigate hostilities, nor does he purposefully create war situations. He does not look for a fight continually, as the inferior warrior does. The virtuous Warrior goes to war only as a last resort, when all diplomacy has failed, and then he fights without hate.

The virtuous Warrior, through years of profound meditations, has attained Peace; therefore he does not fight wars of conquest and attrition, wars of wanton destruction and arrogance. The war the Warrior fights is truly a Holy War, not for his own merit or gain, but for the good of all and to liberate the masses from oppressive evil forces.

How do you fight your wars, my friend? Are you angry and hateful towards people, or are you a Warrior of the Light?

Peace on Earth 1304
Peace of Heart 1595
How to have a Peaceful Mind 1244
How to deal with Crisis situations 1435

Be Tranquil

Ambition is the mark of an evil warrior. Contentment is the mark of a Spiritual Warrior.

The evil warrior is ambitious, proud, arrogant. The Spiritual Warrior is peaceful, simple, does not hanker after name and fame, does not continually seek honours and favours from others. The Spiritual Warrior prefers a simple, quiet life, acting only out of Duty, when Righteousness requires it.

Far off are the Pavilions of our King, but close is His Presence

The true Warrior prefers Tranquillity over war. War happens when Duty calls. The evil warrior likes war all the time to feed his or her ambitions.

Far off are the Pavilions of our King, but close is His Presence. Keep Tranquil, my brother.

What business do you have, my brother, but to serve the King, the Supreme Commander of the Heavenly Hosts, the King of Kings, the Lord of Lords, the Chief of Chiefs, the Ancient of Days?

In the midst of war, be Tranquil.
In the midst of the fight, be Tranquil.
In the midst of arguments, be Tranquil.
In the midst of the chaos of the world, be Tranquil.

Discover, through profound meditations, the Tranquil Light within you that no outer war can disturb, that no outer chaos can perturb, that no outer evil can touch.

Tranquil Mind 1503
The Righteous Fight 1092
Cultivate Silence of the Mind 1239
Transformations of the Mind 1242

Mind in Body

Your body is a receptive instrument, not an originator of events.

Your body is propelled by your mind and emotions; on its own it cannot do anything.

Mind and emotion are not simply activities of the brain and nervous system

Your mind or emotions propel the life-breath within your body, which in turn activates the body. That is how you move.

The life-breath within the body is activated by mental energy or emotional force; desire or intention moves the life-current, and hence the body obeys the desire or intention.

Thus, all action is born out of desire or intention.

∞

Mind and emotion are not simply activities of the brain and nervous system as the ignorant materialists believe. The brain and nervous system simply *respond* to the vibrations of your mental body (mind) and your astral body (emotions). Your emotional (astral) body interpenetrates your etheric-physical body, and your mental body interpenetrates your emotional body. The life-force is contained in the etheric-physical body, which interpenetrates your dense body of bone, flesh, and muscles. It is important for you to be clear about this, for strength depends on it.

You may have noticed that when people are furious they have greater physical strength. This is because fury is an intense emotional vibration which activates the life-breath violently, which infuses the body with extra strength. Can you have strength with a quiet mind? This requires a different training.

You must also know that every thought and feeling *registers* on the brain and nervous system of the body, thus changing it according to the vibration or quality of the thought or feeling.

A lack of harmony in your mind and emotions produces a lack of harmony in your physical body. Mind and emotions come first, the body follows after. Learn this!

The Personality Complex 36
Mind and Brain 79
Mind and Desire 235
Consciousness 1370

Skill in Action

The Master Warriors of old had calm bodies. Why? Because they spent lots of time in calm meditations. A tranquil mind produces a tranquil body, which increases mind-body coordination and performance. An agitated mind produces an agitated body, and therefore a lack of proper coordination.

Skill in Action depends on mind-body coordination

Spend lots of time in correct meditations to produce mental tranquillity and emotional harmony. Then you will have no problem training the body.

Skill in Action depends on mind-body coordination. Anxiety, stress and fear in your mind also registers in your brain and nervous system, making your body uncoordinated. If your body is uncoordinated, you cannot have Skill in Action. So, start with your mind first.

Anxiety and fear in your mind interferes with the smooth functioning of bodily movements.

Orderly thinking creates an orderly activity in your physical body and therefore health and well-being. A chaotic mind produces chaotic responses in your brain, nervous system and bodily functions, creating ill-health and weakness.

Whatever you fill your mind with will be reflected back on the health and functioning of your body. Now you will see why the Masters of the Art of the Warrior have spent so much time in tranquillity-meditations and activities that produce harmonious emotions, such as chanting and specific breathing techniques.

Your physical body has a consciousness of its own, called the *Body-Elemental.* The sum total of the consciousnesses of the cells and atoms of your body are "supervised" by the Body-Elemental. If your mind can tune into your Body-Elemental you can learn much about your body and its "instincts"—that is, the work of the Body-Elemental, which can warn you of dangers, evil forces, wrong situations and evil people.

Mind and Body 1374
Mind and Thought 1376
Movement and the Life-force 1020
The Body-Elementals 213

Overactive Mind

To serve the King, you must still your mind

You may be one of those whose mind never stops, whose mind is always restless, active, seeking, questioning or criticizing. Or you may be one of those who is very active physically, rushing here and there, doing lots of sports, physical work or physical activities.

Balance yourself with the Heart. Seek out your Heart through right Heart meditations and *act* from there. You will notice a vast difference in your life and in your ability to serve your family, tribe, nation, and Mankind. For a true Light-Warrior is in the *Service* of the King, the Lord of the World, the Ancient of Days, the King of Kings and Lord of Lords, the Youth of Eternal Summers, the Eternal Commander of the Heavenly Armies, of the Hosts of Angels and Radiant Lords of Power, to Whom the greatest Warriors on Earth and in Heaven with trembling knees do bow down.

To *serve* the King, the Greatest Chief, you must still your mind, stop the activities of your body, become silent, still, alert. Enter your Heart-system and there *await* Instruction. For the Eternal Warrior speaks in Silence only, and leaves an imprint in your Heart, the Eternal Message of Love fulfilled in Action.

The Way of the Warrior is Action—not the action of selfish and self-centred will, but the Command of Divine Will.

Mental Activity 1228
No-Mind and the One Mind 763
The Silence of the Warrior 1008
Heart Action 1331

The 'No-Mind'

No-mind actually means "no thoughts". You cannot *not* have a "mind", for your consciousness, awareness and reasoning faculty are all "mind". Thus, when the Masters say not to have a mind when you perform an action, they mean not to have many thoughts.

Rather, your "mind" is simple, focused, clear, bright, alert, concentrated, fully in the Here and Now, on the subject of your action. You are not disturbed by panicky or irrelevant thoughts and thinking processes. You are not afraid. You are not daydreaming or wishful-thinking. Your thoughts are not in the past, nor in the future, but Now.

Your whole Conscious Awareness is in the Now, performing the action with the total concentration and attention of your Being. There are no superfluous thoughts about other things, nor even about what you are doing. You are just responding to the situation, fully focused, alert, wide awake, with the full power of your Being, from the Soul-instinct level rather than from the calculating, mental, thought-process level of your personality. You are responding from your Intelligence rather than from your normal human thinking-self level. There is a clear difference between the two when you have mastered the "No-mind".

Monks and Disciples

The Age of the monks is over. The Age of the Disciples has begun.

Monks are those who have renounced the world and turned away from worldly responsibilities, who are concerned only with their own Salvation. The Disciples live in the world and are concerned with the Spiritualization of Mankind, fighting materialism and materialistic consciousness, and showing the Way to Spiritual Freedom in the midst of the Battle of Life.

The Disciples meditate like monks but act like Warriors

The Disciples meditate like monks but act like Warriors. They unite the Inner Life with outer life, the Soul with the personality, and they harmonize the male and female within themselves and in outer life.

The Disciples work in group unity, group strength, group togetherness, not in solitary isolation as monks do. Salvation or Liberation is a group purpose, not a personal, private enterprise. Therefore, every Disciple of a Spiritual Group must do his or her utter best for the success of the Group, for the mission, plan, purpose, objective or goal of the Group, which is the Spiritualization of Mankind, the harmonizing of personalities, the balancing or equalization of male and female, and the fusion of the personality with the Soul.

Our task is the Spiritual Regeneration of the world. The Warrior School serves as a focal point for Spiritual Energies, therefore there must be group unity. Unity is strength. Disunity is weakness and chaos. It is not your personality which is important, nor the personalities of other group members. The real task is the Spiritual Regeneration of the world. To that task all personalities must be subordinated.

The Spiritual Regeneration of the world comes about by the right Teaching given to the world regarding the true nature of Man, God and the Universe. Knowledge is Power. When people correctly *know*, that Knowledge will transform their lives, and they will wean themselves away from the forces of materialism and attach themselves to the Forces of Spirit, the Forces of Light. Therefore, to give them the Esoteric Knowledge is your Task and the Task of your group of Warriors. There is no greater help you can give to any person than Enlightenment.

Do not fight with other personalities in your group of Warriors. Work together selflessly for the common good. Your reward will be Happiness, Joy and Bliss, and your group will become a pure channel for the Forces of Light and Evolution on this planet in the Service of the Regent of Light.

Group Work 1146
Qualifications for Discipleship 1149
Relational Consciousness 906
Spiritual Life and Material Life 1118
Cultivate Knowledge 1366

The Law of Action

The Law of Action is a primary Law of the Universe. All beings act, all of the time. Each action produces an effect, a result, and you receive in kind what you give out. This should be consistently taught in schools and universities! The Universe does not function by blind "chance" or "accidents".

A Spiritual Warrior cannot live by the law of hate, but by the Law of Love

Action, however, is not only physical; your feelings are subtle actions (on the Astral Plane), and your thoughts are the subtlest actions (on the Mental Plane). Each brings its own results back to you. Your physical actions are performed in your physical body; your subtle actions (feelings, desires, emotions, moods) are performed by your astral or subtle body; your thoughts and mental activities are performed by your mental body.

Violent actions, feelings and thoughts sent out by you will bring back violent actions, feelings and thoughts directed towards you. Loving actions, feelings and thoughts sent out by you will attract loving actions, feelings and thoughts towards you. Further, your Soul lives in your causal body on the Causal Plane (the formless part of the Mental Plane), and you, as a Soul, reap the results (good or bad) of the thoughts, feelings and actions of your personality. This is such a fundamental and simple Natural Law, yet hundreds of millions of people are unaware of it.

Think about it. Good actions produce beneficial results; bad actions produce evil results. Think about it and see it in life. The good results cannot be escaped, but neither can the evil results be escaped. Whenever there is evil, it is a result of bad actions—maybe by one person, or two, or three, or a family, or a tribe, or a group of people, or a nation or nations. Evil actions produce evil results, producing suffering, pain, misery, sickness and death.

Love breeds Love; hate breeds hatred. Loving kindness breeds loving kindness; antagonism breeds antagonism. Peace breeds peace; war breeds war. When will Mankind learn?

The Spiritual Warrior must have a Tranquil Mind and a Loving Heart. A Tranquil Mind and a Loving Heart are the mark of a true Spiritual Warrior. You, as a Spiritual Warrior, cannot live by the law of hate (the law of the jungle), but by the Law of Love, which is kindness, gentleness, forgiveness, generosity, tolerance, sympathy, healing, understanding and helping others.

Karma: the Law of Action 240
Creating Karma 242
Action (Karma) 1402
From Hate to Love 229

Those materialistic and religious people who live by the principle of "an eye for an eye, a tooth for a tooth" are constantly destroying themselves and the world. If millions of people live like this (by the principle of revenge, hate, war, antagonism, the law of the jungle), then that country or society suffers tremendously and will do so until they change their ways and live by the Law of Love. This Law has been taught over and over again by the great Teachers of the past, but Mankind is incredibly slow to learn!

Your actions, feelings and thoughts influence the whole world

As a person, family, tribe, nation, society or religious group lives, that is returned to them. This is the great Spiritual Law of Action. People of every religion should be taught this from a very early age until death. The evil actions done in the name of "God" by religious groups have produced much suffering for Mankind for hundreds of thousands of years, and are still doing so now, even as we write.

When will Mankind ever learn? There is a density of consciousness in the human species which is unbelievable! Yet basically the Heart of Humanity is good.

Your actions, feelings and thoughts influence the whole world. You influence your family, group, religion, culture, and political decisions also. Everybody impacts on everybody else. Therefore, what a great responsibility you have towards society, Mankind and the Universe in which you live!

Fight Evil with Good

What are *your* actions, Warrior? Are you troubled by the evil affairs of the world? Then fight evil actions with good actions, actions that produce peace, harmony, goodness, openness, tolerance, forgiveness and Love. For such is a Warrior of the Light.

Be fearless, Warrior, for if you die in the Service of the King of Life and Light, your reward is great. But if you die in the service of your own petty self or worldly powers, you will descend to hellish realms.

The greatest Warrior is the Lord of Life and Light who, in the midst of the Battle of Life, the Battle for this planet, stands firm, unshaken, invincible, unconquerable, incorruptible, impenetrable by evil powers. Our Lord and Chief *stands*, even if the whole world crumbles into dust.

Some Human Evils 384
Your Fate is Before your Eyes 246
The Supreme Act of Karma 264
The Law of the Afterlife 410

Action and the Spiritual Warrior

The most important quality for right action is Intelligence

The Way of the Warrior is Action. The Warrior cannot help but to act. Life is one big Action for the Warrior. But herein lies the problem, for your every thought, feeling and physical act produces definite results upon you, your environment, the people around you, and the invisible worlds or spheres that surround us. Thus, a single thought, feeling or physical act can have enormous consequences for you and for the whole world. Herein lies the problem of Action.

The completely materialistic people do not know this Eternal Law of the Cosmos, nor can they appreciate it. You are bound to the Universe and the Universe is bound to you. Feelings and thoughts of hatred produce violent actions in you, in your environment, in the people around you, and in the mass atmosphere of our planet, whereas feelings and thoughts of genuine Love produce Harmony in you, in your environment, in the people around you, and in the invisible realms. This is not a "goody-goody" philosophy; it is an absolute fact of Nature.

The quality of any action depends on the Intelligence of the doer, his or her mind or mental capacities, the right timing or appropriate moment for the action, the emotional energy behind it, the physical skills or equipment of the doer, and how it is tuned-in (or not) with Universal Nature, the Cosmos.

The first and most important quality for right action, for knowing what to do in any set of circumstances, is Intelligence—which has nothing at all to do with your faculty of "thinking"! Everybody "thinks", but not everybody is Intelligent.

Intelligence is *developed*.

Thinking goes on automatically all the time.

Heart Action 1331
Action in the Transcendent 1080
Karma Yoga: Divine Union by Action 1132
The Law of the Higher Life 1134
Silence and Activity 1446

Primordial Balance

The Spiritual Warrior lives by the Law of Equilibrium or Balance. The true Warrior lives a balanced life.

On the level of Pure Being (the Absolute) there is always the state of Equilibrium, Balance, Harmony. The pairs of opposites are at rest. Any action in the Cosmos disturbs this Primordial Balance, swinging it towards one of the pairs of opposites—hot or cold, good or evil, harmonious or disharmonious, pleasurable or painful, healthy or diseased, birth or death, progressive or resisting progress, and so on. In whichever direction the action is moving, Cosmic Nature seeks to redress the situation and bring it back to the Original Harmony of the Absolute Being, into Balance.

The true Warrior seeks to walk the Middle Path, between the two extremes

In every situation, the true Warrior seeks to walk the Middle Path, between the two extremes.

The Spiritual Warrior develops the state of Equilibrium by meditation, breathing practices and the *right attitude* towards life.

You, as an individual, have an impact on your environment, whether you are aware of it or not. You have an impact on your family, your group, your nation, and this is automatic.

The Wise Warrior *consciously* impacts on the environment, and with such actions that are of greatest benefit to All—not for himself or herself, not just for some favourite person, but for *all concerned*. This ability comes from having a larger Vision of the meaning of Life, a vast Understanding in the Higher States of Consciousness. The Wise Warrior acts from the state of Superconsciousness, a superior state of Being. This is *developed* through years of meditation and spiritual training.

For the Spiritual Warrior, Action is an Art—not in the degenerated sense as the word is used today, in which any abomination is called "art", but that which signifies grace, elegance, beauty, truth, harmony, proportion, skill, mastery, orderliness. This is the true meaning of Art. For the Spiritual Warrior, action is such an Art. Through *Skill in Action* the Spiritual Warrior *cultivates* truth, beauty, harmony, goodness, well-being and loving-kindness in his or her life. The Warrior lives a Cosmic Life, in Cosmic Consciousness, *aware* of his or her *responsibility* to the Cosmos.

Balance in Spiritual Life 505
The Active and Passive Way 1011
Between the Two Extremes, Find the Middle Point 1100
The Creative Soul 1692

The Three Forces of the Warrior

There are three mysterious Forces that a Spiritual Warrior can use:

a. Electric Will-Power.
b. Boundless Life-Force.
c. The Serpent-Fire, or the Dragon-Force.

These are three separate, independent Forces, coexisting within the Universe

A materialistic person will have no comprehension of these mysterious Forces, since a materialistic philosophy will simply prevent that person from comprehending invisible realities.

- True Will-Power is the Electric-Force of the Spirit. This Force is electrical in nature. When the great Spiritual Warriors of ancient times mastered the Electric Will-Power Force they had the power of unbelievable endurance, total fearlessness, and a sense of Immortality.
- True Life-Force is the Boundless Ocean of the One Life permeating every part of the Universe, both the visible and invisible realms, including the subtle worlds. This is the Soul of the World. When the great Spiritual Warriors of ancient times mastered the Life-Force they had boundless energy, enthusiasm, and a sense of direction in life and Oneness with the All. Therefore they could comprehend the Divine Plan as it moved through a particular local situation or Time-Space condition.
- The most mysterious of them all is the Serpent-Fire, or the Fiery Dragon, the Serpent-Force or Dragon-Power. This is the Female Force, the Body of the Universe, that is, the Fiery Energy locked up in the structure of matter itself, in forms or bodies. When the great Spiritual Warriors of ancient times mastered the Serpent-Power they possessed many miraculous powers, such as the ability to fly through the air when they leapt up, incredible strength, and the overwhelming feeling of invincibility.

These are three separate, independent Forces, coexisting within the Universe, operating independently from one another, and a Warrior may master any one of them, or two of them, or all three of them.

The Three Gates to God 151
The Holy Trinity 1342
The Kuṇḍalinī Fire 132
Dimensions of the Cosmic Fire 137
The Thread of the Self 491

We are not talking here of some theory, hypothesis, wishful thinking or philosophy; these three Forces are real! They are invisible Forces coming from the Invisible Worlds, or rather, they are drawn down from the Invisible Worlds into this visible Physical World and used here. Don't forget that the Great Invisible is all *around* us and *inside* us, all the time. All of the time!

The Great Invisible is all around us and inside us, all the time

- The most easily attained "supernatural" power (which is not really supernatural) is the first Force of the Warrior, that of the true Will-Power, because most true Warriors are born with it to a certain degree, and this inborn quality can be increased by self-discipline and hard training, perseverance and effort. This includes the field of martial arts training.
- The second Force, the Boundless Life-Force, is contacted through meditation, breathing exercises, sound work, and opening up the Heart Centre.
- The most difficult Force to master is the Serpent-Fire, the Dragon-Force. When mastered, however, this Force gives all the miraculous powers to the Warrior. The Fiery Dragon or Serpent-Fire is a devastating Force and it should never be awakened until the second Force, the Life-Force, has been totally controlled and mastered, and through it Universal Compassion and Wisdom have been attained.

If a Warrior awakens the sleeping Dragon-Fire, the Fiery Serpent, before he has developed the Universal Wisdom and Compassion through the Universal Life-Force, that Warrior will become a devastating Warrior with tremendous occult powers but with no Wisdom to guide him, and the consequences for the Warrior and for the environment (the area, society and life around the Warrior) could be immense devastation and suffering. That is, without the Universal Wisdom and Compassion the Warrior will fight on the wrong side, for the wrong causes, helping the dark side of the Force instead of Those who fight for the cause of Light, for progress, evolution and the Divine Plan.

When Kuṇḍalinī Awakens 157
Awaken First the Heart 428
Beyond the Will 429
Magic: White and Black 364
Awakening the Serpent-Fire 1038

Family and Duty

In most cases your family ties are due to your previous incarnations with members of your family. Sometimes, however, new connections are made.

Your family is a small group of Souls having its own destiny, and the Spiritual Group you belong to is another group of Souls with another destiny. Your Teacher, the Disciples of the Teacher, and your Warrior Comrades are your Spiritual Family. Your Spiritual Family travels along a different Path (except those members of your family who might also be Warriors or Disciples of the Teacher).

Be independent of your family, yet love them deeply and serve them as best you can

Ancient family ties may hinder your progress in Spirituality if you cannot understand the proper place of family in your life. Your family is an opportunity for Service; you can help this group of Souls with your Spiritual Radiance, Knowledge, Strength and Love. Thus, instead of the ancient ties pulling you down, you will lift them up.

Be independent of your family, yet love them deeply and serve them as best you can. If you can aid them to enter upon the Spiritual Path, you have done the best for them.

The Goal of every Human Soul is to become Spiritual. Help them.

The Destiny of the human personality is to become Enlightened by the Light of the Soul. Help your children to achieve this.

The Law of Cyclic Activity 248
Punarjanma: Reincarnation 249
The Law of Death 398
From Bondage to Liberation 422

Reincarnation and Freedom

The Law of Reincarnation or Rebirth is a natural Law. It affects not only the Human Kingdom, but all the Kingdoms of Nature.

Everything comes and goes in cycles:

- Spring, summer, autumn, winter, then spring again.
- The ocean tides come in, go out, and come in again.
- The planets circle around the Sun in regular cycles.
- The suns circle around in rhythm within a greater star system.
- The Universe comes and goes in cycles, Cosmic Cycles. This Universe is not the first, nor the last, but just one of the Cosmic Cycles.
- Your breath also is in cycles.

Things begin, move away, and return to their origin, thus completing a cycle of rebirth. And so Man is born, grows up, grows old and dies, and is born again to a new cycle of life and death. This will be so until you overcome Nature, until you rise *above* the powers of Nature. Only when you break your ties with Nature can you break out of the cyclic whirl of things, into the Everlastingness of Spirit. Time also moves in cycles—Past, Present and Future—but the Spirit is Timeless, Eternal.

All growth and movement in the Cosmos is cyclic, under the Law of the Universal Reincarnatory Process. But when you return to the Centre of your Being, which is Silence, Stillness, Harmony, you will become Free.

Duty is the greatest virtue of the Warrior. Since time immemorial the Warrior has been guided by Duty—Duty to family and friends, to other Warriors, to king and country, and to the Spiritual Teacher or Guide who gave the Light of Understanding to the Warrior. It is fulfilment of Duty which gives the Warrior the quality of Nobility.

A true Warrior is not a monk. A Warrior lives in the world. Be careful: being in the world does not mean that you become worldly. Although you are in the world, your Heart is anchored in the Spirit and your mind is illumined by the Light of your Soul. Your Duty to society is to perfect it the best way you can and to fight evil which wants to stop the progress of Humanity, which ever seeks to bring forth the Dark Ages of Ignorance and the slavery of Mankind.

It is fulfilment of Duty which gives the Warrior the quality of Nobility

The immediate Goal for Humanity is the development of right relationships between its various members. This starts at the family level, spreads to business and workplace, to society, to country, between countries, and to the whole planet. Thus, to help and protect your family is a duty of the Warrior, and you do this in perfect freedom of understanding, not just because you are "supposed" to do so.

To have right-relationship at home you must be Heart-centred. That is, you must function from the Awakened Heart. There is a fashion today among psychologists and sociologists to devise all kinds of intellectual, dry, analytical, cold, mental theories of how human beings should behave towards one another. Without the Awakened Heart, however, all of that is futile and a waste of time, for only the Heart can unite. The mind divides, criticizes, separates people, while the Heart has the quality of sympathy, empathy, tolerance, understanding and true Love. Thus, right relationships can be established only at the Heart level, including group relationships such as your own group of Warriors. Deal with all relationships from your Heart.

There are many tests and difficulties in all relationships: between man and woman, parent and child, relatives, friends, workmates, and your relationships with other Pilgrims on the Way. But the principle is always the same: the Heart.

The solution is always in the Heart. Try it!

Return to Duty 812
Duty and Spirituality 1641
You have two families 1156
The Breakdown of Family 473
Nourishing the Goal of Life 487
Towards Group-Consciousness 186
From Head to Heart 427

Where do you go from here?
Is there a Plan in your Life?

What you do Now determines what you will become

The Goal of Human Evolution is:

1. **Awakening** to the Divine Presence in the Heart Centre, experiencing the Divine Love in the Heart, and its practical consequence of compassionate and loving actions in daily life towards all Mankind and all kingdoms of Nature.
2. **Illumination** of the mind in the Third-Eye Centre by the Divine Mind, which is Pure Light, resulting in the Wisdom and Understanding of Life and the Purpose and Plan of Creation.
3. **The Magic** of the Divine-Will manifestations in the Crown Centre at the top of the head, which are miracles, transformations and transmutations of human nature into Divine Beingness.

Is your life purposeful? What is your purpose? Is it according to the Divine Plan, the Goal for Mankind? Where are you in your Plan? Have you awakened the Heart of Love within you? Is your mind illumined by the Divine Light? Have you become a pure channel for the miraculous possibilities of your Soul-Nature manifesting through your Crown Centre? This is your Goal or Work in life: *responsiveness to spiritual influences.*

The totality of your past lives created your present personality. You are the *result* of your Past.

Your Future is open-ended, and what you do Now, in the Moment, today, determines what you will become.

So, work to the Plan. ≭

Success is Born of Action 256
The Principle of Choice 1380
Time and Eternity: Action and Destiny 1399

CHAPTER 46

Warrior Training

The Warrior Path

These are the means of training for a Spiritual Warrior:

1. Meditation.
2. Breathing.
3. Silence.
4. Sound.
5. Physical action (physical training).
6. Serious study of the Esoteric Tradition.
7. Study and practice of the Spiritual Warrior Code (Aphorisms).

The purpose of meditation is to establish Soul-contact

Meditation

The purpose of meditation is to establish Soul-contact, followed by the integration of the Soul with the personality, and then the fusion of the personality-Soul with the Spirit, the Divine Nature inherent in all men, women and children, in all of Nature and in the whole Cosmos.

Breathing

Various types of breathing exercises help you to control the mind, strengthen the body, increase the Life-force, integrate body and mind, and harmonize yourself with Nature, both inner and outer.

Silence

The practices of Silence bring about purification of the personal self, to help in Soul-contact, to neutralize the impact of the environment upon your subconscious mind, and hence to help you attain Inner Freedom (which is a mark of the Spiritual Warrior), and to harmonize body with mind, and mind with Soul.

Sound

The purpose of working with Sound-structures is to increase your Soul-force, to direct energies, to awaken hidden powers and potentials within you, to harmonize mind and Heart, and to link you up with the inner, invisible realms of Being.

Meditation is Integration 1193
Warrior Breathing 1020
The Silence of the Warrior 1008
The Primordial Sound Language 1025
The Warrior Code 1077

Physical Action

This physical action includes all the various forms of martial arts and bodily training. The purpose of physical action is transformation, to develop within you the following abilities:

- To respond to impacts from your environment in a holistic, cohesive way.
- To respond correctly to the need and urgency of the Moment.
- To flow in the Moment, this Flow being directed spontaneously from *within,* rather than from the calculating, reasoning mind.
- To act in and from Inner Freedom, spontaneously, not hindered by tradition, set forms, culture, rules, regulations, established patterns, past habits and formulas.
- To suspend and overcome limitations.

The purpose of physical action is transformation

The entire physical training of the Warrior is directed towards these ends. Physical action helps you to overcome "tradition", which normally hinders the flow of the Life-force in the Moment. Or, to put it another way, God is ever new Joy, or, the Divine impacts upon the world moment by moment.

The Four Degrees of Knowledge

1. Secular or worldly knowledge
This includes everything you learn at school or university, or at any worldly educational institution.

2. Religious knowledge
This includes rituals, rites or ceremonies administered by the priestcraft for various religious purposes, such as birth, death or marriage, purification rituals, various celebrations of the cyclic procession of time, the seasons, and so forth.

3. Magical knowledge
This can be white magic, black magic or grey magic. It includes the various forms of alternative healing arts, mediumship, spiritism, ancestral worship, communion with the dead, witchcraft, and so forth.

4. The Warrior Knowledge
This is also known as the Kingly Science or Royal Knowledge. It is the Knowledge of the true Spiritual Warrior. This Knowledge does not belong to a particular tribe, race, culture or religion. Its Initiates are beyond all limitations of tribal or national cultures or particular religious creeds. These mighty Spiritual Warriors have inspired countless generations in many lands on all parts of the planet. These Warriors explored the true Mysteries of Existence and found the answers.

Heart Action 1331
True Thought 79
Esoteric Knowledge 1218
Heart Knowing 1286
Cultivate Knowledge 1366

To Enter the Way of the Warrior

Before you can enter the Way of the Warrior, you must have an open mind and an open Heart. You must be willing to learn, nay, *want* to learn the answers to these questions:

- Who am I?
- Why I am here on this planet?
- Is there a meaning to life?
- Why are there conflicts between people, and how can I resolve them?
- What is a True Warrior? Is mere fighting or fighting skills a sign of being a True Warrior, or is there something besides, such as an invisible Field of Power, Knowledge, Wisdom and Love that the True Warrior can tap into and release for the benefit of All?
- What happens after death? Is death the end to it all? Or is there a graded series of worlds where the Soul sojourns after the casting off of the veil of flesh? And how do you get to the Radiant Worlds of Light and Bliss?

Within you already shines with splendid Glory the true Warrior

These are some of the questions answered, along with many others, as you step upon the Path of the Warrior and complete your training. The Way means a life-transformation, a Heart and mind transformation, a vast transformation of your personal self beyond your wildest dreams. For within you already shines with splendid Glory the true Warrior, but you need to learn the techniques, the skills to meet him, to *become* him.

Look out for the One...

For the Spiritual Warrior, the greatest enemy is not outside but *within* yourself. It is the limited, *conditioned* self that you must conquer before anything else. You must be prepared to *learn* from whatever source you can. Do not be proud. You do not have all Wisdom. Not you, nor your family, nor your tribe, nor your nation, nor your culture, nor your religion, have all the Wisdom. Look out for the One who can teach you. Being taught by a Spiritual Teacher is not your "right", it is a privilege. It is a gift from the Teacher to you.

Living Guidance 339

Qualifications for Discipleship 1149
Death and Liberation 397
The Aquarian Teachers 1147
The Approach to Truth 1152

Integrity and Perfection

Before you can make any further progress, you have to attain integrity in the state you are in.

This is a Warrior Principle and a very practical one. Integrity means "wholeness, soundness, completeness, an unbroken state or condition, entire, unimpaired, perfection, honesty, uprightness, sincerity, a sense of morality, virtuous behaviour".

You have to practise everything until you achieve perfection

There are two aspects to this Warrior Principle: first there is *wholeness*, and then there is the natural *morality* or *goodness* that comes out of it. It means that you have to practise everything until you reach perfection, whether it be meditation, sound-work, silence, breathing exercises, or physical techniques and bodily movements.

Perfection in a process will give you a sense of well-being, or wholeness, through which you will naturally feel good about yourself, and therefore in harmony with your surroundings, and therefore well disposed towards others.

This "state you are in" is your present condition. It means any particular process or technique, and your whole life as well. It is because you have not reached perfection in your present situation that it is difficult for you to move on.

The Law of your Being 976

The Practice of Grounding

Sit in your favourite meditation posture, with your eyes closed, and focus your attention into the Base Centre, at the bottom of your spine. Think of the word "Grounding", the idea of Grounding—to come to rock bottom, the foundation, the roots. Think of your connection with Earth, the ground you are sitting on. Make contact in your consciousness with the physical Earth. Feel the solid Earth underneath you. If you can, feel the energies of Earth beneath you. This way you will develop a sense of security and steadiness in the world and in your life, and a strong survival instinct. This is not an intellectual exercise; your mind must be calm, simply focused, aware, with no extraneous thoughts. You may also use the word **LĀṀ**, intoned silently in your mind at the Base Centre. (The word LĀṀ means Earth.)

Internalizing the Semi-Vowels 1044
Personality Integration Chart 1333
The Bīja-Mantra Lāṁ 1544

The Structure of the Warrior School

The proper structure for a Warrior School is as follows:

Members of a proper Warrior School must be progressive

The One

The *One* is the Source, the Inspiration, the Knower of the Plan. This is represented by the Teacher, the Sage, who is universal, not bound by tradition or culture or time or space.

The Two

The *Two* see duality, opposites, polarity, good and bad. They understand the cause of enmity and conflict, and they embrace the inspiration and objectives of the *One*.

The Three

The *Three* seek balance, the resolution to opposition and conflict. "The Warrior seeks Peace, not War". This is represented by the *Two*, along with a third person who is progressive, open-minded, willing to learn, and willing to evolve spiritually.

The Seven

The *Seven* are the backbone of the Warrior School. They work under the *Three*. They are the foundation, the pillars upon which the Warrior School rests. They have to be solid, trustworthy.

The Twenty-One

The *Twenty-One* are the body of the School, the building blocks. They work under the *Seven* who work under the *Three*, who work under the *Two*, who work under the *One*. They have to be loyal and they form the Protector Shield.

The Many

From here the Warrior School can be extended to many classes, many locations, many peoples, many grades and levels of the Teaching, including people from the community who are interested in the aims and objectives of the Warrior School as a Spiritual Path.

Members of a proper Warrior School must be *progressive*, not bound or limited by past tradition. Past tradition is very limited owing to the fact that it becomes crystallized and the inner Warrior Knowledge is lost. The Sage can only work with open-minded and

The Sage 973
Monks and Disciples 991
The Mystery Schools and Āśramas 1148
Traditionis 379

open-hearted people who understand the need to recover the Warrior Knowledge—which is more than just fighting skills.

It is very important that they have not been involved in witchcraft, magic or psychism and are not connected to deceased people whom they call upon, as any psychic disturbance will throw them off the Path and be a danger to the School for Warriors.

It is also important that they do not mix up mythology with facts. Myths, legends, mythologies are for children; facts are for grown up people. All tribes and nations have mythologies and legends about their Heroes, their founders or ancestors. Most of it is exaggerated imagination, elaboration or wishful thinking. Many tribes, nations and religions think that these myths are the sacred "facts".

The Teacher distinguishes facts from legends

The Teacher, or Sage, distinguishes facts from legends, and the true greatness of a Spiritual Warrior, the true Hero, from the popular "warriors" and "heroes" of the masses who, in most cases, were simply enjoying fighting and killing. The true Hero is very rare and is the noblest of the noblest, the greatest of the greatest of Mankind.

What is Initiation?

Initiation is a recognition of the *attainment* of something, which allows the initiated one to start a new beginning, a new venture, a new enterprise, a new state of Being.

Initiation is very ancient and has been used by every religion and culture since the beginning of Consciousness on this planet. There are many forms of Initiation, greater and lesser, according to the evolutionary development of the one to be initiated.

Initiation can take place in many forms: with or without an outer ritual, silently or aloud, with a Word of Power or without it, on the Physical Plane or in the Inner Worlds, verbally or by mind-to-mind transmission, on the personality level or on the Soul level.

You can be initiated by a Living Teacher in a physical body, or by your Soul, or by the Spiritual Hierarchy of the Invisible Worlds.

Initiation is a transmission of Energy of a particular type which allows for further development along a line. There are many types of Energy in the Universe.

Initiation is the unfolding of a new type of consciousness or awareness within you, allowing you to have new powers and abilities, and new states of Being.

Truth and Mythology 7
Where are the Heroes of old? 274
Where are your Wisemen? 387
Causes of Group Disruption 1154
The True Teachers 1694

The Silence of the Warrior

The Spiritual Warrior spends a lot of time in Silence—Silence within himself and in silent places, in Nature, away from the crowds.

Why does a Warrior need Silence? Silence is the natural state of your mind. When you return to Silence within yourself, it feels as if you have returned Home, to your base, to your true Self.

When you choose an action with an agitated mind, it is bound to be wrong

Mental activity agitates your mind. After you have been in true Silence within, you will experience mental activity as disturbing Inner Harmony and Peace, and you will wonder why people are endlessly "thinking", relentlessly churning out ideas which disturb their Inner Poise, Balance and Peace.

Inner Stillness gives you Poise, Balance and Peace. It is the source of Harmony within you, and therefore the Power to choose correctly in a situation. When you choose an action with an agitated mind, it is bound to be wrong.

Because of your over-active mind, Silence does not come by itself. Silence within you needs to be *cultivated*. You cultivate Silence by taking as many opportunities as you can in a day just to be Still.

Connecting to the Silent Source of Creation

The practice of Silence is vital for a person who wants to become a true Spiritual Warrior. It covers many aspects:

- Not criticizing others.
- Speaking no ill of others and not communicating or spreading evil gossip about a person.
- Spending time in periods of Silence, which means no talking and no thinking, just being in Silence with yourself and with your environment. This practice can be done in your own private room or in Nature, but not for long periods—a half hour or one hour at a time, otherwise you will become too passive.
- Group Silence. This is group-activity done in Silence. This fuses the group energy into a subtle, constructive force-field.
- The Silence of deep meditation. This is transcending the three lower realms of Creation into the Eternal.

Zen Silence 790
The 'No-Mind' 990
Stillness before Battle 1095
Cultivate Silence of the Mind 1239
The Silence of the Deep 1355
The Practice of Silence 1443
The Evil of Criticism 1156

Cosmic Sensitivity

The ONE is the Unity-Field of Being in which all opposites and polarities take place simultaneously, mutually interdependent and in Harmony with each other. This Unity-Field is the Cosmic Force of Love, *God's Love.*

We need to develop sensitivity to the Feminine aspect, as the world is too Masculine-oriented and unbalanced. Through the correct balancing out of the Male and Female forces and energies comes Health, Harmony and Perfection.

When the Male and Female are in perfect Balance within us, then is the state of TAO: Oneness, Unity, Divinity.

Love is the Law 25
The Law of Polarity 164
Yin, Yang, Tao 476
What is Tao? 772
The One 1686

POLARITY
The Creative Process

Feminine	Masculine
Heart Centre	Head Centre
Subconscious Mind	Rational, logical mind
Female of the species	Male of the species
Astral Plane	Mental Plane
Feelings, emotions, desires	Thoughts, ideas, mental constructs
Buddhic Plane (the World of Unity)	Nirvāṇic Plane (the World of Origins)
Passivity, Sensing	Action, Describing
Receptivity, Attraction	Dynamism, Repulsion
Stillness	Sound
Female Potentialities and Powers	Male Potentialities and Powers
Negative	Positive

The ONE

The Unity-Field of Being

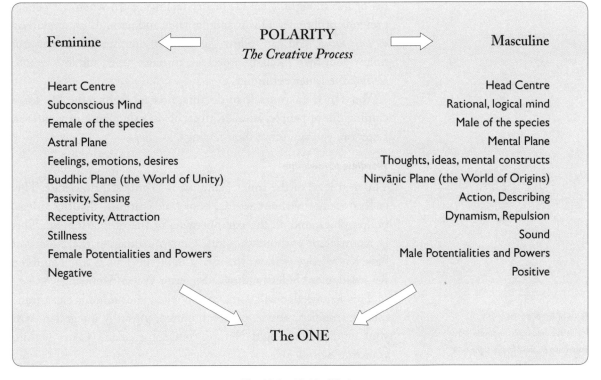

Getting in Touch with your Inner Feminine

To *consciously* get in touch with your Inner Feminine you must become passive, silent, reflective, receptive, open to the invisible atmosphere around you and inside you. You must cultivate inner Silence, Stillness, and a motionless mind. An overactive mind cannot register the impressions coming to you from the Inner Feminine. The Inner Feminine is a sure Guide if you can follow It.

The Inner Feminine is a sure Guide if you can follow It

Instinct

Instinct is the lowest manifestation of your Inner Feminine. This is primeval and ancient. Instinct will warn you of danger, or that something is not right in your environment or not right with a person. Obey it. Do not use your "rational" mind to override it or you will regret it later.

Telepathic Feeling

The next level of the workings of the Inner Feminine is psychic ability, that is, when you can read another person's mind, pick up his or her thoughts, feel his or her feelings, even when the person pretends otherwise. This is spontaneous and natural, *not a construct of your mind*. You can follow the mind of another just as you can follow your own thought-processes, through inner, subtle *telepathic feeling*, the Inner Feminine.

You can train yourself to do this, first by feeling the life-force coming out of people, animals, trees, birds, fish, plants, or whatever. Later on, you can sense their feelings.

Wordless Knowledge

The next level of the Inner Feminine is Wordless Knowledge. This is Knowledge without words, books, definitions, theories, ideas, philosophies, and all the paraphernalia of the ordinary mind. This is Knowledge without thought. Can you imagine that? Do you have Knowledge without the use of thought? This is true Feminine Knowledge or Understanding, a Superior Way of Knowing.

This Knowledge will come to you when your mind is clear, tranquil, untroubled, serene, peaceful, united, inwardly integrated with your fundamental Light-Nature, your Imperishable Glory within, your true Self.

Types of Telepathy 346
Intellectus, Intuitionis, Inspiratio 375
Inspiration by the Mind of Light 1113
Super-Knowing 1242

This Knowledge is the experiencing of your mind in its pure, original form, before it became polluted and confused by objects of the outside world. What is your mind like when it has no objects of thought in it?

Spiritual Intuition

The next level of the Inner Feminine is Realization, or Intuitive-Consciousness. This is *not* what is commonly called "intuition", which the ignorant use for the word "instinct". This is infinitely higher than instinct. It may be called *Spiritual Intuition*. It is a Field of Unity-Consciousness wherein all things are One. This Oneness is perceived as Feminine in nature.

What is your mind like when it has no objects of thought in it?

This Feminine Consciousness is above your personality level. It is the Source of Revelation and the direct Knowledge of Reality, of Man, God and the Universe.

The Active and Passive Way

The Way of the Spiritual Warrior is a combination of the Contemplative Life and Active Life.

This means being established in the Transcendent, yet active with full Consciousness in this ever-changing, impermanent, temporary world.

The Way is both active and passive.

Meditation, breathing exercises, silence, sound-work and the study of the Esoteric Tradition enable you to contact and establish yourself in the Transcendent, the Eternal, the Real.

Physical action (physical training) and the practice of the Warrior Code, or Warrior Aphorisms, are for your active life in this world, in the world of ever-changing and passing events, unstable currents, states and situations.

The Way is both, experienced not separately but simultaneously.

It is important that you understand this if you want to become a Spiritual Warrior. This is the unique state or condition of a true Spiritual Warrior:

The Inner Silence fused with the outer noise of the world.
The Stillness of the Eternal swiftly expressed in irresistible motion.

This is the Warrior.

What is Intuition? 328
Balance in Spiritual Life 505
Relational Consciousness 906
Saints of Action 1134
Silence and Activity 1446
The Twofold Way 1465

Meditation and the Joy of Living

The Kingdom of Happiness lies within us, but most people do not know about it, nor do they know how to access it. Meditation is the Path to discovery of this lost Kingdom and the Bliss therein.

Meditation is the Path to discovery of this lost Kingdom

Most people try to find happiness in objects and things outside themselves, which may give some temporary satisfaction, but which later turn sour or disappointing. Is there a permanent Joy, Happiness, Satisfaction, which does not fade away, which does not wear out, which does not disappear?

The answer lies in the discovery of the Self, the Eternally Blissful Original State within us. This can be contacted only through the Science and Art of Meditation, the regular practice of which gives you ever more Peace, Joy, Calmness, and leads you to the ultimate discovery of who You really are, the Bright Eternal Spirit who shines by its own Light in the Realms of Eternal Bliss and Joy, forever and ever. This is known as Self-Discovery or Self-Realization.

It is an error to think that you are merely your physical body. It is error to think that you are your "psychological self", that is, your personal make-up and characteristics, your personal sense of "I". All these things are simply coverings over the Real, the true Self that you are: the Eternal Soul and the Boundless Spirit.

Before you can meditate, you need to understand why you should want to meditate.

The Goal of Meditation is the Eternal, the Transcendent, the Absolute, the Godhead, the Truth (many words for the same Reality).

Today in the Western World the idea of meditation has been degenerated by materialistic thinking. Materialists think that meditation is about simple bodily changes. People are taught to meditate to reduce the stress of living, to increase work output, to study better, to get better jobs or better grades, to improve physical health, longevity, and so on. The Transcendent, the Real, is simply forgotten in the effort to have a better physical life, relaxation, or a healthier physical body.

This is like trying to breathe without air. This is a great betrayal of the noble purpose of meditation. The true purpose of meditation is to increase Spirituality, the Spiritual Condition, not the materiality in Man and in society.

Happiness Exists Within 1381
In Search of Reality 1174
Entering the Lost Kingdom 1176
Meditation Degenerated 1180
The Work of Meditation 1440

Your life will become more joyous the more you are in touch with the Spirit, the Real, the Eternal, the Being of the Universe and Yourself. This can be done only through the right kinds of meditation. Merely "thinking" about God, or the Transcendent, or Being, or the Absolute, or the true Self, will not lead you there. Nor will psychology, philosophy, education, metaphysics, religion, science, politics or social revolutions, which rely merely on "thinking" about things, or ideas, or the Truth. No amount of "thinking" will lead you there, no matter what kind of "thinking". This is why the Kingdom of God is closed to the hundreds of millions of people.

No amount of thinking will lead you there

By correct practice, stop "thinking", and the gates to Bliss, Joy and Happiness will be open for you. The Joy of Living, the Joy *in* Living, is already inside you. As a human being (of the Man-species) it is your true Nature, but the process of endless "thinking" prevents you from experiencing it. This is a simple fact, but with great consequences.

Thinking has its function in relationship to this world, but it has no function at all in the True, the Eternal, the Ever-Blissful.

How to find Peace and Joy through Meditation

Peace comes when all the warring feelings, emotions, desires and hopes are absorbed in the Radiance of the Heart.

Joy comes when you have definitely managed to link up with your Soul and the Divine Self within you, your Lord and Master in your Heart, and you know that you are "walking with God"—that is, you feel the Divine Presence in your life.

Happiness comes when your mind (head) is at rest, when your thoughts have settled down, when there is no more conceptual-thinking-activity in your mind, when there is no more "striving" in your mind to attain this or that, when you are no longer influenced by your own thoughts or the thoughts of others, when your mind is at rest in the Ultimate Reality.

Bliss is the direct experience of Reality, beyond words, ideas, concepts and the mind, in a No-mind State, in a Transcendental Consciousness in which the Self is the All, and All is the Self, and your little ego (your normal "self") has died.

For meditation to have real meaning in your life, you have to have the *right view* of life. You have to know that you are more than your physical body, that the world is more than what it appears to be, and that there is a Goal or Plan of Evolution that you must undertake.

Towards Bliss-Consciousness 423
Return to Primeval Happiness 1179
How to have a Peaceful Mind 1244
The Way to Bliss-Consciousness 1246
Peace of Heart 1595

Resting in the No-Mind State of the Absolute

A Passive Meditation Form

This is a most important practice for the would-be Spiritual Warrior. It has infinite ramifications.

Resting means that you do not do anything

Resting...

No-mind State...

The Absolute...

Resting means that you do not *do* anything. Your personality-ego is at *rest* (which normally is full of emotions, thoughts, plans, desires, ambitions and aggression).

No-mind State means that your mind is disengaged from activity, from striving, seeking, planning, manoeuvring, calculating, and manipulating the situations of your life.

The Absolute means the Boundless All, the Universal Life, the One Self of the Universe, the Infinite Mind, the Root, Source and Foundation of All that exists in the Cosmos. It is *your own* Source, Life and Original Condition, from which you *descended*, and to which you will return upon the completion of your true Warrior training, when you have become a Warrior of the Light.

Each of these three—Resting, No-mind State, the Absolute—will have ever new and profound meaning for you as you progress upon the Path of the Warrior.

∞

The *'No-Mind'* 990
No-Mind and the One Mind 763
Clouds of Unknowing 704
Suspended Mind 1209
What is Reality? 1175

Stage One (sitting meditation)

Begin as you are, at whatever stage of Spiritual Evolution you have reached. Sit down in a meditation-posture, on a chair, on the floor, on the ground outside, in Nature, wherever you will. You may also take any of the cross-legged positions or sitting-on-the-heel positions. Close your eyes and *rest*.

Stage Two

You can be at rest in the Absolute, and yet spontaneously act without an ego

As you develop yourself through meditation, breathing, silence and sound-work, you will experience periods of the No-mind State. You will experience an intense Stillness and Quiet in your mind, and a sense of all-enveloping Peace. Space will appear to be open and infinite, and you will begin to sense, with interior faculties, the Universal Life all around you. This is the No-mind State.

Stage Three

As you progress further in the process of Inner Development of the Warrior, you will begin to sense or have glimpses of the Absolute Condition, the Divine Condition, the truly Holy and Sacred. You will notice that things actually begin inward and move outwards into manifestation. You will sense Inner Guidance and you will sense that there is a Plan, Purpose and Direction in your life and in the life of Humanity, of our planet and the Cosmos in which we all live. The Divine is hidden inside All and is seeking to manifest the great Plan. You will sense Light everywhere with your super-sensory senses, and you will sense that this Light is the Guiding Force of the Universe.

Stage Four

In this state, "Resting in the No-mind State of the Absolute", you have *merged* the Inner and the Outer, the Active and the Passive, Motion and Stillness, Silence and Sound, Infinite Space and local conditioning, human nature and Divinity. You can be *at rest* in the Absolute, in Infinity, and yet *spontaneously act* without an ego, for the Good of All, without disturbing your Inner Harmony. You have reached a cohesion between Action and Non-Action, a poise between Inner Life and outer life, between Heaven and Earth, between God and Man. You have become a Spiritual Warrior, a Warrior of the Light, in Service of the King, the Invisible Regent of our planet, the Awesome Warrior of Irresistible Light.

The Law of the Higher Life 1134
God-Consciousness is the Wholeness of Life 504
The Warrior of the Light 984

From Action into Stillness
From Stillness into Action

Before action, return into Stillness. From Stillness, go into action. This is balancing out the active and passive principles and it makes all the difference.

The Way is in still-action and active-stillness

The Way is in between, in the middle, in still-action and active-stillness. This is the Hidden Way, the Concealed Road, the Secret Path, like your breath when it is neither going out nor coming in, nor is it restrained. Then is the Moment—the Way, the Truth and the Life—which is timeless, eternal and harmonized.

The Way of the Warrior is Watchful Alertness: Alertness in Action, Alertness in Stillness; Watchfulness in Motion, Watchfulness in Meditation.

The Warrior is an Observer of Life, an Observer of people, events, feelings and thoughts.

The Warrior is the Watcher of his or her own feelings, thoughts, impulses, desires and actions.

The mind of the Warrior is ever Awake, Alert, Watchful, watching inwardly (thoughts, desires, feelings) and outwardly (actions, plans, purposes, people and events).

When the mind is totally Awake, there comes Stillness, Silence and Peace, and then all actions are Powerful.

Remember that everything always begins from the point of Stillness or Silence within you. You must be Still, Silent, before you even move an inch. This is why you need to develop Stillness first, before any Action.

Now, apply this Principle to your life. The life of a Spiritual Warrior is based on Silence, Stillness, Aloneness, Solitude, attunement with Nature and the Cosmos and within himself or herself, and then moving into Action according to the appropriateness of the Moment.

When the Mind is Still 768
Stillness before Battle 1095
Action and Stillness: the Supreme Way 1083
Karma Yoga: Divine Union by Action 1132
Silence, Solitude, Peace 1386
Silence and Activity 1446

Mindfulness

The Warrior Within

1

Sit in your meditation posture. With your eyes closed, calmly watch what goes on in your mind, in your feelings, in your body and in your environment (you "sense" the environment around you). The Warrior Within watches and observes. This Observation includes everything: your thoughts, feelings, moods, breathing, body, and the space around you (with your eyes closed). Your Awareness is passive, choiceless, non-judgmental; it is simply being Aware of everything, as if you are ready for action, but without doing anything. It is simply Awareness that registers how things are in the Moment, in you and around you.

The Warrior Within watches and observes

2

Standing with your feet slightly apart and your eyes closed, take hold of your weapon. Hold it in front of you, at the level of your chest and head. Practise Mindfulness as above. What difference does it make to have your weapon in your hand?

3

Execute slow physical movements while practising Mindfulness as above. What difference does it make to your Mindfulness that you are in a state of motion?

Take your weapon and move it slowly, while practising Mindfulness. This means that you are Aware of everything (as in the first practice, above), while at the same time you are aware of the movement of your weapon. What difference does this make to your Mindfulness?

4

In the next exercise of Mindfulness, you practise fast movements physically. Can you still be Aware, in the state of Mindfulness?

5

In the next stage you practise Mindfulness with your weapon moving fast, swiftly, precisely. Can you still be completely in the state of Mindfulness?

Mindfulness is the moment-by-moment Awareness of your mental, emotional and physical states of being. This is a most important practice for the would-be Spiritual Warrior. This Awareness is practised by the Warrior within you. At first it is extremely difficult, but it becomes a habit for the accomplished Warrior.

Vipaśyanā Yoga 1222
Awareness Meditation 1656

Open-Eyes Meditations for the Warrior

Just Sitting

Sit in your favourite meditation posture. Keep your eyes open and look at a spot a few feet in front of you. Just *sit.* Your attention is in the body, on the body; you are aware of your whole body as it rests on the ground or chair. You are concentrating on your posture, relaxed but fully alert. If thoughts or feelings come, let them come and go, but do not act on them or follow them or fight them. Be aware of your environment also, the space around you, remaining relaxed but alert. This is being Here and Now, using the physical body as the Point of Awareness. You don't have to *do* anything—just sit.

Just Breathing

Sit in your favourite meditation posture, keeping your eyes open all the time. Focus your attention in your Solar Plexus Centre, the seat of your emotions and your astral body (the body of feelings). Breathe in slowly into your solar plexus, Sō, and breathe out slowly, HĀNG. Focus totally on your breathing cycle, in and out. Let thoughts and emotions subside into the breathing process. Think neither of the Past nor of the Future. Be Here and Now. That is all you have to do: breathe in and breathe out, keeping your attention in the solar plexus. Practise this for a while and you will have *calm confidence* in yourself.

Controlling the Mind through Breathing 1059
Rest in the Great Breath 1654

Just Seeing

Sit in your favourite meditation posture with your eyes open. Look in front of you, either a short distance or a long distance, or see generally all around. Your eyes should not be roving, nor should they be fixed. Just *see,* with your mind relaxed, with no mental chattering and commentary, with mind and emotions *still.* Do not analyse or interpret what you see, nor daydream. You do not need to do anything else—just *see,* with your mind *alert.*

Just Hearing

With your eyes open and focused slightly in front of you or towards the ground, just *hear.* Your mind is calm and silent, with no thoughts or commentaries interfering. Just directly experience hearing all the sounds you hear, that is all.

Just Doing

When you are doing something, you are Aware that you are doing it, that is all. In all circumstances you do what *needs* to be done, what is *essentially right* in the situation. You experience the good and the bad, the pleasant and the unpleasant, the joys and the vicissitudes, the positives and negatives, *just doing.*

Quietly Seeing 786
Zen Listening 787
Heart Action 1331

Meditation in Action

Exercise 1

This practice can be done fully and correctly only when you can function in Transcendental Consciousness. It is *Spontaneous Action as required by the Moment*, with no previous planning of attack or defence, with no ego involved, with no fear of life, death or pain, with no thought of loss or victory. It is *Action flowing from Higher Consciousness without judgment*, without concern for consequences or results.

In this Unitive State your ordinary, wakeful, self-conscious mind is non-functional, quiet, alert yet at rest, and the Field of Action is totally open to the Superconscious Mind, the Eternal Mind, which is beyond reason, logic and limited thought-patterns. There are no thoughts of any kind moving in your "normal" self-conscious mind, and no images flashing into your awareness from your subconscious mind. You are totally at One with the Transcendental Mind, the Wisdom Mind. You are serene, calm, centred. Your lower ego, your personal "I", does not dictate results. Your actions are simply movements in the Folds of the Transcendent, enfolding upon Itself, disappearing within Itself. It is performed by the Eternal. It is absorbed by the Eternal.

Realms of the One Mind 492
Action and the Spiritual Warrior 994
Action in the Transcendent 1080

Exercise 2

If you are not in Superconsciousness, or have not yet been able to function in the Formless Condition, then before going into Battle (a physical, verbal or emotional conflict, or a situation that you cannot avoid, or a circumstance that has been forced upon you), remember the following:

- Stay calm.
- If you can, empty your ordinary mind of all thoughts.
- Approach the situation or conflict (verbal, mental, emotional or physical) with an open mind. Do not have set, rigid rules about how you should act.
- Do not try to win, but do not aim to lose either.
- Do not resist the situation and do not put up a desperate fight against it. Accept it as a fact that you have to deal with it.
- Meditation in Action is just Action, just doing what needs to be done. It is the simplest form of action that is required in that particular situation, whether the action is verbal, emotional, mental or physical. It is Action Meditation. Your action becomes your meditation.
- Have no thoughts for yourself. Try to see the best for all. Make it a selfless act, dedicated to the Absolute.
- You mind is peaceful, your emotions calm.

Action Zen 802
How to deal with Crisis situations 1435
Silence and Activity 1446

Warrior Breathing

There are many forms of breathing techniques in the arsenal of the Warrior. Some are for energizing, others are for calming. Some are for focus and sharpening the attention. Some are for uniting the inner and the outer, and some are for balancing the psychic energy streams within the Aura, your Invisible Shield.

Breath connects your physical body to your mind

Breath connects your physical body to your mind (which is *not* the brain and nervous system as the ignorant believe!). Your mind can function apart from your physical body, and You, as a Soul, can function apart from your body *and* your mind.

Breath is the invisible Life-current you receive from the planetary atmosphere. While you are breathing, your mind is connected to your body. If you stop breathing, the connection stops between your Soul-mind and your body, and then you stand free of your body in your Soul-mind structure.

The Subtle-Breath unites your mind-structure (mental body) to your Soul. Therefore the Subtle-Breath is a gateway to your Soul, that is, to *realize* yourself as a Soul, called Self-Realization, Knowing Yourself, locating the Ground of your Being, Returning Home, and so on. The Subtle-Breath is the advanced training for the Warrior.

Baptism and Rebirth 722
Mindfulness of Breathing 794
Prāṇāyāma-Vidyā 1553

Movement and the Life-force

How you move is very important. There is a direct connection between your bodily movements, your breath, your life-force, your emotions and your mind. They all affect each other.

When you watch today's "rap" and "hip hop" singers and dancers, jazz music and dancers, and so-called contemporary music and dancers, you notice one particular quality in all of them: intense, chaotic, jerky and sometimes mechanical movements (which seems to be accepted in today's civilization as "normal"). Parents are quite happy to see their children jerk their bodies in all directions, and the teachers at schools smile benignly upon them. This is modern civilization!

Jerky movements are short, quick, beginning and ending abruptly, twisting, turning, twitching, spasmodic, as if your body was having an epileptic fit. To be able to do this, first you have to make your mind jerky, to "think" jerky. Your mind dictates the jerkiness to your breath, the breath to your emotions and life-force, and the life-force compels the body to move in such a way. Thus, your whole personality functions in a *disintegrating* way, and your life-wave or life-pattern manifests accordingly.

Warrior Calming Breathings

1

- Stand with your feet comfortably apart, knees slightly bent, hands in front of your chest (at Heart-level), palms facing downwards, fingertips touching.
- Exhale while pushing your hands downwards towards the Earth. (Your palms always remain facing downwards.)
- After completely exhaling, inhale and at the same time lift your hands up (palms facing downwards), until you have completely breathed in.
- Repeat this process slowly, calmly, focusing on pushing the Life-force back into the Earth while exhaling, and lifting the Life-force up from the Earth while inhaling. This Life-force is the invisible, subtle energy-field of the planet. You will feel this in your hands.

In this breathing you open your Heart to the Universe

2

- Stand as before, with your hands folded across your Heart Centre. Both palms are facing your Heart, one on top of the other.
- As you breathe in, open your arms wide, as far as you can (palms facing forward).
- As you breathe out, bring your arms back, with your palms facing the Heart Centre.
- In this breathing you open your Heart to the Universe (in-breathing), and you bring the universal (cosmic) Energy into your Heart (out-breathing). Do this slowly.

3

- Stand as before, with your hands by your sides.
- As you breathe in, lift your arms high above your head. As you breathe out, return your arms to your sides. The arms move in a snake-like motion, with the hands and fingers being the head of the snake.

Warrior Breathing Techniques to Develop Internal Strength

Reverse Breathing in Sitting Position

Sit in the thunderbolt posture (sitting on your heels which are tucked under your buttocks, with your back straight, head held high, hands resting on the top of your thighs).

Breathe slowly and deeply.

Inhale slowly and *contract* your abdominal muscles; that is, pull the abdomen in and upwards (this is the reverse of what you would normally do when deep-breathing). When you exhale, *push* the abdomen out (the whole navel region and below it) as far as you can. Do this very slowly, consciously: breathe in, hold the breath, breathe out, hold the breath out, and so on. Do this very calmly, with concentration.

Reverse Breathing in Standing Position

Stand with your feet pointing outwards about forty-five degrees, your hands in front of you, fingertips touching, with palms up. At the starting position the hands are in contact with your navel (solar plexus).

Inhale slowly as you raise your arms up sideways until your fingers touch above your head, with palms down facing. As you exhale, return your arms to the starting position in front of you. Do all this while breathing very slowly and with full attention and concentration.

Breathing from Horse Position

With your feet wide apart and facing forward, squat into the horse position (as if you were riding a horse without a saddle). Your fists are clenched and held together, slightly pressing into your abdomen (solar plexus).

Inhale slowly and straighten your legs, exhale slowly and squat back into the horse position. The fists remain clenched at all times, touching your solar-plexus or navel.

Withholding Breath in Lotus Position

This means you are sitting cross-legged on the floor, the right foot on the left thigh and the left foot on the right thigh, or the reverse. The knees should touch the floor if you can. You may also sit in the half-lotus posture if that is easier.

In this sitting posture you breathe in deeply and *hold* your breath. Holding your breath you bend forward as much as you can, as if you wanted to touch the floor with your head, then move towards the left knee as if you wanted to put your head on your left knee, then move towards the right knee doing the same, then back to the centre. Then straighten up while breathing out. This is one round of the exercise.

Then adjust your breathing. This means you breathe evenly, deeply, until your breath is calm again. Then repeat the exercise.

Warrior Energizing Breathings 1060
Three Kinds of Breathing Meditation 1220

The Significance of Warrior Greetings

Originally, the various forms of greetings between human beings had meanings, which often become forgotten over a period of time.

Handshake

White European. Facing the person in front of you, clasp the other person's hand in a firm handshake. This means that you offer yourself in friendship. You are ready to mix your life-force with the person you shake hands with. Your two separate paths in life have come together.

Open palm

American Indian. Facing the person in front of you, lift your right arm to about a 45-degree angle from your shoulder, your palm facing the person. This greeting means that in your hand there is no concealed weapon, that you are open, sincere, and have no devious plans in your mind. You are open and receptive.

Closed fist

Chinese. Clench your right hand into a closed fist and press it into your left palm, which closes over your right fist, in front of you at about chin-height or slightly lower. This means that you greet the person in front of you as if he or she was your brother or sister, and you are ready to defend him or her and to give that person protection, brotherhood, comradeship.

Salutation

India. Facing the person, put your two palms together in the prayer position, in front of you, in the middle of your chest, and slightly bow your head towards the person. This means, "I acknowledge the Divine within you, which is the same Divine Being who lives in my Heart."

Third-Eye touch

New Zealand Māori. Facing the person, the two foreheads are brought together. (Nowadays the nose and forehead touch.) The original intention of this greeting is highly esoteric. In the middle of your forehead is the invisible Third-Eye. When awakened it can channel power and personal magnetism. This means that you are willing to share your power and magnetism with the person you are greeting. (The nose has no esoteric relevance to this process; the nose touch came about when the esoteric meaning of the Third-Eye touch became forgotten.)

Heart touch

The Spiritual Warrior. You embrace the person to your Heart. You enfold the person in your Heart Centre or Heart-radiation-field. When the Heart is awake in you this will stimulate the Heart Centre in the person who you embrace or hug, resulting in blessings and Love.

The Heart and the Energy Centres 1332
The personal greeting of old India 1703

Understanding your Work in Silence

The Path is measured in terms of Light, Love, Bliss, Silence, Music, Harmony, and At-One-ness with all things. This is all *within* you.

Before you can Work in Silence you must accustom yourself to *being* in Silence. You must feel that Silence is your natural state of Being.

Our Work in Silence consists of using Mantra

There are the NIRMĀNAKĀYAS on the Planes of Light who Work in Silence, modulating the Universal Boundless Light Vibrations which pervade the Infinite Inner Space. And there are the GANDHARVAS who Work in Silence with the Colour Vibrations of the Inner Sounding Space, modulating the lower Light-Sound frequencies which give rise to the Inner Music of the Spheres, which you can hear when you have transcended your body and mind.

Our Work in Silence consists of using MANTRA, or structured Sound-Vibrations, in a Group Unified Field, to build a Group-Bridge to Light whereby individually, and as a group, we may ascend to the Realms of Light and experience Love and Bliss and the Transforming Light for ourselves and all Humanity.

Sound is the Structured Vibrations of the Creative Powers of the Cosmos.

Mankind is making lots of noise but does not understand the Liberating and Transforming Power of Sound. Sound is the Creative, Sustaining and Destructive Energies of the Creative Hierarchies of the Universe. This includes the human-type hierarchies, the angelic types, the Archangels, and the Kingdom of the Gods, the Great Builders of Cosmic Forms. They all create, sustain and destroy by the Power of Sound-Vibration.

Sound-work training occupies many years in the life of a trainee Warrior, for there are healing sounds, soothing sounds, constructive sounds, energizing sounds, evil sounds and destructive sounds.

The Warrior of the Light uses only sounds which create health and harmony in the environment, which liberate people, which increase the Life-force in himself or herself.

The Dark Warrior, the Black Magician, uses evil sounds for the purpose of destroying and limiting others in their life-waves. Such ignorant Dark Warriors have their rewards already in the negative structures of the invisible interiors of the planet, places of darkness and evil foreboding, to which they go after they die.

The Creative and Destructive Power of Sound 201

The Gandharvas 200
Meditational Service of the Buddhas 393
Works of Silence 1643
Magic: White and Black 364
The Law of the Afterlife 410

CHAPTER 47

The Primordial Sound Language

The Ancient Primordial Language of Sound-Vibrations

The letters of the Sound Language are simply Sound-Vibrations

There is a language which predates all the known historical languages, a language composed not of words but of pure Sound-Vibrations. The power of this language is in the sounds of its letters or syllables, which form the basis of all the later ancient tongues, the Sacred Languages, and all the many modern tongues. Knowing this language, the Ancient Warriors of the Dawn of Time understood all Nature and acquired many powers.

The Original Language of Humanity, the Primordial Language, is not used as a language of ideas, concepts, or descriptions of objects. Rather, it involves working *intelligently* with the effects of Sound-Vibrations. Each vowel has a specific quality of Sound-Vibration, and thus a specific effect. Similarly, each consonant, each semi-vowel, each nasal sound, has a specific effect. The conceptual or intellectual mind is not involved at all.

Today we "think" about thoughts, ideas, concepts, and physical things and objects, and "language" names and describes these. But the letters of the Sound Language are simply Sound-Vibrations, and the "words" of this language (the combination of the various sounds into various structures) are but combined Sound-Vibrations. They are not thoughts, ideas, concepts or "objects" of the Physical World or of any world.

When you "think" in the Primordial Sound Language, you "think" Sound-Vibrations, and this is not dependent on any outside objects or any conceptual thoughts.

This language predates any of the ancient languages (including Sanskrit) by countless thousands of years, and it has the same effect on every human being on this planet who can respond to Sound-Vibrations. It is the one Original Primeval Language of the Man-species on this planet.

From out of this Primordial Language of pure Sound-Vibrations developed all the ancient tongues and modern languages, with their *modified* and *altered* vowels, consonants, semi-vowels, nasal sounds, and so forth. But with these languages came concepts, ideas, and the arbitrary naming of things. The words in all subsequent languages are

The Primordial Language of Sound is not a language of ideas, of concepts, of objects, but of Sound-Vibrations. Does that surprise you? This may be difficult to comprehend for this "modern" generation, for the Ancient Wisdom has been lost to them.

Vibration and Mantra 1518

arbitrary; they are consensus languages, no longer based on the understanding of Sound-Vibrations. You can call anything by any sound.

Exceptions exist in the ancient Sacred Languages, such as Hebrew, Arabic, Sanskrit, Chinese, Māori, Egyptian and Hungarian, in which some sacred and secret words are pure Sound-Vibrations—a memory of the lost Primordial Language of Sound-Vibrations.

Example 1

Take, for instance, the English word "cow". It is an animal. In the Original Language it would be the sound **KEA**. Now, irrespective of what you think is a cow, in the Original Language it is a vibration of sound, **KE** and **A**. The sound **KE** is **KA** modified to sound the vowel E. The pure vowel A is added, and all are glided together.

The Sound-Vibration has its own effects without you having to "think" any thoughts about it

Example 2

Take another simple example from modern English: "I am God". This is an idea, a concept, a thought. In the Archaic Sound Language it is the following sounds:

AI EM GĀD

When you intone these as pure sounds (according to the Primordial Sound System), separately then all together, you introduce a very powerful Sound-Vibration into your system—physical, psychic, mental and spiritual. That Sound-Vibration has its own effects or results without you having to "think" any thoughts or ideas about it. It works by Sound-Vibrations alone.

Example 3

Another simple example is the Hungarian phrase:

ISTEN URAM (My God)

In the Archaic Primordial Language this would be the sounding of:

ĪSH	TEN	Ū	RAM
in-breathing	*out-breathing*	*in-breathing*	*out-breathing*

This sequence of sounds has a very pronounced, soothing, calming effect on the breathing system.

Don't pronounce any of these sounds as in English, but according to the Primordial Sound System! You may use the Sanskrit soundings as a guide to the correct pronunciation.

The Primordial Sound Alphabet

Here I shall indicate the basic alphabet of this timeless language. But remember, this alphabet is *not* pronounced in the same way as the English alphabet. You must never read the Ancient Code as if it were English, as generally the English letters don't correlate with the sounds they indicate.

Never read the Ancient Code as if it were English

Pure Vowels

A E I O U

These Pure Vowels can be short, long or prolonged. This indicates the duration of pronunciation. *Short* is the normal pronunciation, *long* is of longer duration, and *prolonged* means as long as required, with no set time limit.

Combined Vowels (Diphthongs)

AI EI OI AU OU AE OA AO EU etc.

Nasal Sounds

Closing-down sound:	M (MA)
Nasal:	Ṁ
Deeper nasal:	Ṅ (NG)

Consonants

Gutturals:	KA (K)	GA (G)	NA (N)
Palatals:	CA (C)	JA (J)	ÑA (Ñ)
Cerebrals:	TA (T)	DA (D)	ṆA (Ṇ)
Labials:	PA (P)	BA (B)	MA (M)

Semi-Consonants (Semi-Vowels)

HA (H) YA (Y) RA (R) LA (L) VA (V) FA (F)

Remember that here we are dealing with the sounds of the Original Primordial Sound Language of Humanity, and the innumerable later variations and adaptations are not included.

Sibilants

SHA (SH) SA (S)

Aspirated Breath Sounds

HA (Ḥ) AH (H:)

The Source of the Primordial Sound Language

You must understand where the Primordial Language comes from.

Creation begins from the Silence of the Absolute Unmanifest Being (you may call it the Primeval Godhead, or the Absolute Creative Intelligence of the Pre-Cosmos). From the Silence of the Unmanifest Absolute Being arises Sound, the Word, the Voice, the Divine Speech, an immeasurable, almighty Sound-Vibration which projects the Cosmos into being through a graduated series of sound-structures. God "speaks" and the Universe becomes.

God "speaks" and the Universe becomes

Thus, the Primeval Sound is actually the "stuff" or "matter" of the Universe (the *Universe* includes all the many invisible worlds, planes and dimensions of the Cosmic Being). Thus, the Cosmic Sea of Universal Substance is actually the Word, or Universal Sound-Vibration.

The Primordial Sound Language of the Man-species on this planet is but a part of the Universal Cosmic Sound Language, the Original Word-Vibration.

Every "object", whether it be physical or belonging to the invisible realms, is made up of Sound-Vibrations of the Original Word. Your physical body, your mind (your mental body), your feeling nature (your astral body), you as a Soul dwelling in your Soul-body (the causal body), and you as a Monad, or Spark of Divinity, all are Sound-Vibrations of the Original Word, which is the Language of the Godhead or Absolute Beingness.

You are simply a manifestation of the Absolute Sound, the Word, and so is everybody else, and so is the whole Universe. Everybody has the One Father-Mother, the Universal Word or Primeval Sound.

When you use sounds from the Primordial Sound Language of Mankind you are creating vibrations of sound which affect your physical body and all your subtle bodies (your "emotions" and your "mind"), as well as You as a Soul (when the sound is vibrating on the Causal Plane). Your "speech" becomes the Creative Word.

Since each single letter has a specific Sound-Vibration, each letter or combination of letters into Sound-words has a specific effect. This the initiated Ancients knew. Thus, in this Primeval Sound Language you have Sound-words, not conceptual words or names of objects.

The Logos: the Word of God 114
Vāk: the Divine Speech 118
The Voice of God 864
The Word, Logos, Voice, Name 1646
The Action of the Primordial Sound 165

The Vowels

The Cosmic Elements 26
Symbols of the Cosmic Elements 362

Vowel	Element	Quality
A	**Spirit**	All-Pervading, Expanding
E	**Air**	Moving, Strengthening
I	**Fire**	Inspiring, Activating
O	**Water**	Mellowing, Focusing
U	**Earth**	Solidifying, Stabilizing

The Pure Vowel Sounds

A	E	I	O	U
AE	EA	IA	OA	UA
AI	EI	IE	OE	UE
AO	EO	IO	OI	UI
AU	EU	IU	OU	UO

The Combined Vowel Sounds

When the Vowels are combined, or glided together, they have the powers of both. For example:

AE	is Spirit-Air	EA	is Air-Spirit
AI	is Spirit-Fire	EI	is Air-Fire
AO	is Spirit-Water	EO	is Air-Water
AU	is Spirit-Earth	EU	is Air-Earth

And so on, for the other combinations. The Combined Vowels can be pronounced in various ways:

- As a single short sound. For example: AE
- Or they can be long, of equal lengths: A...E...
- Or one Vowel can be longer than the other: AE... or A...E

The longer Vowel Sound will then have the predominant quality or effect.

Pronouncing the Pure Vowels

A	as in f**a**ther
E	as in th**ere**
I	as in mach**i**ne
O	as in g**o**
U	as in f**u**ll

The Seven Mystic Vowel Sounds

In the Beginning the Creator uttered the Seven Mystic Vowel Sounds (Great Waves of Primordial Energy) and the Seven Great Planes of Being were formed.

Human beings on this planet can utter only five Pure Vowel Sounds. Each of the five Vowels corresponds to the development of one of the five Root-Races on the planet. The sixth Vowel Man will utter in the future, during the sixth Root-Race, and the seventh Vowel in the very far future, during the seventh Root-Race of Earth's evolution. The sixth and seventh Vowels will be absolutely distinct and human beings of the present day could not pronounce them.

Planes and Subplanes 14
The Descent of the Word 118
Human Evolutionary Epochs 176

The Seven Mystic Vowels uttered by the Creator God at the beginning of Time are the Seven Great Creative Potencies. Their interplay and combinations yield the 49 (7x7) subdivisions or subplanes within the Seven Great Solar-Systemic Planes, which encompass all the worlds and realms of Being, from the gross to the subtle realms to the subtlest Light Worlds.

Since the human species on this planet can utter only the five Pure Vowels and their combinations, a human being on this planet has access to 25 (5x5) subplanes or energy combinations when that person has undergone the necessary training in the perception and use of the Sounding-Light Language of the Creator God.

The five Pure Vowels are thus part of the sevenfold Creative Potencies, or part of the Word or Name of the Absolute Reality (God) which created and is manifesting the Universe now and until the end of Time (until Cosmic Dissolution). Thus, the Vowels are creative energies, forces, powers, qualities. When awakened in a human being, he or she will become God-like, that is, possessing the 25 Powers out of the 49 Cosmic Powers.

Similarly, there are actually seven Elements (types of Manifesting Forces), but the human being of today can only possibly perceive or experience five. That is why we work with only the five Elements.

Modern Vowels

Remember, when we speak of *Vowels* in this teaching we refer to the Pure Vowels, *not* the English pronunciation of the vowels. The English alphabet does have all the proper sounds, but the alphabetic indications of the sounds are a mass of confusion and therefore misleading.

The many *modified* vowels of the English, French and other modern languages are not different vowels; they are just alterations of the five Pure Vowels of the Original Sound Language of Man. The problem with the modern French and English is that *their alphabets do not match their sound systems*, as well as the many nuances of vowel manipulations, although they do have the five Pure Vowels within them if you care to dig them out.

Remembrance of the Five Pure Vowels in some Ancient Languages

By the time of what we call the "Ancients" (more than 8,000 years ago) they had forgotten the complete, pure Primordial Language of Sound-Vibrations which started in Lemurian Civilization and continued in Atlantis.

I	O	U	E	A	Greek (Ancient)
A	E	I	O	U	Latin (Roman)
A	E	I	O	U	Māori (New Zealand)
A	I	U	E	O	Pali (Ancient India)
I	A	O	U	E	Hebrew (Ancient)
O	E	A	I	U	Senzar (Pre-Sanskrit)
A	I	U	E	O	Asian (Ancient)
A	E	I	O	U	Hungarian
A	I	U	E	O	Sanskrit (India)
A	I	U	E	O	Chinese (Ancient)
A	I	U	E	O	Zend (Pre-Persian)
A	I	U			Persian and Arabic
A	I	O	U	E	Slavic (Old)
A	E	I	O	U	Germanic (Old)
A	I	U	O	E	Teutonic (Pre-English)

The ancient Persian and Arabic languages had only three Pure Vowels; the E and O were already forgotten.

The Name of the Deity

If you are aware of world religions, you might recall that the Polynesian and Māori word for the Supreme Deity was **IO**, and to the ancient Greek civilization it was **IAO**, and to the peoples of the old Indian subcontinent it was **AUM**, and to the later Mystic Sages of India it was **ŌM**. These are just fragments of the Ancient Sound Language *remembered*, the rest being forgotten. For:

The Name of the Deity is Sound Itself.

That is, the original pure Sound Language embodies the Deity Itself (the total Sound Language, not just the fragments remembered by a few ancient races).

What is the Name? 1259

Sounding the Vowels

1

For outward growth, expansion, harmony, holistic health, healing, overcoming negative states and negative emotions (such as anger, depression, stress, tensions, the "blues"), you or your group should practise first the five Pure Vowel Sounds:

Sounding the Vowels has a tremendous healing effect

A E I O U

Intone long, drawn-out vowels, loud and clear, brightly and purposefully. This has a tremendous healing effect on you or the group. It makes you or the group feel whole, complete—not fragmented as before, not "lonely", not "isolated". It puts your personality or the group-personality "together".

Next, you or the group should do this silently, mentally:

A E I O U

2

The next stage of this practice is to intone the Combined Vowel Sounds:

First:	AE	AI	AO	AU
Next:	EA	EI	EO	EU
Next:	IA	IE	IO	IU
Next:	OA	OE	OI	IU
Next:	UA	UE	UI	UO

Working with the Pure Vowel Sounds of the Ancient Primary Language, the mother of all languages, which is pure Sound-Vibration, gives you the following powers:

A	Opening up, expanding, widening.
E	Strengthening, energizing, directing.
I	Penetrating, dynamic, activating.
O	Concentrating, focusing, sharpening.
U	Protecting, enclosing, deepening.

The Vowels in the Heart 1303
Cosmic Tuning-In: the 'I' Sound 1652

IAO

The Pure Vowel sequence **I A O** is the connection between the Spirit, the Soul and the physical body:

I	=	Spirit
A	=	Soul
O	=	Body

IAO is the connection between the Spirit, the Soul and the physical body

3

Begin with the prolonged **I** sound, the sound of Pure Spirit. The Spirit is the Transcendental Nature, the Eternal, the Absolute at the highest levels of Creation, just before the Unmanifest Condition.

- First practise physically the prolonged **I** sound (or, as a group, the continuous **I** sound). At the same time, your attention (or the group's attention) is focused on the Spirit.
- Having practised the Pure Vowel Sound **I**, aloud, singly or as a group, practise it silently; that is, intone the pure **I** sound mentally, prolonged. In a group this would be group mental intonation of the continuous **I** sound.

Do each of these practices for 10 or 20 minutes. Then remain absorbed in Silence, the Silence of the Pure Spiritual Nature within you, within the group, within the whole Universe.

4

Having practised with the **I** Vowel Sound, proceed in the same way with the Pure Vowel Sound of **A**, the sound of the Soul and the intermediary dimensions and realms of the Cosmos. This time your focus of attention is upon yourself as a Living Soul in the intermediary Light Worlds. When you do this with the group, however, the group's attention is on the Soul of Things, that is, the Invisible Universe.

Silence Seals

After each practice, you (or the group) must remain in Silence, because during the practices there are Internal Transformations and Connections with the Invisible Realities, and Silence seals or confirms.

The Silent State 1554

5

Next, singly or as a group, practise in the same manner with the Pure Vowel Sound of **O**, the sound of the physical body and of the physical universe.

6

Having practised separately the Pure Vowel Sounds **I**, **A** and **O**, now you (or the group) are ready for the first combination: **I A O**.

- First, intone **I A O** physically. When working alone, intone the prolonged **I A O** sound. As a group, intone the continuous **I A O** sound.
- Then the same practice is done silently, mentally only, singly or as a group. In the group practice the silent sounding of **I A O** is continuous.

This practice unites Spirit, Soul and body into One

This practice unites Spirit, Soul and body into One. As an individual you become an integrated, complete human being, while the group becomes a single integrated Humanity.

7

Next, you or the group practise in the same manner with **A I O**.

8

Next, you or the group practise in the same manner with **O I A**.

9

Then practise **I A O A I O O I A**.

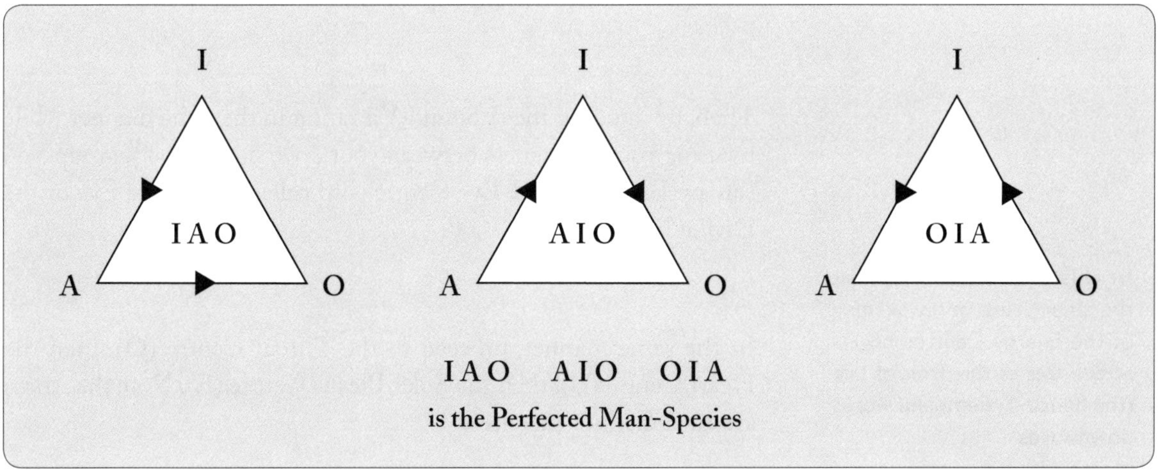

IAO and the Perfected Man-Species

The Vowels in the Energy Centres

The Pure Vowel Sound-Vibrations are also used to activate the subtle invisible Energy Centres in your Aura, your invisible Energy-Field.

The Pure Vowels are also used to activate the Energy Centres

Pure Vowel	***Energy Centre***
I	Crown (top of the head)
A	Third-Eye (between the two physical eyes)
O	Throat
U	Heart (not the physical heart)
E	Solar Plexus

Remember that the physical body references are only a reference to space, that is, to the regions where you find these Energy Centres. The body parts themselves are *not* the Energy Centres!

10

Sitting in your meditation posture, focus your Awareness at the top of your head, in the Crown Centre. Intone aloud the prolonged **I** Sound-Vibration while concentrating in that area, and try to register the **I** Sound-Vibration there. This **I** Sound-Vibration will stimulate the Crown Centre into activity.

You can also do this silently, intoning the **I** Sound-Vibration mentally while focusing at the top of your head. You may do this also as a group exercise, with the whole group focusing above the head.

11

Then, by intoning the **A** Sound-Vibration in the same manner while focusing your Awareness between your eyes, singly or as a group, you can awaken the Third-Eye Centre, also called the Single Eye or the Divine Eye.

In this practice, notice that the energizing or awakening of the Energy Centres begins at the top of the Tree of Life (the human system) and works downwards.

The Heart and the Energy Centres 1332

12

In the same manner, proceed to the Throat Centre (**O**), then the Heart Centre (**U**), then the Solar Plexus Centre (**E**). Note that these are each distinct exercises.

Awakening the Higher Centres

Ordinary Humanity, the masses, work from the Base Centre (at the bottom of the spinal column) and the Sex Centre, along with a lower (reactive-emotional) expression of the Solar Plexus Centre.

The Sex Energy Centre is ordained by Nature to ensure that the human species survives on the planet; thus the intense sex drive in humans. At the moment, however, it is completely out of control and its purpose or nature is completely misunderstood. Humans no longer know how to manage this powerful force of Nature. Wrong social attitudes and religious teachings on the subject are holding Mankind in the grip of an evil attitude towards the Sexual Energy as part of the total Auric Energy-Field, causing immense suffering, conflict, anger and rage in generation after generation of human beings on this planet. Psychology, science and religion deviated from the path of understanding Nature—that is, the complete Nature, not just the fragment seen and sensed by the physical senses.

The higher Energy Centres are not open in the masses of Humanity

The Base Centre is responsible for keeping the human being in touch with this dimension, the Physical Plane or physical universe. The higher Energy Centres are not open in the masses of Humanity; hence the intense materialism prevalent in society. When the higher Centres become open, one's whole view of Life changes fundamentally.

Energy Centres	Powers
Crown	Universal Consciousness, Cosmic Consciousness, Infinite Consciousness, Boundless Light
Third-Eye	The Light of the Soul, Vision into the Inner Worlds and Invisible Dimensions
Throat	Creative Intelligence, Intense mental, artistic and skilful activities, arts and crafts skills
Heart	Infinite Love, the Power of Compassion, Union with All Life, At-One-ness
Solar Plexus	The complete control of the personality

Powers of the Awakened Centres

The Human Cakras 44
The Ascent of Kuṇḍalinī 152
Creating Karma 242
Śauca: Purity 570
To Understand Sex 917

13

A more advanced form of activating the subtle, invisible Energy Centres is as follows:

The sound that connects you to the Base Centre is HU

I	Crown Centre
I A	Third-Eye Centre
I A O	Throat Centre
I A O U	Heart Centre
I A O U E	Solar Plexus Centre

Use the Pure Vowel vibrations to active the centres: **I** for the Crown Centre, **I A** in the Third-Eye, **I A O** in the Throat Centre, **I A O U** in the Heart Centre, and **I A O U E** in the Solar Plexus Centre.

As before, intone these sounds physically in these centres, aloud, then silently, mentally, alone or as a group. You should do this systematically, working downwards, starting first with the Crown Centre.

Remember that the Crown Centre is your connecting point to Divinity, your Heart Centre to your Soul, the Solar Plexus Centre to your personality, and the Base Centre to your physical body.

14

The Kuṇḍalinī Fire 132
When Kuṇḍalinī Awakens 157
The Three Forces of the Warrior 996

In the Primordial Language, the sound that connects you to the Base Centre, and to your physical body consciousness, is **HU**.... It is practised in the same manner as the Vowel Sounds.

Awakening the Serpent-Fire

The sound **HU** is also used in the Primordial Language to awaken the Serpent-Fire situated inside the Base Centre system, but a different technique is employed. The Serpent-Fire, or Fiery-Serpent Energy, was well known to the Ancient Warriors, and it gives many miraculous powers to those Warriors who master it.

For the reader, however, it is better not to know much about it, as the mishandling of this Primeval Force results in extreme danger to the personality mechanism. It is also best for the reader not to know the sound used to awaken the Sexual Centre into greater activity, as most people already have enough trouble with the Sexual Energy.

The Serpent-Fire Energy is a subtle, invisible Energy or Force working normally through the Base Centre and Sex Centre. When properly developed and used, however, it bestows upon the Warrior tremendous psychic, magical and occult powers.

The Serpent, the Dragon and the Lion were symbols for this ancient Force.

The Development of the Mind through the Five Pure Vowel Sounds

15

The Pure Vowels are also excellent for Mental Training. Sound them out aloud, and also silently. Each has a particular quality for Mind Training.

Each Vowel has a particular quality for Mind Training

For example, if you want to increase your mental capacity, comprehension, expansion, use the A Vowel. Intone aloud:

A (short)

Ā (long)

$\overset{\infty}{A}$ (prolonged)

Practise short A-s and long Ā-s (2 measures), and separately the prolonged $\overset{\infty}{A}$ sound.

In the same manner you can practise the Vowels one by one, in order:

A, E, I, O, U

Or, focus on the Vowel which you think you especially need for your mental development.

Vowel	Mental Effect
A	Opens up the mind, makes it larger, expands its capacities
E	Gives strength and power to the mind, stability and equilibrium
I	Dynamizes and activates the mind, gives it mental energy
O	Gives the ability to focus and concentrate, sharpens the mind
U	Protects the mind and makes it whole and fused and united

The Pure Vowels for Mental Training

The Prolonged Vowels:

$\overset{\infty}{A}$ $\overset{\infty}{E}$ $\overset{\infty}{I}$ $\overset{\infty}{O}$ $\overset{\infty}{U}$

The sign of infinity (∞) means that the sound is endless, with no time measure given.

Personal Development through the Five Pure Vowel Sounds

On the personality level you are made up of the Five Elementary Qualities

The five Pure Vowels can be also used for your personality development and strengthening. Spirit, Air, Fire, Water and Earth are the Elementary Qualities of the Solar System. The planets represent the Regulatory Forces of the Solar System.

You are not isolated from the Cosmos. On the personality level you are made up of the Five Elementary Qualities, the Five Cosmic Elementary Substances, and through you flow the Planetary Energies of the Solar System. You are a part or fragment of the whole Solar System and you can consciously invoke the Elements and Forces of the System at will to *increase* some Quality or Force within you.

For example, the Pure Vowel A *increases* the Elementary Quality of the Spirit within you, as well as the forces represented by Uranus and Neptune.

16

The Cosmic Elements 26
Children of the Sun 1590

To use the Vowels to develop and strengthen your personality, sound a Vowel and think of the corresponding Quality or Force you want to develop.

Vowel	Element	Force	Quality
A	Spirit	*Uranus, Neptune*	Bliss, Origin, Expansiveness, Transcendence
E	Air	*Mercury, Jupiter*	Mental Control, Thought-Power, Wisdom, Communication
I	Fire	*Sun, Mars, Pluto*	Activity, Assertiveness, Life-force Transformation
O	Water	*Moon, Venus*	Imagination, Art, Union, Subconscious Force
U	Earth	*Saturn, Earth*	Solidity, Shape, Form, Structure, Organization

Forces and Qualities of the Vowels

The Two Directions of Sound

The Primordial Sound Language can be applied in two directions:

a. Towards manifestation, growth, expansion, strengthening, empowering outwardly in the world, and developing powers and abilities.

b. Inner transformations, returning your consciousness to inner planes, realms and states of Being, and to reconnect you to Being Itself, the Timeless, the Eternal, the Absolute, the Unconditioned Godhead, which is your Source and the Source of the whole Universe. That is, to reunite you to the Whole, the Complete, the One.

Thus, there are two ways to use the Ancient Sound Language:

The technique for growth, expansion, gathering powers and abilities, and so forth, is to use the long Vowels and the prolonged Vowels.

The technique for reconnecting to the Source, for moving deeper inside yourself, is to shorten the Vowels by the M, Ṁ or Ṅ (NG).

The **Ṁ** is sounded in the nose as a humming sound, *"mmmm…"*, the humming vibration striking the Third-Eye Centre, the Single Eye, the Eye of Spiritual Vision, between the two physical eyes in the forehead. This Eye is not physical but ethereal—that is, etheric-physical.
The Third-Eye Centre 49

Open Sounds	Closed Sounds		
Pure Vowels	1 *With Consonant*	2 *Nasal*	3 *Deeper Nasal*
A	AM	AṀ	AṄ (ANG)
E	EM	EṀ	EṄ (ENG)
I	IM	IṀ	IṄ (ING)
O	OM	OṀ	OṄ (ONG)
U	UM	UṀ	UṄ (UNG)

Internalizing the Pure Vowels

AEM	EAM	IAM	OAM	UAM
AIM	EIM	IEM	OEM	UEM
AOM	EOM	IOM	OIM	UIM
AUM	EUM	IUM	OUM	UOM

Internalizing the Combined Vowels

The closing 'M' can be the consonant **M (MA)**, or the nasal **Ṁ**, or the deeper nasal **Ṅ (NG)**, according to what degree you are directing the sound inwards.

Although all sounds can be turned either inwards or outwards, there are some sounds that are better used for certain purposes, which we will teach you as we go along.

Powers of the Primordial Sound Alphabet

The Consonants

Gutturals

KA (K) Activating, initiating movement, dynamism, creative power, inception.

GA (G) Improves memory, densifies, solidifies, attracts materiality.

NA (N) Negating, opposing.

Palatals

CA (C) Softening, feminine, gently activating.

JA (J) Softly densifies, brings materiality more gently, feminine.

ÑA (Ñ) Softening, mellowing, not so harshly opposing.

Cerebrals

TA (T) Liberating, delivering, strengthening.

DA (D) Strongly protective, builds up strength.

ṆA (Ṇ) Overcoming, healing, resisting.

Labials

PA (P) Explosive, destroying capacity, directing energy, controlling, energizing, male.

BA (B) Strengthening, building up.

MA (M) Resistance, endurance, stopping, densifying, maternal, female.

Aspirated Sounds

HA (Ḥ) Can be used as an energetic, virile sound; fiery, aggressive, male, produces courage, increases Life-force,

AH (H:) Releasing, relaxing, letting go, out-breathing, dissolution.

Nasals

Ṁ Harmonizing, uniting, integrating, all-including, leading to the Transcendent.

Ṅ (NG) Overcomes diseases, harmonizing, healing, produces Wholeness, leads to the Transcendent.

You must remember that when we talk of Vowels, Consonants, Semi-Vowels, and so forth, we are not talking of some pretty calligraphy or human speech in modern languages. We are talking of an ancient science of Sound-Vibrations, which you do not learn today in educational institutions.

The Vowels, Semi-Vowels and Consonants, and the various other sounds of the Original Sound Language of Humanity, are forces, energies, powers, which do affect you and your environment in many ways if you learn to understand them and use them correctly.

The Primordial Sound Alphabet 1028

The Semi-Vowels or Semi-Consonants

17

HA YA RA VA LA

Intone this aloud, *fast*. The emphasis is on the first sound:

HA YA RA VA LA, HA YA RA VA LA...

These five sounds are part Vowels and part Consonants

This has the dual impact of the Vowels (steadying) and the Consonants (energizing, activating), because these five sounds are part Vowels and part Consonants. They are neither Pure Vowels nor Pure Consonants, but in between.

18

Intone, singly or as a group, in the *prolonged* way:

HĀ... YĀ... RĀ... VĀ... LĀ...

This will have the balancing effect of all five Elementary Qualities within you. You, or the group, will become a "balanced" person or personality (or group personality).

This exercise also can be done mentally, silently, in your mind.

Semi-Vowel	Element	Elementary Quality
HA (H)	Spirit	All-pervasiveness, all-inclusiveness
YA (Y)	Air	Motion, movement, locomotion
RA (R)	Fire	Expansion, aspiring upwards, growing, developing
VA (V) ←	Water	Contracting, simplifying, smoothness, evenness
LA (L)	Earth	Resisting change, cohesion, solidifying
FA (F) ←	Water	

Powers of the Semi-Vowel Sounds

FA (F) is a variant of **VA (V)**. The Semi-Vowel/Consonant **FA (F)** can be used aggressively for projecting, emphasizing, manifesting, striking, expressing.

Internalizing the Semi-Vowels

When you close down (internalize) these sounds, they become:

From this group of sounds, only one was remembered

Semi-Vowel	Stage 1	Stage 2	Stage 3	Stage 4
HA	HĀMA	HĀM	HĀṀ	HĀṄ (HĀNG)
YA	YĀMA	YĀM	YĀṀ	YĀṄ (YĀNG)
RA	RĀMA	RĀM	RĀṀ	RĀṄ (RĀNG)
VA	VĀMA	VĀM	VĀṀ	VĀṄ (VĀNG)
LA	LĀMA	LĀM	LĀṀ	LĀṄ (LĀNG)

The Internalized Semi-Vowels

From this group of sounds of the Primeval Language, only one was remembered in ancient days, **RĀMA**, which was the Name of God in India more than five thousand years ago. The rest were forgotten.

The Internal Use of these Sounds

Each sound, taken inside and reduced with the **M**, **Ṁ** and **Ṅ** (NG), will switch your attention from Outer Awareness (of the world) to the Inner Awareness of the Self (that is, Yourself, who you really are).

The Elementary Qualities

Remember that the words *Spirit, Air, Fire, Water* and *Earth* represent the five Primordial Elementary Qualities active on the Creation levels—the Physical Plane, the Astral Plane (or subtle plane), the Mental Plane (or subtler plane), and the Unity Plane (above the Mental Plane). These qualities are ways in which the Universal Energy or Force expresses itself, symbolized in human language as the words Spirit, Air, Fire, Water and Earth. They represent types of energies or forces which matter assumes when impelled by the Cosmic Sound-Light Vibrations of the Universal Language or Word of God.

Great Incarnations of Divinity 1270
The Seven Elementary Qualities 28
Use the Powers of the Five Elements 1172

19

To further integrate your personality, or the group personality, sit in your meditation posture.

First focus at the base of your spine (the Base Centre region) and there intone silently:

LĀṀ...

Then move up to the Sex Centre region and intone silently:

VĀṀ...

Then move to the Solar Plexus Centre region and intone silently:

RĀṀ...

Then move to the Heart Centre region (in the middle of the chest) and intone silently:

YĀṀ...

Then move up to the Throat Centre region and intone silently:

HĀṀ...

Do this once through, one after the other, moving up the spine, silently, internally. Then repeat the whole process. Do this exercise for several minutes. This is the equalizing of the Elements within your Microcosm, the Aura, using the Primordial Sound Language.

This is the equalizing of the Elements within your Microcosm

Semi-Vowel	Element	Energy Centre
HĀṀ	**Spirit**	Throat Centre region
YĀṀ	**Air**	Heart Centre region
RĀṀ	**Fire**	Solar Plexus (navel) region
VĀṀ	**Water**	Sex Centre (sacral) region
LĀṀ	**Earth**	Base Centre region

Internalizing the Semi-Vowels in the Energy Centres

Transformation of the Centres 1333
Potent Vibrations: Bīja-Mantra 1544

The Semi-Vowels combined with the Pure Vowels

In this tablet, each line represents a Semi-Vowel and how its sound is modified with a Pure Vowel Sound, giving it a different effect.

From these sequences of sounds, only HŪ was remembered

H	HA	HE	HI	HO	HU
Y	YA	YE	YI	YO	YU
R	RA	RE	RI	RO	RU
V	VA	VE	VI	VO	VU
L	LA	LE	LI	LO	LU

The Semi-Vowels combined with the Five Pure Vowels

From these sequences of sounds of the Primordial Sound Language, only **HŪ** was remembered. **HŪ** is a Name of God in Arabic. But, as we mentioned earlier, every sound of the Primordial Sound Language carries the Energy of God.

These sounds can be internalized with the Stopping Sound **M** and the Nasal Sounds **Ṁ** and **Ṅ (NG)** (represented here by the **M**):

H	HĀM	HĒM	HĪM	HŌM	HŪM
Y	YĀM	YĒM	YĪM	YŌM	YŪM
R	RĀM	RĒM	RĪM	RŌM	RŪM
V	VĀM	VĒM	VĪM	VŌM	VŪM
L	LĀM	LĒM	LĪM	LŌM	LŪM

The Semi-Vowels with the Pure Vowels and the M, Ṁ and Ṅ

Sūfī Mantras for Meditation 874
The Bīja-Mantra Hūṁ 1546

From this system of Semi-Vowels, Pure Vowels, Stopping Sounds and Nasal Sounds, the sound **HŪM** was remembered by the Ancients. To the ancient Tibetans, the sound **HŪM** represented the Transcendent, the Timeless, the Eternal—that is, the Godhead.

20

Practise sounding the following sequences, one sequence at a time. When you (or the group) practise these sound sequences you are combining the vibrations of the Semi-Vowel Sounds with the Pure Vowel Sounds; that is, you are combining energies, potentials, possibilities. Each sequence will have a different effect. In each case, notice the different effects upon you.

Each sequence will have a different effect

HA HE HI HO HU, HA HE HI HO HU...

YA YE YI YO YU, YA YE YI YO YU...

RA RE RI RO RU, RA RE RI RO RU...

VA VE VI VO VU, VA VE VI VO VU...

LA LE LI LO LU, LA LE LI LO LU...

HA YA RA VA LA, HA YA RA VA LA...

HE YE RE VE LE, HE YE RE VE LE...

HI YI RI VI LI, HI YI RI VI LI...

HO YO RO VO LO, HO YO RO VO LO...

HU YU RU VU LU, HU YU RU VU LU...

21

The next practice is to sound the same combinations of Semi-Vowels and Pure Vowels with the internalizing M, Ṁ and Ṅ (NG) sounds added. For example:

HĀM HĒM HĪM HŌM HŪM... etc.

HĀM YĀM RĀM VĀM LĀM... etc.

Practise each of the five rows (horizontally) and each of the five columns (vertically), one sequence at a time.

Remember that the Sacred Language of Primordial Sound-Vibrations are expressions of the God-power or God-force in Creation or Manifestation. They therefore increase your own life-force and powers, but they can also lead you back to the Source, the Godhead.

The Consonants with the Vowels

22

Practise this tablet of the Consonants with the Five Pure Vowel Sounds, progressing across (horizontally) and downwards (vertically).

Note the following pronunciations:

C as in *church.*
J as in *jaywalker.*
Ñ as in *señorita.*
Ṇ as in *none.*

Consonants	Pure Vowels A	E	I	O	U
K	KA	KE	KI	KO	KU
G	GA	GE	GI	GO	GU
N	NA	NE	NI	NO	NU
C	CA	CE	CI	CO	CU
J	JA	JE	JI	JO	JU
Ñ	ÑA	ÑE	ÑI	ÑO	ÑU
T	TA	TE	TI	TO	TU
D	DA	DE	DI	DO	DU
Ṇ	ṆA	ṆE	ṆI	ṆO	ṆU
P	PA	PE	PI	PO	PU
B	BA	BE	BI	BO	BU
M	MA	ME	MI	MO	MU

The Consonants combined with the Pure Vowels

From this table of the Consonants with the Vowel Sounds, only **MU** was remembered as a "sacred" sound, by the Zen (Chān) Patriarchs of China.

Terms of Awakening 766

The Consonants with the Vowels and the Final M and Nasal Sounds

23

Practise across the lines, as well as down the columns.

Remember that the **M** in this tablet represents three things:

a. The Final **M** or Stopping Sound.

b. The **Ṁ** or Nasal Sound.

c. The **Ṅ (NG)** or deeper Nasal Sound.

	Pure Vowels				
Consonants	A	E	I	O	U
K	KAM	KEM	KIM	KOM	KUM
G	GAM	GEM	GIM	GOM	GUM
N	NAM	NEM	NIM	NOM	NUM
C	CAM	CEM	CIM	COM	CUM
J	JAM	JEM	JIM	JOM	JUM
Ñ	ÑAM	ÑEM	ÑIM	ÑOM	ÑUM
T	TAM	TEM	TIM	TOM	TUM
D	DAM	DEM	DIM	DOM	DUM
Ṇ	ṆAM	ṆEM	ṆIM	ṆOM	ṆUM
P	PAM	PEM	PIM	POM	PUM
B	BAM	BEM	BIM	BOM	BUM
M	MAM	MEM	MIM	MOM	MUM

The Consonants with the Vowels and the M, Ṁ and Ṅ

From this table of the Consonants with the Vowels and Final Stopping Sound, only **GAM** and **DUM** were remembered, by the Sages of India. **GAM** they attributed to the god of fortune and material success, and **DUM** they attributed to the goddess which overcomes all obstacles.

The rest of these sounds were forgotten by the time of the Ancients. In actual fact, they *all* are sacred sounds, and *they depend on Sound-Vibration, not on mythology or imagination.*

The Sibilants

The Sibilants are the Hissing Sounds, or the Snake Sounds. They have the following qualities:

The Sibilants are the Hissing Sounds

SHA (SH)	Subtle feminine energy, Inner Fire, purifying, cleansing.
SA (S)	Gives subtle feminine energy, repels evil forces.

24

First, practise the following, singly or as a group:

SHA SA, SHA SA, SHA SA...

Then:

SH...

Observe what effects the Hissing Sounds have upon you. Then:

SH... S..., SH... S....

25

Then combine the Hissing Sounds with the original five Pure Vowel Sounds. You will observe that the Hissing Sounds will be modified differently by each of the five Pure Vowel Sounds, producing different effects upon you.

SHĀ	SHĒ	SHĪ	SHŌ	SHŪ
SĀ	SĒ	SĪ	SŌ	SŪ

26

Then practise the following, each prolonged:

SHĀ..., SHĒ..., SHĪ..., SHŌ..., SHŪ...

SĀ..., SĒ..., SĪ..., SŌ..., SŪ...

27

Then practise these sounds with the Closing Sound **M** and the Nasal Sounds of **Ṁ** and **Ṅ** (**NG**). The effect is different again:

SHĀM	SHĒM	SHĪM	SHŌM	SHŪM
SĀM	SĒM	SĪM	SŌM	SŪM

In China, the word SHĪ was used for the Spiritual Warrior

In the ancient Egyptian language, one sound was remembered from this group of sounds of the Primordial Language of Mankind: **SHŪ**. **SHŪ** was the night sky god or goddess—that is, the Unmanifest Unborn Deity.

The ancient Chinese language also used several of the **Sh** and **S** sounds with Pure Vowels, because the Sages of Old China remembered a little of the lost Atlantean teaching on the Language of Sound (before words and concepts).

Thousands of years ago in China, the word **SHĪ** was used for the Spiritual Warrior. **SHĪ** is one of the sounds of the Primordial Sound Language. The Sounds **SHĪ** and **SHŪ** have tremendous powers for spiritual development of the human being.

In ancient China, **SHĒN** was the word for Spiritual Energy, Spiritual Mind, Subtle Energy, or Subtle Mind. This is a direct remembrance of that sound from the Primordial Sound Language. **SHĒN** is Spirit in action, Spirit in motion outwardly.

Remember at all times when reading this material that the Primordial Sound Language is not a language of words, ideas and concepts. It is Sound-Power, the effects of Sound used *internally* and *externally*.

When intoning the Sound Language you do not have to think of any thoughts or ideas. Just concentrate on the Sound-Vibrations you are making and produce the pure sounds of the Original Primordial Sound Language of Mankind. It is Sound which does the work for you or the group, not your ideas or thoughts. And remember that these sounds are particles of the Ineffable Name of the Ultimate Reality, the Ultimate Unity of all things.

The Creative and Destructive Power of Sound 201

The Bīja-Mantra Śaṁ 1551

Centring and Deepening SHĪ and SHŪ

28

Go ever deeper inside yourself with the SHŪ... sound

Sit in your meditation posture (if you can, in the thunderbolt posture, or the lotus posture, or the easy posture). Be still. Intone the sound **SHĪ**, prolonged, inside you:

SHĪ...

First, your attention is in the Base Centre, at the base of your spine. As you *intone* the prolonged **SHĪ**... sound, *visualize* it as a golden, orangish, reddish energy stream moving up your spine, all the way up your back, through your head and out above your head through your Crown Centre. The energy streams upwards continuously with the upward-moving sound of **SHĪ**...

29

Sit in your meditation posture and continuously intone the **SHĪ** sound mentally and just *listen* to it.

(These two meditations on the **SHĪ** sound are for centring your consciousness inside you.)

30

Sit still in your meditation posture and intone the prolonged **SHŪ**... sound deep inside yourself.

SHŪ...

Go ever deeper and deeper inside yourself with the **SHŪ**... sound. Mentally produce it and, at the same time, *listen* to it and *move* your consciousness deeper and deeper until there is no longer *you* left, only **SHŪ**, the Spirit moving through the Mother Deep of the Cosmos. Listen to that Spirit and become Cosmic Oneness.

Shining from Within
The Moment of Shining. Mind Shining
MĀ RA MA

MĀ RA MA (MĀRAMA)

RĀ MA (RĀMA)

RĀM

The Vibration of RĀM produces the Moment of Shining within you

The Vibration of **RĀM** in the ancient Primordial Sound Language of Mankind produces Luminous Bliss.

MĀ – RA – MA produces Light in you.

RĀ – MA produces Light filled with Joy.

RĀM produces shining Bliss inside you.

The Vibration of **RĀM** produces the *Moment of Shining* within you. When you shine within yourself, success is yours in all endeavours. You accomplish all your tasks, duties and chosen goals with ease, and you are Radiantly Happy.

31

Sit in your meditation posture. Silently, mentally, with ease, say in your mind:

MA... RA... MA..., MA... RA... MA...

Leave intervals, pausing before each repetition. This will stop your mind from chattering.

After a while you will feel that you only need to say:

RĀ... MA..., RĀ... MA...

This will take your mind deep inside yourself. You begin to *Shine.* After a while you will feel that you only need to say:

RĀM... RĀM...

This will lead you to Blissful Awareness, a Field of Boundless Joy inside you.

RĀM: the Warrior Power 1068

Sound-Words

Sound-words work miracles in transforming Consciousness

Up to this point we have been dealing with the *single sounds* of the Primordial Sound Language. When these single sounds are *combined* in various ways, we have *Sound-words*. For example:

HRĪM, SHRĪM, KRĪM, KLĪM,
STRĪM, SHYĀM, SAIṀ, SVĀHĀ

And longer combinations, such as:

KĀKĀKA - BISANMA - EI - SŌHA

GA-TE GA-TE PA-RA-GATE
PA-RA-SAM-GA-TE BO-DHI SŌ-HA

Sound-words are Sound-Vibrations and are not dependent on artificially contrived "meanings". Their power lies in Sound itself and, when used internally in meditation, they work miracles in transforming Consciousness, purifying the subtle bodies (the emotional and mental bodies), and harmonizing and healing the physical body.

The Sound-Word KRĪM

For example, the Sound-word **KRĪM** is composed of the following sounds:

a. The Consonant **K** (**KA**), which is activating, dynamic, initiating action.
b. The Semi-Vowel or Semi-Consonant **R** (**RA**), which is fiery, producing expansion, aligned to the Sun.
c. The Pure Vowel Sound **I**, which is the Fire Element of the Vowel Sounds, activating, moving, developing.

Thus, the sound **KRĪ** (with the long **Ī** sound) is the most effective activating sound. It is used for the following purposes:

- To produce action, to change conditions.
- To destroy old and outgrown patterns, ideas, habits or lifestyles.
- For protection and fearlessness amidst opposition.
- For vitalizing, energizing, growth, positivity, beginning new projects.
- For control of situations and events.

Potent Vibrations: Bīja-Mantra 1542
Understanding your Work in Silence 1024

Meditation on KRĪM

32

Practise the Sound-word **KRĪ** *aloud*, with the long **Ī** sound and then with the prolonged **Ī̃** sound.

33

This Sound-word will break down your limitations

Then practise it *silently*, mentally.

34

When you add the Stopping Sound **M**, this changes the vibration.

KRĪM
KRĪṀ (nasal)
KRĪṄ (KRĪNG) (interior nasal)

Practise this *aloud*.

35

When you use this for interior meditation, do this *silently*, in your mind:

KRĪM (KRĪṀ, KRĪNG)

When you repeat this Sound-word silently, as your inner meditation, it will increase activity inside you, on the inner planes, on the inner dimensions, as well as on the outer plane of your physical life. It will break down your limitations.

You may also use this sound to reach the Source of your Mind, the Higher Self or Soul within you, by gradually *reducing* the mental vibration of the Sound-word until you arrive at Stillness, non-activity, in Union with the Passive Self of you and the Universe, the Source of Bliss.

Pure Being
IĒNG (YING-YENG)

What are you without your thoughts, feelings, desires, plans, goals, activities? What is the real You? The real You is Pure Being.

You must learn to move from the Shadow to the real You which is boundless

What were you before your physical body was formed, before your mind was formed? What were you before you became *conditioned* by your parents, relatives, schoolteachers, tribe, nation, religion, and so-called culture? All that you know yourself to be *now* is what you have been *conditioned* to believe about yourself. But what is the *real* You? The unconditioned You?

The real You is a timeless, formless, boundless, unconditioned, absolute, blissful *Pure Being,* within which lies all potential to become anything, to be anything, to create anything. This is Pure Being, the real You. The real You knows no pain, no sorrow, only Bliss, Love and Eternal Existence. The conditioned you is all that you know about yourself now, what you have *identified* yourself with.

To become the Spiritual Warrior you must learn to *experience* the real You and to distinguish it from your Shadow, the Time-Space bound self that you think you are now. The real You is vast, fathomless. The shadow-you is limited by necessity to your conditioning factors. So you are two: the Real and the Shadow. You must learn to move from the Shadow to the real You which is boundless. For this you must go through a gradual process of *deconditioning* to discover who you are.

Are you interested in the Mystery about your Self? The Mystery of who you are?

In this process you have to go beyond your physical body, your emotional body (your feelings and desires) and your mental body (your thoughts and thinking processes and plans and ideas) and establish yourself in Pure Being, your Eternal Formless Self, and discover how that Eternal Formless Blissful Self, which is all Joy, all Love, all Intelligence, is *related* to your present evolutionary conditioned self that you mistakenly believe yourself to be.

Pure Being is beyond Time and Space, beyond all thinking processes, feelings and physical causes and effects. This is on the level of your Soul and the level of You as pure Spirit, beyond the Soul.

Understand your Predicament 892
The Law of your Being 976
Know Thyself 1389
Who is 'I AM'? 1418

The Journey to Pure Being is essentially no Journey at all; rather, it is just being what you already are, Pure Being. If there is any Journey at all—or way, or method, or path—then it is learning to *dis-identify* yourself from your Shadow and to *identify* yourself with the Real.

36

For the purpose of *dis-identifying* yourself from your limited, conditioned self and *identifying* yourself with Pure Being, or the Spiritual Soul that you are, boundless and timeless, the Primordial Language of Sound uses the Vowels as follows:

The Journey to Pure Being is essentially no Journey at all

- **I, E, A** if you are a Warrior or an Administrator, or are living in the world.
- **O, U** if you are a monk, a renunciate or a recluse withdrawn from the world.
- **M, Ṁ** and **Ṅ** (**NG**) are used for termination with the Vowels alone or with sympathetic Consonants combined with these Pure Vowels.

The Sound-Vibration is a means or medium or tool to draw your attention away from your conditioned self, allowing yourself just to *Be*, thus going beyond your physical body, emotional nature and thinking process. You sink into the Essential Self that you are, allowing yourself to experience the Timeless Condition, which is your Root, Source and Inner Strength. Experiencing the Warrior within you, you develop tremendous confidence, integrity, healing and balance.

Allow your attention to move deeper and deeper inside with the Sound until the Field of Silence is reached—Pure Being.

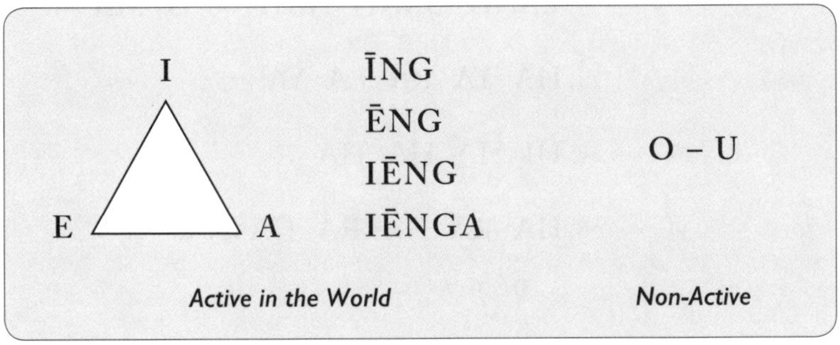

Sounds for Identification with Pure Being

Beyond the Veils 894
Trapped Spirits 1240
The Three Identifications 1369
The Essence of Wisdom 1680

Tremendous Sound-Structures in the Primordial Sound Language for the Development of Humanity

1. SHĪ VA YA NA MA HA

2. KĀ E I LA HRĪNG
HA SA KĀ HA LA HRĪNG
SA KĀ LĀ HRĪNG SHRĪNG KLĪNG

3. Ā Ē Ū AI O

4. Ū Ā Ē AI O

5. Ē Ō Ū Ā AI

6. E U A E O

7. E U A AI O

8. Ā Ē Ū Ē Ī Ō

9. Ā Ē Ū Ī Ā Ō

10. HA SA RA KA LA DA

11. Ī HĀ

12. HĀ U

13. HĀ Ī

14. A HA

15. HA SA O MI TO FU
TSONG KA PA
RA RE RA RA

16. YA RA LA VA
SHA SA AH HA

17. KA KHA GA ÑA CA JA
TA THA DA ṆA PA BA
YA RA LA SHA SA HA

18. HA HĀ HE HI HO HU
KA KĀ KE KI KO KU
MA MĀ ME MI MO MU
RA RĀ RE RI RO RU

19. KA KHA GA GHA
CA CHA JA JHA
TA THA DA DHA
PA PHA BA BHA

20. RA RĀ RE RĒ RI RO RU
PA PĀ PE PĒ PI PO PU
TA TĀ TE TĒ TI TO TU
NA NĀ NE NĒ NI NO NU

21. SA RE GA MA PA DA NI SA

22. A I U RI LI E OI OU O

23. A I U NA RI LI KA
O ONGA EO CHA
HA YA VA RA LA TA
LA GA
EANH UANH NAH NAH MA

24. HA YA RA LA VA

25. HI HA HA HA

26. HA RA HA RA HA RA

Controlling the Mind through Breathing
SŌ–HĀNG, HŌNG–SAU, HA–SA

In the ancient Primordial Sound Language the sounds **SA** and **HA**, a Sibilant and a Semi-Vowel, along with two Pure Vowel Sounds and one Nasal Sound, **SŌ-HĀNG (SO HA NG)**, describe the cycle of your breathing, its connection with the Life-force of the planet, and its connection with your mind (mental body).

The breathing is natural, with no artificial forcing

	in-breathing	*out-breathing*
	SŌ	HĀNG
or:	HŌNG	SAU
or:	HA	SA

37

Sit in your meditation posture and watch your breathing. As the breath enters your nostrils, *sound mentally* the sound **SŌ**.... As you breathe out, sound mentally ...**HĀNG**.

You are doing two things simultaneously:
a. You are watching your breathing.
b. You are making the sounds in your mind.

The breathing is natural, as it comes, with no artificial forcing. In this lies a world of discovery for you.

The Life-Force 589
Gāyatrī (Sun) Breathing 1553
Rest in the Great Breath 1654
Education for Life 484

The Pre-Ancients, the Initiates of Atlantis, knew of the connection between the mind, the Life-force, breathing and the Primordial Sound Language. Modern materialism is ignorant of all this. According to modern intellectuals the mind is but the physical brain and nervous system. As for the Life-force, they don't consider it, not even theoretically. As for breathing, it is automatic and the intellectual is not conscious of it. And the Primordial Sound Language? Well, who has ever heard of such a thing?

It cannot be truthfully said that in school or university you were properly instructed in these matters. Instead you *memorized* lots of details about objects and things, so called, "animate" and "inanimate" objects *outside* yourself. This *memorizing* of information about myriads of outer objects you were told was "knowledge" and "learning". But what did you learn about the *real* Knowledge, about your subtle invisible mind-field or vibration, or the vibrations of your subtle, invisible emotional field, or the invisible Life-force permeating the planet and your connection to it via your breathing? What did you learn at school and university about your Cosmic Life?

You are more than what you *appear* to be and the Universe is more than what it *appears* to be to physical science—much more. The Universe devolves out of the Cosmic Mind until it becomes "physical" and thus "perceptible" to physical science. But what is before?

Warrior Energizing Breathings

38

Begin in the horse position (feet apart, knees bent), your hands and arms in front of you, elbows bent, palms facing forward.

Practise rapid breathing of the Primordial Language Sounds of:

Your arms and hands move rhythmically with the breathing of the sounds

HI HA HA HA HI HA HA HA...

Your arms and hands move rhythmically with the breathing of the sounds, as if you were pushing energy away in front of you. The emphasis is always stronger on the first sound (**HI**).

As you establish the rhythm of breathing the sounds and moving your arms, you can hop forwards and backwards in small hops, bending your knees, still in rhythm with your breathing sounds. Then you can take greater leaps, forwards then backwards. Then you can leap high just with the sound **HI**.

39

Stand in the horse position. As you raise your hands upwards, sound **I**, then slam the backs of your hands on your thighs with the sound **HA**! Thus, the complete sound is:

I HA!

It is an exclamatory sound. Do this in rhythm. As your hands move upwards with the sound **I**, straighten your knees slightly. As you slam the backs of your hands hard on your thighs with the sound **HA**! the knees bend deeper. Start off the movement slowly and then go faster and faster. The force explodes at the contact of thighs and hands.

40

Stand in the horse position. Breathe out the Primordial Sounds of:

RA RE RA RA RA RE RA RA...

As you breathe out **RA**, push your right arm across towards the left side (as if you were knocking something over), the palm facing forward. As you breathe out **RE**, push your left arm towards the right side.

Warrior Breathing 1020

Then breathe out twice, **RA RA,** each time pushing both hands forward in front of you.

Then repeat with your right hand, then the left, and so on. Start off slowly, then do it faster and faster. It is as if you were trying to knock down a wall with the palms of your hands.

41

For developing stamina, use the Primordial Sounds HU-HĀ

Stand with your feet comfortably apart and your arms lifted up in front of you.

Swing both arms to the left, with your body twisting to the left as you breathe out the sound **HA**. Then swing both arms to the right, with your body twisting to the right, as you breathe out the sound **RA**. Then swing again to the left with the sound **HA**, then to the right with the sound **RA**, and so on. All of this is done in a rhythmic, breathing-sounding motion.

HA RA HA RA HA RA...

The open palms of your hands are like two swords in this action, blocking and cutting at the same time. The arms and wrists twist and turn simultaneously with each movement, left and right, as if you were fending off a crowd or wading through a crowd.

42

For confidence-building, use the Primordial Sounds of:

HU-RĀ HU-RĀ HU-RĀ...

Have your two arms raised (elbows bent), fists clenched, or with weapons in your hands.

43

For developing stamina, use the Primordial Sounds of:

HU-HĀ HU-HĀ HU-HĀ...

Small strike on **HU** and full-strength strike on **HĀ**.

The Semi-Vowels combined with the Pure Vowels 1046

A Connecting Breathing
RŪ - HĀ

44

Stage 1: Connecting the Inner and the Outer

The physical air you breathe is but the covering over the real Breath

The purpose of this breathing is to make you aware of the Breath-current that pervades the planet, your absorbing energy from it into your system, your personal transformation of that Life-force, and your returning that energy back into the planetary energy field. This makes you aware of your relationship with Mother Earth, or Nature, and develops in you the ability to draw larger and larger amounts of energy into your Life-stream. Hence you will be able to do more, perform better, and live longer.

Remember that the physical air you breathe is not the Breath; that is but the covering over the real Breath, which is subtler than air, but you can access it with physical breathing. (Later on, you can breathe, on subtle-dimensional levels, the True Breath.)

The formula for this Connecting-Breath is **RŪ-HĀ**:

RŪ	HĀ
in-breathing	*out-breathing*

- Mentally follow the sound **RŪ** with your in-breathing and the sound **HĀ** with your out-breathing.
- With the **RŪ** in-breathing you enter deeply into yourself; with the **HĀ** out-breathing you go out of yourself.
- With each in-breathing you penetrate deeper and deeper into yourself, and with each out-breathing you go further and further out of yourself.
- Then there comes a balance when you are neither in nor out of yourself, a poise, a suspension of your breathing. Then you have joined Heaven to Earth, Earth to Heaven.
- Then you can choose to penetrate ever deeper into yourself with the sound-breath **RŪ**, or expand yourself ever larger outside into the world with the sound-breath **HĀ**.

The Holy Breath 1340
Memory Breathing 1345

You may practise this breathing in any sitting or lying-down posture, or you may practise it standing up, but the best postures for this technique are the sitting-on-heels postures.

The initial focus-area for this breathing exercise may be in the Third-Eye region, or the Creative Centre region (Throat Centre), or in the Spiritual Heart Centre. As the exercise develops, however, the focus may shift or change according to the *spontaneous need.*

This breathing unites the cold and hot currents

45

Stage 2: Uniting Male and Female

This breathing unites the cold and hot currents, passive and active energies, or the inner female and male qualities.

RŪ	–	HĀ	RŪ	–	HĀ
breathe in right nostril		*breathe out left nostril*	*breathe in left nostril*		*breathe out right nostril*

This is one cycle of breath. Repeat this for five minutes. Gradually build up to ten minutes. Control the flow of breath in the nostrils by the thumb and middle finger.

46

Stage 3: Uniting the Base Centre and the Crown Centre

Repeat in the pattern shown below. This shows one cycle of breath.

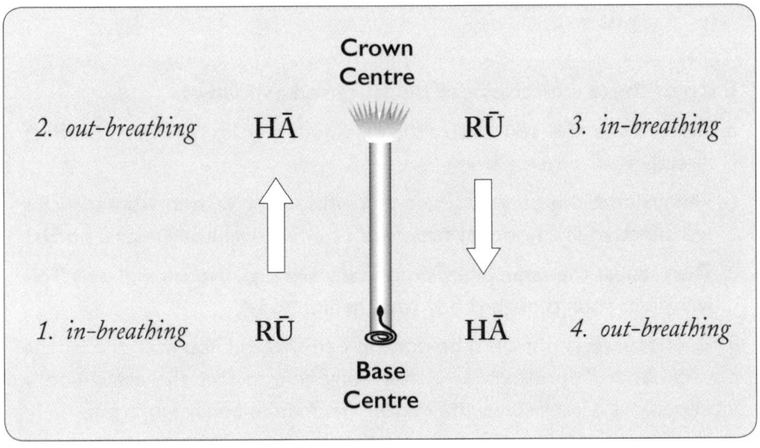

RŪ-HĀ Breathing in the Base and Crown Centres

Baptism and Rebirth 722

Healing Sound-Vibration Formula
HRĪṀ HRĀṀ HRŪṀ HRAIṀ HREIṀ HRĀH

This Sound-formula will give you energy, youth, life and health

This Sound-formula will give you energy, youth, life and health.

Vowels:	**I A U AI EI ĀH**	
Semi-Vowel:	R	- fiery energy of the Sun.
Aspirated:	H	- a strong, breathing sound.
Nasal Sound:	Ṁ	- sounded in the nose as a humming sound.

- The Vowels **I A U** are the primary sounds of the ancient Universal Language of Humanity, the ancestor of all Sacred Languages and all languages.
- **AI** and **EI** are the basic Combined Vowels (gliding into each other, called *diphthongs*).
- **ĀH** is the long drawn-out sound of breath leaving the body.
- The **R** sound is a forceful **RA** sound, with the **R** rolled.
- The **H** sound is **HA**, forceful breathing with the emphasis on the **H**. (Remember to pronounce the pure **A** sound.)

Each of these exercises will have effects on you and the group on the physical, emotional and psychological levels. You always have effects when you work with sound. Observe these effects, then you will know what sounds can help you in which way.

Each of these exercises can be practised as follows:

a. First intone the sound-structures aloud, physically. This will affect directly your physical body.

b. Then repeat the same practice at a whisper or with low-breath. This will affect your emotional structure or emotional body (astral body).

c. Then repeat the same practice mentally, silently, in your mind only. This will affect your thought-body (the mental body).

This, of course, is not all to be done in one session! You master first the physical bodily vibrations; at a later stage you master the astral bodily vibrations; at a later stage you master the mental bodily vibrations.

The Personality Complex 36

The Primordial Sound Alphabet 1028
The Inner Healer 1454
The Healing Sun Mantra 1599
Solar Meditation in the Cakras 1640

47

You can start by intoning the three primary Vowel Sounds, **I A U**, prolonged:

I... A... U...

The Vowels increase your life-force and are excellent for producing a general sense of health inside you.

Listen to the sound you are making, and observe the effects it has on you

48

Then you can practise the primary Vowels one by one:

I..., A..., U....

Begin by intoning the **I** sound many times.

When you intone a sound, *listen* to the sound you are making, and *observe* the effects it has on you—on your physical body, on your mind, on your emotions.

When in a group, intone the **I** sound continuously for 10, 20 or 30 minutes. Listen to the sound you are making, then listen to the group and *merge* your consciousness into the continuous **I** sound of the group. Then listen *inside* the group **I** sound and try to reach the inner dimensions of it. The continuous **I** sound, chanted continuously by the group, has a tremendous, transforming effect on your consciousness.

At another time you can do the same with the **A** sound, either by yourself or sounded continuously by the group.

At another time you can do the same with the **U** sound.

The continuous $\overset{\infty}{\bar{\mathbf{I}}}$ sound, the continuous $\overset{\infty}{\bar{\mathbf{A}}}$ sound and the continuous $\overset{\infty}{\bar{\mathbf{U}}}$ sound each will have very specific effects on you and the group.

49

Then sound all the Vowels in this formula, one after the other:

I A Ū...
AI EI ĀH...

There is a slight pause between the sounding of **I A Ū** and **AI EI ĀH**, and the **Ū** and **ĀH** are prolonged longer than the other sounds.

Sounding the Vowels 1033

50

Next you can practise the nasal **Ṁ** sound or humming Sound-Vibration.

The Ṁ has an intensely unifying effect upon you

Then practise also the prolonged group humming sound of **Ṁ** for 10, 20 or 30 minutes, nonstop. This has an intensely unifying effect upon you and unifies the group into one whole, massive energy field. The group will have the sense of Oneness as the separated individualities disappear into the One Power.

51

Next, you (or the group) can practise the **HA** (**H**) sound:

HA HA HA HA...

These are strong, powerful out-breathings, done fast. This is very energizing.

52

Next, you or the group can practise the **RA** (**R**) sound:

RA RA RA RA...

This is done fast, with the **R** rolled. This will generate Fire in you and in the group, and is also very energizing.

53

Next, combine the two:

HA RA HA RA HA RA HA RA...

This is done fast. If you (or the group) do this for 10 or 20 minutes you will be on Fire.

54

Then you can work with each individual part of this healing Sound-Vibration. For example:

HRĪṀ...

The Semi-Vowels 1043
The Bīja-Mantra Hrīṁ 1547

You can prolong the **Ī** sound, or you can prolong the **Ṁ** sound, or you can sound the **Ī** sound and the **Ṁ** sound with equal length. Each will have a different effect on you and the group.

In the same way, you can practise all the other sounds, each separately:

HRĀṀ..., HRŪṀ..., HRAIṀ..., HREIṀ...

55

The HRĀH sound generates lots of energy

Then, you or the group can practise:

HRĀH HRĀH HRĀH HRĀH...

This is done slowly at first, then faster and faster. It is important that the **HR** sound is pronounced clear and strong, with the strong breathing **H** sound merging into the rolling **R** sound. The **HRĀH** sound generates lots of energy.

56

Then, you or the group can practise the complete formula:

HRĪṀ HRĀṀ HRŪṀ HRAIṀ HREIṀ HRĀH...

57

You may have noticed that this general healing formula does not employ the Pure Vowel Sounds **O** and **E**. The long **Ō** and the long **Ē** are missing from this Sound-formula. This is intentional.

To complete your practice you may intone the long **Ō** sound and, as a group, the continuous **Ō͡** sound. This has an intensely unifying effect, inwards and upwards upon the Planes of Being. This will make you and the group whole, complete, integrated, unified, harmonized.

Next you may practise intoning the **Ē** sound and, as a group, the continuous **Ē͡** sound. This Pure Vowel has the opposite effect to **O**. This is an outgoing sound, outward bound into the world and into the subtle realms around you. It gives you and the group power, strength, energy.

The Art of Warriorship

Understanding even this one Sound-Vibration formula gives you a little insight into the power of the Ancient Primordial Sound Language, which the Initiated Warriors of olden days could use to develop various powers and attributes within themselves.

You gain virtues (abilities) by consciously developing them. Nothing comes by itself. The Warrior trains in the Art of Warriorship from childhood until the end of his or her physical life.

Integrity and Perfection 1005

The Supreme Mantra of the Spiritual Warrior RĀM: the Warrior Power

The Primordial Sound-Vibration **RĀM** is the supreme Word of Power of the Spiritual Warrior. In it is contained all things the Warrior needs, and the Spiritual Warrior Path from beginning to end.

In RĀM is contained all things the Warrior needs

Qualities of the Divine Sound of RĀM

Active goodness, positive energy, goodwill, compassion, helpfulness, service to all.

Constructive activity, progressiveness, evolutionary Force, success, accomplishment, overcoming all obstacles and challenges.

Healing, life-giving vibration; nourishing, sustaining vibration.

Warrior skills; the sense for fairness and justice; perfection, courage, fearlessness, righteousness; physical, mental and spiritual strength.

Intelligence, Wisdom, Bliss, Peace, Spirituality, Kingliness, Divinity, the meeting of Man and God as one.

The Dynasty of the God-Kings or mighty Spiritual Warriors, Emperors and Rulers all over the planet and of all times.

Solar Dynasty, the Sun, the Solar Logos, Spiritual Radiance, Majesty, Divine Glory, the Power of Light-Vibration.

The Presence of God, Cosmic Mind, Pure Consciousness, Liberation, Self-Realization, Enlightenment.

The Force of the Spiritual Hierarchy; invincible Will-power, purpose and plan; Divine Government; the active, saving Force of Divinity.

The Warrior Power (**RĀM**) applies to:

a. The Individual.
b. The Group.
c. The Planet.
d. The Cosmos.

Rām: the Universal Name 1273
The Bīja-Mantra Rāṁ 1544

58

Practise first the sounding of the pure **Ā** sound, prolonged, physically then mentally. Sense the all-pervading pure **Ā** sound.

59

Practise next the **RĀ** sound, physically then mentally. The **Ā** sound is prolonged. Feel the **RĀ** sound as an *opener*, *initiator* or *commencer* of energies. It *opens you up* from within yourself, into the Energy-Field.

Allow the sound of RĀM to arise in you spontaneously

60

Next, practise the **RĀM** sound, first physically, then mentally:

RĀM, RĀM, RĀM...

The **Ā** sound is long, but *not* prolonged (only for 2 or 3 counts). Feel the *opening up of energies* inside yourself with the **RĀ** sound, and let them go with the **M** sound. With the **RĀ** of **RĀM** you generate energy; with the **M** of **RĀM** you relax or let go of the energies. (Tension and relaxation, action and letting go of action. This principle is important in daily life.)

61

Next, practise **RĀM RĀM RĀM...** to *build up energy* inside you.

62

Now you are ready for the next stage. At first, repeat **RĀM, RĀM, RĀM...** mentally, *intentionally*. Then stop the intentional repetition and relax, and allow the sound of **RĀM** to arise in you *spontaneously*, **RĀM... RĀM... RĀM...**, at intervals. When you can do this, you will begin to experience waves of Bliss or outbursts of Joy.

63

Next, begin with *intentional* repetition mentally a few times, **RĀM, RĀM, RĀM**, to set up the Energy-Current, or to link up with the Sound-Current. Then reduce the sound to shorter and shorter wavelengths, until you see, hear or sense Light-Vibration *inside* you.

Light 978
Shining from Within 1053

64

Next, go through the same stages as before until you see, hear or sense the Universal Light *within* you and *around* you. This is the Cosmic **RĀM** Vibration, the Mind of the Absolute Deity.

65

Your Thought becomes merged with the Power of RĀM

When you Sense **RĀM**, the Mind of the Solar Logos, or the Universal Deity in Cosmic Space, you can do two things:

a. "Listen-in" to the Divine Plan and help to manifest it on Earth.
b. Consciously invoke the Deity for a Plan to be manifested by you, for now you are a Spiritual Warrior of Light.

66

Because of the Magical Potency of the Sound of **RĀM** in Human Consciousness, you can also use it to *develop* any or all of the qualities listed previously (the qualities of the Divine Sound of **RĀM**).

In this process you mentally meditate, **RĀM**, **RĀM**, intoning it at intervals, while *simultaneously thinking* of the quality you wish to awaken or develop in yourself. You hold the Thought of that quality in your mind while you are tuning into the Power of **RĀM**, the Universal Light-Vibration.

For example, if you want to develop fearlessness, then meditate on **RĀM** *simultaneously* with the Thought "fearlessness". Do not "think" about "fearlessness", that is, do not get your mind *thinking* about fearlessness; simply hold onto the Thought "fearlessness".

In this way the Spiritual Warrior develops many "miraculous" powers. Your Thought becomes *merged* with the Power of **RĀM**, the Infinite Light-Field, and **RĀM** backs up your Thought with tremendous Power and Creative Force to *manifest* your Thought. This is the Science of Miracles known by the Great Warriors of olden days.

67

When used by the Group as a group meditation, apart from the individual benefits, it develops all these qualities in the Group-Soul and builds and nourishes the Wall of Light in the planetary atmosphere.

To Worship the Sun 1586
Warriors of the Sun 1618
The Warrior of the Light 984

68

The Word of Power of the Warrior can also be used to develop Heart Radiation. You irradiate your Heart Centre with Light by the internal mental repetition of **RĀM, RĀM, RĀM** in the Heart region, with Devotion, Love and Longing for the Divine. For **RĀM** is the manifest God, God-in-Incarnation, God-in-Creation, as the all-powerful, miraculous, Sounding-Light Vibration *within* your body, the planet, the Solar System, the Universe.

The Sunshine inside you will drive away all your negative emotions

As you repeat with Devotion, **RĀM, RĀM, RĀM**, in your Heart, you will attract the Light of God to yourself and you will *feel* the Presence of God, the Nearness of God, the Immanence of God *within* yourself and within all things. This will bring about a great Transformation, a great Transfiguration within yourself.

69

RĀM is also used by the Spiritual Warrior for *character training*, for the development of virtues and for overcoming negative tendencies.

The repetition of **RĀM, RĀM, RĀM**... inside you, silently, mentally, produces the phenomena of Sunshine (not symbolically but actually): Heart-Sun, Solar-Systemic Sun, Spiritual Sun, Universal Sun. The Sunshine inside you will drive away all your negative emotions, such as fear, insecurity, worries, hatreds, aggressive tendencies, stress, doubt, anger, the "blues" or "melancholy", and wrong habits.

Glorious indeed is RĀM.

God is the Chanter, the Chanted and the means of Chanting.

The Absolute Reality is you (you are a part of It), It is the chanted (the sounds you make, whether audibly or inaudibly), and It is the means of chanting (the power, life and energy by which you chant or intone). All is the One, the *That*, the inexpressible Absolute Being. When you *realize* this as you work with the Sacred Primordial Language of Sound, you will at once attain Self-Realization and God-Realization, and you will *know* that you are *That*, the Sacred, the Eternal One, and that in fact all is in *That* and issues forth from *That*, including the Sacred Language of Sounds.

The One 1686

The Presence of God 1396
The Manifested-God 1589
The Self-Generating Light 1594

Meditations on Aspects of RĀM (Sanskrit)

1. Śrī Rām
   The Holy Power (the Miraculous Power).
2. Śrī Rām Namah
   Glory be to God (the Divinization Power).
3. Śrī Rām Sakala Namah
   Glory be to Rām who is the All (who is within All).
4. Śrī Rām Ādi Puruśāya Namah
   Glory be to Rām the Primeval Lord.
5. Śrī Rām Parakaśāya Namah
   Glory be to Rām the Supreme Radiance.
6. Śrī Rām Sarvadevāya Namah
   Glory be to Rām the All-Shining Power.
7. Śrī Rām Sarveśāya Namah
   Glory be to Rām the All-Manifesting Power.
8. Śrī Rām Sarvajñāya Namah
   Glory be to Rām the Omniscient.
9. Śrī Rām Anandāya Namah
   Glory be to Rām who is All-Bliss.
10. Śrī Rām Jaya Rām Jaya Jaya Rām
   Glory be to the All-Conquering Power.

The Ten Cosmic Powers of the RĀM Primordial Sound-Vibration

1. Holiness and miracles.
2. To make all things Divine.
3. To Perceive the Divine Presence in All.
4. Eternity and Timelessness.
5. Radiant Glory.
6. The Universal Light-Vibration.
7. The All-Controlling Power.
8. Omniscience.
9. All-Bliss.
10. The All-Conquering Power.

After you have established yourself in the **RĀM** Vibration of the Cosmic Sound through the practices previously described, then you can develop the Cosmic Powers of **RĀM**. This can be done when you are in Higher Consciousness or Superconsciousness (in Causal Consciousness or above). You are in your Living-Soul-Consciousness, with your normal rational mind function suspended, all mind-chatter having been stopped naturally. You are in the Inspired State, the State of Inspiration, and in that state you can use any one of the ten extended versions of the **RĀM** Sound-Vibration.

This can be done when you are in Higher Consciousness or Superconsciousness

Examples

For instance, if you want to acquire the Power of Holiness, or the Power of Miracles, you first enter the State of **RĀM** with your previous **RĀM** meditation practice, then, in your Inspired State or Causal Consciousness, you meditate upon (repeat):

ŚRĪ RĀM...

As you repeat the mantra, you simultaneously hold the Thought in your mind, "Holy Power". This is a curious state of your mind. You are in the Transcendental State, yet simultaneously you re-engage your mind on one Thought, "Holy Power".

Or, for example, if you want to develop the Power of Omniscience, you enter the **RĀM** State, the Transcendental State, and in that state you meditate upon (repeat):

ŚRĪ RĀM SARVA JÑĀNA NAMAH

...while holding the Thought "Omniscience".

Or, if you want to develop the All-Conquering Power, in that state you meditate upon (repeat):

ŚRĪ RĀM JAYA RĀM
JAYA JAYA RĀM

...while holding the Thought "All-Conquering Power".

Follow the same procedure with all ten aspects. Another way to go about this is to start with any one of these extended aspects of **RĀM**, go through all the stages to Causal Consciousness and, in that state, meditate upon that aspect of **RĀM** as described above.

Saṁyama 582
Esoteric Knowledge 1218
Action while in Samādhi 1331
The Seven States of Consciousness 494

The Warrior of the Heart
ŌM RĀM KLĪM

ŌM RĀM KLĪM are three Sound-Vibrations from the Primordial Sound Language.

The Bīja-Mantra Ōṁ 1542
The Bīja-Mantra Rāṁ 1544
The Bīja-Mantra Klīṁ 1549

With the **ŌM** sound we *penetrate* into the Heart.
With the **RĀM** sound we *expand* the Heart.
With the **KLĪM** sound we *unify* the Heart.

70

Stage One: **ŌM...**

Stage Two: **ŌM - RĀM...**

Stage Three: **ŌM - RĀM - KLĪM...**

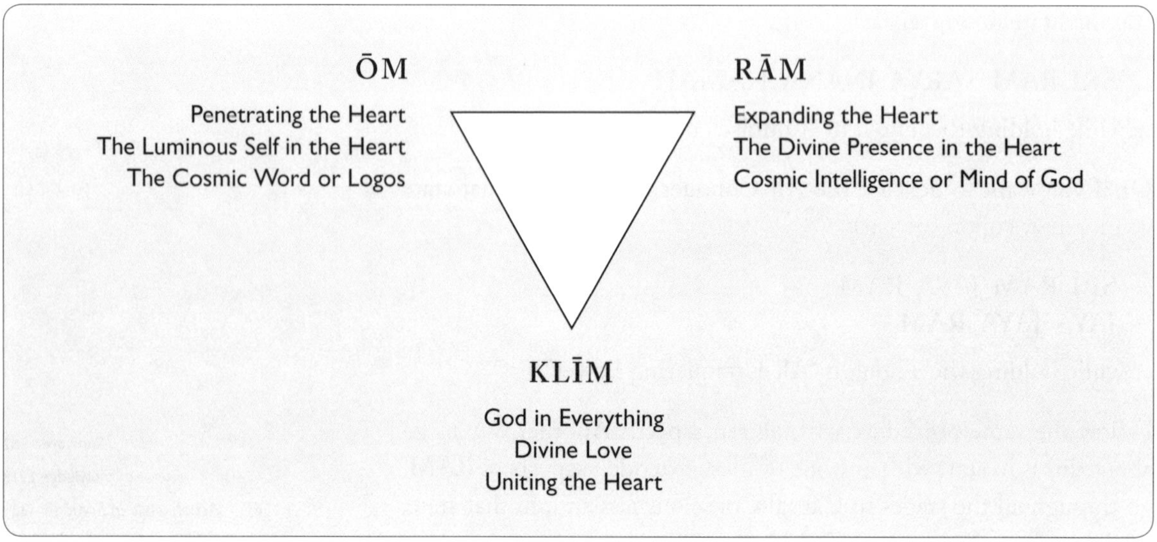

The Warrior of the Heart

The Creative Power of the Primordial Language of Sound

The Primordial Sound Language of Primeval Mankind is a language of Sound-Vibrations from the total Sound-Vibration of the Word, the Logos, the Name of God. It vibrates in the Universal Aether, Space, and by using it you release tremendous spiritual forces into your auric-field which will change and transform you, and ultimately will liberate you from the limitations of material consciousness.

By using the Sacred Language you enable the God-Power to act within you

Behind all the sounds of the Primordial Sound Language, behind all the Vowels, Semi-Vowels, Consonants, and so forth, there is the Original Universal Field of Pure Sounding-Light Vibrations, the one and only True Name of God. This Universal Single Field of Sounding-Light Vibrations is the basis of all Creation, the Foundation of the Universe. When you practise this Science of the Universal Sound Language, after a while you will reconnect to the Source of the sounds you are making both internally and externally, and you will see, hear, taste and smell That which is Sounding-Light, Blissful Being and Boundless Love-Wisdom, the Primeval Godhead.

The Powers of God, the Absolute Being within the Universe, are locked up in this language, because God and the Name (Sound-Vibration) are One. By using the Sacred Language you enable the God-Power to act within you and through you into the environment and into all Creation. This is the Secret of it.

The Sacred Language has the Power to open your Heart to the Universal Vibration of Divine Love and the Vibration of Infinite Wisdom. It speeds up your evolution, and by its Power you can consciously enter the Higher Evolutionary Stream.

The Secret is this:

You can do all things through God, whose Power is working through you by the Power of the NAME. ≮

What is the Name? 1259
God's Cosmic Symphony 1649
The Way of the Heart 1249
The Worship of the Goddess 1481
The Yoga of the Sun 1583

CHAPTER 48

The Warrior Code

A Guide for Living

In reality, this planet Earth is a School for Warriors. The Warrior Path deals with the advanced meditational practices of the true Spiritual Warrior living the Spiritual Life.

This chapter is a guide for *practical* living in the world, where the Spiritual Warrior must live. You may meditate on one Aphorism each day, or you may choose to meditate on an Aphorism for as long as you wish.

This Way of the Spiritual Warrior is not a worldly wisdom

The Aphorisms may also be used as a source of guidance in times of crisis, trouble and opposition in your life. When problems seem insurmountable and the enemy is attacking you, simply open a page at random and instruction will come your way. After a while you will find a *solution* to all problems and conflict situations. The Spiritual Warrior will give you indications of what to *do*. Sometimes it is *action* that is required, while sometimes it is precisely *inaction* that is the appropriate Way.

This Way of the Spiritual Warrior is *not* a worldly wisdom. You will be guided by another Light. May that Light bring you through the Valley of Tears and Death to the mountaintop of Wisdom, Insight and Skill in Action.

∞

The beginning Warrior must learn Virtue.

The advanced Warrior must learn Meditation and the Spiritual Life.

The perfect Warrior must apply his Spiritual Realizations and Insights in daily life.

The Master Warrior must live in the Eternal and act from the Transcendental State.

Aphorisms of the Spiritual Warrior

Your greatest Power
is at your point of Focus.

*

Order in the midst of chaos.
Love in the midst of hate.
Light in the midst of Darkness.

*

Walk away with your dignity intact,
even if you lost the Battle.

*

Go to the Battle not only to fight,
but to win.

*

Listen, rather than fight,
as often as you can.

*

Justice, Compassion and Charity
are the marks of the good Warrior.

*

Study your opponent to win.

*

Determined, positive, self-confident:
that is the Warrior.

*

For the Warrior,
Focus is a matter of life or death.

*

Control your temper.
Do not become angry over unimportant things.

The Warrior fights for God
and the Cause of Righteousness.

*

Your Battles are not always won,
but the Spirit within you is always Victorious.

*

The Warrior-Spirit is
the sense for Duty and Honour.

*

Your Future is in your own hands;
let no one take it away from you.

*

Persistence and Patience
is the key to Victory.

*

Conquer your fears *before* your Battle.

*

Warriorship and Nobility are identical.
A true Warrior is a Nobleman or
Noblewoman at Heart.

*

The Path of the Warrior is the Path of Struggle,
but the Fearless Spirit conquers day by day.

*

Some things are just not worth fighting for.
The Wise Warrior often forgives.

*

A Warrior must endure great hardships
without any complaints.

The Quest for the Holy Grail
is a Quest for your Self.

*

Don't hold yourself in too high esteem,
lest you fall too hard.

*

Avoiding confrontation hinders your growth,
but the War you fight must be a fight
for true Righteousness.

*

Knowing your Enemy is the
most important part of your Battle.

*

Attack and defend yourself simultaneously.

*

Be confident like a general who knows
his army is going to win the War.

*

Don't argue against superior forces,
or when your vitality is low.
Be cautious.

Strength and Dignity
are the mark of a Warrior.

*

Make an alliance with the Sun.
The Sun is your Strength.

*

To overcome a deadly opponent, you must
become like him. Respect your enemy,
learn about his nature *before* the Combat.
Know his every move and master his every skill.
Thus shall you Win.

*

Fight for the best.
Be prepared for the worst.
Thus, draw the Middle Line.

*

Being a Warrior is not about War,
but about Peace.

*

A Warrior is fearless, calm, confident,
physically fit, mentally strong,
and cool under extreme pressure.

Action in the Transcendent

The Transcendent pervades All. The Eternal is all around us and within us. This means that all things, beings and situations are included in the Eternal Oneness. In the Transcendent, all merge. A Warrior who can function *in* the Transcendent and *from* the Transcendent is *One* with the enemy, with the opposition, with the attacker. For the Spiritual Warrior, One with the Spirit, One with the Eternal Transcendent, there is no enemy, only the necessary Action to be taken.

In the Oneness of the Transcendent, the actions of your enemy are but part of the complex web of Total Action. You are not moved by life or death, living and dying, pain or suffering. What has been Ordained *is*. You merely participate in the *Is-ness* of what is happening around you in the Moment. It could be your life. It could be your death. Inwardly you are calm, centred in the Eternal, alert, ready for all possibilities, without fear or favour. Then you *Act*.

When you fight with anger or from fear,
you will lose the Battle.

*

The fear of anything
is ultimately the fear of God.

*

When there is nothing for you to be afraid of,
you have reached the Ultimate State.

*

The good Warrior knows when to retreat
and when to advance.

*

When you are under attack,
find a Weapon to defend yourself with.

*

Sometimes, to go forward
you need to take a step back.

*

Can you sacrifice your high Principles,
O Warrior?

*

If you make mistakes, Warrior,
learn from them.

*

The Spiritual Warriors are equal to each other.
Each has a voice to speak with and a hand
to act with. They fight for Justice and Truth.
Together they carry the Banner of Light.

*

The Path is about Responsibility.

In the Warrior Code of Honour
it is wrong to sacrifice another life
to save your own life.

*

Never underestimate your Enemy,
nor disrespect his skills and abilities,
for then you will be conquered by him
instead of being the Conqueror yourself.

*

Take time out to study your Enemy.
Learn from him.

*

To defeat your Enemy you must know him
like your brother or your father.

*

Fight with your Heart for what is Right,
not with anger, nor with fear.
Then you are Victorious already,
even if you lose the Battle.

*

You will never become a Warrior
unless you have Virtue.

*

Merely to have a destructive urge does not
qualify you to become a Spiritual Warrior.

*

The greatest Victory is victory over your
own mind and your own physical senses.

*

Only Total Awareness can protect you
from sudden surprise attacks.

Life is your Battlefield and
living day by day is the Battle.
Each day conquered and masterfully
lived is a Victory for you.

*

The Warrior loves ceremony
and appreciates protocol.
He honours his leaders
and Spiritual Guides.

*

Remember the King of Kings,
the Lord of Lords, the Omnipresent,
the Supreme Commander who Watches us all.

*

Seeking Warrior,
there is no Quest without
pain, trouble and suffering,
if you desire to own the Great Price.

*

Enlightened Chiefs and loyal Warriors
fight together for Victory.

*

Your choices are limited
by your opponent's skills
and your own weaknesses.

*

Fight, work, pray:
this is your Duty until your last Battle,
O Tender-Hearted Warrior.

*

Prayer is your most important weapon,
O aspirant to Warriorship.

If you make a mistake,
there are lessons to be learned from it.

*

The School of Wisdom
and the School of the Warrior
work together hand in hand.

*

Never be without your Spiritual Guide,
O Understanding Warrior.

*

Be firmly rooted in the Spirit,
Victorious Warrior.

*

When you have Conquered yourself,
you will become the Perfect Warrior.

*

You are the great Hero and Inspirer,
O Perfect Warrior.

*

Integrity shines from you,
O Virtuous One.

*

The Path of Clarity is fraught with danger,
for the Opposition never rests.

*

Channel all your energies at One Point;
thus you will become Mighty and Powerful.

*

Self-sacrifice is a great Virtue
for the Honourable.

The Master brings out the best in you.

*

Don't compromise your sense of Direction,
Vision or Goal, O Masterful Warrior.
Know your Self.

*

You will never become a prisoner,
Powerful Warrior, if you remain
Free in your Spirit.

*

Don't dismiss an Idea or Plan until you have tested
it out and proven it right or wrong.

*

Heroic Warrior, you continually
test the limits of your Endurance.

*

Your Brave-Heart is made of Fire and Steel.

*

Don't allow pride, O Noble Warrior,
to blind your Good Judgment.

Don't bear a grudge against anybody,
O Loving Warrior, nor hate anybody,
for life is too short to waste it on negative energy.

*

Your fervent desire is for Glory and Honour.

*

Brave Warrior, let your Strong Heart
be tempered by Wisdom.

*

First listen to your Heart,
then listen to your Mind,
O Warrior of the Noble Spirit.

*

Motivation and Commitment
is the key to your Victory.

*

Your Survival depends on your Will to Live.

*

Your Sword is only as sharp
as your Awareness.

Action and Stillness: The Supreme Way

Life consists of positive and negative situations and circumstances. Accept them both with an equal mind. Face negativity and unpleasant people with Courage, Strength, Patience, Love and Understanding. The positive and negative, the energies of Love and hate, Serenity and intense Activity commingle eternally in the Oneness of Cosmic Duration. It is a great Play. Live in the Transcendent, even Now.

The Supreme Way consists of paying equal attention to body, mind and Soul, to worldly affairs and matters of the Spirit, to Action and Stillness, to happiness, joy, success and progress, and to opposition, misfortunes, enemies and tragedies. In equal attention there is no split, no divisions in the Way, for all is One. Perils, dangers and negative circumstances are accepted equally and worked through, as much as all pleasures and positive circumstances. There is only Action, there is only Stillness, and the two are One in the Timeless.

The Infinite Supreme is everywhere.
God is in everything.

This is the Way of the Spiritual Warrior.

There is no limit to
your Courage and Endurance,
O Lion-Hearted Warrior.

*

Mighty Warrior,
Persistence is your Virtue that unlocks
your Limitless Strength.

*

Your Indomitable Spirit is already Victorious,
O Unconquerable Warrior.

*

I invoke the Strength and Fearlessness
of the Warrior Spirit.

*

I salute you, O Noble Warrior of the Heart;
all praise and glory be to you!

Conditioned Thinking

Conditioned thinking arises when you think in grooves or patterns established by your religion, culture or tradition. Education, psychology and politics are also conditioned. A person's arguments may seem reasonable and logical, but that person's mind may still be heavily conditioned. People's motives control their thinking. They project these outside of themselves and, if you are not careful, they trap you in their thoughts.

In conditioned thinking there is no Freedom. If your mind is conditioned by techniques, processes, traditions, theories, models, beliefs or ideologies, then Spontaneity of the Spirit becomes impossible and the chance of success in your War or Struggle is very limited. When you commit yourself to an ideology, your mind is trapped and you go around and around in a circle, like a mouse on a wheel.

Discipline is your Superior Virtue.

*

Dignity is yours.

*

Spiritual Warrior, ceremony,
pomp and Power belong to you.

*

Life and Death are your Gift.

*

In the Jungle of Life,
constant Vigilance is the key to Survival.

*

The true Warrior is not afraid to lose his life
for Honour and the Love of Truth.

*

The accomplished Warriors
are masters of Themselves.

*

Military music stirs your Heart to Bravery.

*

You can also choose to lose if your
Noble Heart prompts you, for a greater Good.
Self-Sacrifice is your hidden Strength.

*

Believe in yourself and believe in the
great Brotherhood of Enlightened Warriors
and you will succeed in your Quest.

*

The True Warrior chooses Duty
instead of selfish, personal satisfaction.

As a Spiritual Warrior you are one
with the Universe. You can meet all
the other great Spiritual Warriors on
the Plane of Enlightened Mind.

*

Don't give in to the Darkness,
nor to gloom and despair.

*

Pain, Self-Sacrifice and hard work are
the lot of the Warrior. Dare to Succeed!

*

Focus on the Goal to be accomplished;
thus you will generate the Vital Power.

*

Push the limits of your Endurance;
thus you will acquire Virtue, Valour and Virility.

*

Remember your Commitment, which is to
serve the King of Kings, the Lord of Lords.
And, on your Journey back to the Kingdom,
remember your Companions on the Way.

*

Fortune favours the Brave Warrior.

*

Listen to the Old Warrior about
great Battles won and great Battles lost;
but the last and greatest Battle is
to Conquer Yourself.

*

Your disciplined Will-Power
can generate limitless Energy
and miraculous feats of Strength.

The Power of the Warrior
resides in Indomitable Will.

*

Mental discipline and sharp Focusing
of the Will is the training of the Warrior.

*

You will have Challenges from within
yourself and Challenges from without.
But each Challenge overcome is a
Victory for your Deathless Self.

*

A Warrior becomes the Hero
after having conquered the Self.

*

The secret of the Warrior's Strength
is a Masterful Will-Power.

*

Through mistakes and challenges
you grow to Perfection.

*

The Quest for the Holy Grail is
the Quest for the Kingdom of God.

*

You are a perfect Warrior when
you have conquered your Anger.

*

The Warrior fights only at the right time
and only for the right reasons.

*

There is a Warrior in each one of us;
often it is dormant and lies asleep.

The Warrior that is motivated
by ego is not a true Warrior.
The true Warrior has no self-interests.

*

Teach me what I need to know to become a
Warrior, and give me the Strength to be one.

*

Incredible Patience is yours,
O Great Warrior.

*

Life and Death are a *choice* for the Warrior:
to sacrifice a life or to sacrifice oneself.

*

Pain makes the Warrior stronger.

*

The Warrior's Destiny is
to do Battle for the *Just Cause;*
then you become Immortal.

*

The Way of the Warrior is
Fearlessness and performing all duties
on the Righteous Way.

*

The secret of the Warrior is to
control mental and physical energy.

*

The Warrior tests the limits
of human pain and endurance,
suffering and will-power.

*

To survive, maintain your Mental Balance.

A weapon is only as good as
the Spirit of the Warrior who uses it.

*

Strength, courage, honour and loyalty
are the signs of the True Warrior.

*

It is in the nature of things that Evil must
be opposed by the Spiritual Warrior.

*

Obedience brings Victory to you.

*

Loyalty is not a choice for the Warrior.
You are born with it. It is your life.

*

Self-Discipline and Will-Power are
the greatest assets of the Warrior.

*

Do not fight always brute force with brute force;
learn the Art of Subtle Manoeuvre,
the invisible side.

*

A Warrior lives by *respect:*
respect for his Teachers and Elders,
respect for his Opponents,
and respect for himself or herself.

*

The Warrior is determined,
resolute and hard-working;
that is the key to the Warrior's Success.

*

Turn your Weakness into Strength.

For the sake of Righteousness, sometimes you
must use Fire to fight fire, Force to fight force,
so that Truth and Justice may prevail.

*

Sometimes you have to sacrifice a little now
to gain much, later on.

*

The planet Earth is a battleground between
the opposing forces of Heaven and Hell.
Humanity is the Prize to be won.
Be established in the Light.

*

The Spirit within you is Fearless and Deathless.

*

May honesty, sincerity and courage be your Way.

*

You must always be Ready and Alert.

To eradicate anger,
cultivate its opposite: Calmness.

*

Every Defeat is a seed for a future Victory.

*

Every mistake you make is simply
another opportunity to improve yourself.

*

Listen to the *Ancient Warrior.*

*

Sometimes the Path of Least Resistance
is the best way to act.

*

Sometimes the old-fashioned way is the best.

*

Power, Choice, Decision, Victory.

Facing the Evil Mind

Evil exists and there are people with evil minds. There are times when they will make an offensive to try to engineer your downfall. They will engage in devious plans, machinations and personal attacks against you. The question is: What do you do with evil people?

Sometimes your enemy is just a misguided human being, or sometimes he is consciously malicious and has a purposeful evil mind to destroy you. On their own terms, in their own sphere of Cosmic Repercussion, they have already condemned themselves to suffering in this life or in lives to come. But what should *you* do?

The Superior Warrior is one who is unshaken, unruffled, undaunted by the attacks of enemies, always Peaceful, Serene, accepting them as they are, inwardly Free of condemnation, yet facing them bravely, courageously, without fear or anger, without succumbing to negative energy, doing what he can to rectify the situation, being established in the Solid-Foundation-Consciousness which is all around, all of the time.

Don't let them get to you. Watch your steps. If you are easily riled by your enemy's attacks, you make yourself an easy target for further attacks. The more you react, the more weapons they will hurl against you. Be patient and self-controlled. Every Battle comes to an end. Be patient with difficult people. This is a test of your Faith.

Enter the Sphere of the Boundless, the Timeless Sphere which is Cosmic Intelligence, wherein all actions fuse and melt. Be not afraid. Pause, be silent, be receptive, allow the Supreme Warrior to get ahold of you, and then, without an ego, *Act.*

The key to winning the Battle is preparation,
hard work and total Commitment.

*

Discipline develops Virtue,
and Virtue gives Peace and Happiness.

*

Bring out your *Inner* Strength, Authority and
Power, for you are a Child of God, the *Sun*.

*

With your Will-Power you can
stay always Calm and in Control.

*

Do not be afraid of the larger Life,
for you are destined to be Great and Glorious
by your Creator-God.

The Power of Yielding

The secret of the Warrior is yielding to opposition, not using direct force against it, not using aggression against aggression, but modifying it with your own energy, force, power, so that it cannot harm you. Your aim is to *create harmony* in the situation, to balance out the opposing force.

When you are about to be attacked physically, emotionally or mentally, when you are in danger or in a life-threatening situation, when you are in crisis and do not know what to do, don't panic. Include your opponent into yourself. Do not oppose him or her. Put yourself in the State of Awareness, yield to the oncoming force or energy, blend with it, then change its direction with your energy.

Include, accept, yield, merge, blend, and then change the situation by moving your energies in the direction of Harmony, Balance, Peace and Power.

Great Strength of Will comes to you
when you dedicate yourself to the
Service and Progress of Humanity.

*

Believe in your Self,
for the Strength of God lives within you.

*

A Warrior's Power lies within his own Mind,
and Peace within his own Heart.

*

Courage comes in all sizes,
but do not tempt your Enemy.

*

Respect your Enemy,
but don't give in to him or her.

*

Amidst chaos and destruction,
Calm and Confident is the Warrior's Spirit.

*

Virtue gives great Strength to the Warrior.

*

Whom does the Holy Grail serve?
The Warrior who is pure in Heart,
strong in Spirit, and fearless in Battle.

*

The True Warrior does not fight
for worldly glory and fame,
but for the Cause of the Spirit.

*

The quality of the Sage is Wisdom.
The quality of the Warrior is Strength.

Scatter not your energies in all directions,
but focus on the events at hand.
Yours then is the Crown of Victory.

*

If you become angry,
your mind gets confused and you
cannot make the right decisions.
Be Calm.

*

The most important weapon
of a Warrior is the Focused Mind.

*

Observe courtesy and etiquette,
but be Fearless.

*

If you take advantage of a person
weaker than yourself, then you are not
a true Warrior of the Spirit.

*

Keep your Dignity and Self-esteem always,
O Warrior of Light.

*

A Warrior fights for what he or she believes in.
But consider, is your belief Righteous?

*

There are some Wars you cannot win,
Peaceful Warrior, but that is all right too.

*

Fearlessness, Calm, Confidence, Humility:
these are the pillars upon which you stand.
Quiet, Peaceful, Determined and Fearless
is the Peaceful Warrior.

Set aside your reputation and
pride in yourself. Overcome all fears,
even the fear of death itself.

*

The Warrior meditates on Death every day,
for where there was a beginning there will
be an end. Death surely comes to all of us.
The Warrior is always ready to leave the body
and enter the Great Circle of Light.

*

The Warrior lives in the Moment,
for only in the Moment do all
Transformations take place.

*

The true Warrior unconditionally
respects all human beings, but
he never becomes enslaved by them.

*

Intense Awareness in the Moment
is the Way of the Warrior.

*

The Warrior without self-discipline
is a danger to common Peace.

*

Freedom, Fearlessness, Self-dependency.

*

When you meditate,
lay down your weapon and your warring mind,
and you shall find Peace within yourself.

*

If there is no discipline,
there is no achievement, no success.

I draw Strength and Guidance
from Discipline.

*

The Path of the Warrior is a Spiritual Journey,
a Quest for Divine Consciousness.

*

Whenever there are two extreme opposing views,
there is usually some truth in both of them.
Take the Middle Way.

*

Bear no grudges or discontent against
your enemies, nor be disappointed in people.
Settle your Heart in the immediate Peace
of the Now. Let the Past dissolve in
the mists of ancient times.

*

Listen to the Sound of a flower;
it will teach you how to become a true Warrior.

*

Hardships breed Strength and Character.

*

Self-control gives you Strength.

*

For a Warrior,
mind-wandering can prove costly.
Focus your Life-current.

*

That which is Real in you
is forever unharmed.

*

Patient endurance in times of trouble.

Never give in to feelings
of helplessness and defeat,
nor to bewilderment and despair,
for the Will of the Warrior is the
all-conquering Spirit.

*

There is no such thing as defeat for
a Warrior, only a temporary setback.

*

A Warrior's Mind is unmoving,
like a rock around which all else moves.

*

A Warrior's Mind is
focused in Intense Awareness,
as at the height of a mortal combat.

*

Centre yourself
and it will happen naturally.

*

A Warrior's Mind is rooted in
Peace—vigilant, alert, intense—yet moves
effortlessly in Action, firm in all situations.
This comes through practising the Art
of Warriorship and Meditation.

*

The Warrior meditates for long periods of time.
This makes his body and mind firm.

*

By constant practice comes Success.

*

The Way of the Warrior is Awareness:
Awareness in Action, Awareness in Stillness.

Sit Still in the Thunder Posture,
or in any comfortable posture,
with eyes closed, and be totally *Aware.*

*

The Spiritual Warrior lives life
without an ego, without selfish interests,
and without interpretation of events.

*

Turn to face your opponent
like a lion unafraid of his prey.

*

Find Peace within the Storm.

*

What you have promised, you must perform.
Do not give promises lightly.

*

Every tribe has its own protocol.
Although you follow the protocol,
stand Free within.

Any chance is better than no chance.

*

Have no fear of death.

*

Even if it hurts, control your emotions.

*

If you are fearful, you are ineffective.

*

In the midst of battle and the chaos of being
attacked, stay Focused, Centred, Calm.

*

An angry Warrior is a no-good Warrior.

*

Calm and Alert.

*

No thinking, no reflecting,
just Perfect Awareness.

Stand in the Void

The Ultimate Reality (God, the Absolute) is Formless, which appears as Emptiness because of its Infinite Expanse and Boundless Measurement, incomprehensible to the human mind. The All-inclusive Everything-ness is the Transcendental Consciousness, which is experienced as Emptiness, like the sky, but it contains all things as the sky contains all clouds. It is empty, like the sky, but It is the perfect Fullness because all bodies, forms, worlds, realms and beings are contained in It. This is the Primal Cause in the state of Pre-Manifestation and Manifestation simultaneously. I am in That. You are in That. Our opponents and enemies are in That. Everything gets done by the Transcendent.

Understand that all actions are intertwined. There is no such thing as a separate self—that is only an appearance. All selves are interconnected and all actions are interfaced. Your destiny is not different from the World Destiny which your enemies and opponents also share. Your destiny is part of the destiny of the Whole. Therefore, place your Consciousness in the Whole, the All-Perfect, the Transcendental Self, the Living Boundless Intelligence, the Formless dimension within which all bodies and minds arise.

Yes, stand in the Great Void, collect yourself and, without passion, *Fight*.

Do not act when you are flustered
or in confusion or muddle-headed.
Over-hasty action often precipitates disaster.

*

Great power means great responsibility.

*

The Path of the Warrior is to
go about in the world with open eyes,
but centred in the Spirit.

*

If you do not want to fight, don't go to war.
That is, be clear in your mind about
what you want to achieve so that
you don't have future regrets.

*

Standing in the Transcendent,
free from thoughts and emotions,
act in the Moment, spontaneously.

Victory is for the Warrior who has
no ego and no thought of himself.

*

Self-consciousness, or ego,
is the hindrance to the Realization
of the Boundless State.

*

If you have no ego,
then it does not matter
what people think of you.

*

Your daily life and War are not separate.
The Battlefield is life.

*

See everything happening
and be not anxious about the outcome.
This is to view things as they really are:
in the Transcendent.

The Righteous Fight

If you are a Light-Warrior, you will take action to make things right that were wrong, and there will be *consequences* of that action. If you are a Warrior, it is an honour for you to fight a Righteous Fight.

The true Spiritual Warrior does not engage in arguments or gossip, nor slander or criticism of others, nor does he spread evil rumours or create divisions and separation due to differences of opinion. Love and Unity are his watchwords. Forgiveness and Generosity are his actions toward those who have made a mistake. Instead of blaming others, he ever works to perfect himself.

The Master Warrior has no ego, no self-centredness. He is Spontaneous in action, being just himself, responding to the need of the situation. Doing nothing with his ego, avoiding friction and conflict as much as possible, unyielding to oppression yet never oppressing others, he is dispassionate, quiet and calm within. Accepting what is inevitable, he adapts spontaneously and responds to each situation perfectly. He is always in the Moment, never looks back to the Past, nor bases his hopes or dreams in the Future. His actions are effortless for they are derived from the *calm mind.* He remains *centred* at all times, has no fear of any situation, never forces, commands or dictates any person or event. He is Awake in *Being,* the Heart of the Universe.

The Warrior's Way is to act, but without getting attached to the results of the actions. Offer all your actions to God and let God take care of results.

Action and inaction,
inaction and action,
is the Way of the Warrior.

*

The Warrior who has mastered the
Art of Meditation and re-focused into the
Transcendent (the formless Supra-Existence)
becomes filled with Light, Power
and Compassion.

*

When the Transcendental Reality is not
experienced, your mind's inherent Peace
is shattered by the ceaseless activities
of thoughts and physical actions.

*

If you have many questions,
seek the answers within yourself.

*

Unless you have a Spiritual View of life,
you are lost.

*

Cast your mind into the Great Sign,
the Totality, the all-pervading Active Power
of God the Absolute, the Name that pervades
you and your environment, and you will have
strength to deal with all situations.

*

In the midst of action,
rely on the Stillness which
is everywhere present.

*

Vigorous physical action
relieves emotional tensions.

Accept a tiger as a tiger
and a mouse as a mouse.
Don't try to turn a tiger into a
mouse, or a mouse into a tiger.
Thus avoid a lot of emotional conflicts.

*

Don't move directly against the person who
is attacking you, but go with his movement.
Using his energy and movement,
deflect his power and establish your
own control of the situation.

*

Know the Stillness that leads to Freedom
where there is no more Fighting.

*

When you have no thoughts of self,
no fear of death, no fear of injury, pain or defeat,
when victory and defeat are the same for you,
then you are a Spiritual Warrior.
This can happen only after you have established
yourself in the Transcendental Absolute.

*

You cannot control
everything and everyone.
Relax.

*

Be Centred where you are
and results happen by themselves.
Take results as they come.
Have no disappointments.

*

Patience and diplomacy
can often correct a situation,
avoiding the need for an all out conflict.

Life will often bring negative
situations that you will have to deal with.
Understand the relative significance of each.
They cannot touch the Eternal within you.

*

When you can endure insults and
ill-treatment with Equanimity of Mind,
you are a Master Warrior.

*

When you never become angry,
then you have become a Master Warrior.

*

Deal with one problem at a time,
one enemy at a time, otherwise
you will be overwhelmed.

*

Adapt like water.

*

Many times it is better
not to interfere with situations,
but to let them evolve by themselves.
It is Wisdom to know when to act
and when not to act.

*

You will become a Master Warrior when you *know*
that Stillness in Meditation and Dynamic Action
in the field of Battle are one and the same.
Meditation and Action are One
in the Transcendent.

*

That State which includes
Sound and Silence, Stillness and Action,
that is the Transcendental State.

Wakefulness, being alert, awake, ready,
is the Way of the Warrior.
Wakefulness in Action,
Wakefulness in Meditation.
The Warrior's Mind is clear, sharp, bright.

*

Decrease your pride, Warrior.

*

The Great Way is to accept victory and defeat
as if they never happened.

*

In the Ultimate Reality there
are no separated bodies and minds,
no separate entities, just as the fish
are not separated from the sea.

*

All bodies, names and forms
are but momentary Transformations
in the Field of the Transcendent.

*

The First Cause is that which
sets all things into motion.
It is Divine Mind.
Although in ceaseless Motion,
It hasn't moved anywhere at all.

*

Why re-invent the wheel?
The Ultimate Truth has been known
all the time and That has not changed.

*

The Ultimate Mystery of the Universe
surpasses all human language, all definitions,
all thought-processes, all human actions.

To understand the Way
you have to use the Suprarational Mind.
Your ordinary mind cannot grasp It.

*

The Original Way has
no qualities or attributes,
yet all qualities and attributes
are contained within It.

*

The Way is indefinable.
It is spontaneous and natural.

*

That which is the Real is
both Action and Inaction,
Manifest and Unmanifest.

*

The Primordial Unity
is both male and female,
aggressive and passive,
yet transcends both.

*

The Ineffable Absolute
is hidden (Unmanifest)
and open (obvious in Creation).

*

When you are Still,
you are in the Nameless.
When you are Active,
you are in the Nameless.

*

Consciousness is the ground of Being.
Your State of Consciousness
determines your actions.

All action proceeds from the Stillness,
all that is manifest from the Unmanifest.

*

That which is the Real is Transcendent
and Immanent simultaneously.

*

The Eternal Formlessness
is the Mother of all forms.
The Bodiless Spirit is the Father of all forms.

*

The Way of the Warrior is a way of life
to seek the Permanent in the
ever-changing field of Actions.

*

The Timeless is all-pervading.
It is Active-Stillness.

Stillness before Battle

Correct action—physical, emotional or mental—can come only from the state of Stillness. Before any action, to cultivate the state of Rest is paramount. That is why the Wise Warrior enters Interior Quiet and Silence before each Battle, before each important action, before each important decision. There, in that state of Interior Silence, he waits patiently. When the time is right, the correct decision and the correct action will emerge spontaneously, without using his will-power or thinking faculty.

In the Stillness of the Warrior's Silence, when all weapons are laid down to rest, when you have stopped fighting without and within, when there is no analysing, dividing or criticizing in your mind, just Silence and Stillness, then the Great Path of Victory opens up inside you and the Unshakeable Unity is revealed unto your innermost Soul, bathed in Light, filled with Adoration.

Negative thinking produces fear.
Conquering fear is a prerequisite
for becoming a Spiritual Warrior.

*

Free your Mind from fear.

*

Focus on the Transcendental Reality
and merge your mind into It;
then you will have no fear and
your actions simply become
the Divine Will in motion.

*

Watch the Energy Flow.
Hence comes Wisdom in Action.

*

The Way of the Advanced Warrior
is non-aggression, non-assertiveness.
The way of the unskilled Warrior
is aggression, self-assertiveness,
anger, violence and hate.

*

Have no regrets in failure
and rejoice not in success.
Keep an *even mind.*

*

When you have attained
Spontaneous Consciousness in the
Transcendental State, all of your actions
are motiveless—without a selfish ego.

*

The Ultimate Warrior is
One who protects all beings
through the Power of Love.

Treat your enemy like a crying baby.

*

Love has no boundaries.

*

Love is a state of the Heart.

*

Doing nothing with the ego,
the action gets done.

*

Calm and repose is the best weapon.

*

If your breath is even, your life is even.
If your breath is disturbed, your life is disturbed.
Therefore, practise calm breathing exercises.

*

Develop Calm and Inner Peace
in your solar plexus by deep breathing.

*

Swallow your pride, swallow your knowledge.
This is the hardest lesson.

*

The most dangerous attitude is
"I am an invincible Warrior".
Be always on your guard.
Be ever watchful.

*

Don't be quick to judge.
Hold your peace.

*

True friendship counts most.

The Art of War is to know who your Enemy is.
Sometimes it is yourself.

*

You are a victim of your own desires.

*

When a person is always critical
and judgmental of others, that person
is still in worldly consciousness.
The Consciousness of the Warrior on
the Way is inclusive, tolerant, and comes
from a wider Inner Understanding.

*

The thirst for vengeance poisons not only
the mind, but also the physical body.

*

Don't see things as "either or", as black and white,
positive and negative, good and bad.
The Way includes both.

*

There are other traditions than yours,
other protocols, other forms of action.
Be flexible.

*

Respect and Honour are the
virtues on the Way.

*

Fear, anger, hate and conflict
lead to death and degeneration.
The Way of the True Warrior is
Love, Gentleness and Peace.

*

You are in Control when you respect Life.

Warriors are made by effort and discipline.

*

The Warrior advances by
self-sacrifice, effort and perseverance.

*

The greatest skill of the Warrior
is the art of Patience.

*

Have Patience to maintain Focus.

*

To become a great Warrior
you must have strong Will.

*

Indomitable Will and Confident Power
come from the Higher Self within you.

*

The true Warrior never quits.

*

A strong body and a sharp mind
are the first step for the Warrior.

*

Stay strong.

*

Refuse to limit yourself.

*

Make the impossible into fun.

*

Move forward always.
Don't keep looking back.

A temper controlled is channelled strength.
Physical strength and endurance
make you self-assured and confident.

*

If you cannot run, jump internally.

*

Things change. Change is good.

*

You cannot stop changes from happening.
The very nature of the Universe
is constant Change.

*

Resistance to Change creates tensions,
and ultimately circumstances will
force Change upon you.

*

It is the Journey itself that is the reward
in your Quest for Enlightenment.

*

Out of adversity and opposition
comes Wisdom and Understanding.

Struggle makes the Prize more valuable.

*

Have the Courage to stand up
for your convictions.

*

What matters is how you see yourself,
how you feel about yourself,
not how others judge you.

*

Have self-respect and self-esteem.

*

True Joy is not self-centred,
but Universal.

*

Take your point of view from the Sun.
Be Sun-centred, not earth-centred.

*

Keep in touch with the Sun.

*

All actions derive from the Sun.

Beyond War

War is the product of wrong thinking and accumulated psychological stress in an individual, group, society or nation. Both wrong thinking and psychological stress can be corrected by the Art of Meditation. Thus, the true Warrior is also a Master of Meditation.

War arises when individuals, groups and societies are unable to function in the Light—that is, in the Order, Coherence and Positive Energy Waves of the Divine Mind. Thus, war is prevented when the people are educated in the Art of Meditation, which is a tuning into Higher Consciousness, into higher regions of one's Being and of the Universe, wherein the only Law is Love, Coherence, Unity and Togetherness.

The whole Human Family on this planet is one Unit. Therefore, when you Fight, you are fighting against yourself. To become Aware that you are a part of the Whole, and not independent of the Whole, is to Realize the grandeur and dignity that is Humanity.

The further away you are from the Sun,
the greater the chaos in your life.
The closer you are to the Sun,
the greater your Peace and Security.

*

Pay Homage to the Sun.
Meditate on the Sun.
The Sun is your Life,
Virility and Strength.

*

The Word you hear in Silence.
The Light you see in the Dark.
You are Born in the Spirit
when to your self you Die.

*

The Living-Force of the Universe
is all around you and within you.
That Cosmic-Intelligence is
your Protection and your Guide.
Harmonize your mind and emotions with It.

*

If you respect your weapon,
your weapon will respect you.
If you respect your Teacher,
your Teacher will respect you
and can be of great benefit to you.
Disrespect towards your weapon or
your Teacher shows that you are
not yet ready to follow the Way.

*

The Teacher works by
Spontaneous Intuition,
or Innate Wisdom.

Reality is where your Focus is.
If you focus on the Material, you are material.
If you focus on the Spiritual, you are spiritual.
If you focus on conflict, you are conflict.
If you focus on Peace, you are Peace.

*

The Essence of the Spiritual Warrior Path
is to become simple—simple in thought,
in feelings, in action and in Silence.
When you become totally simple in your
whole life, the Way opens up for you by itself.

*

A Warrior is masculine outside
and feminine inside.

*

The Stillness in Stillness
is not the Skilful Stillness.
Stillness in Movement is the real Stillness.
Establish yourself in Stillness before action,
then perform your actions as if
they were deep meditation.

*

It is only through practice that you
can come to know the Art of the Warrior:
practice in meditation, practice in action.

*

Each Moment is a fragment of Eternity.
In reality there is no time and space
as perceived by your bodily senses.
Real Time and Space is Eternal,
Boundless, Measureless, Everlasting.
Within your Inner Core of Being,
you are THAT.

∞

Between the Two Extremes, Find the Middle Point

Tension arises when extreme views are held.

Nature works by the Law of Harmony, which balances out the pairs of opposites.

Learn to overcome the pairs of opposites by transcending them both

You must learn to overcome the pairs of opposites by transcending them both. That is the Middle Point, the Transcendent.

And how can you get to the Transcendent? By abandoning the pairs of opposites in your life through humility and simplicity in your life, by renouncing ambition, by giving up wilful conflicts with others, by unselfishness, by desiring nothing for yourself, by true Love and Forgiveness, and by returning to your Source, the Transcendent, in profound meditation, and there listening to the Sound of Dharma which pervades the Universe.

Listen to the Sound of the Dharma.

What does that mean, O Warrior? The word DHARMA has been translated as "the Law, Truth, Life, the Way, Religion, the Principle of Right Action, Righteousness". All of these meanings are correct. But the profound esoteric meaning will be revealed to you only in deep meditation, when you have reached the Transcendental State, your fundamental non-ego Self, beyond your mind.

In that State, Listen to the Sound of the Dharma, then do your Duty and let come what may come.

On this Journey you move not alone. In the beginning it appears that you travel for yourself only, but later on you know that you travel because of the Self, which is the Self of All.

Primordial Balance 995
Dharma: the Law of Being 244
Destiny (Dharma) 1407
Listening to the Sound of the Dharma 789

Persevering to the End until Final Liberation

The *Journey* of the Spiritual Path is a *process*. It begins in Spiritual Ignorance, in materialistic consciousness. It ends in Spiritual Illumination, which is Liberation. It is an ongoing Journey. It appears to have a beginning, but it ends in an endless End of everlasting Spiritual Progress.

Many people on the Path are under the delusion that there is a *final* stage or state beyond which there is no further to go. For example, when they have united the inner and the outer, then they think they have reached final Liberation; or when they attain to true Nirvāṇa they think that is the End-State. Not so: the State of Unity with all things, and even Nirvāṇa itself, are simply stages upon the Infinite Way of Evolution.

You must bravely battle with all the opposing, obstructing and disintegrating forces

Progress is a Journey *towards* the Light.

Having perceived the Light, the progress is *in* the Light *towards* the Greater Light, and *within* the Greater Light *towards* the Light of All Lights, the Inconceivable Reality.

Each stage is preceded by troubles, problems, tensions, crises and readjustments within and without. This is part of the Journey. You must bravely battle with all the opposing, obstructing and disintegrating forces that try to hinder you and throw you off the Path.

Success is Born of Action 256
Rely on your Inner Self 1226
To Succeed in your Quest 1330

The Code of the Spiritual Warrior

No fear.
No anger.
A calm mind.
A friendly Heart.
A constant readiness to serve and to help
in the working out of the Divine Plan on Earth.

Respect for the Teacher.
Respect for the Teaching.
Respect for the Group one travels with on the Path.

To follow one's inborn Destiny.
To live nobly and Free.
To overcome all difficulties with dignity and strength.
To persevere upon the Path until the end,
until Mastery and Perfection are gained.

This is the Code of the Spiritual Warrior.

**Let this be your Guide,
your Inspiration,
and your Strength.**

Farewell

Our Journey must end here. We have tried to indicate the Noble Path of the Spiritual Warrior. Many things we have said, and still many things remain unsaid.

∞

Who can sing praises for the Noble Warrior?

The Way of the Warrior is a struggle: struggle with the self, with the environment, with the human condition on this planet. It is a struggle towards the Light, towards Wisdom, Understanding and final Peace.

The Warrior senses a great Destiny which he or she must accomplish, which will affect many people, sometimes a whole nation or the whole world.

In the end comes the Great Sacrifice, the laying down of one's life for one's fellow men and women—for Humanity. This Great Sacrifice may be accomplished in one big battle, or in years of Service for the cause of Light, Progress, Evolution and Enlightenment of the planet.

Who can sing praises for the Noble Warrior? Who can sing praises for one who lays down his or her life so that, by that Sacrifice, many others will benefit, evolve, progress and know greater happiness?

Like an unshakeable rock, the Warrior stands dignified and noble in the stormy seas of life. When the Warrior lays down the Sword finally, then comes Peace—full, complete, unending.

See Volume III
TRANSFORMATION